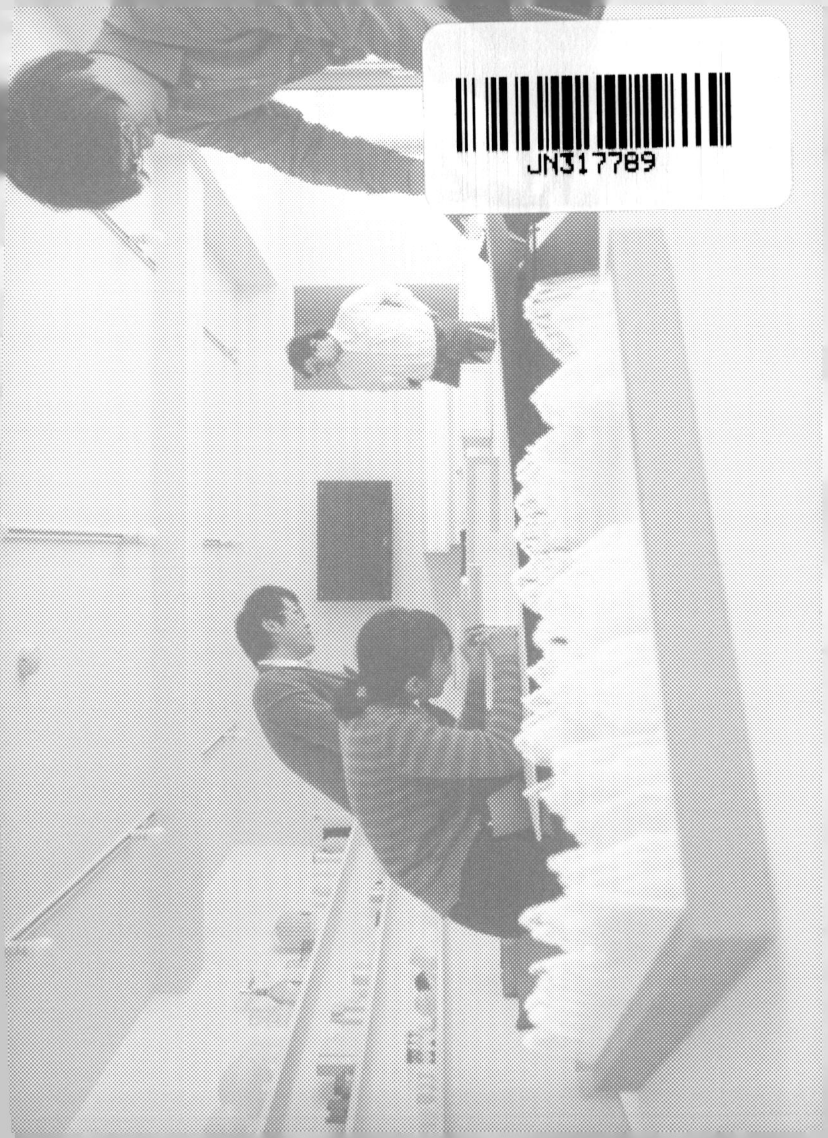

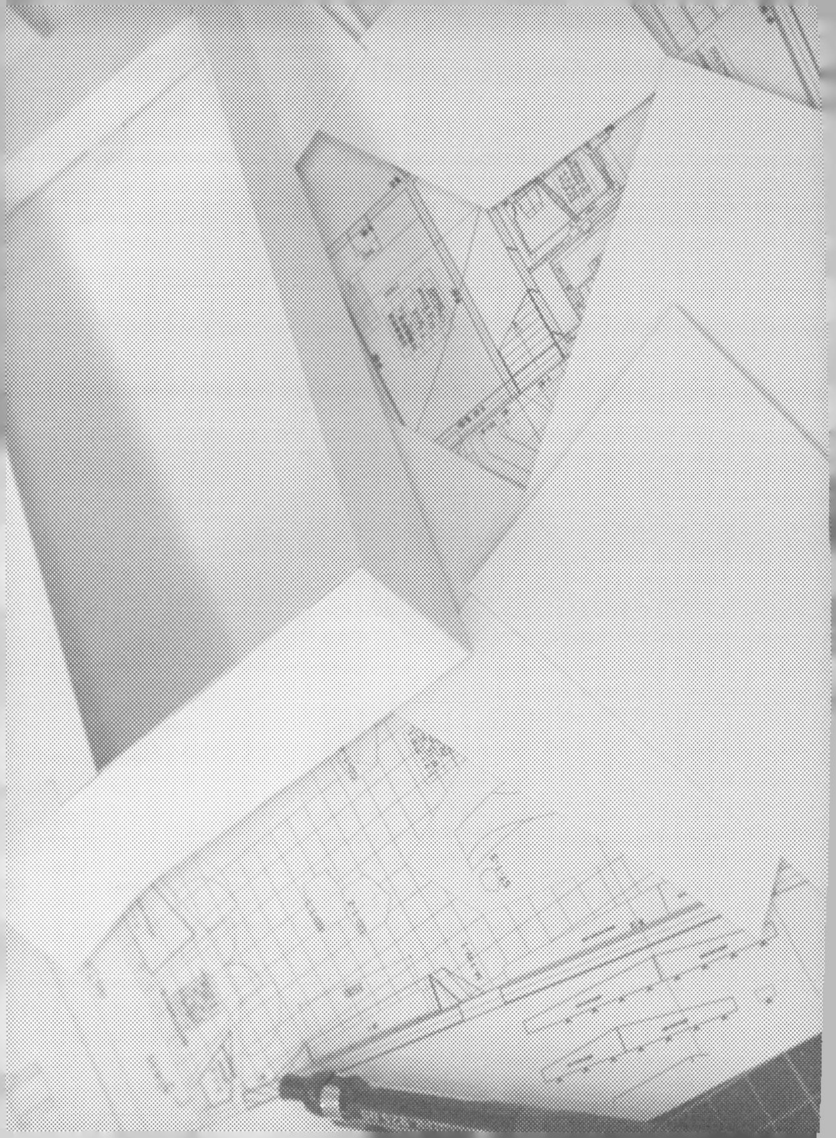

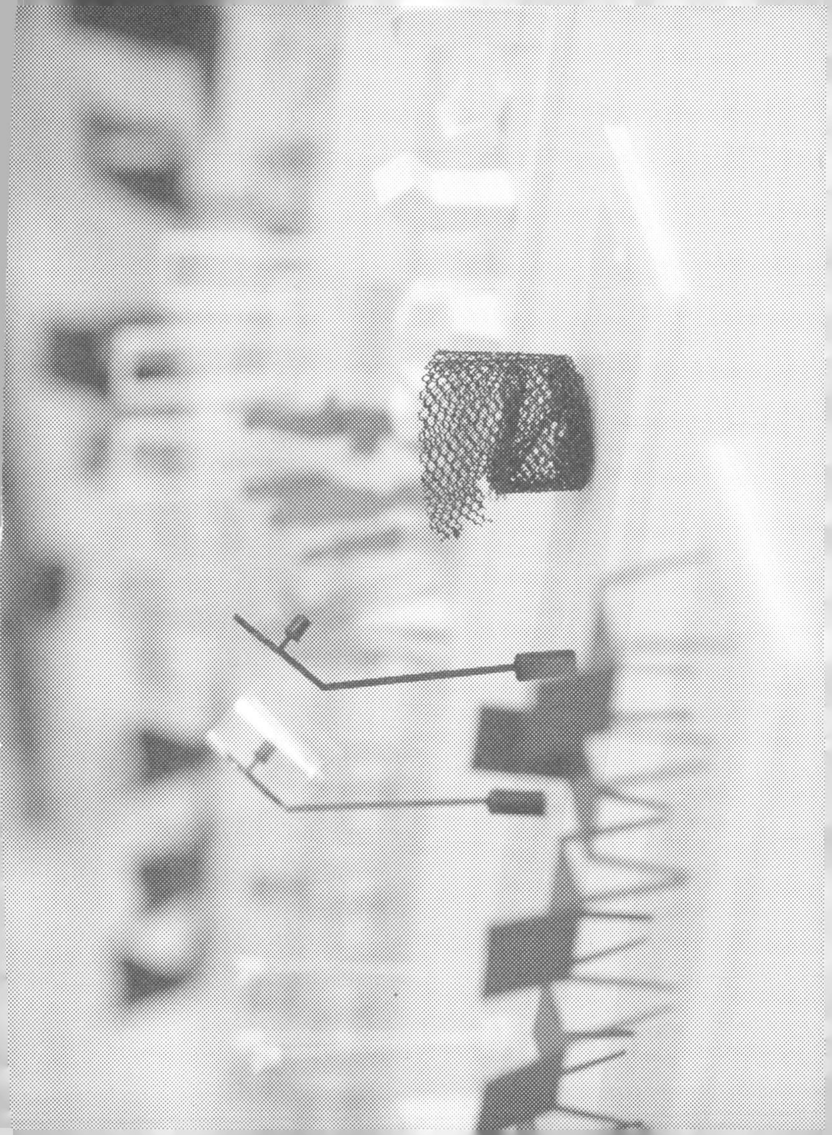

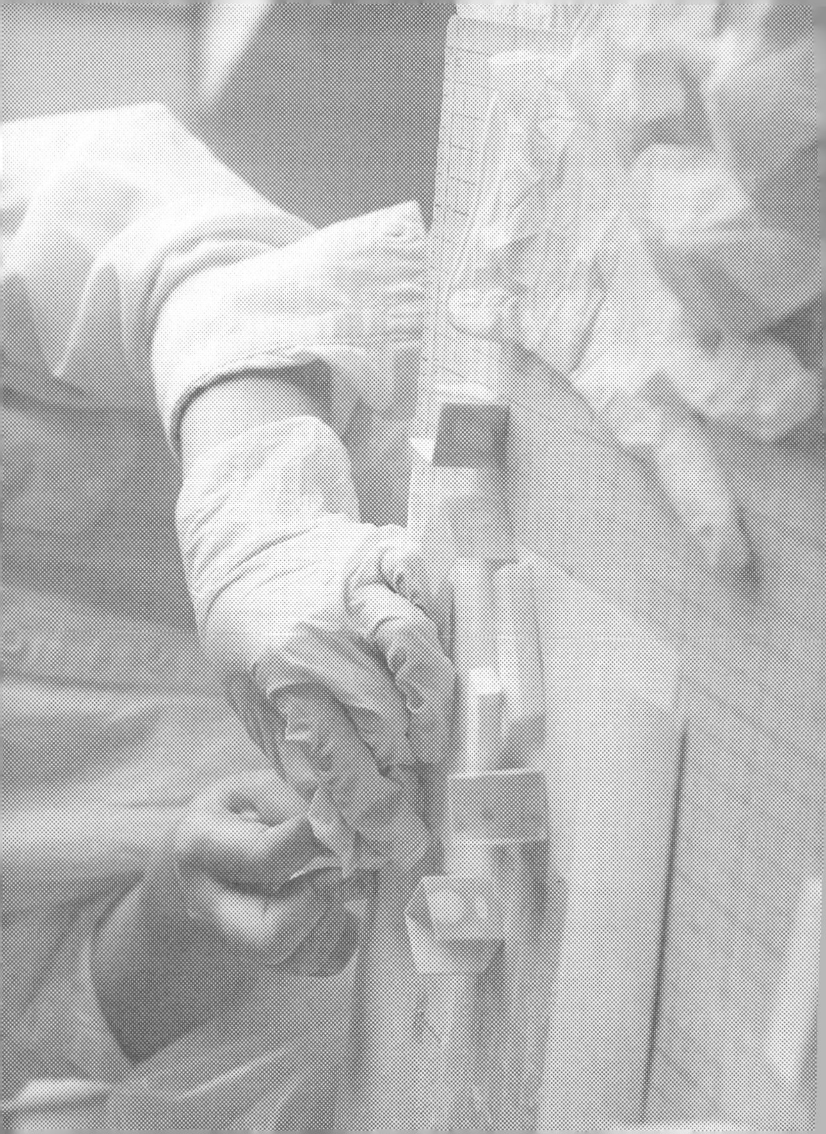

nendo
in the box

ADP

nendo: in the box

Date of Publication: April 16th, 2014

Author: nendo / Oki Sato
Photo: Hiroshi Iwasaki
Book Design: Yoshiaki Irobe, Akiko Uematsu
(Irobe Design Institute, Nippon Design Center Inc.)
Printing Direction: Yuki Ura (i Word Co., Ltd.)

Publisher: Keiko Kubota
Publishing House:
ADP Company / Art Design Publishing
2-14-12 Matsugaoka, Nakano-ku,
Tokyo 165-0024 Japan
Tel: +81-3-5942-6011   Fax: +81-3-5942-6015
http://www.ad-publish.com

Printing & Binding: i Word Co., Ltd.

©nendo 2014
Printed in Japan
ISBN978-4-903348-41-4 C0072

All right reserved.
No part of this publication may be reproduced
or transmitted in any form or by any means,
electric or mechanical, including photocopy,
or any other information storage and retrieval
system, without prior permission in writing
from the ADP company.

Contents

- 10   Alice's Tea Party
- 18   ASOBIO Channel One
- 32   ASOBIO Cloud Nine
- 40   BEIGE,
- 52   bird-apartment
- 58   Camper New York
- 68   Camper Paris
- 78   CATALOG Beijing
- 90   COMPOLUX
- 102   Established & Sons@LDF
- 110   ghost stories 2nd chapter
- 118   HALSUIT
- 136   Hermès wandering forest
- 144   HIRATA NO BOSHI
- 154   hitogaki
- 162   ILLOIHA OMOTESANDO
- 170   INDULGI
- 182   International KOGEI Triennale
- 196   International KOGEI Triennale Pre-event
- 202   JAPAN: Tradition. Innovation.
- 214   karaoke-tub
- 218   kisala
- 226   MD.net Clinic
- 232   meguro office
- 244   mimicry chairs
- 318   moss house
- 324   PUMA HOUSE TOKYO
- 332   Rinascente Milan
- 342   spicebox office
- 352   Starbucks Espresso Journey
- 362   Theory
- 436   thin black lines + dancing squares
- 448   tokyo baby cafe
- 456   Yii exhibition
- 464   1% products@IFFT
- 474   1% products@Interior Lifestyle
- 482   24 ISSEY MIYAKE
- 488   80 sheets of mountains

nendo: in the box

Alice's Tea Party

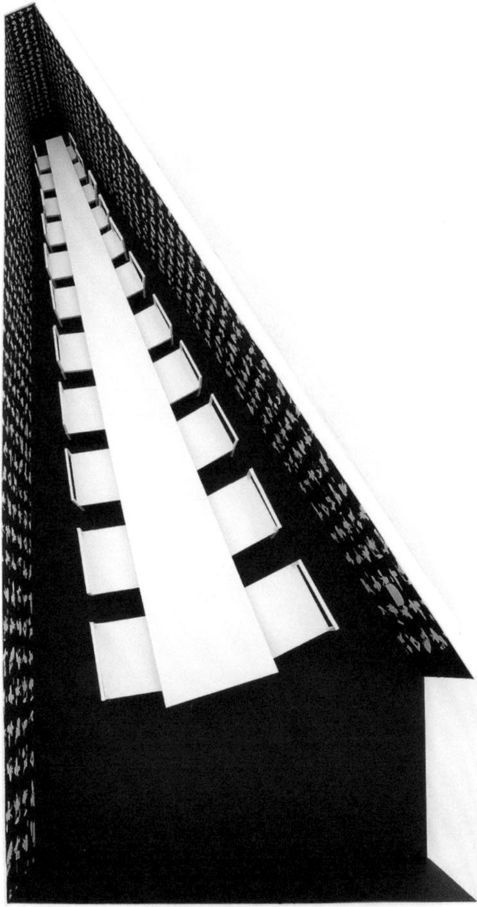

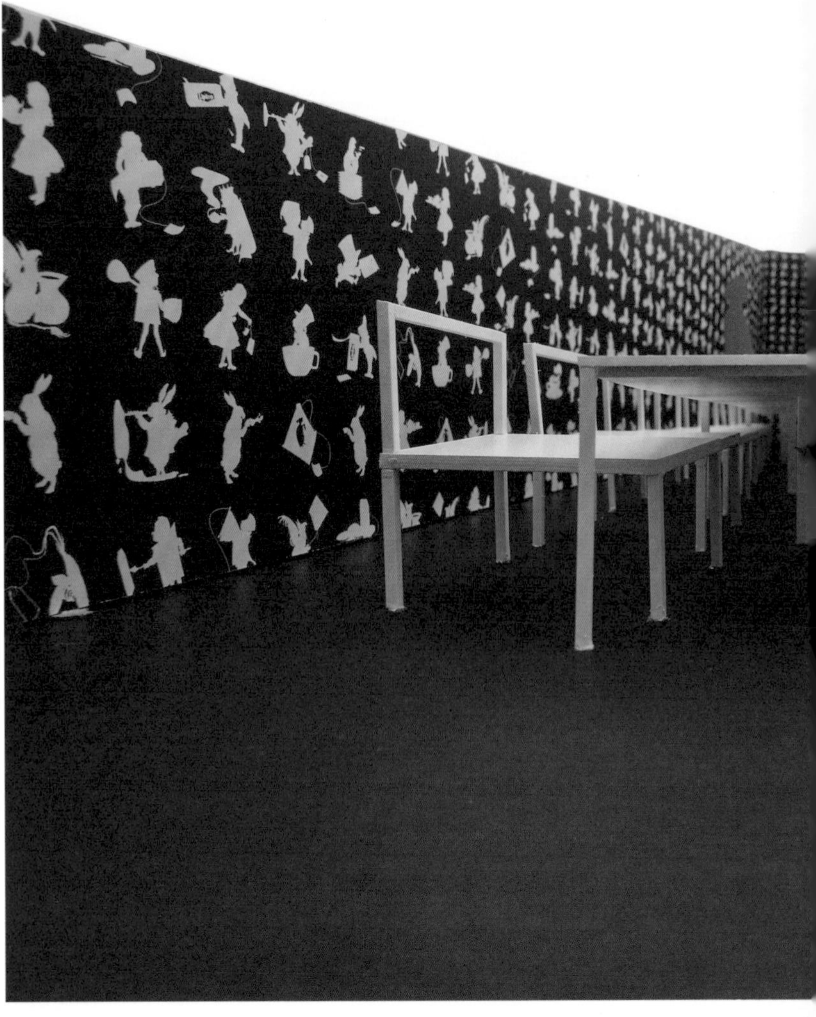

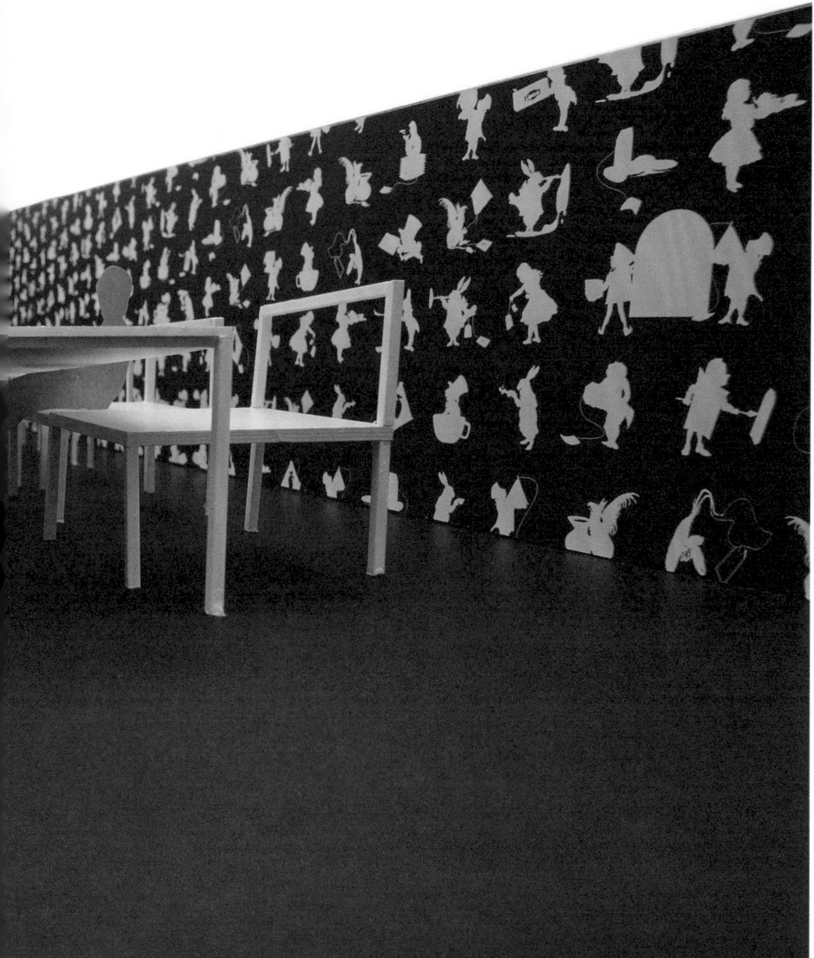

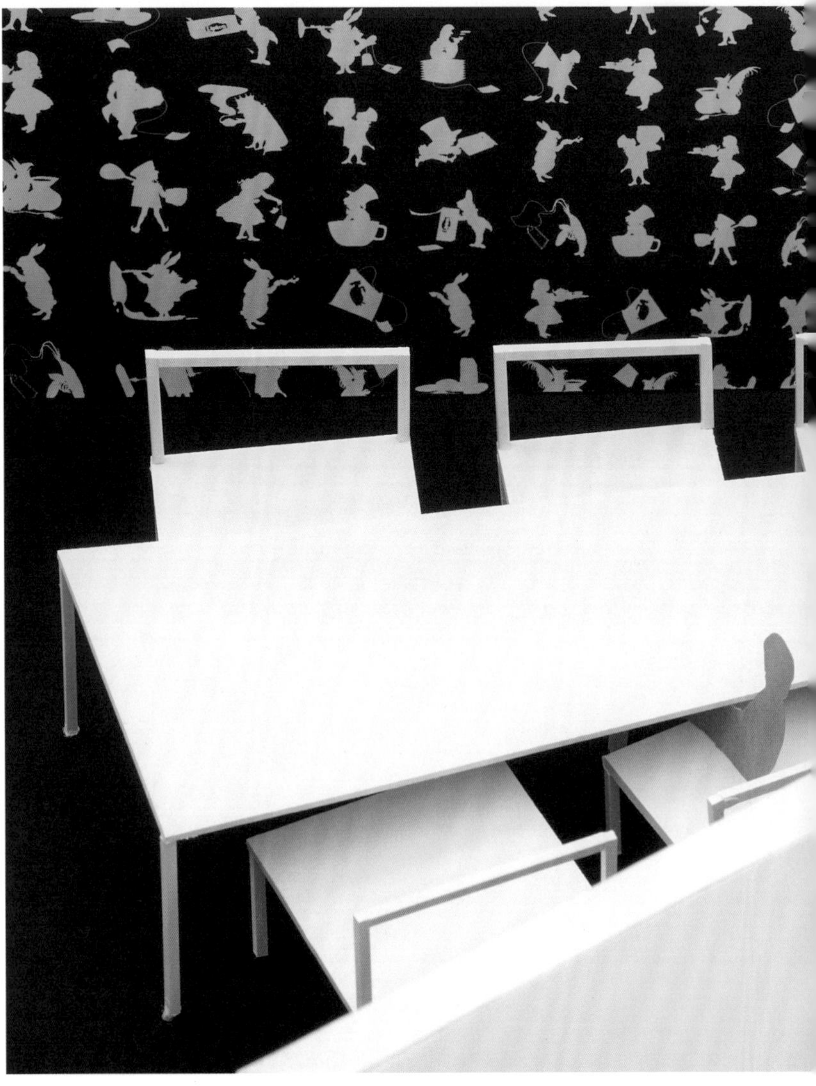

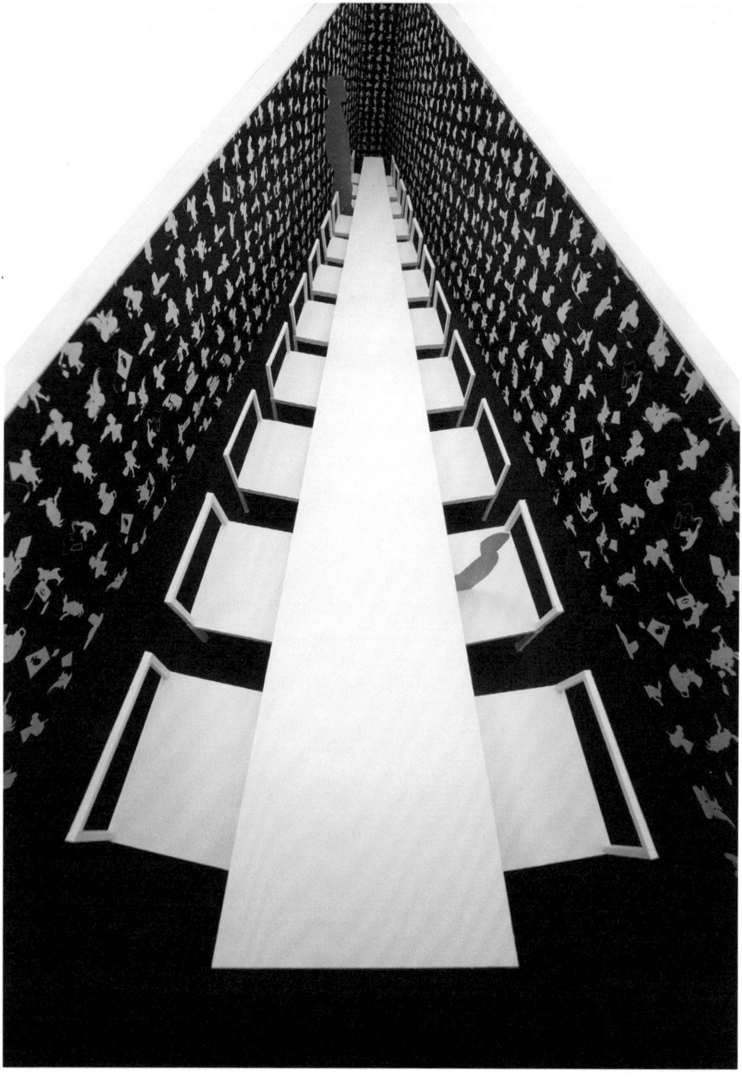

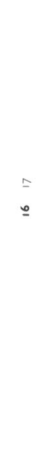

Alice's Tea Party

ASOBIO Channel One-IF

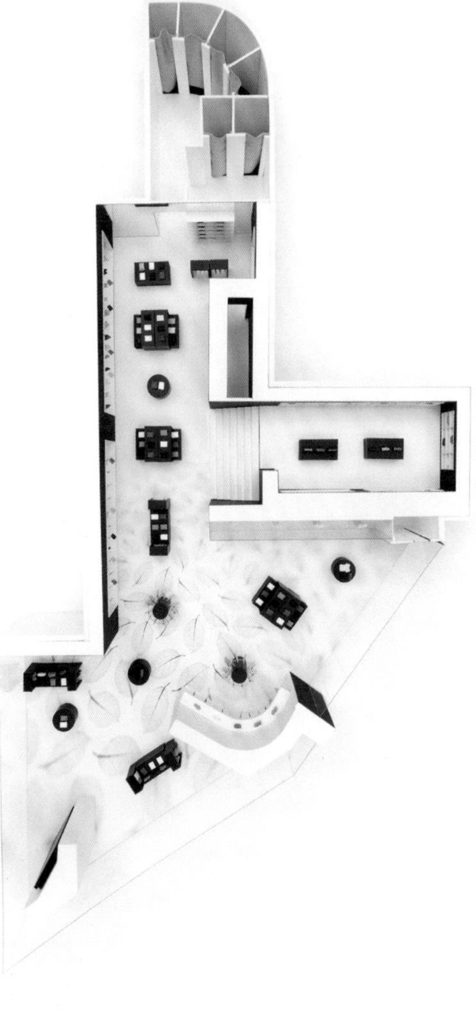

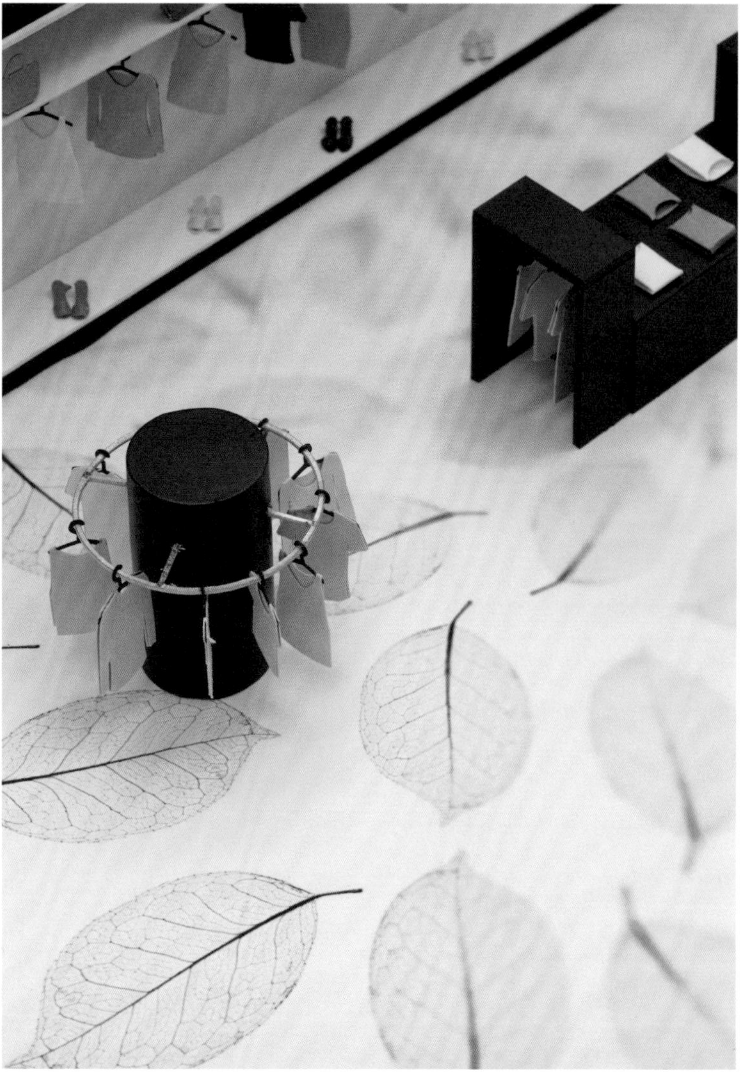

ASOBIO Channel One-IF

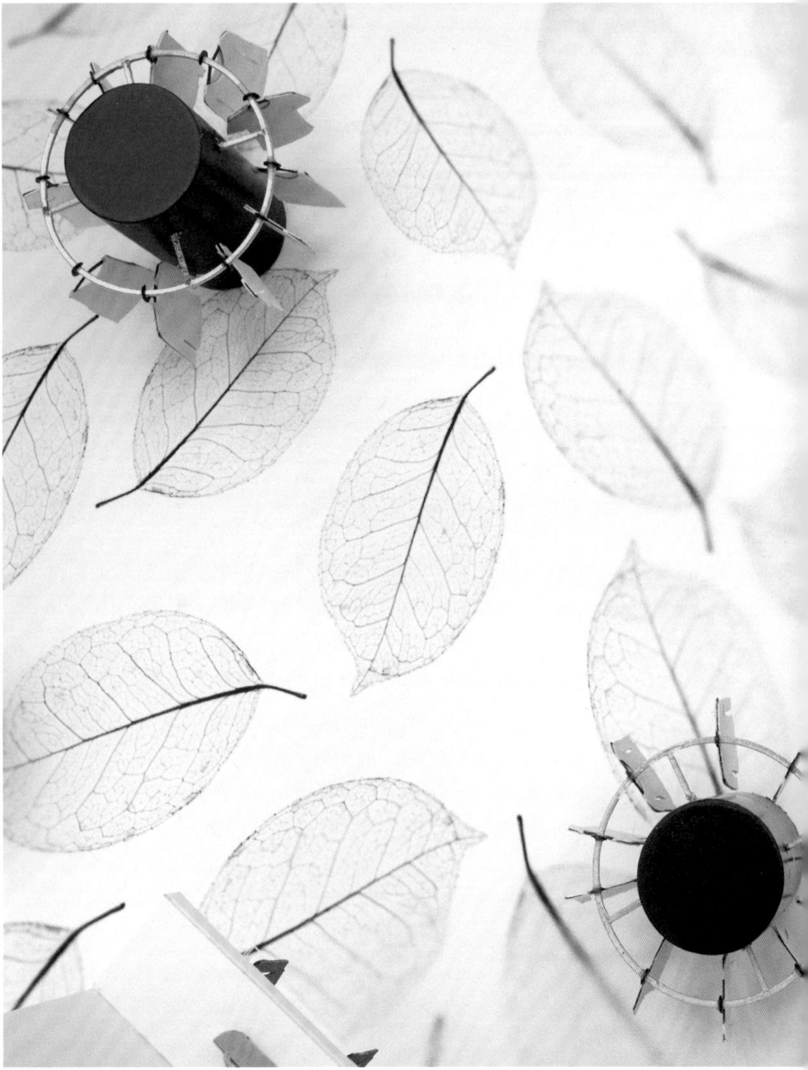

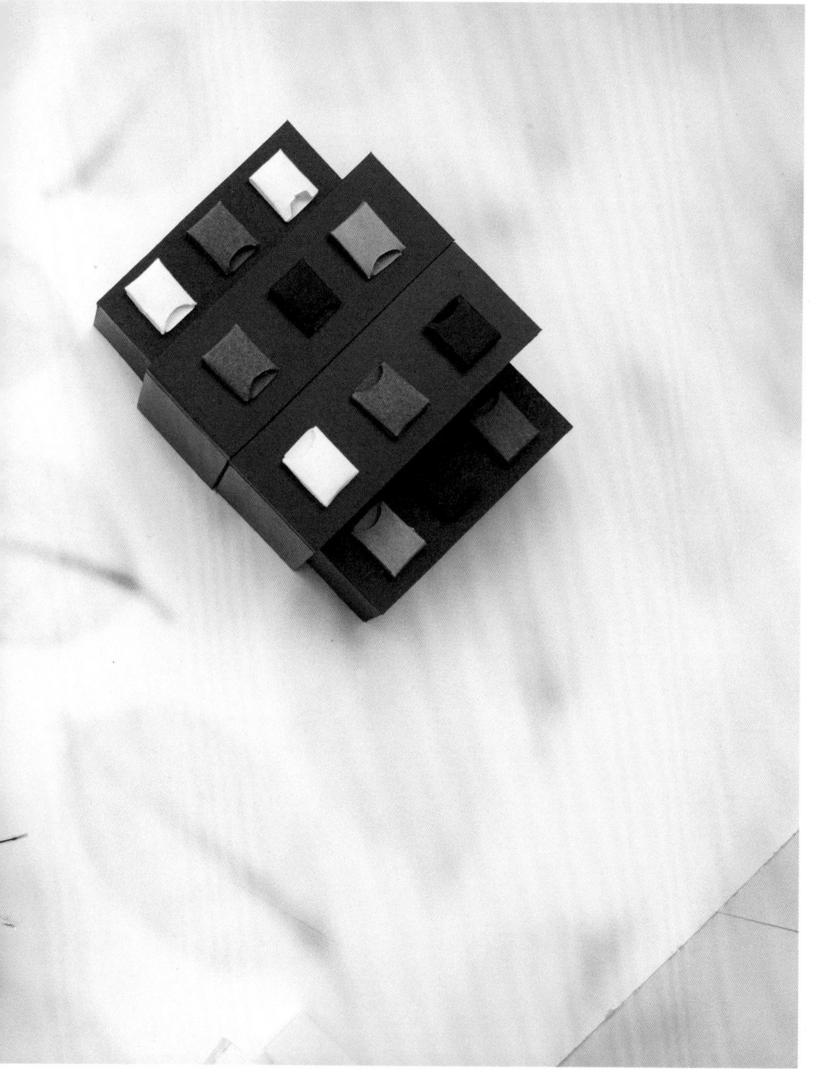

ASOBIO Channel One-2F

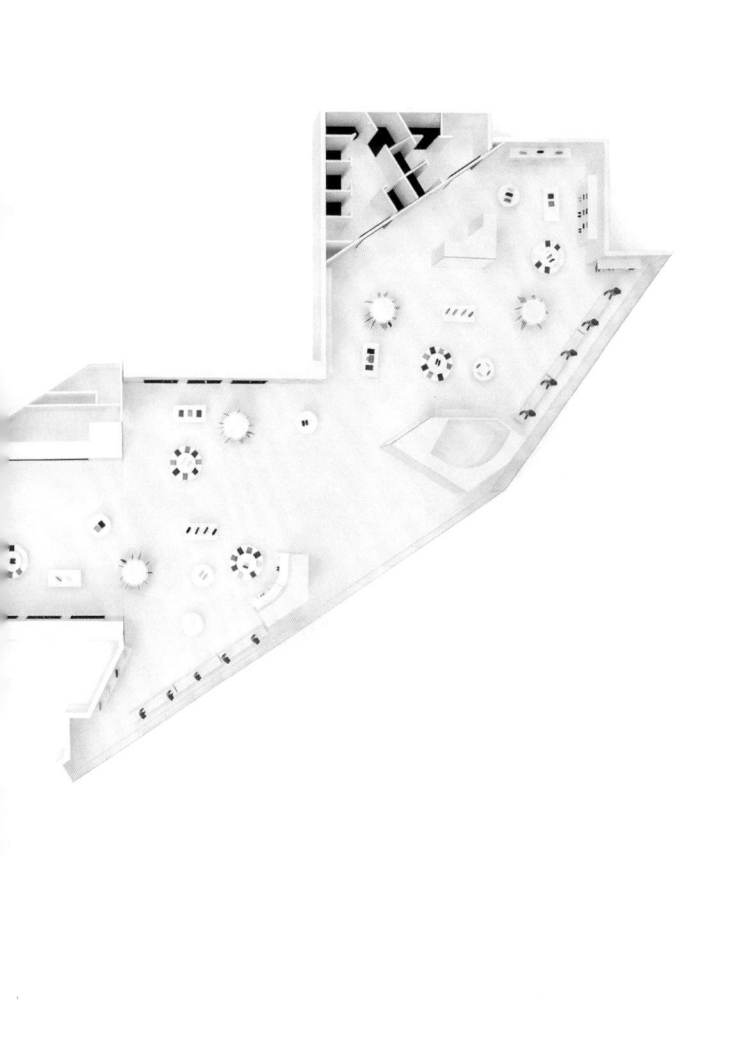

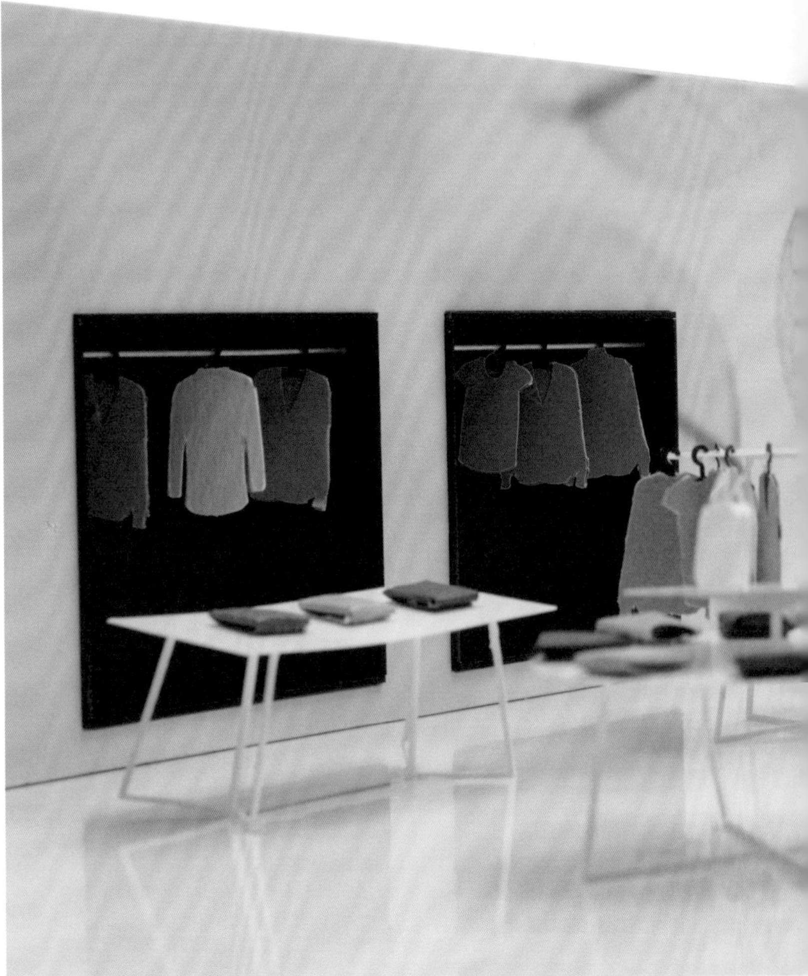

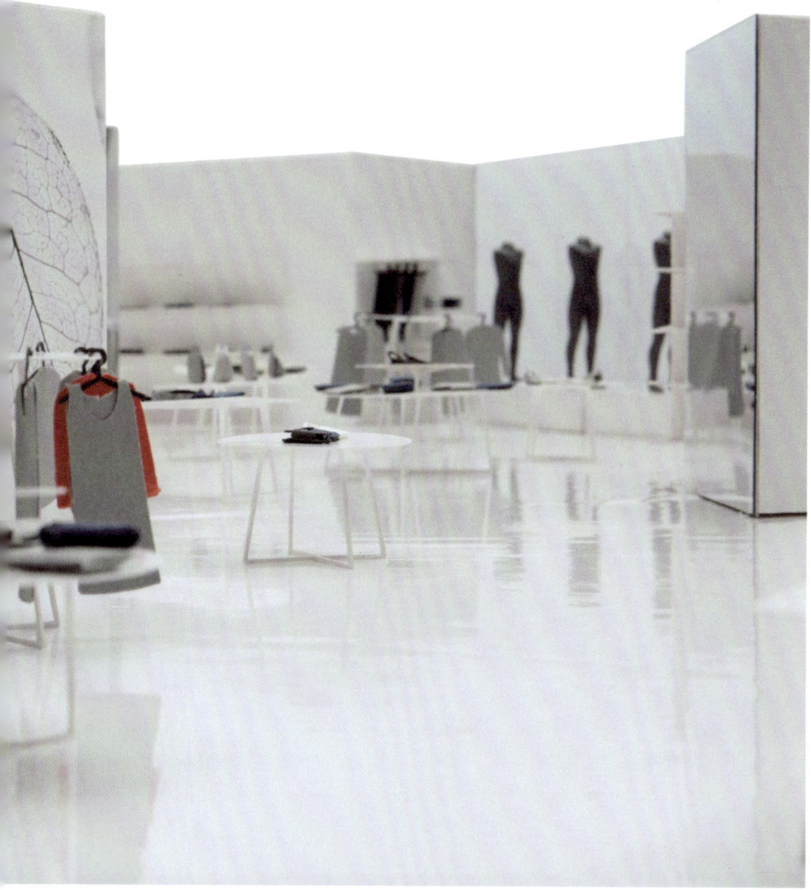

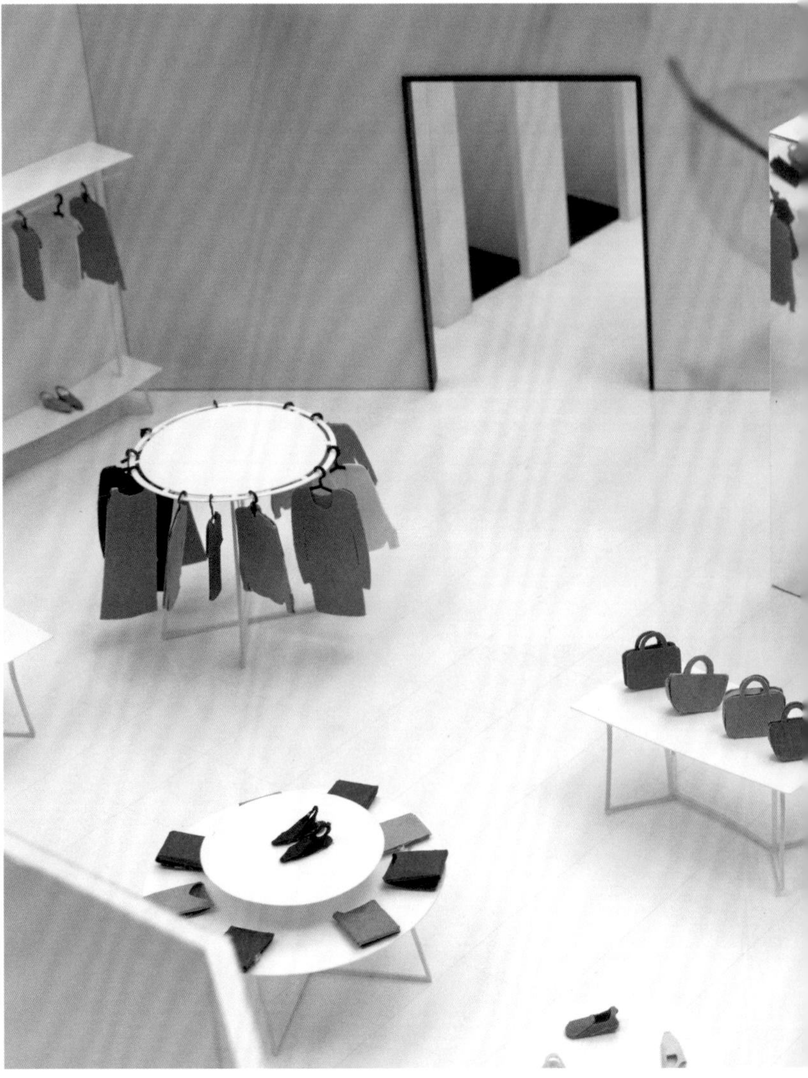

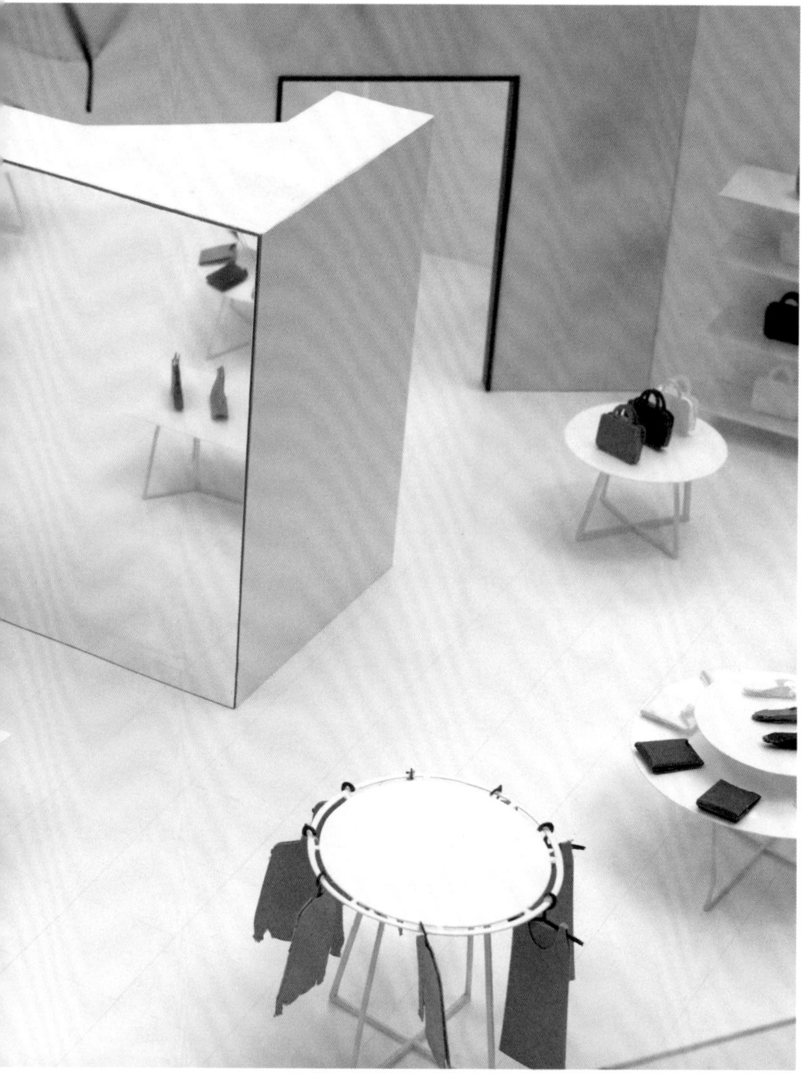

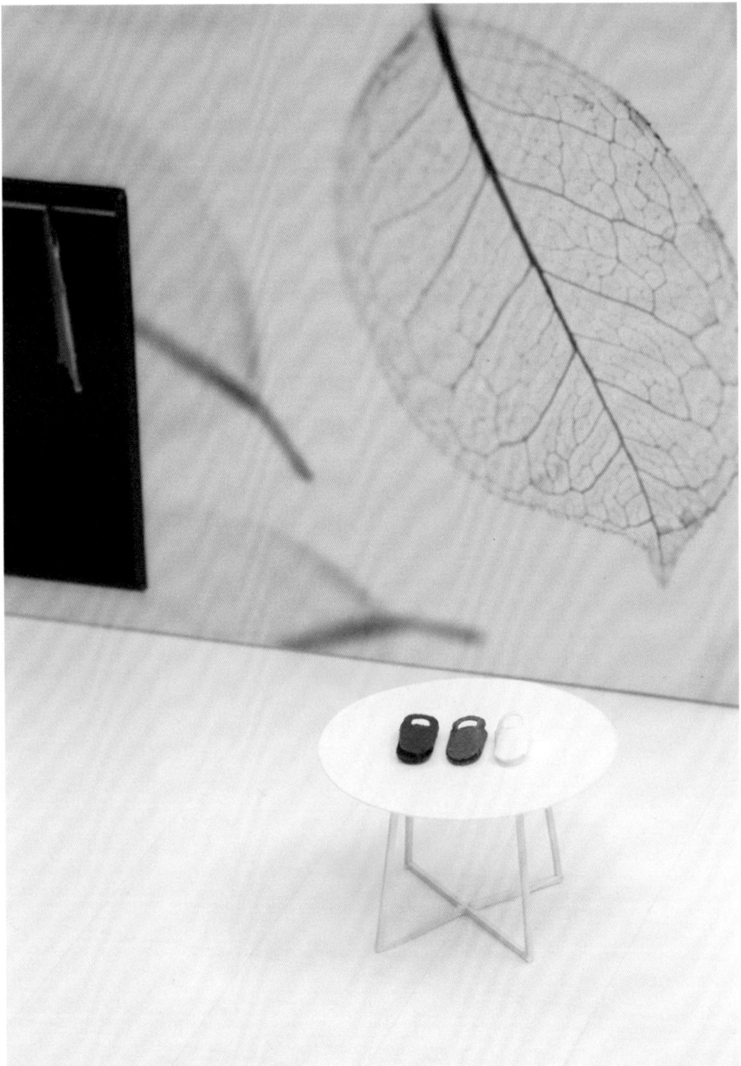

ASOBIO Channel One-2F

ASOBIO Cloud Nine

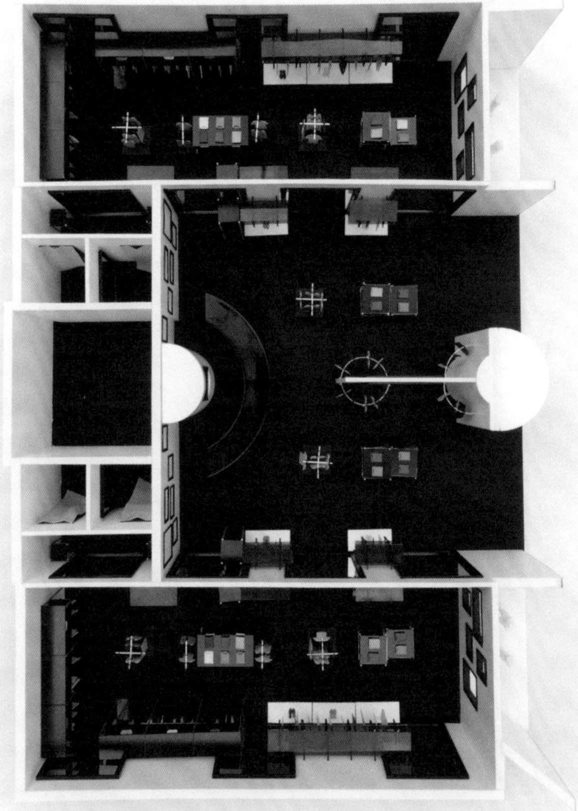

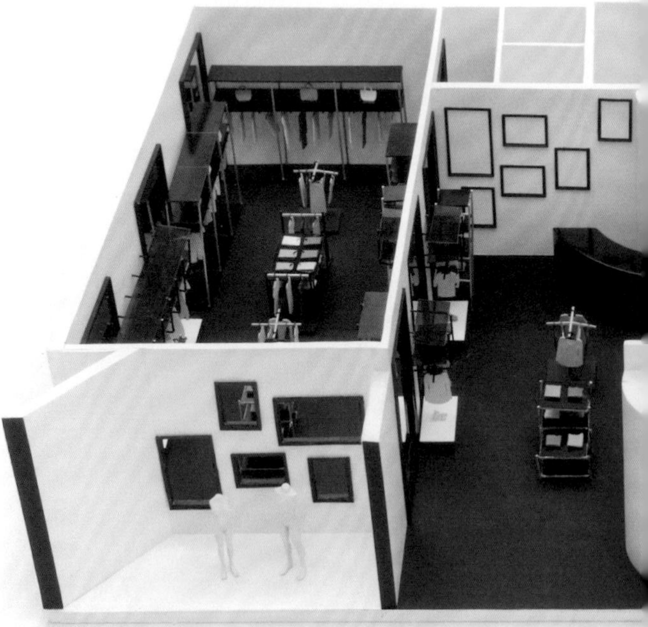

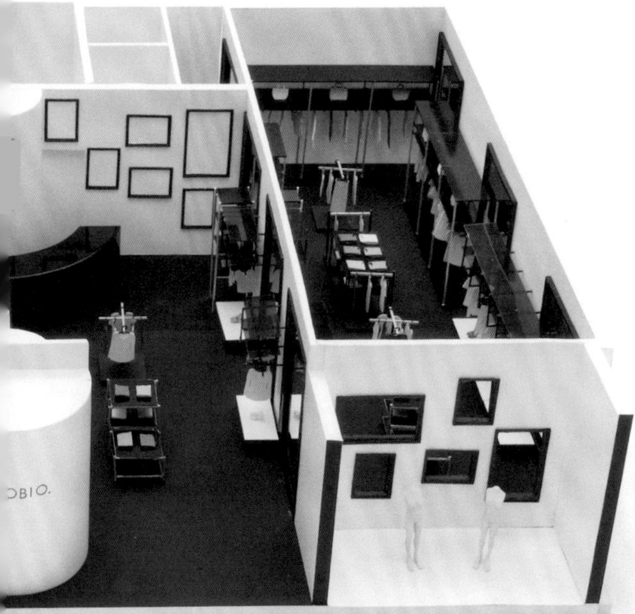
OBIO.

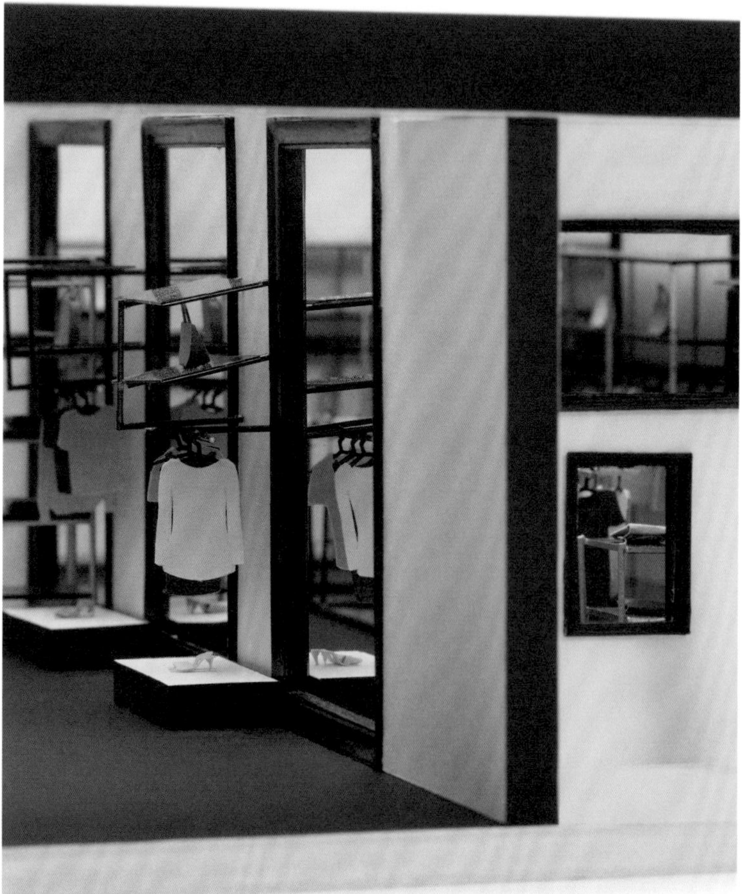

ASOBIO Cloud Nine

38 39

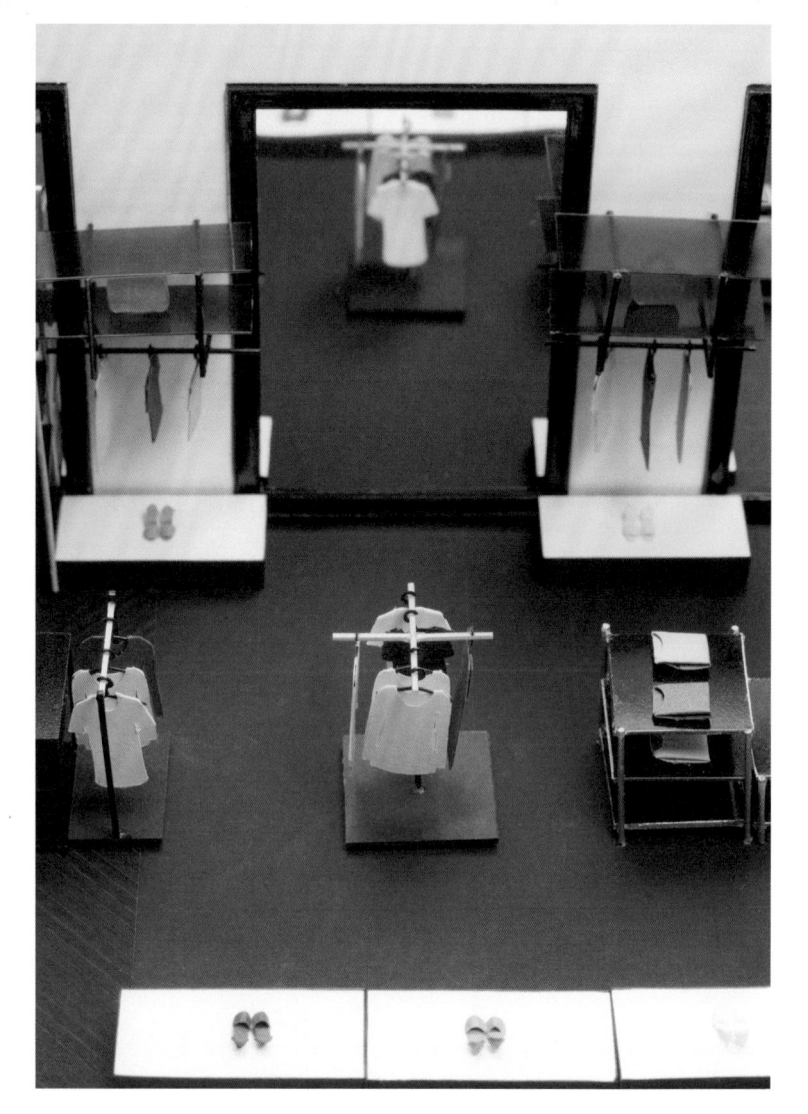

ASOBIO Cloud Nine

BEIGE,

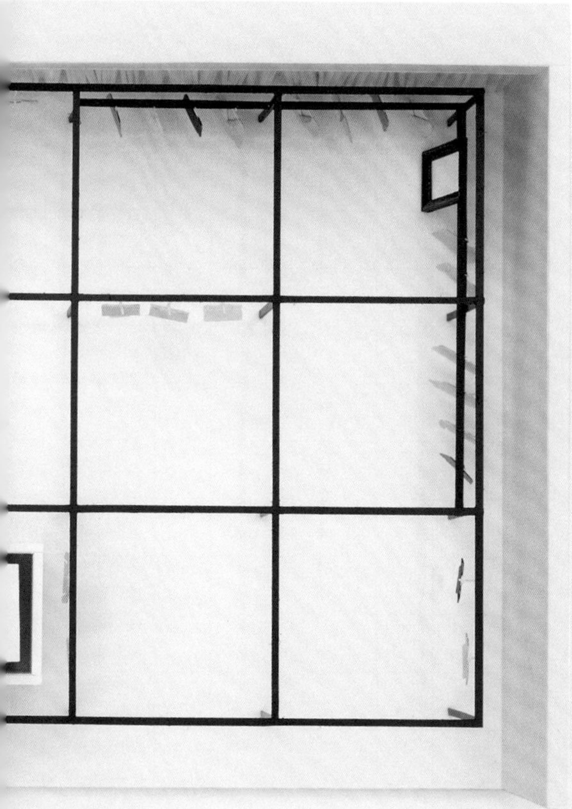

BEIG

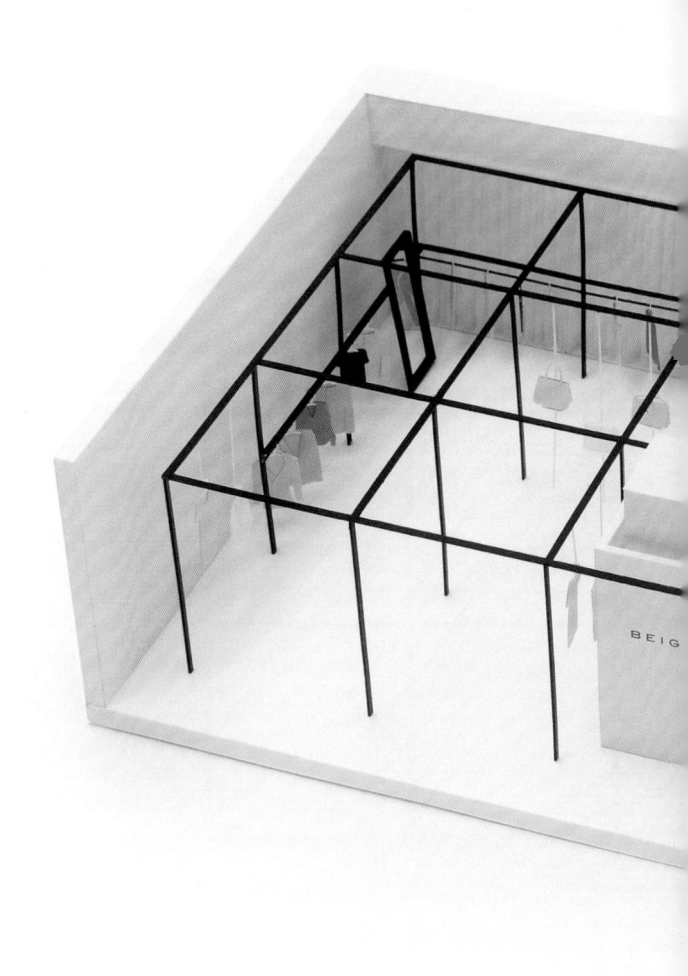

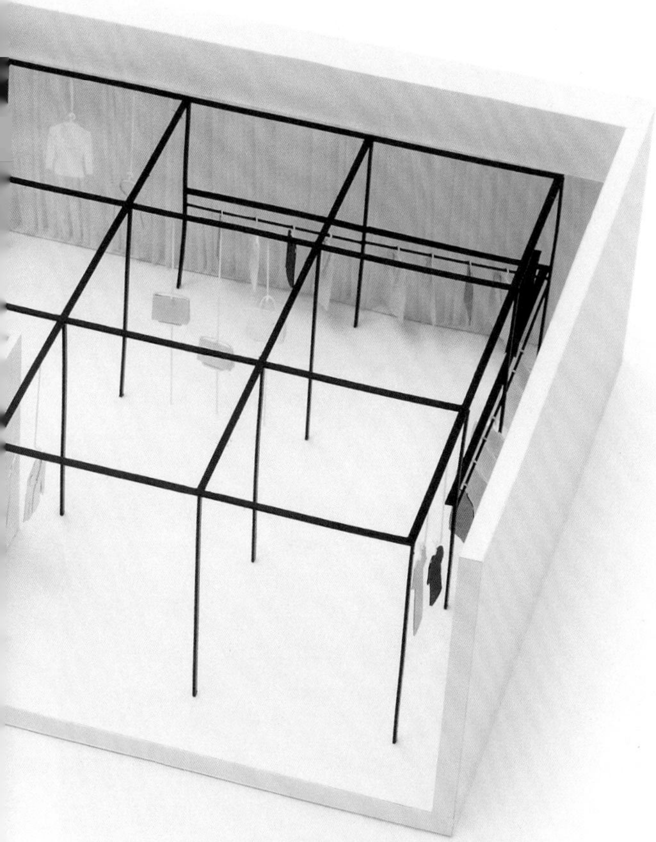

BEIGE,

BEIGE.

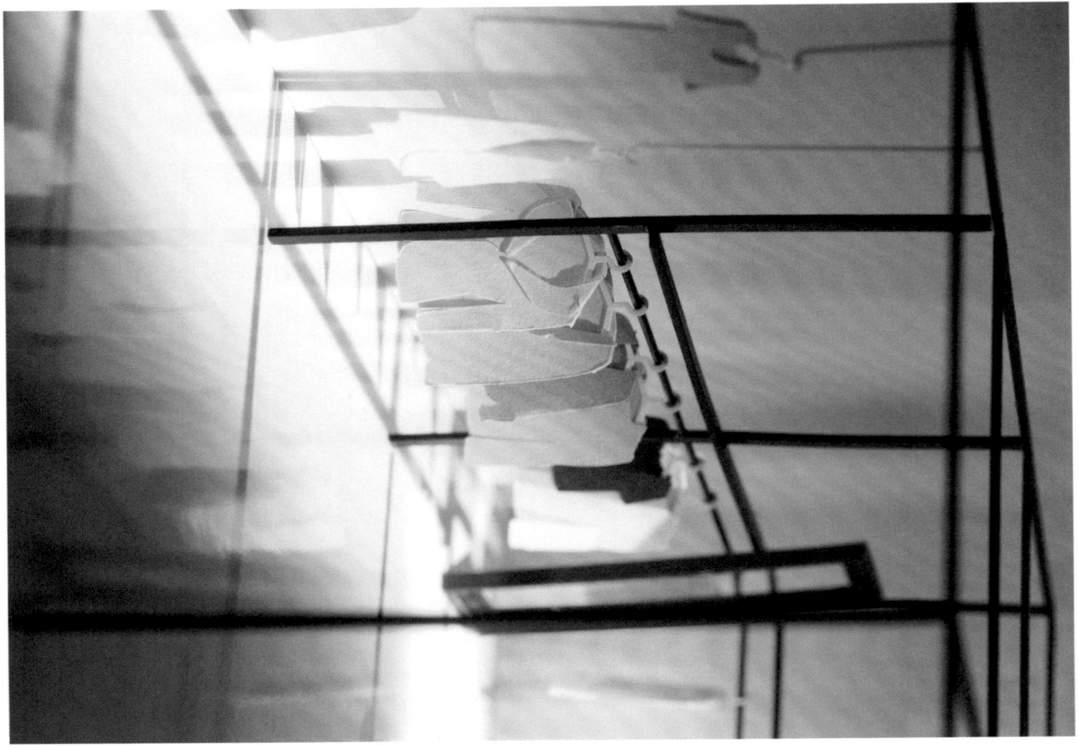

BEIGE.

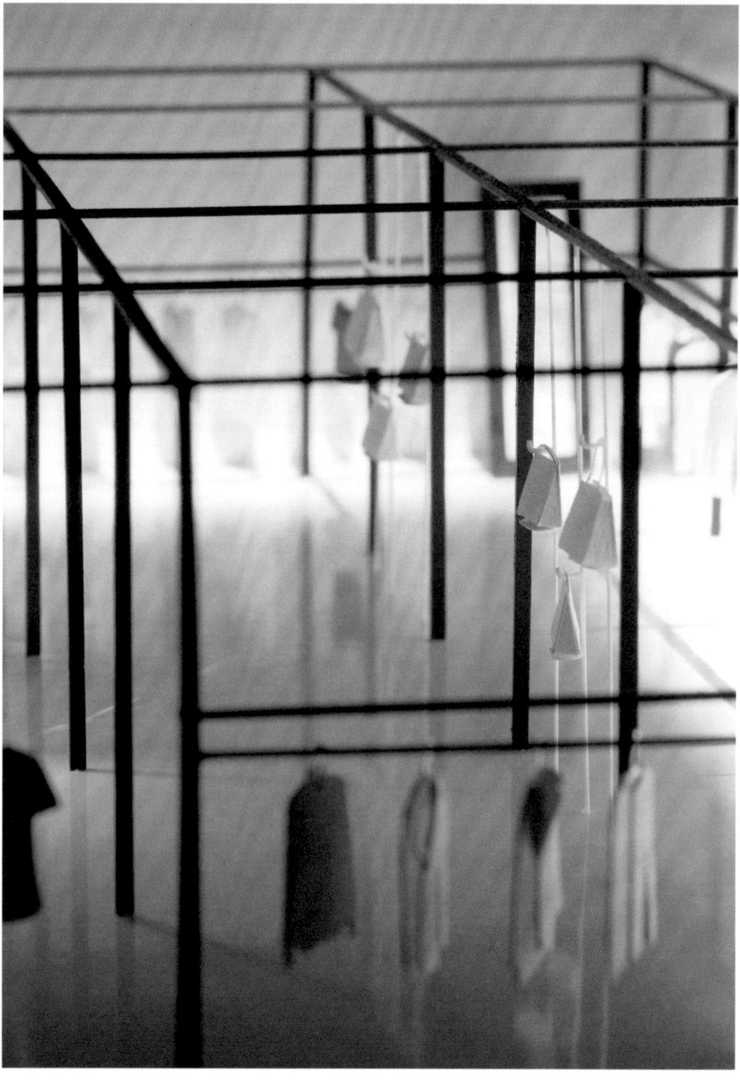

BEIGE.

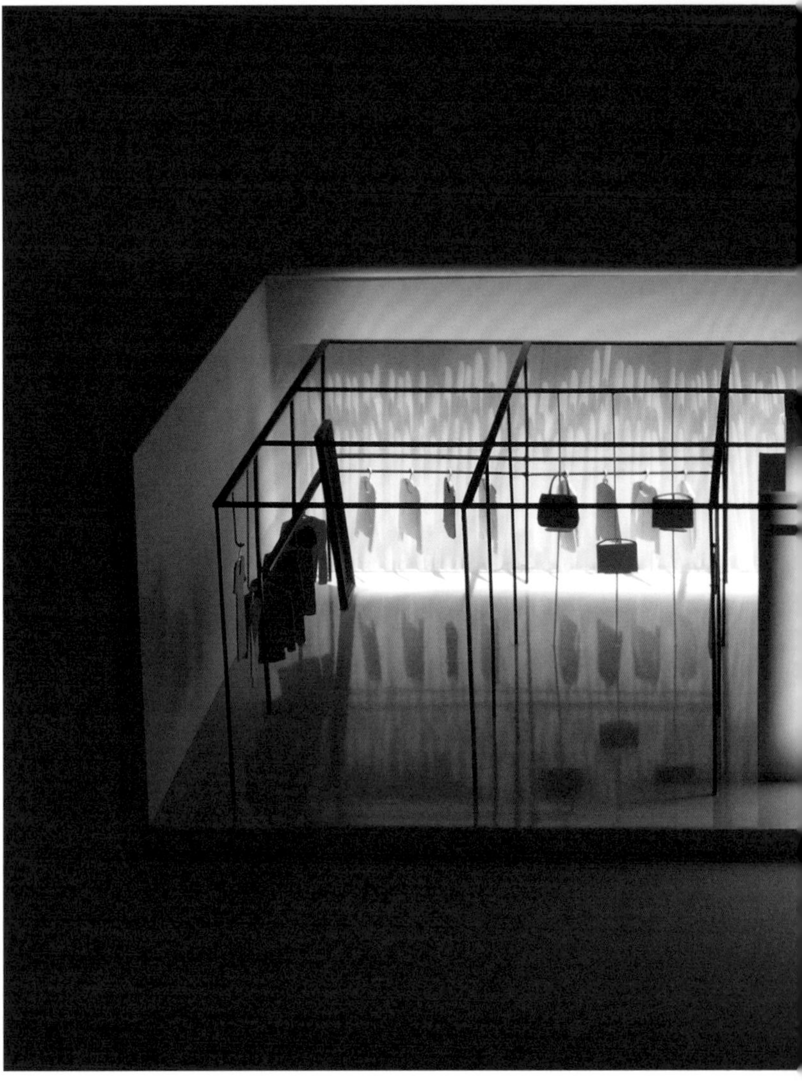

E,

bird-apartment

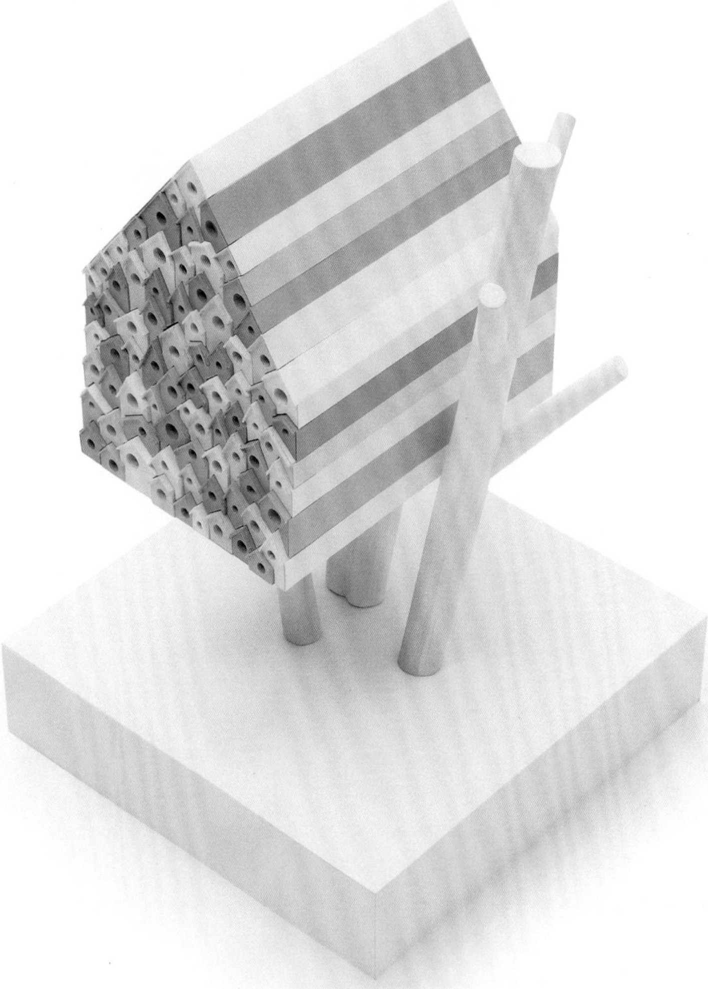

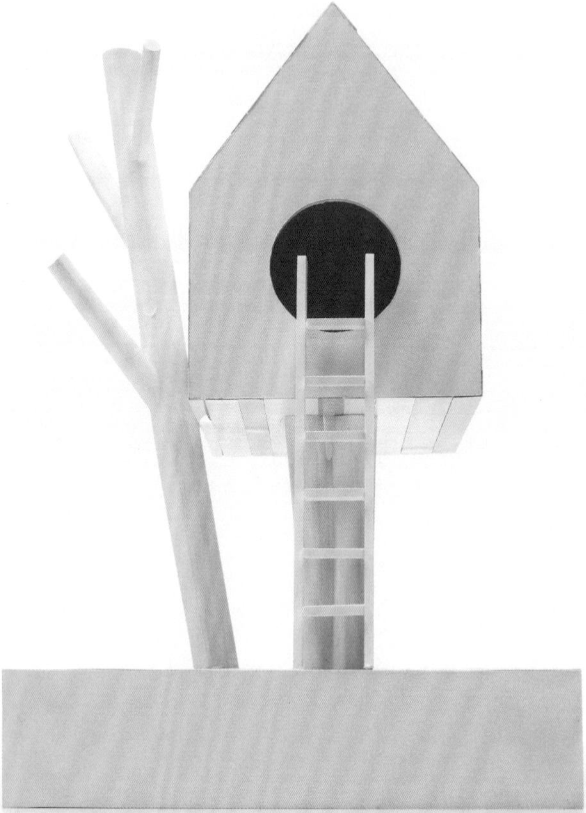

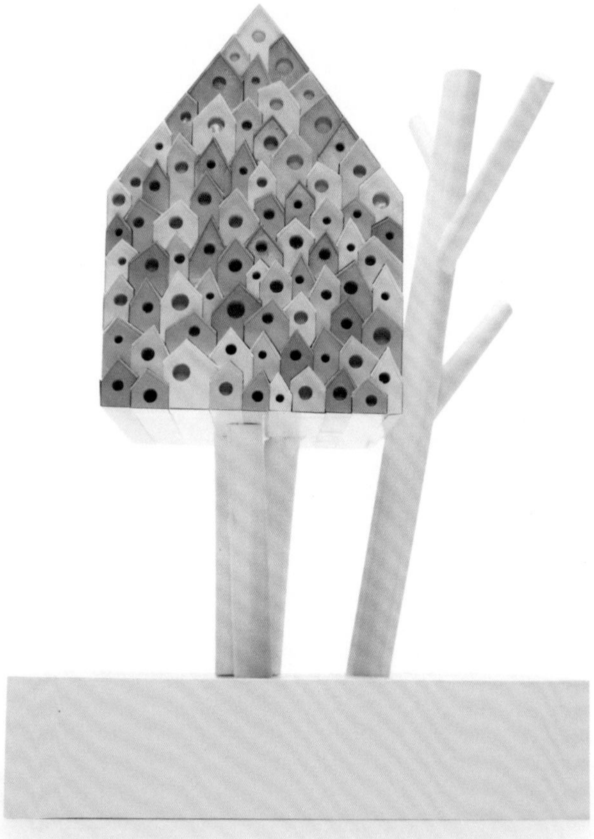

56 57

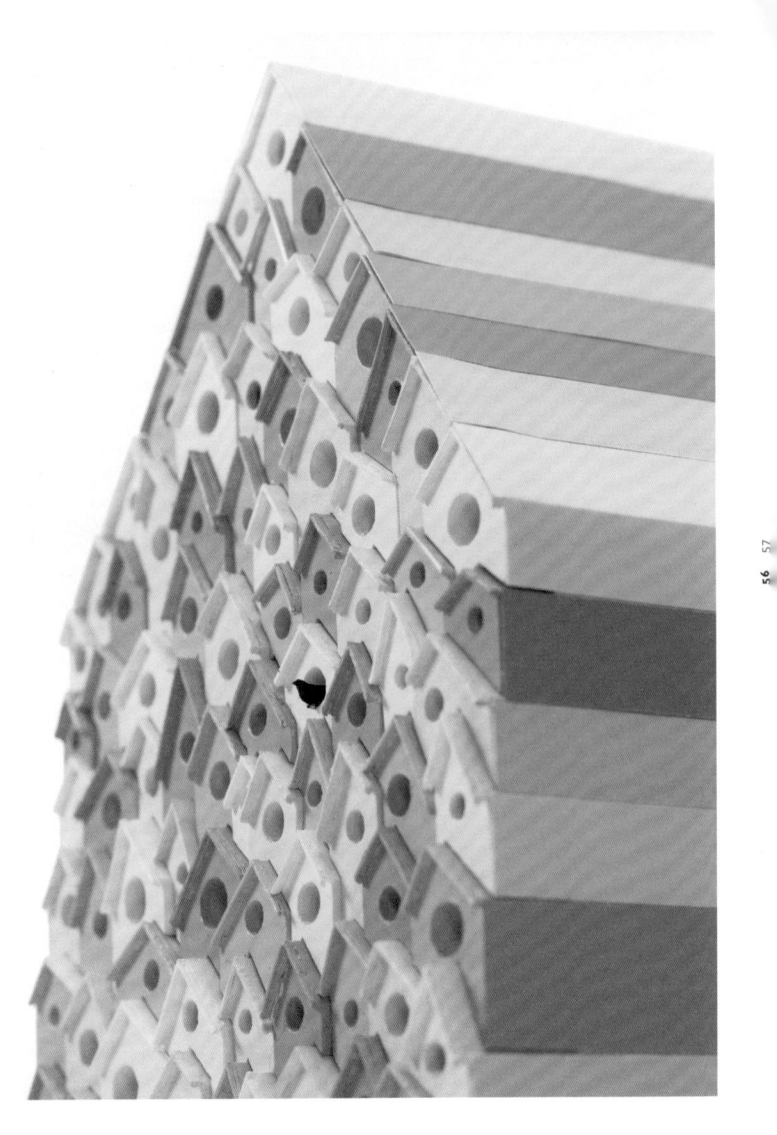

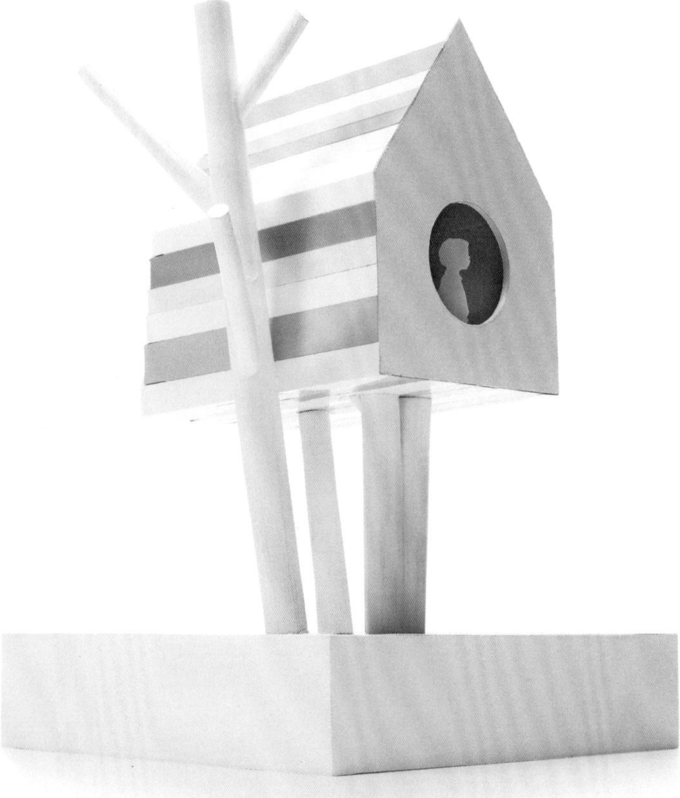

Camper New York

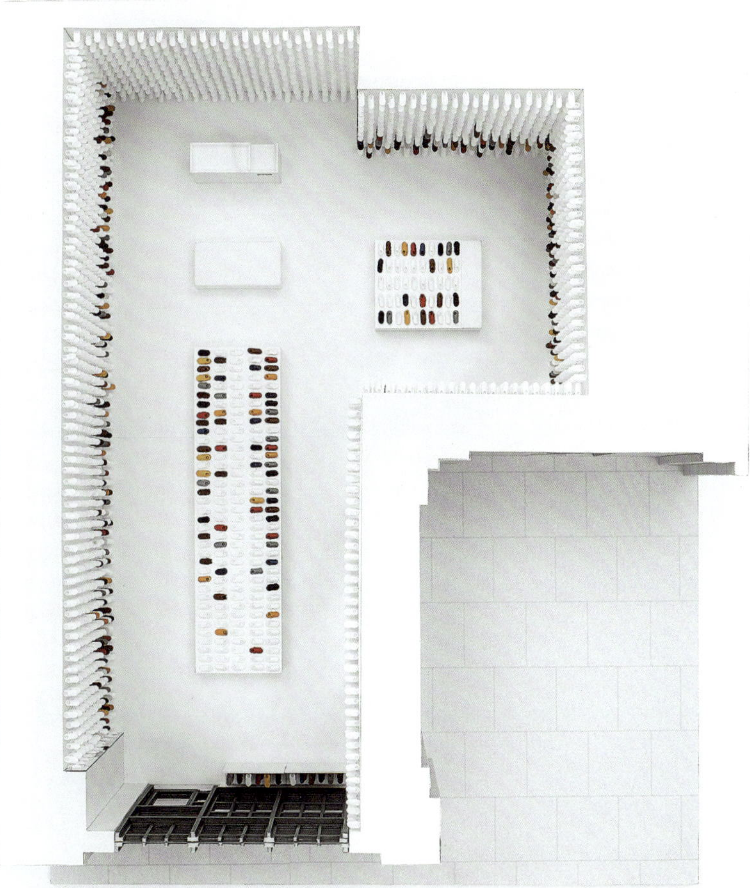

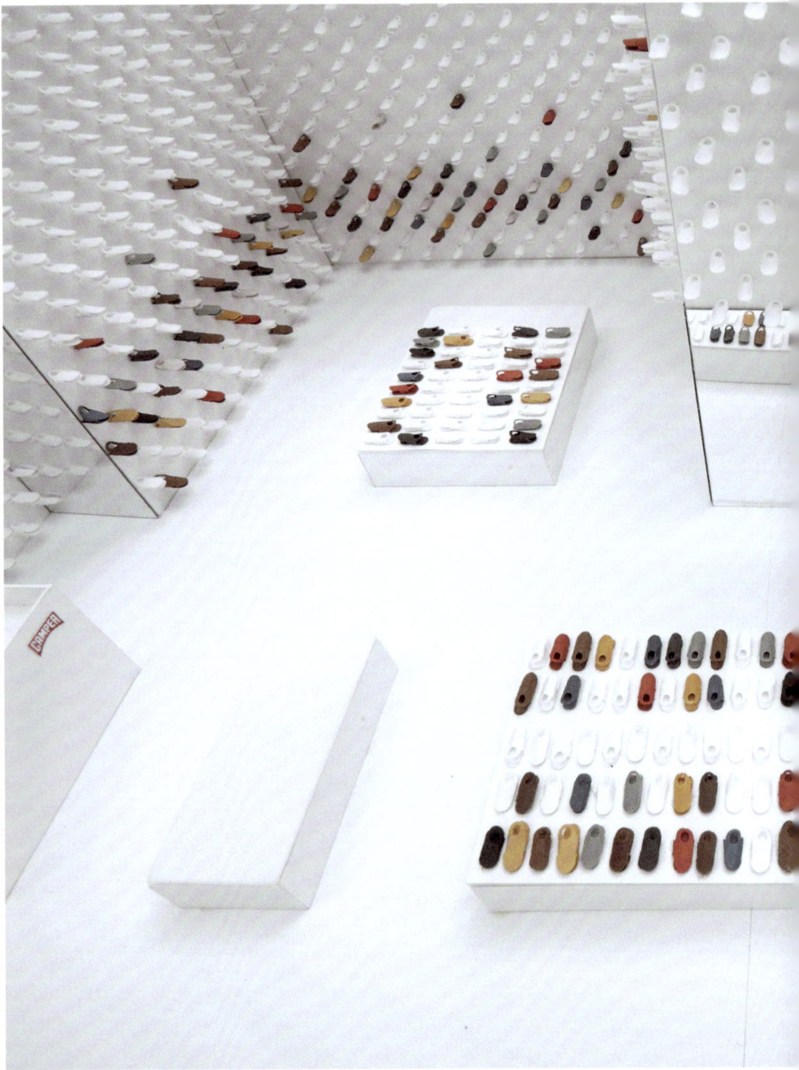
CAMPER

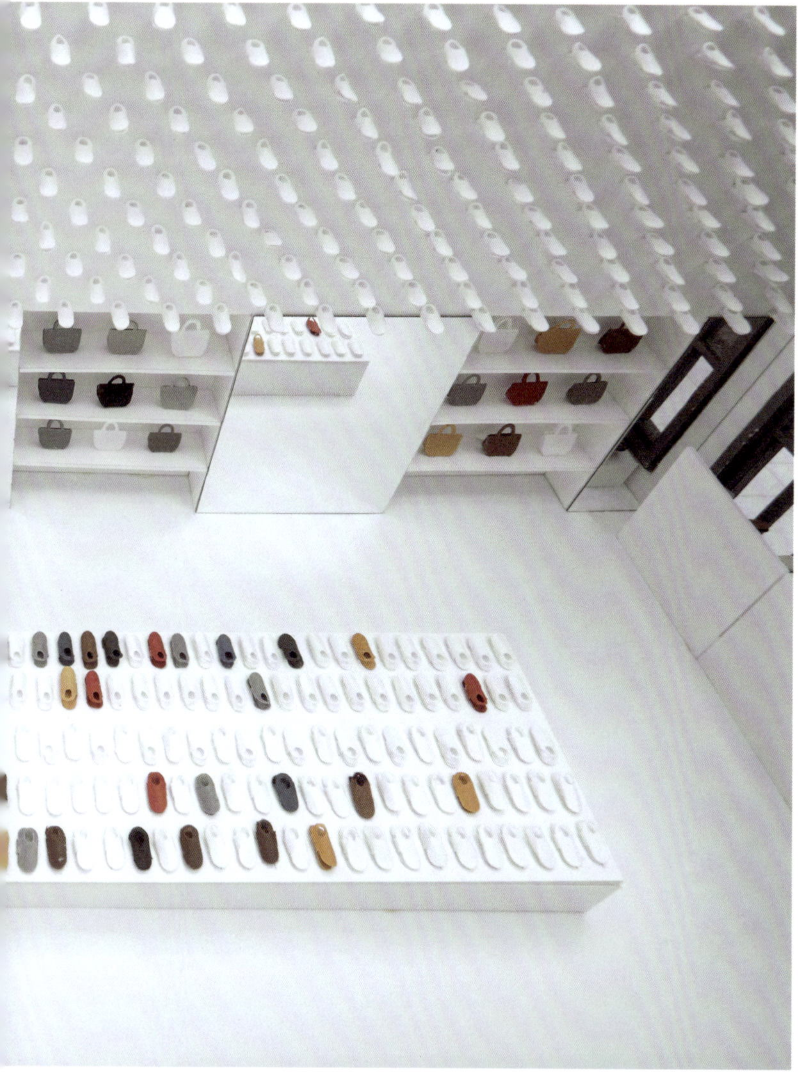

62 63

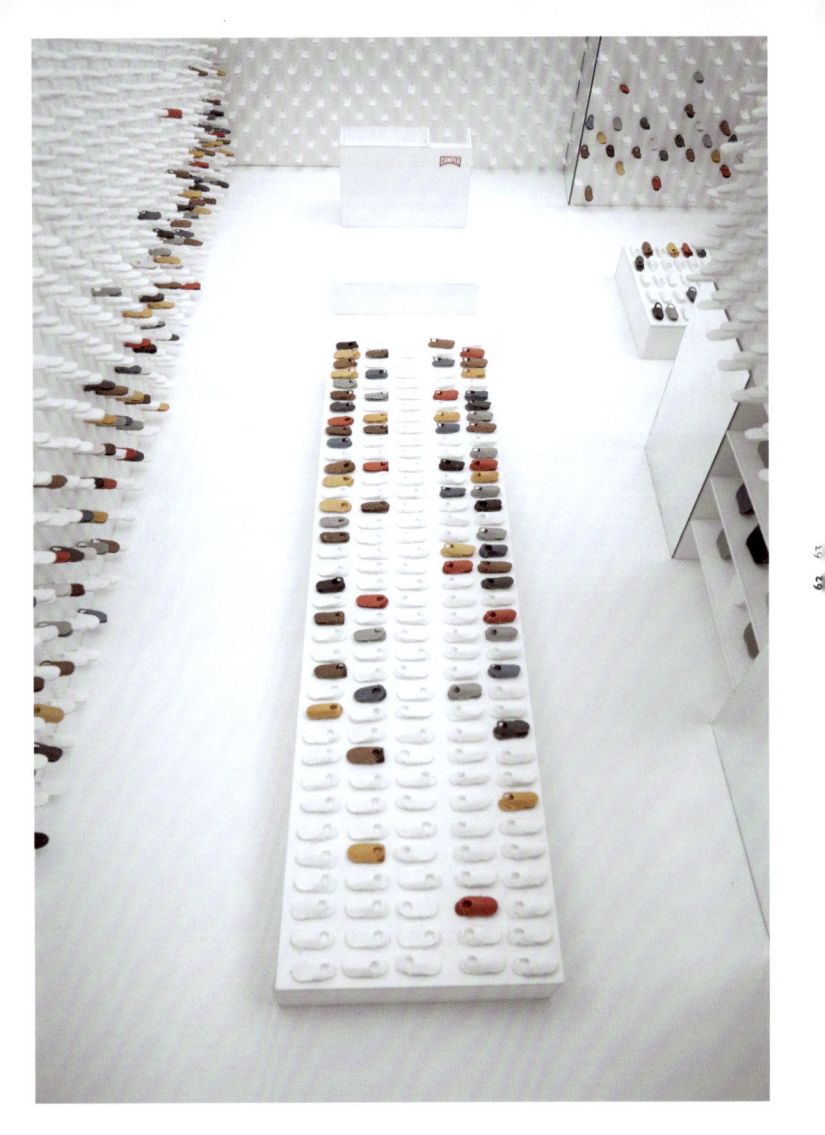

Camper New York

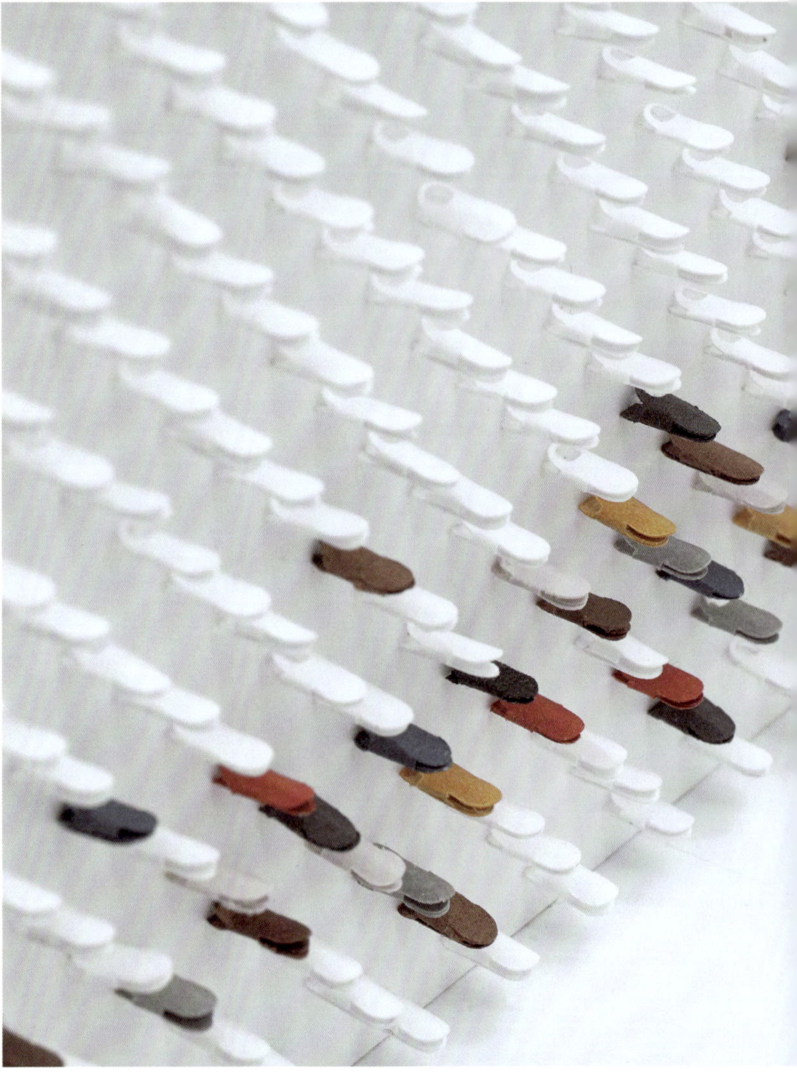

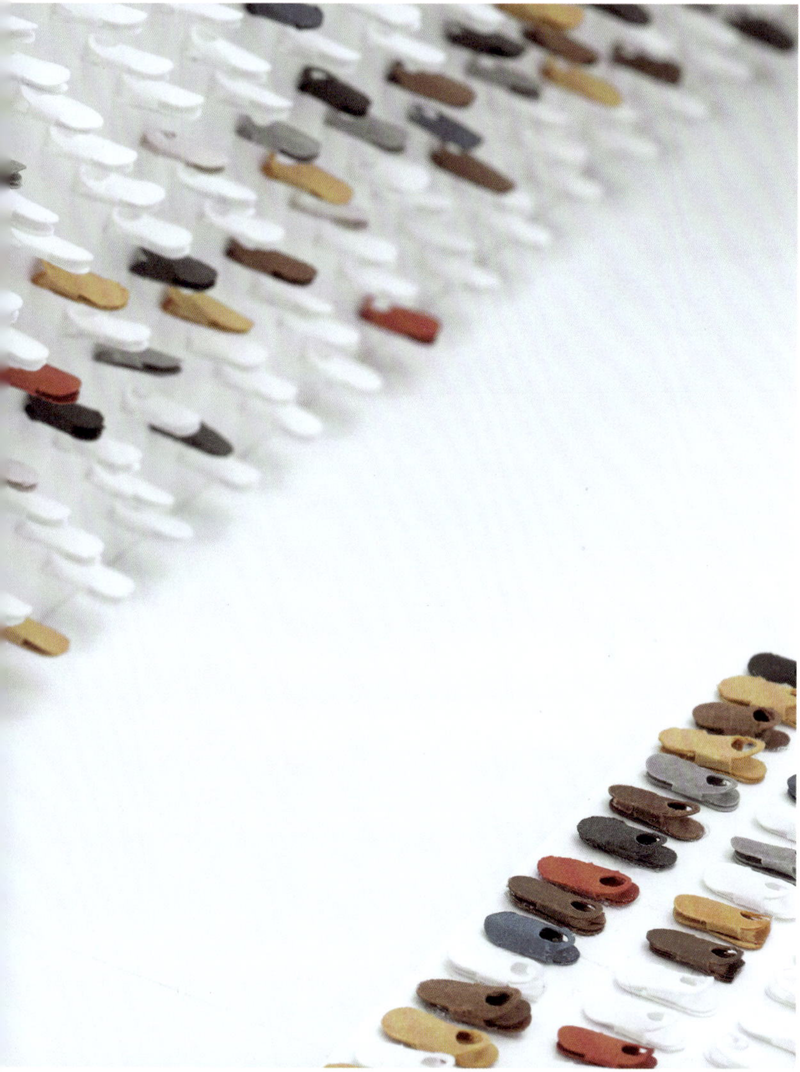

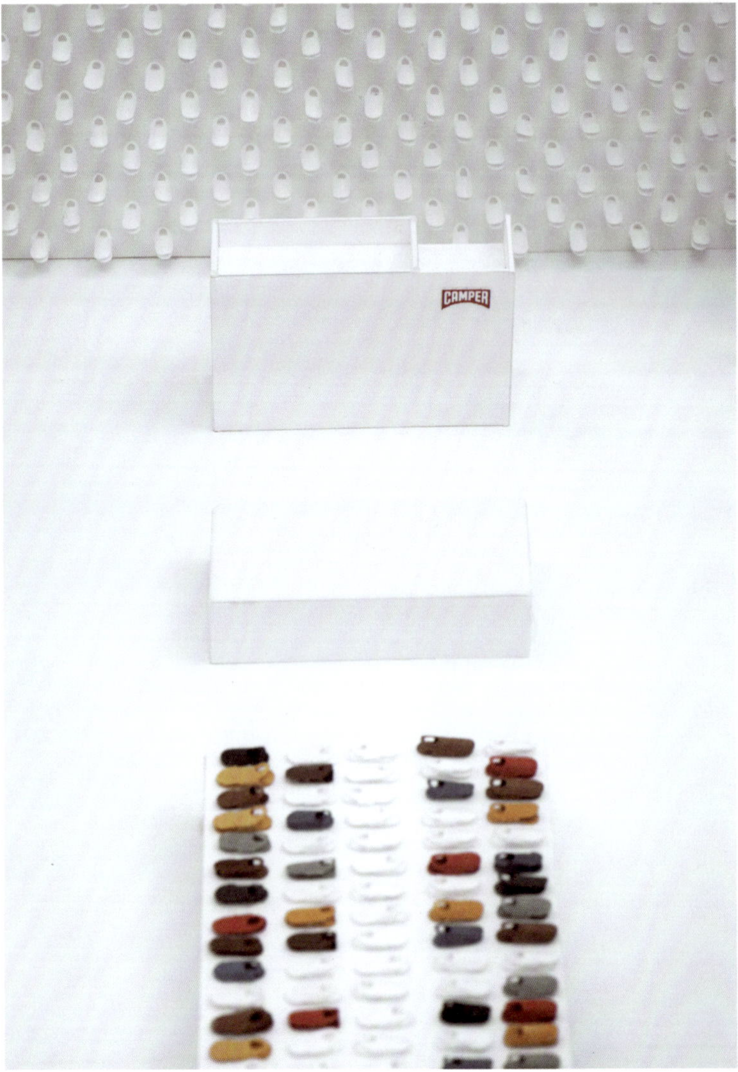
CAMPER

Camper New York

Camper Paris

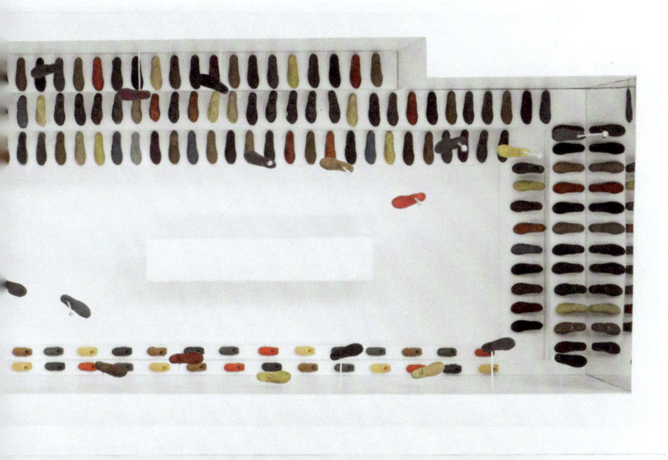

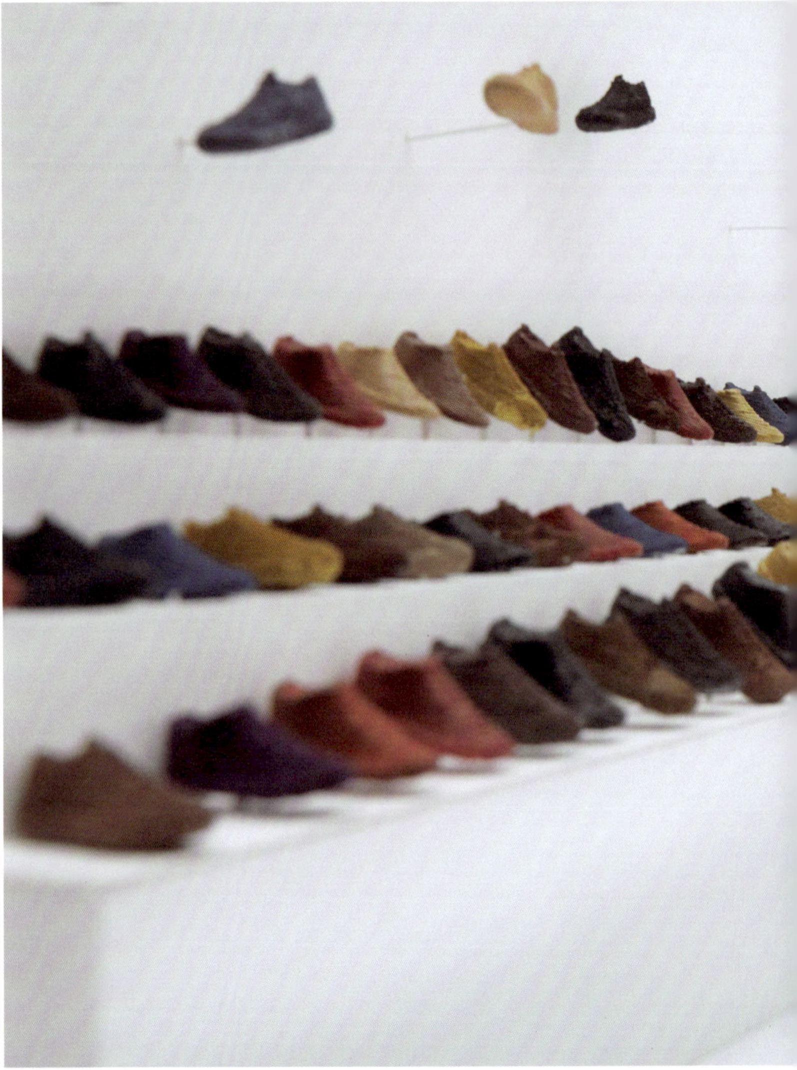

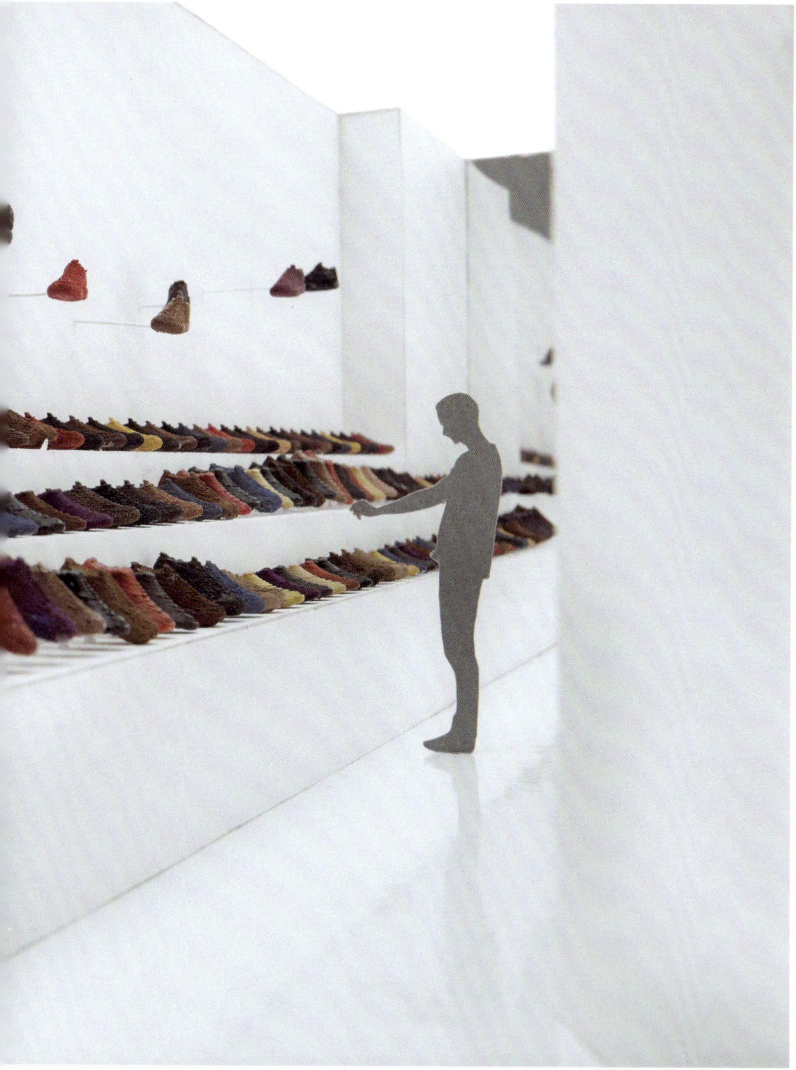

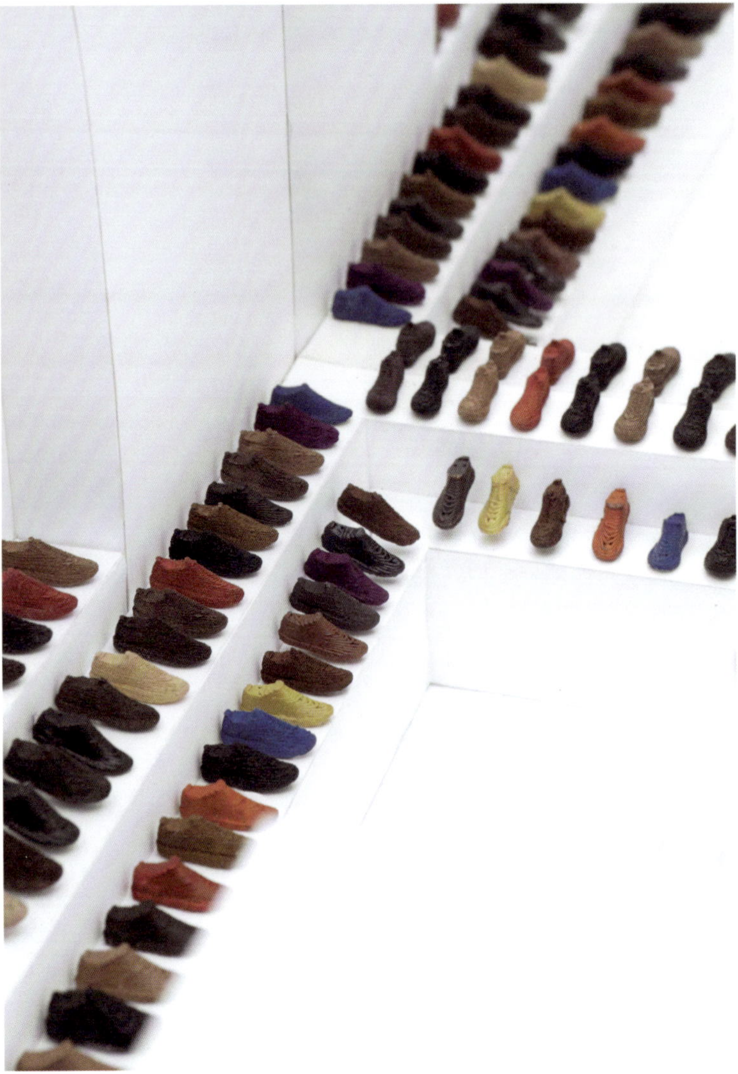

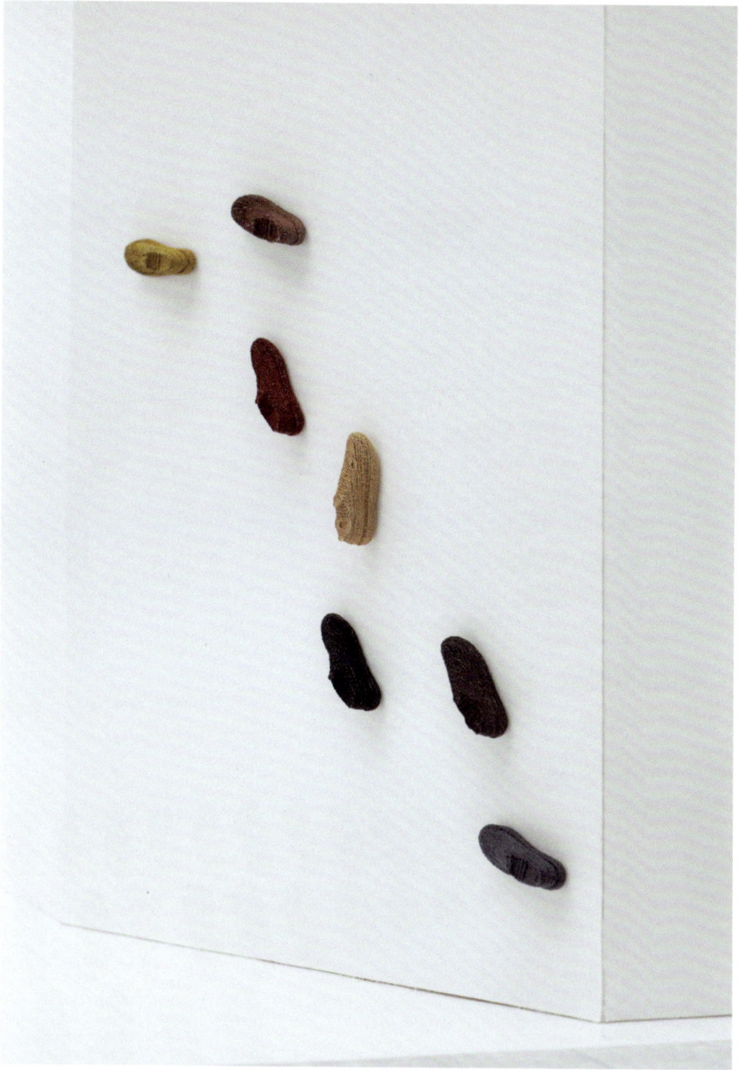

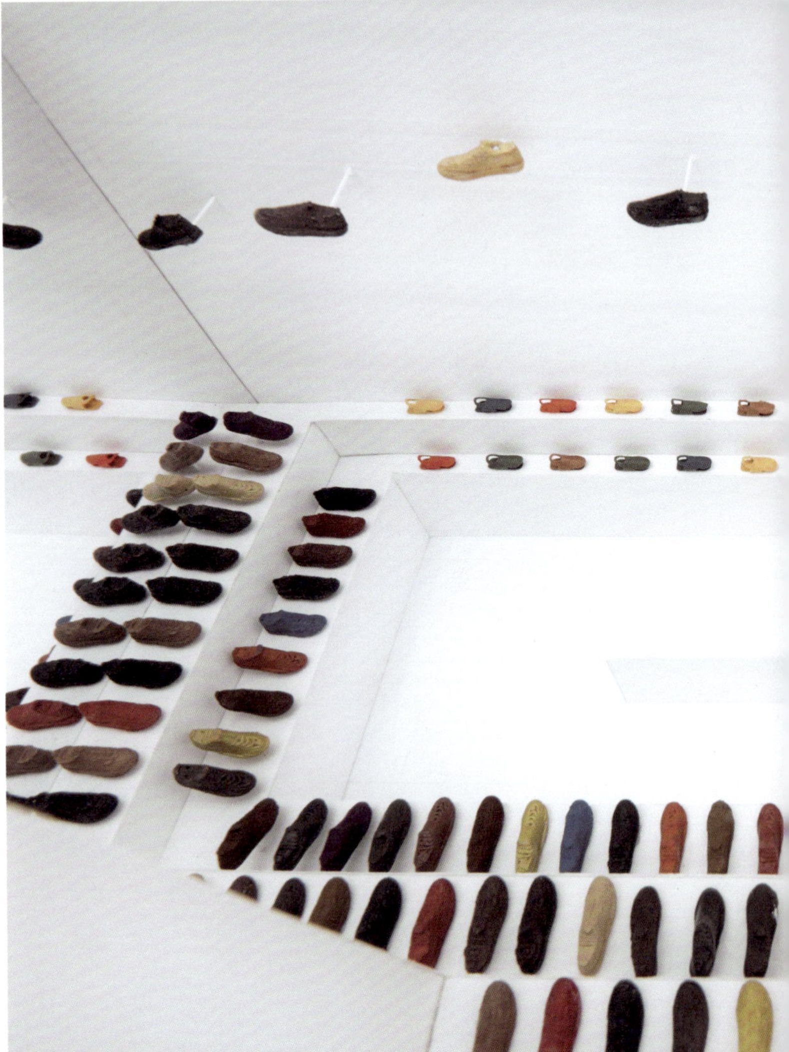

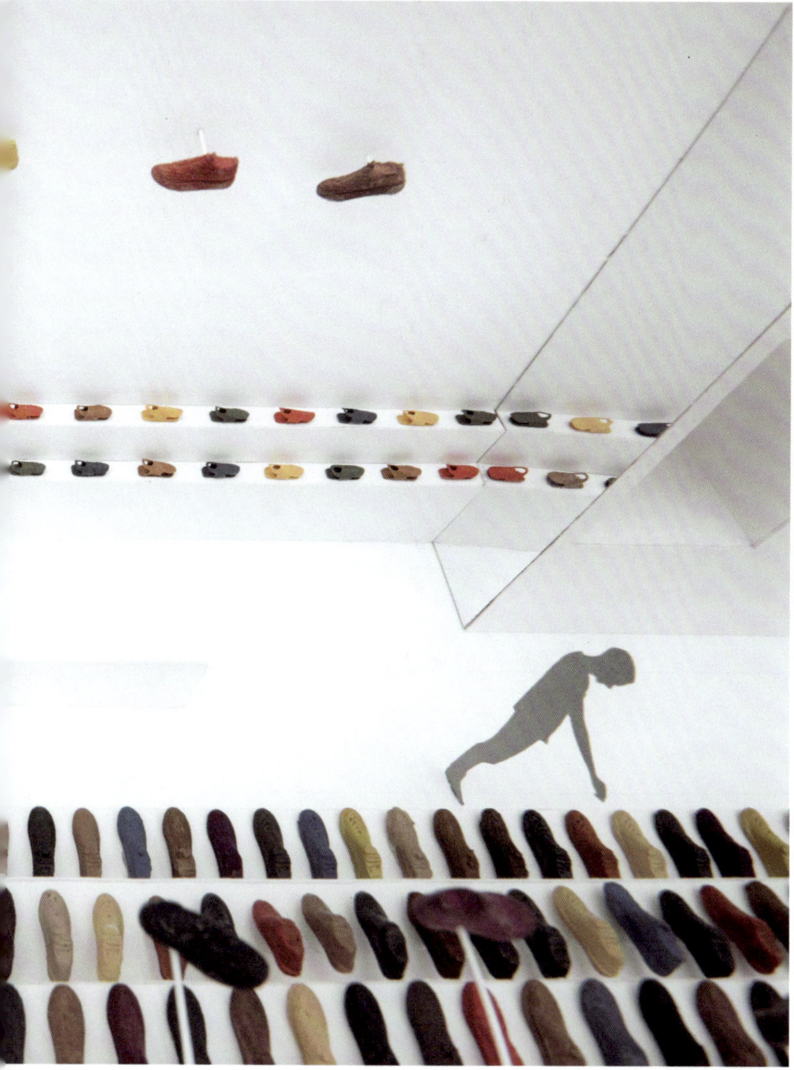

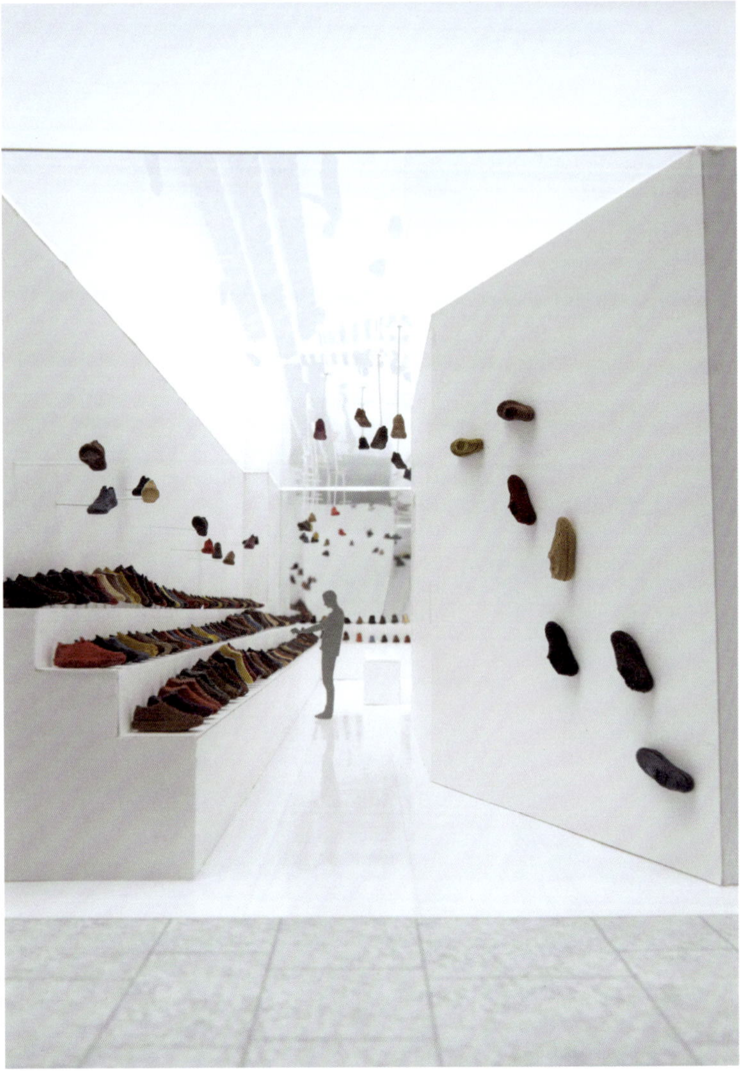

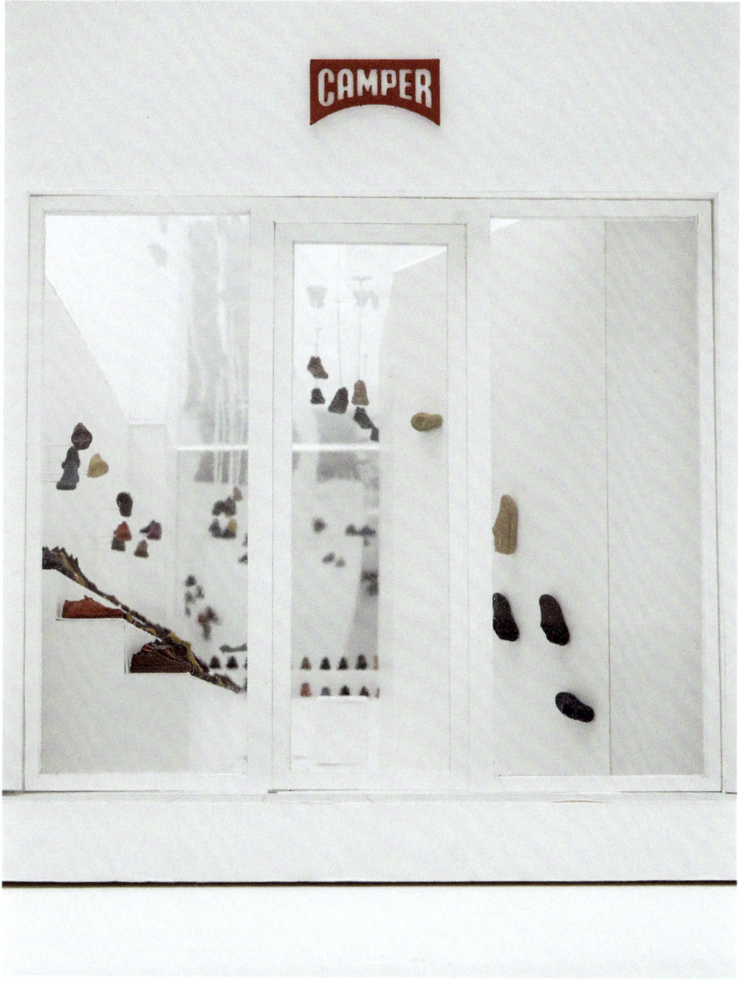
CAMPER

CATALOG Beijing

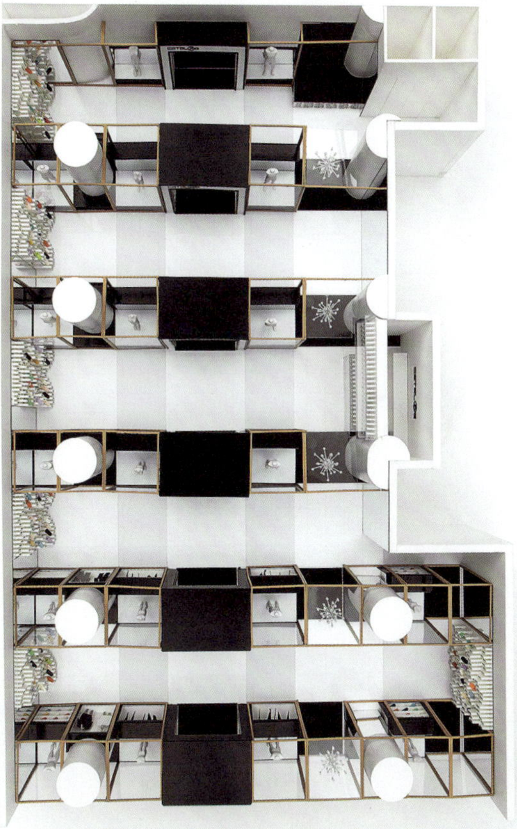

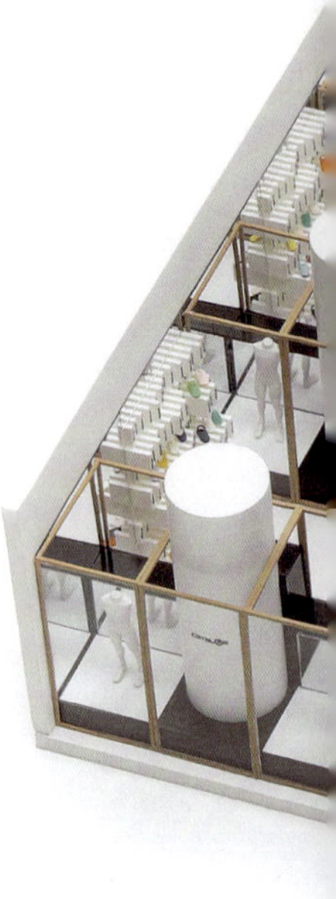

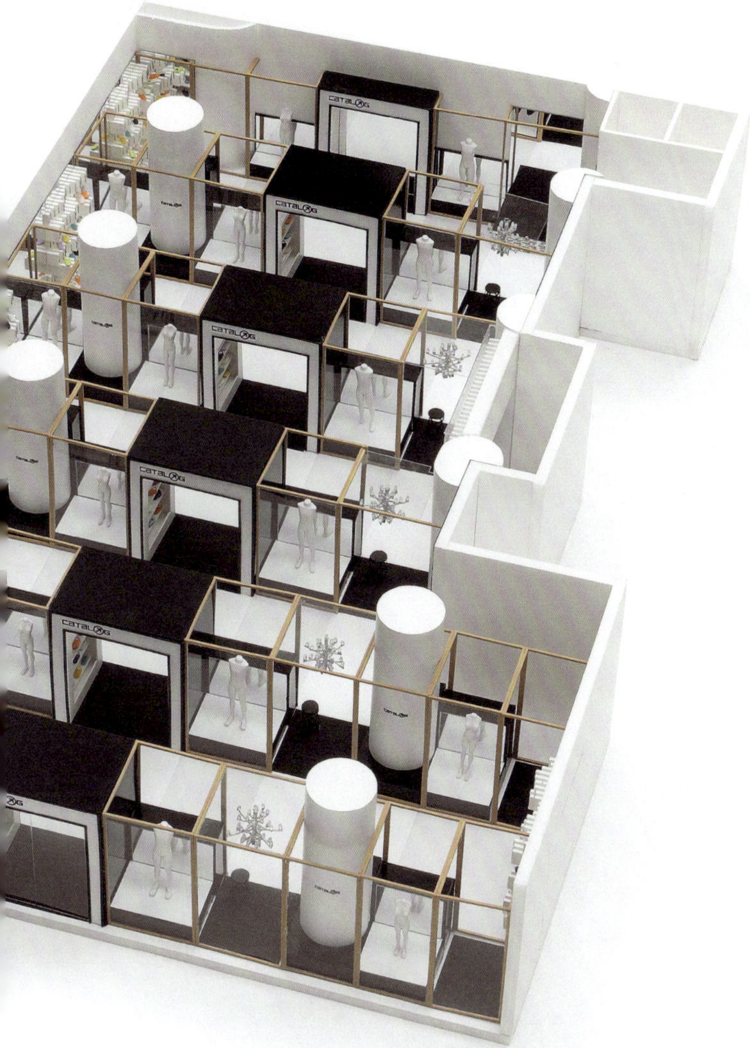

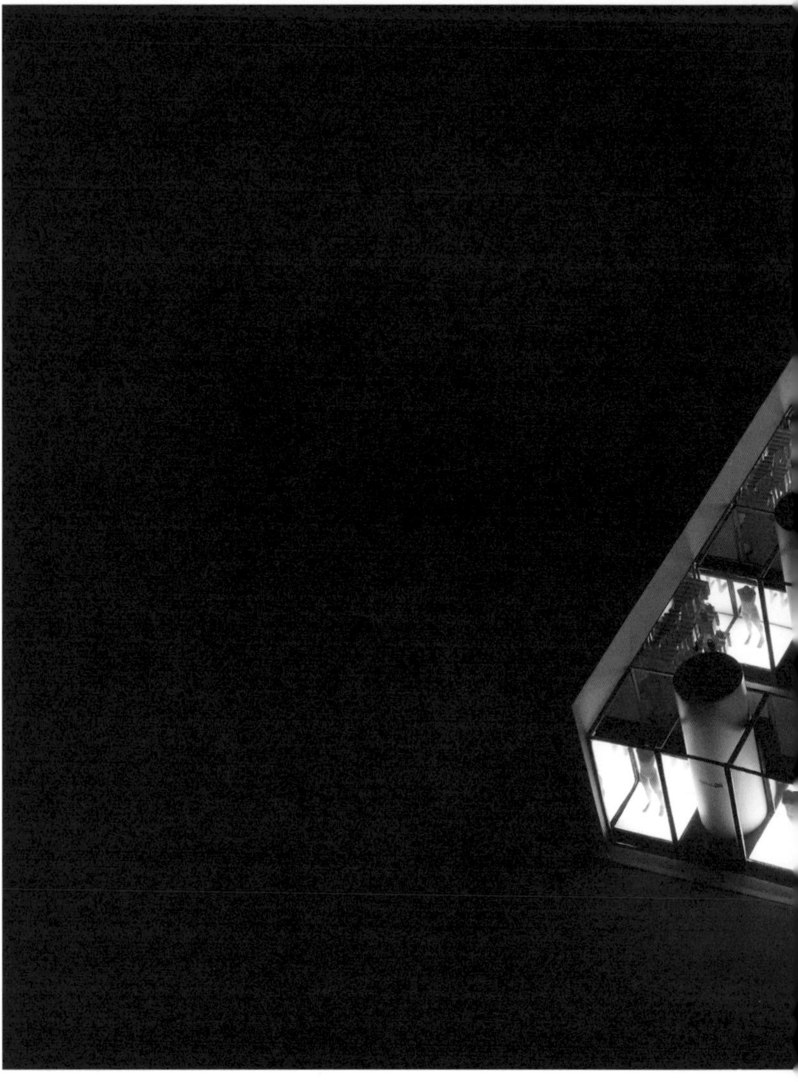

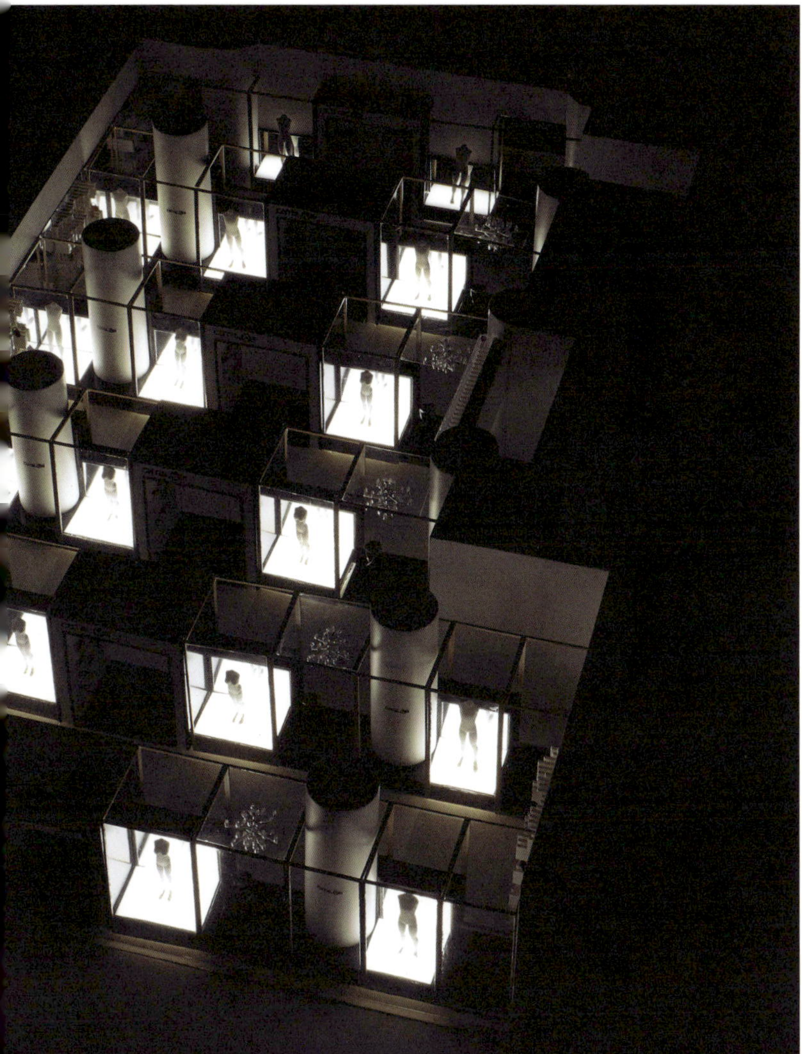

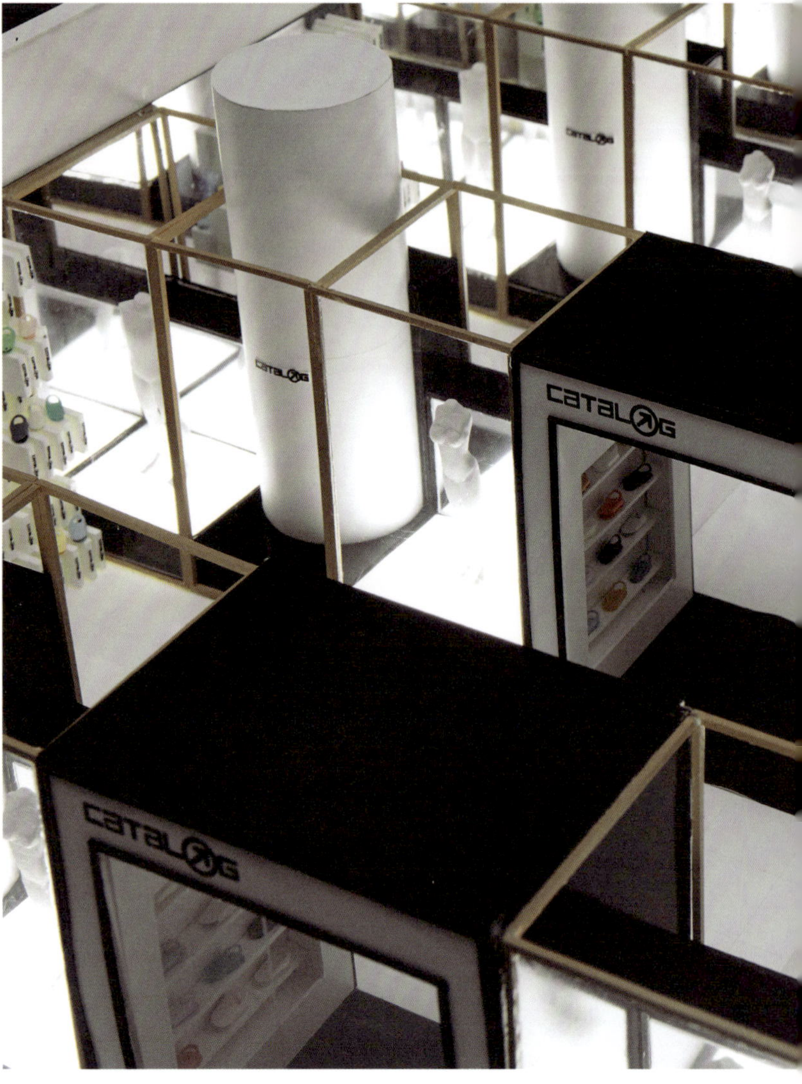
catalog

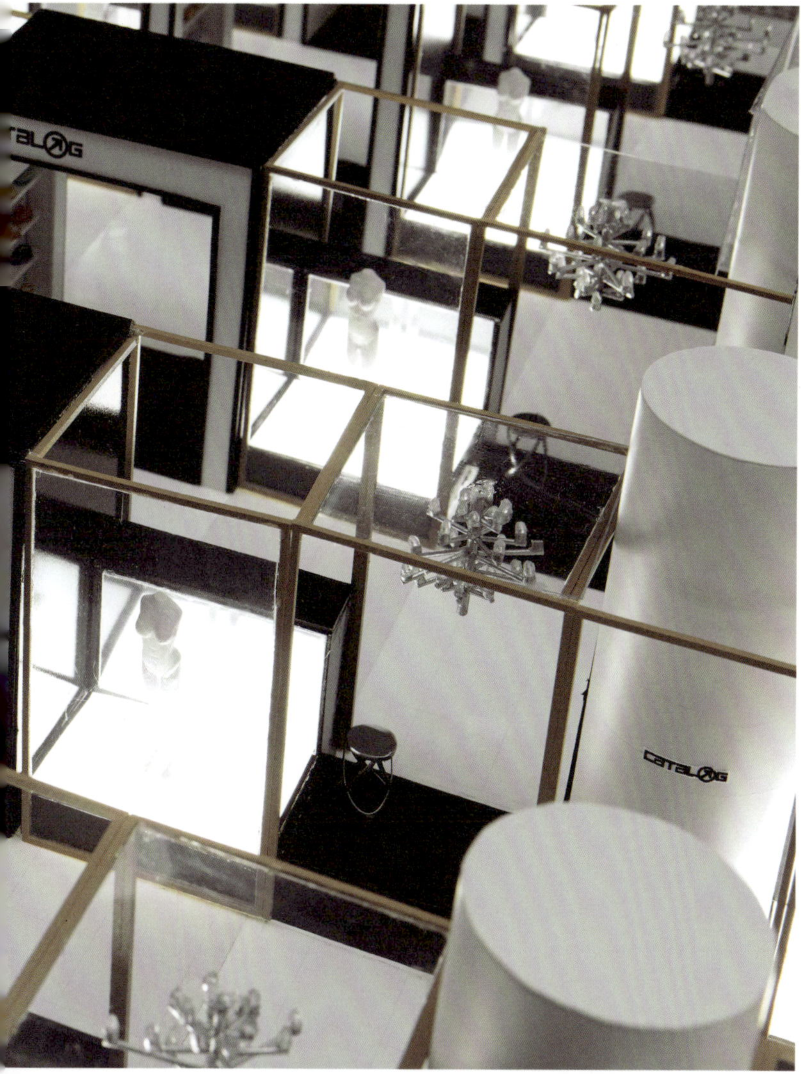
catalog

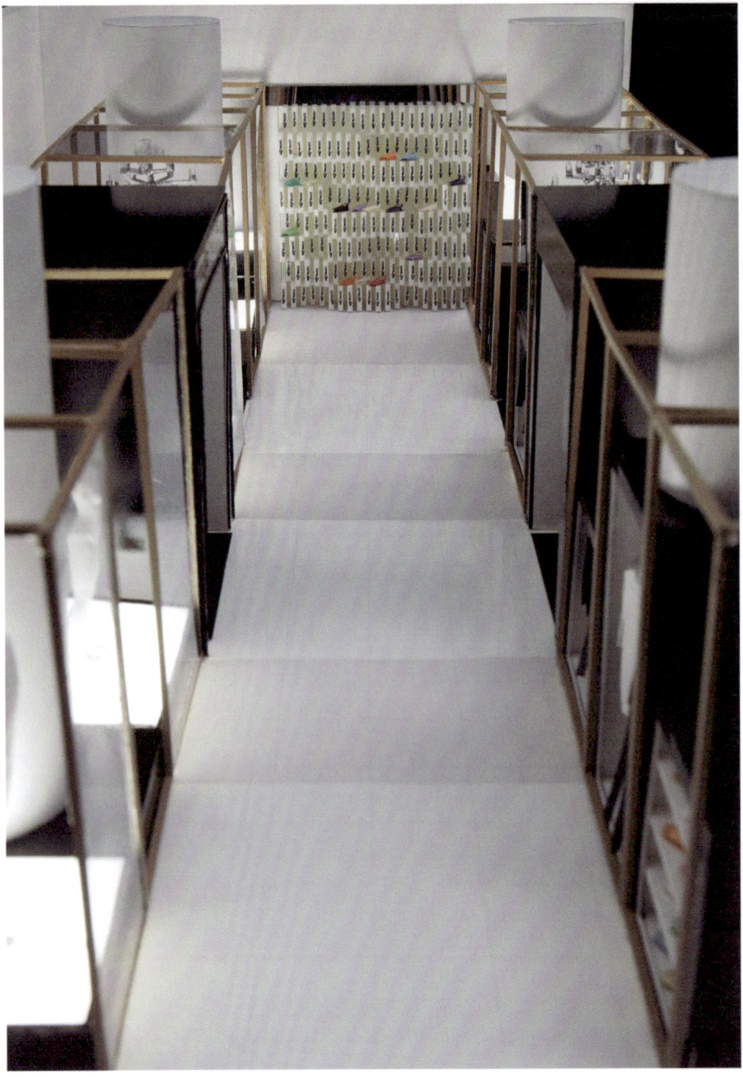

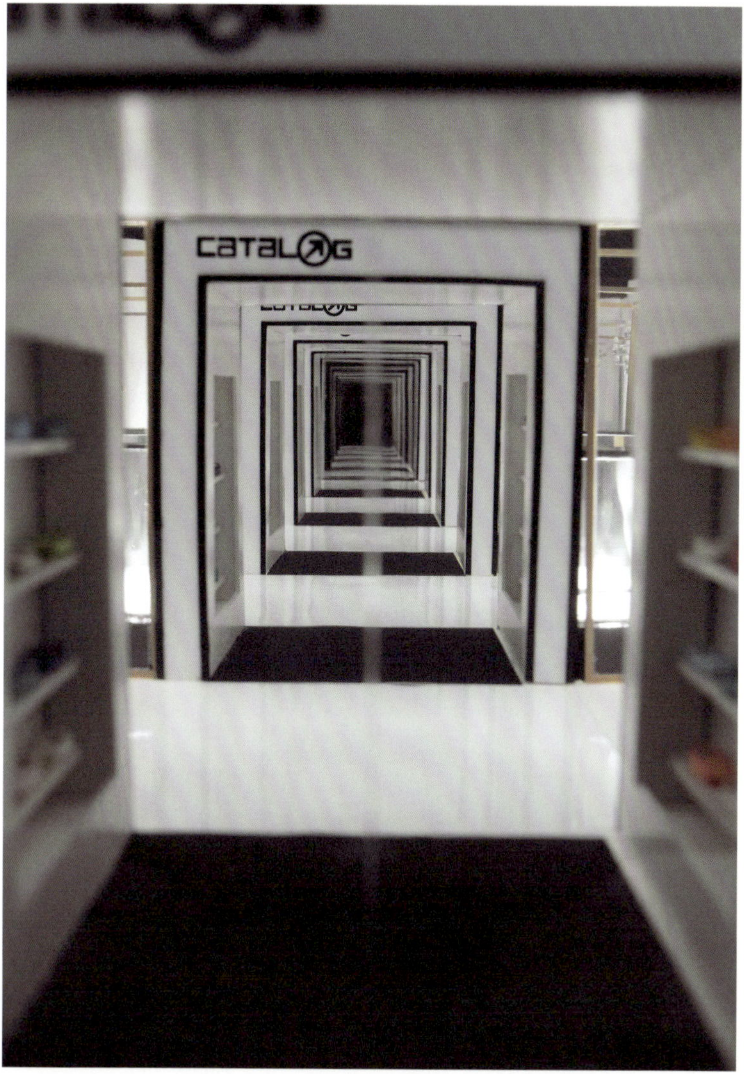
CATALOG

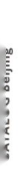

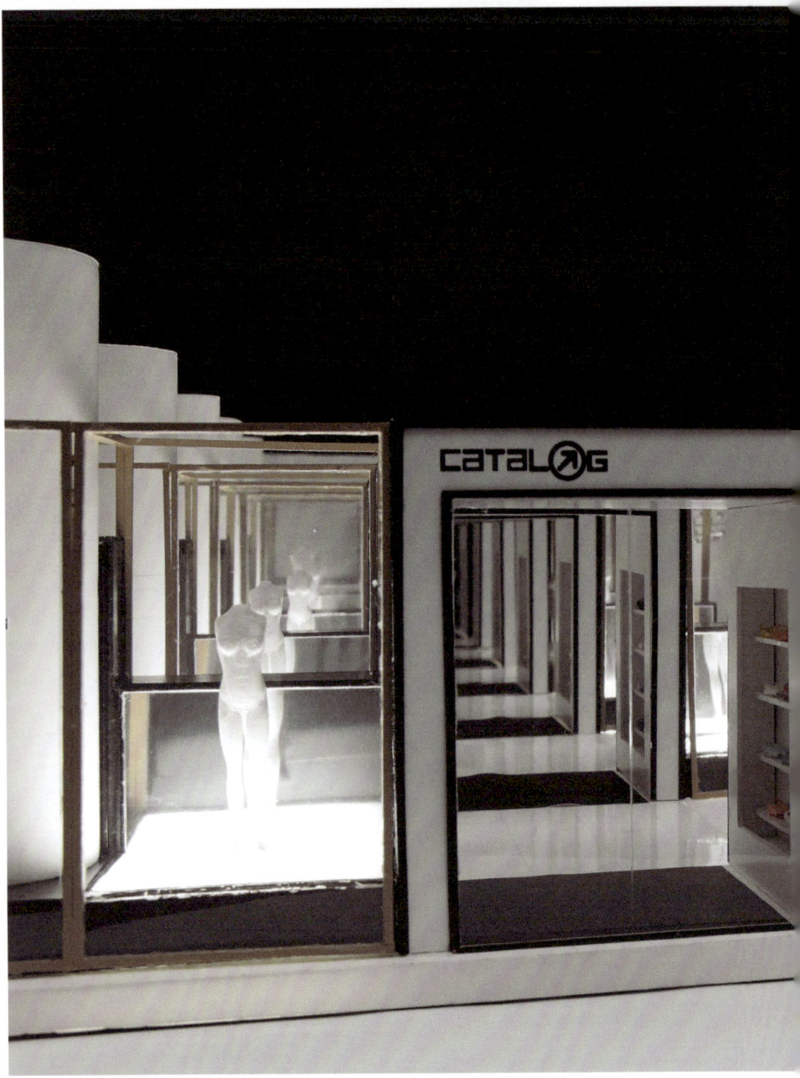
CATALOG

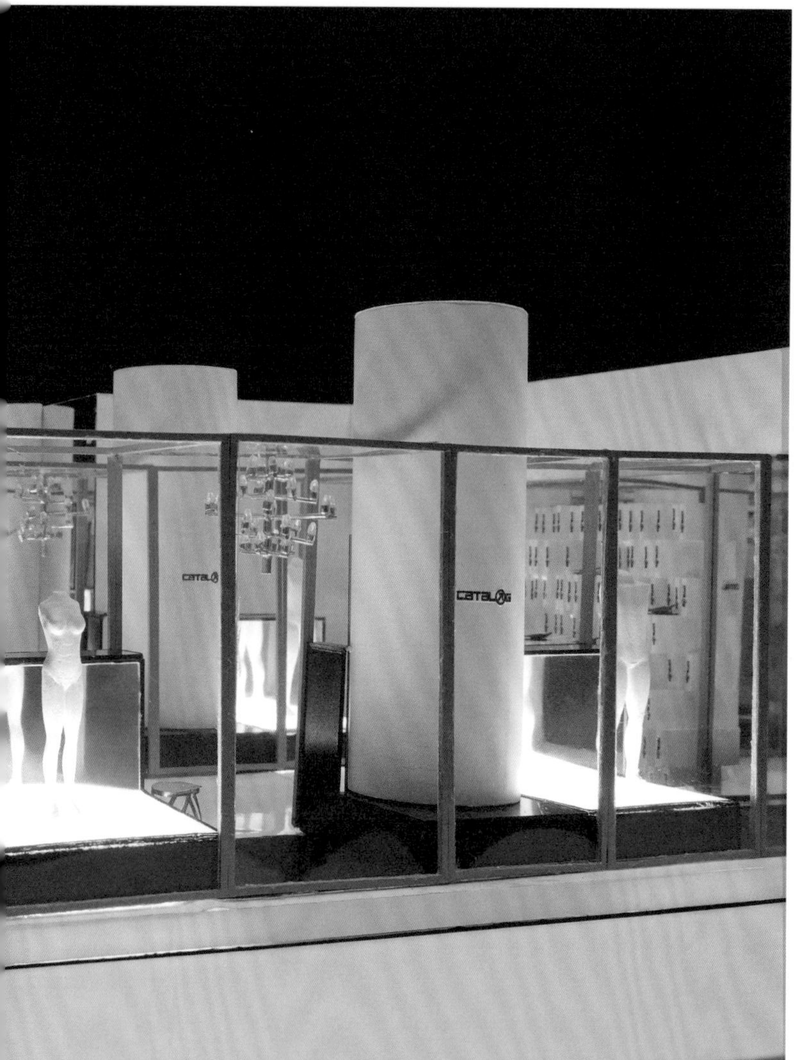

COMPOLUX

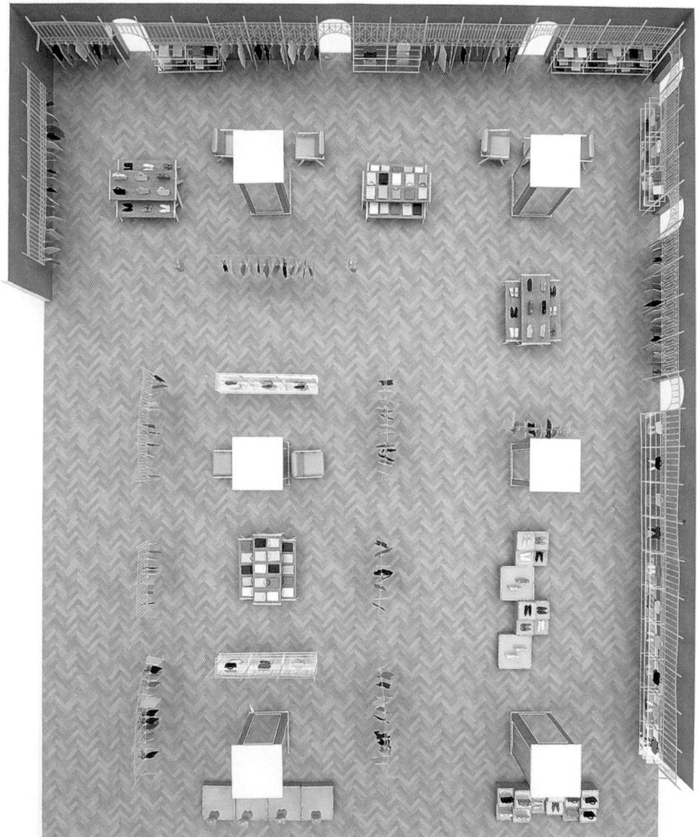

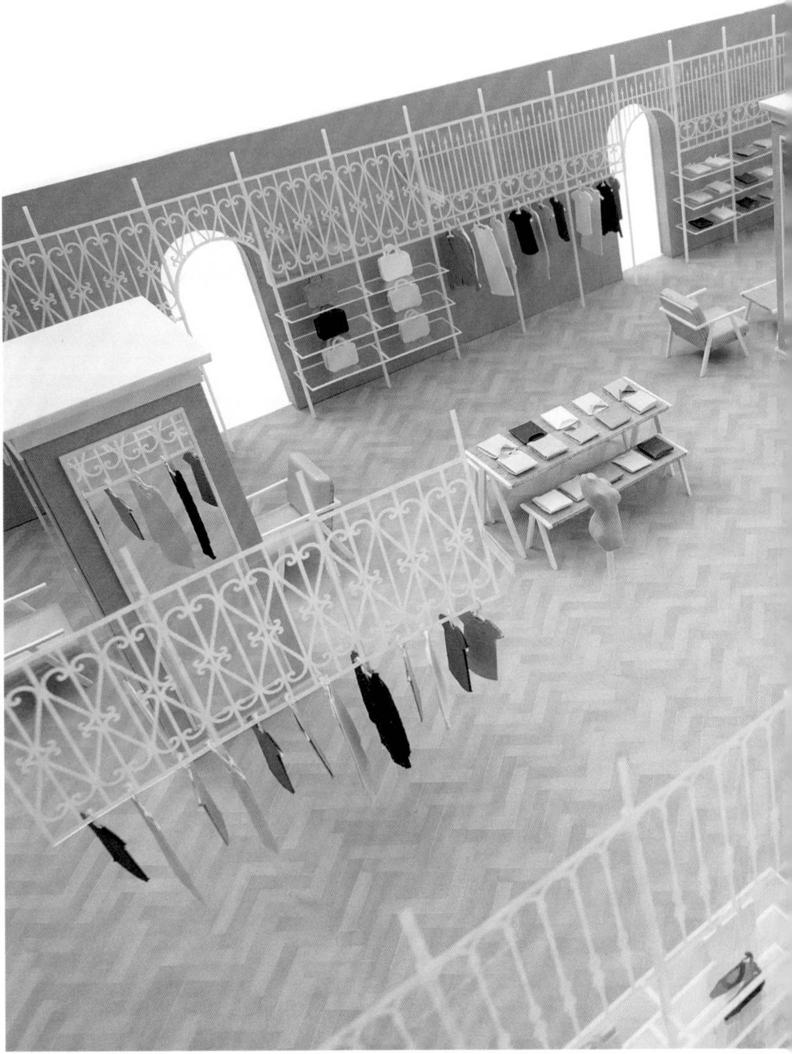

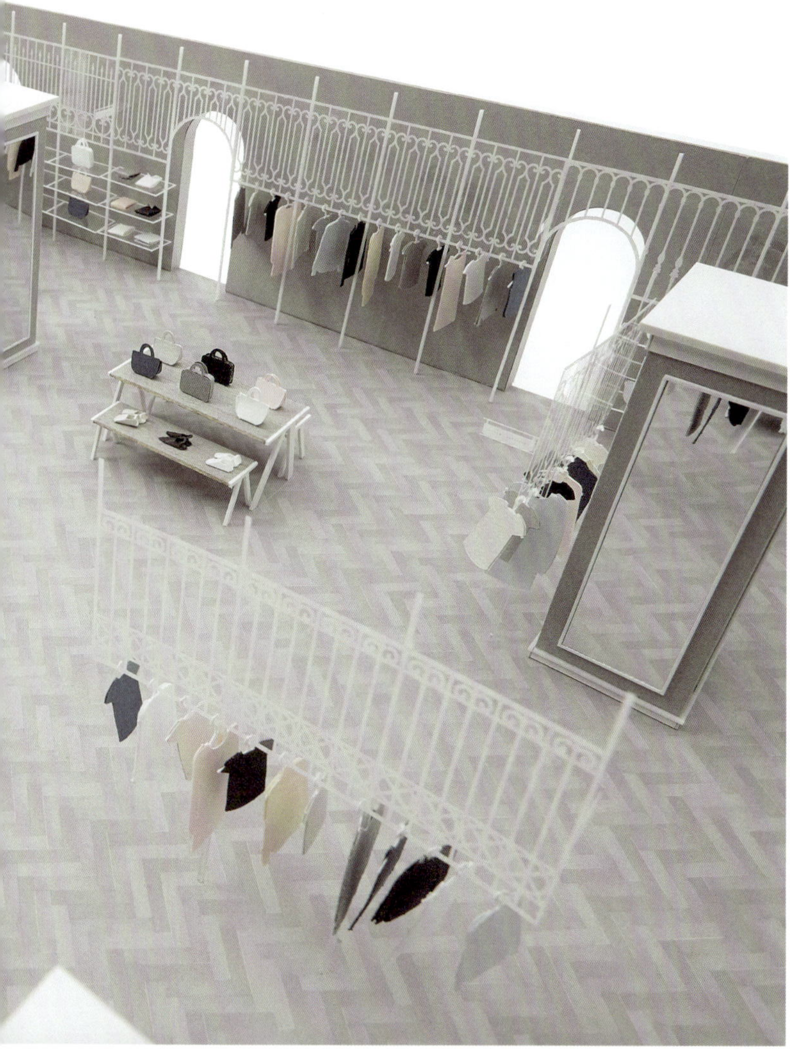

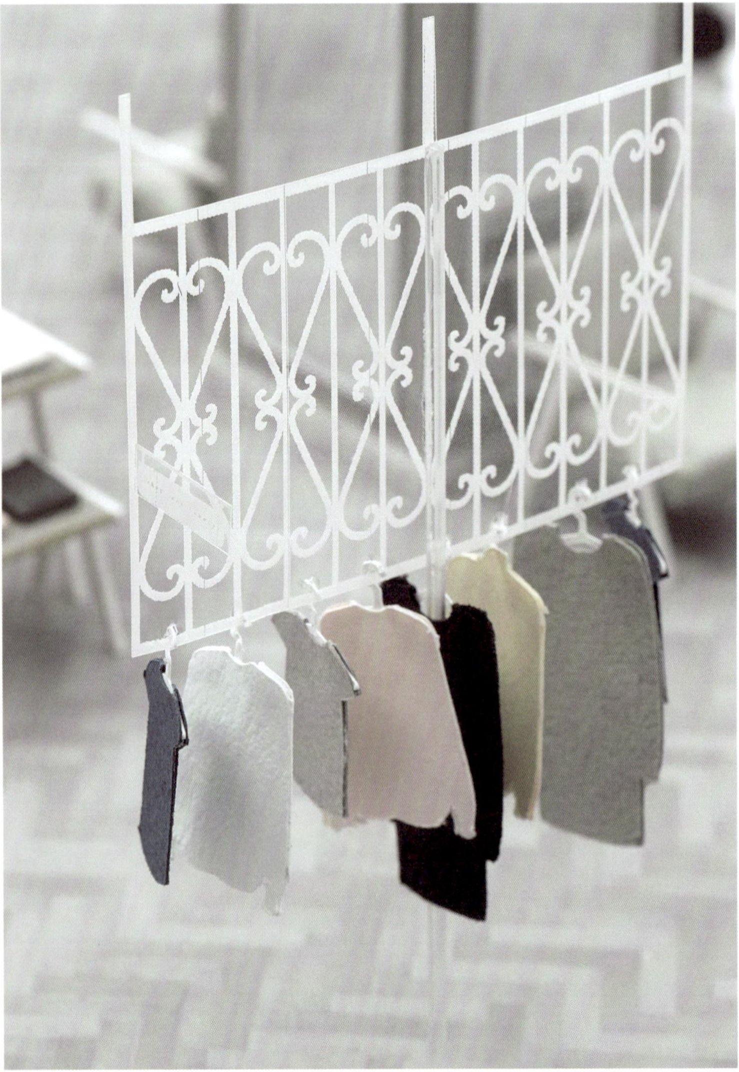

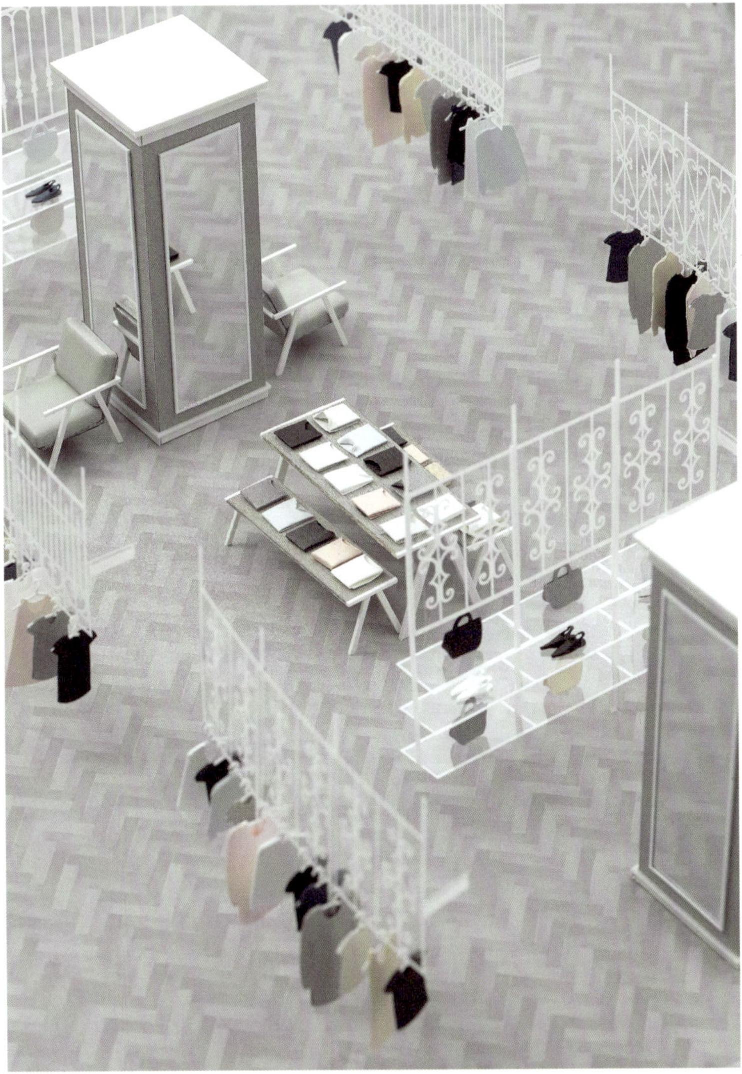

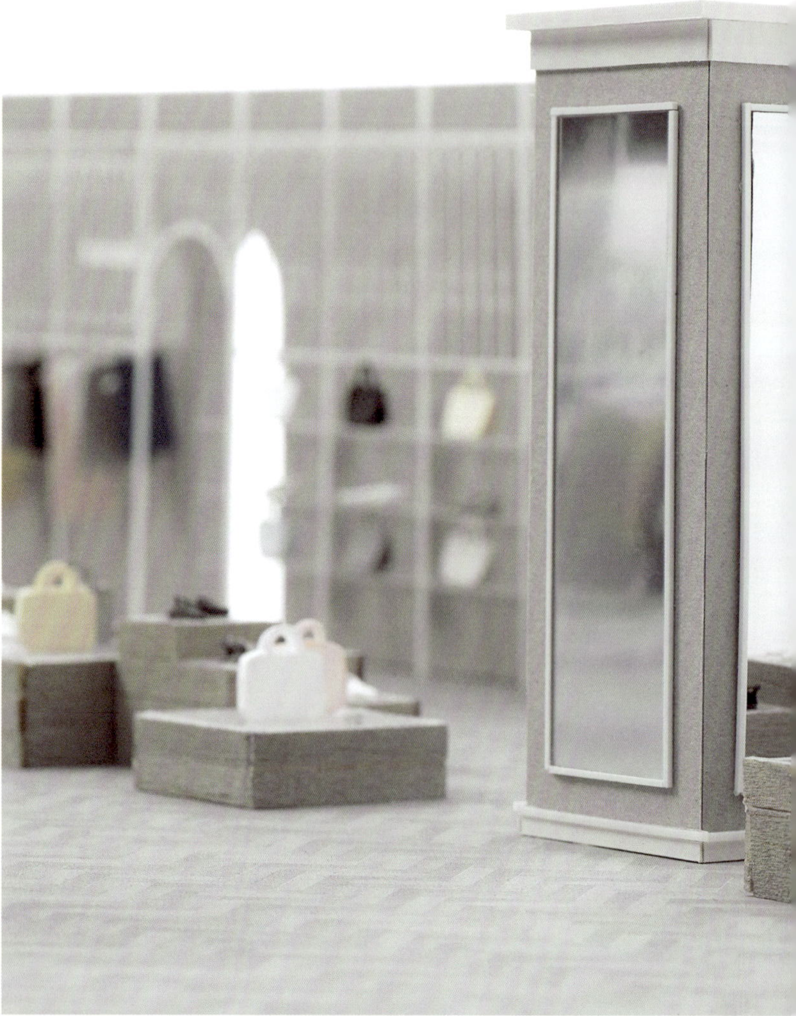

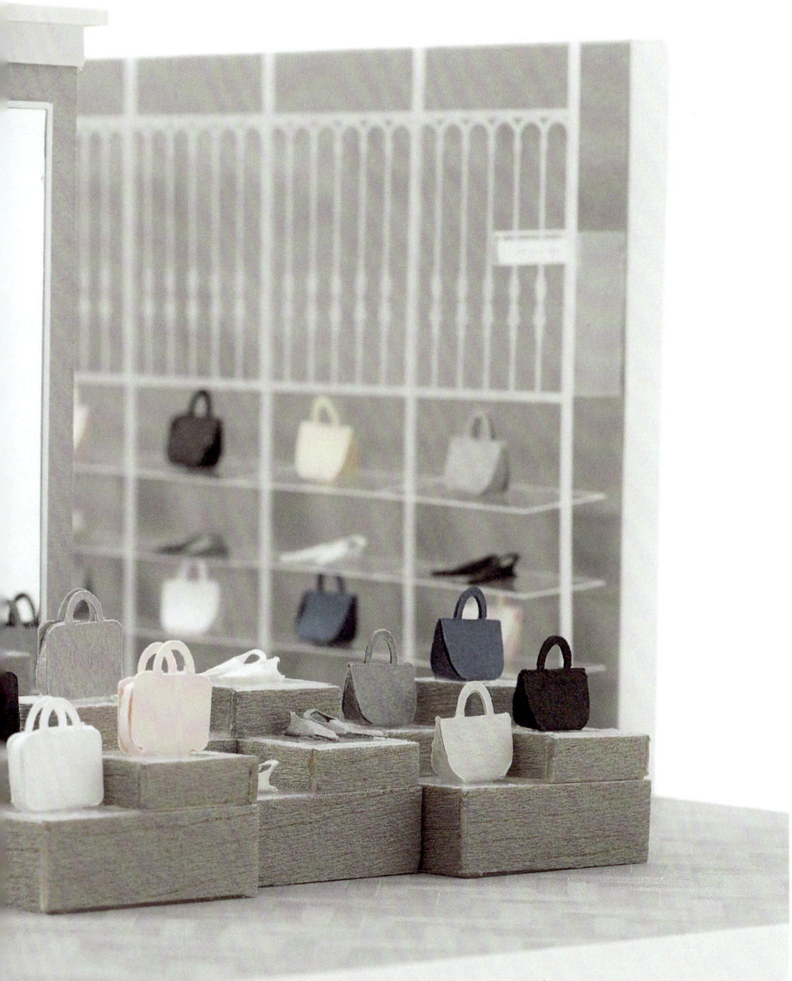

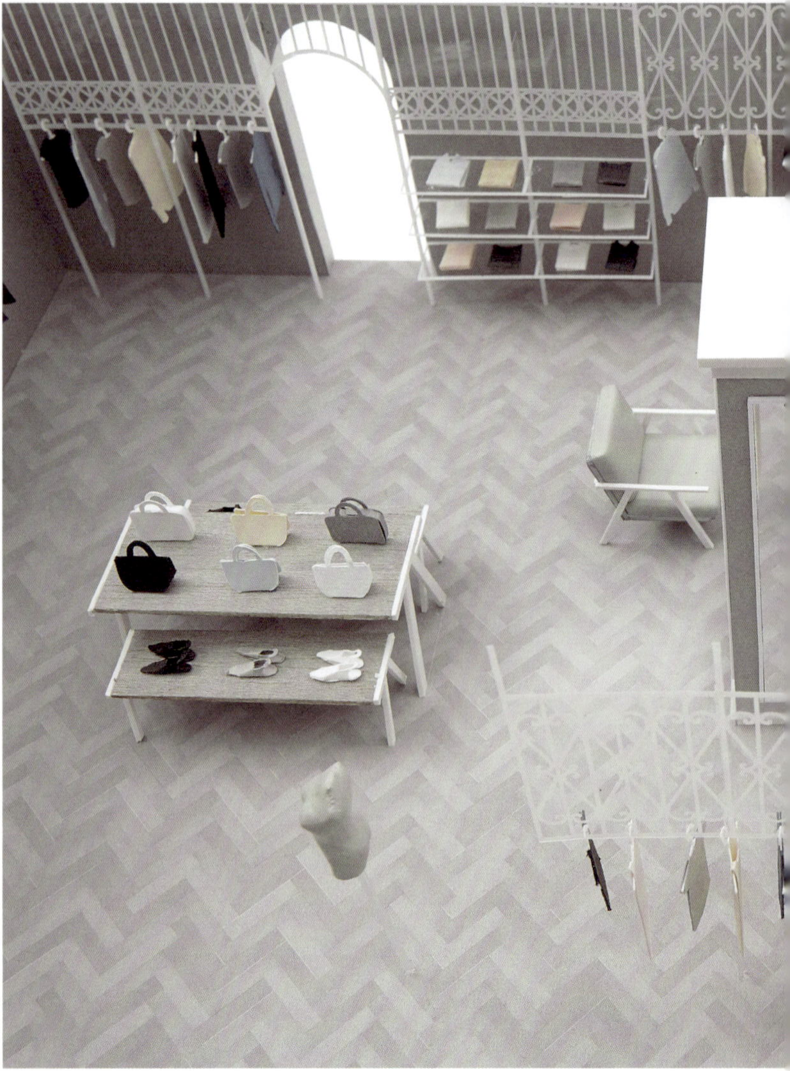

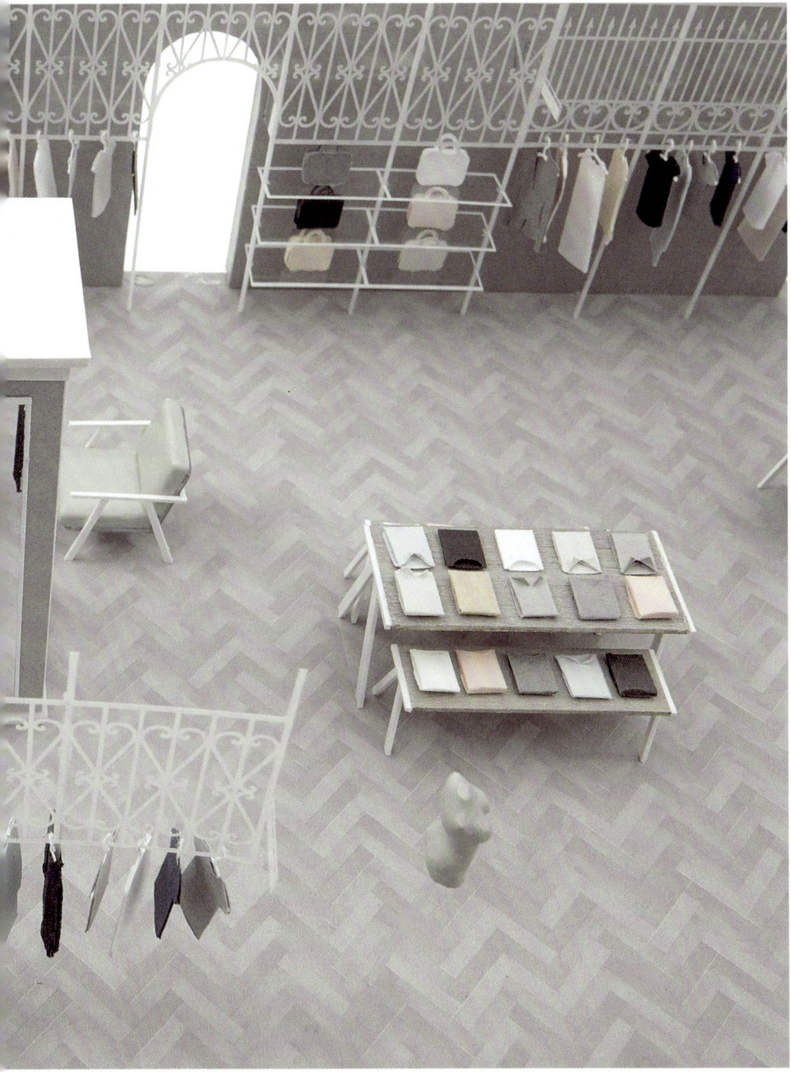

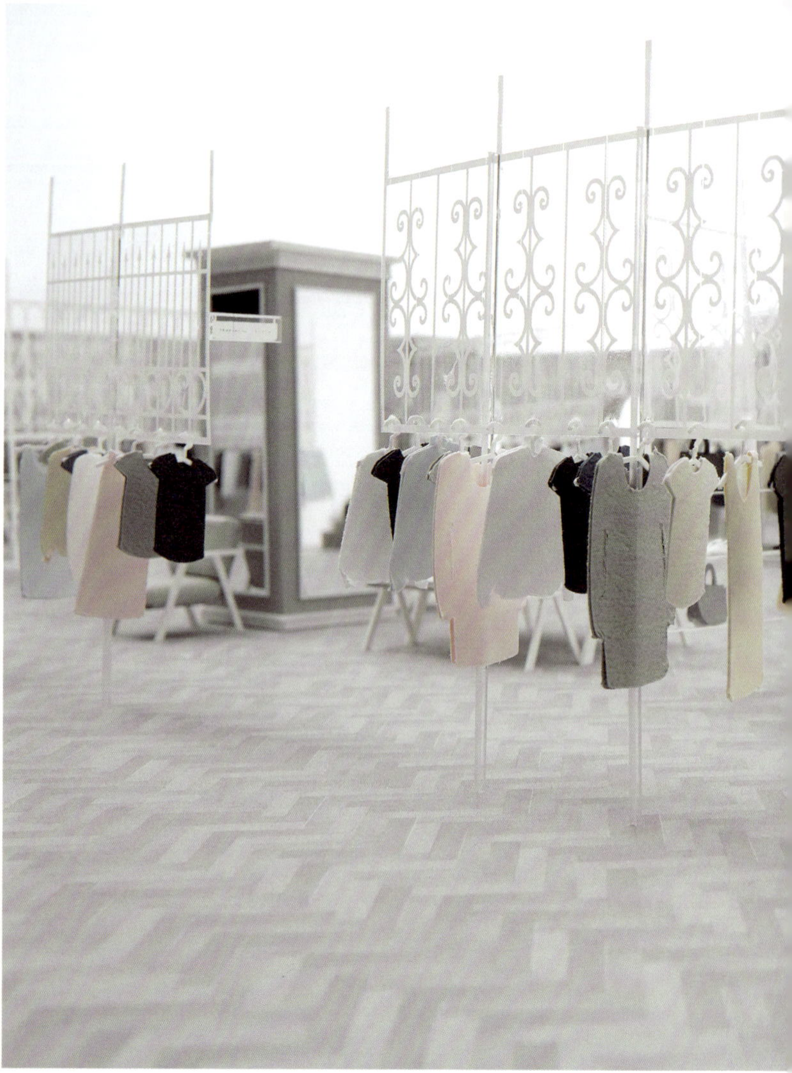

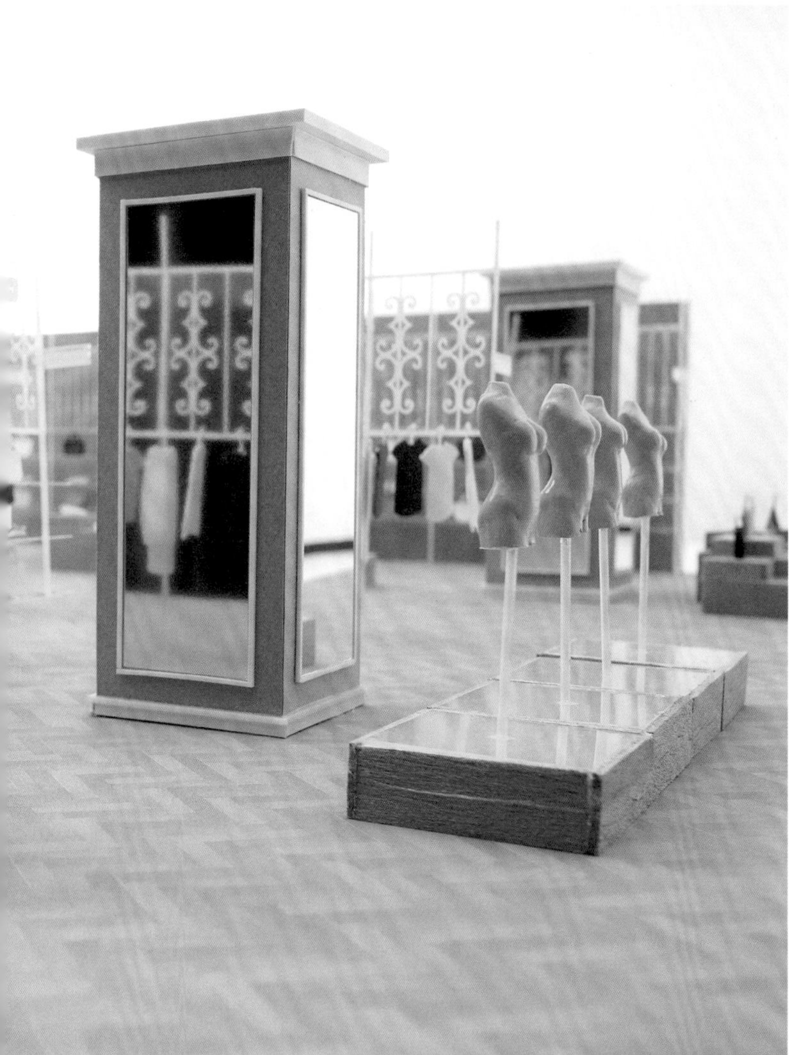

Established & Sons@LDF

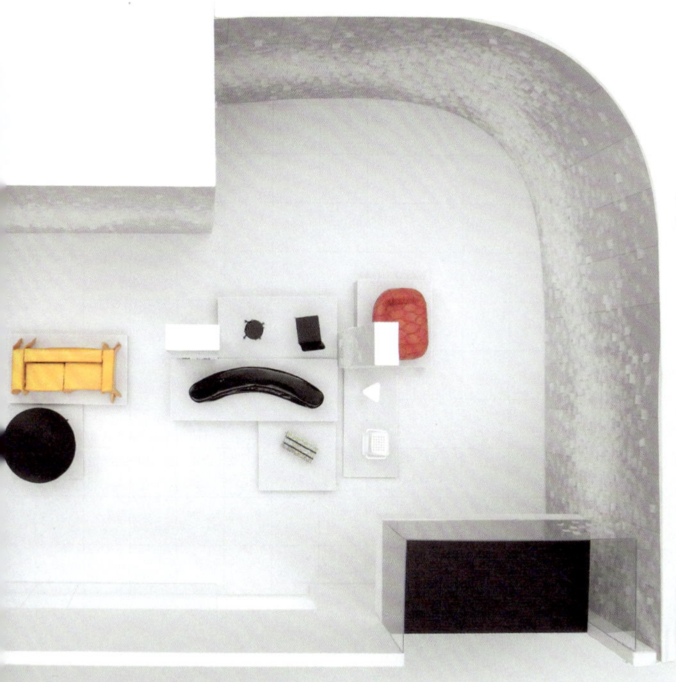

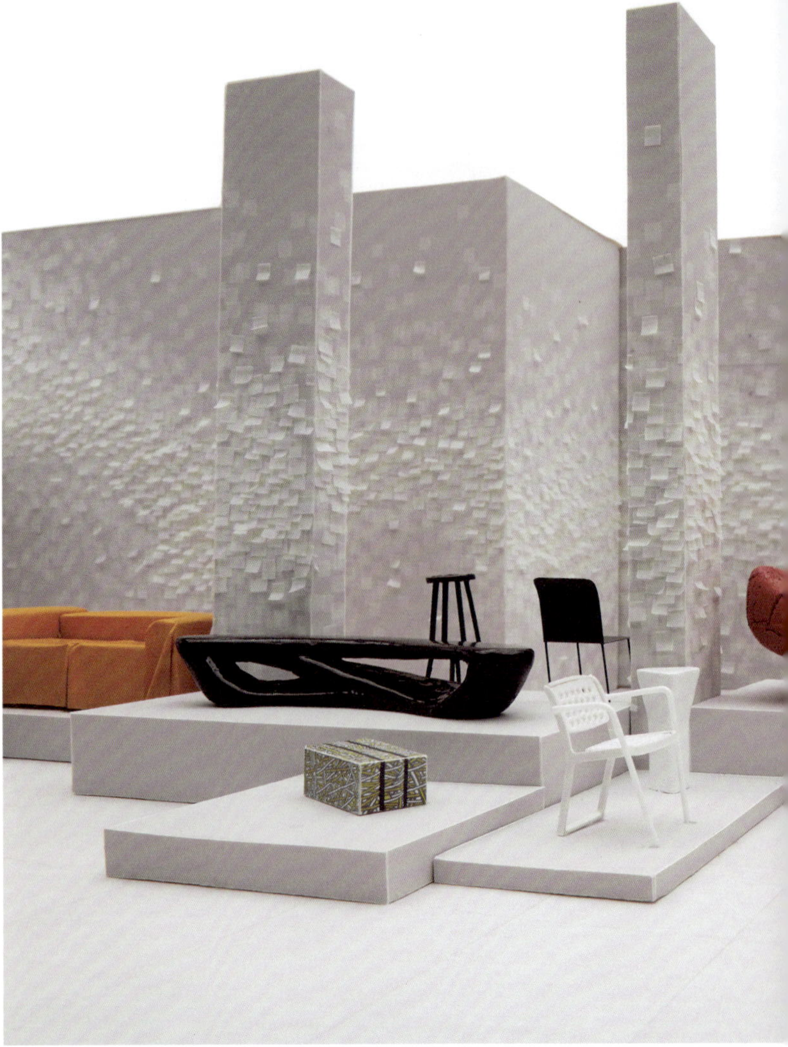

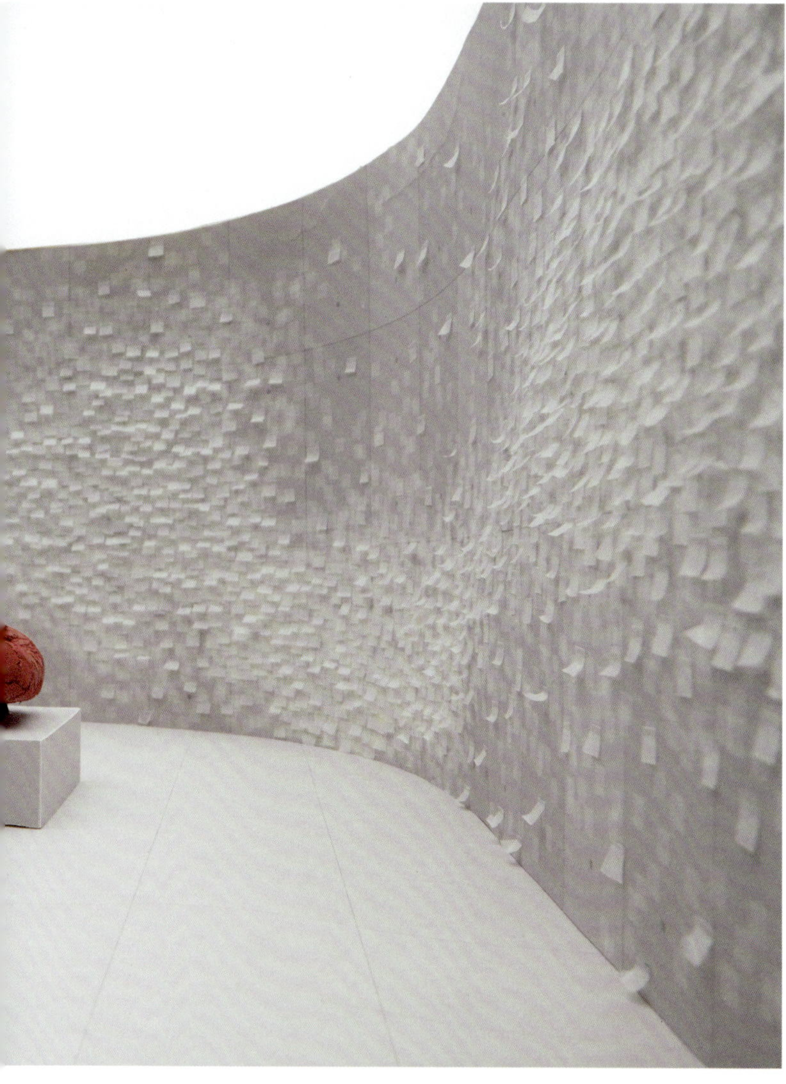

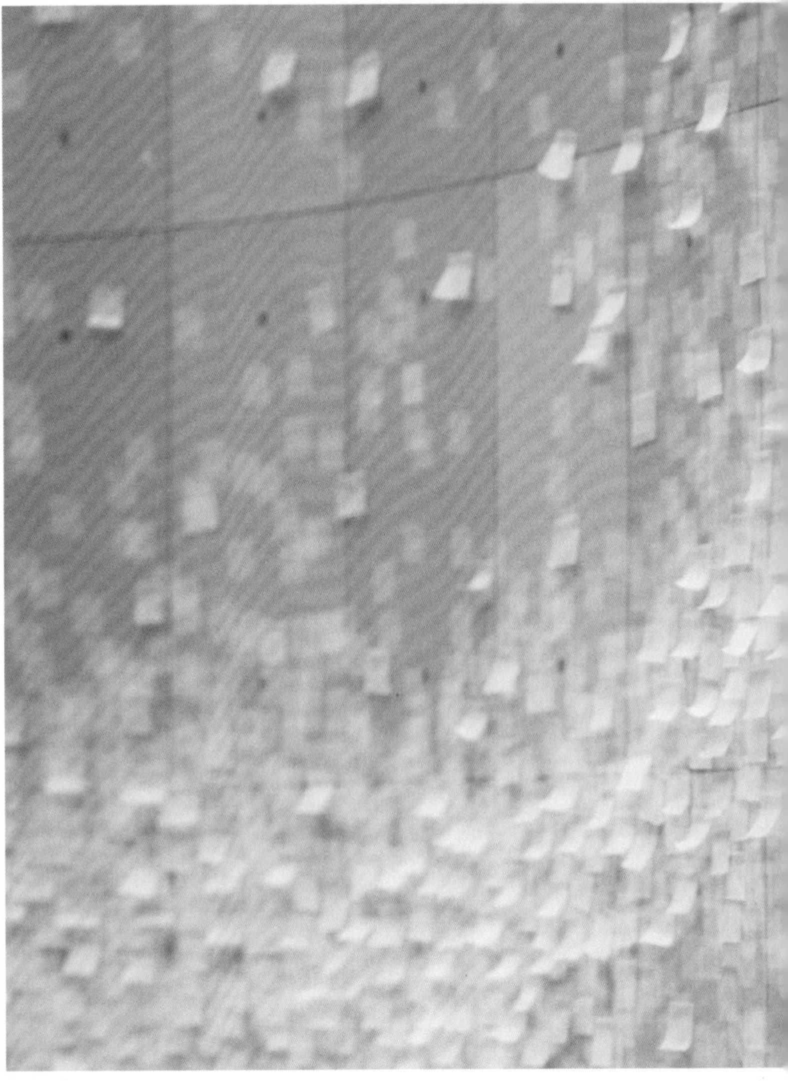

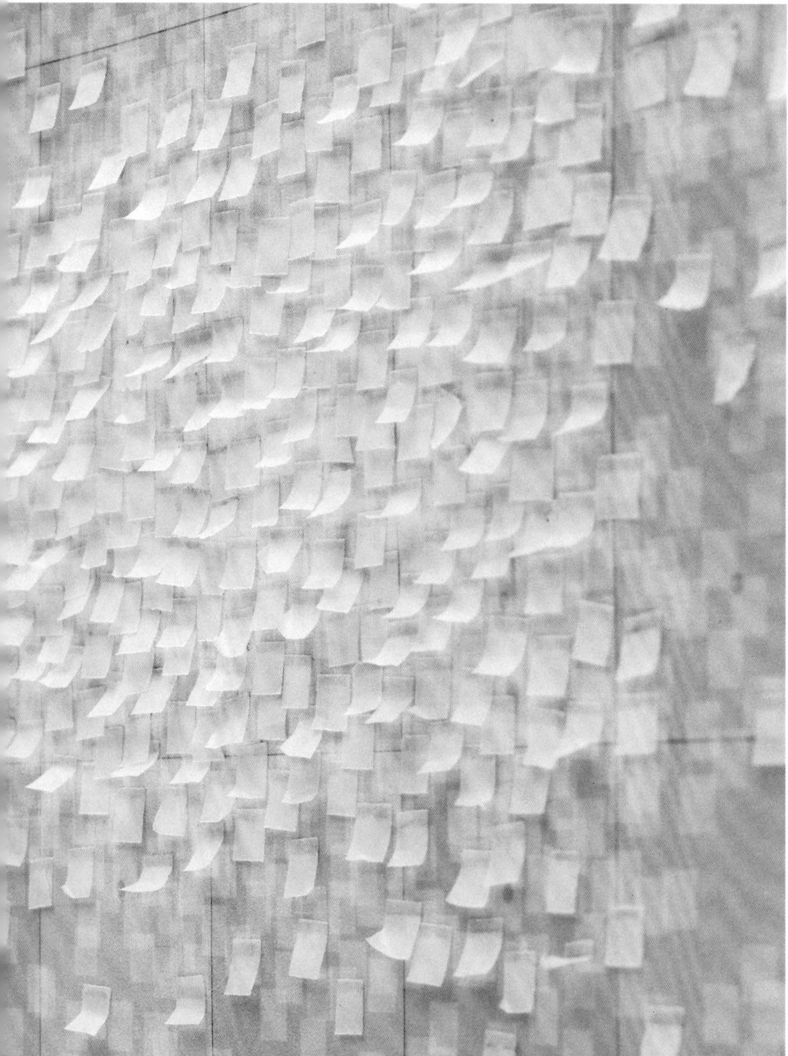

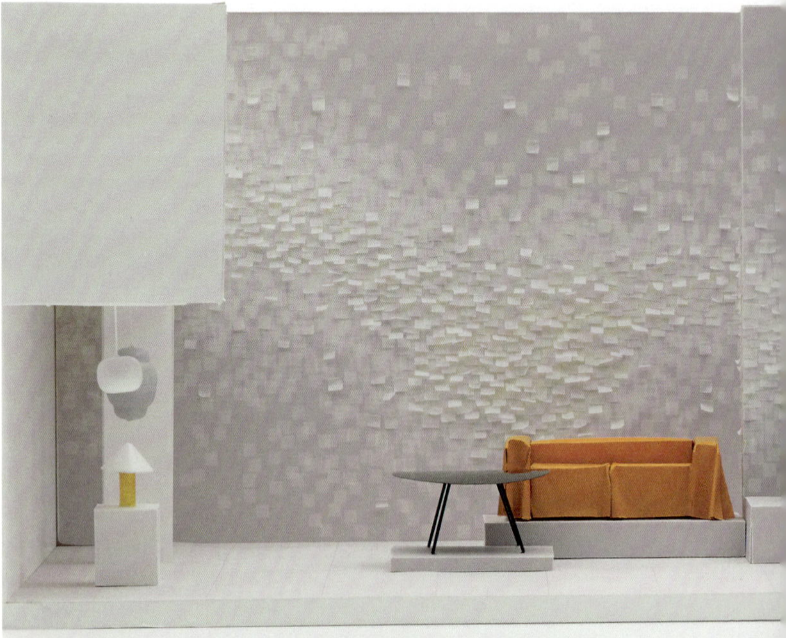

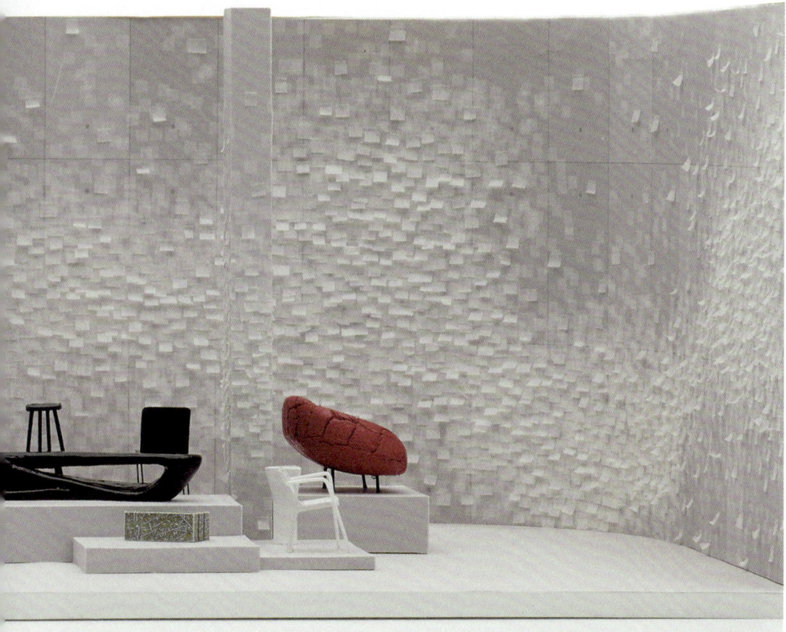

ghost stories 2nd chapter

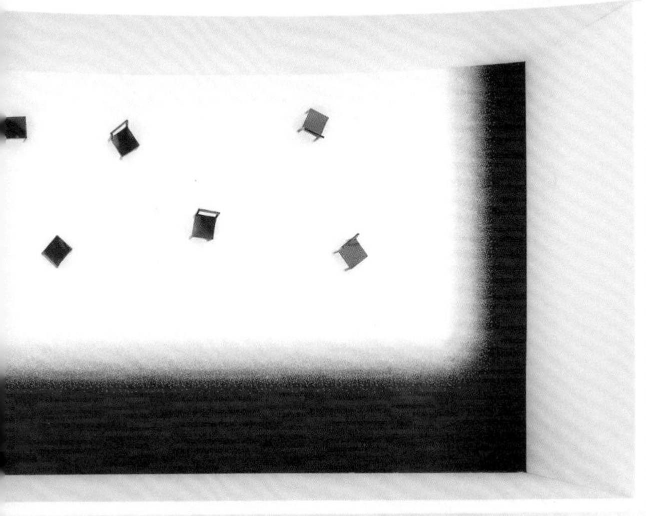

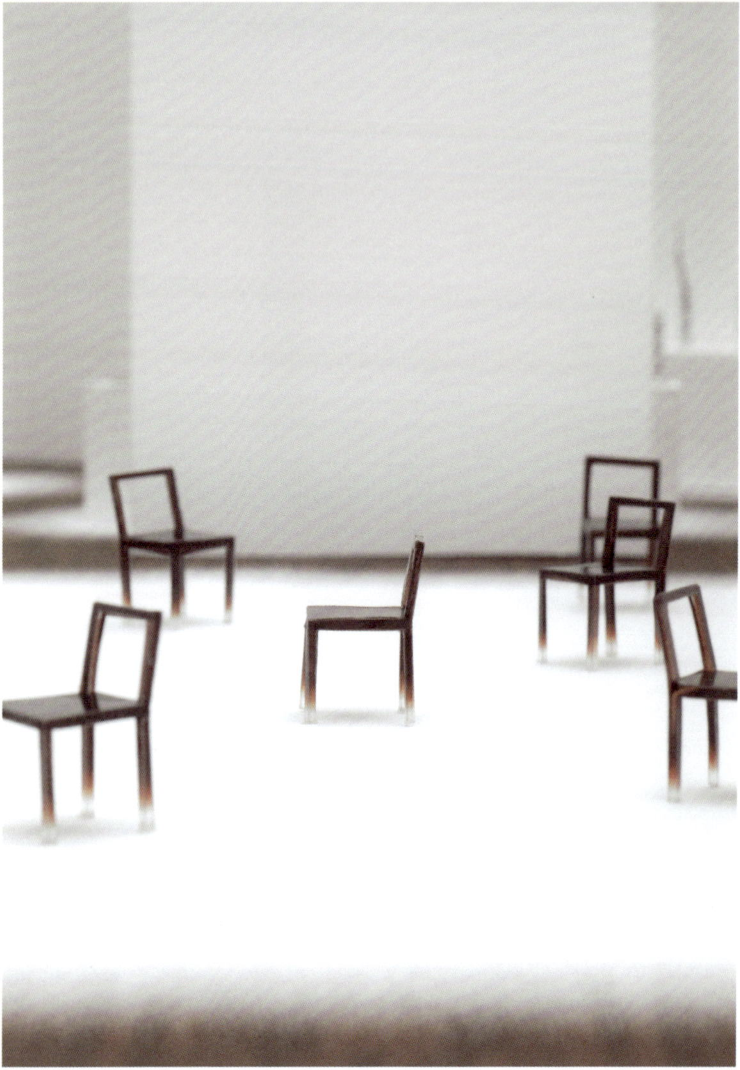

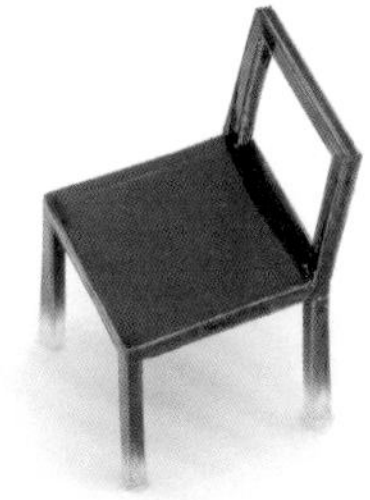

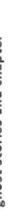

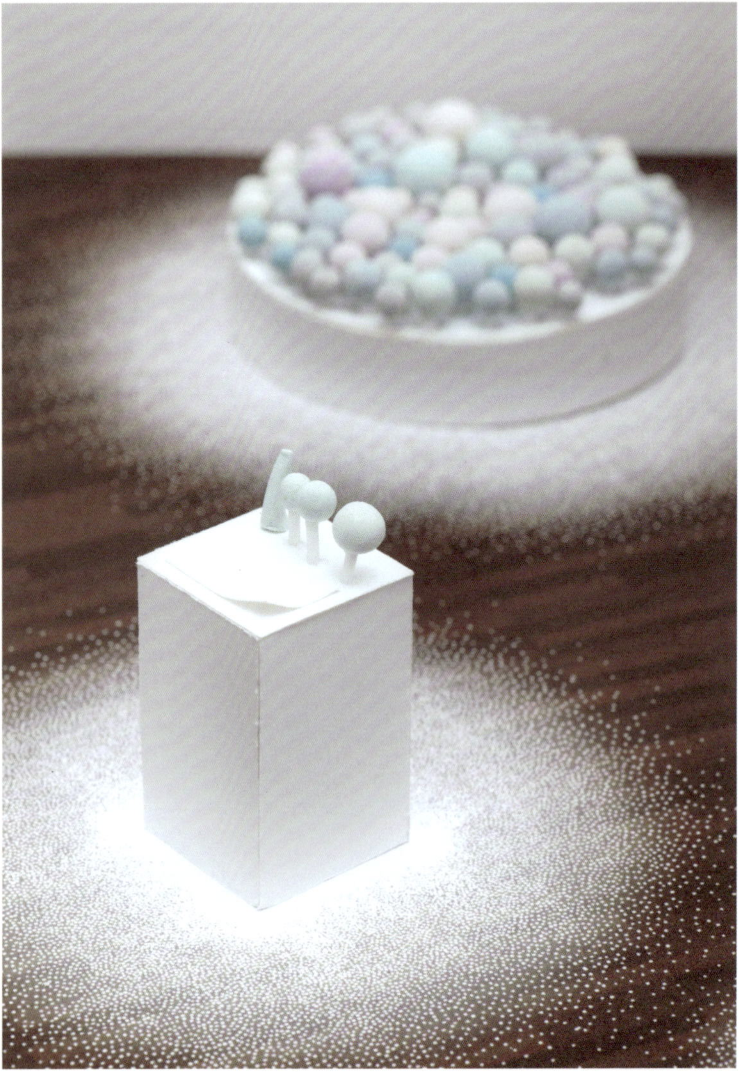

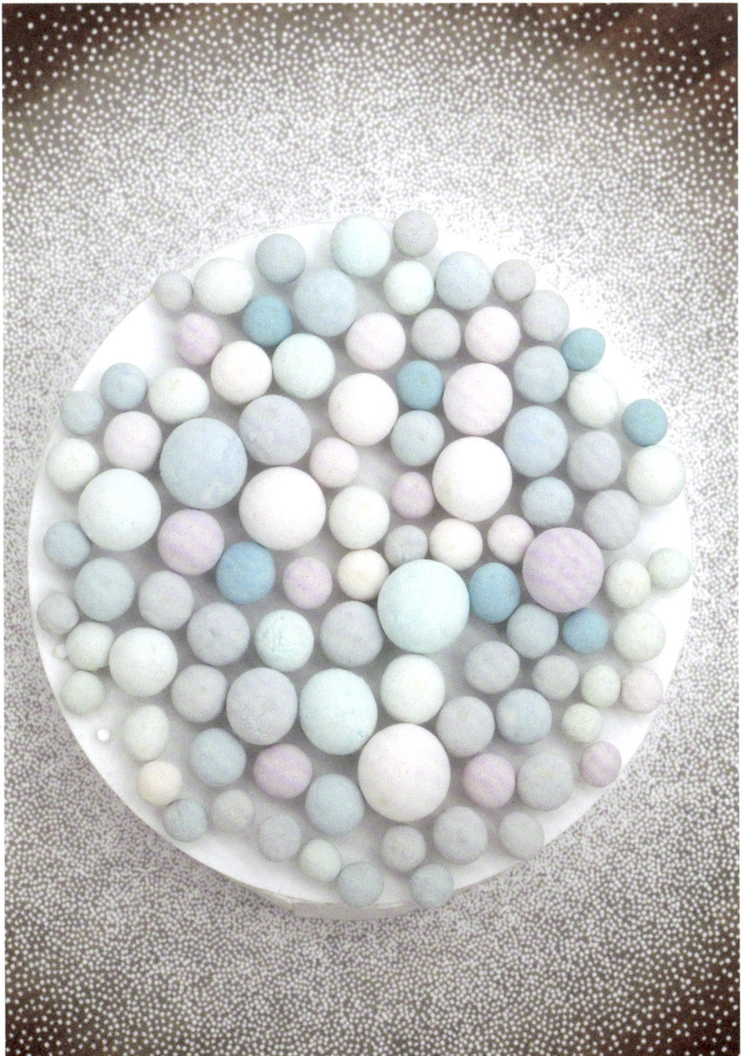

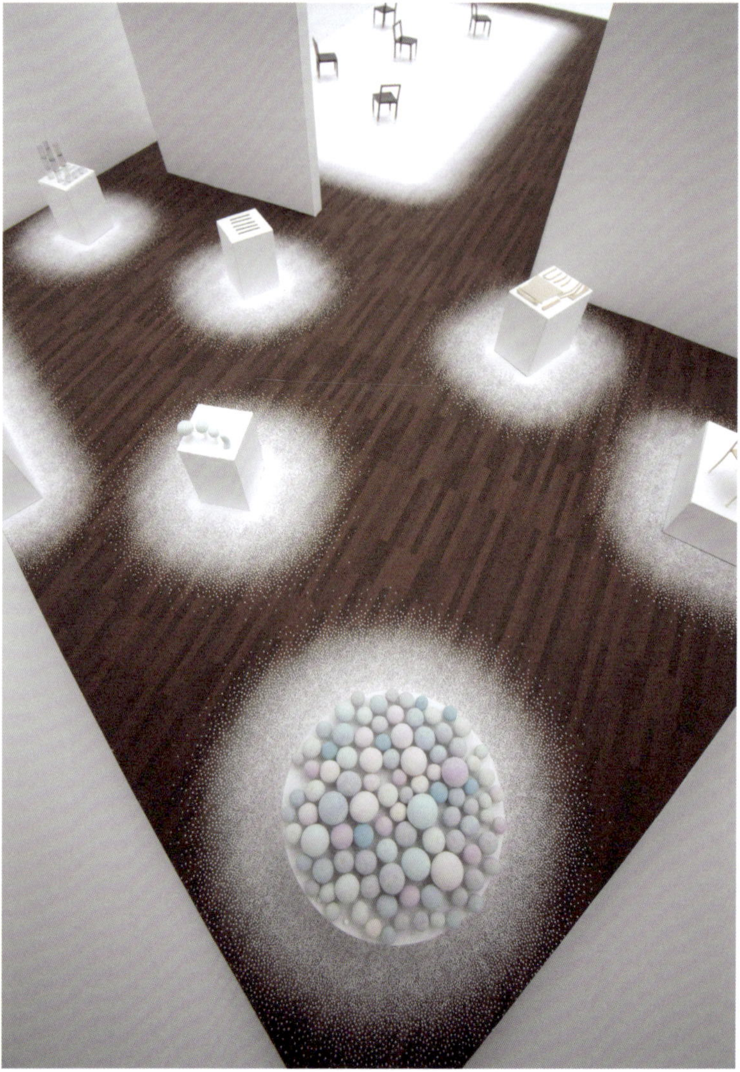

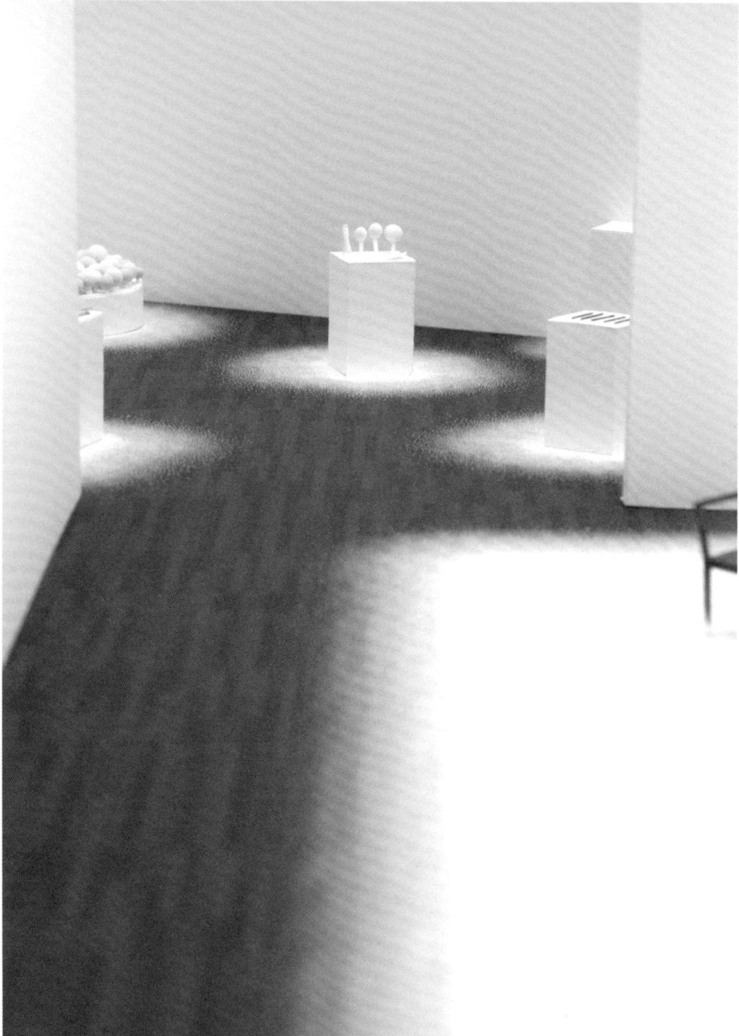

HALSUIT

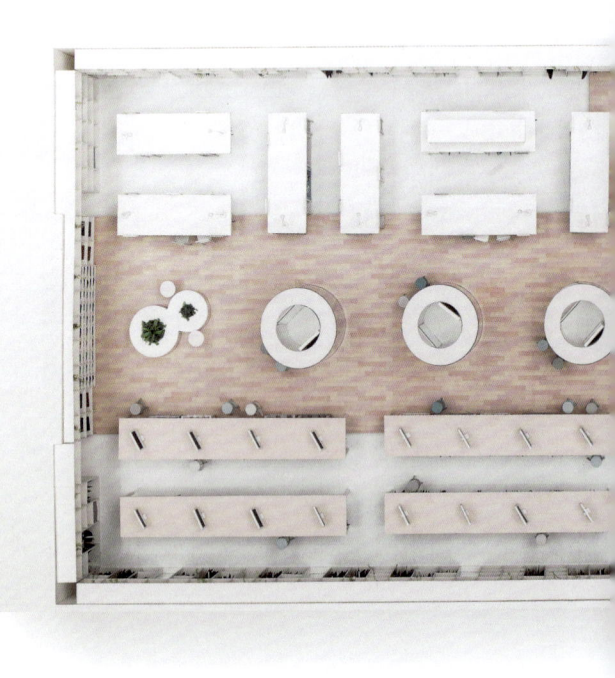

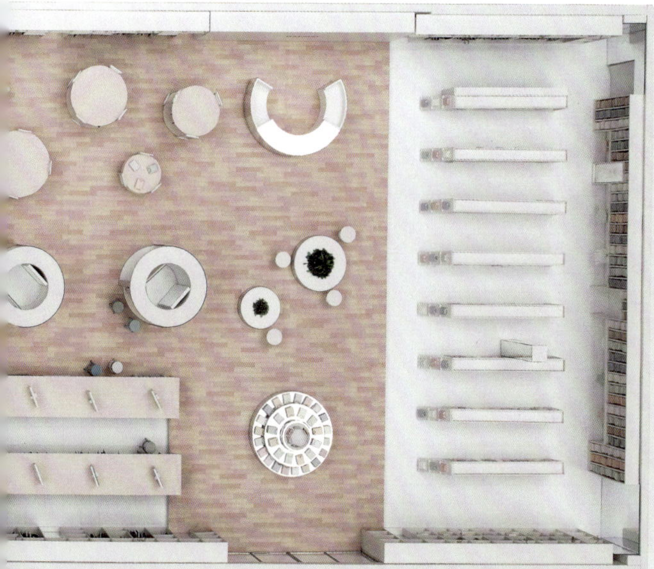

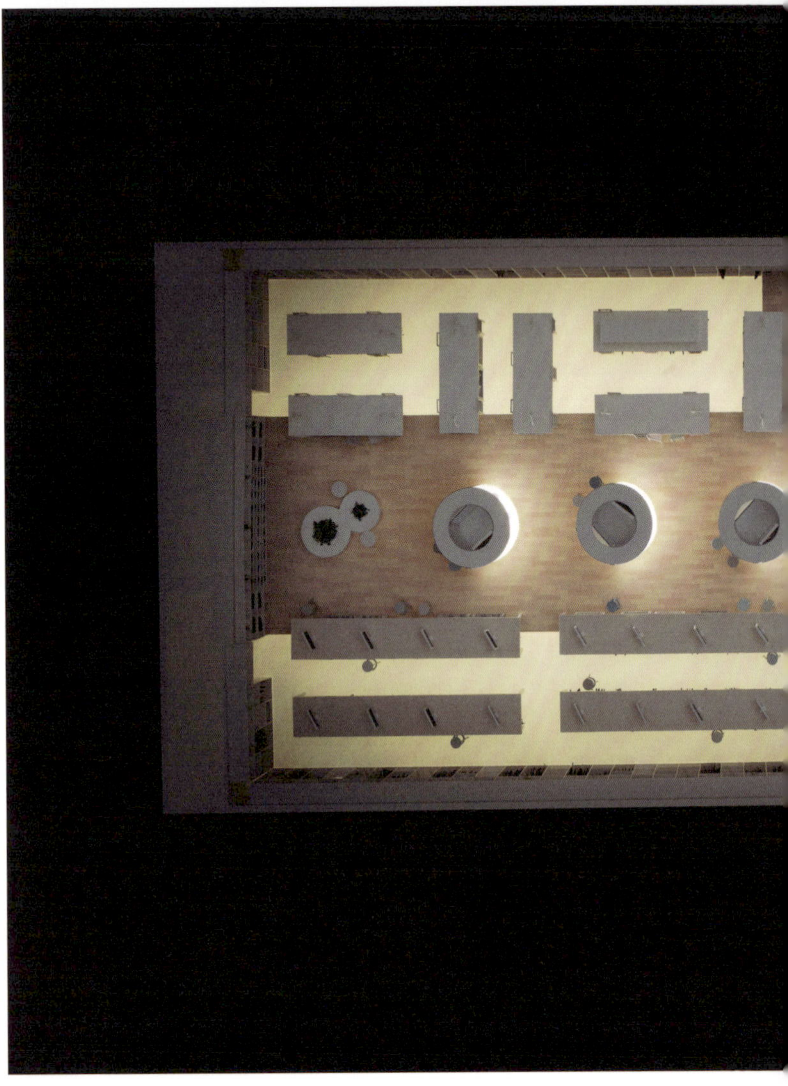

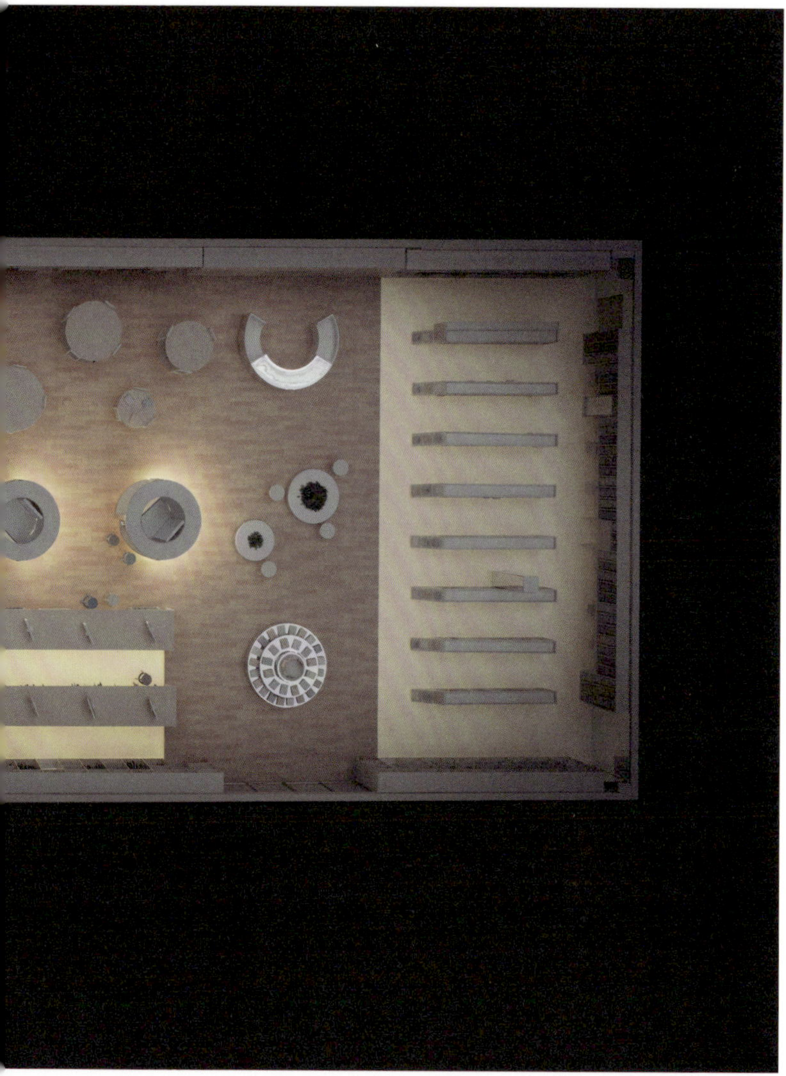

HALSON

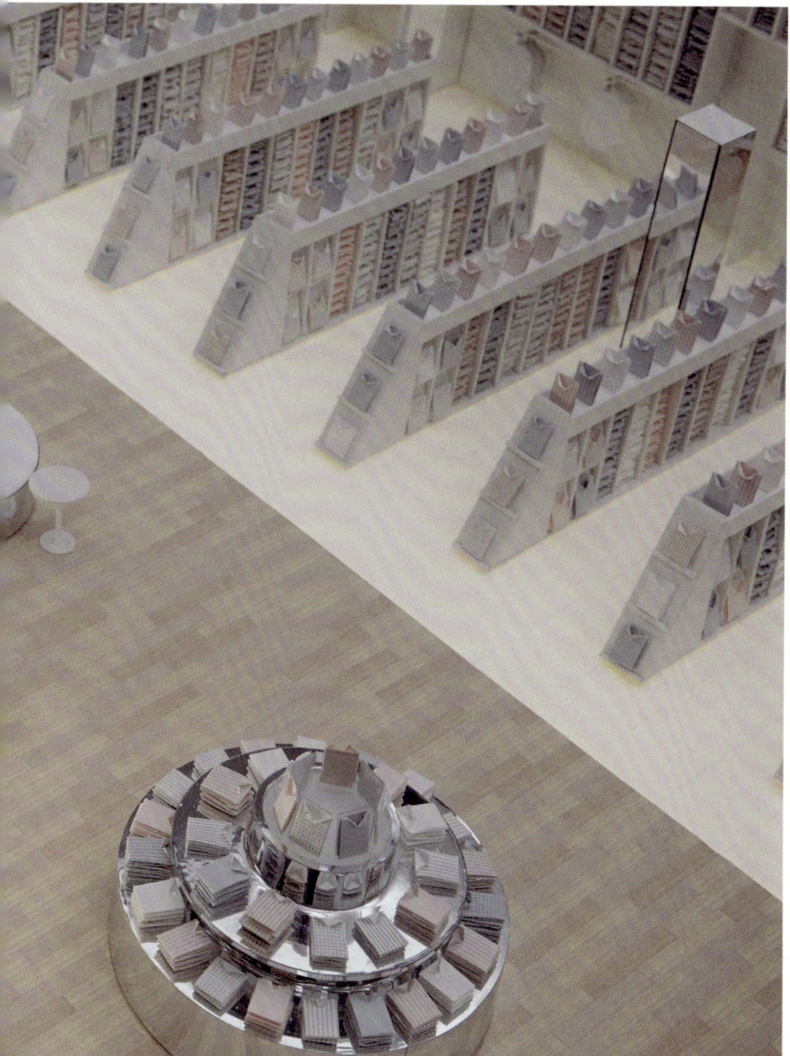

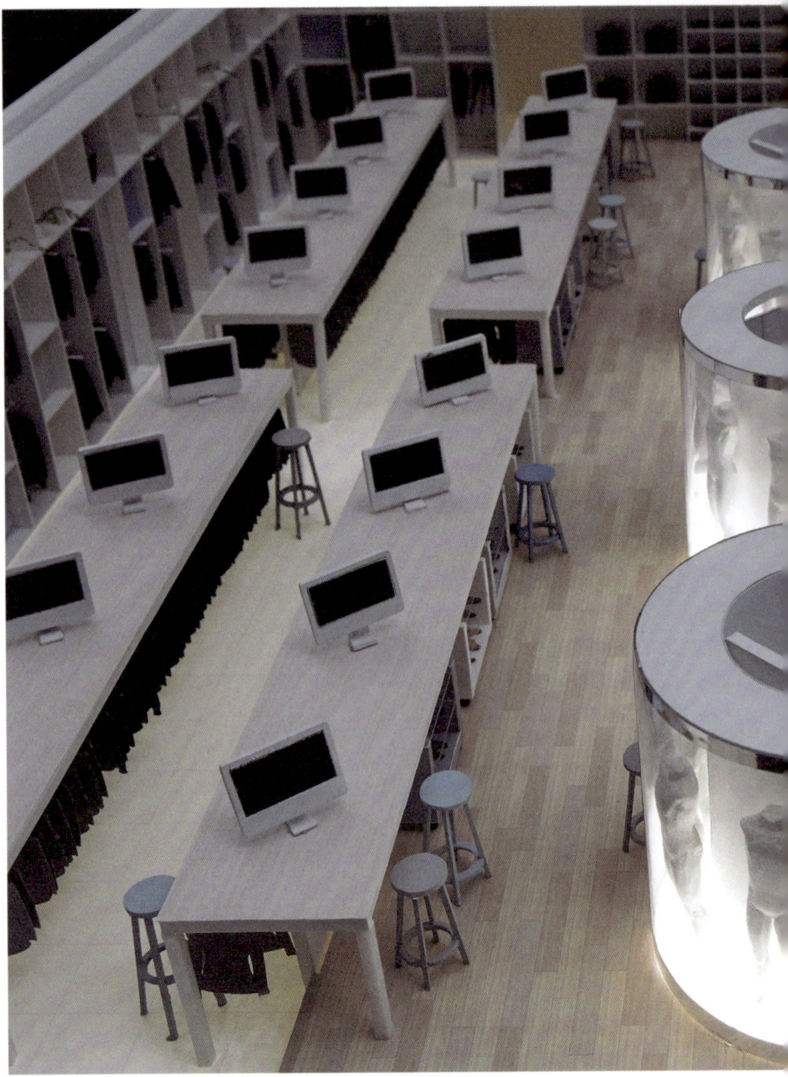

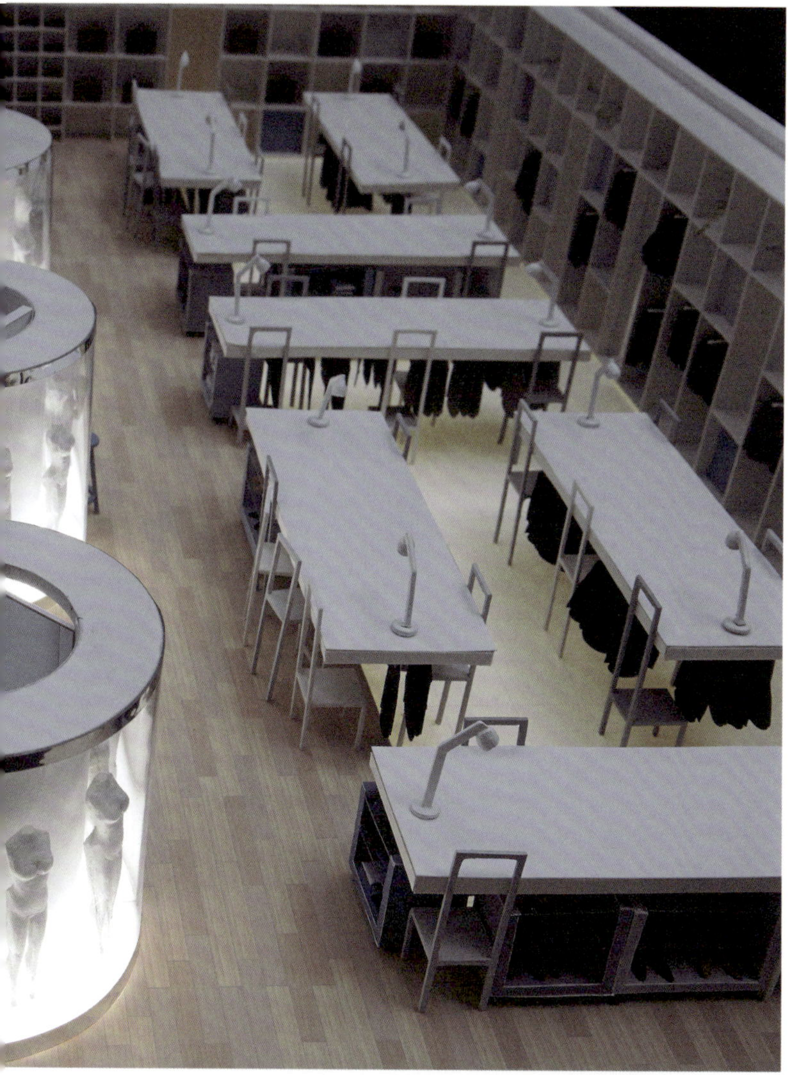

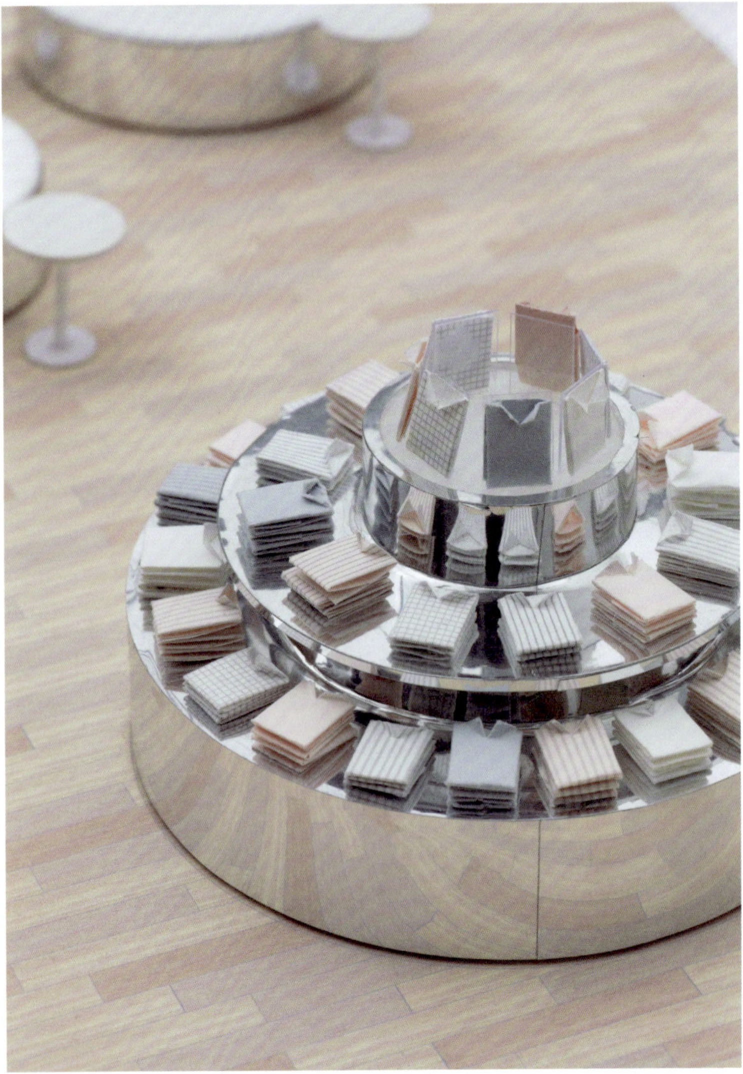

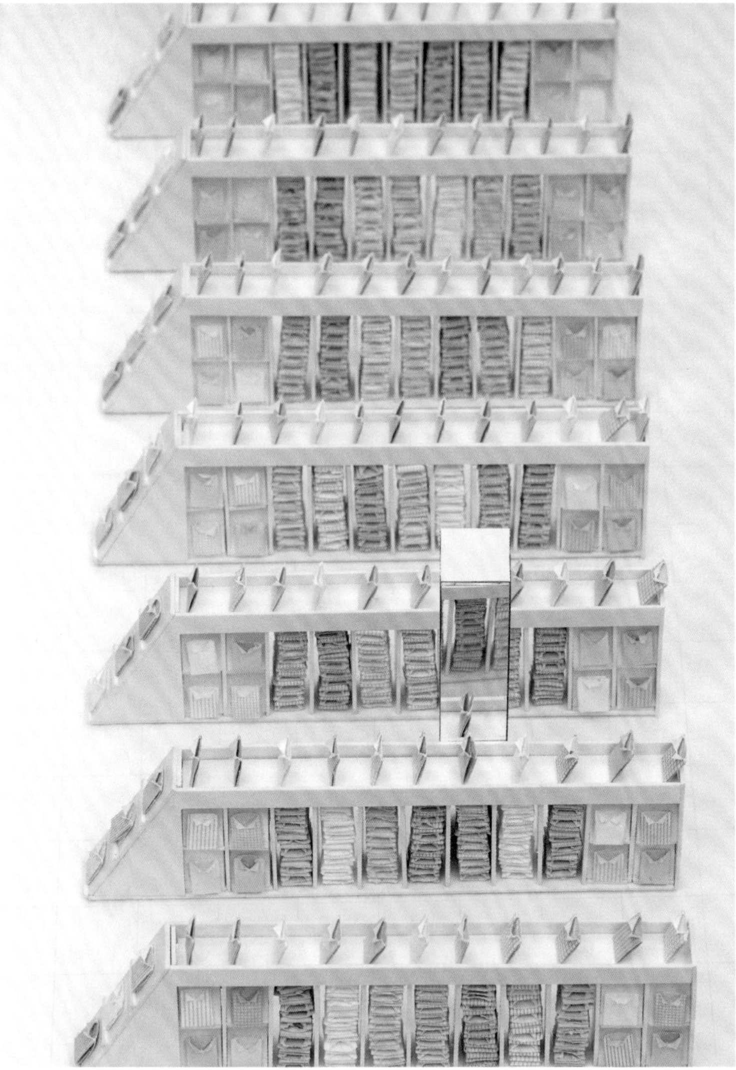

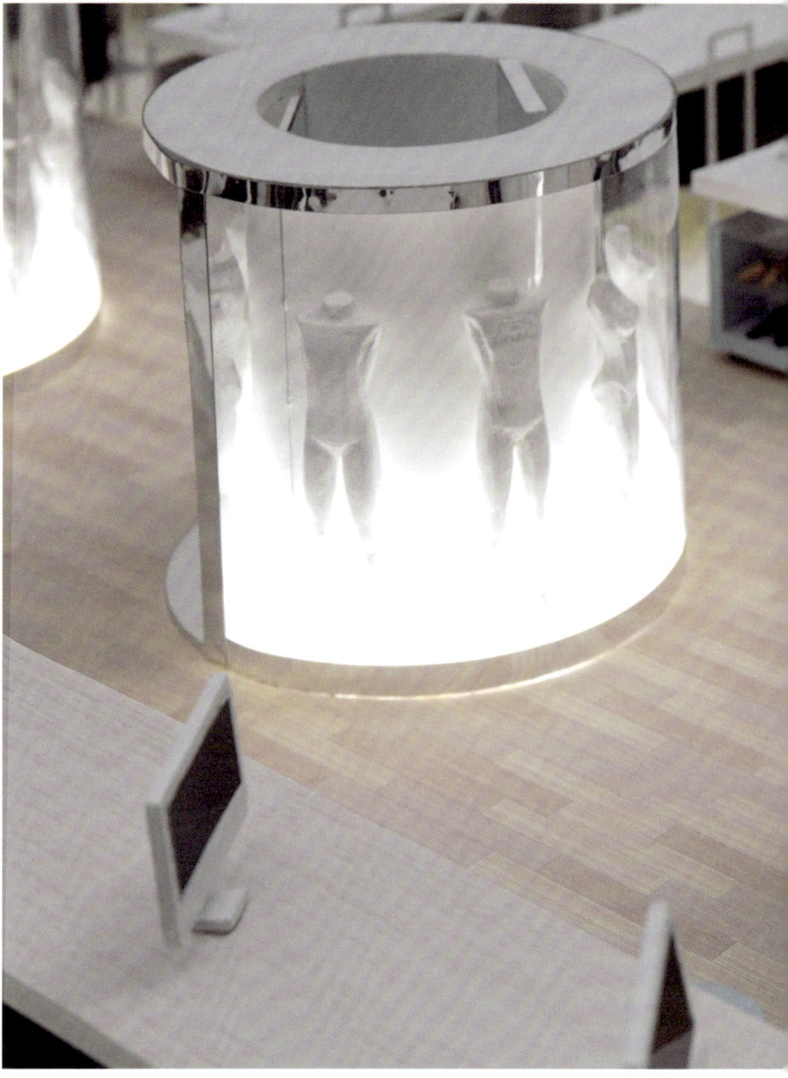

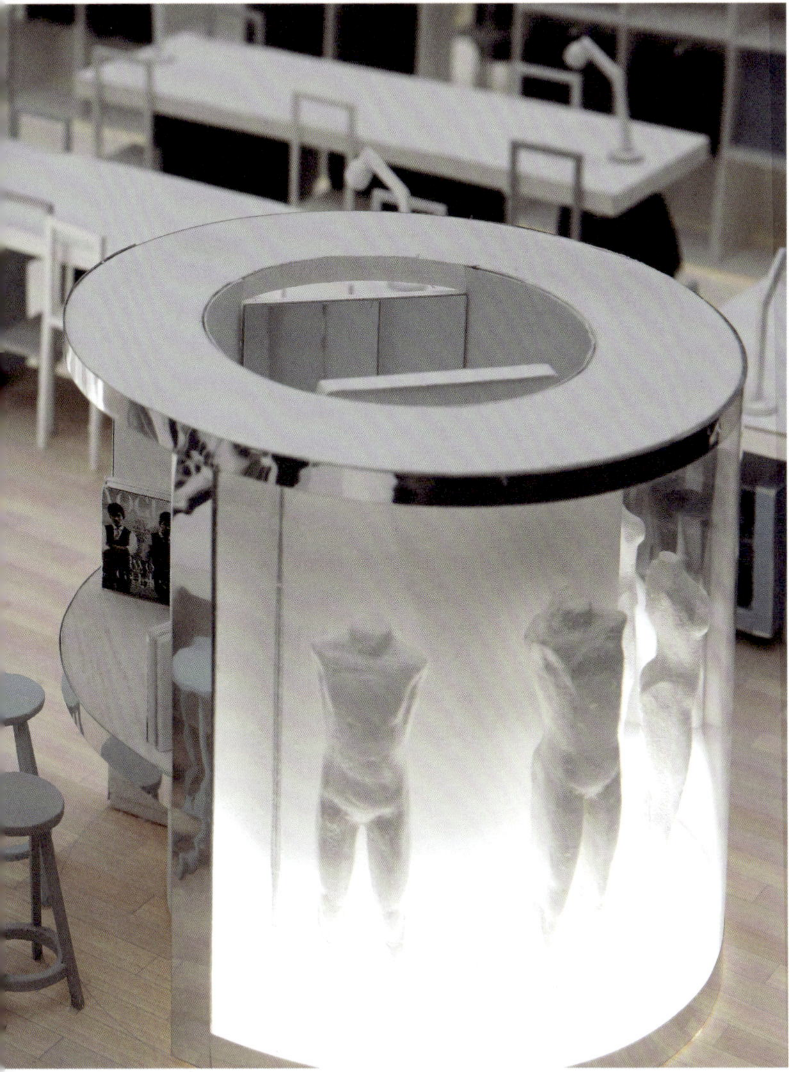

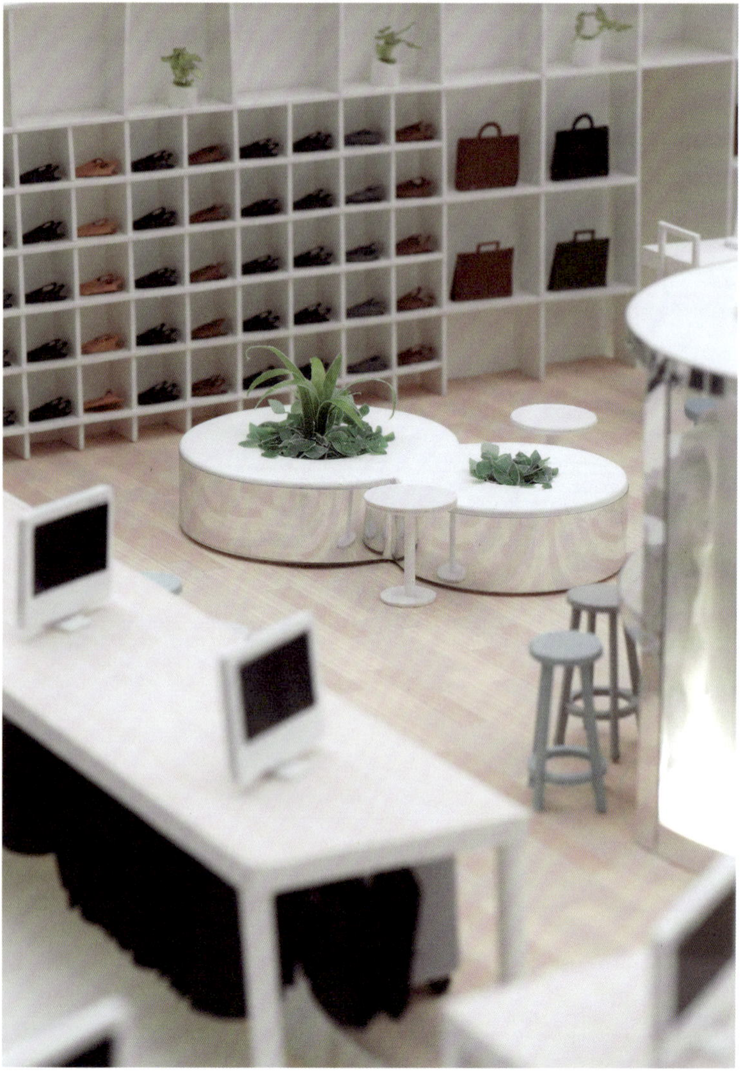

HALSUIT

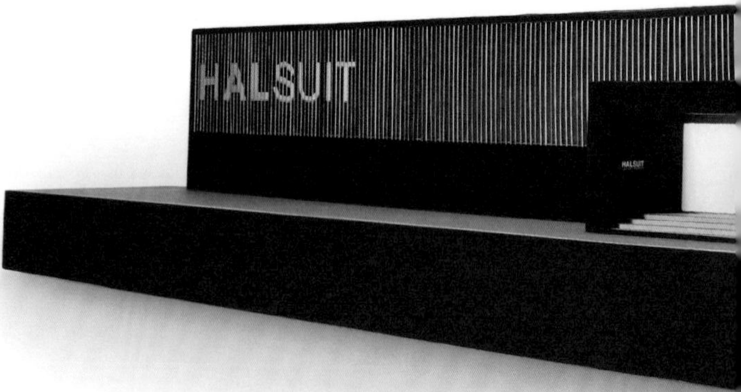
HALSUIT
HALSUIT

HALSUIT

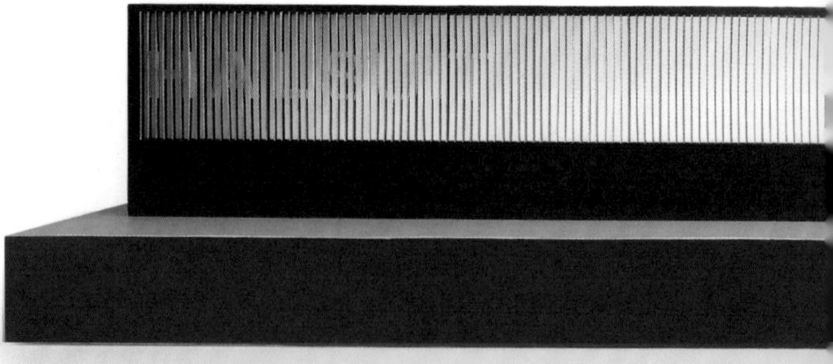

HALSUIT
HALSUIT
suit
shirts
accessories
shoes
bags
underwear

Hermès wandering forest

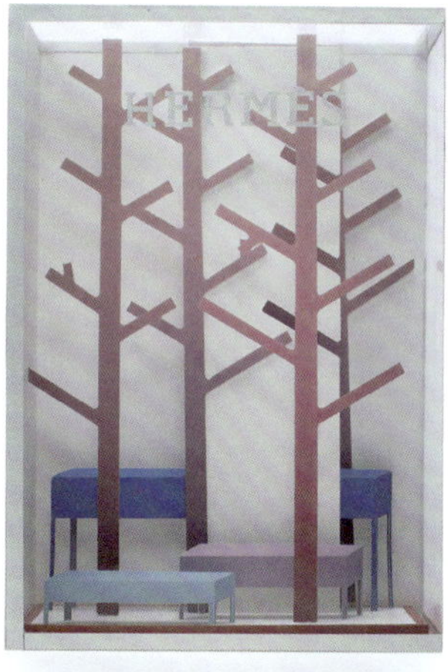
HERMES

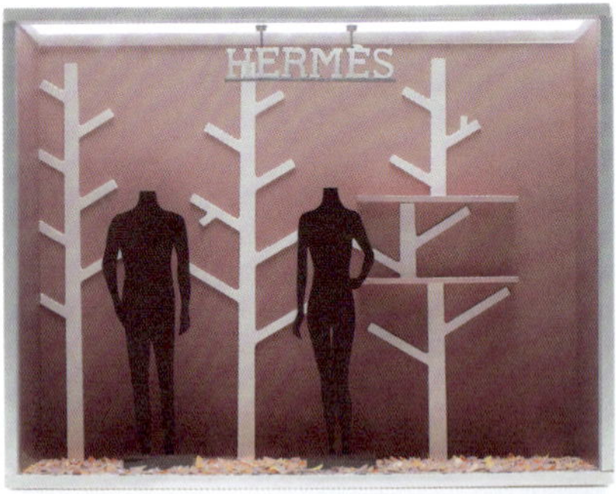
HERMÈS

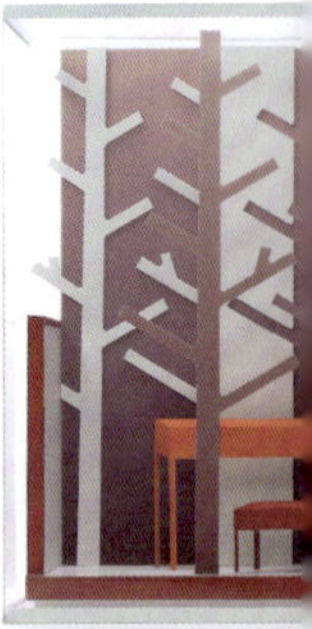

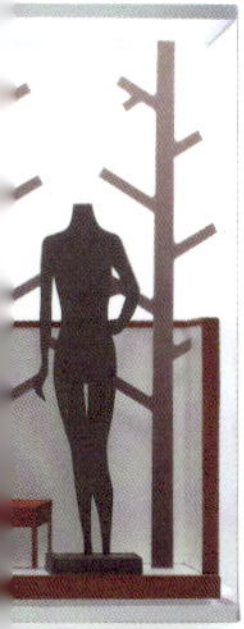

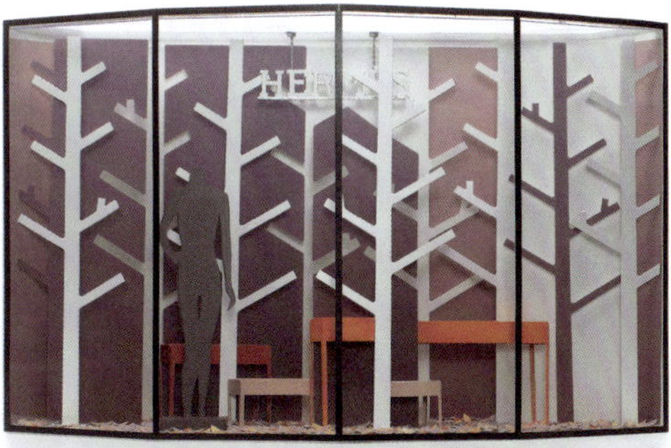

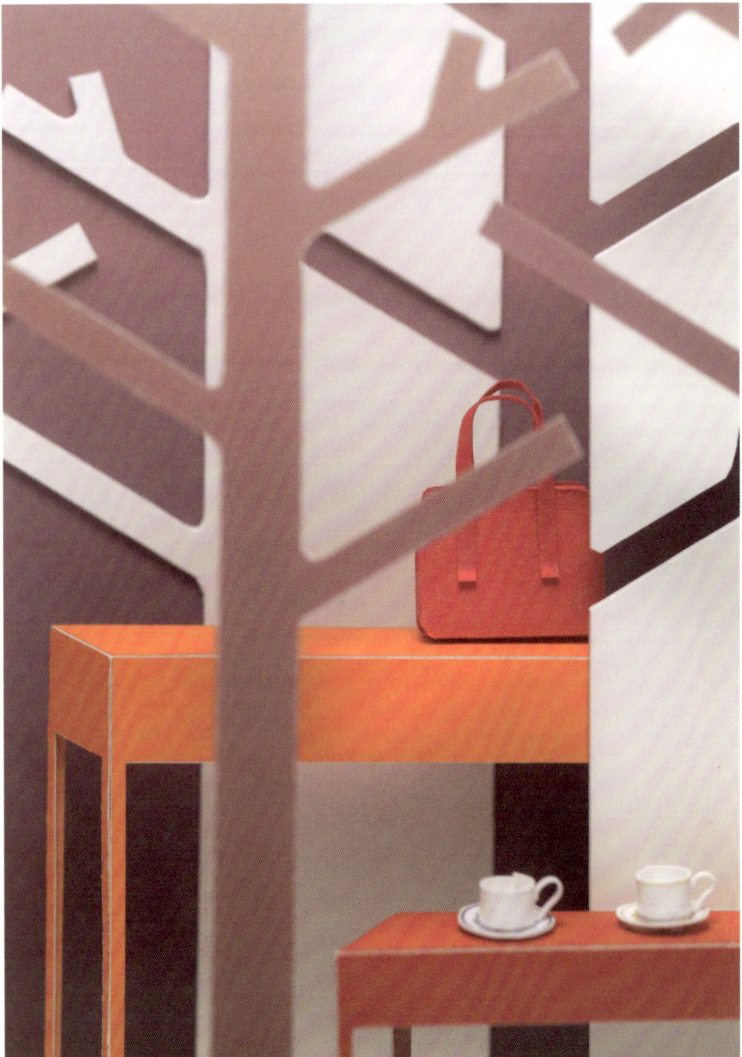

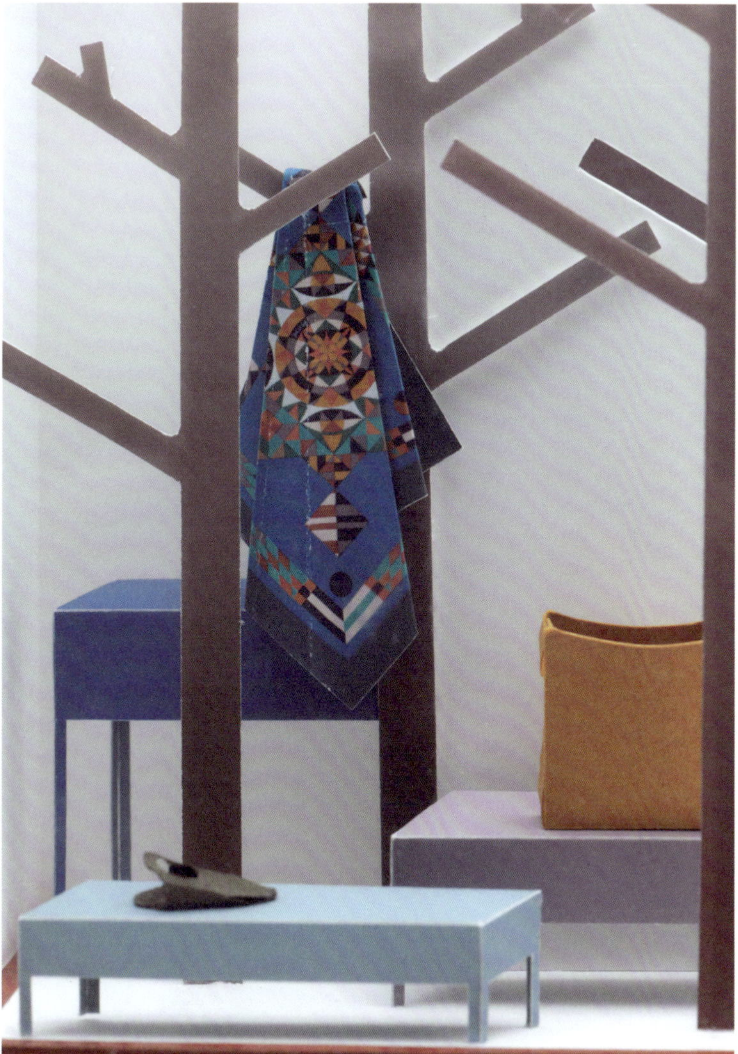

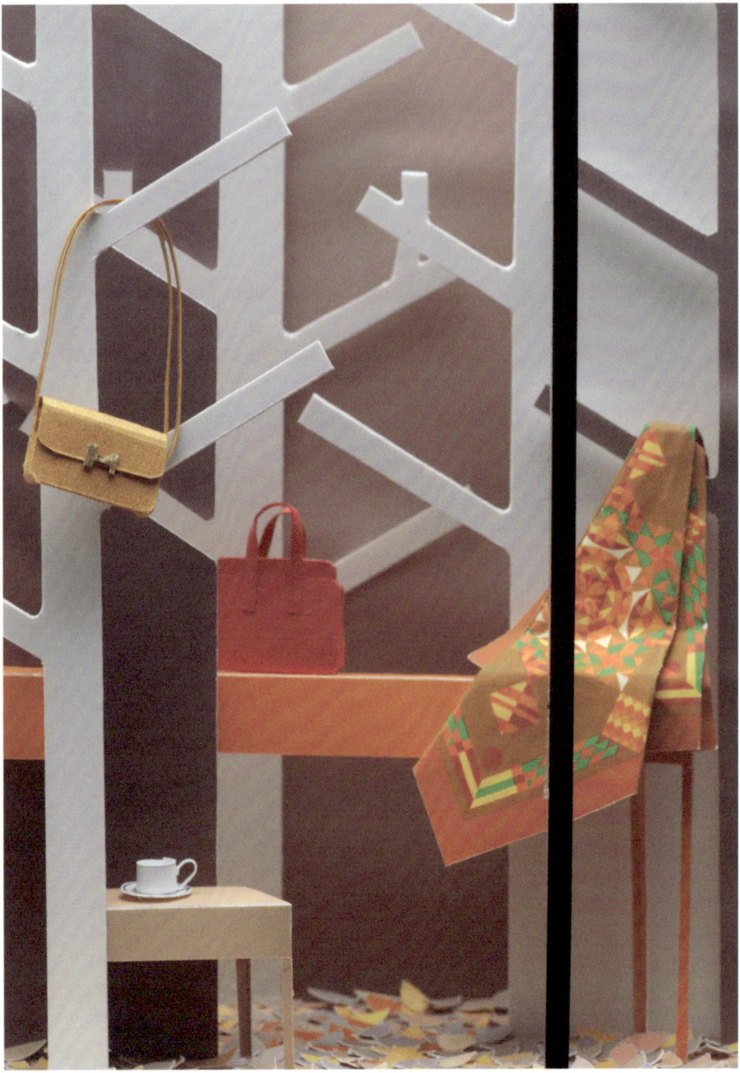

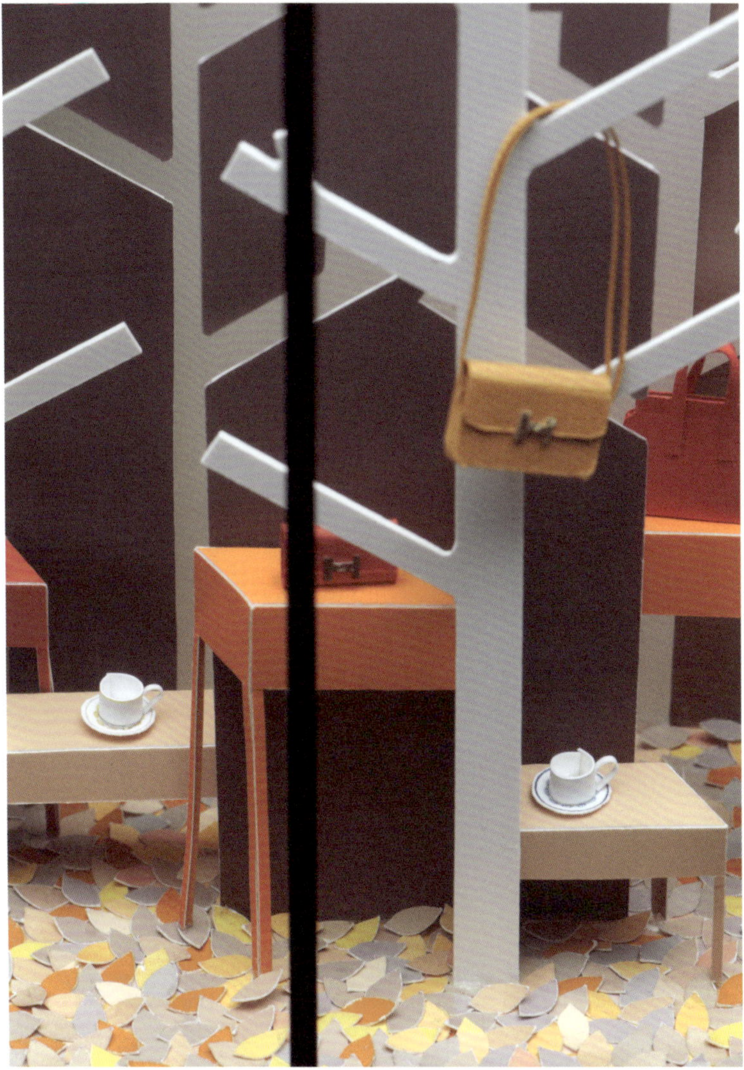

HIRATA NO BOSHI

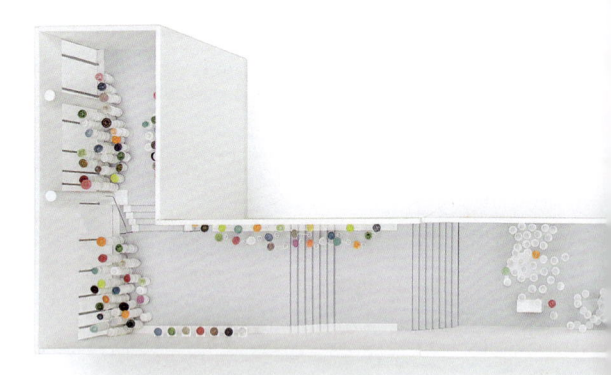

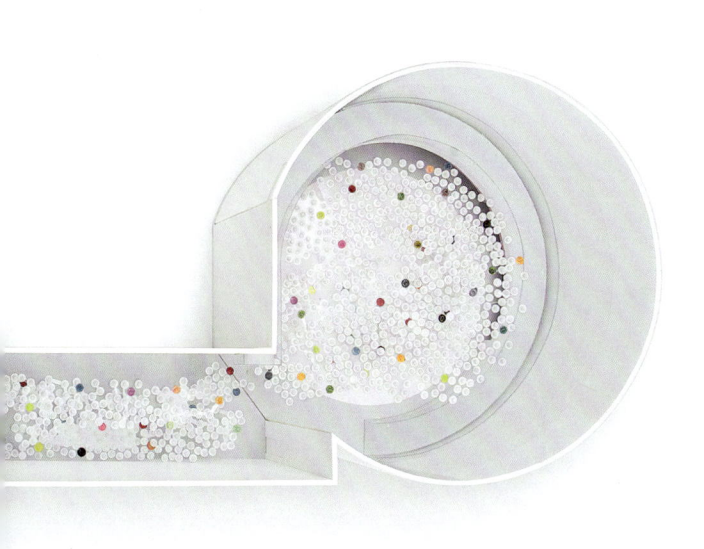

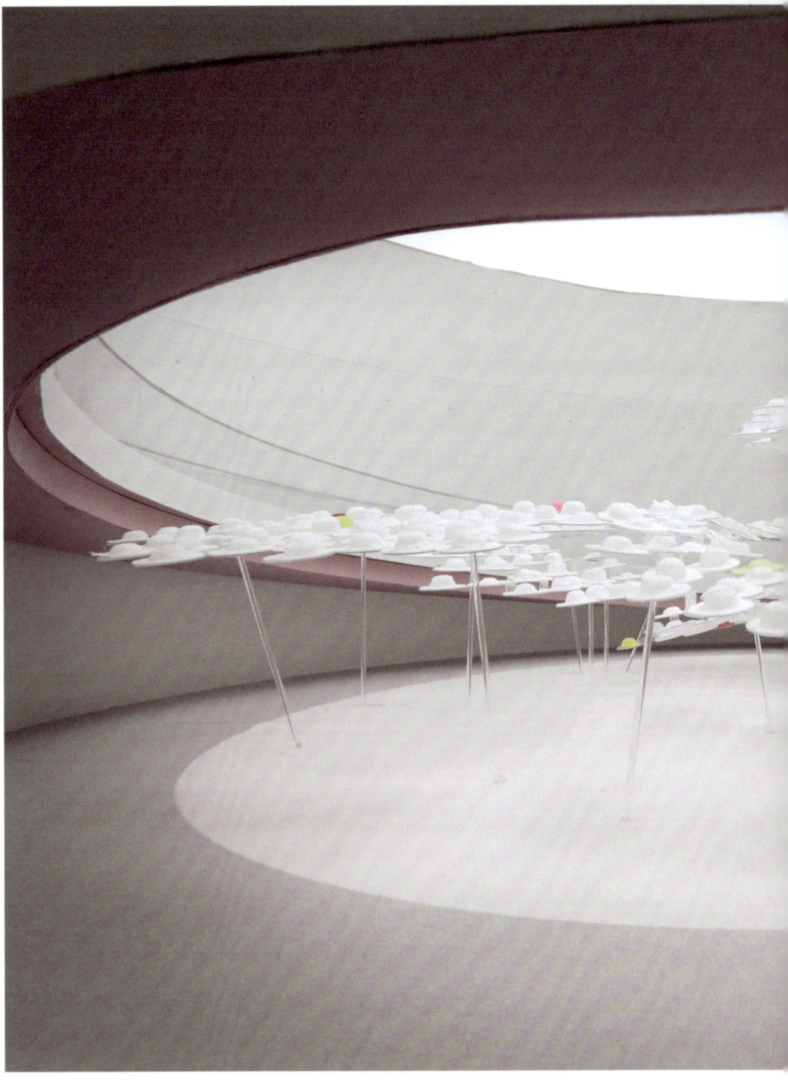

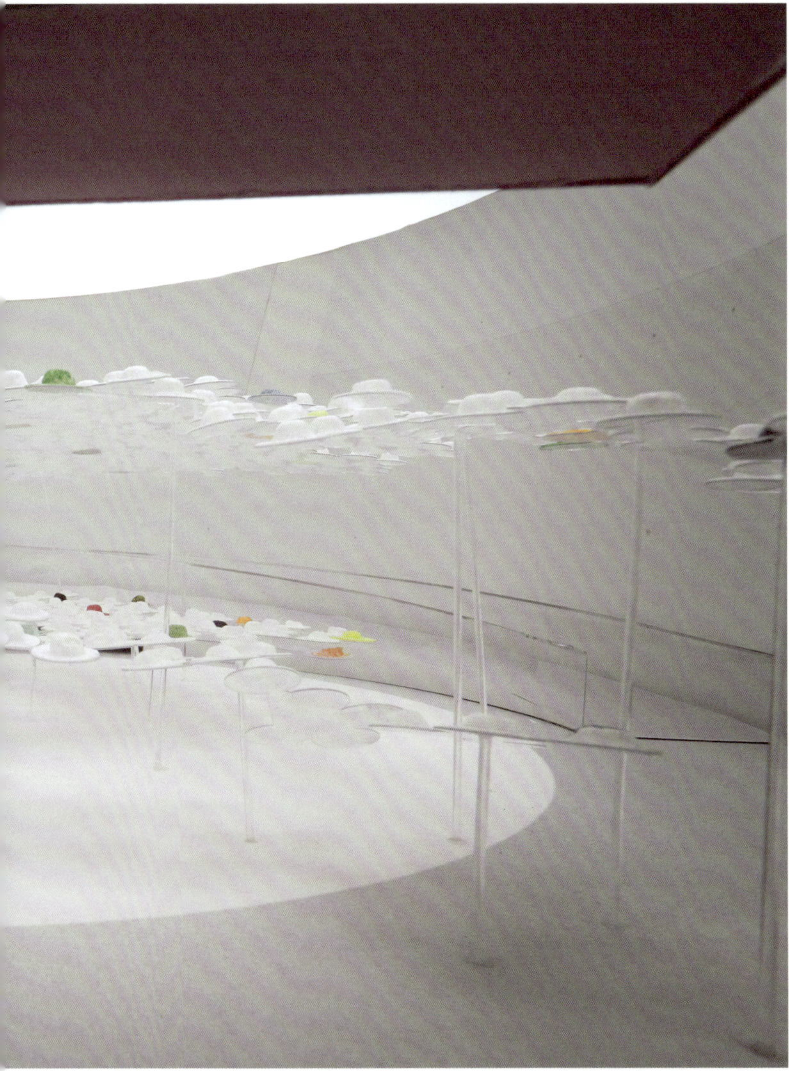

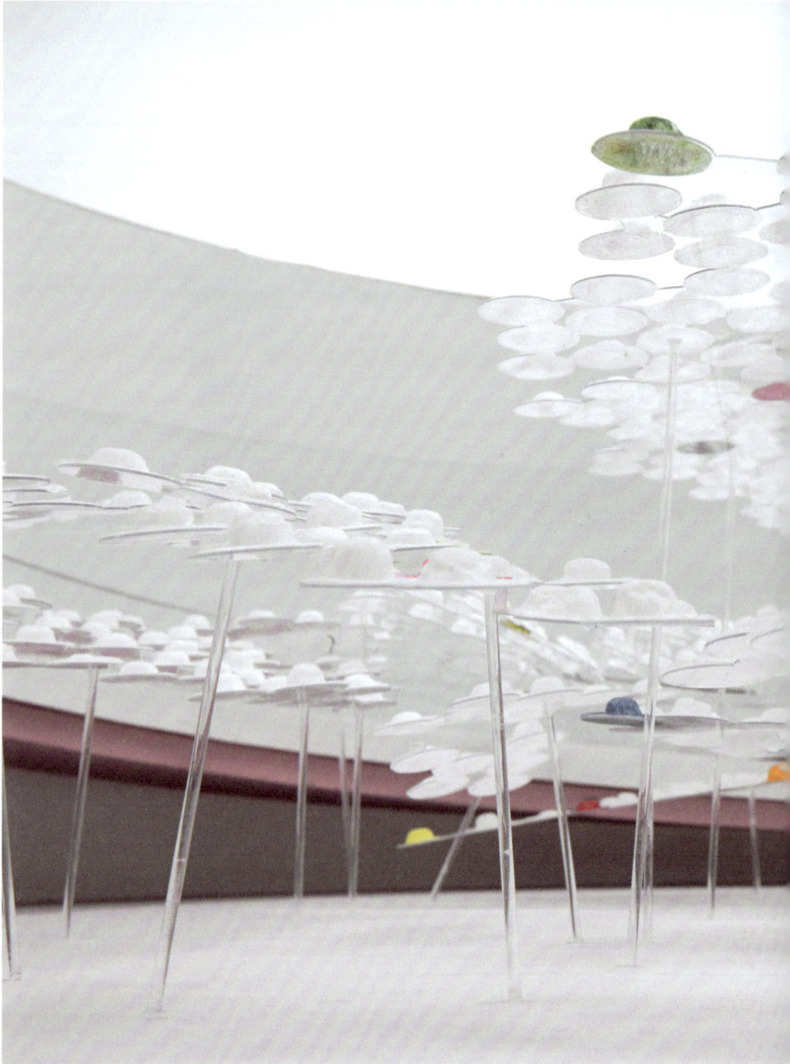

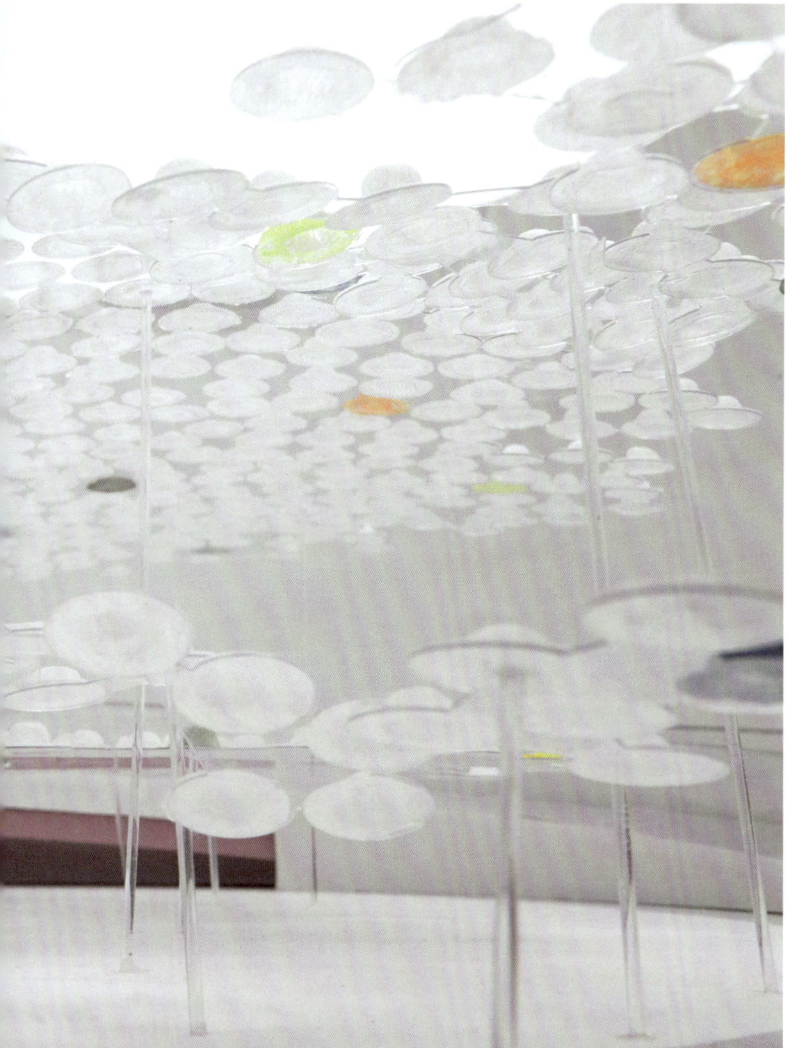

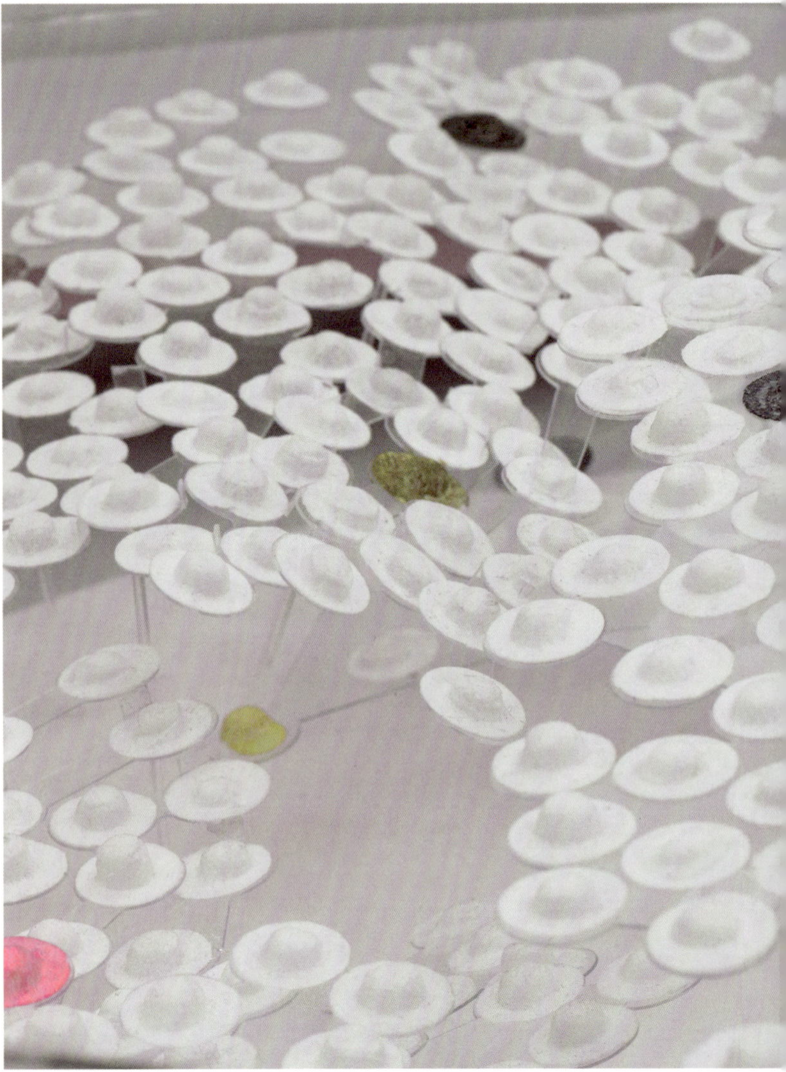

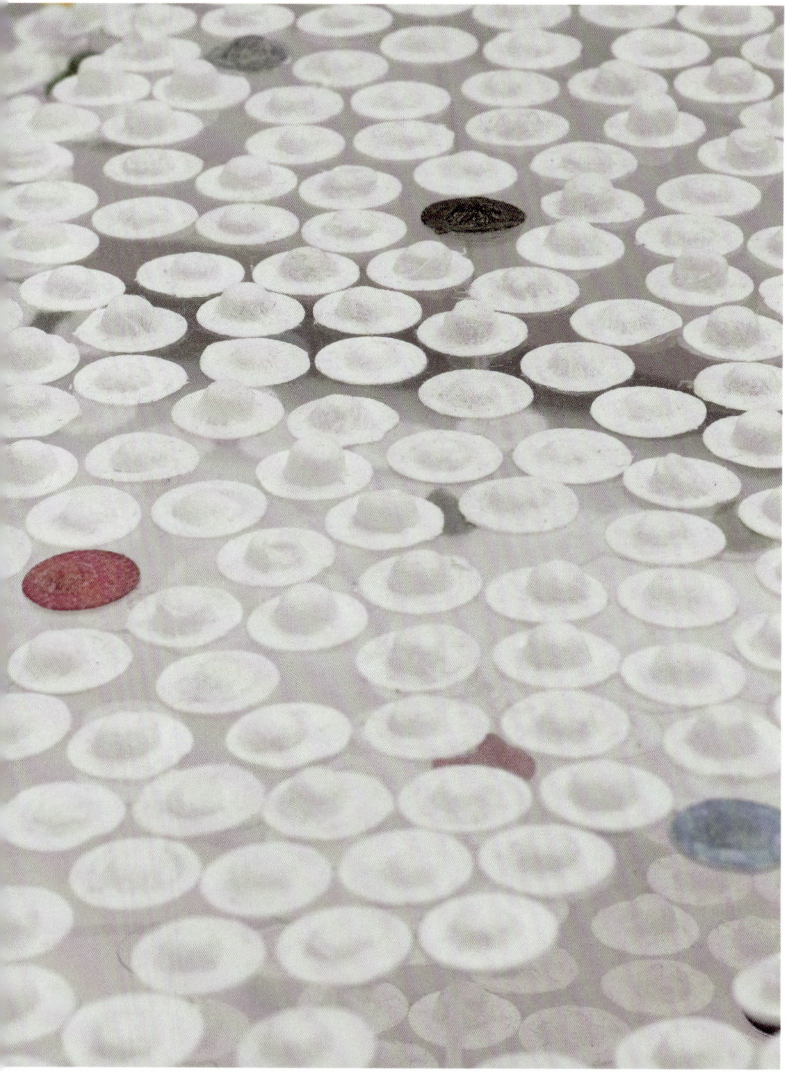

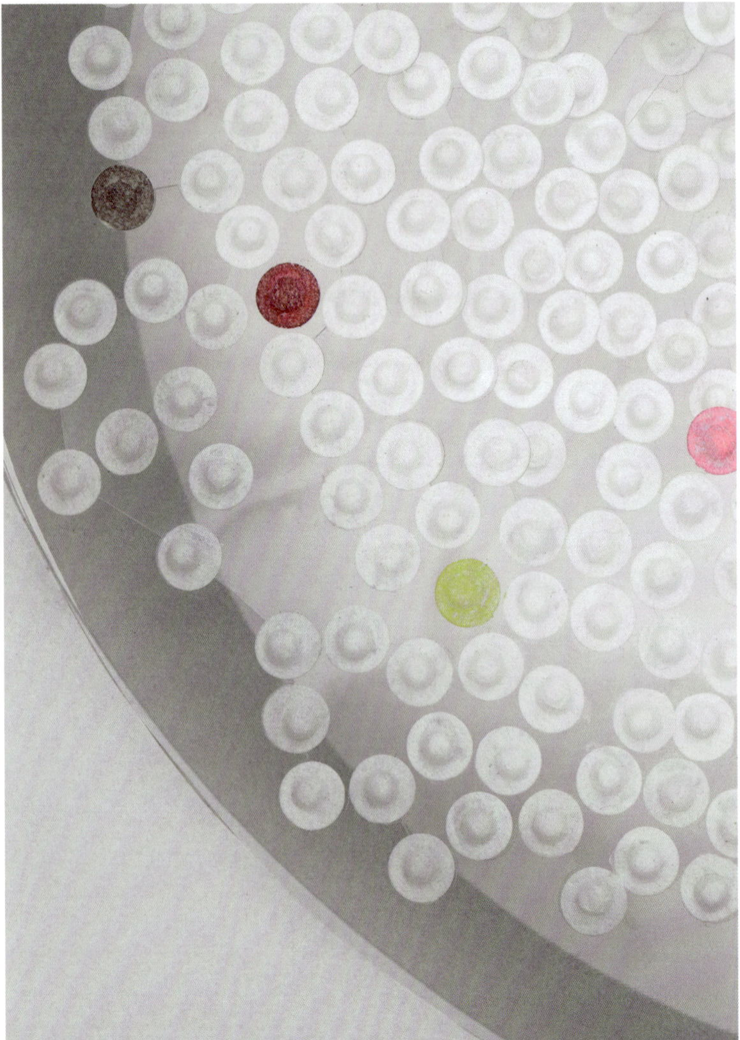

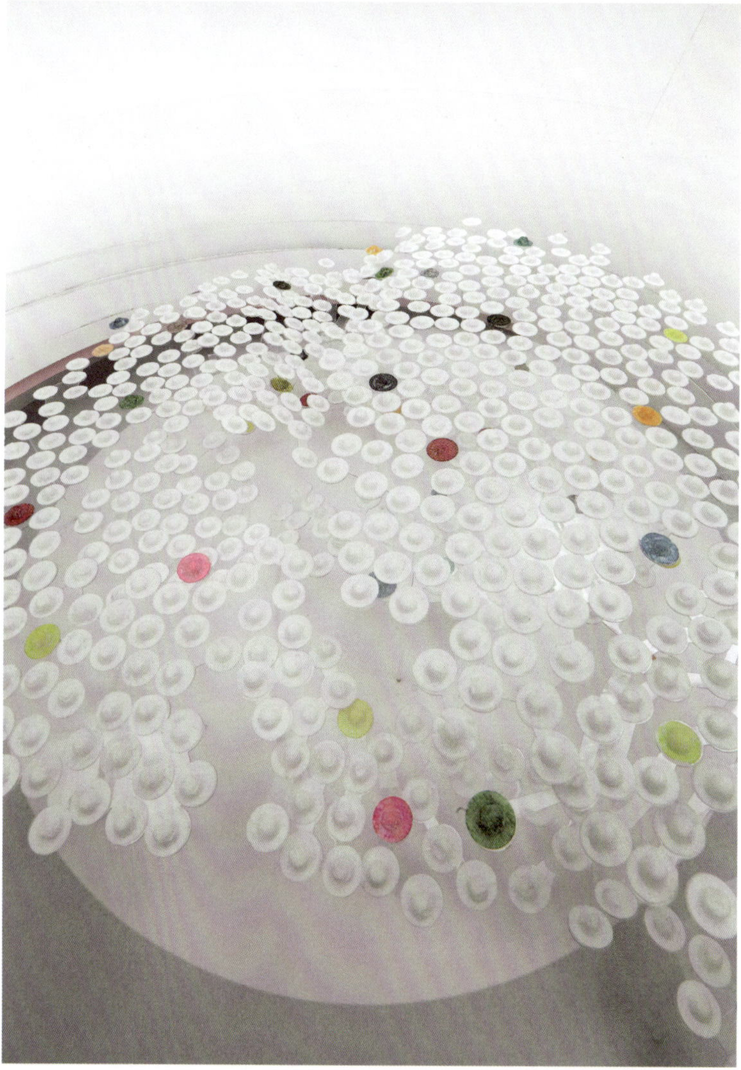

hitogaki

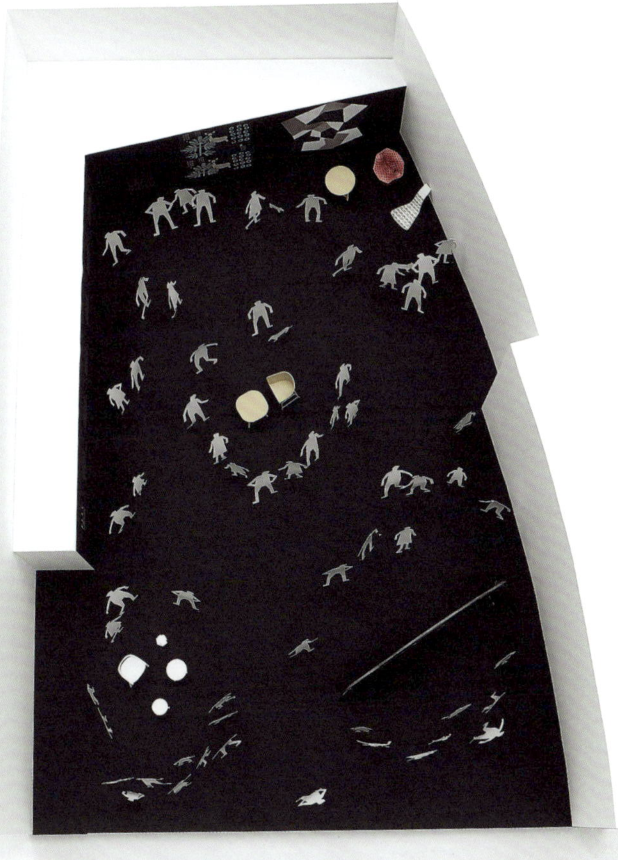

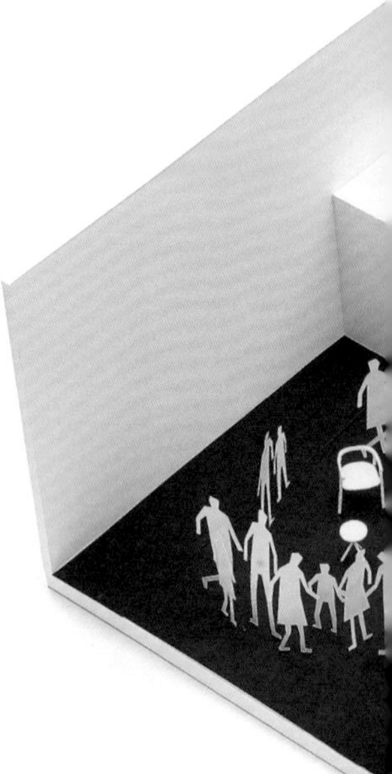

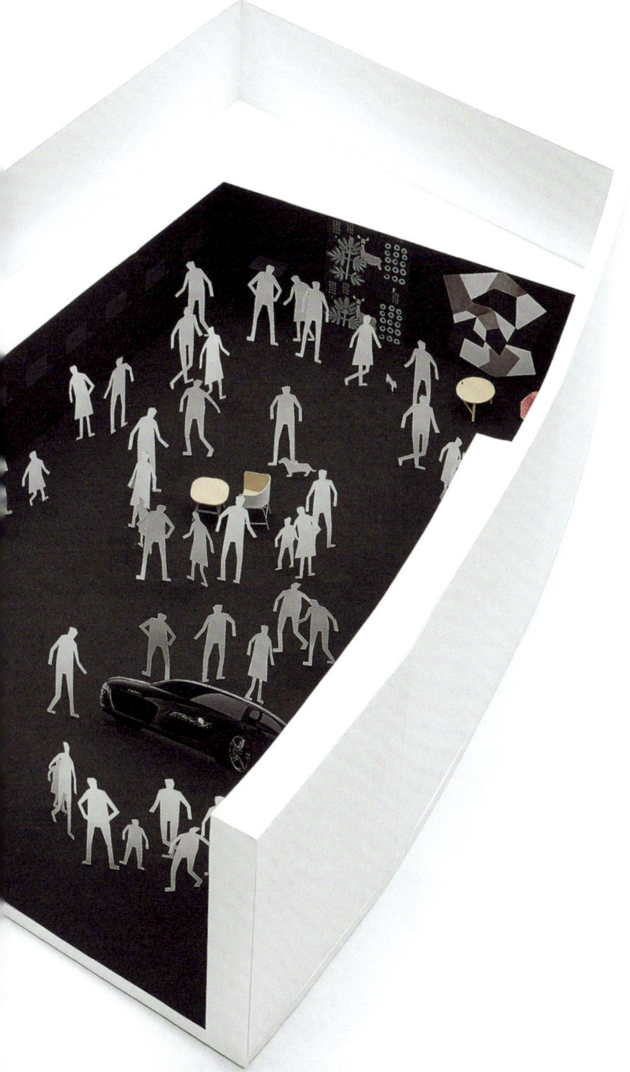

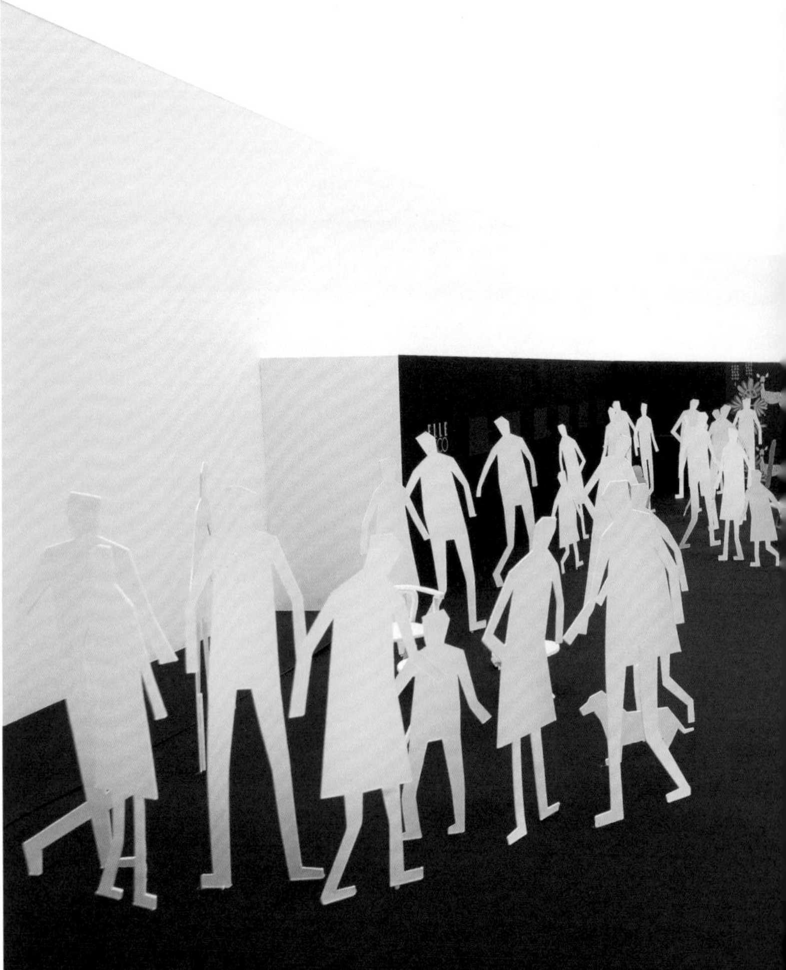

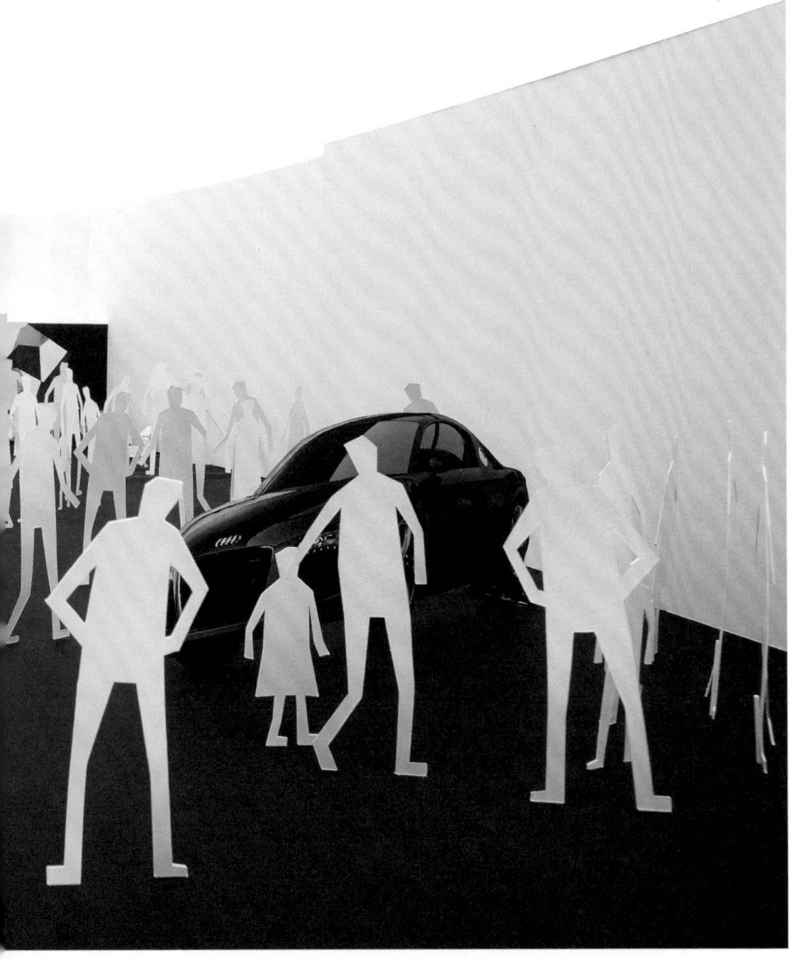

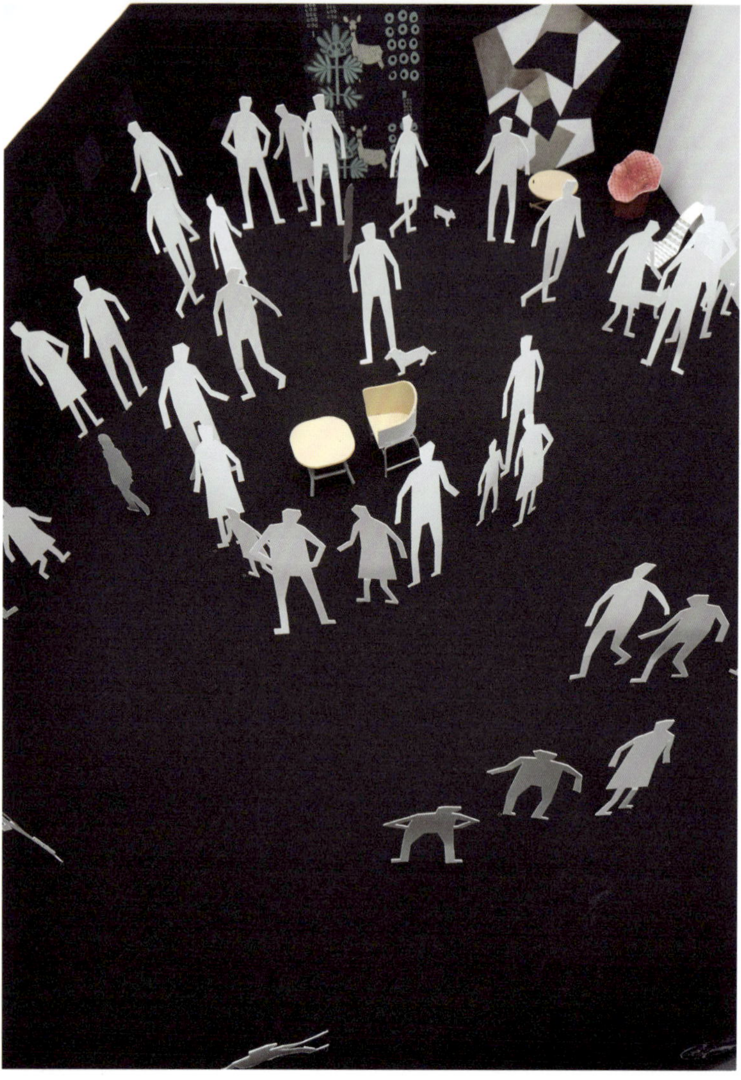

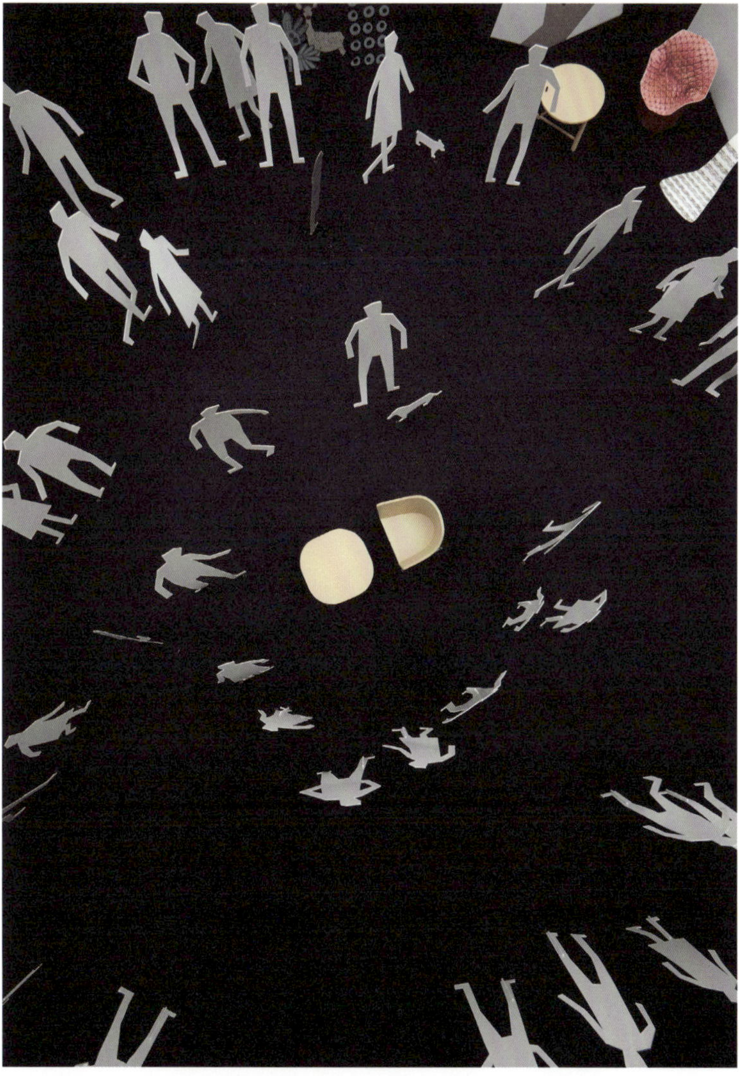

ILLOIHA OMOTESANDO

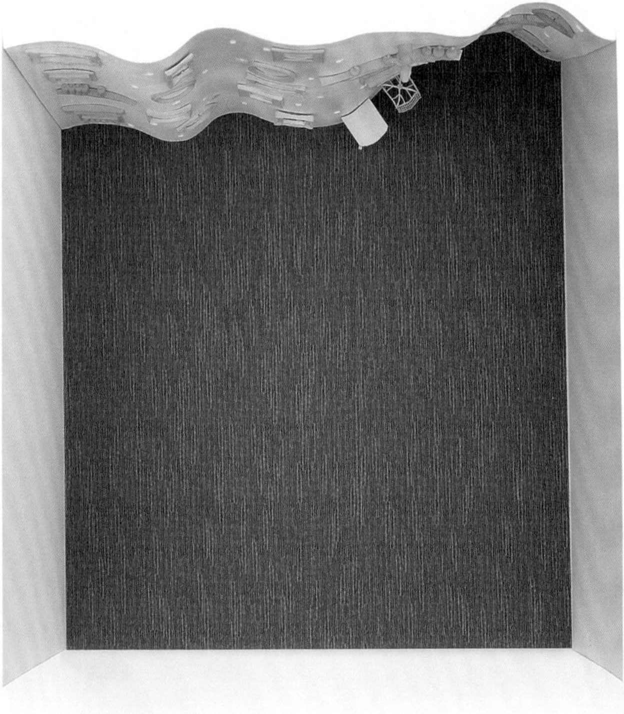

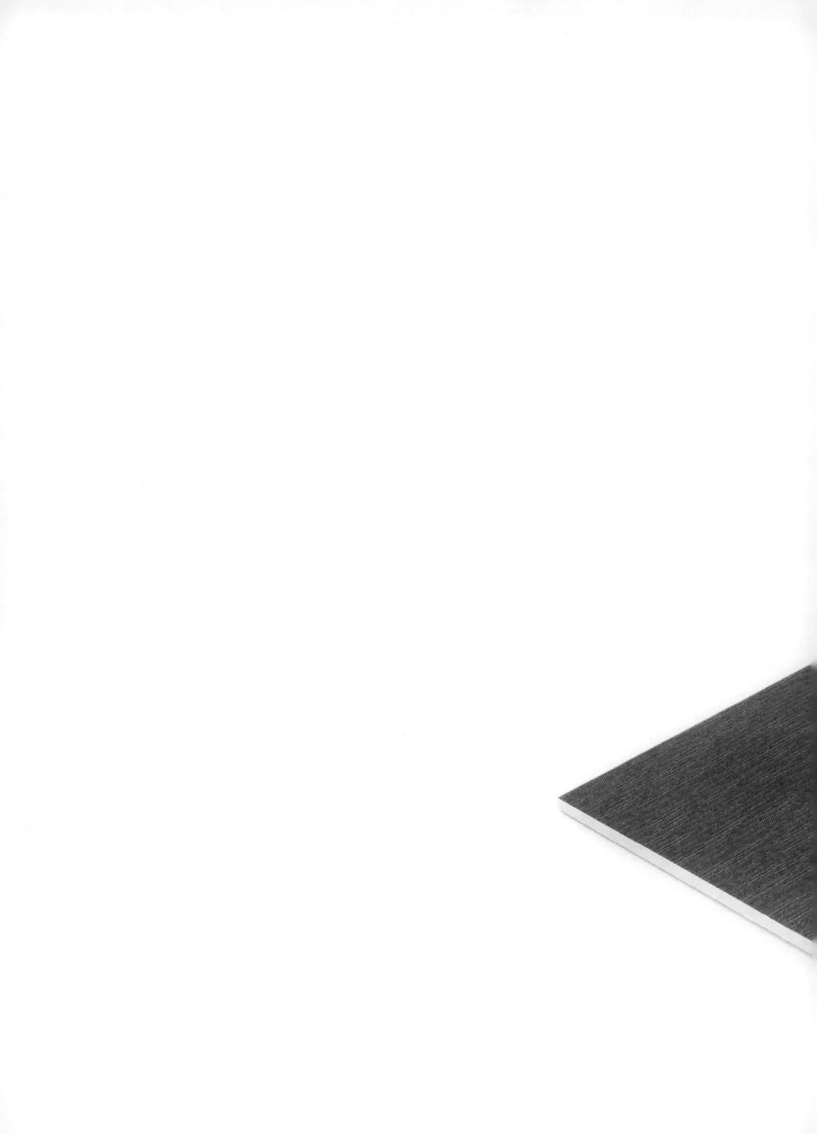

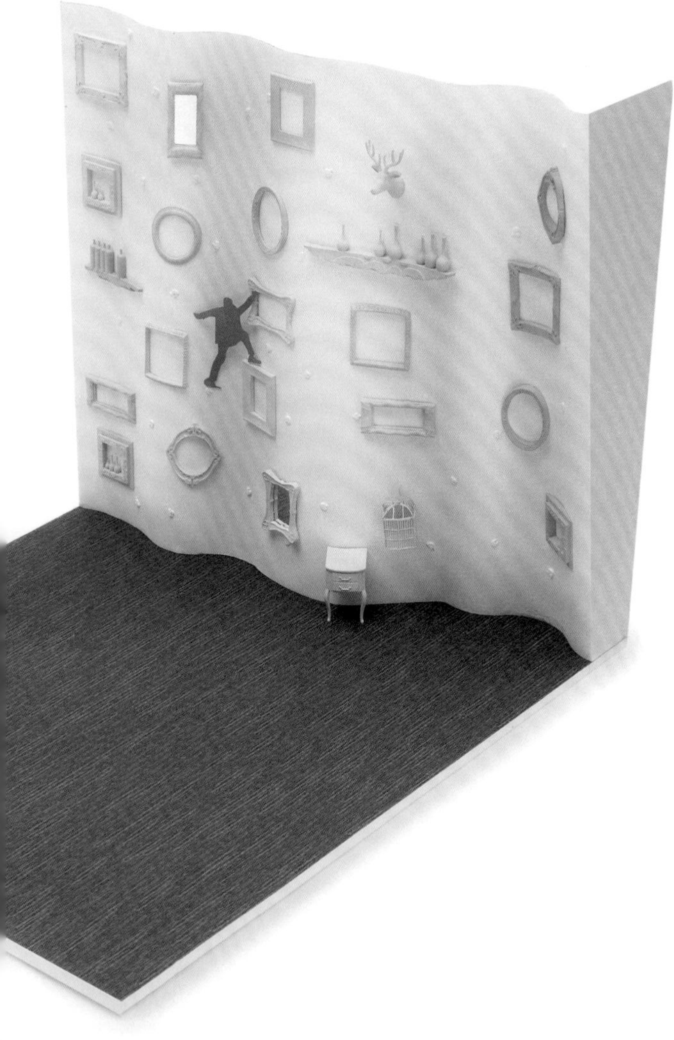

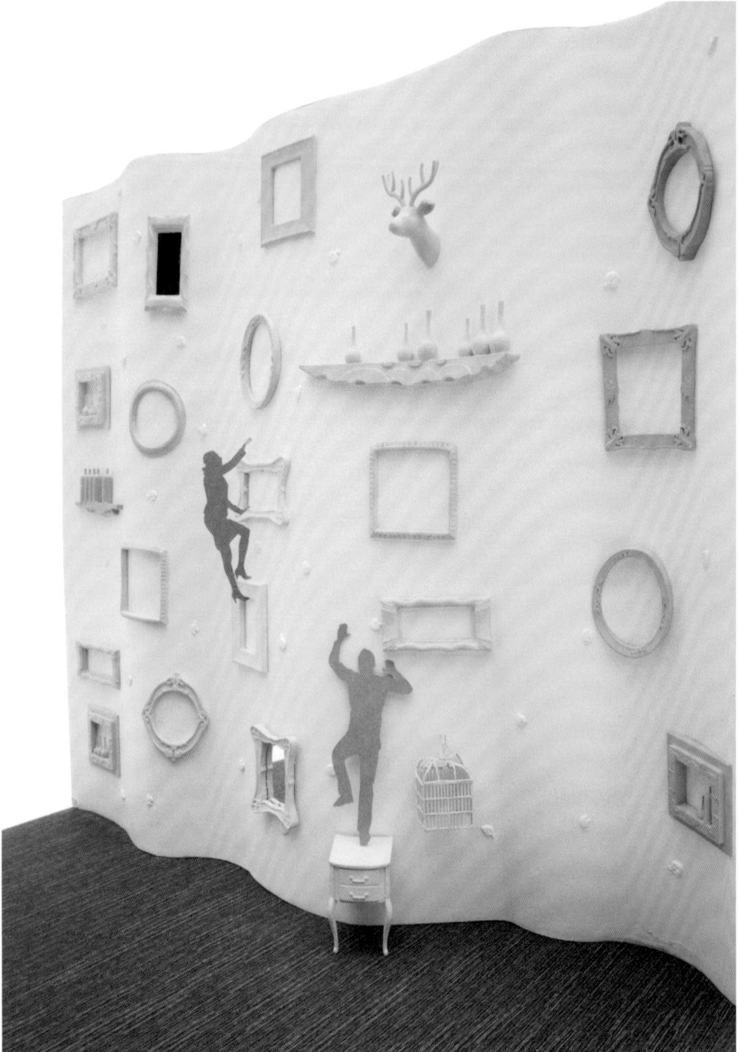

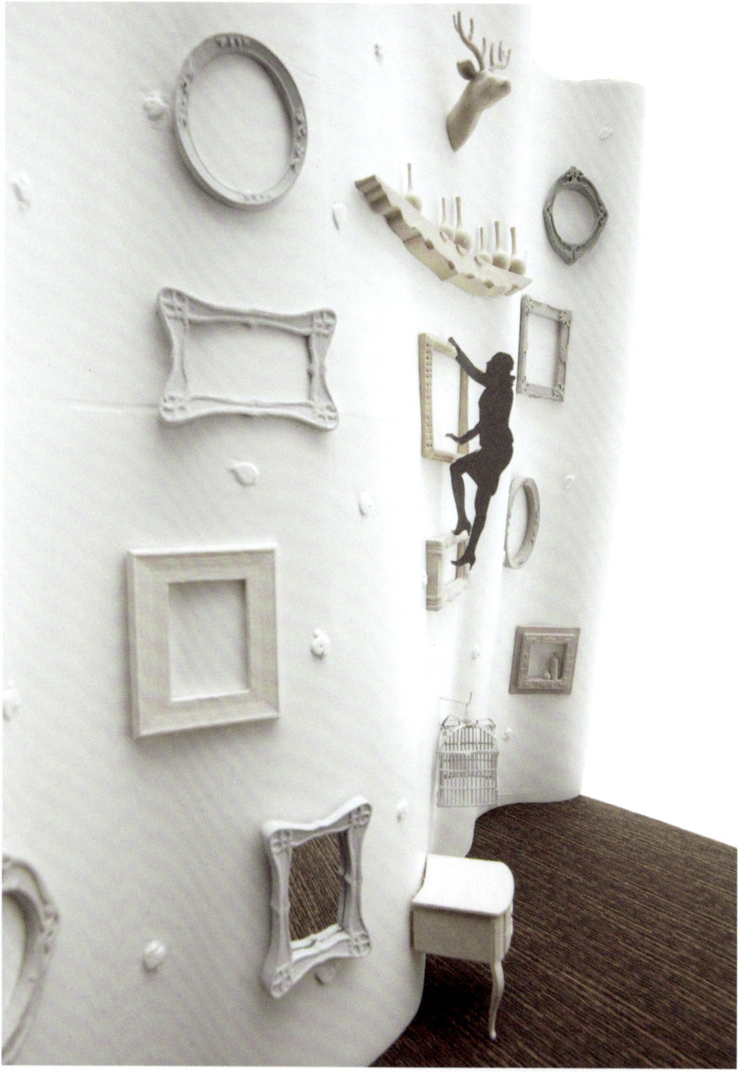

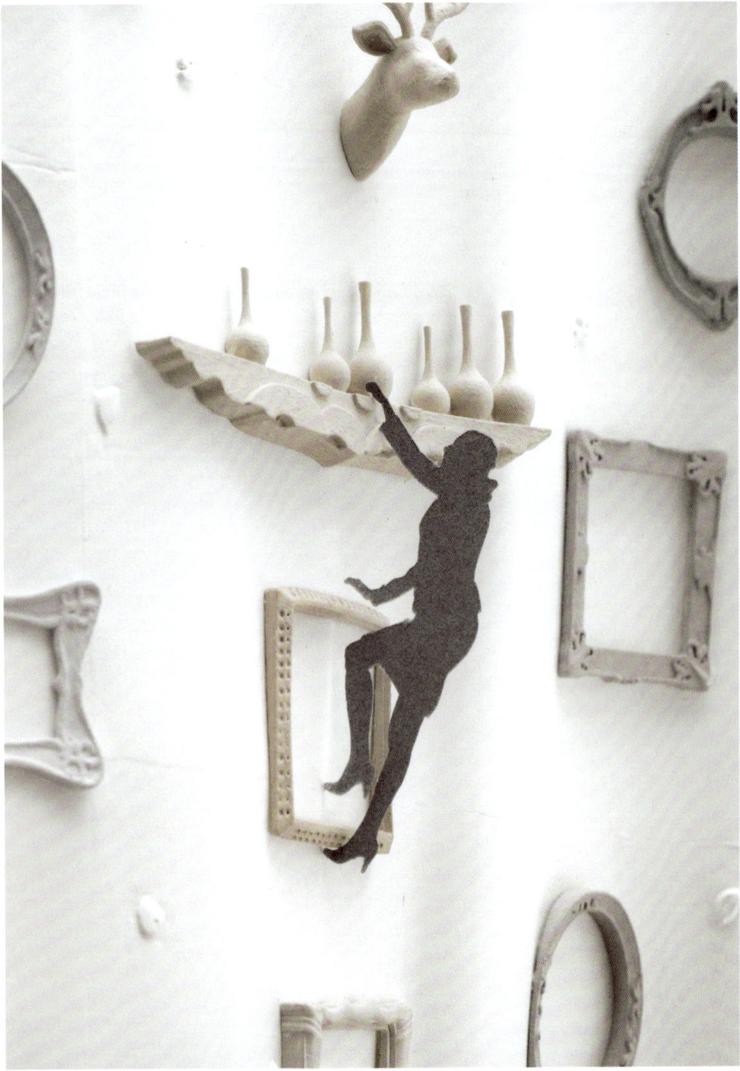

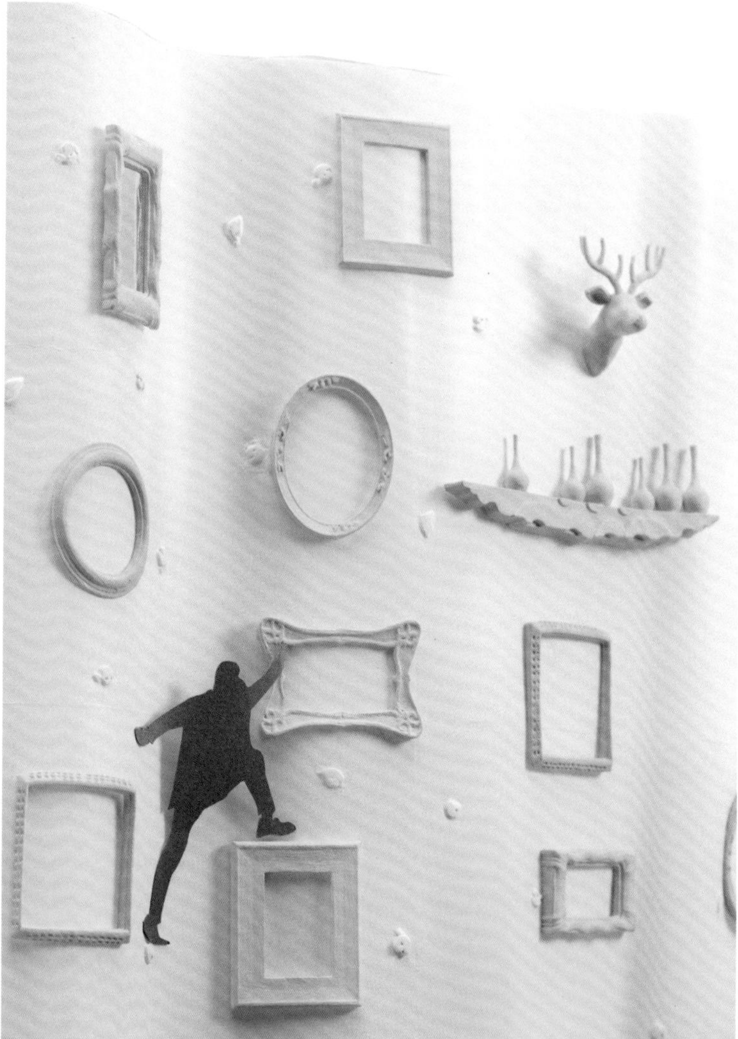

INDULGI

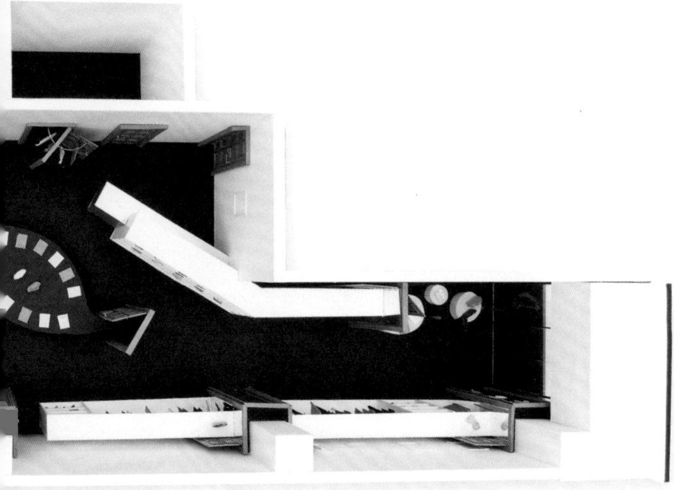

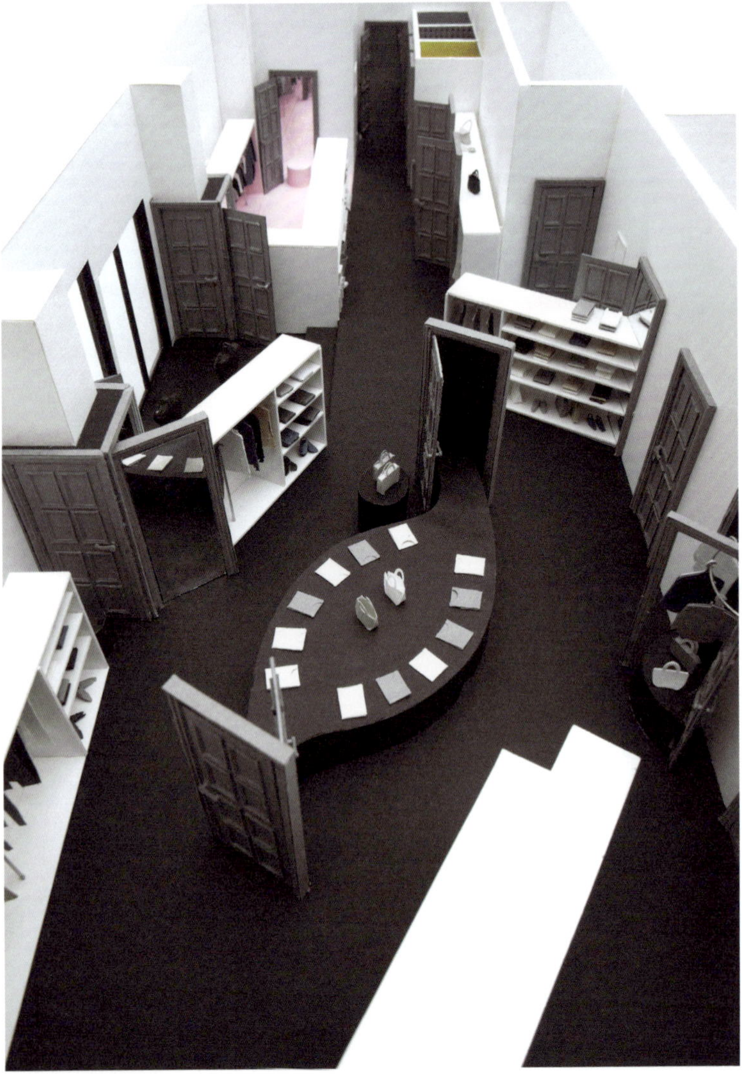

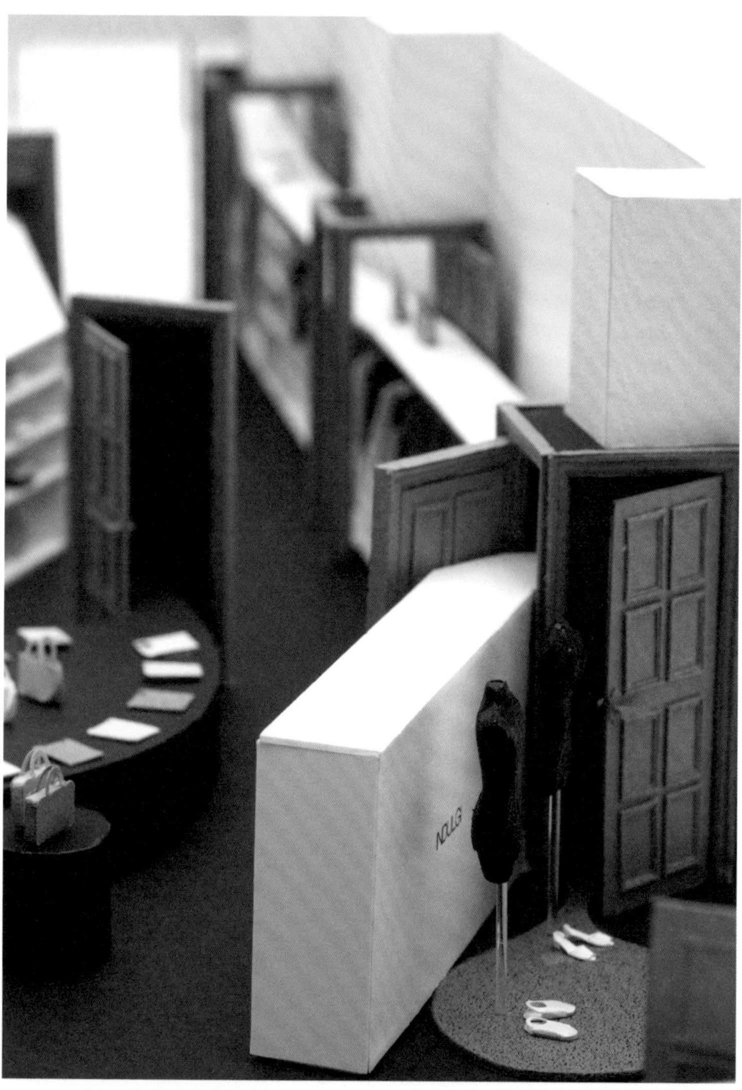

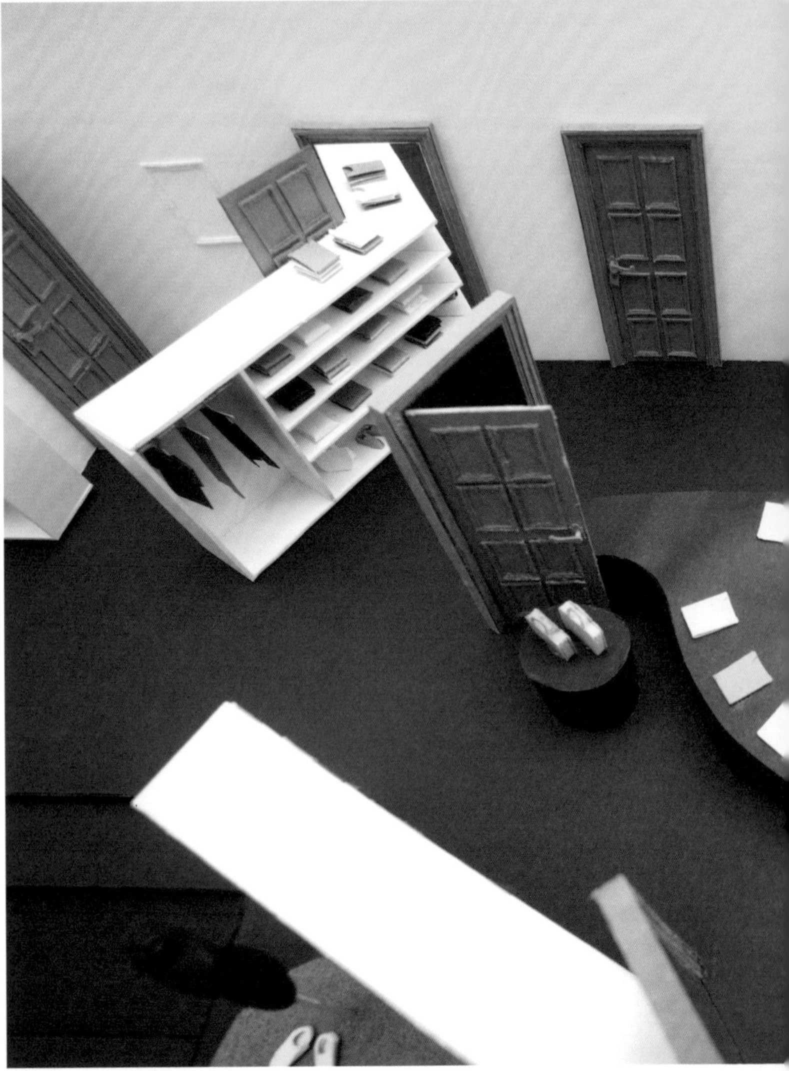

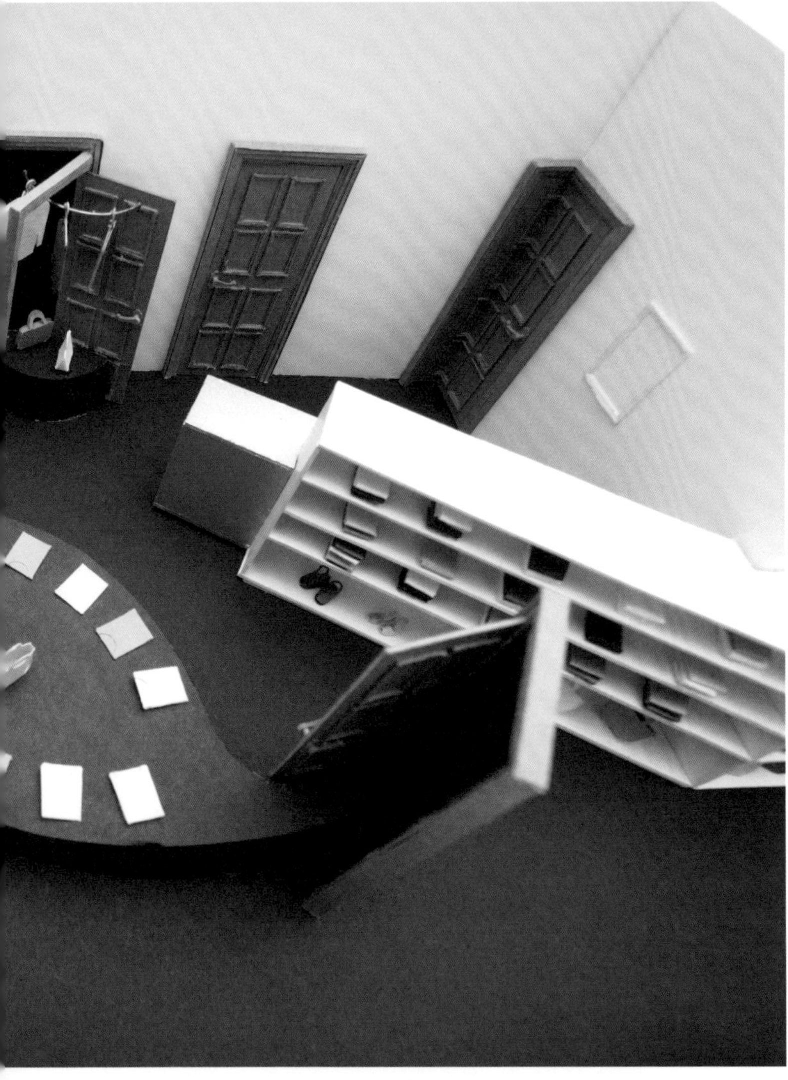

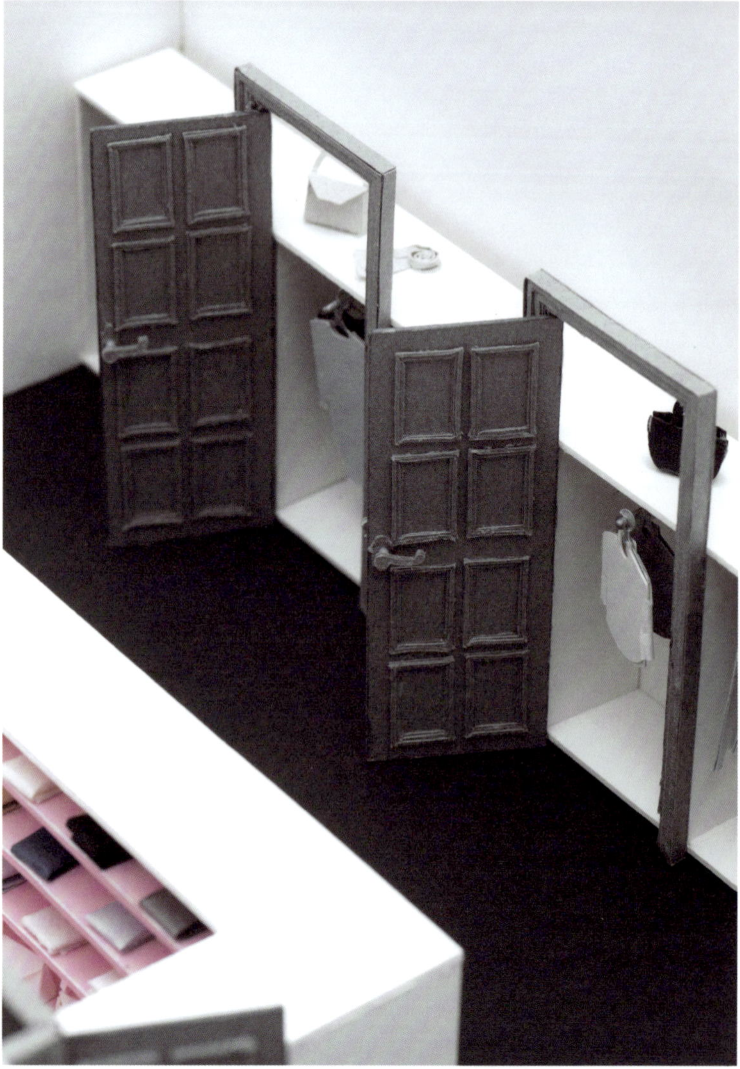

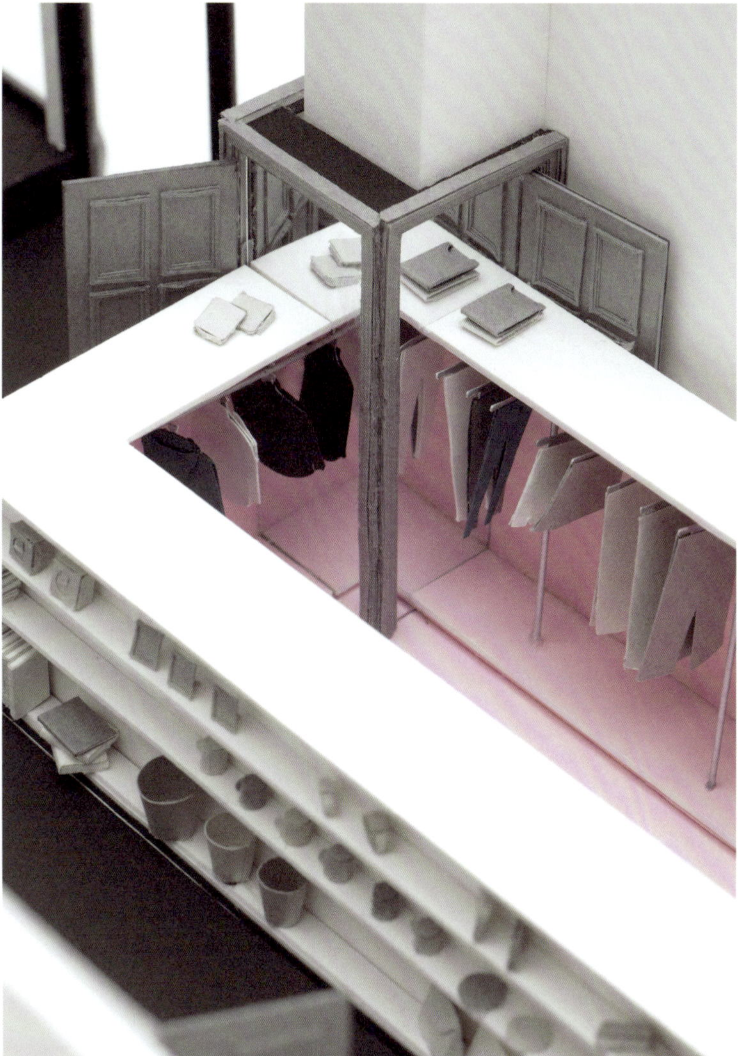

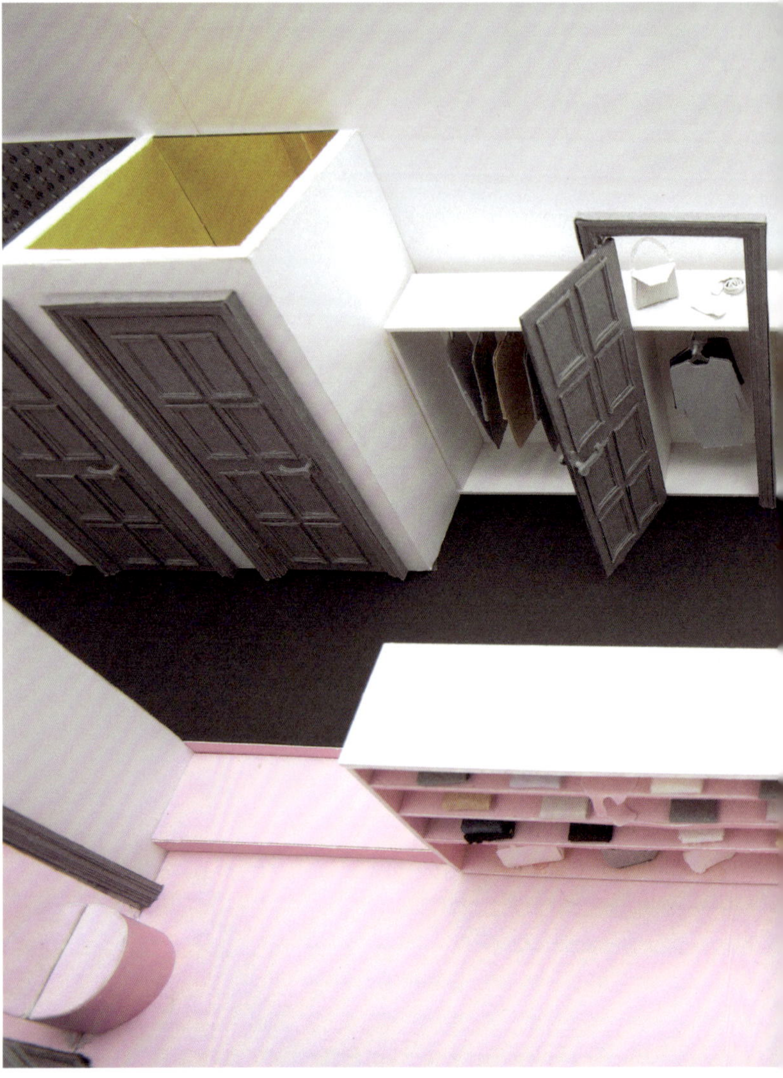

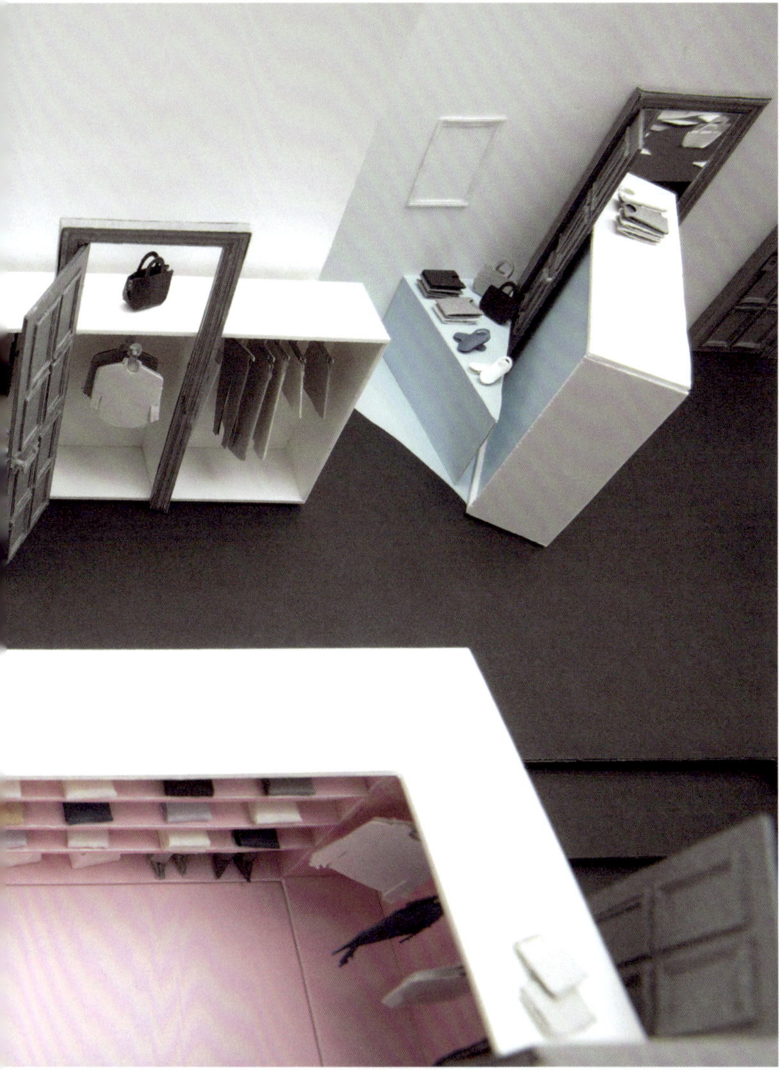

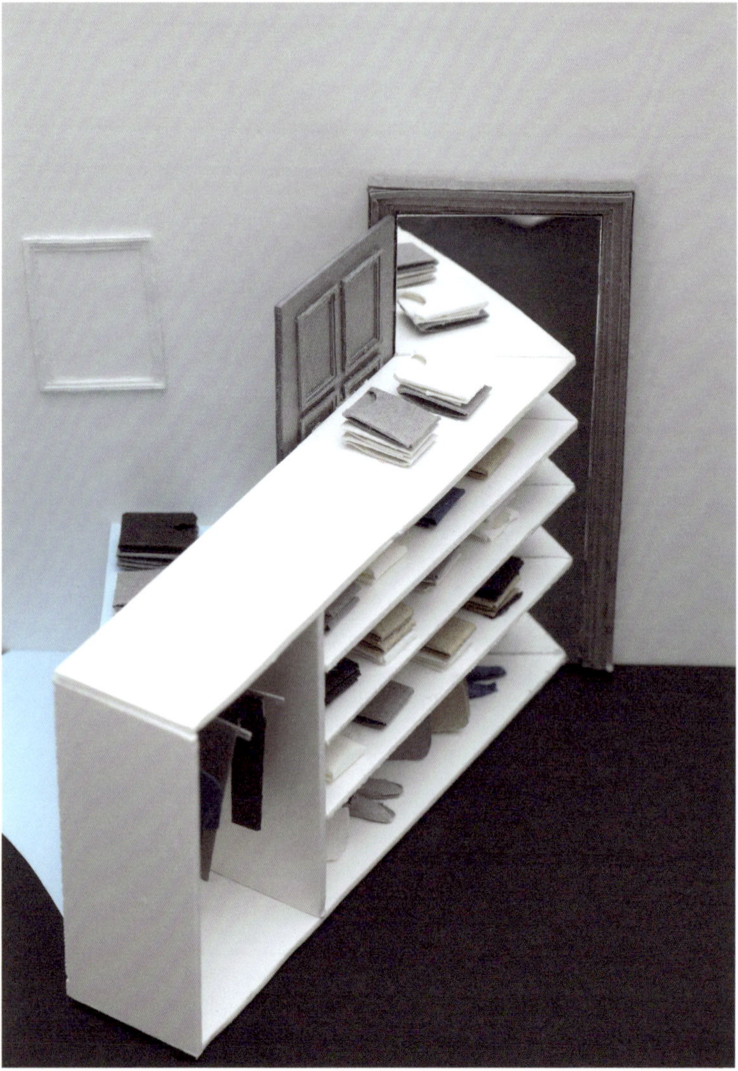

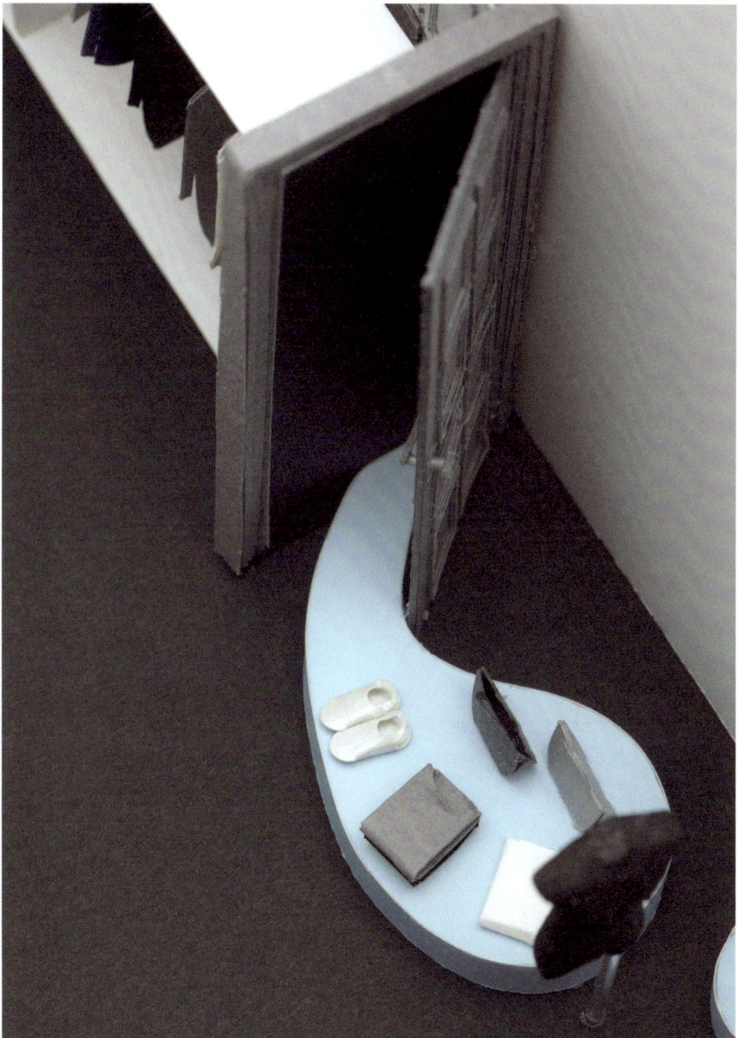

International KOGEI Triennale

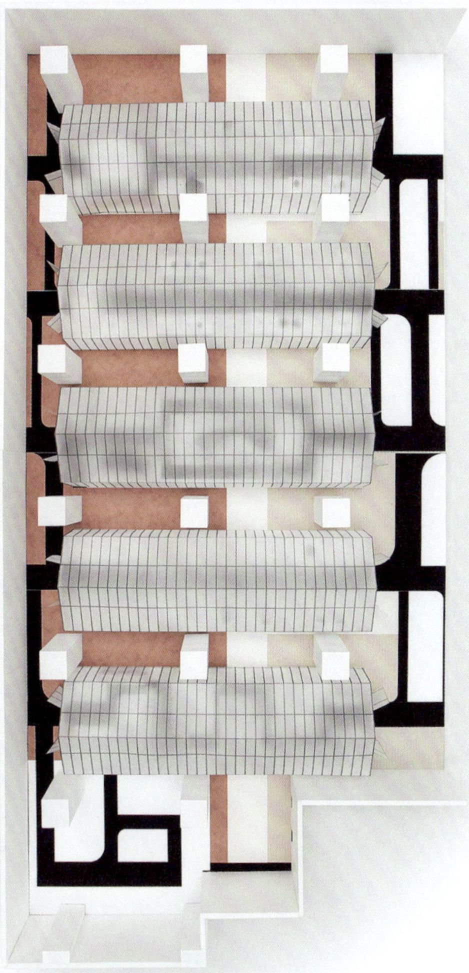

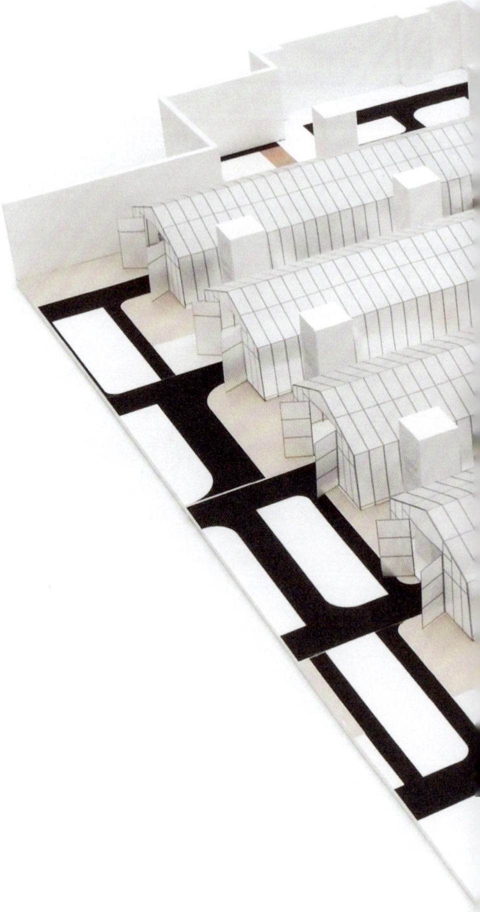

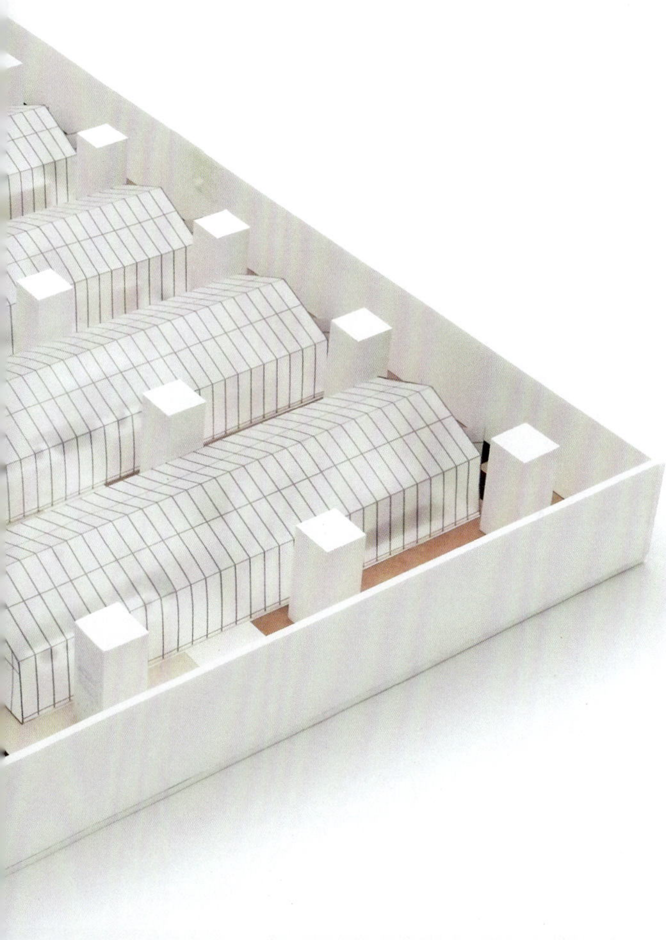

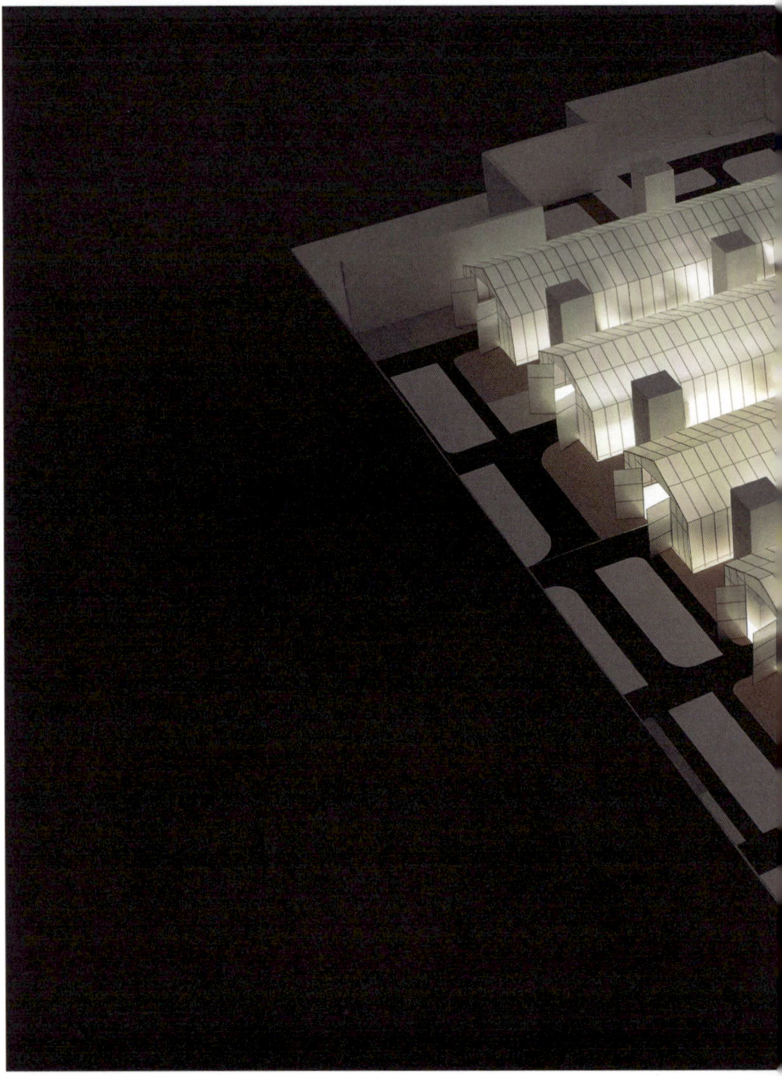

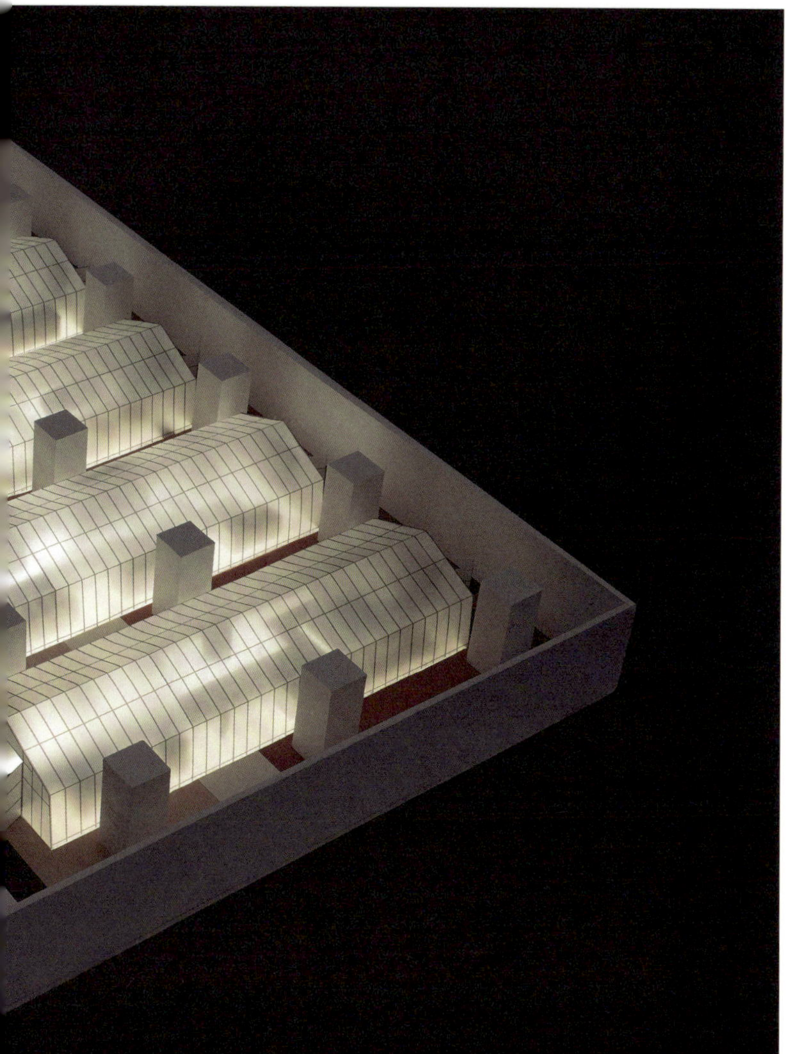

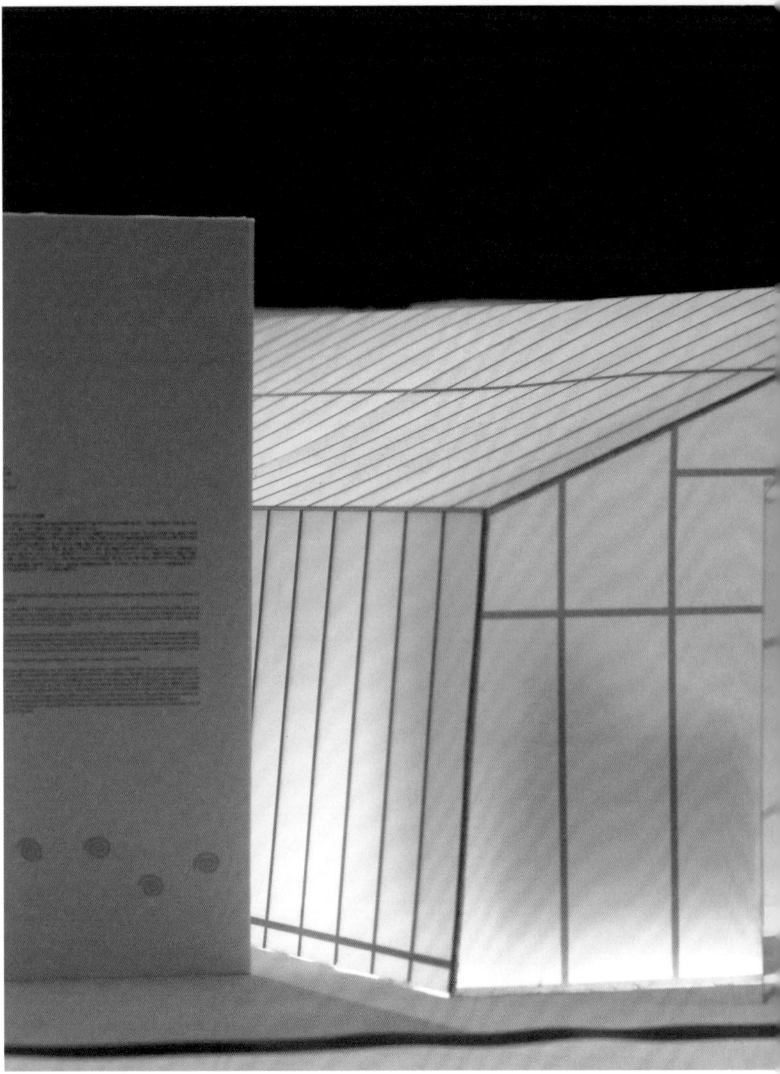

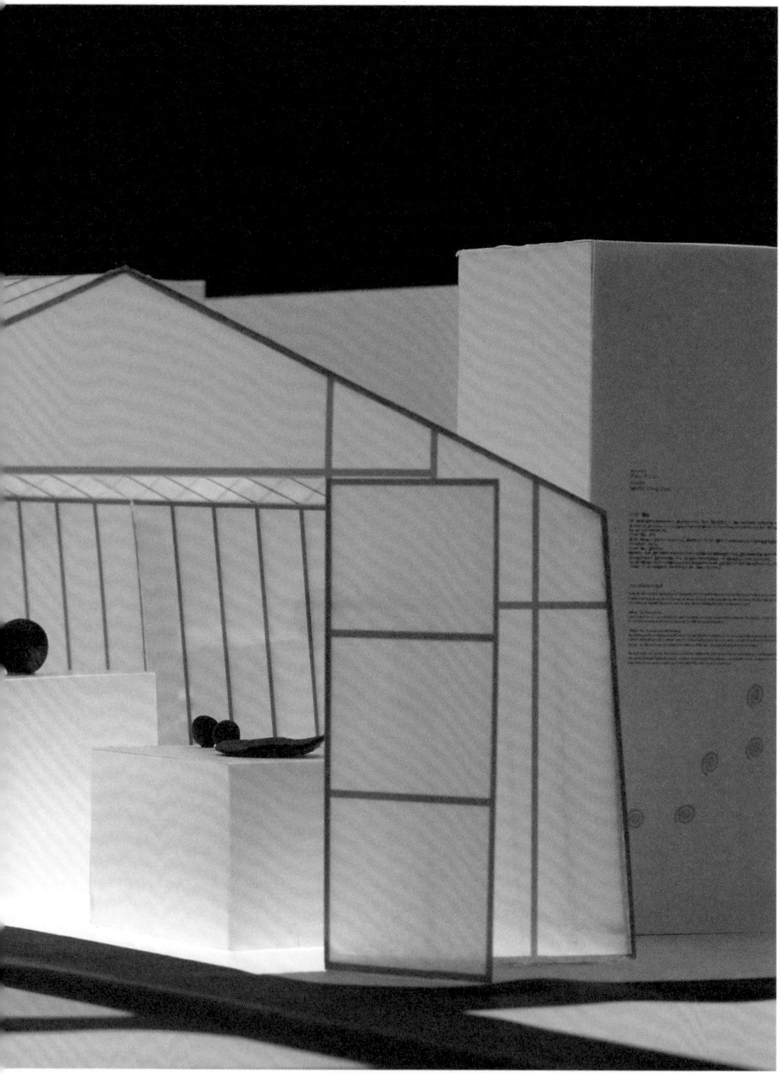

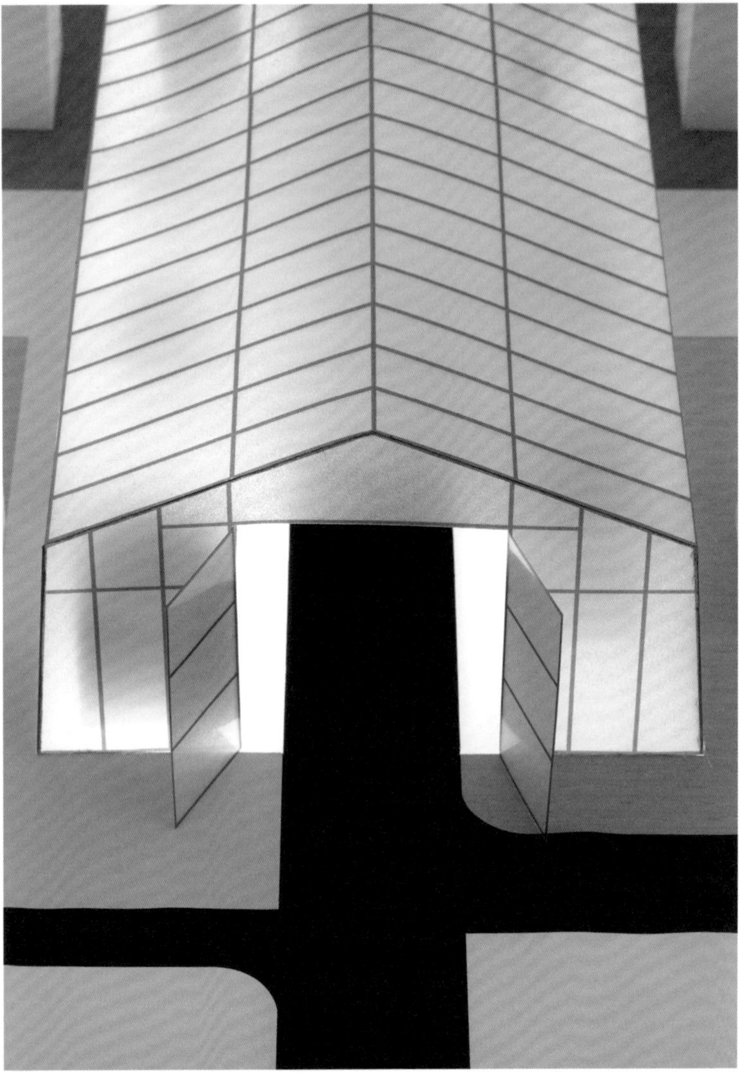

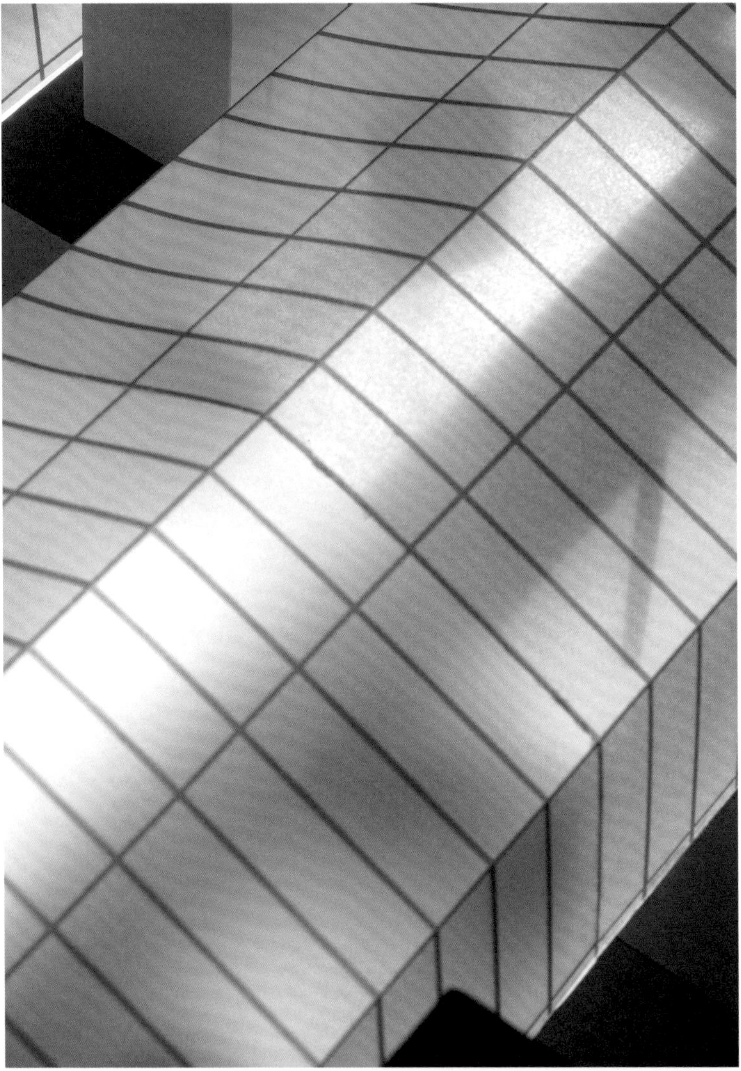

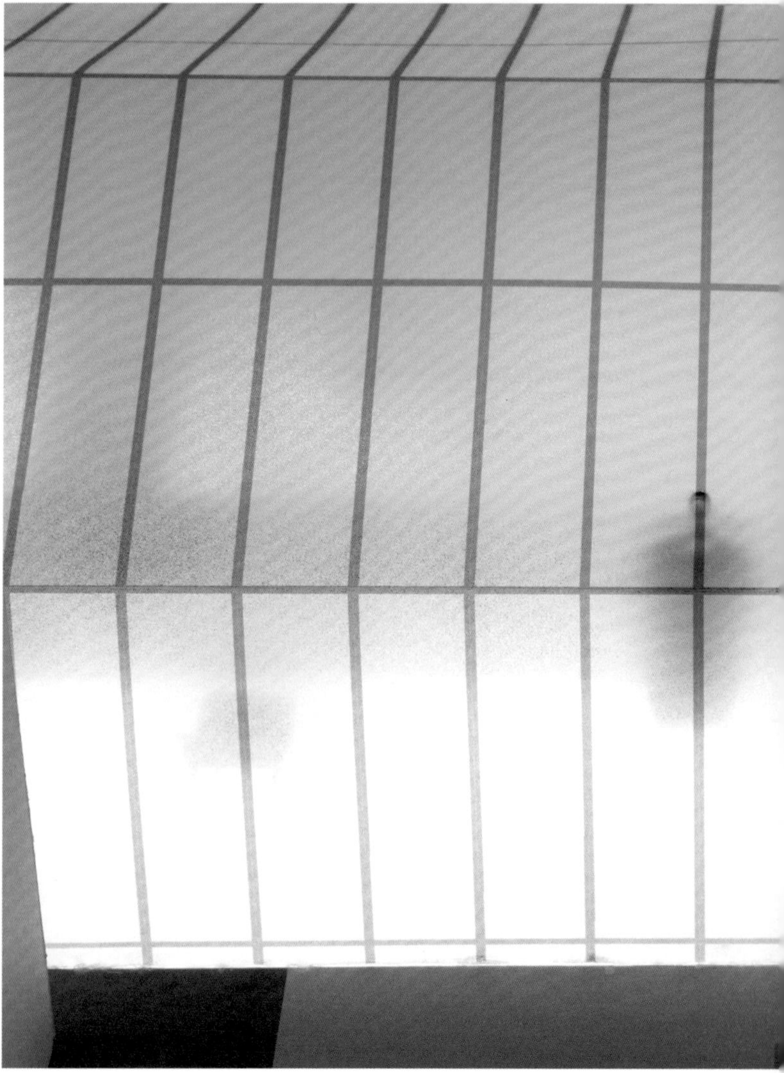

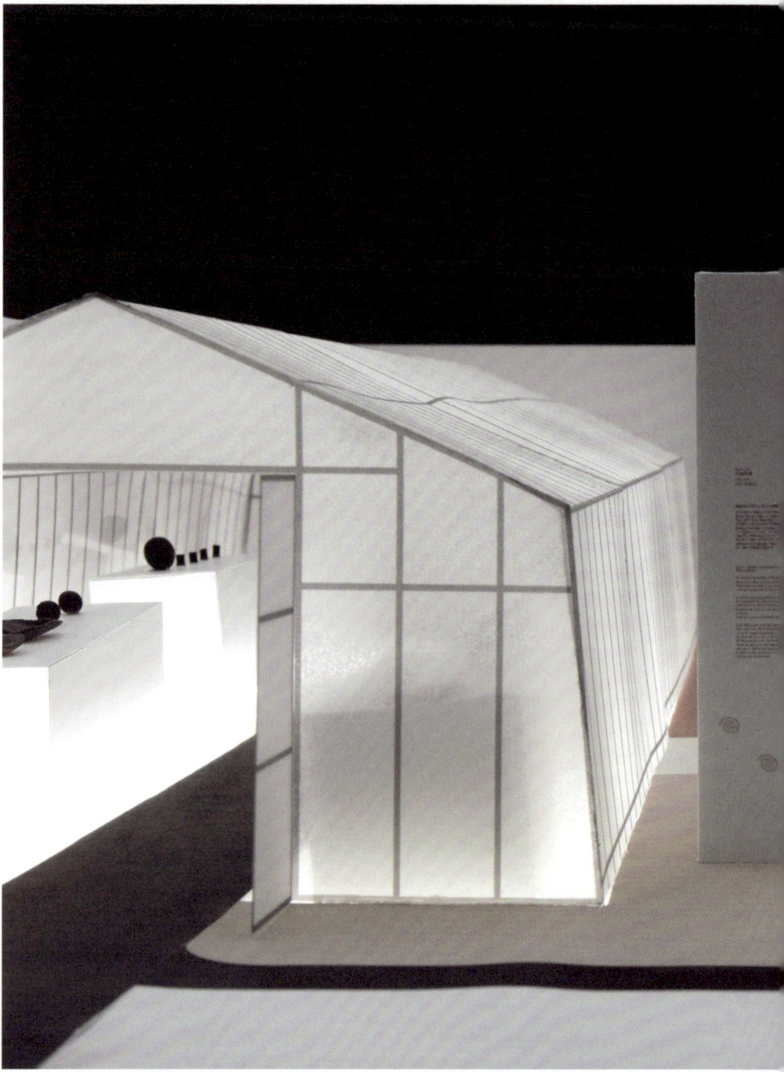

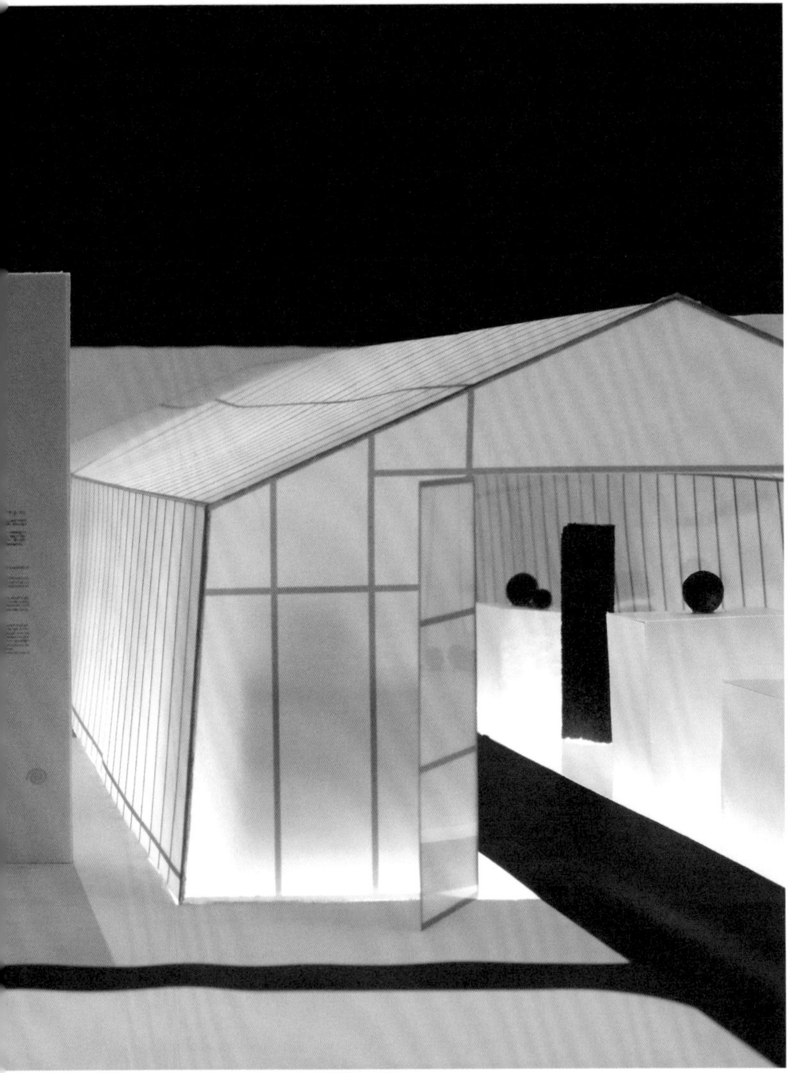

International KOGEI Triennale Pre-event

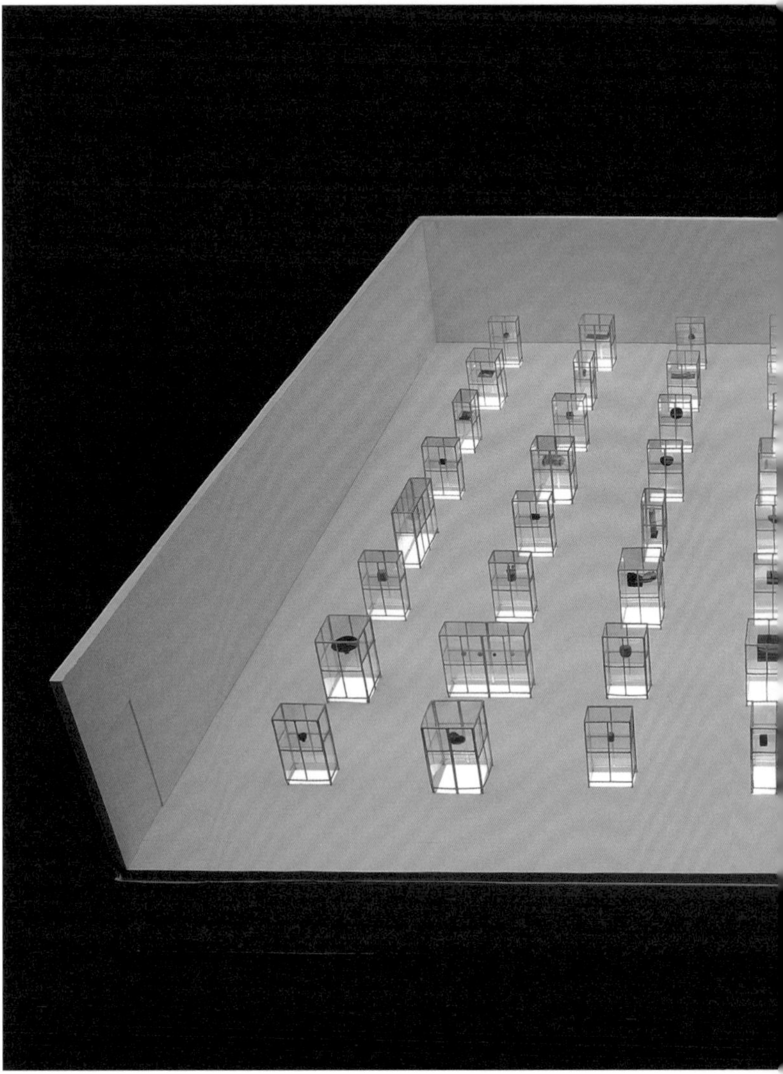

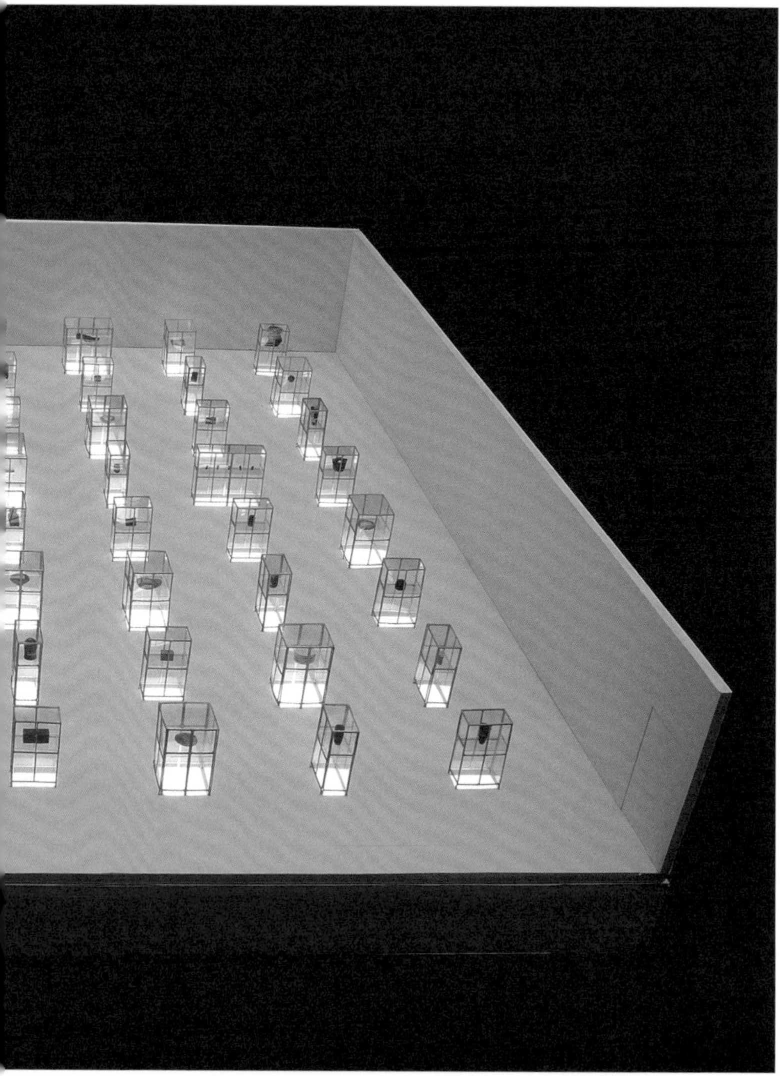

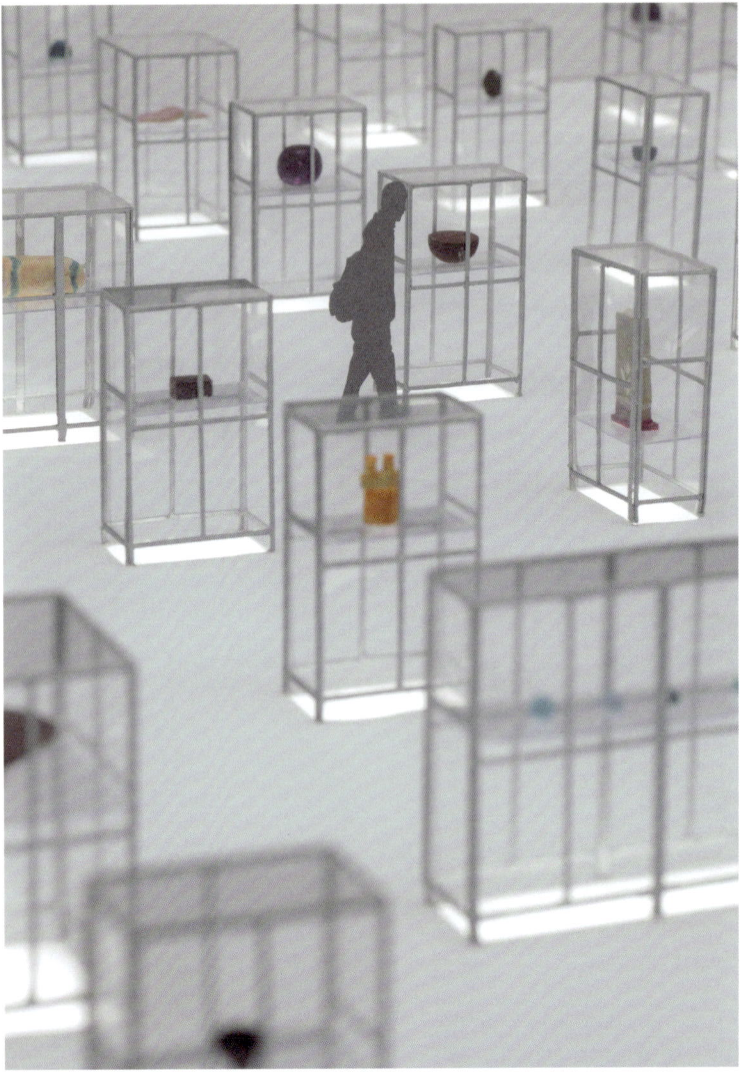

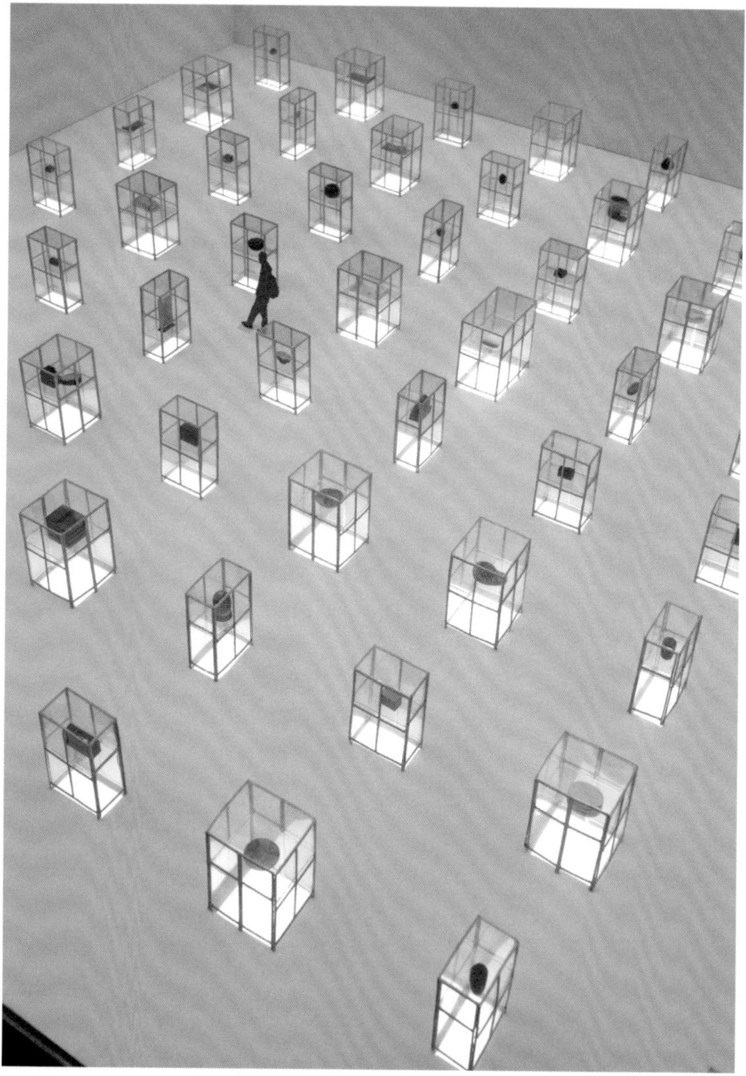

JAPAN: Tradition. Innovation.

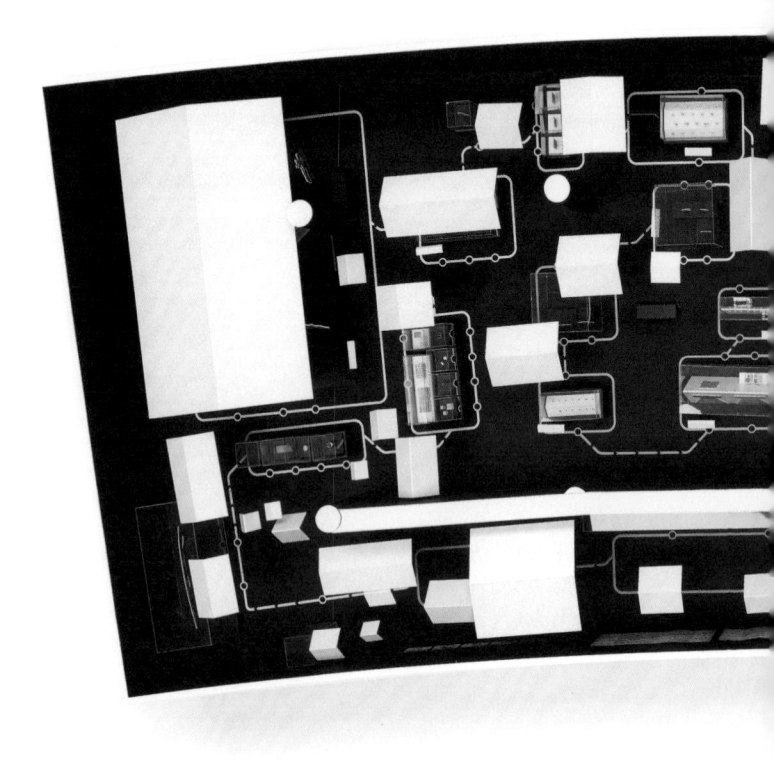

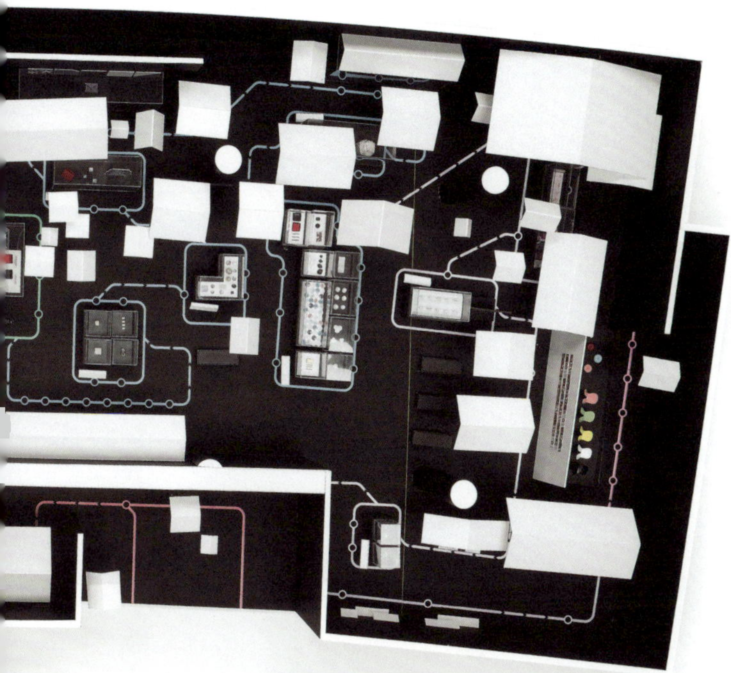

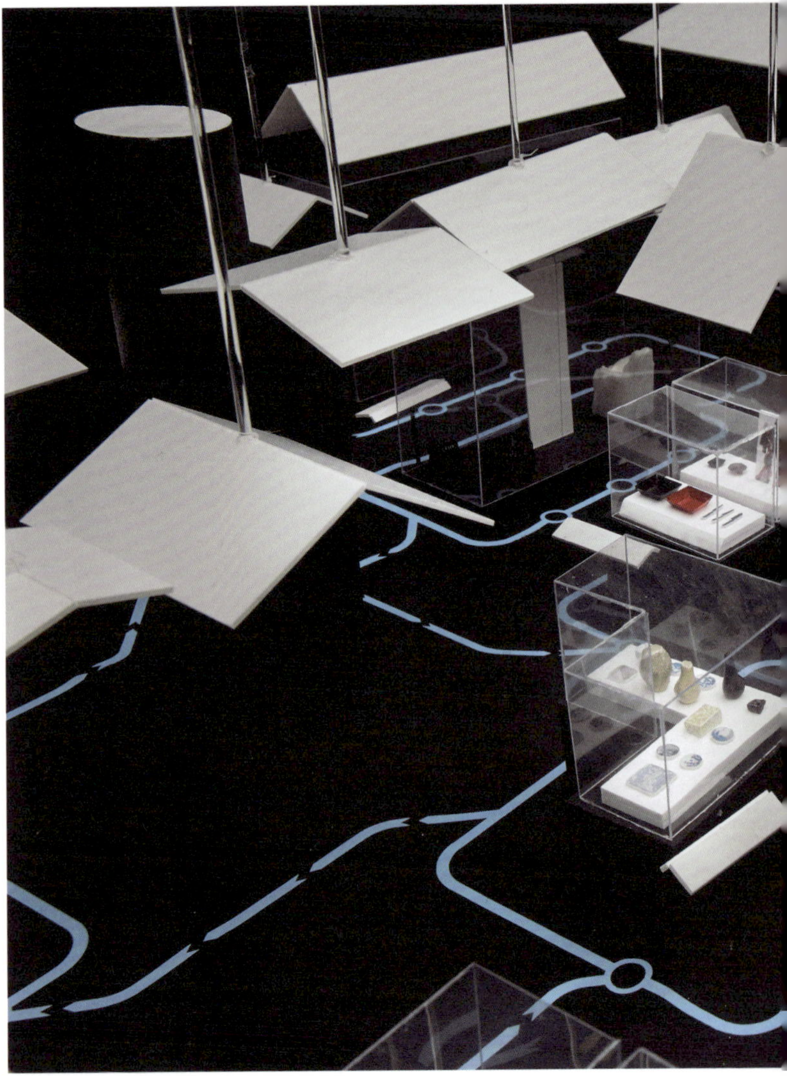

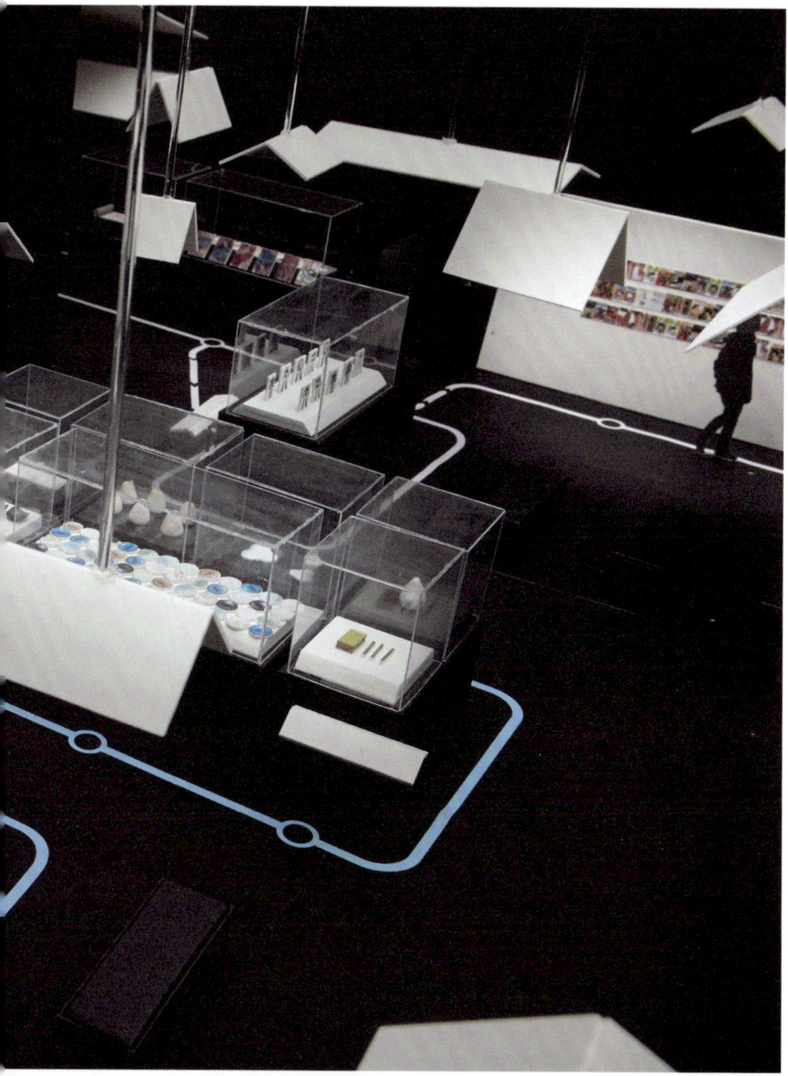

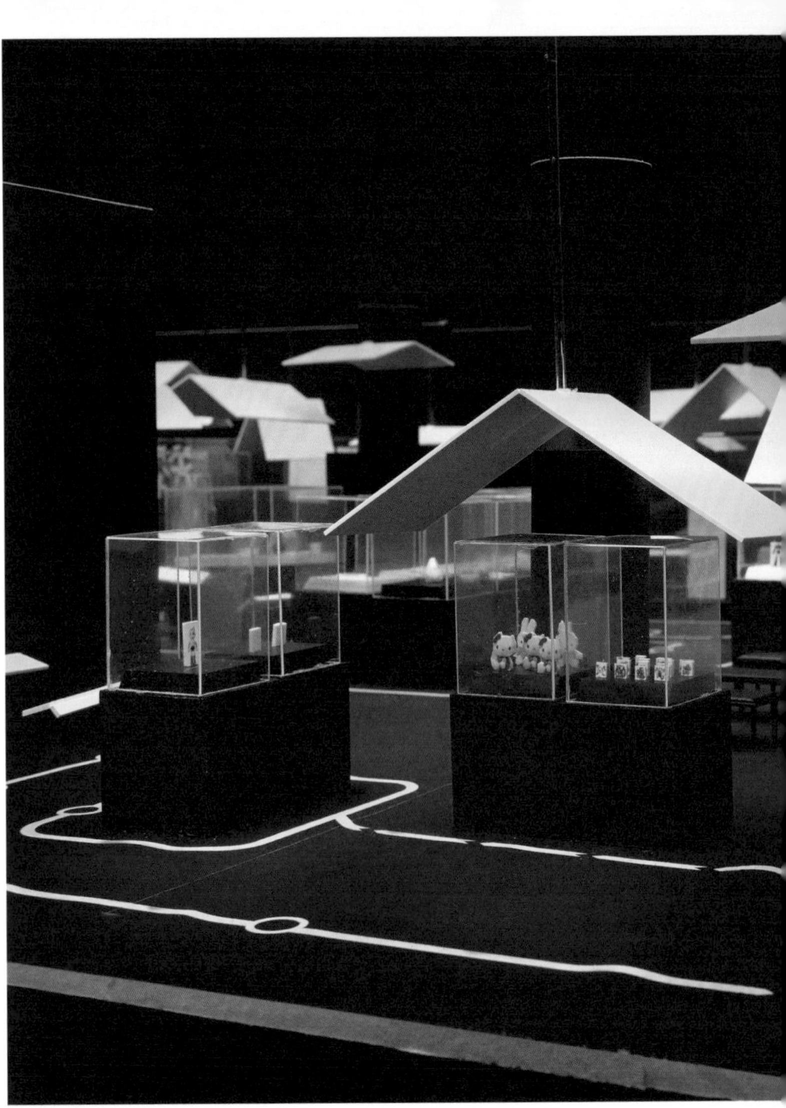

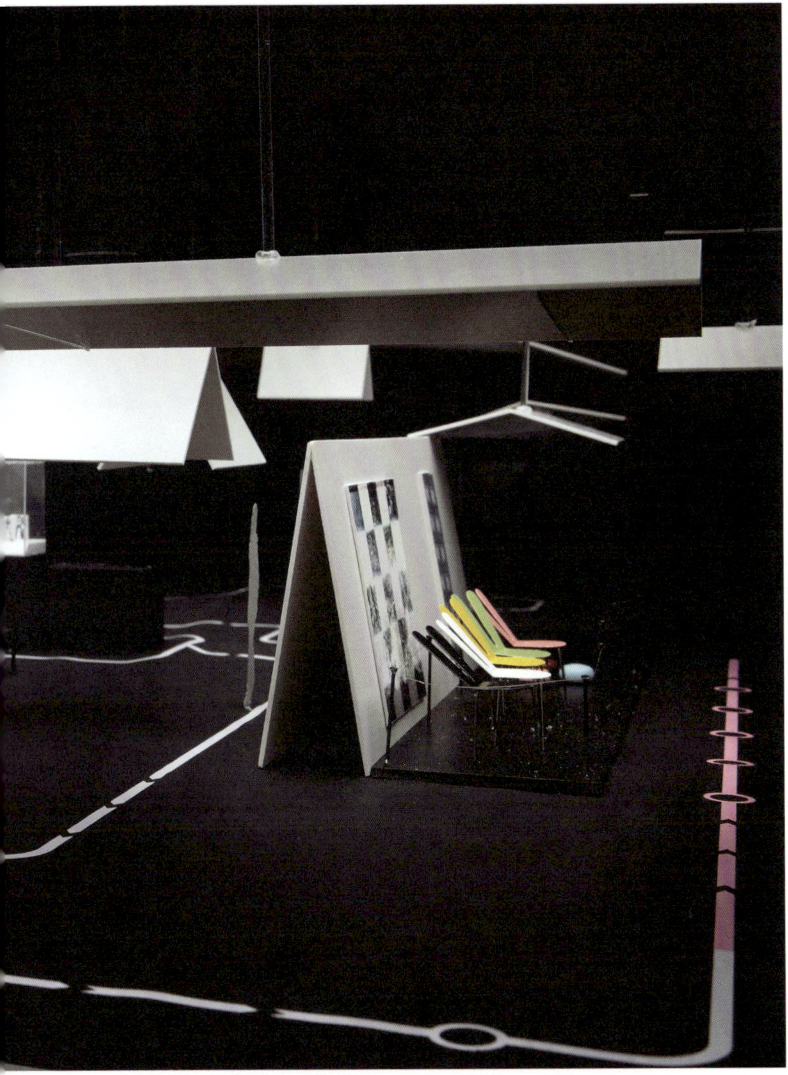

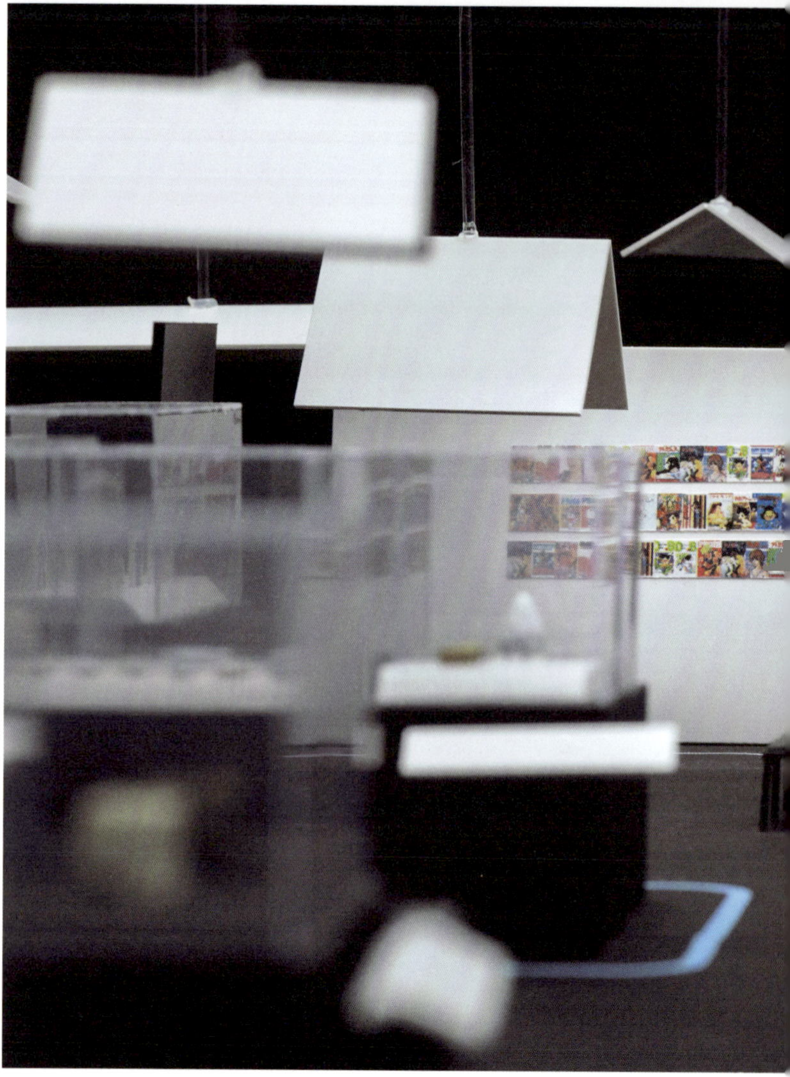

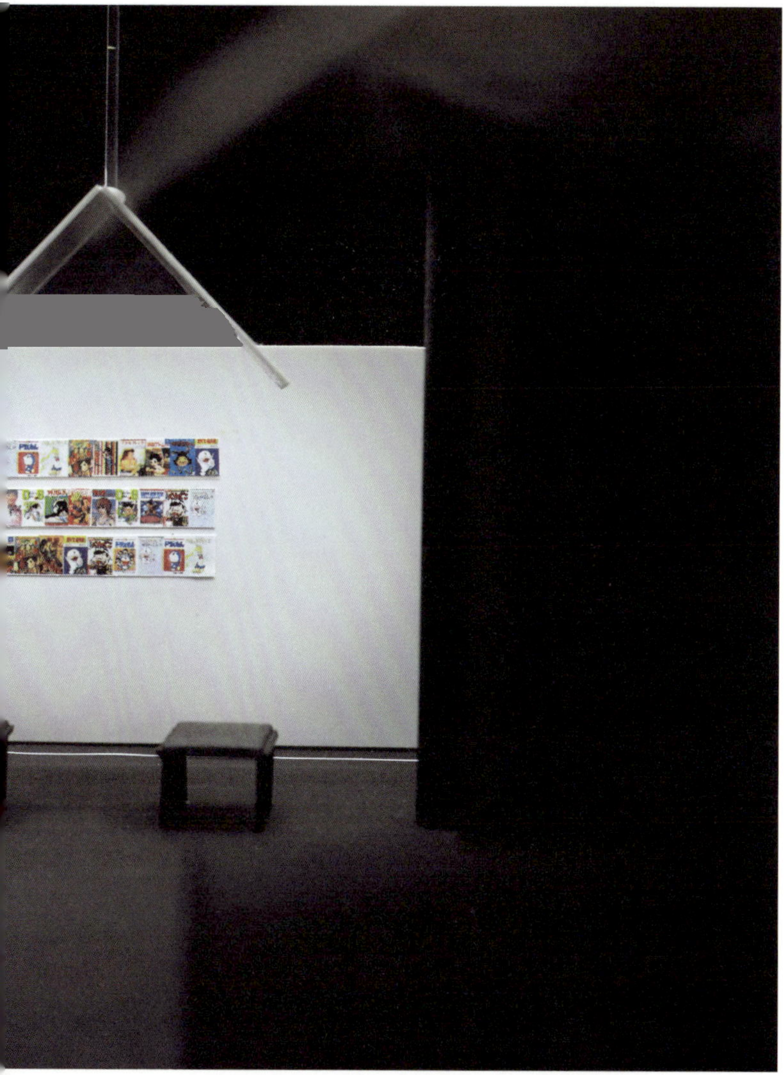

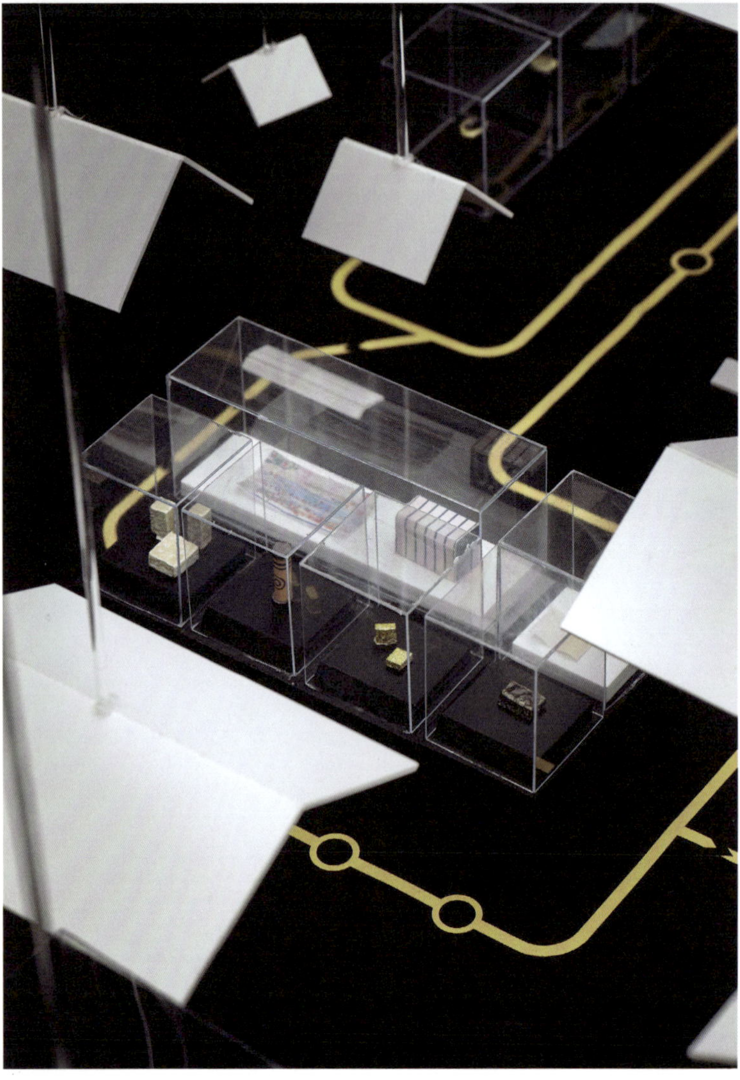

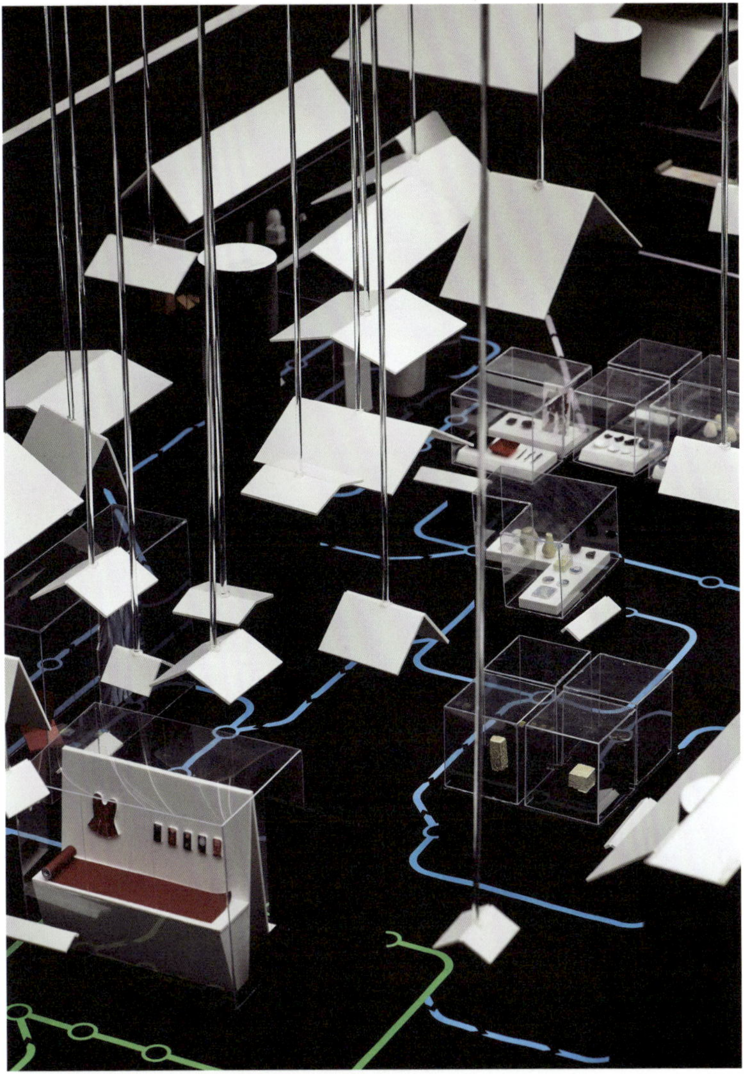

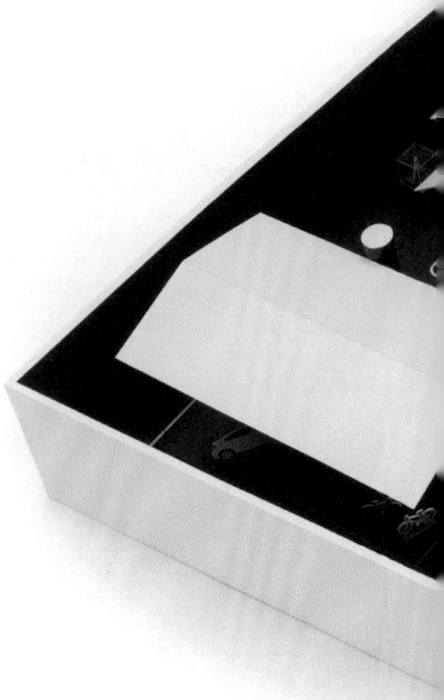

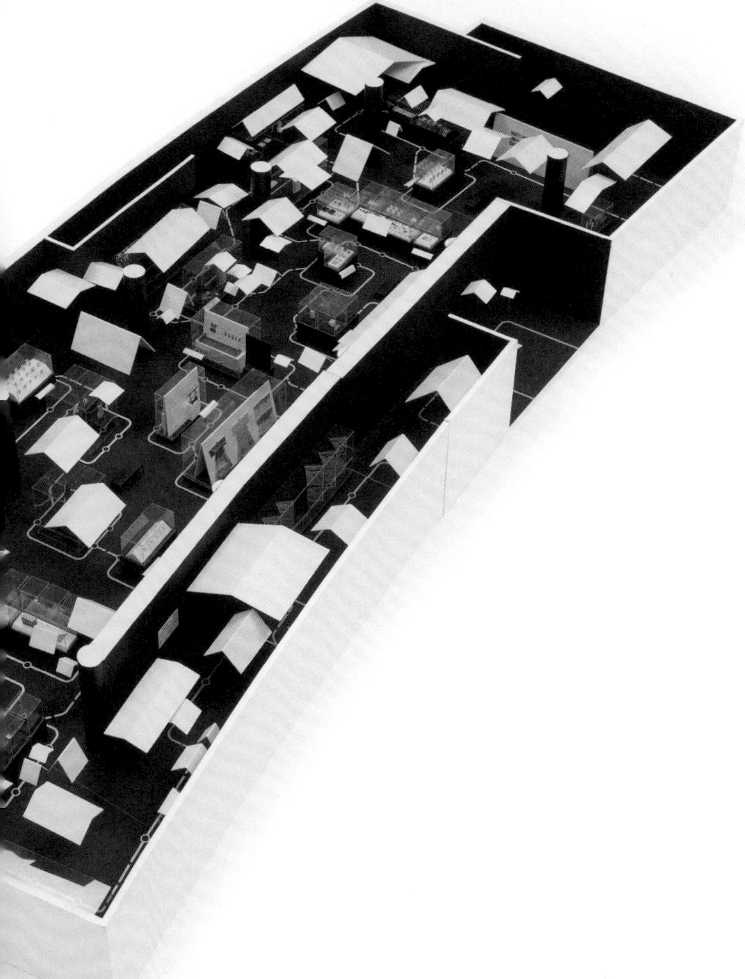

karaoke-tub

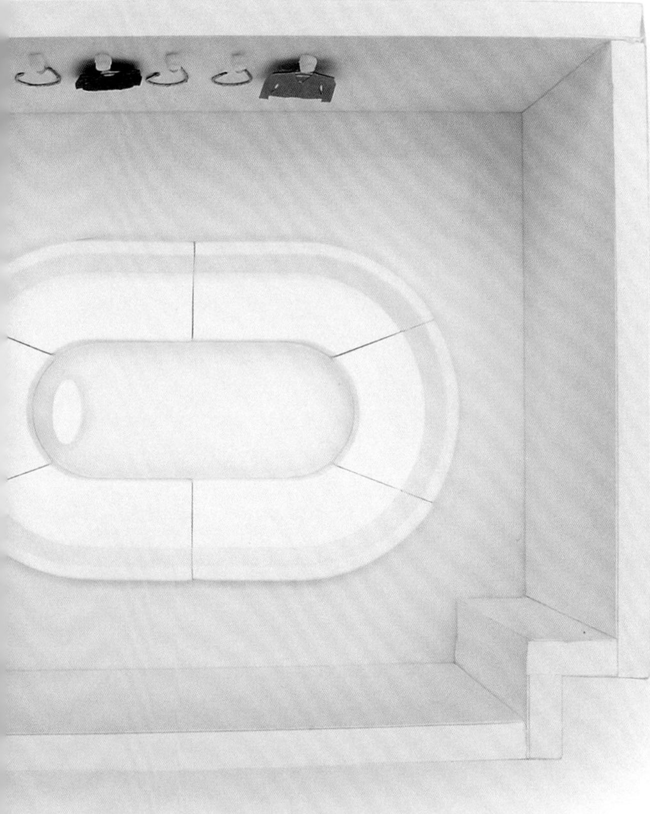

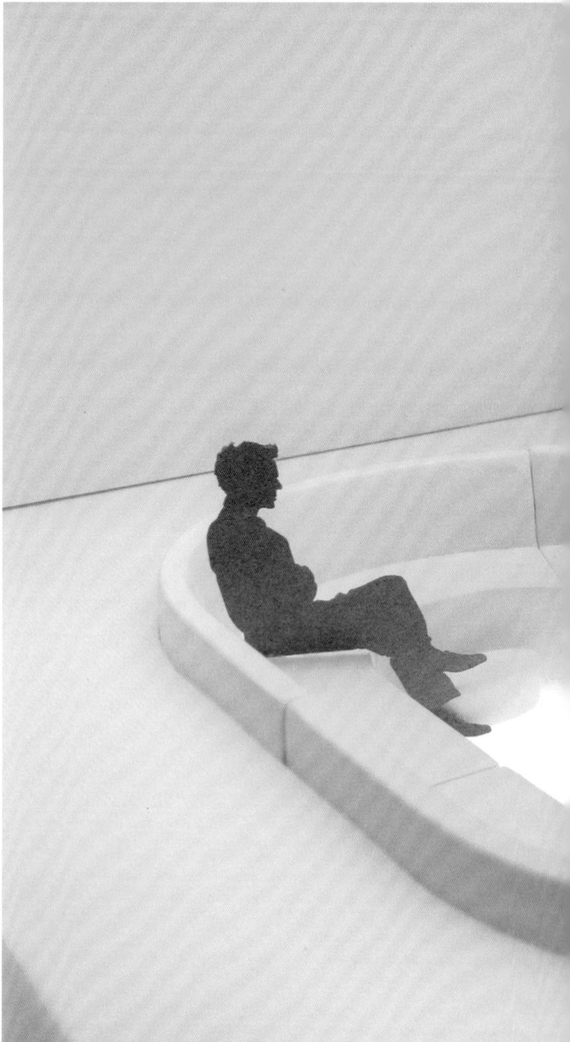

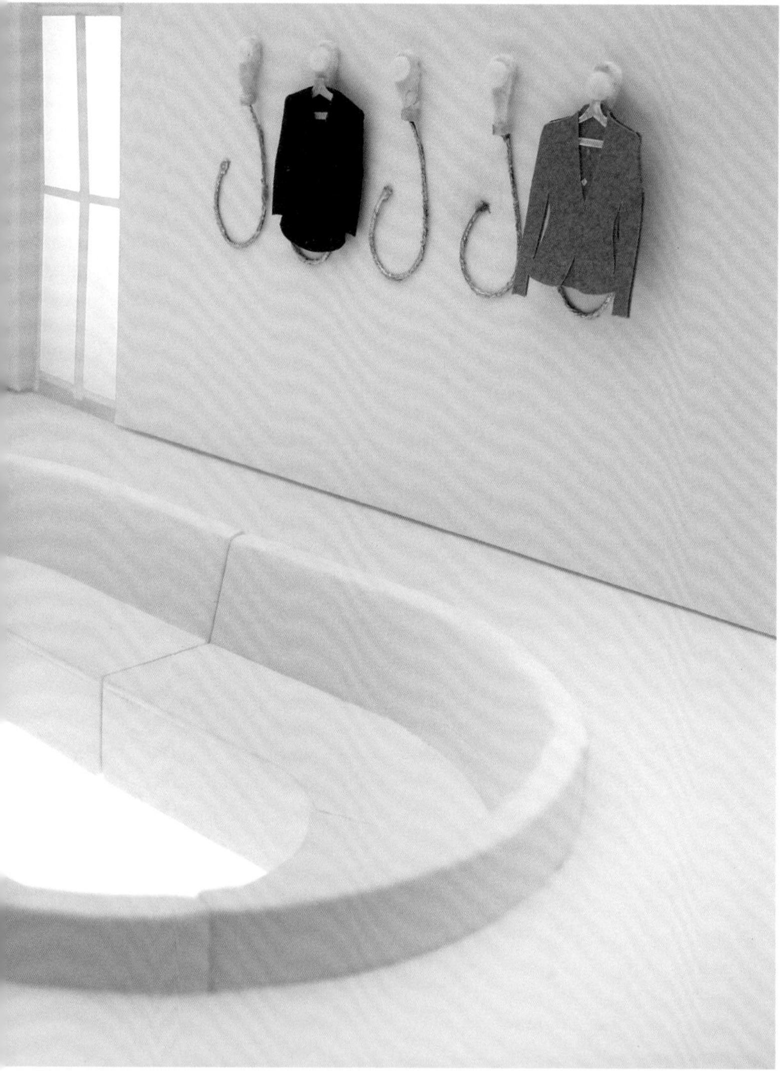

kisala

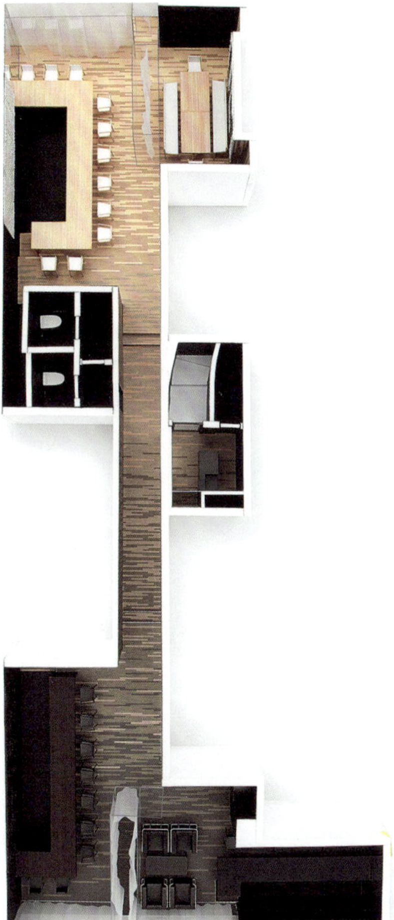

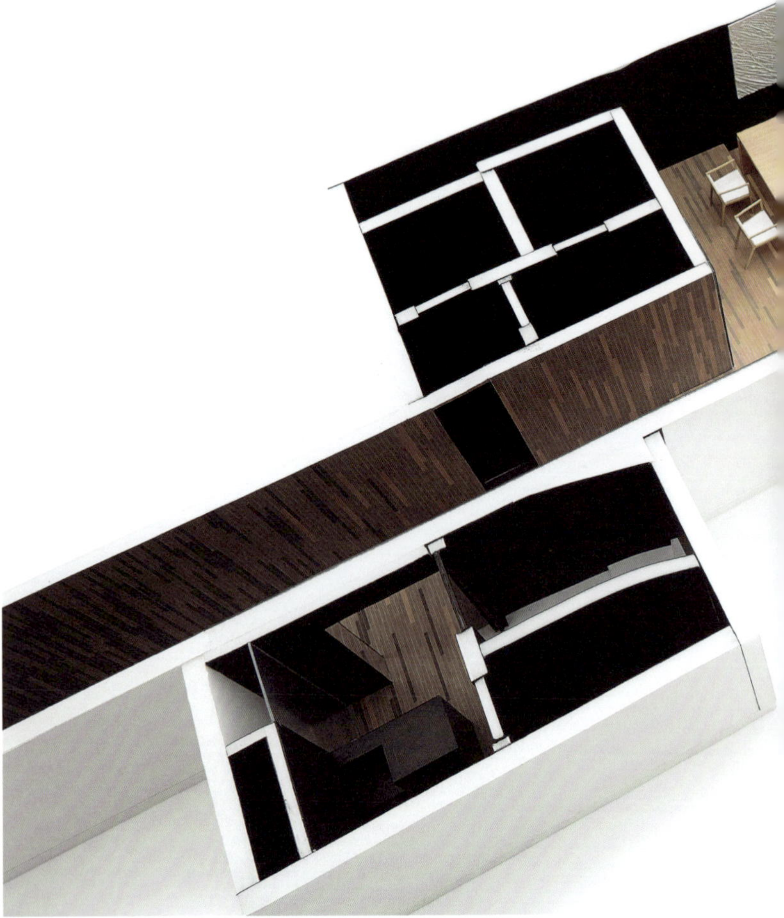

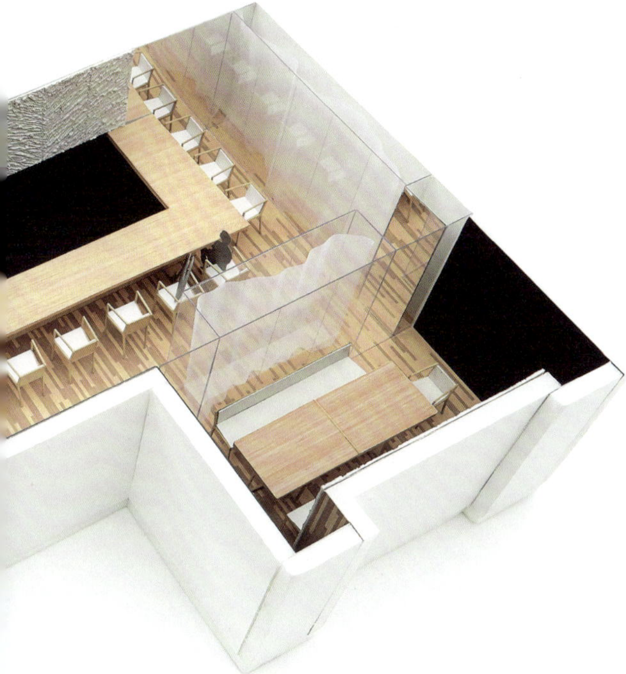

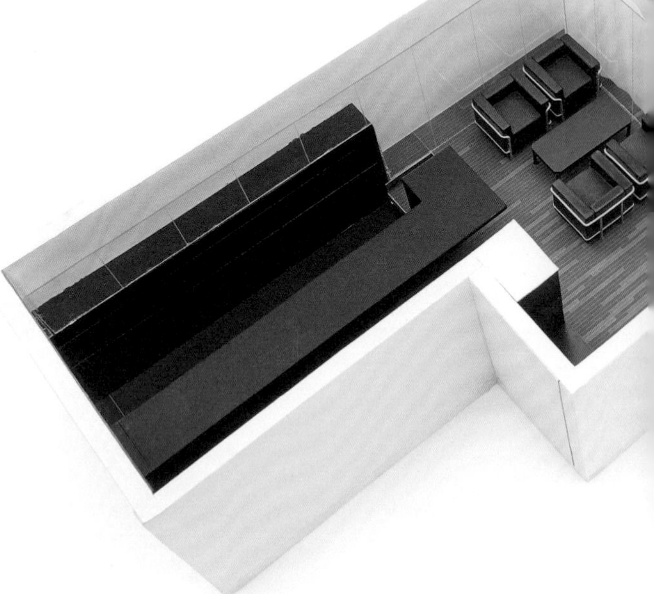

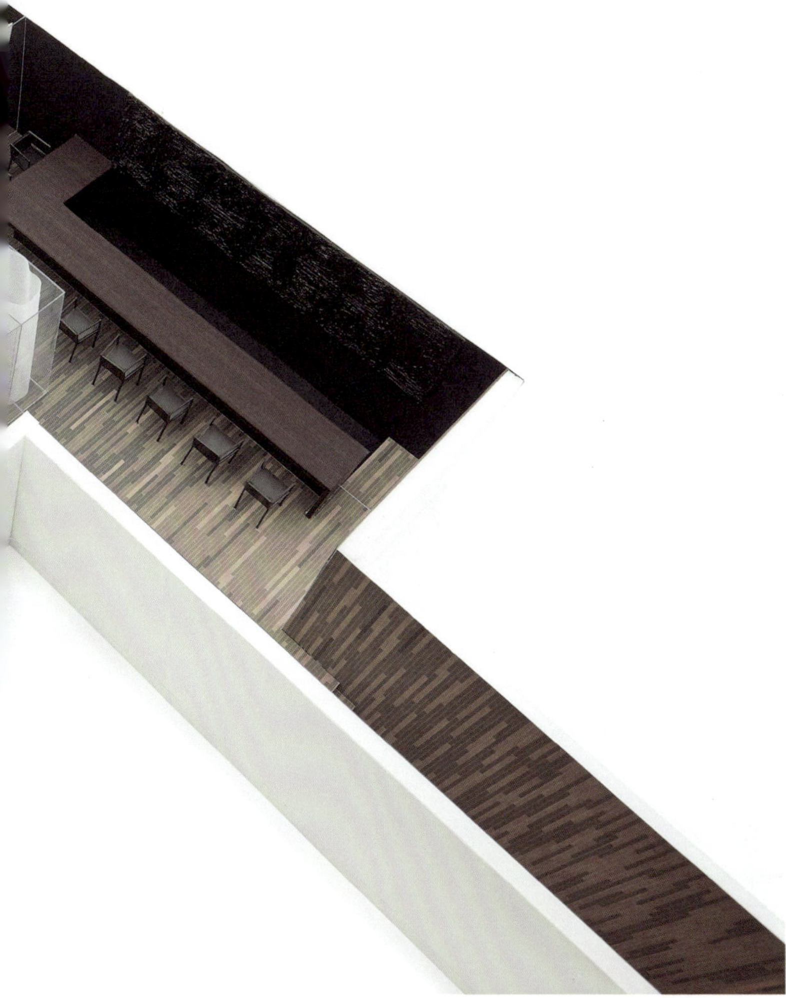

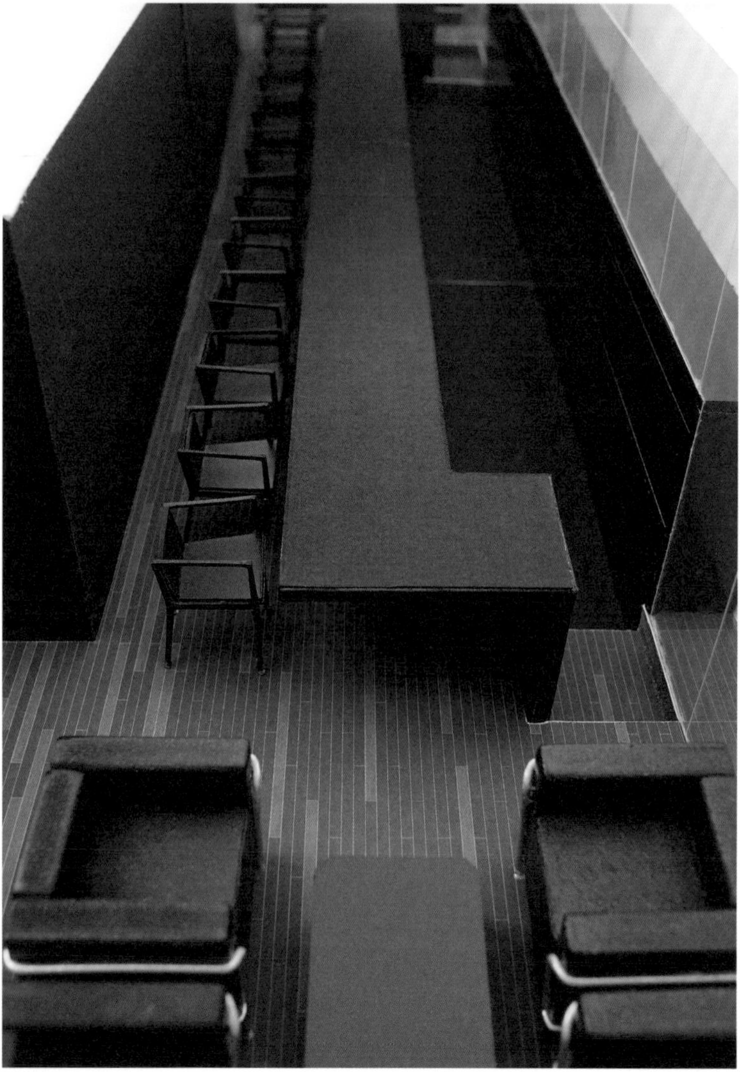

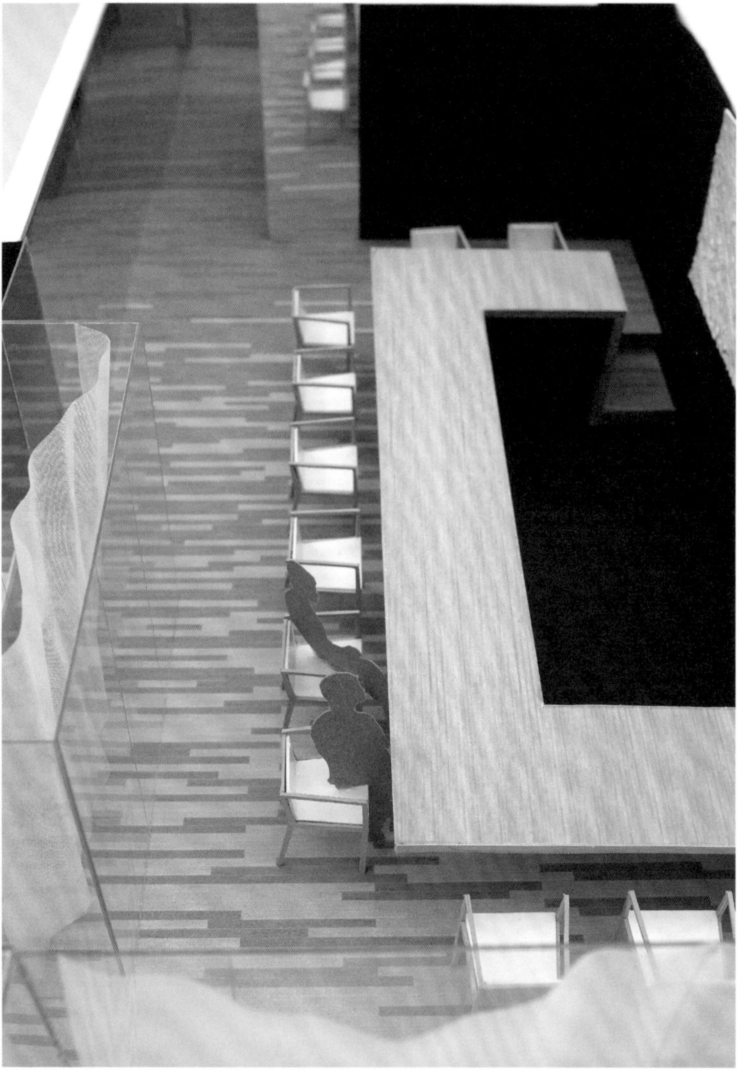

MD.net Clinic

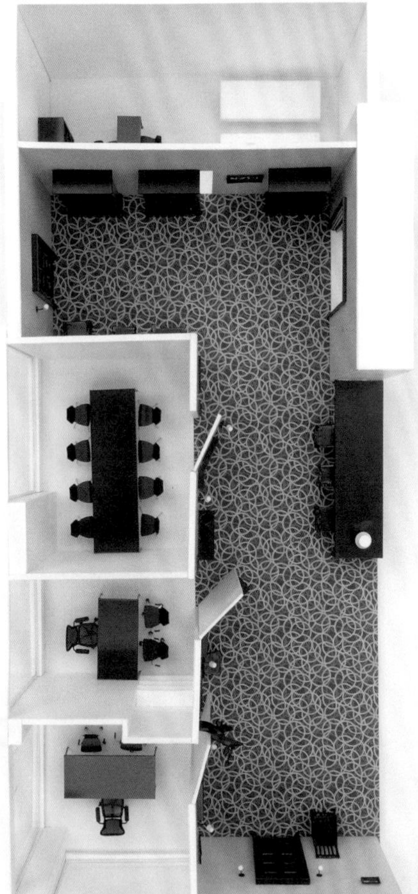

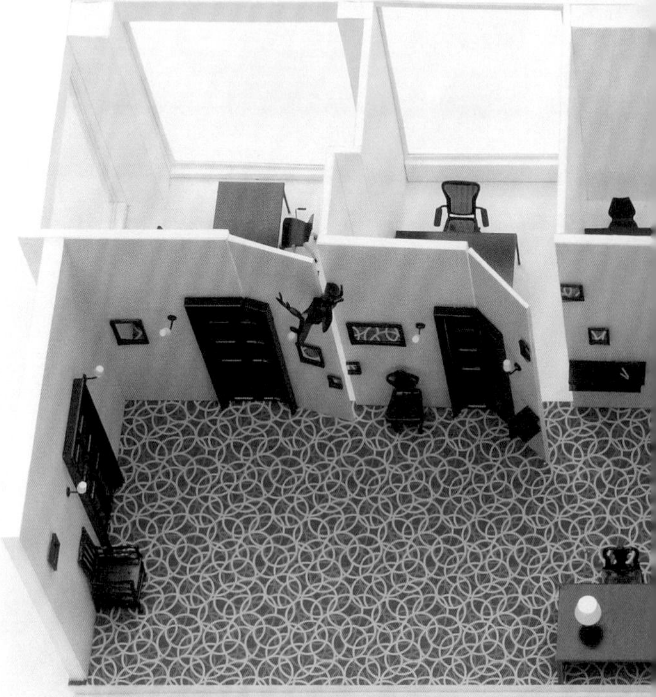

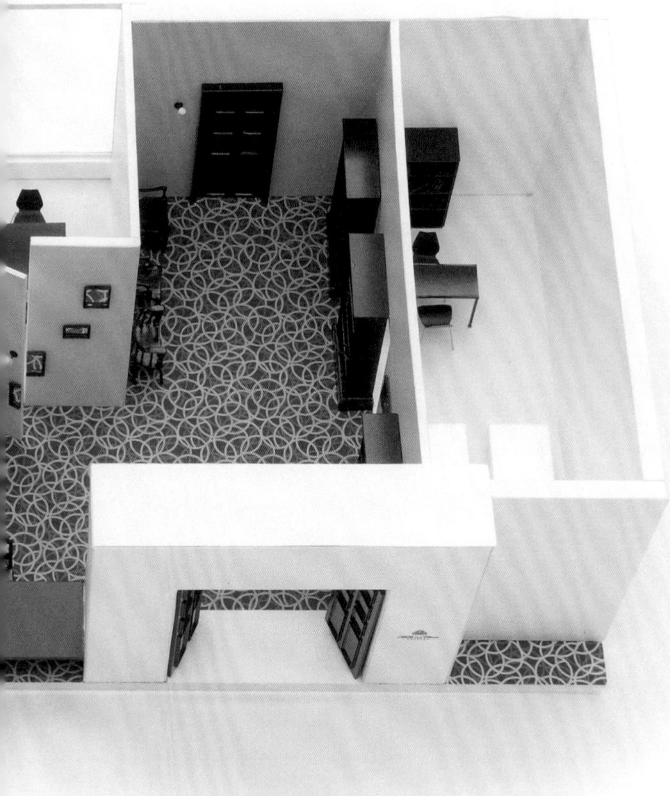

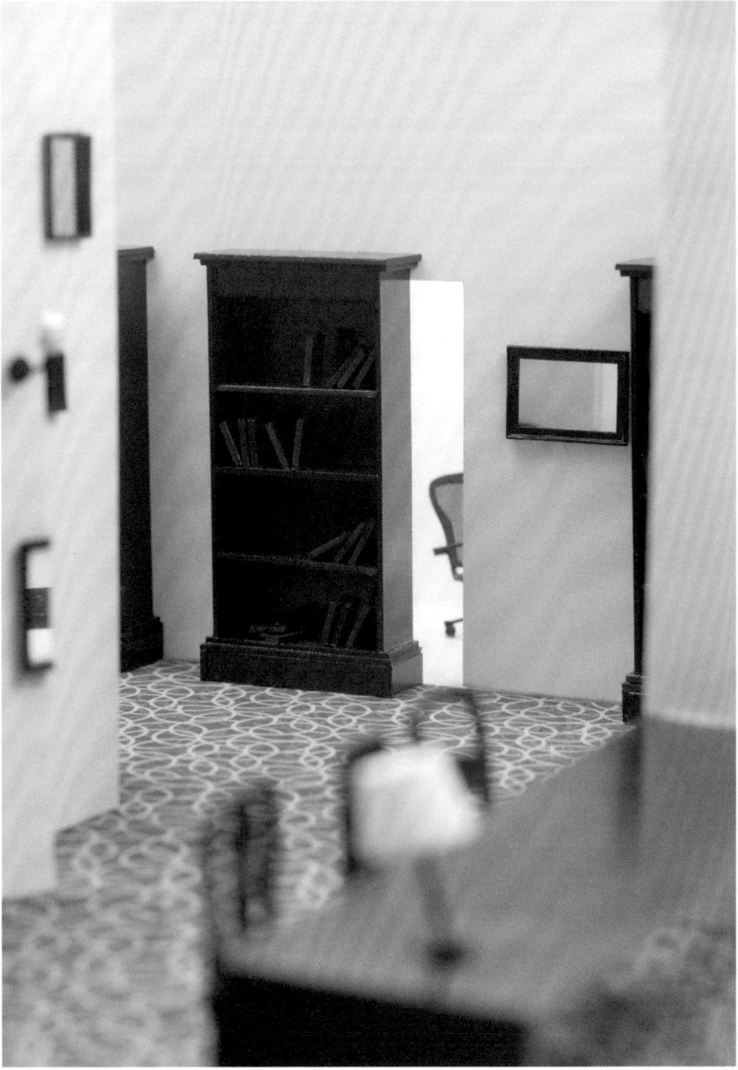

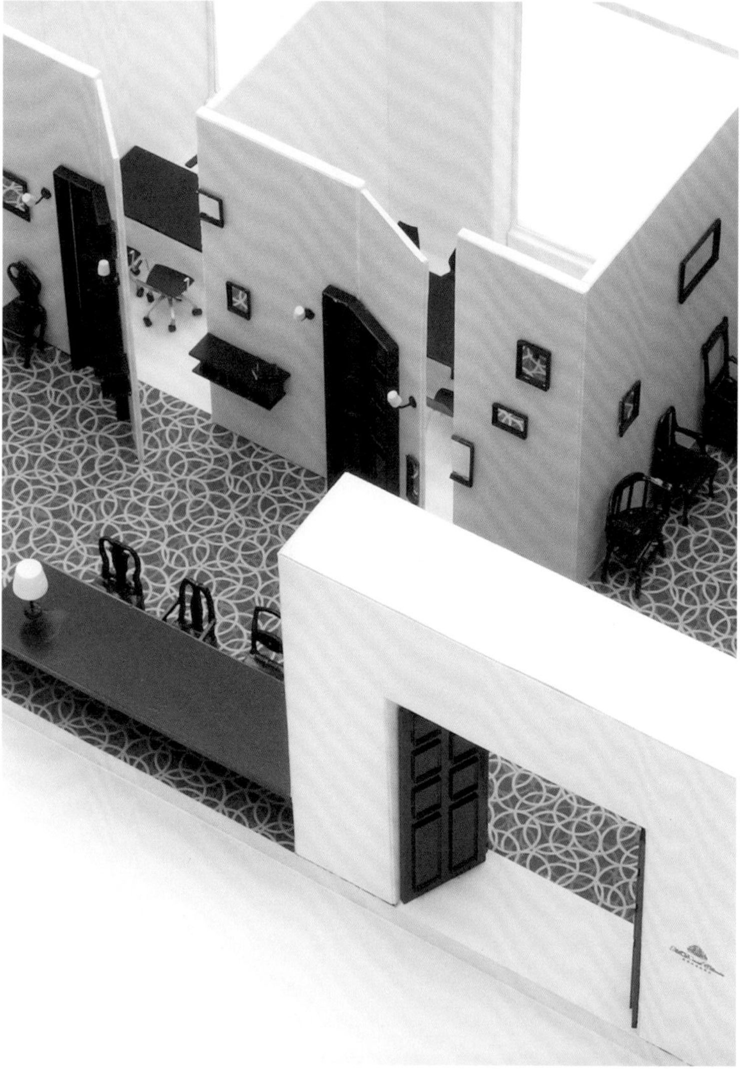

meguro office

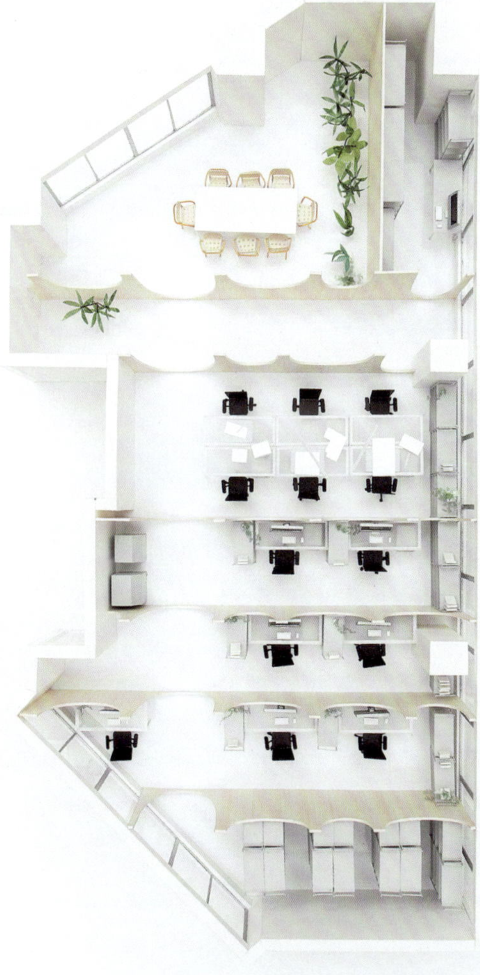

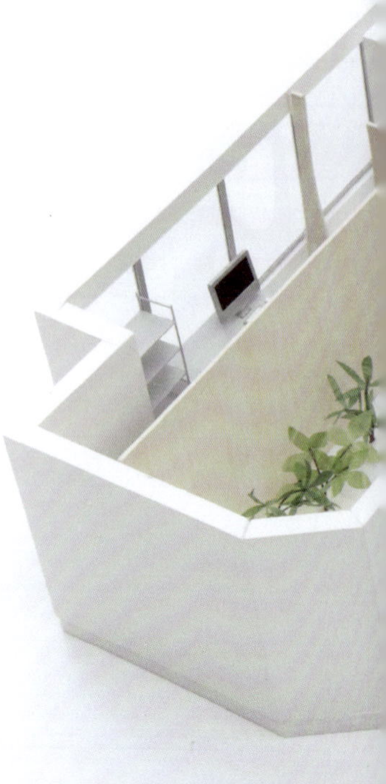

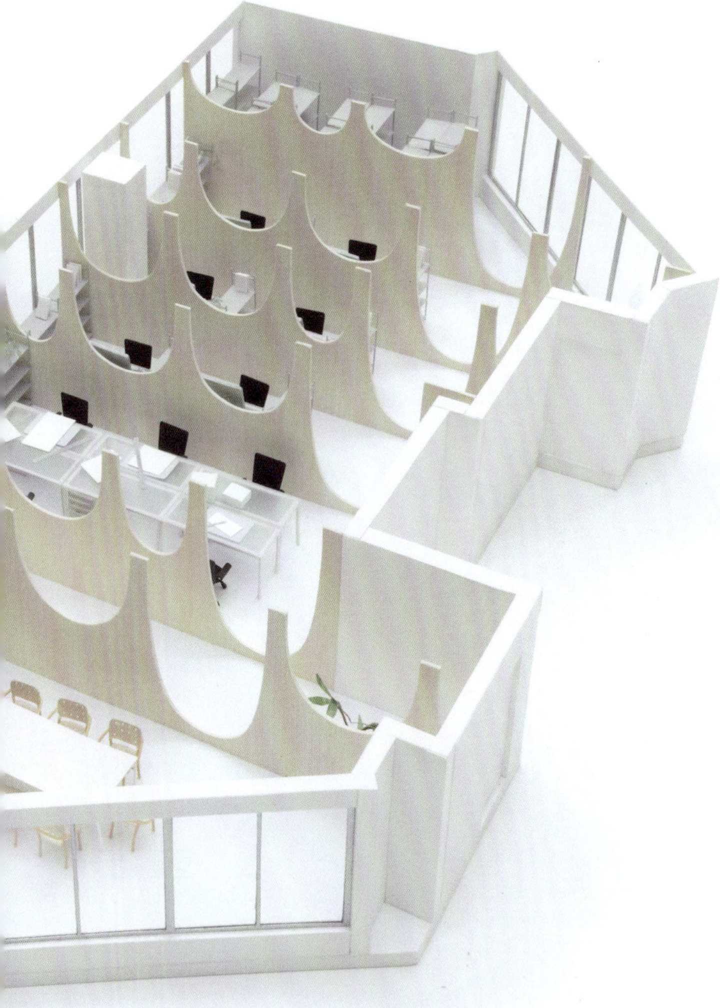

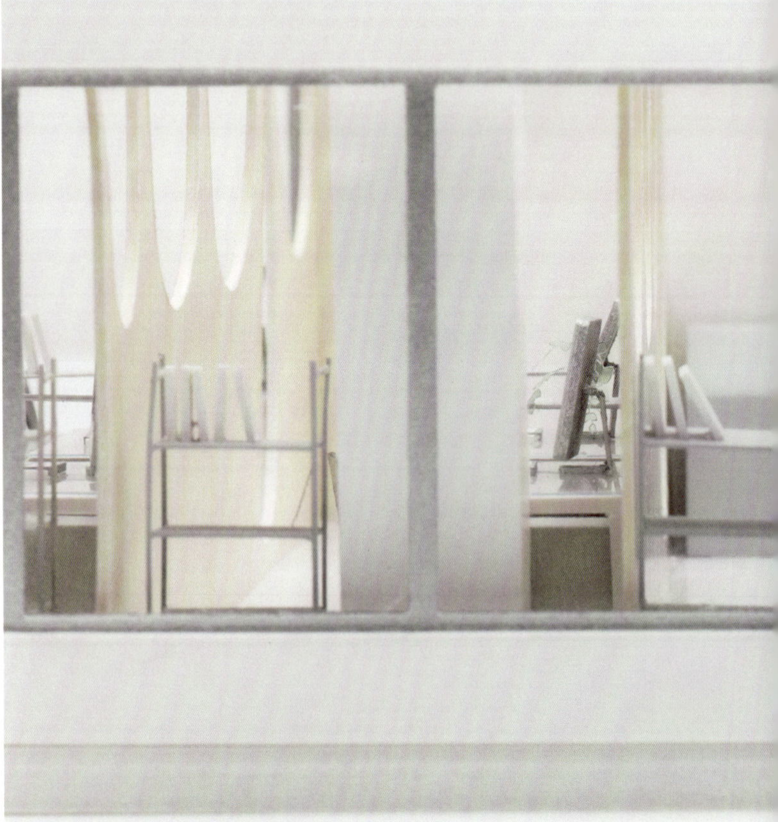

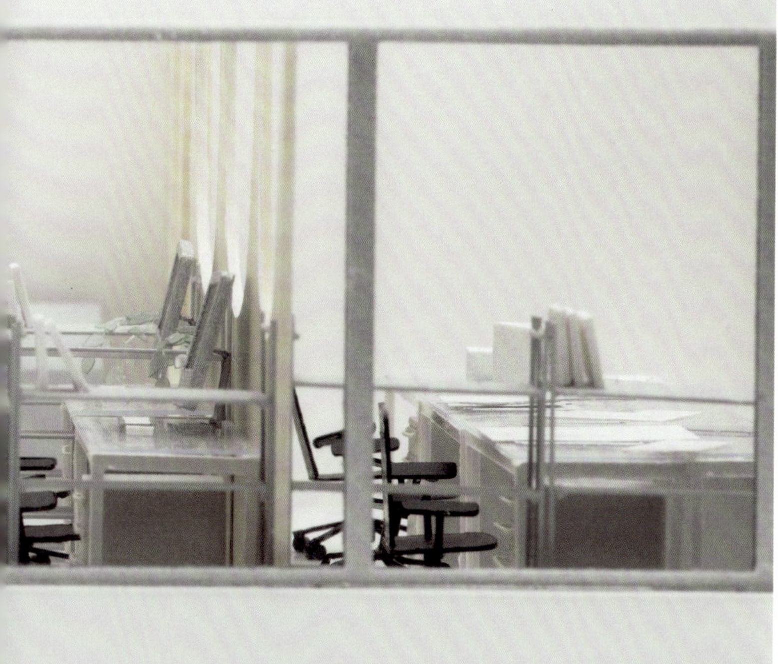

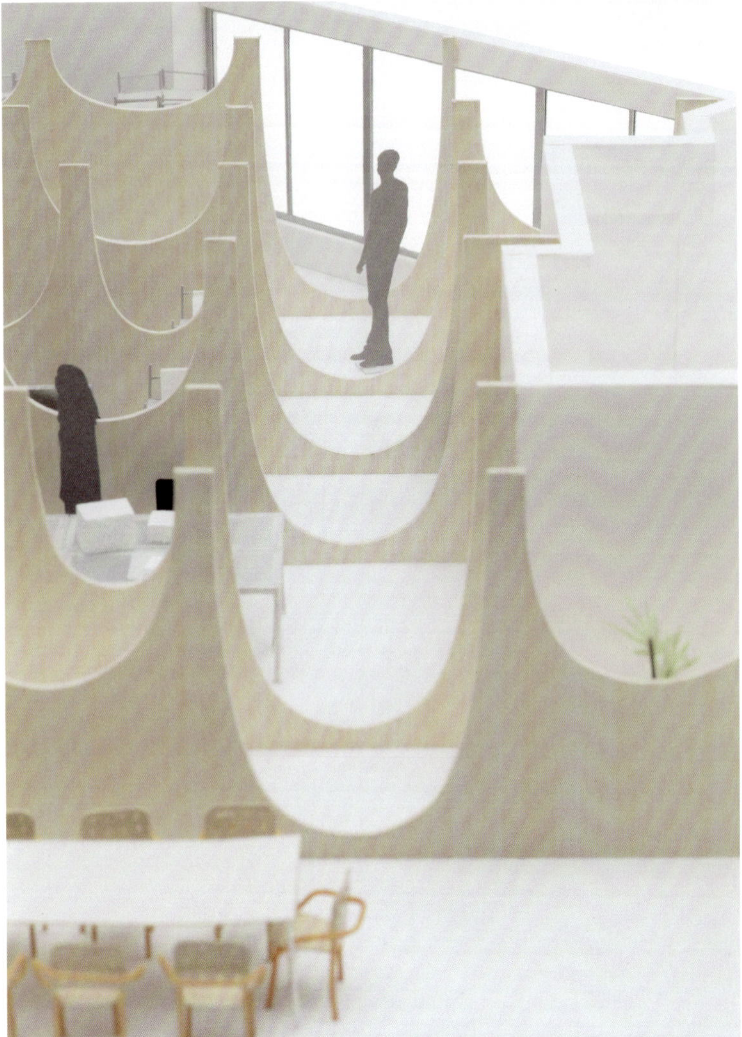

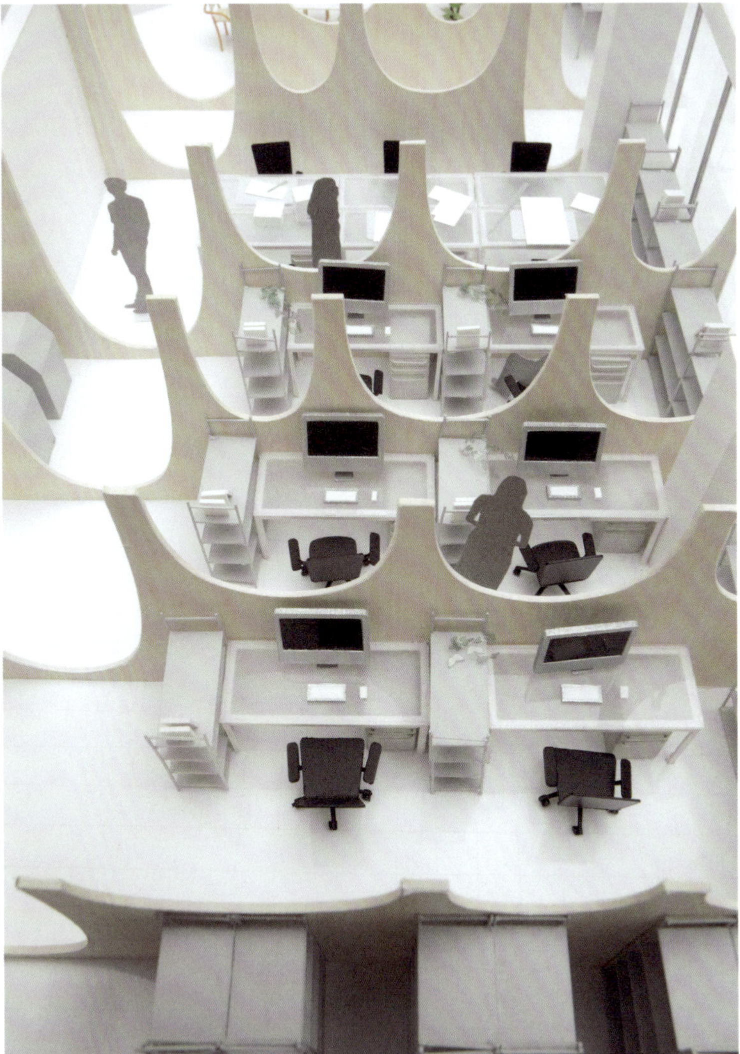

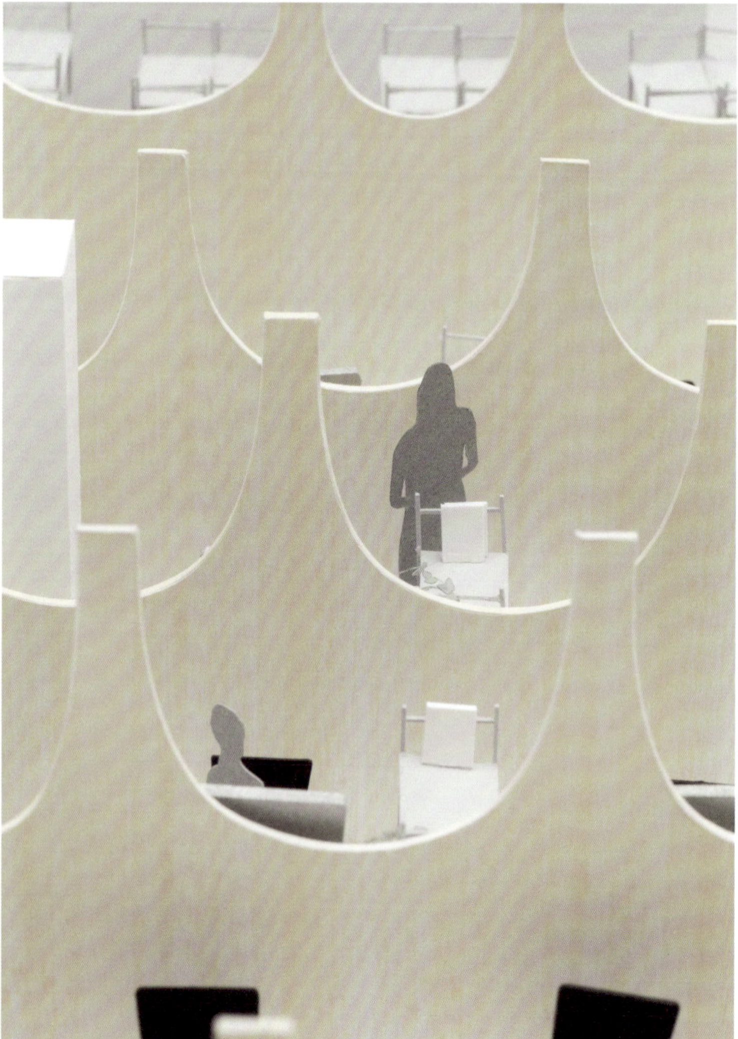

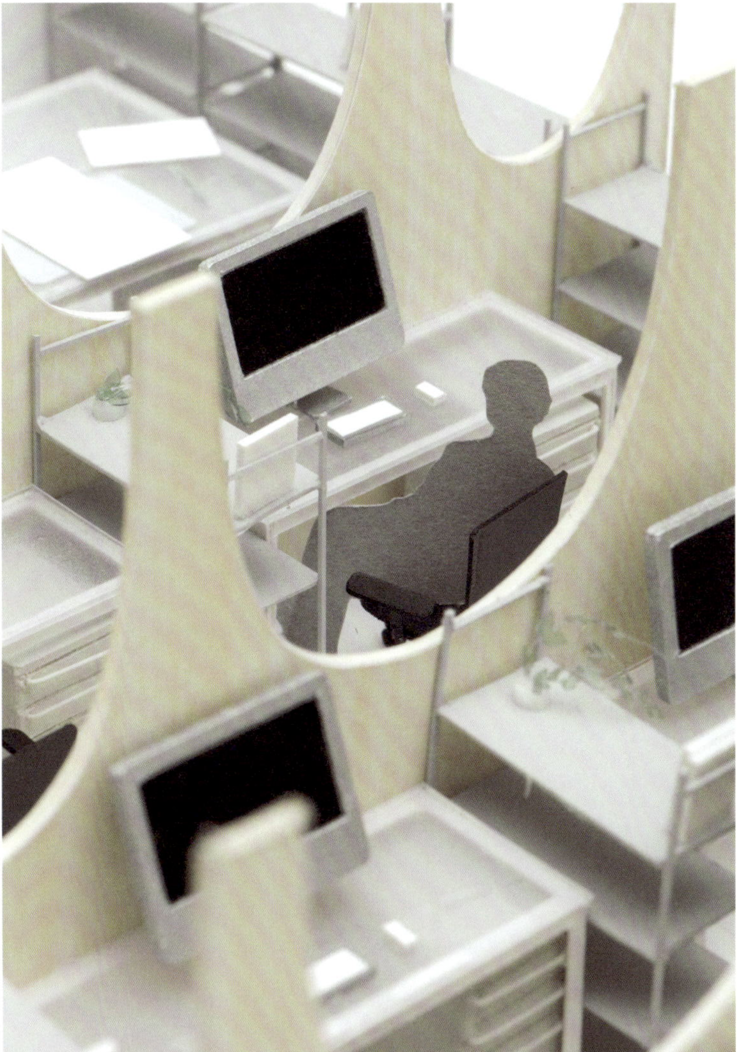

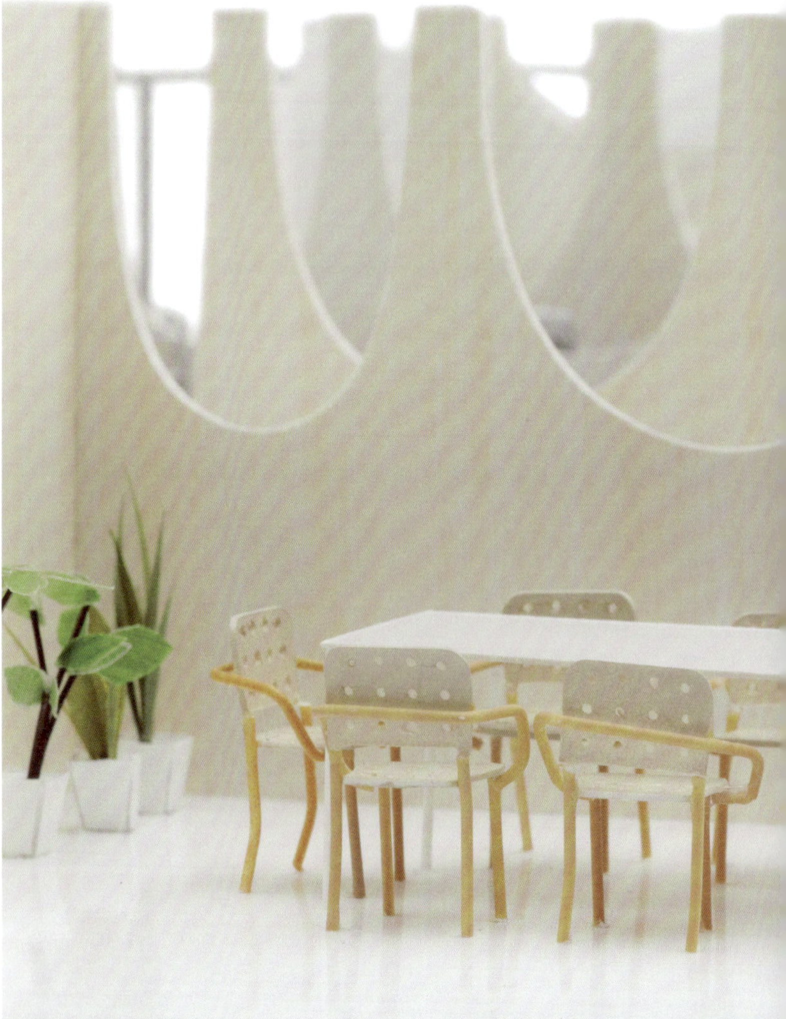

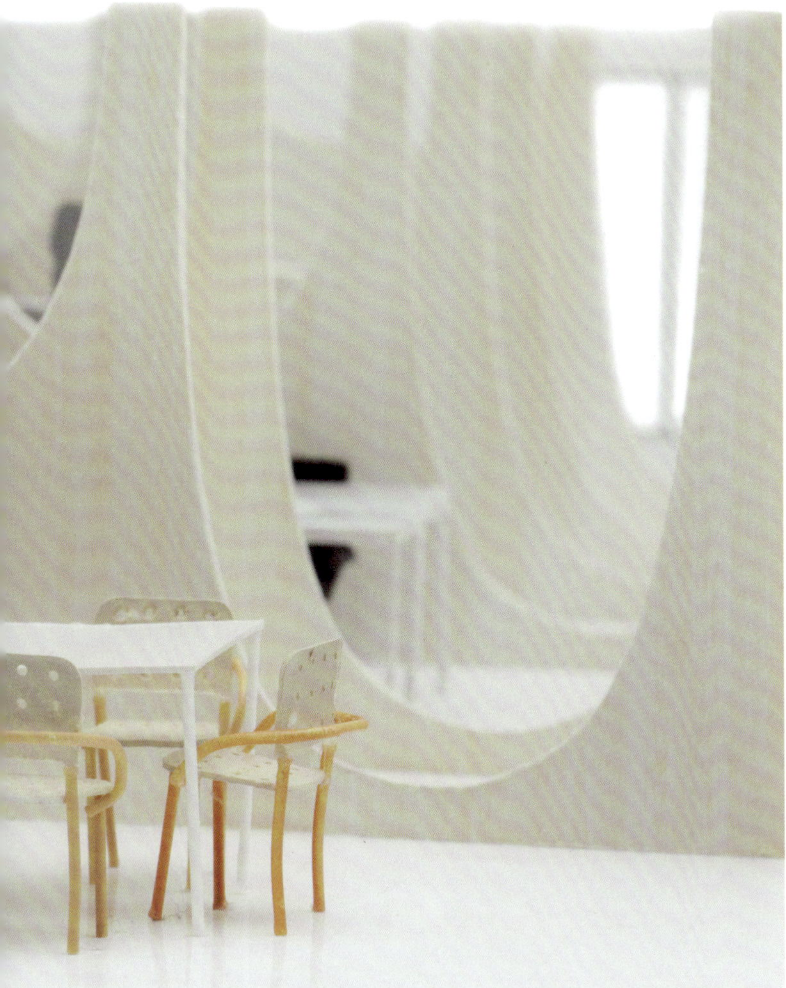

mimicry chairs

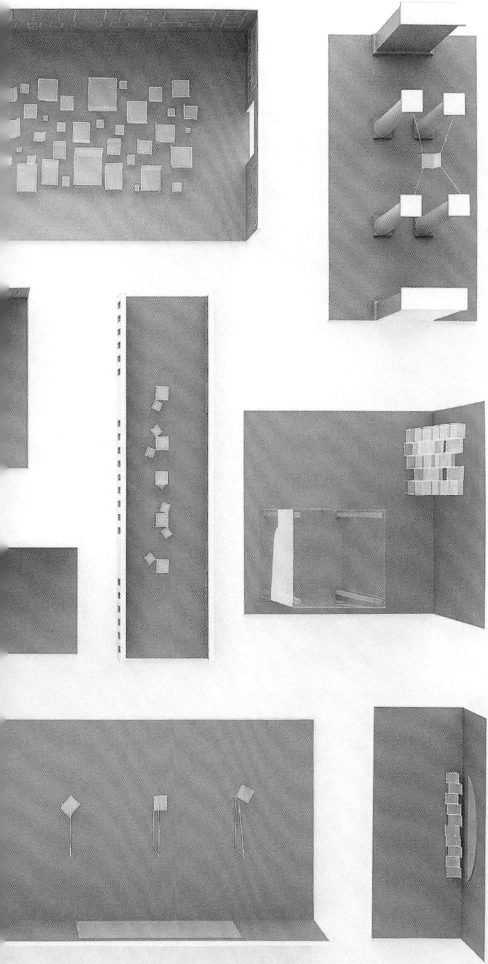

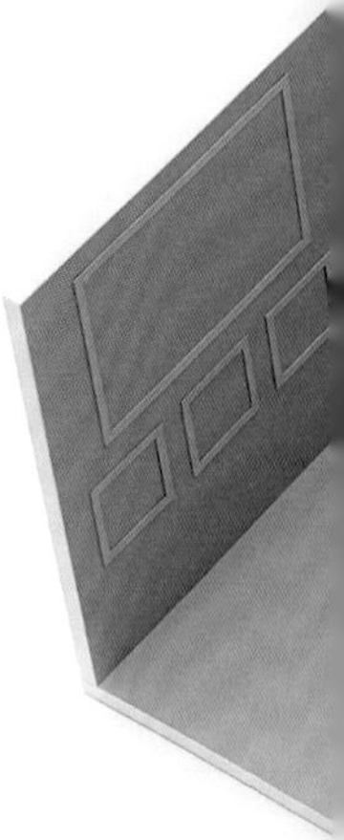

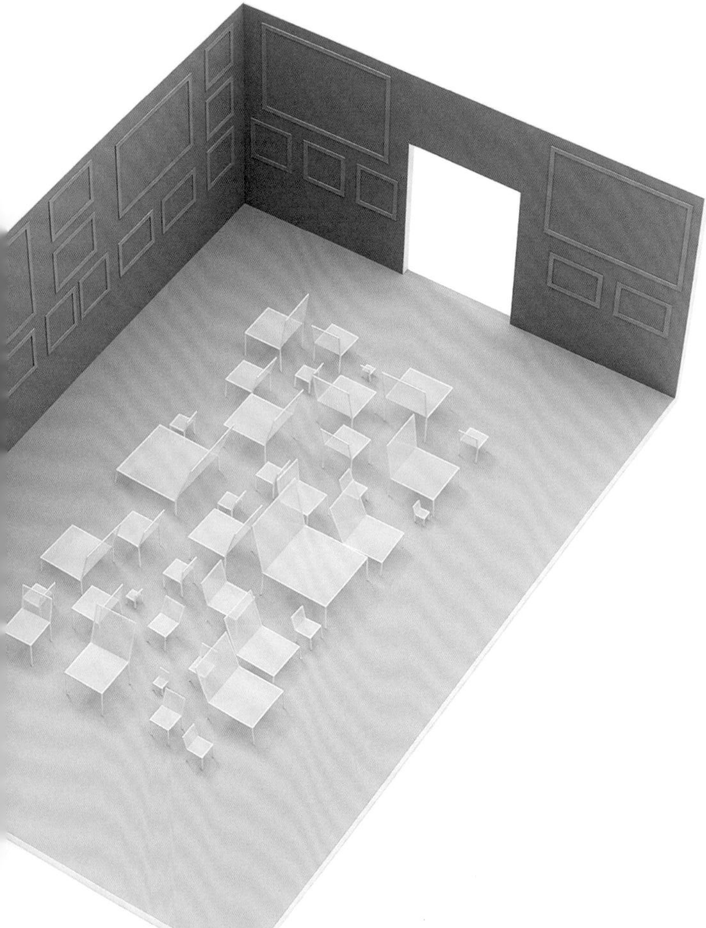

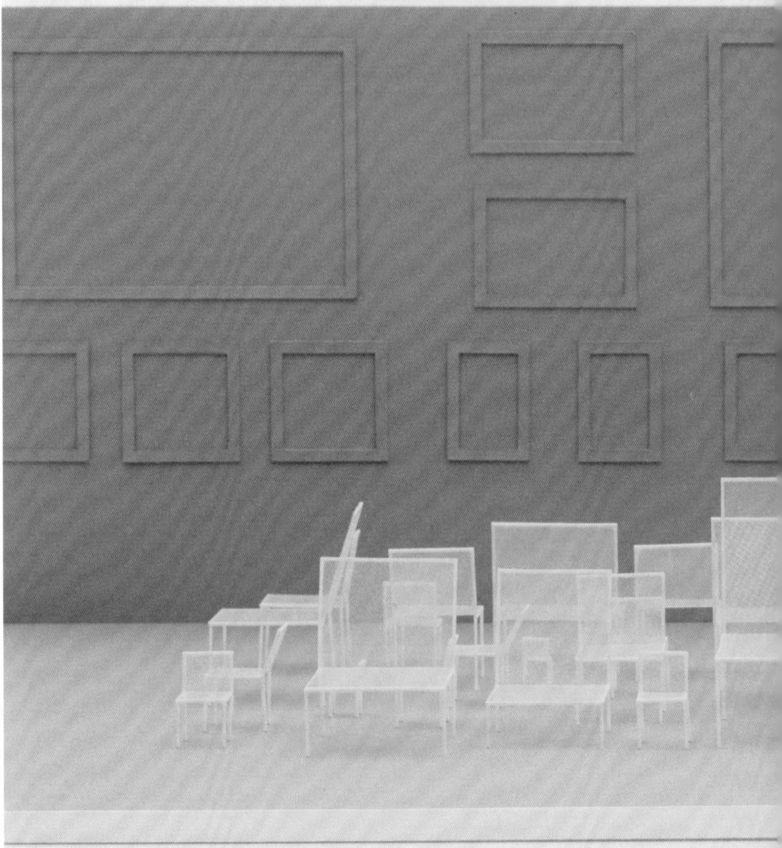

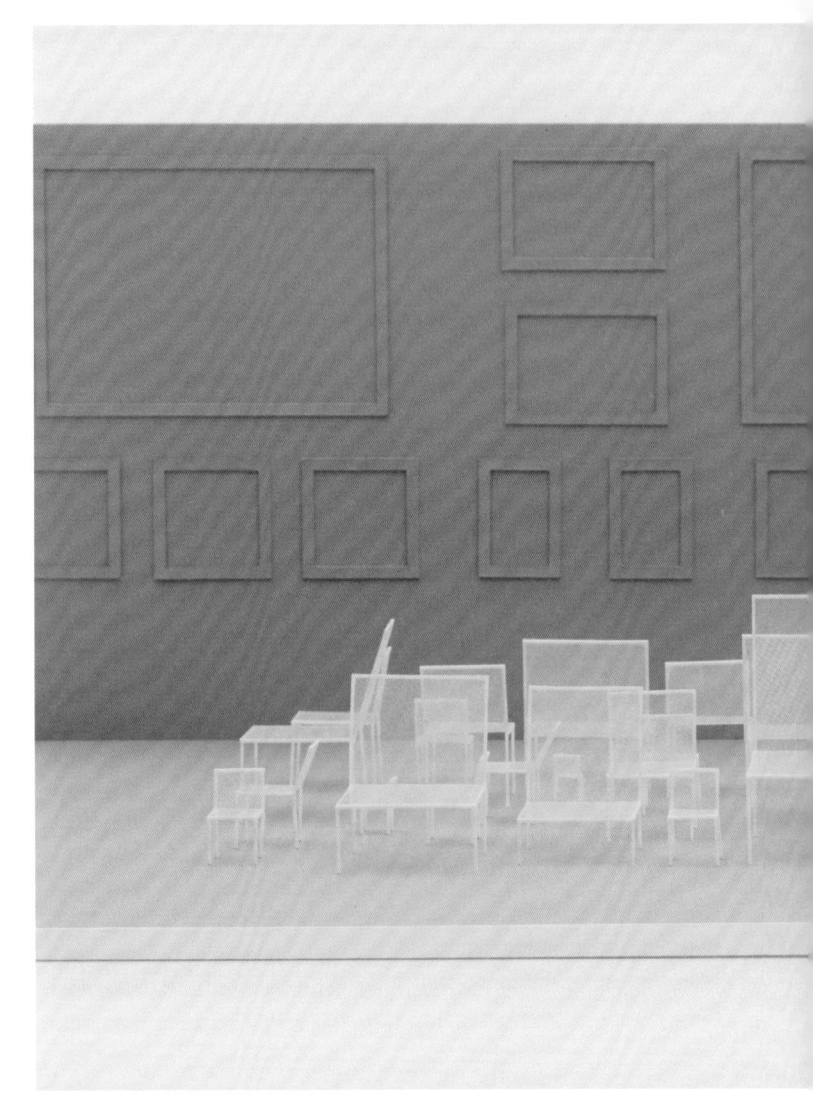

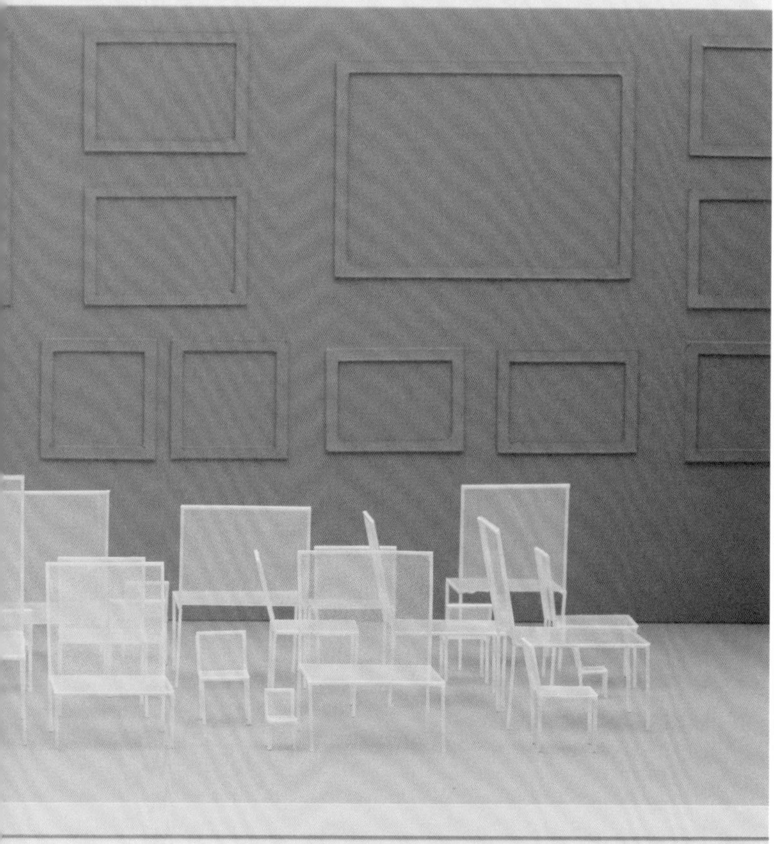

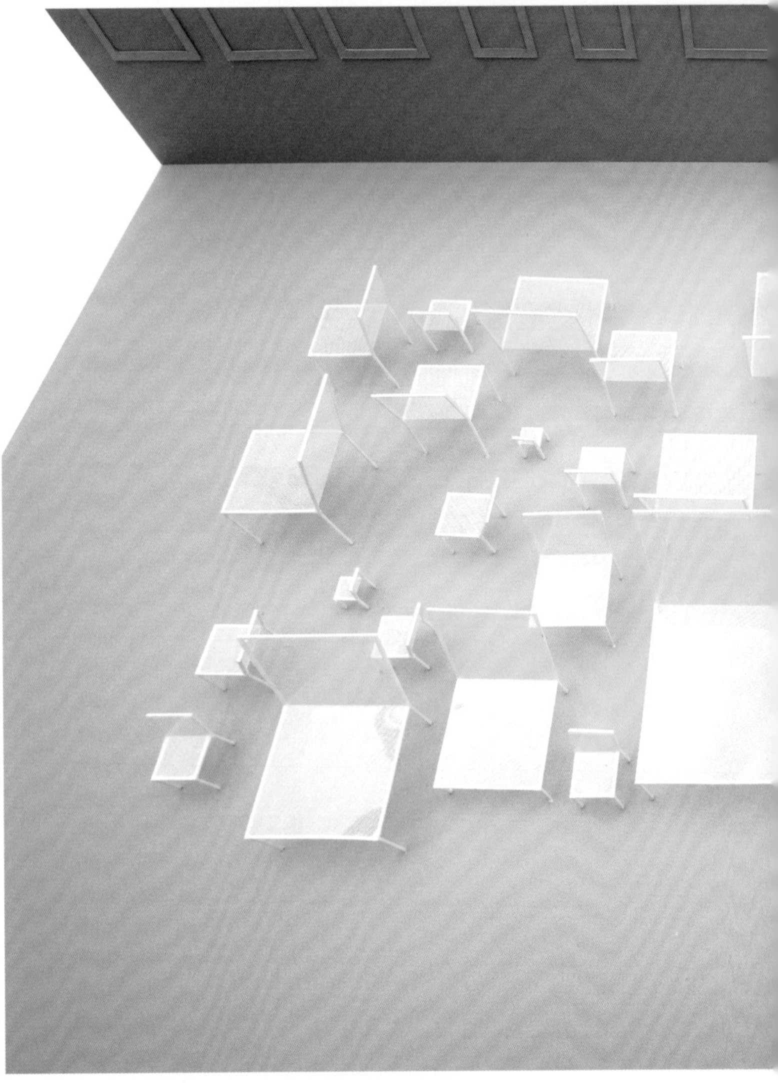

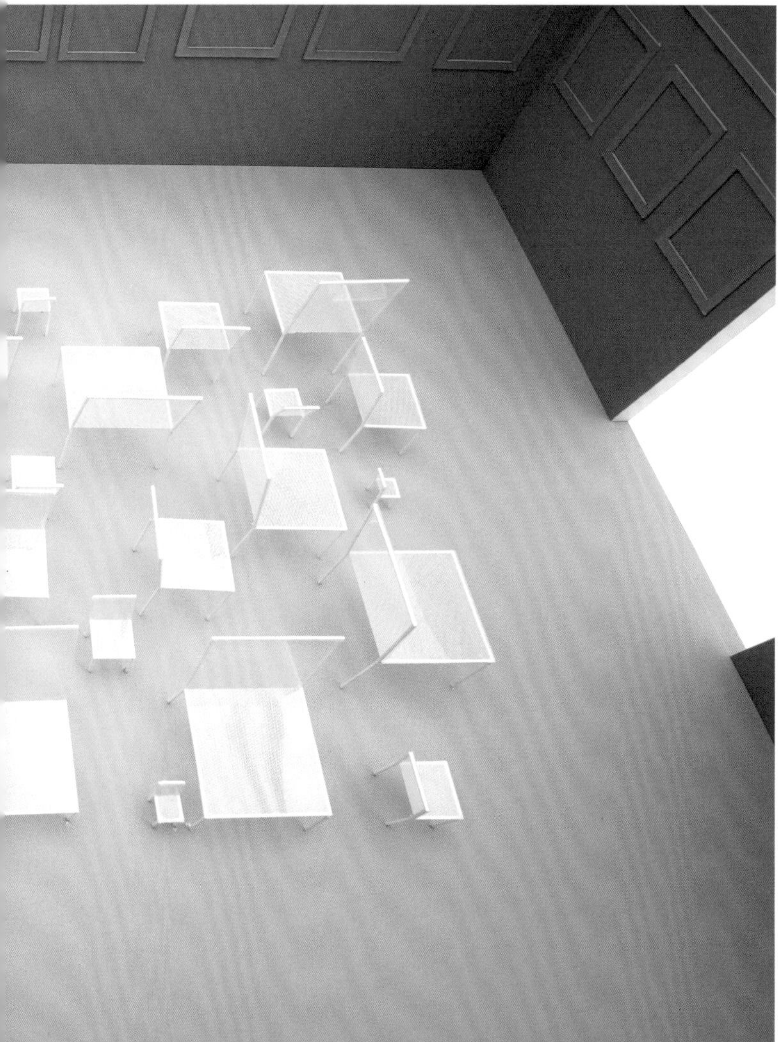

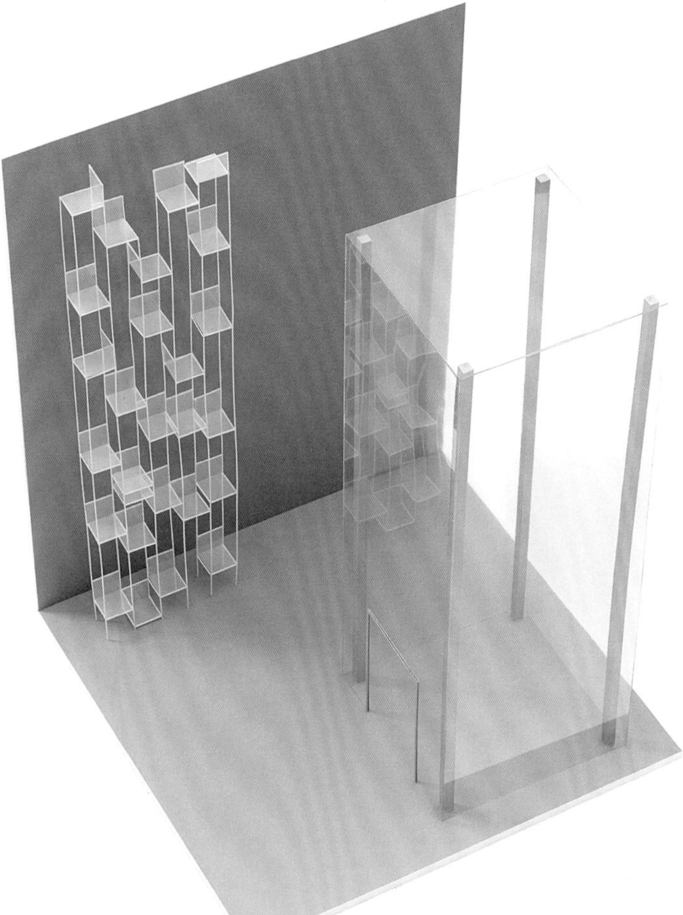

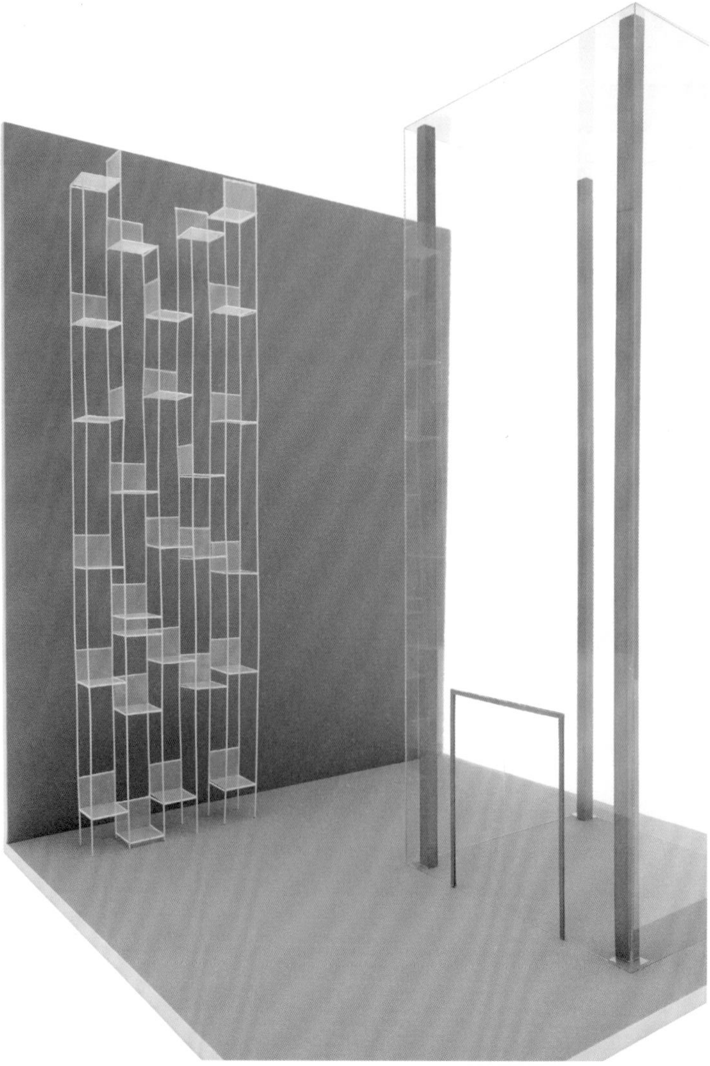

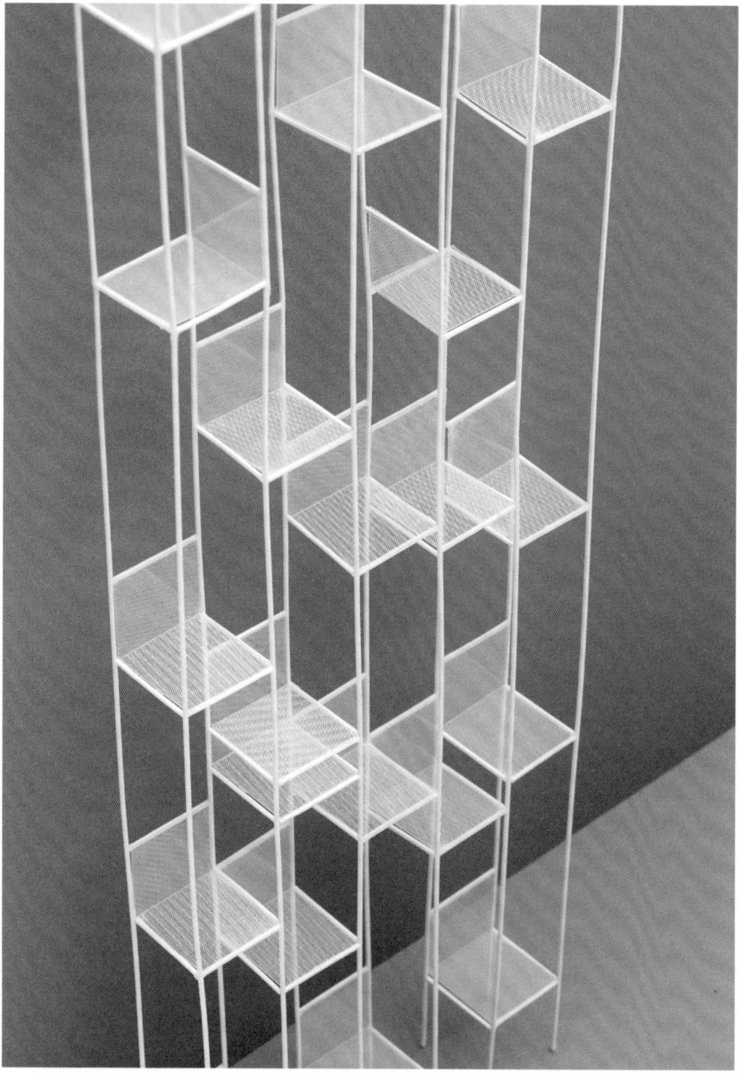

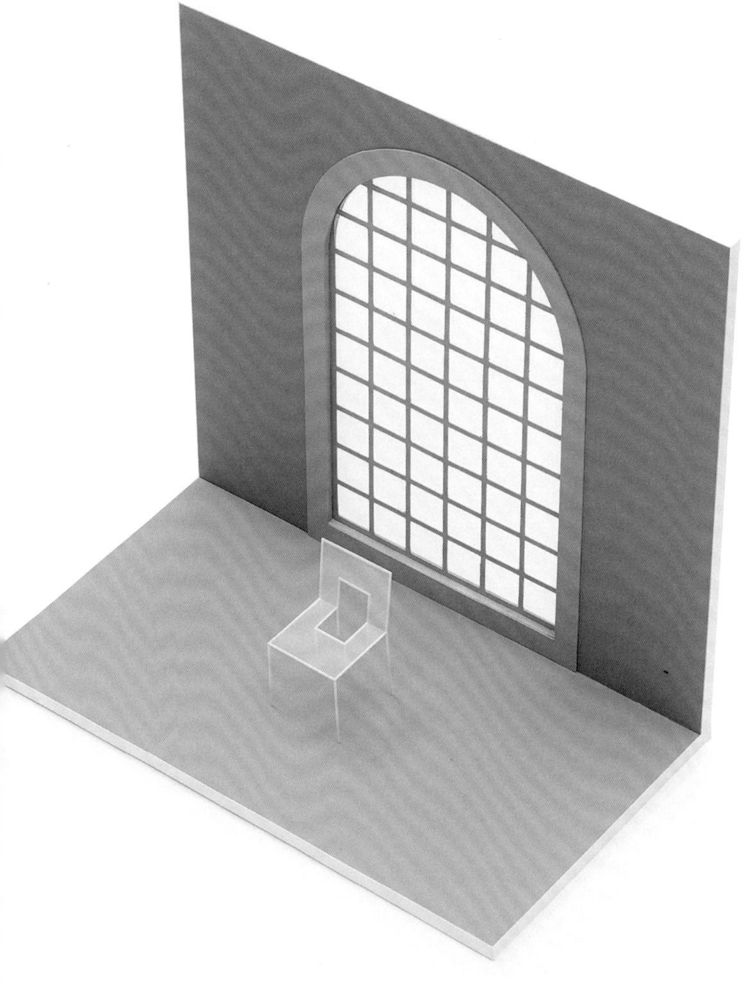

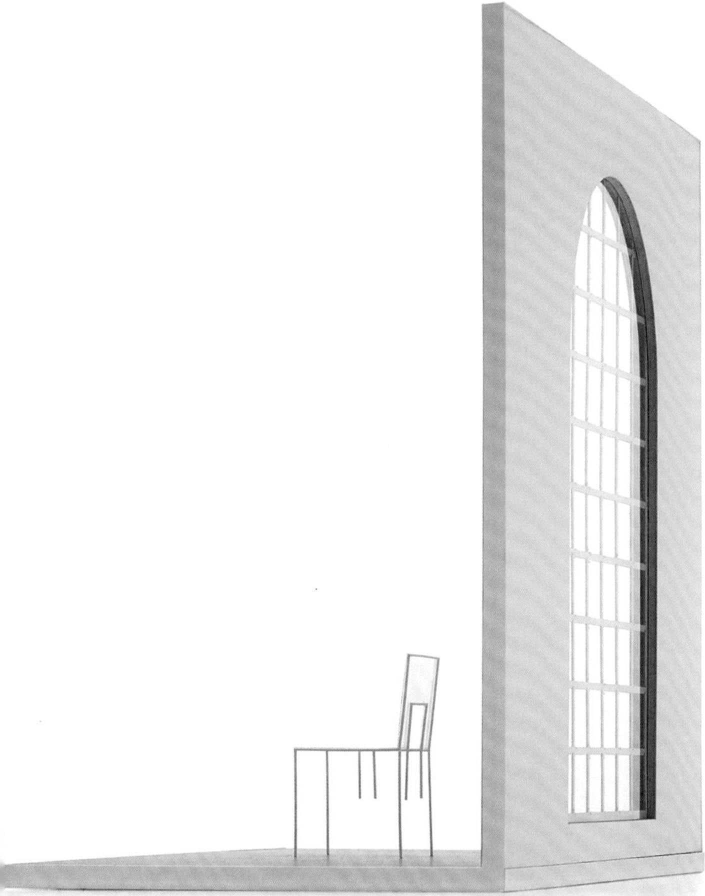

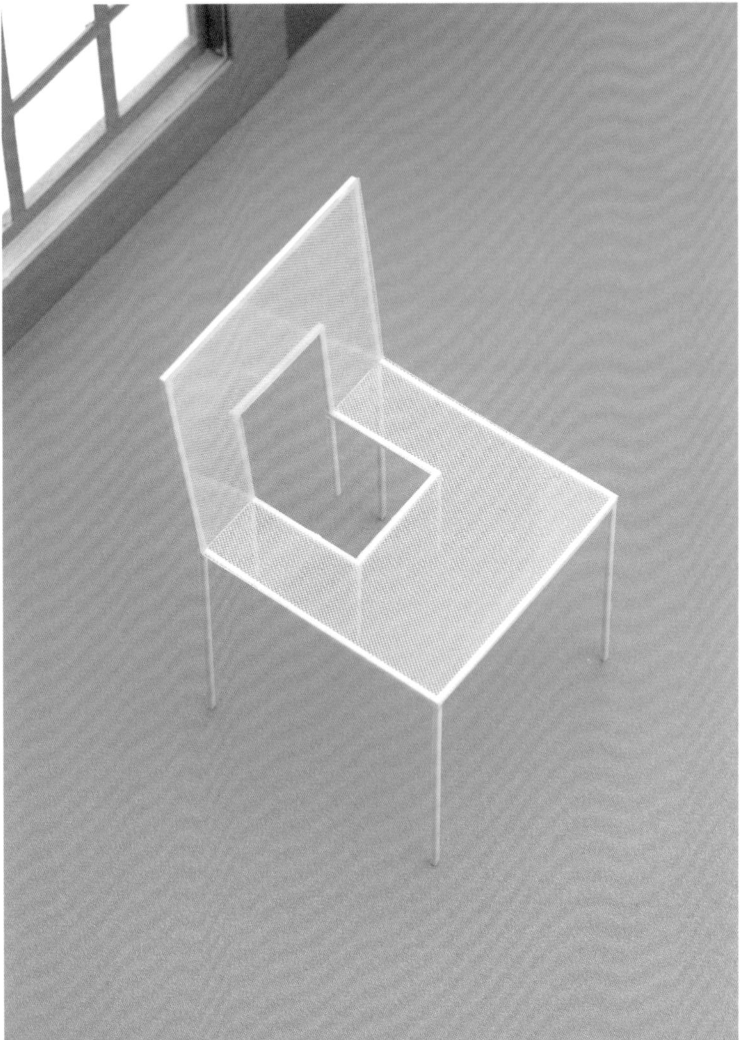

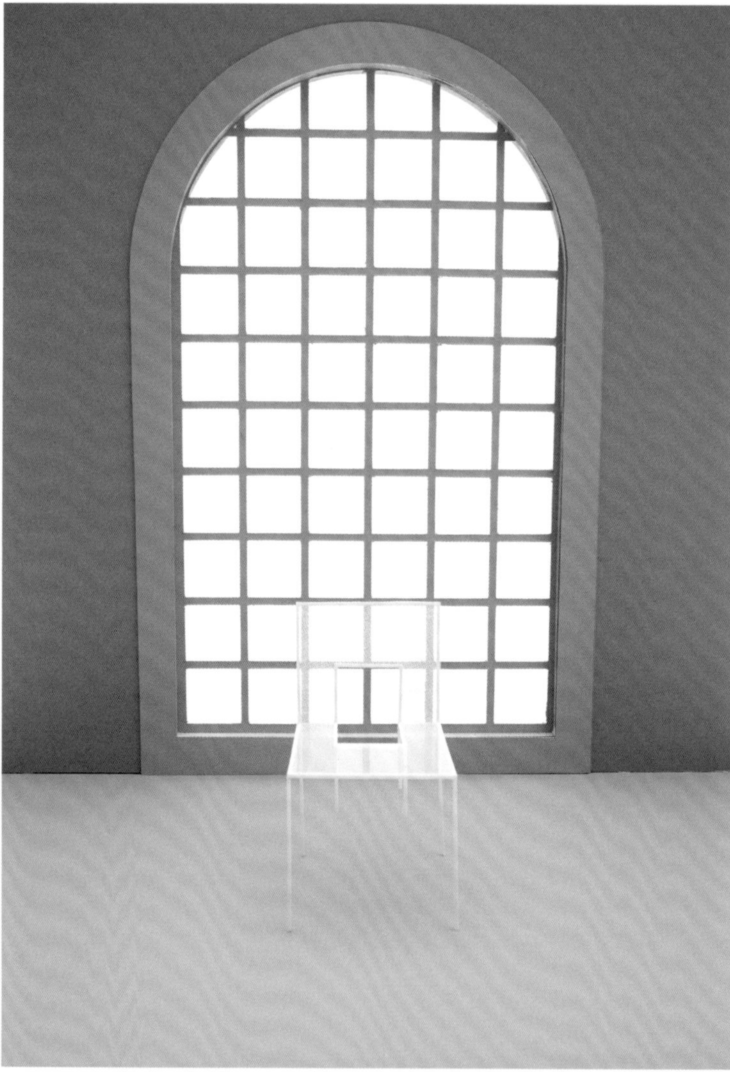

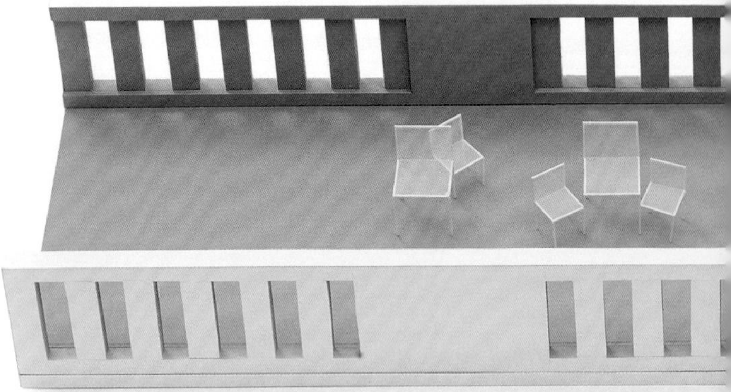

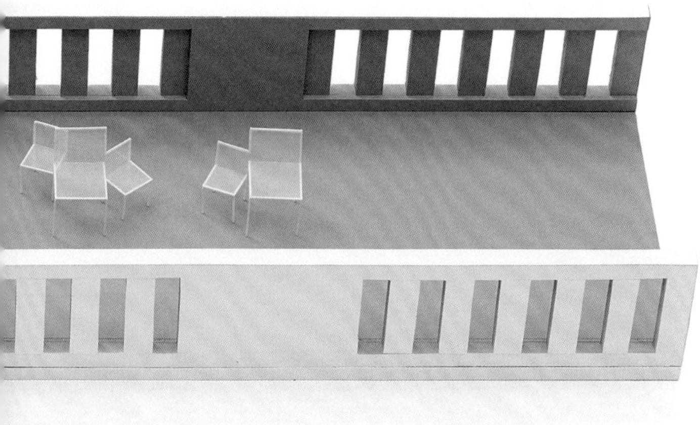

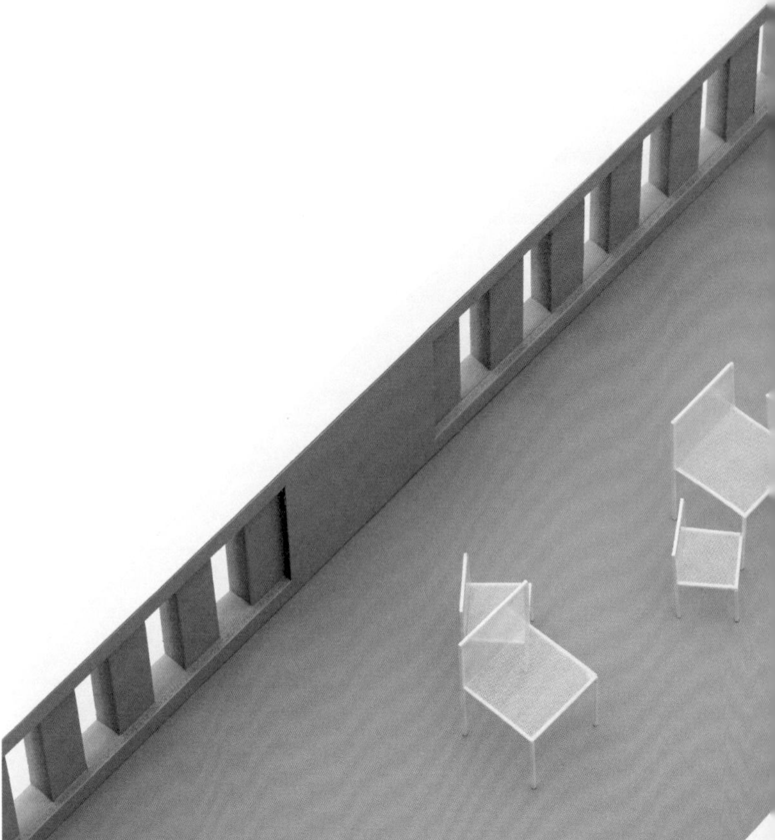

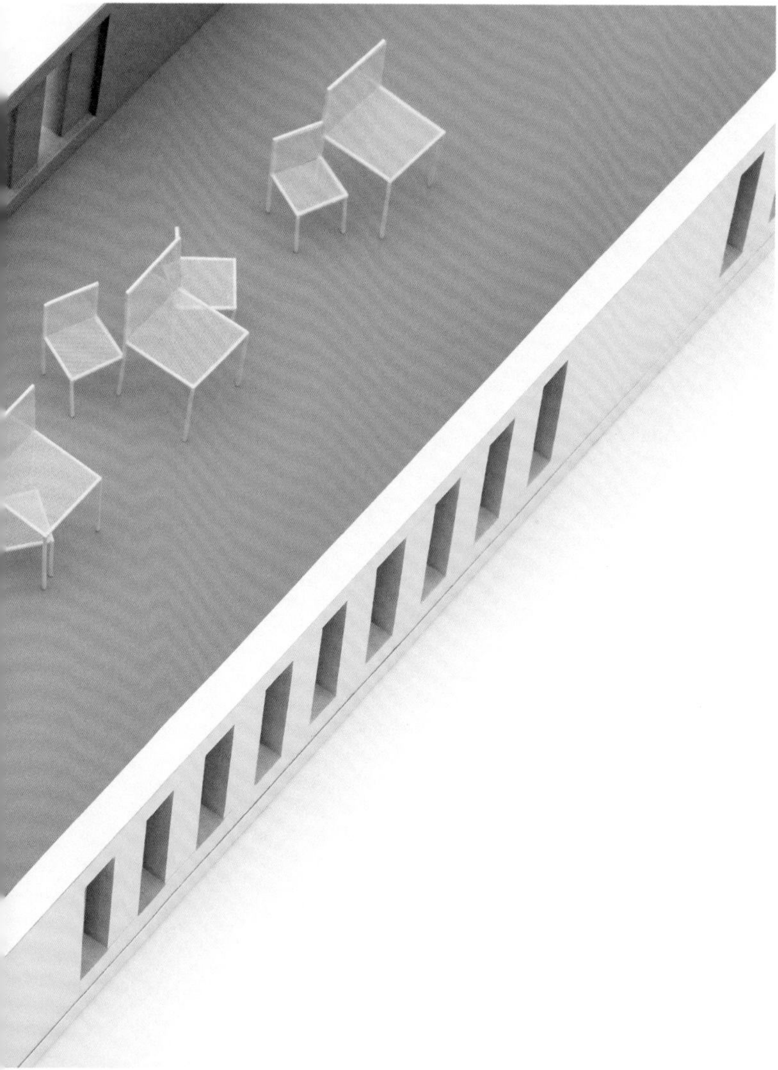

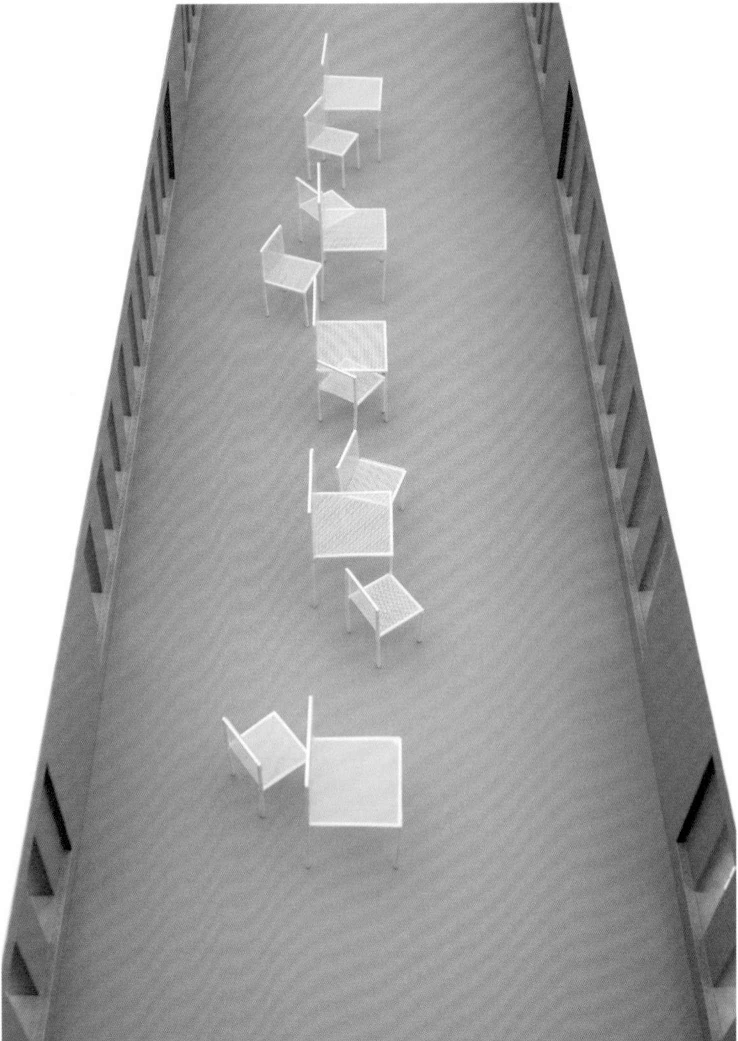

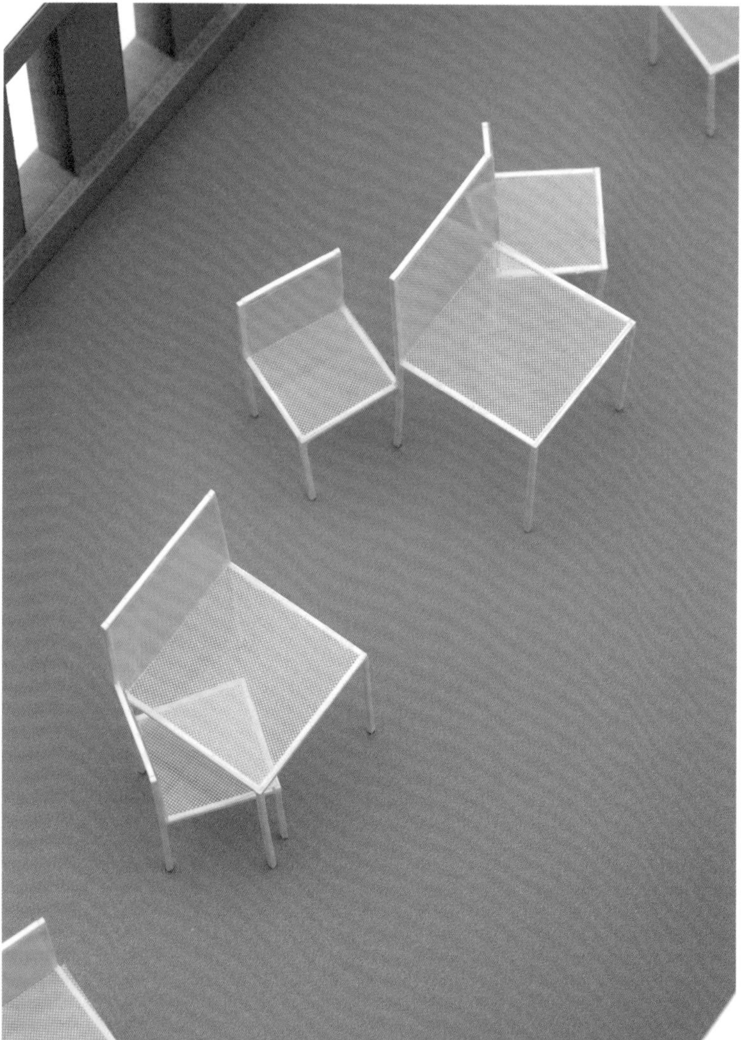

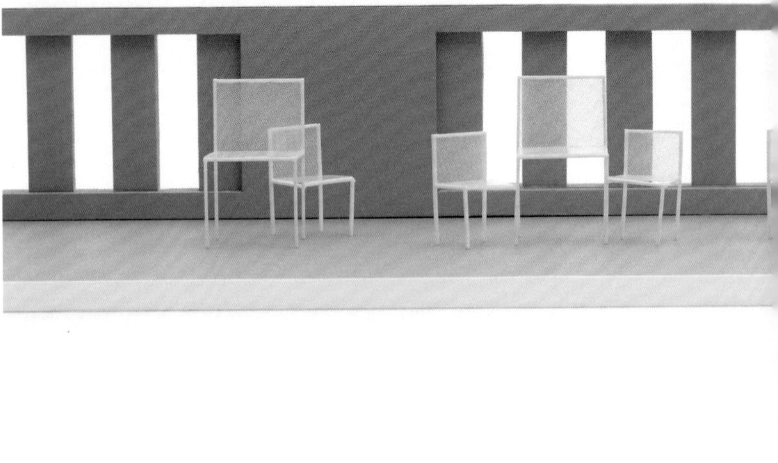

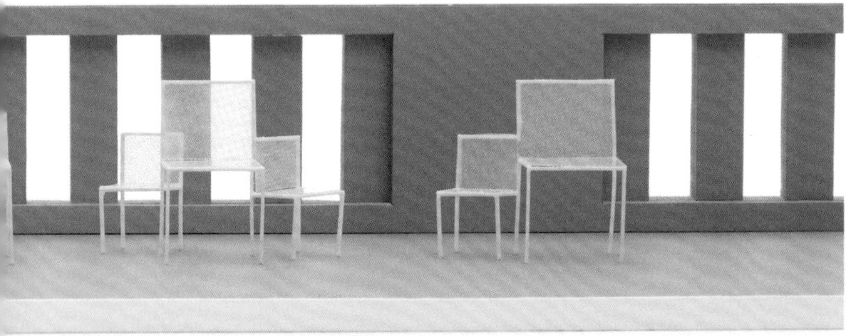

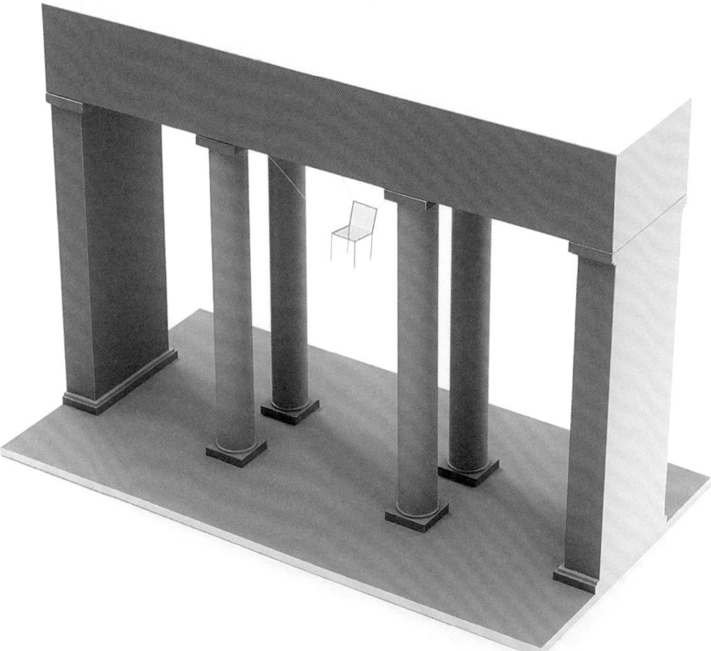

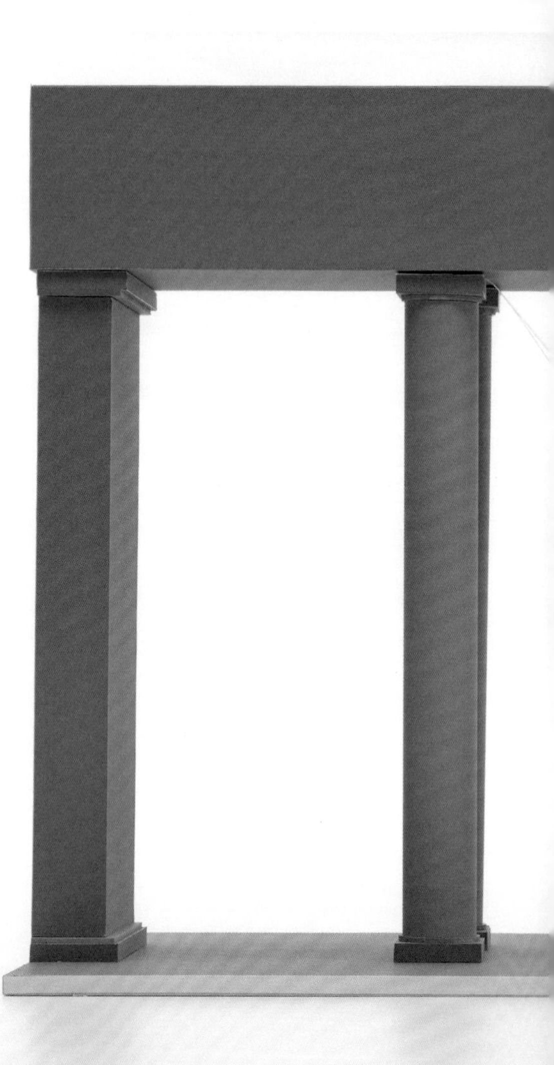

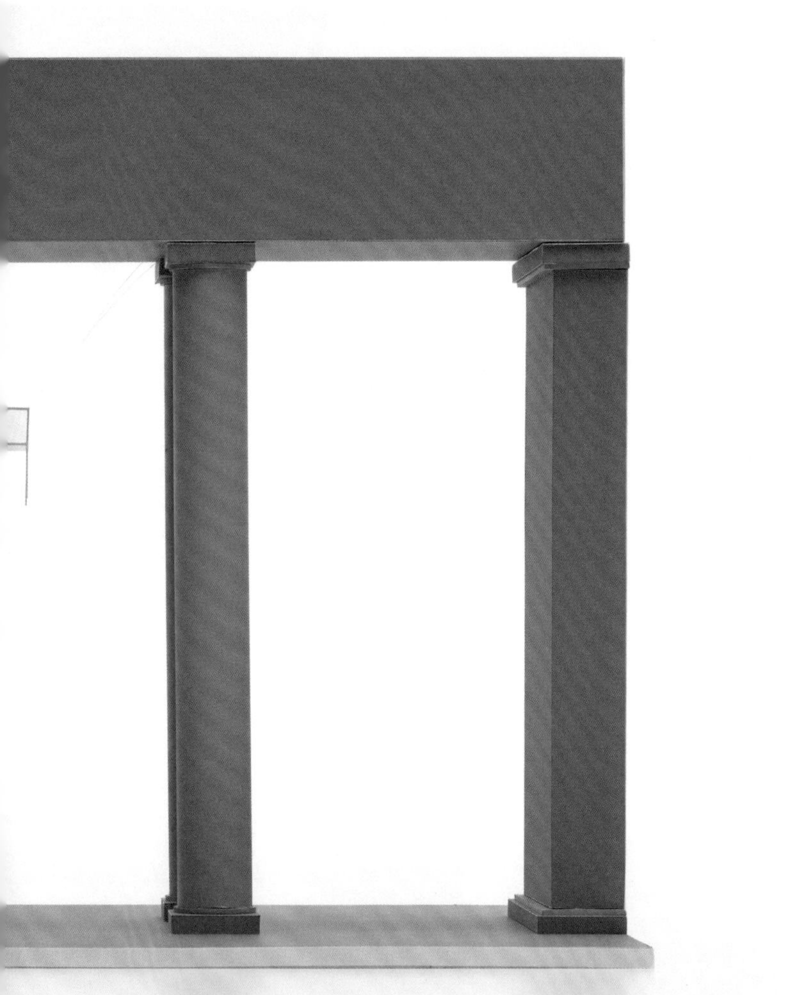

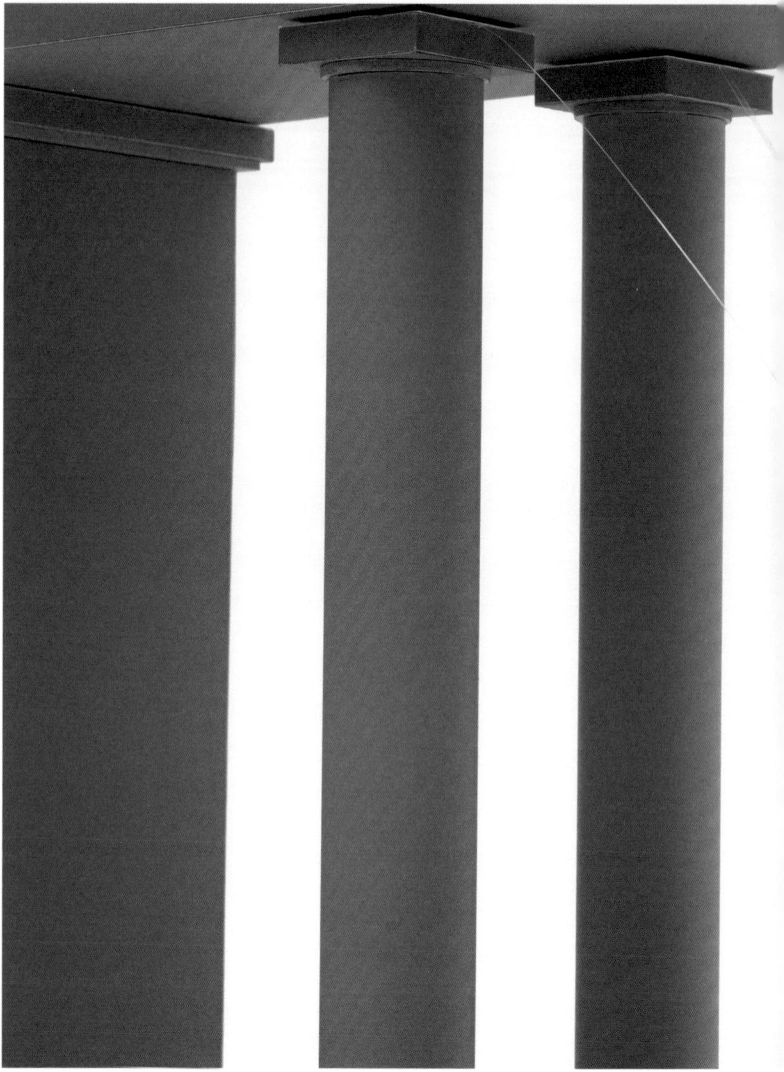

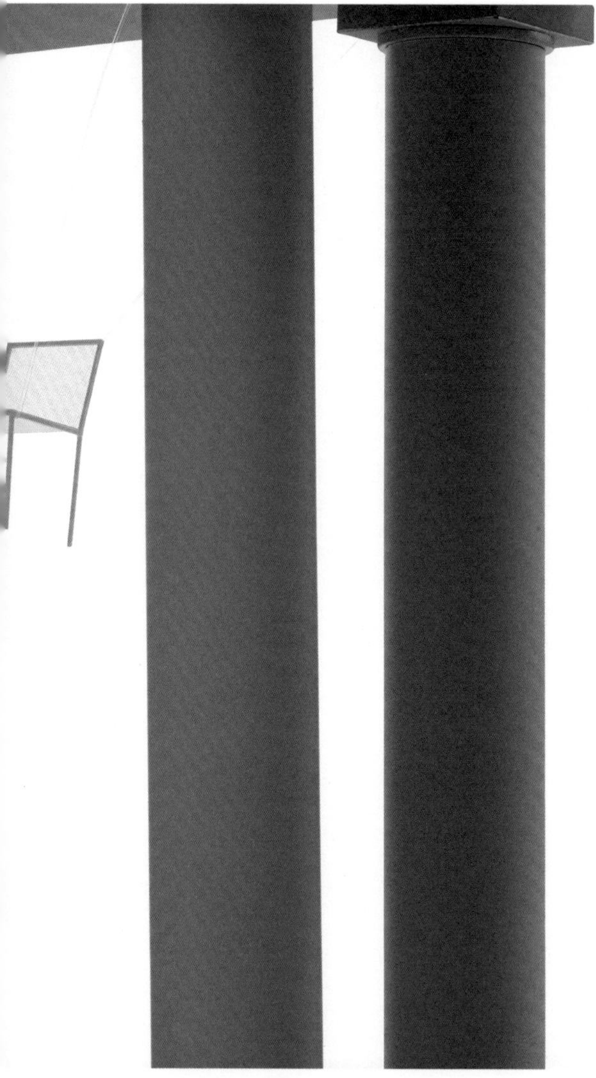

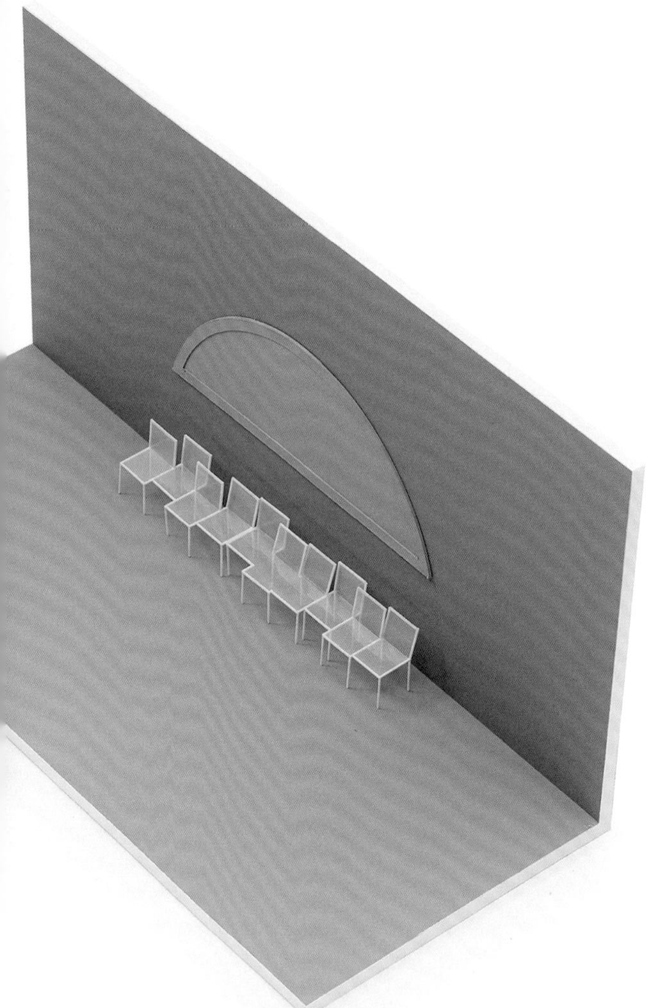

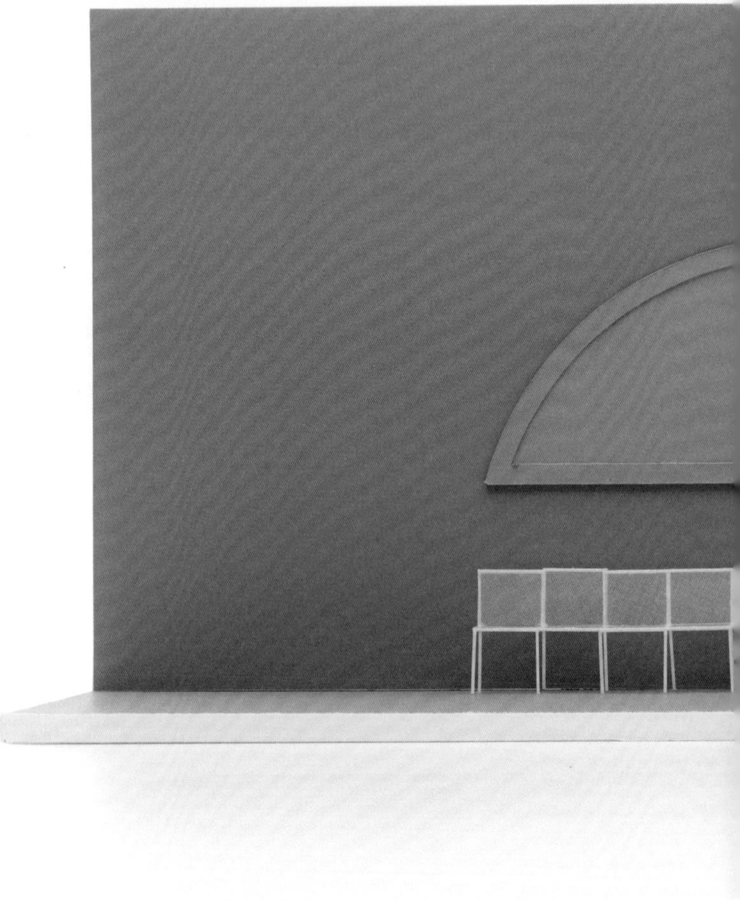

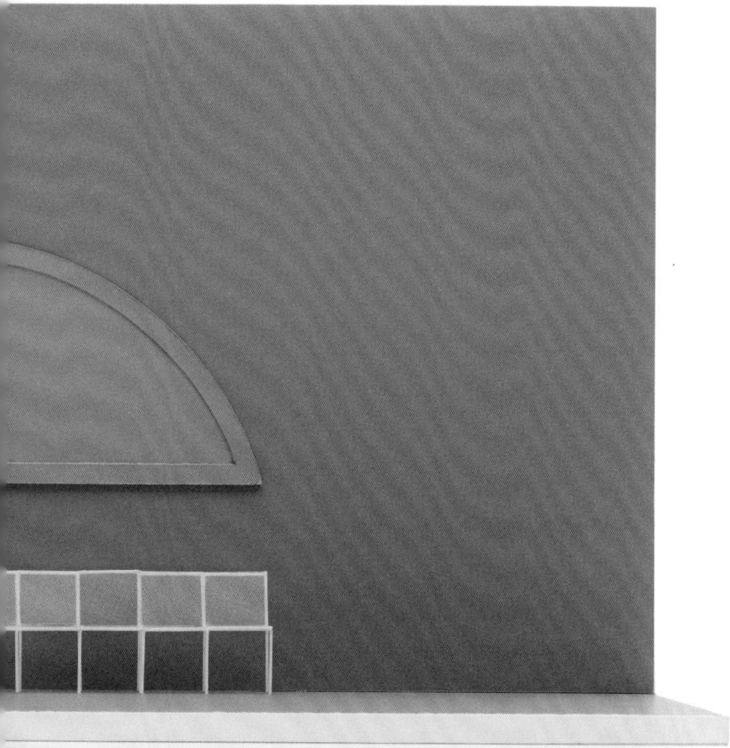

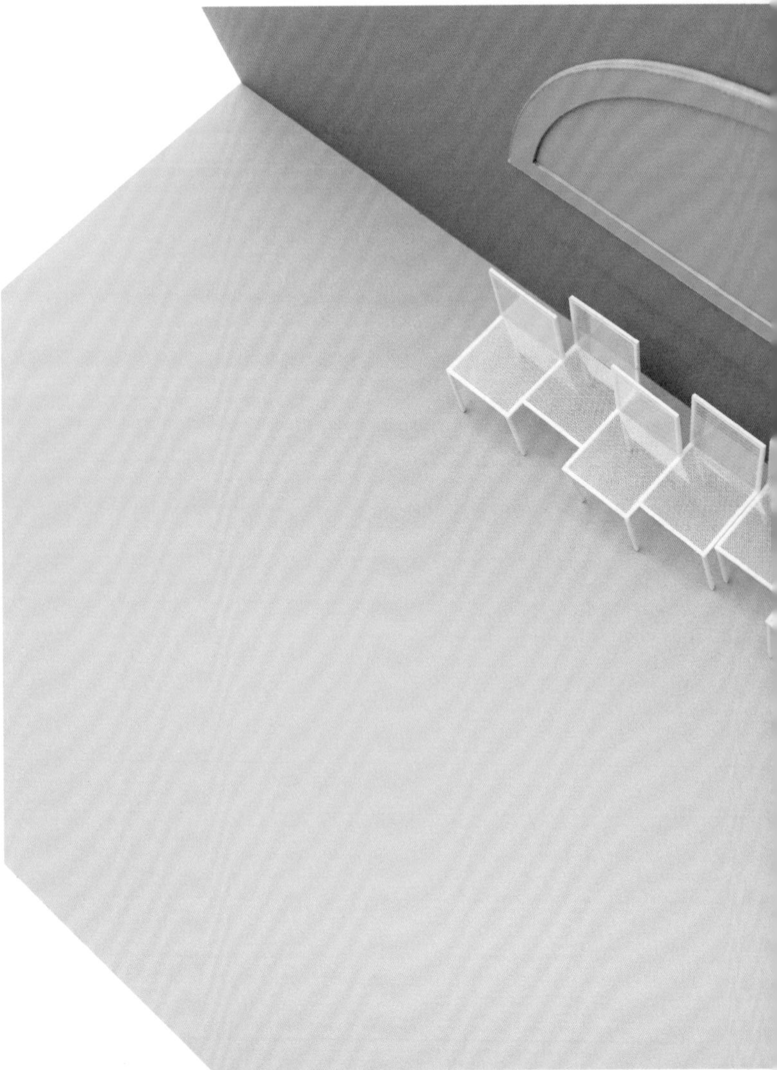

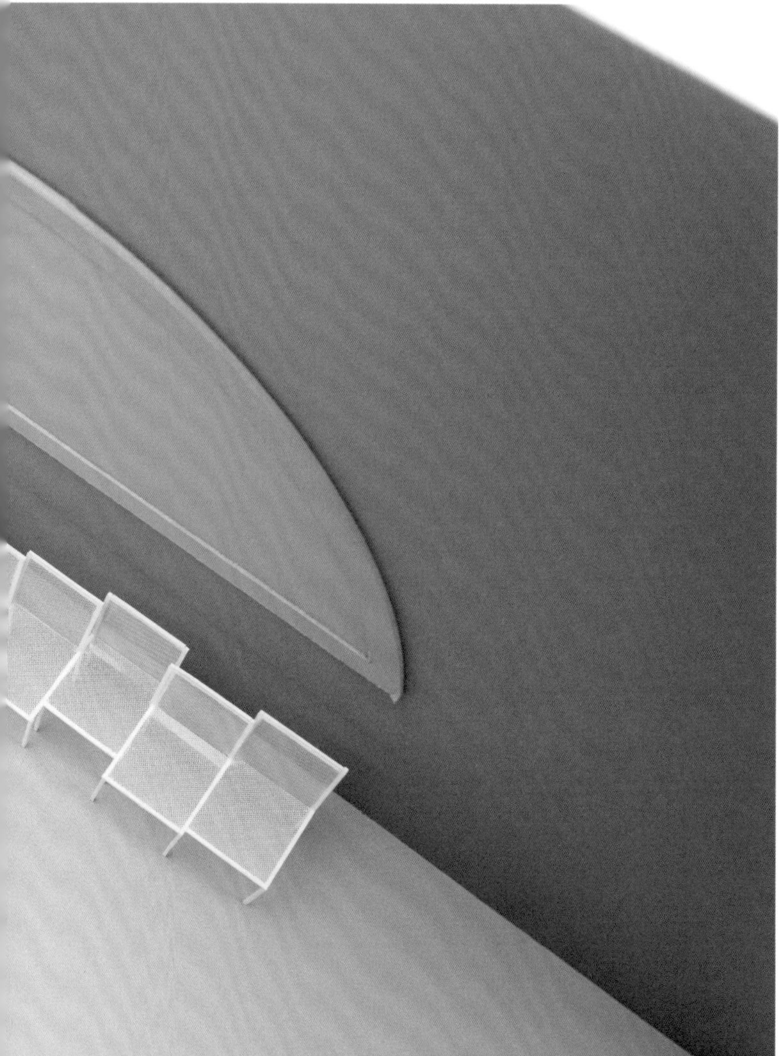

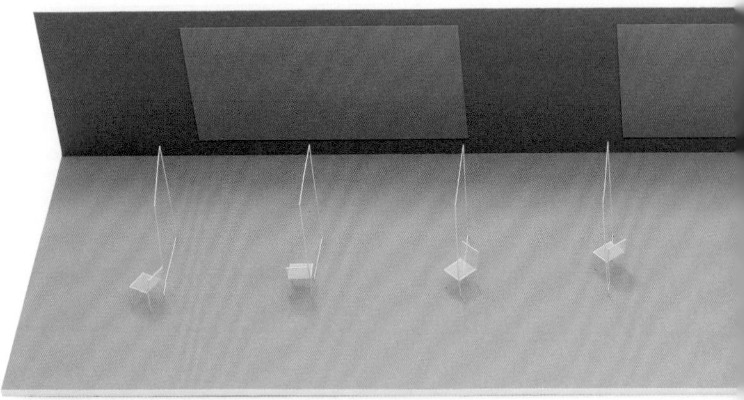

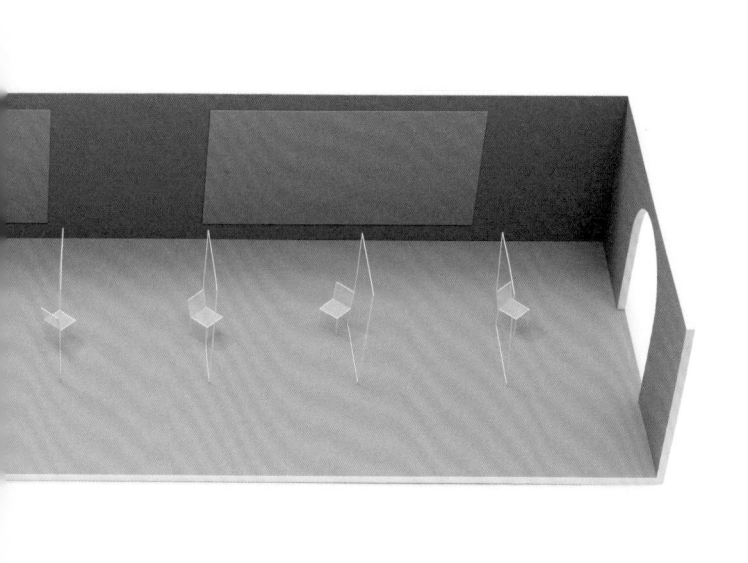

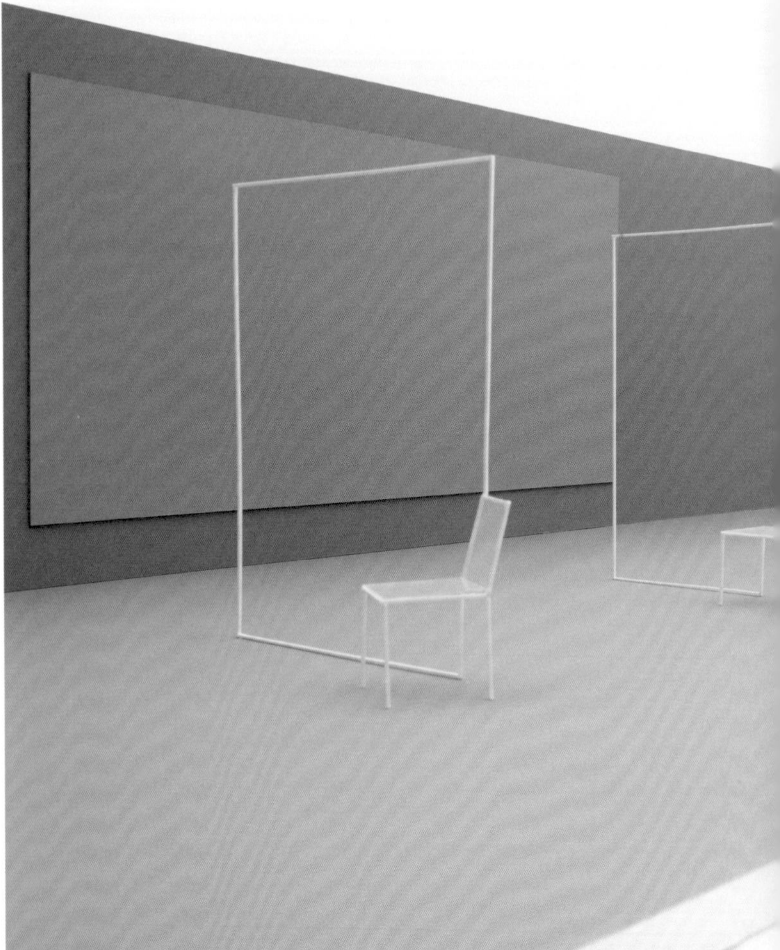

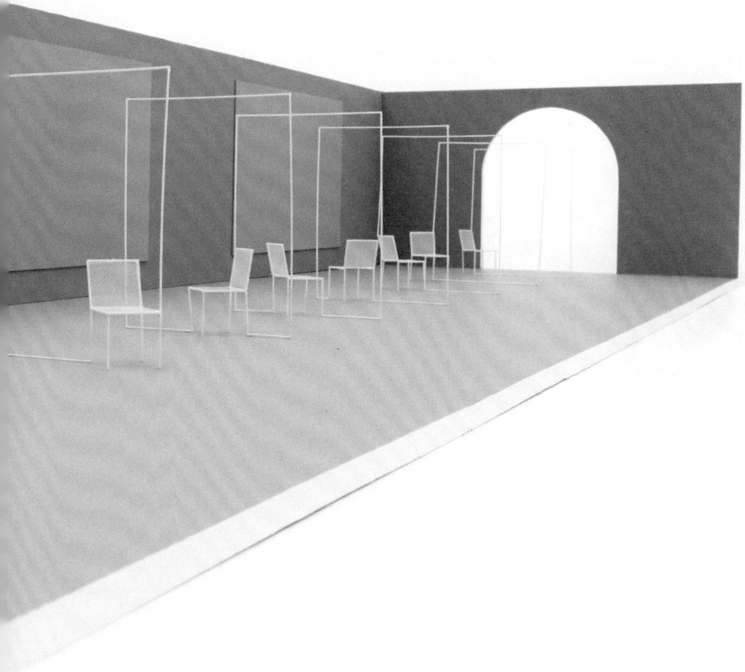

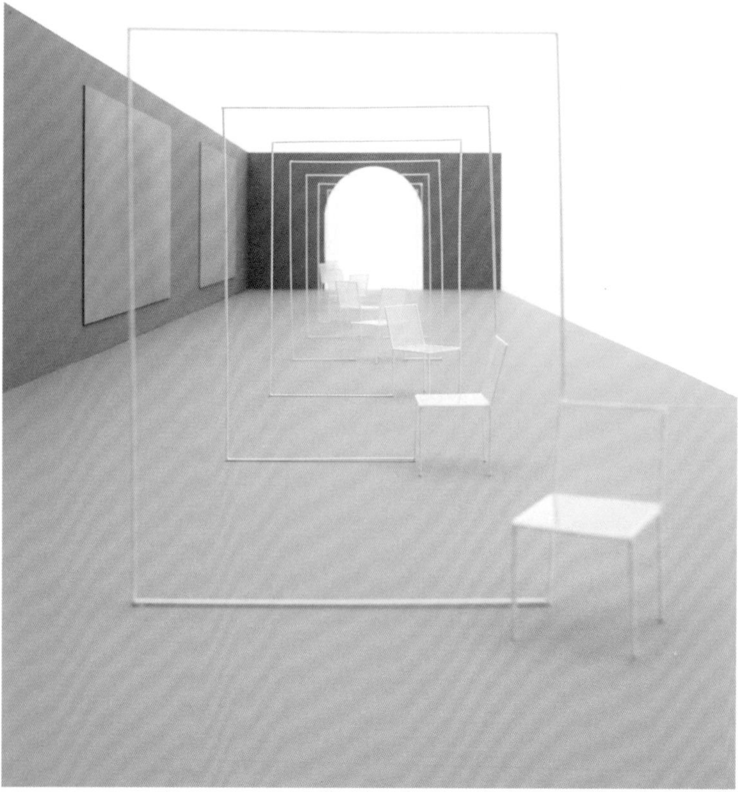

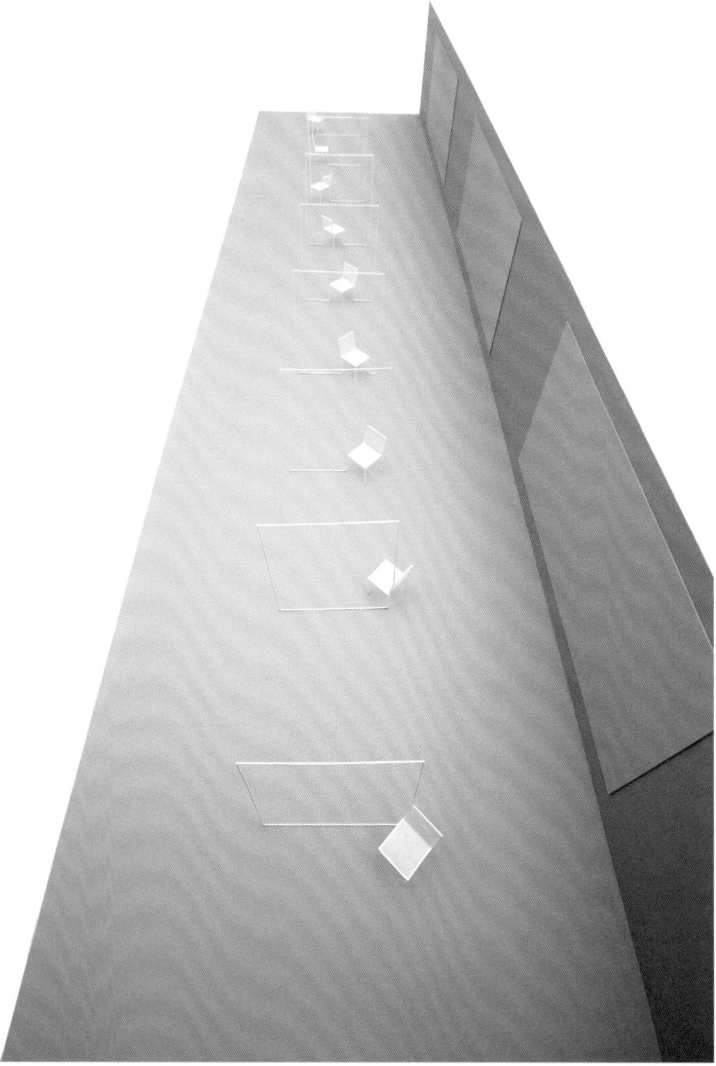

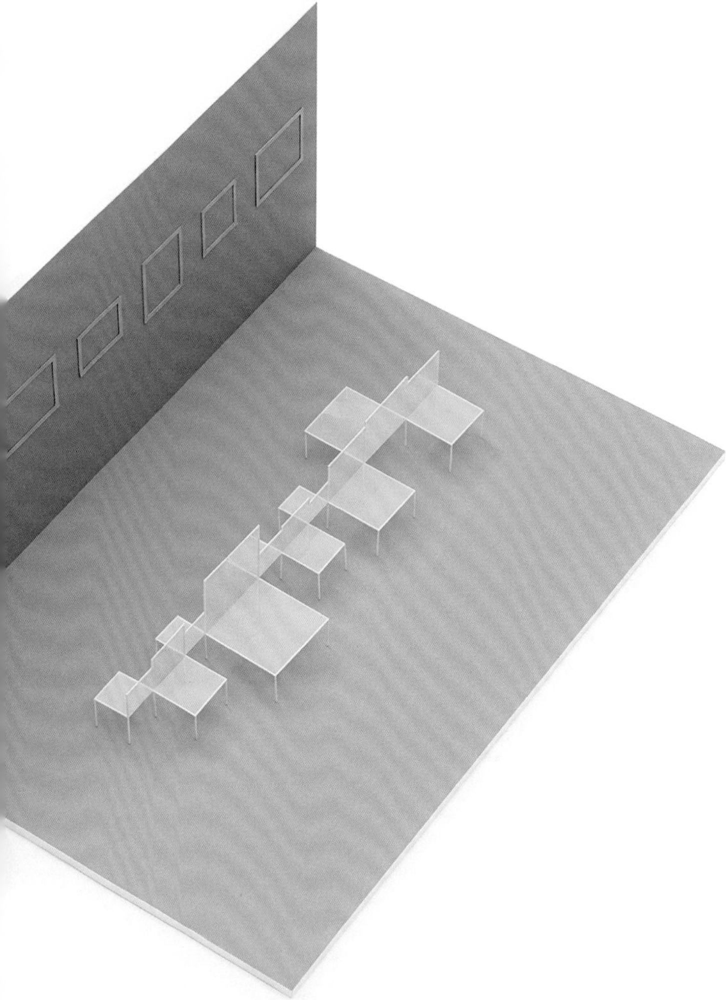

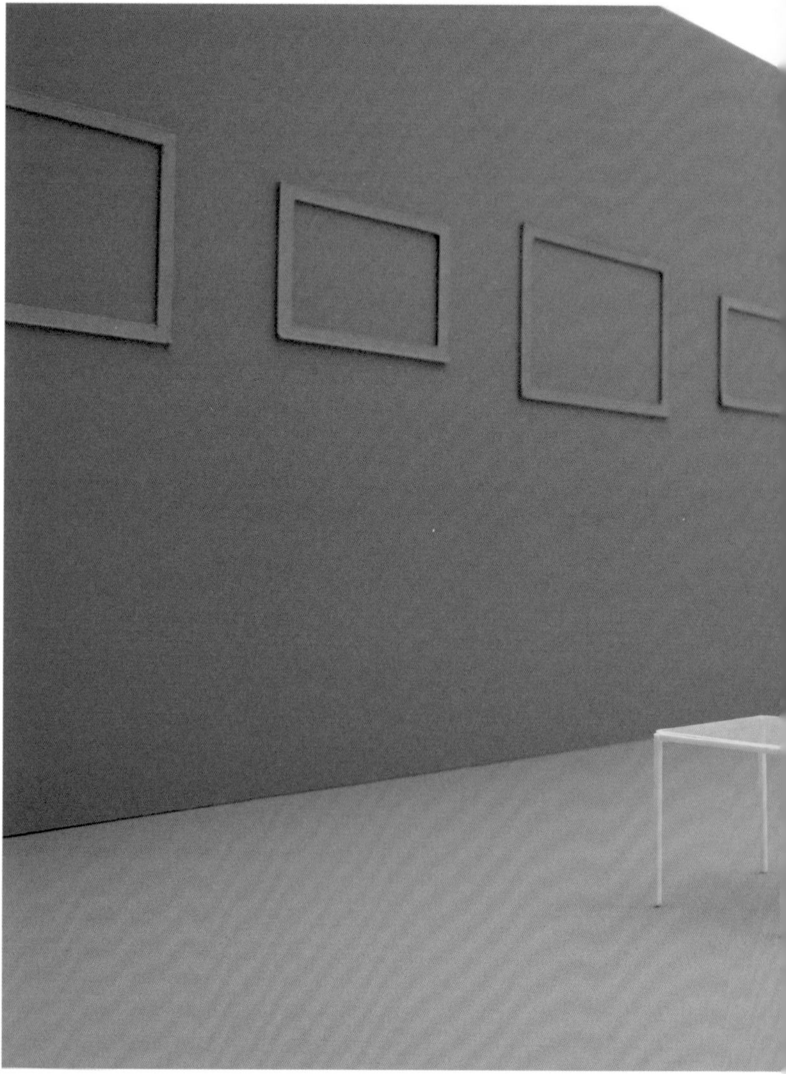

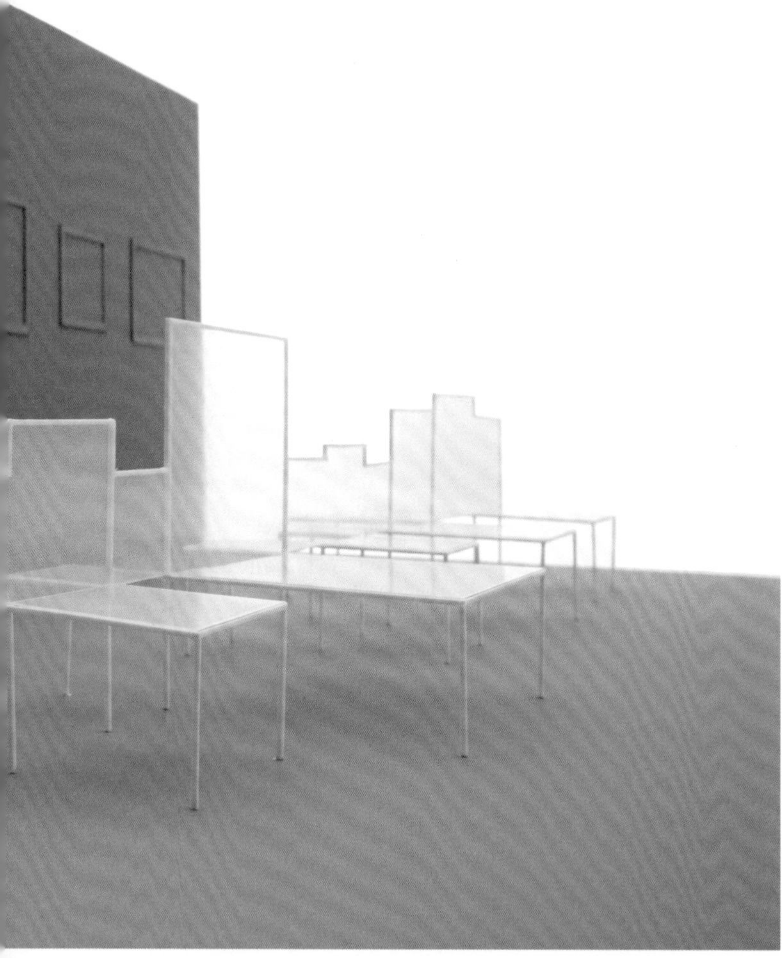

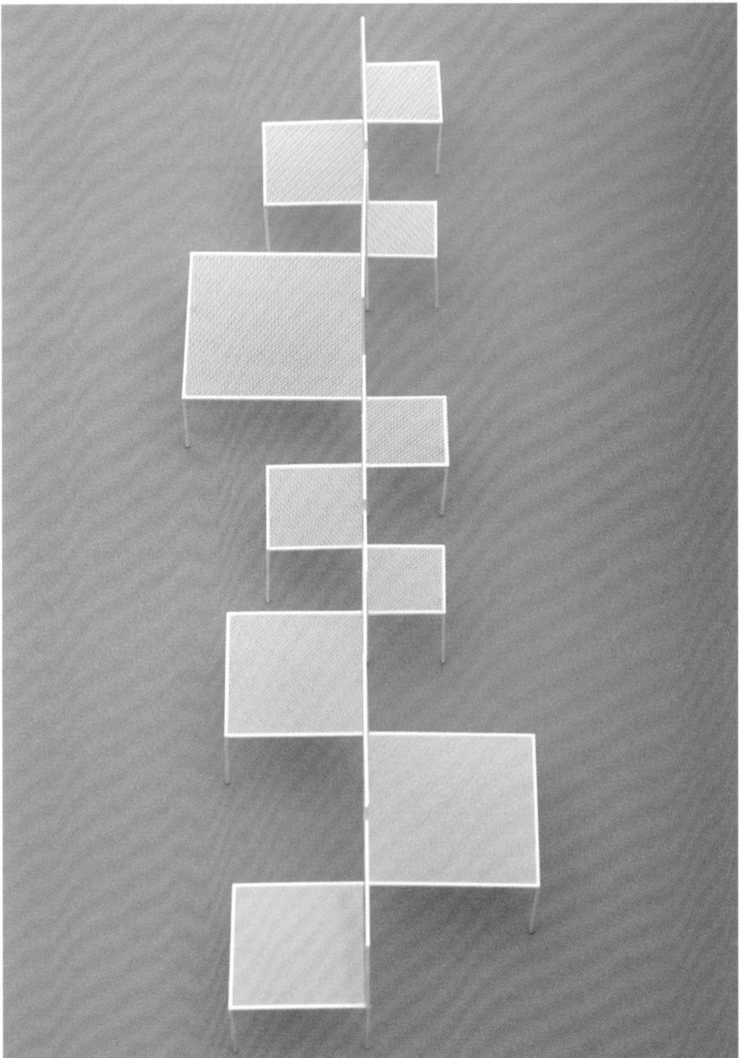

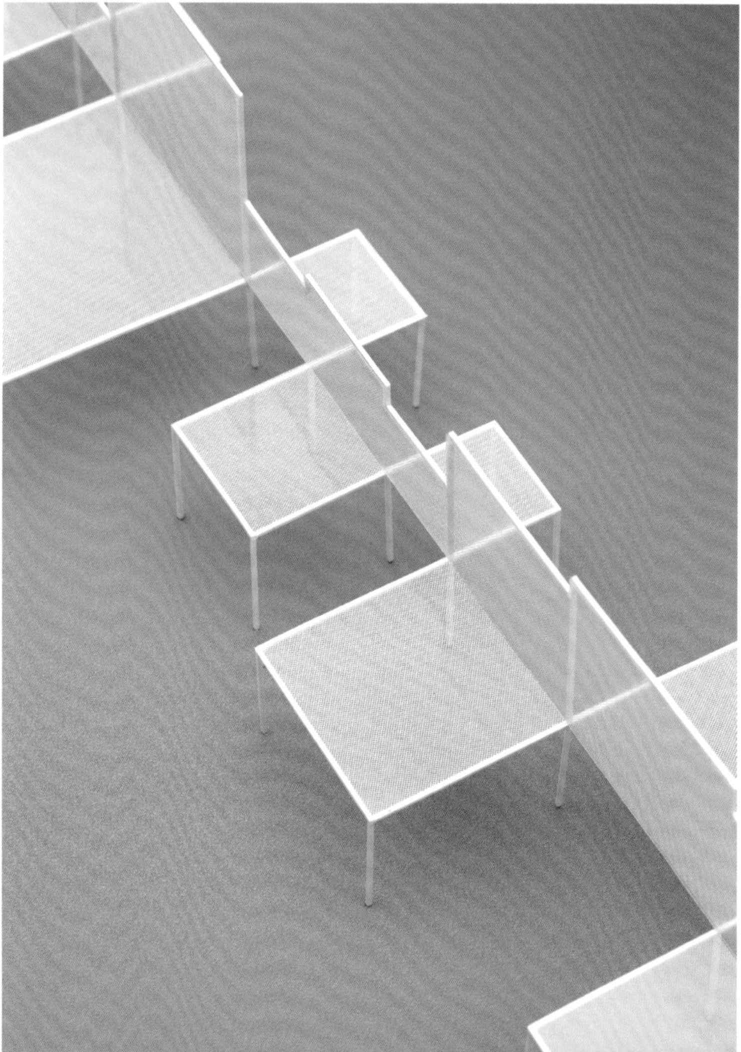

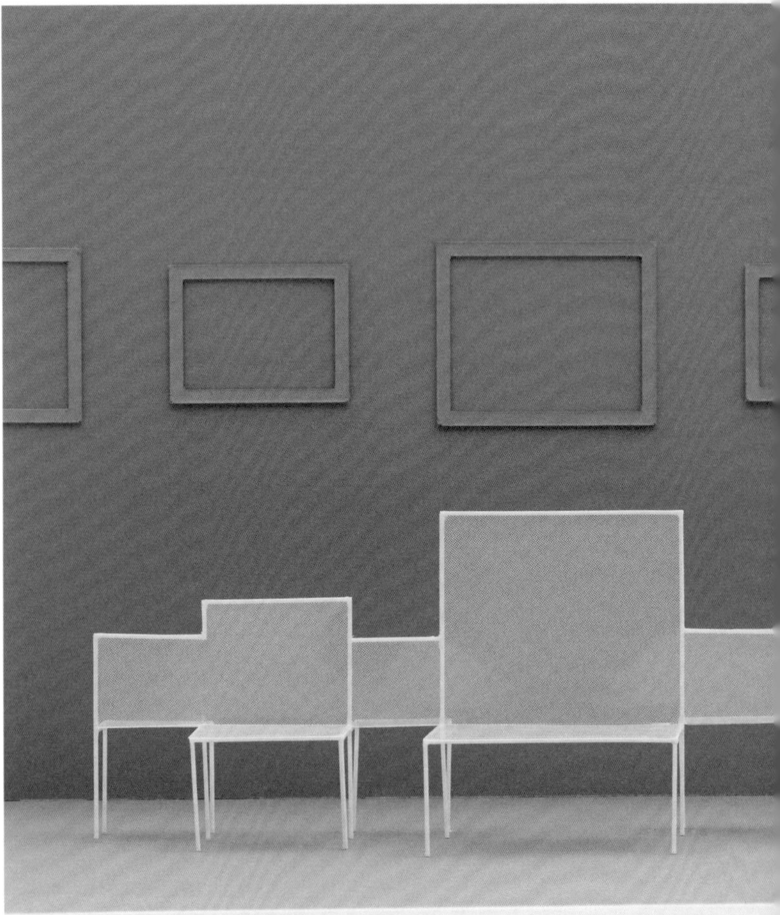

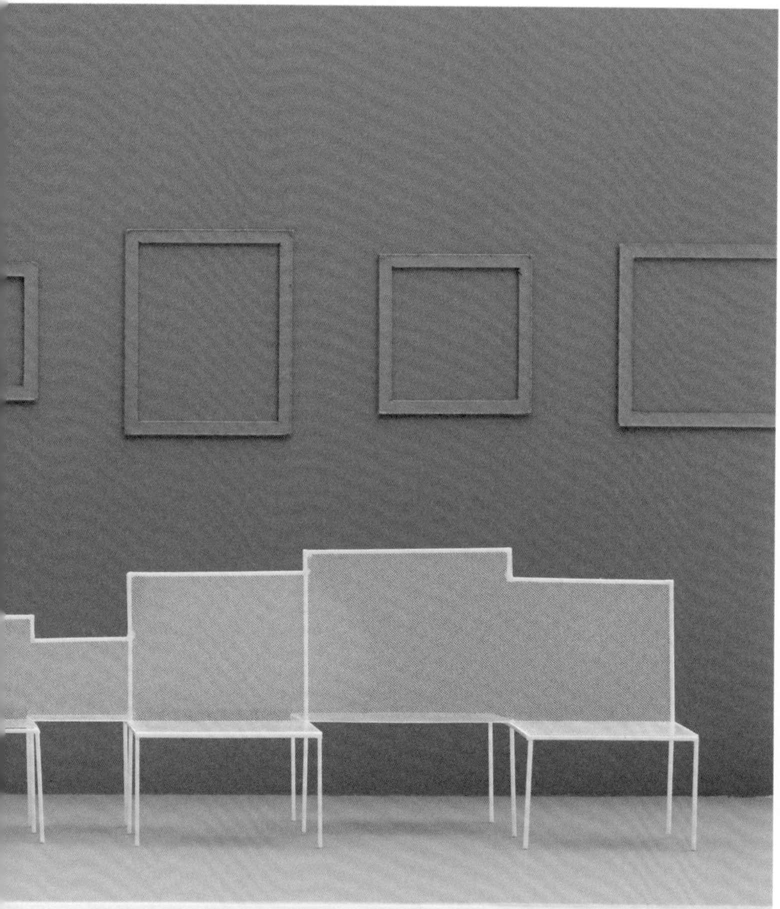

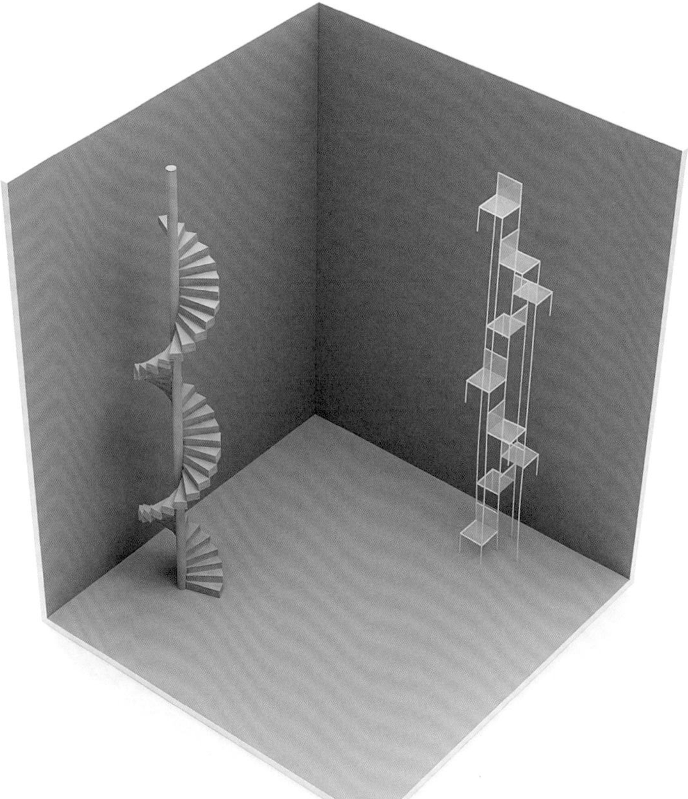

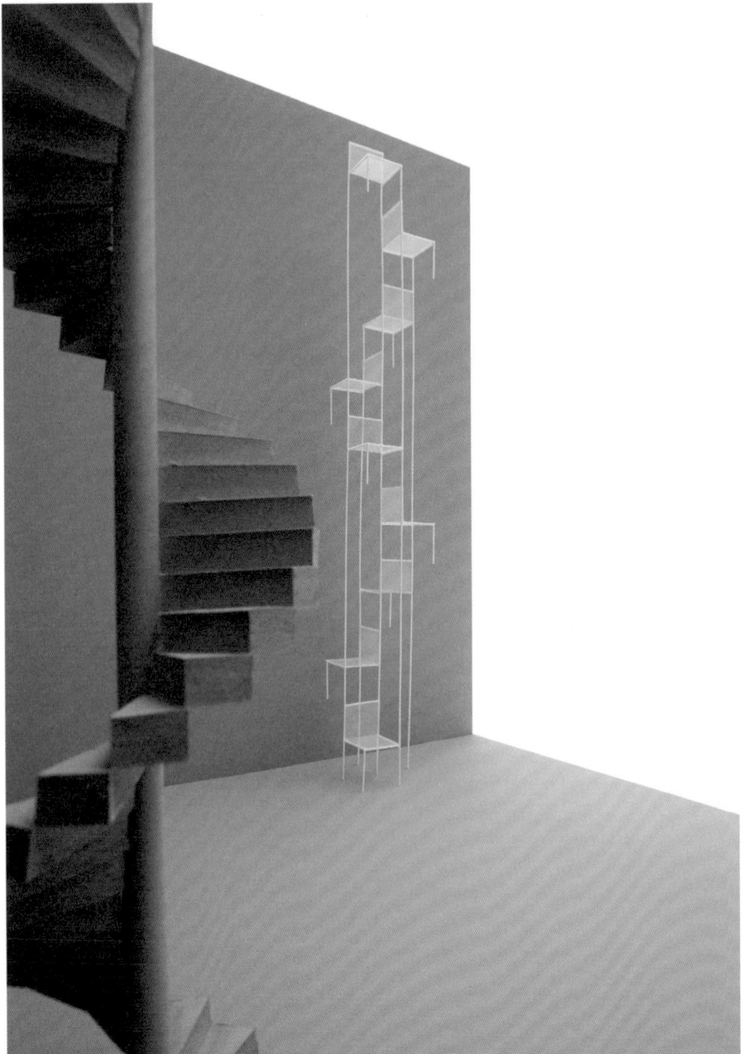

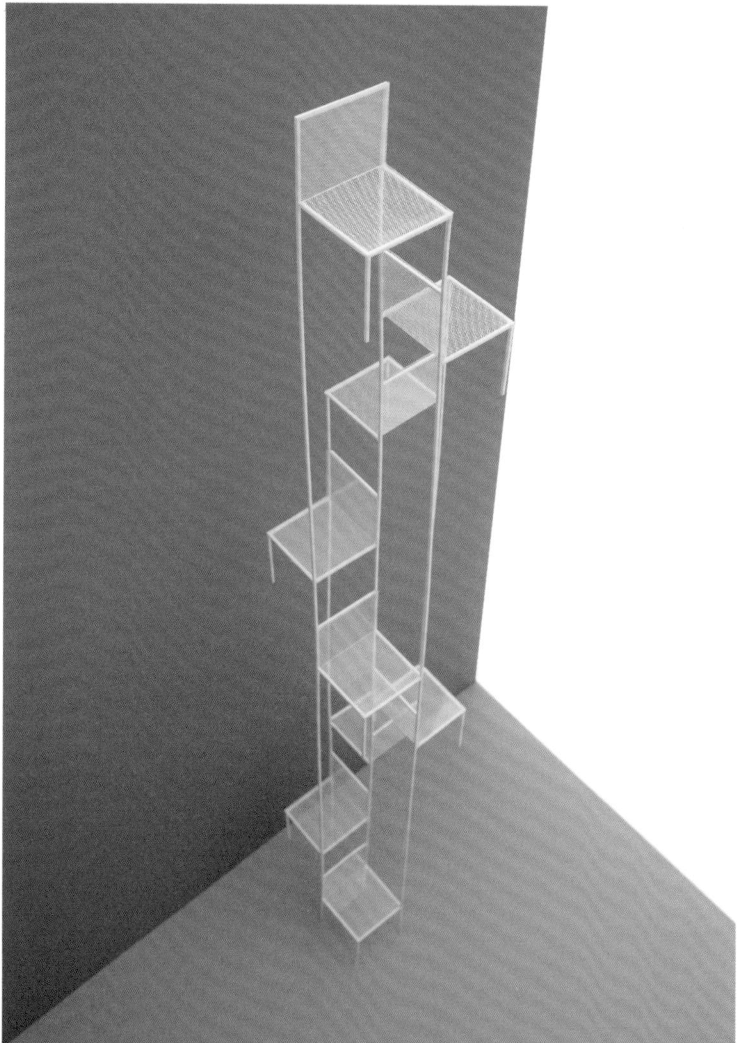

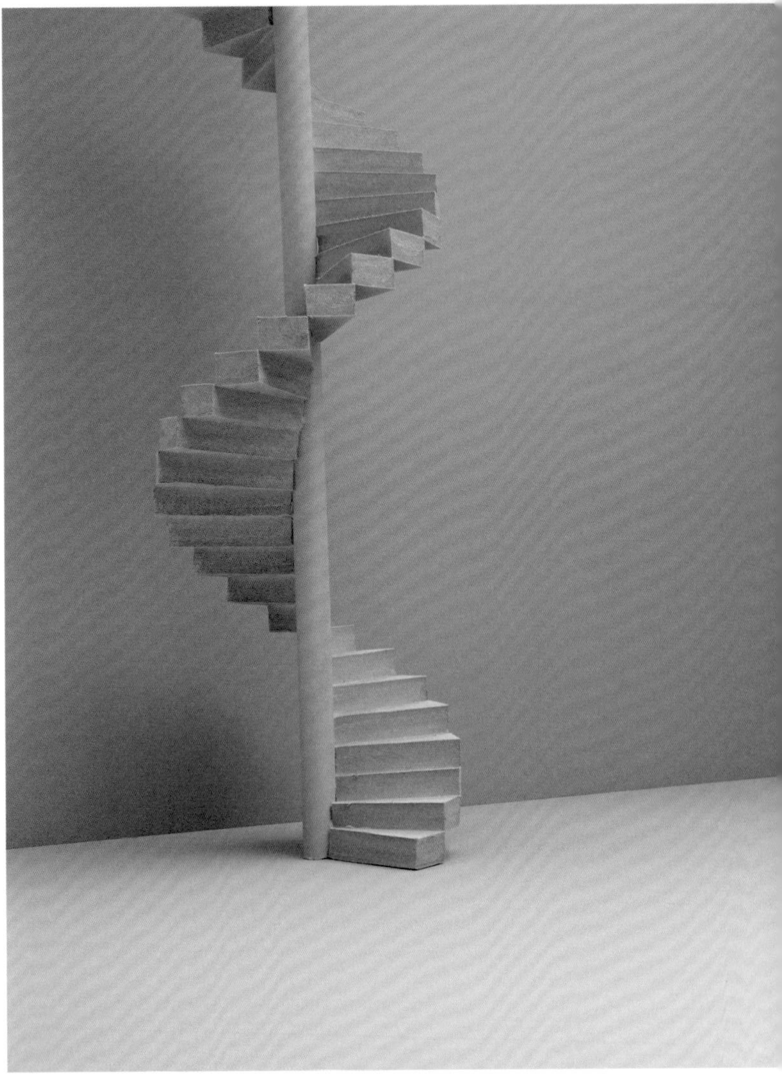

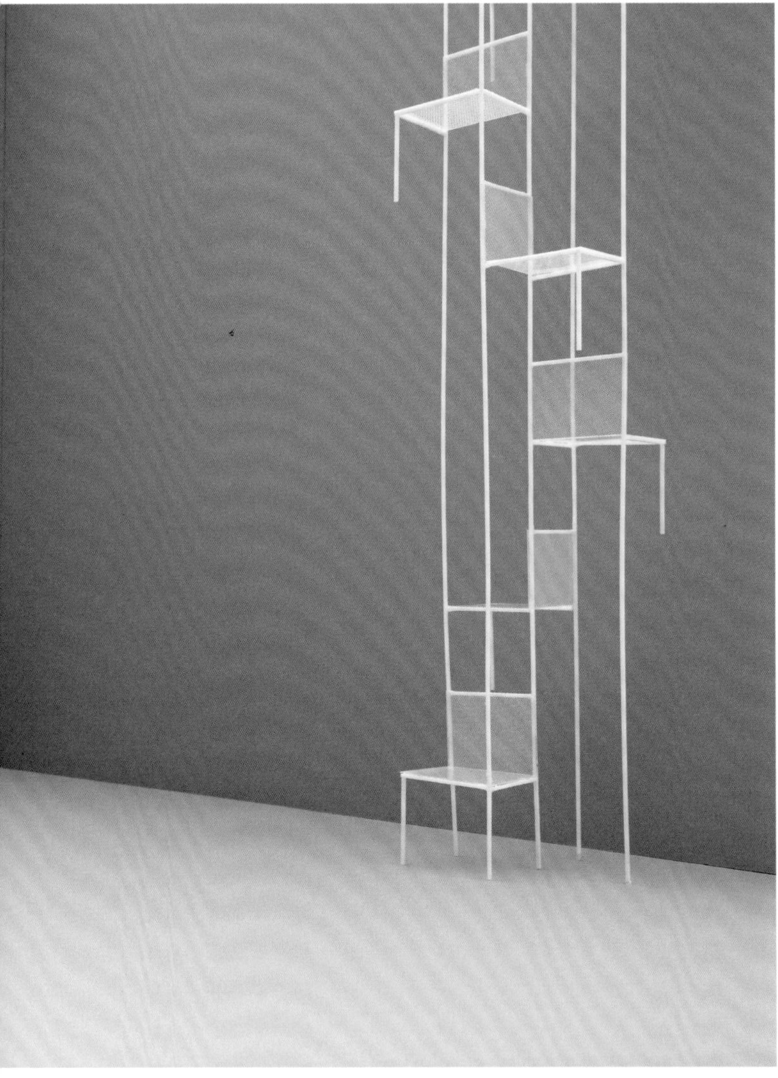

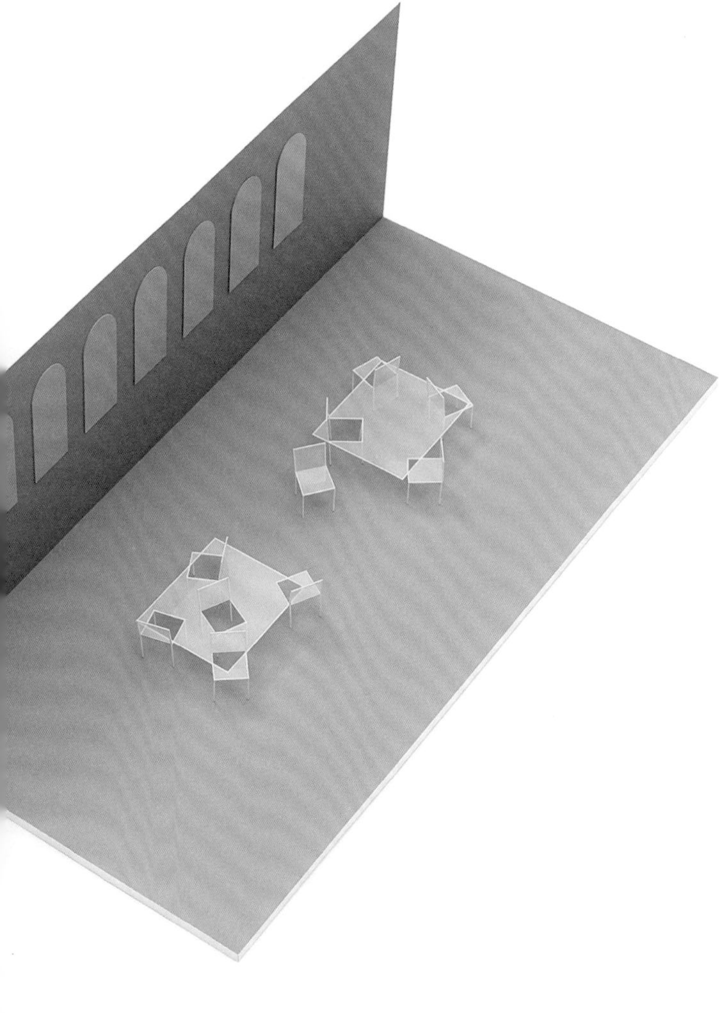

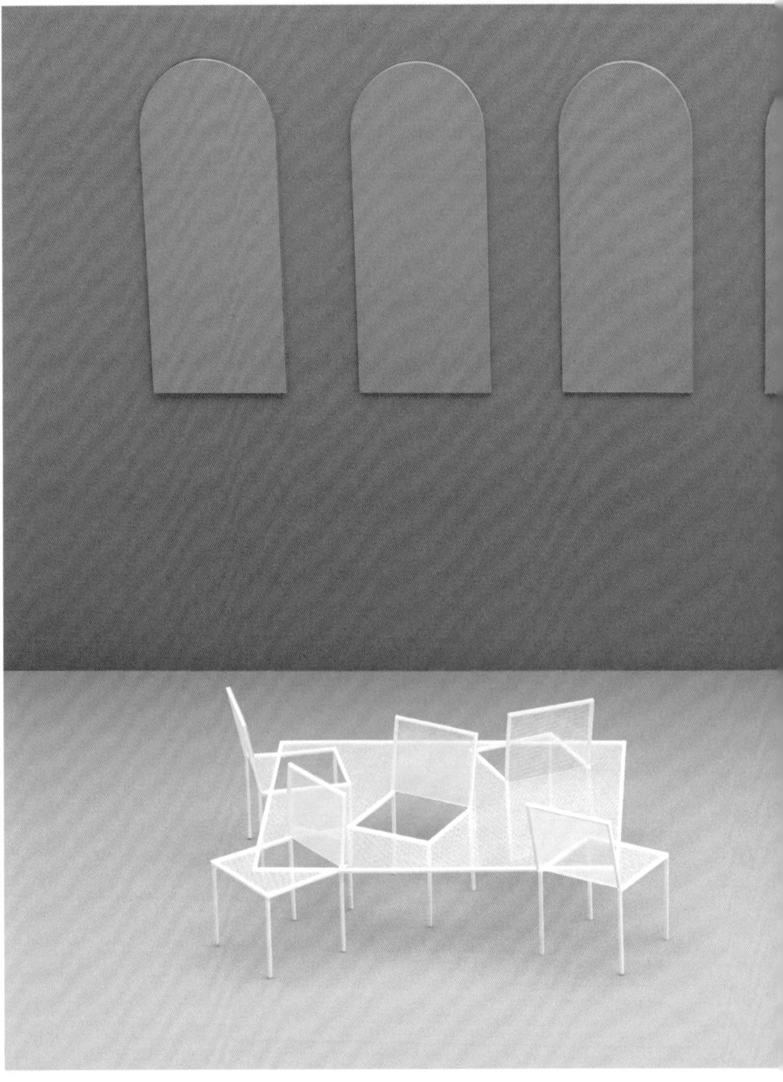

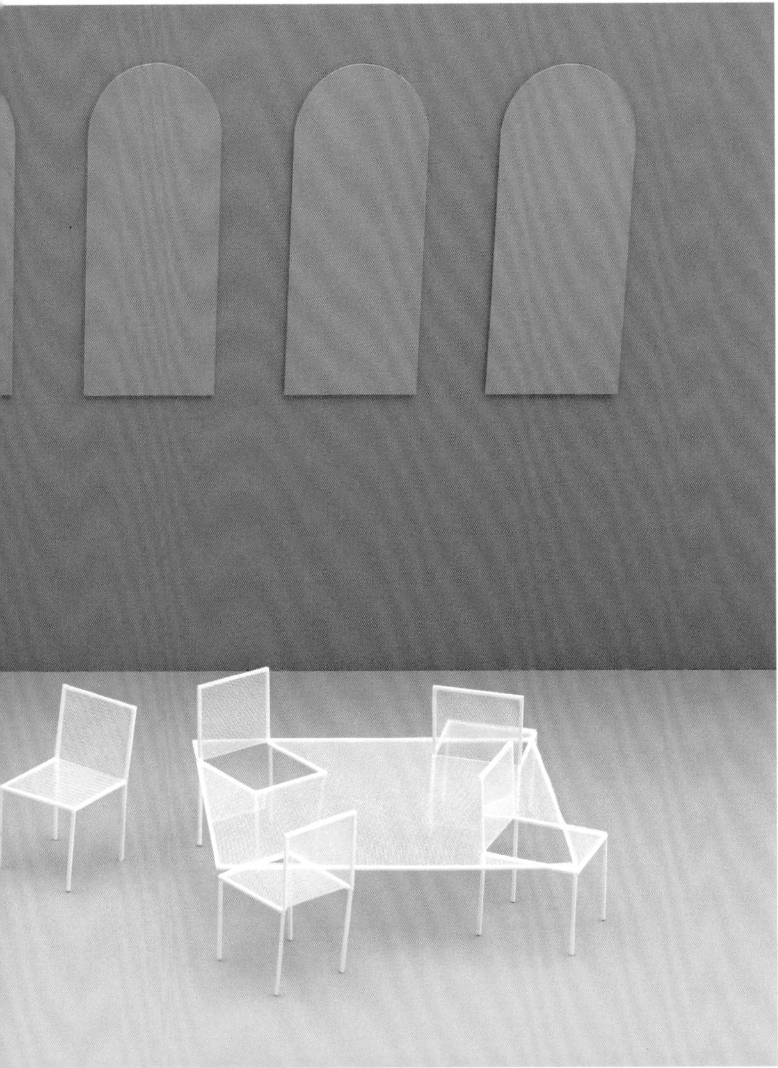

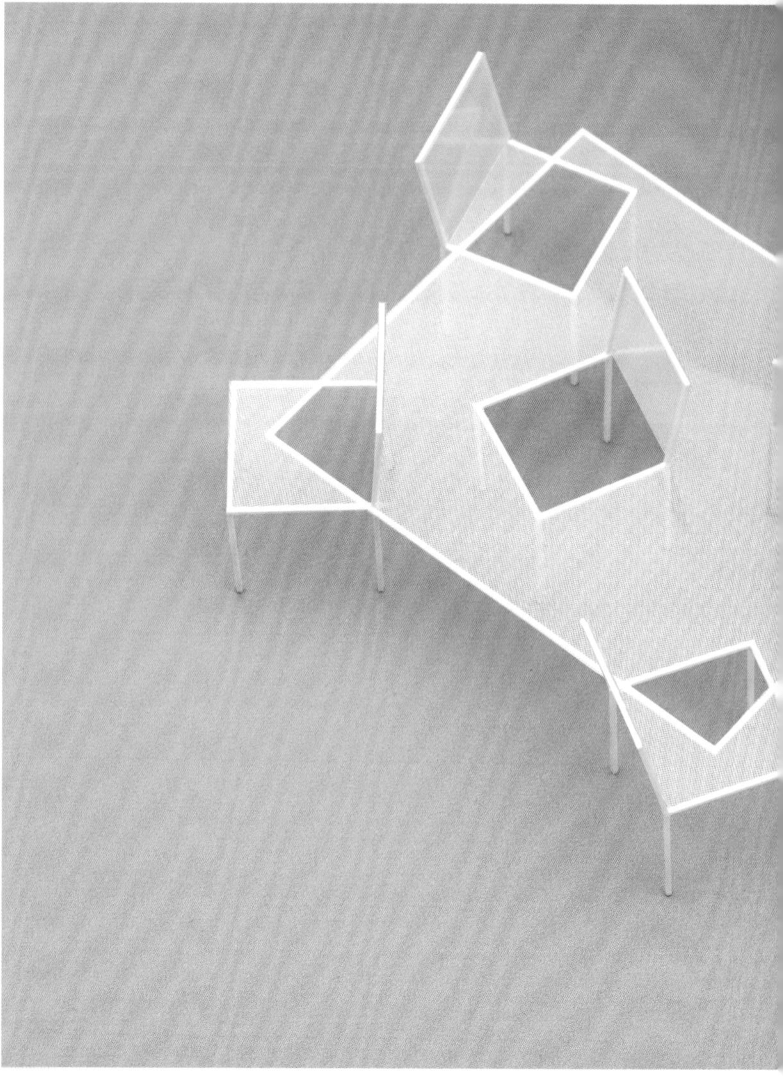

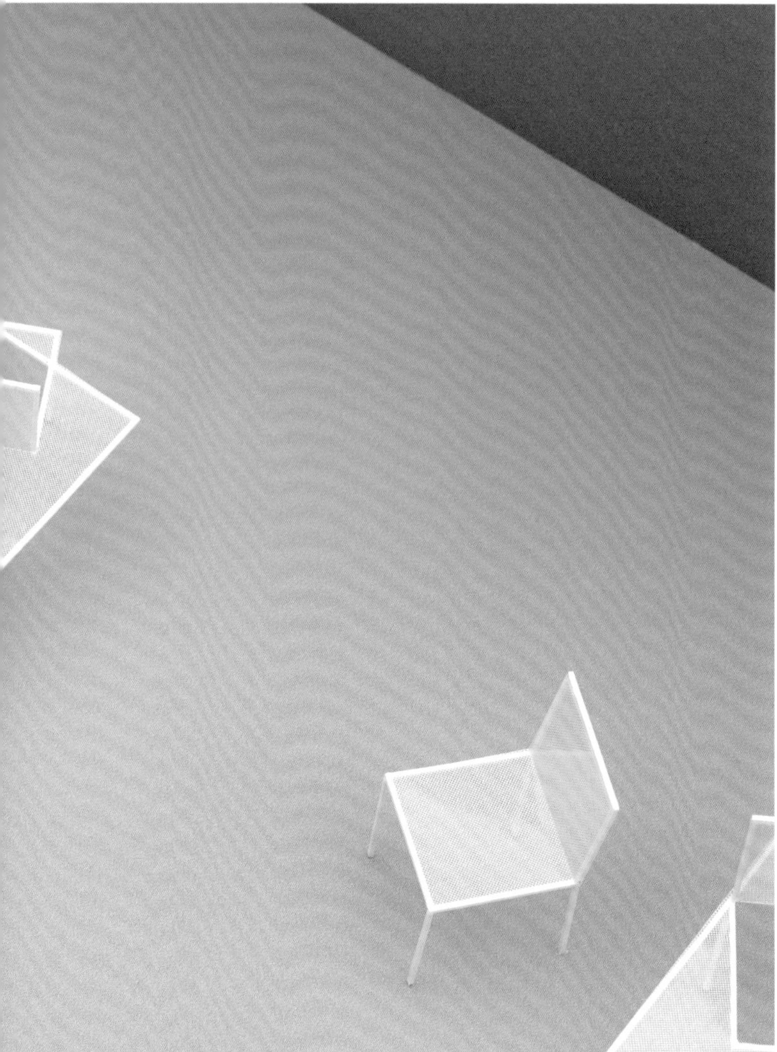

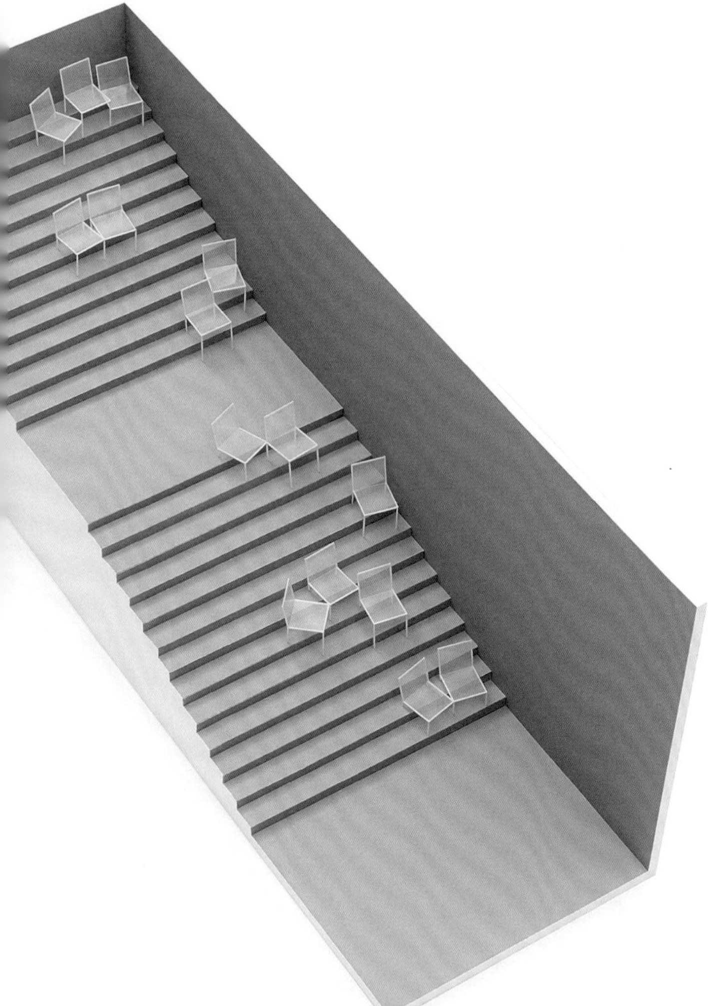

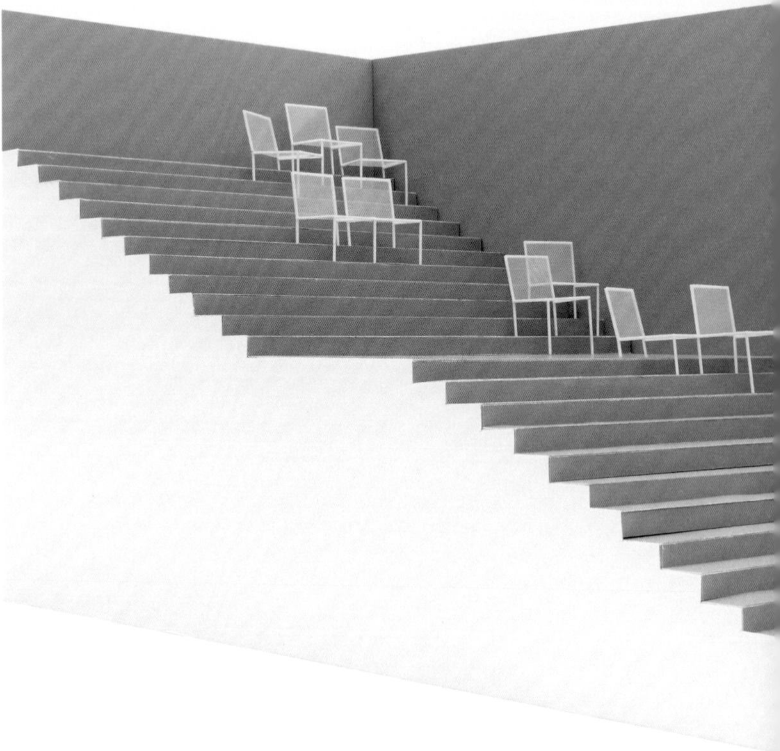

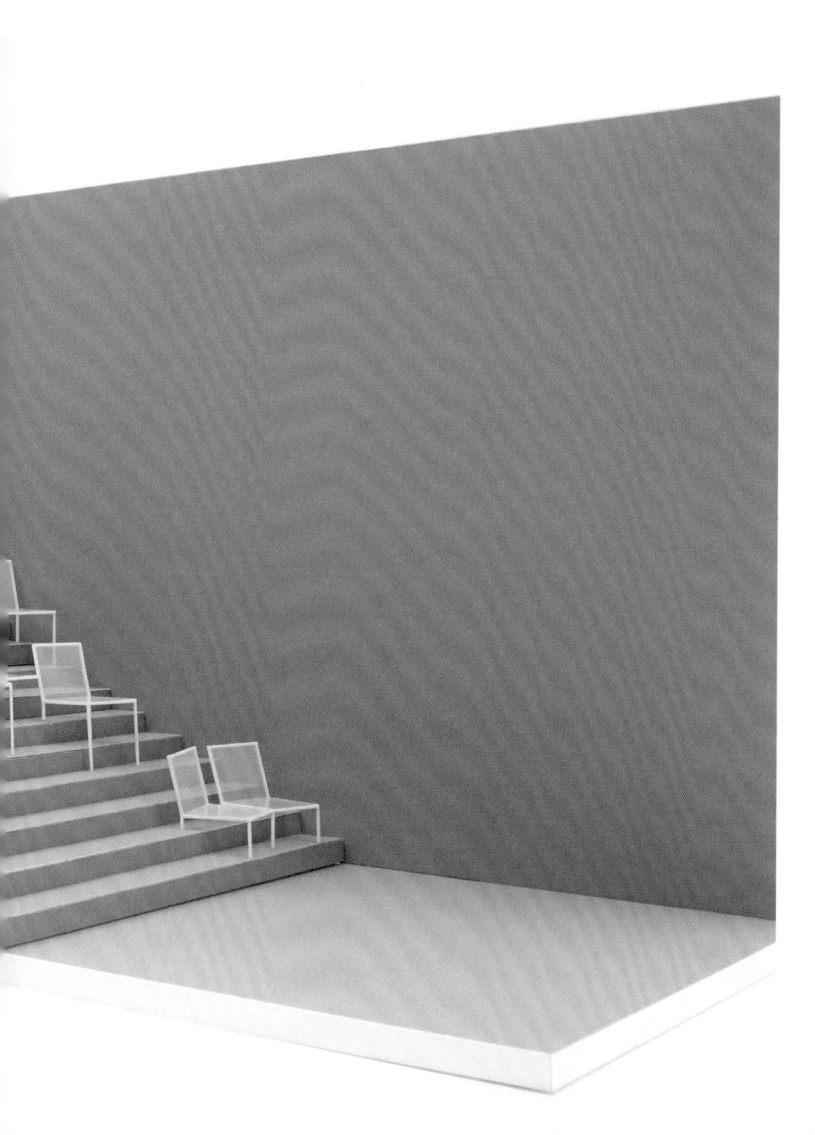

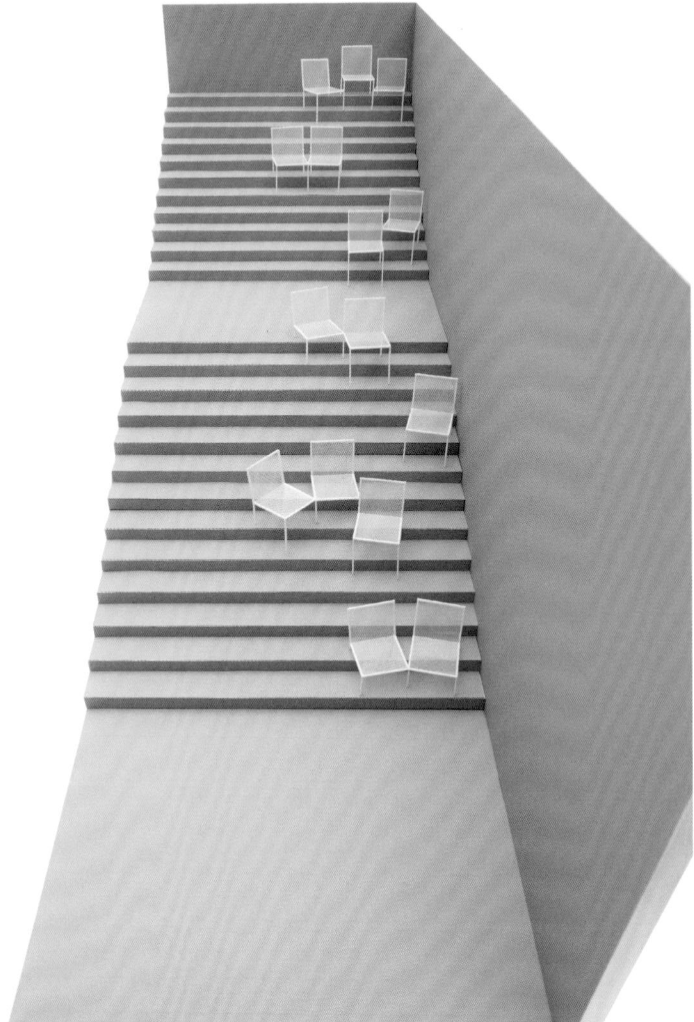

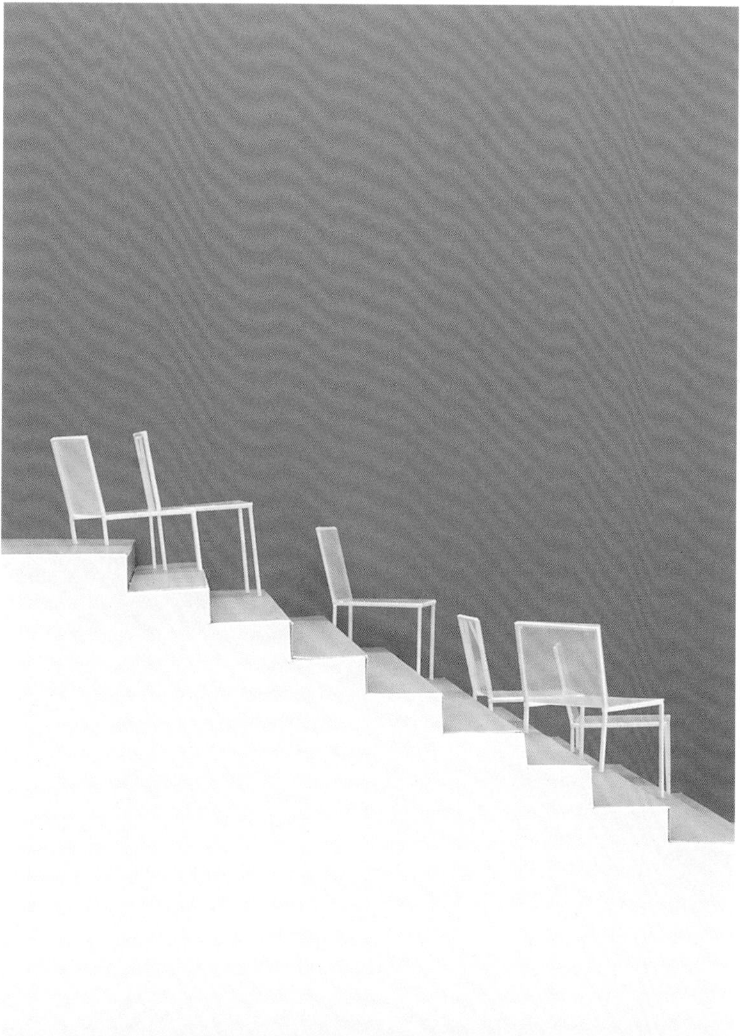

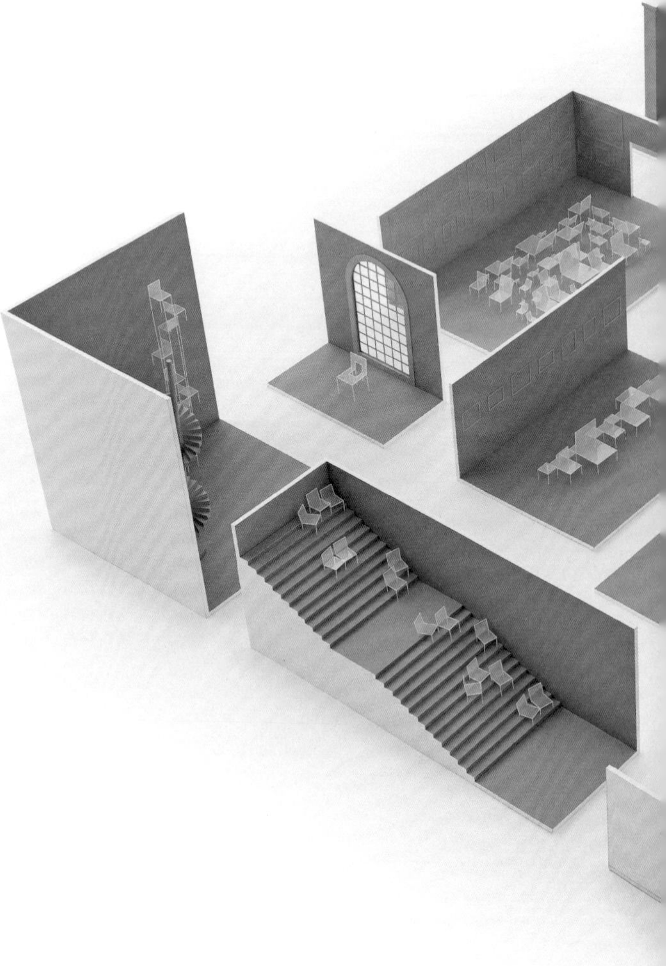

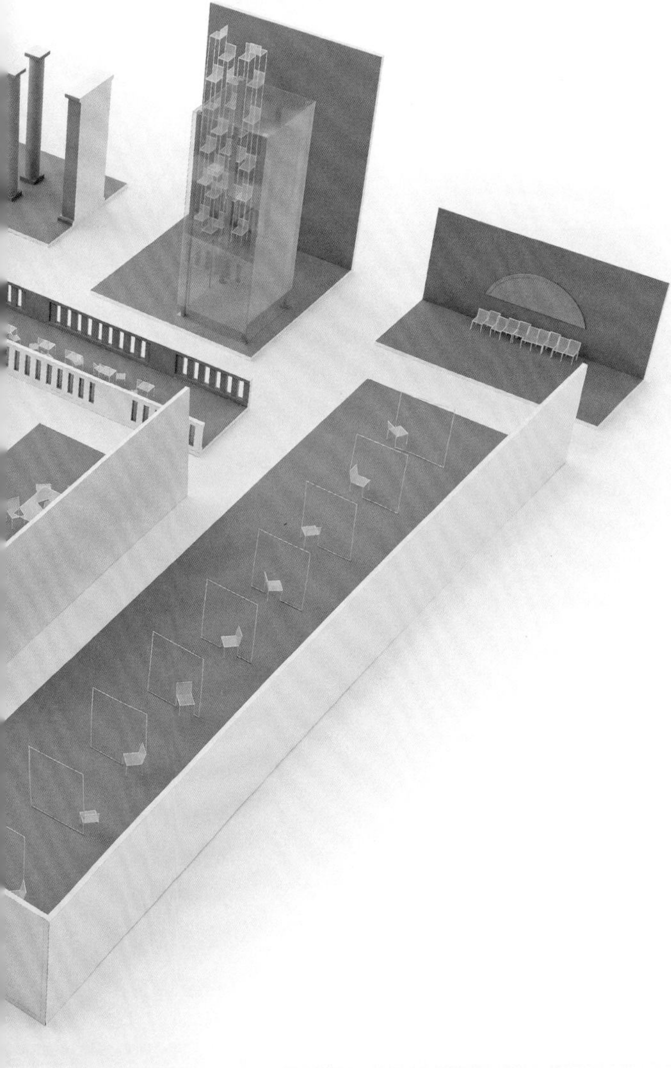

moss house

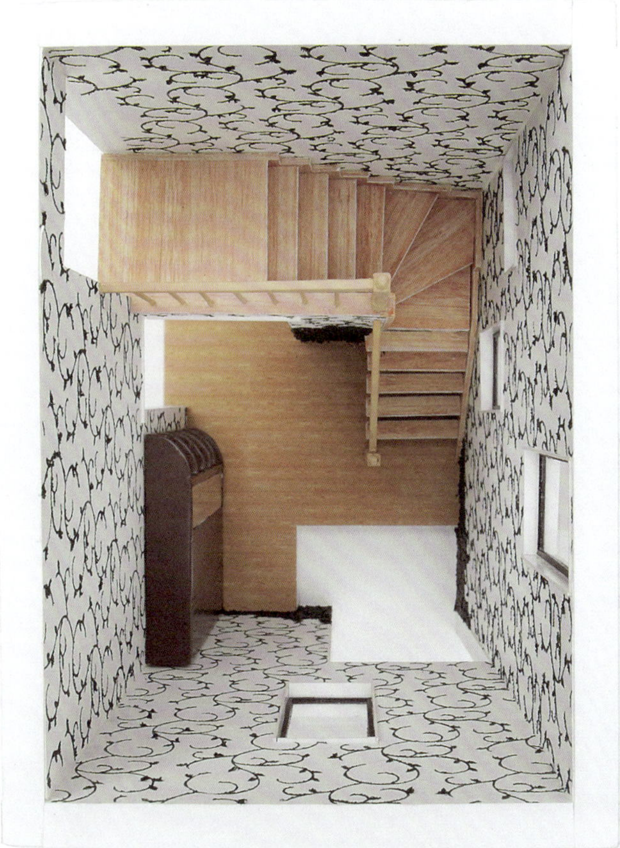

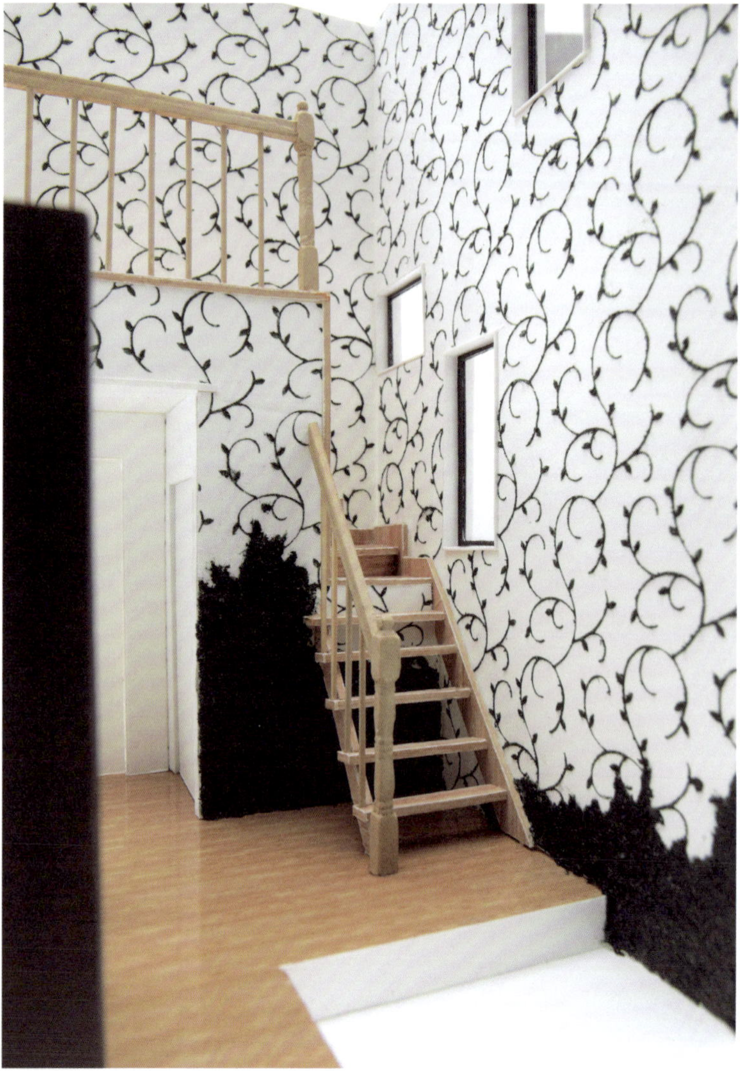

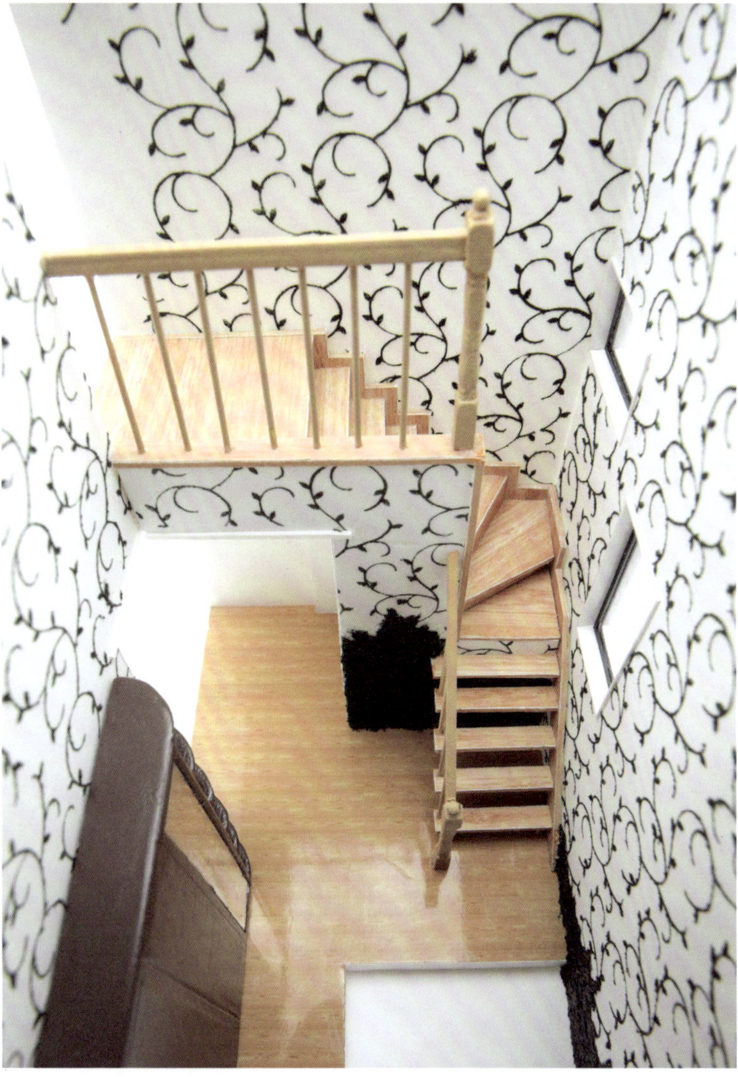

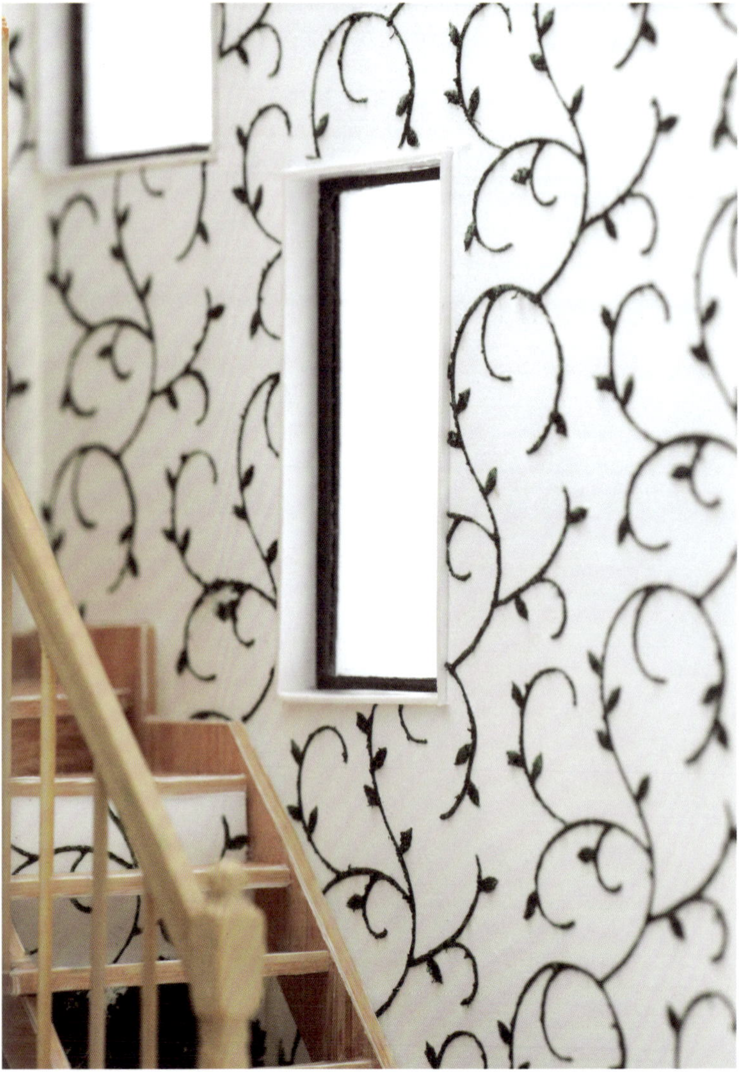

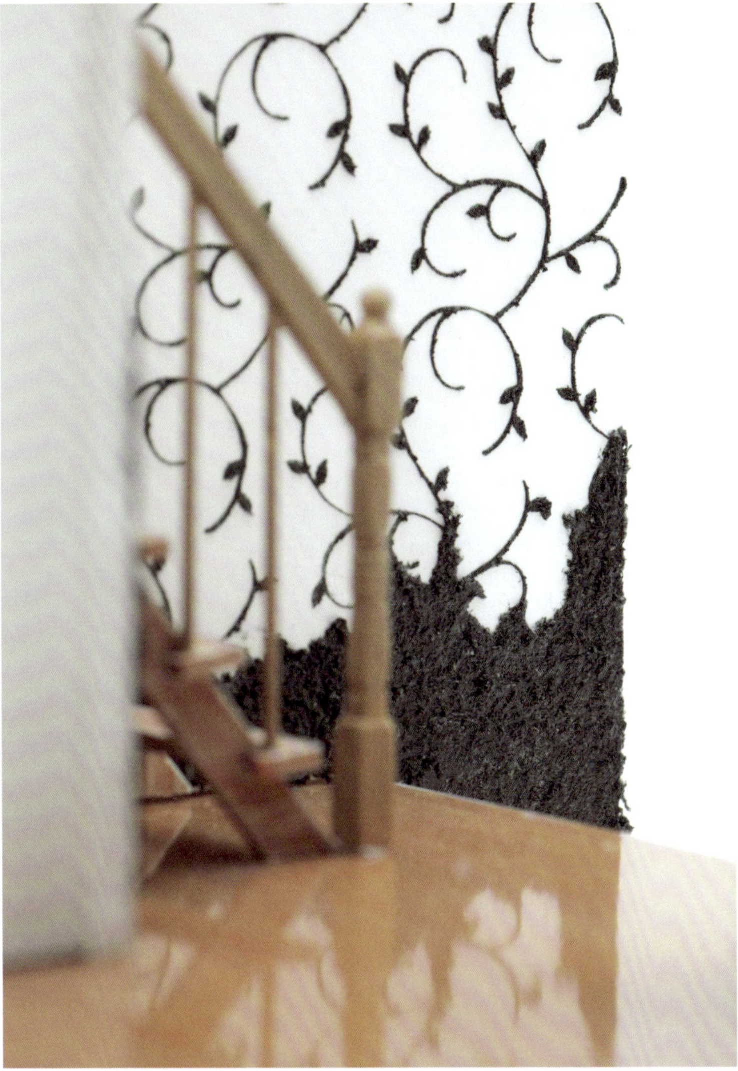

PUMA HOUSE TOKYO

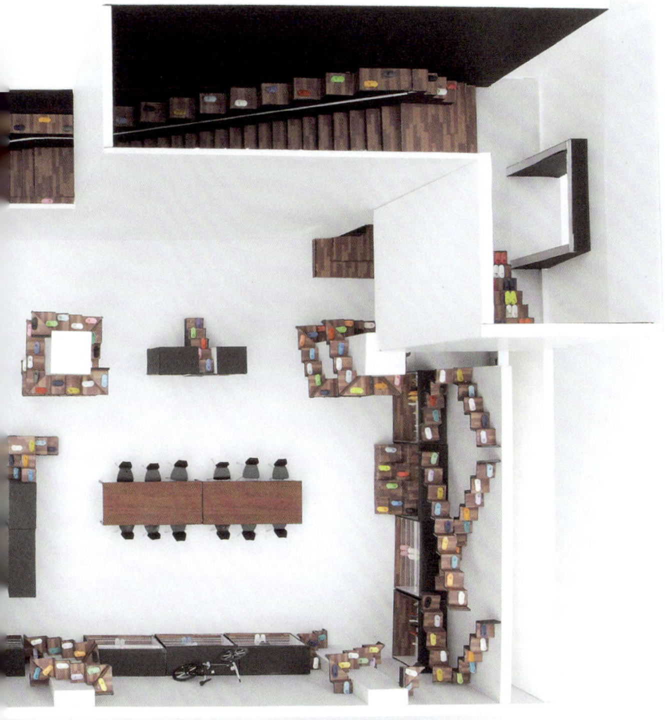

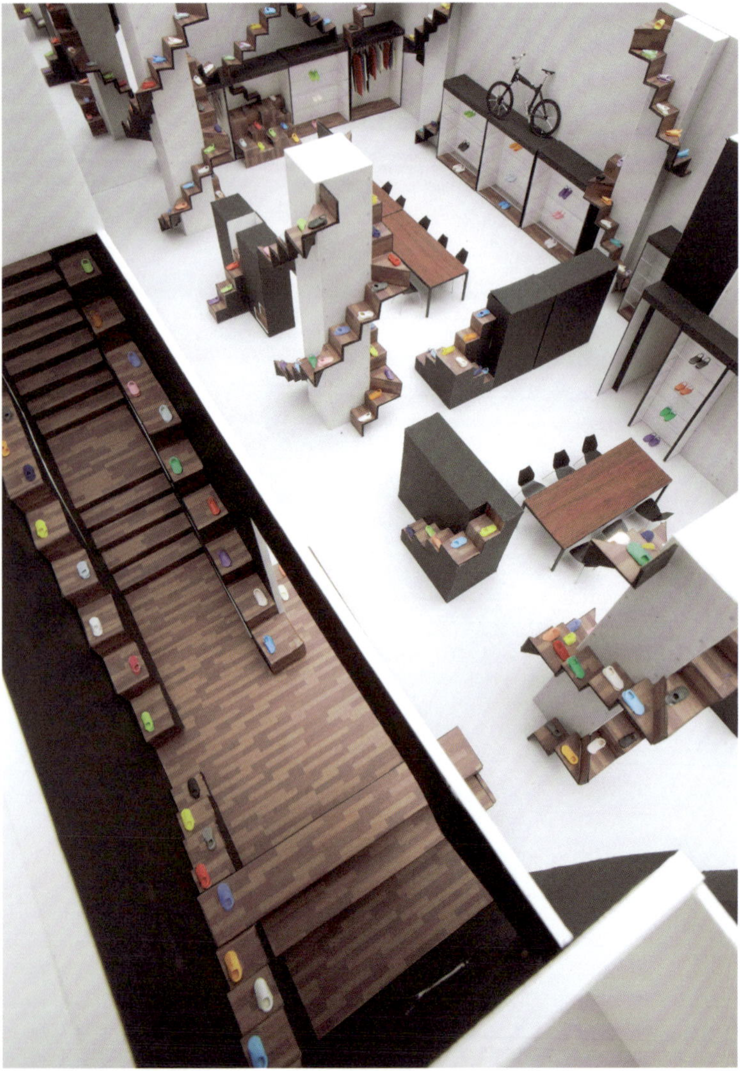

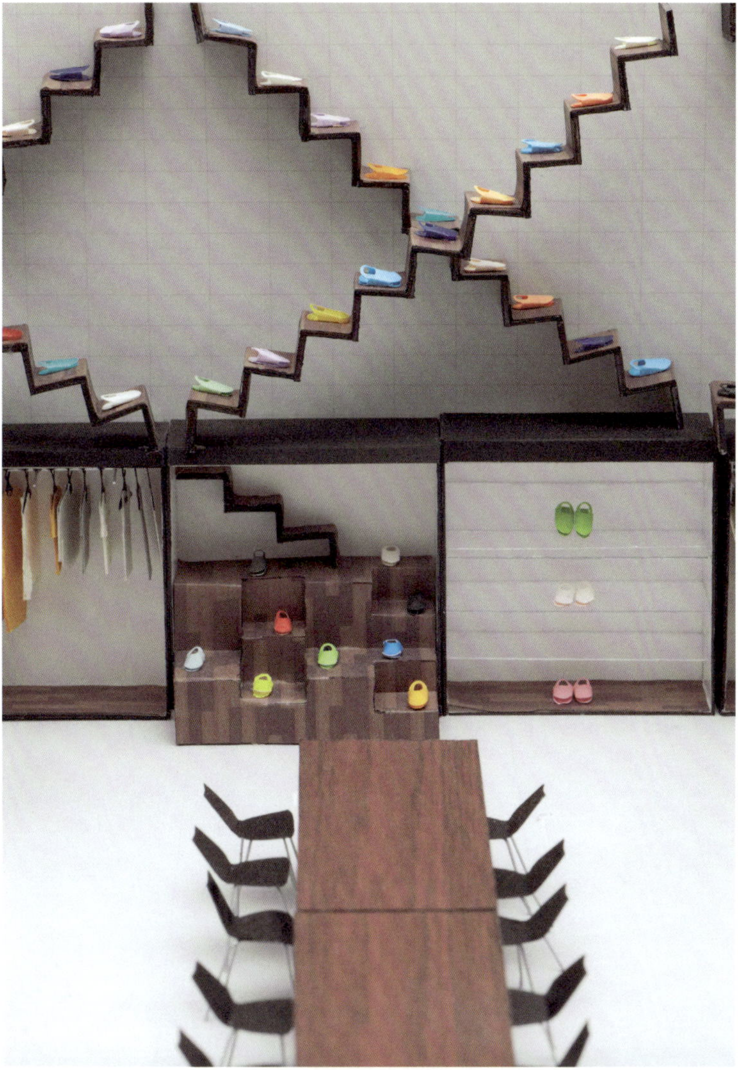

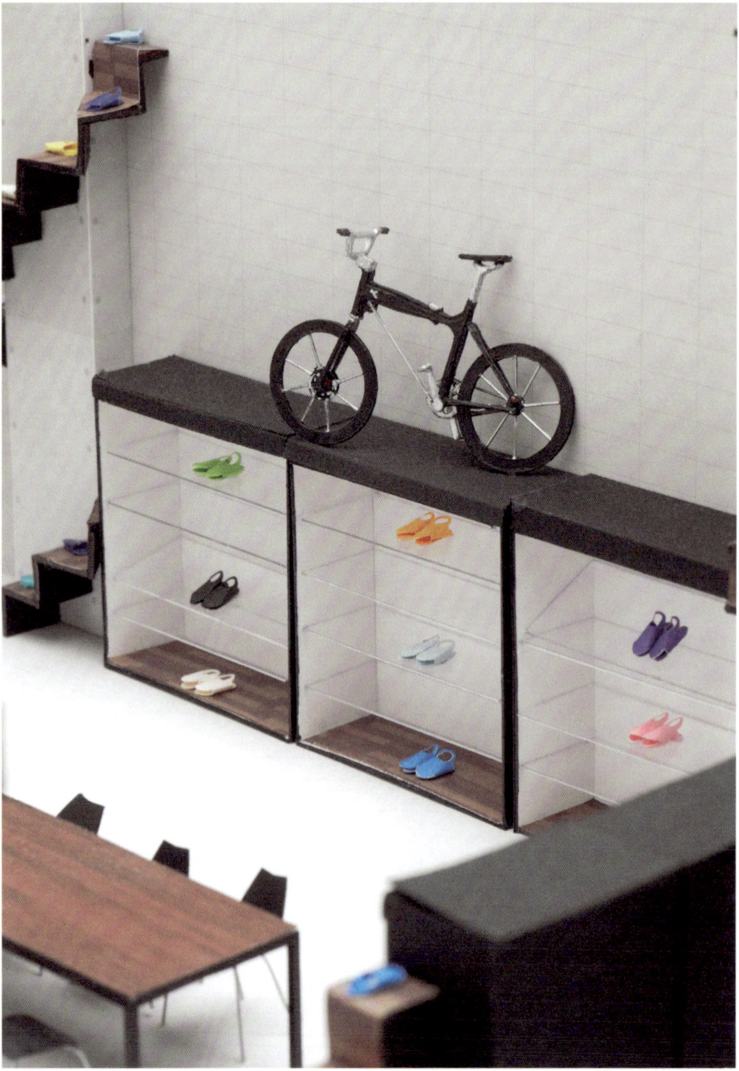

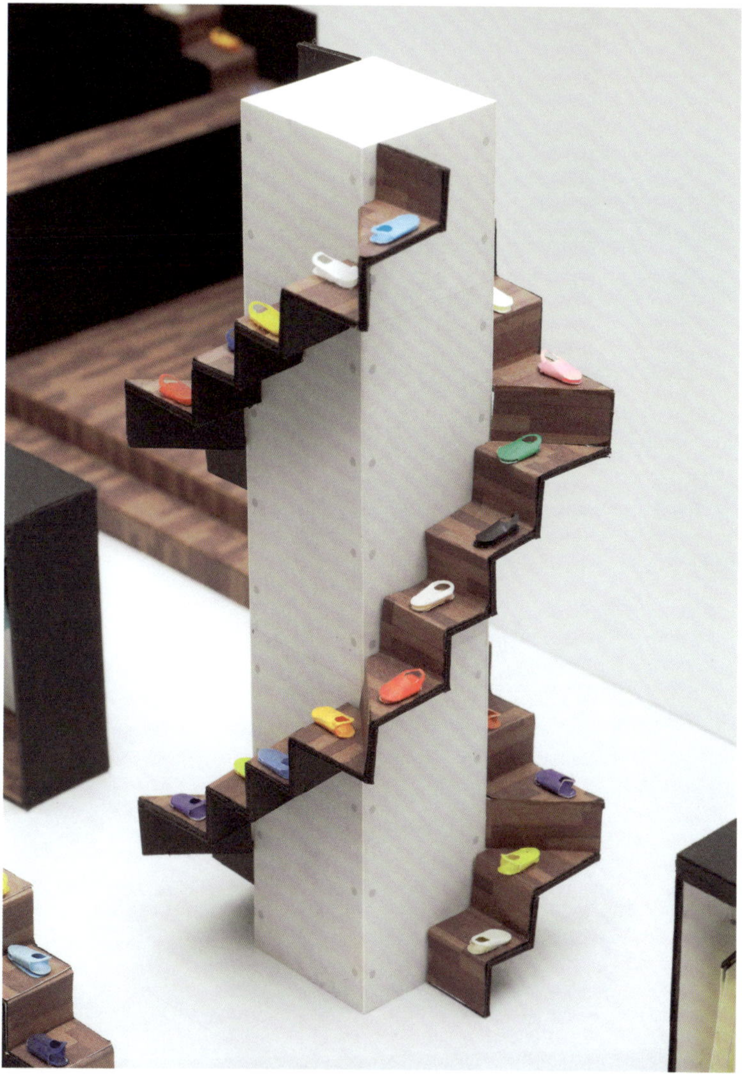

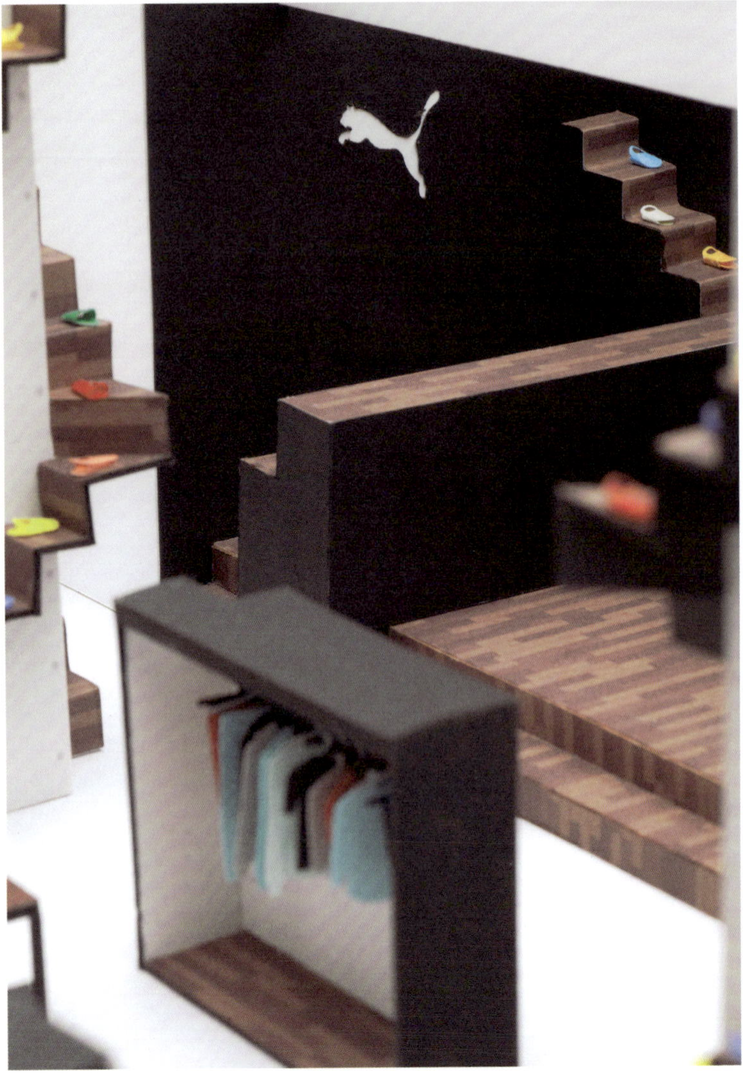

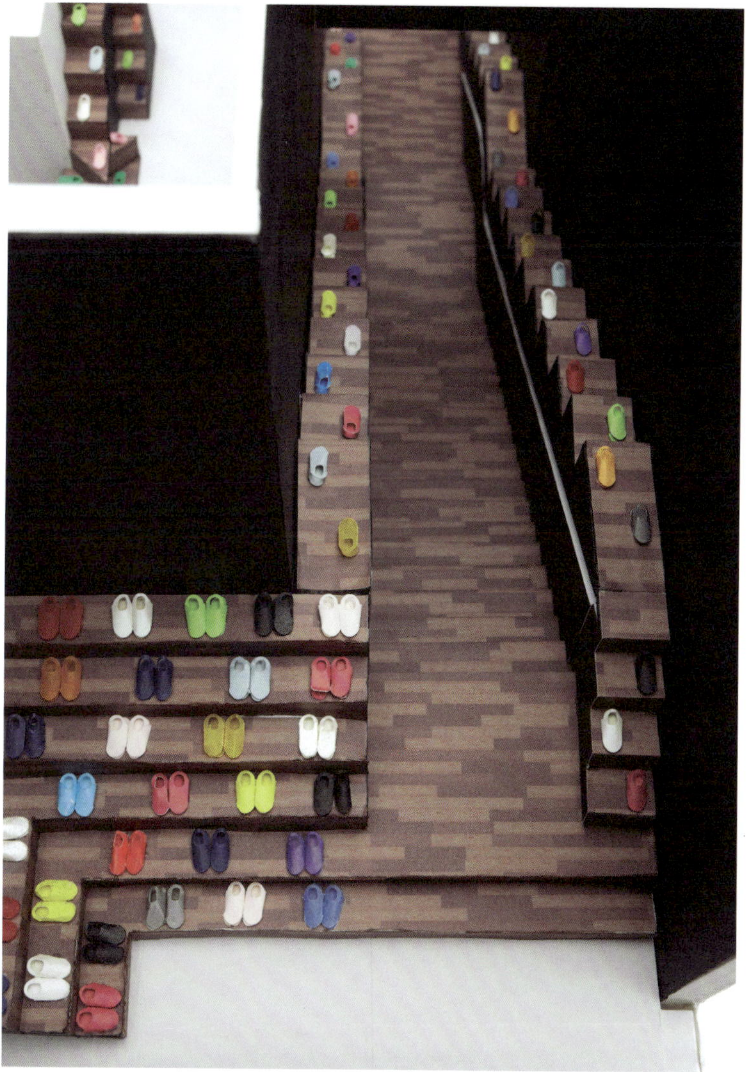

Rinascente Milan

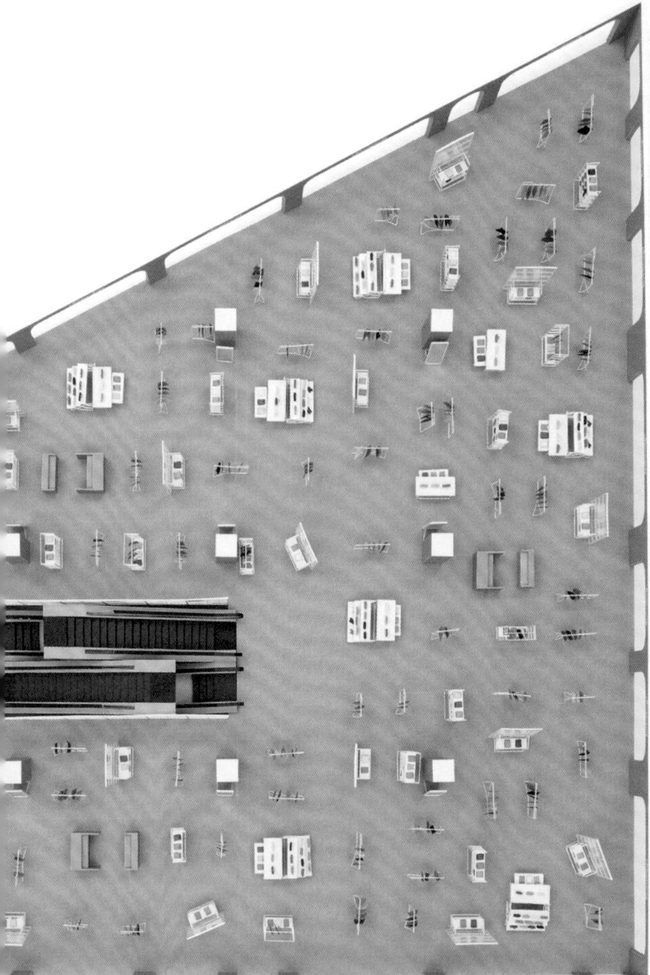

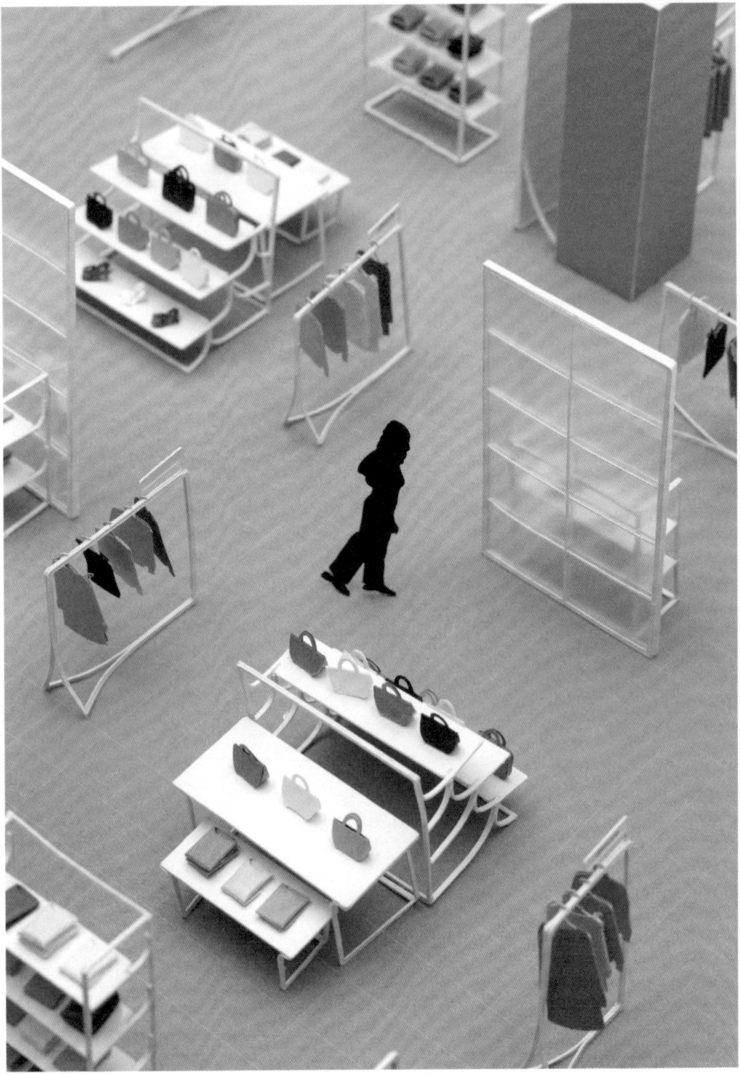

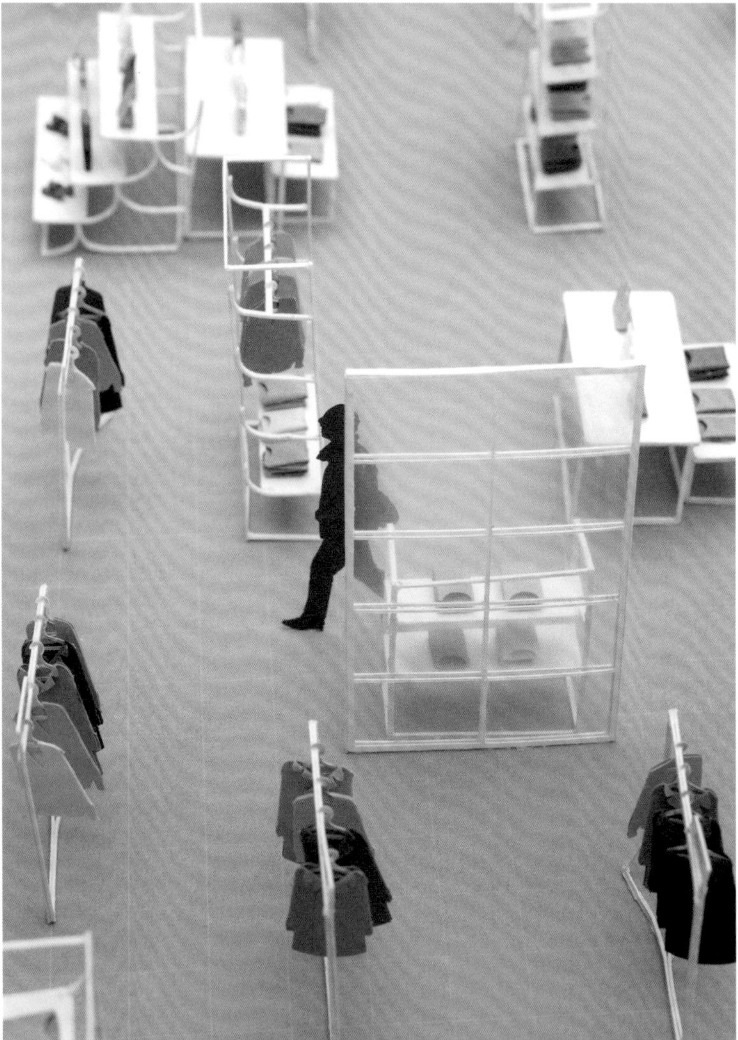

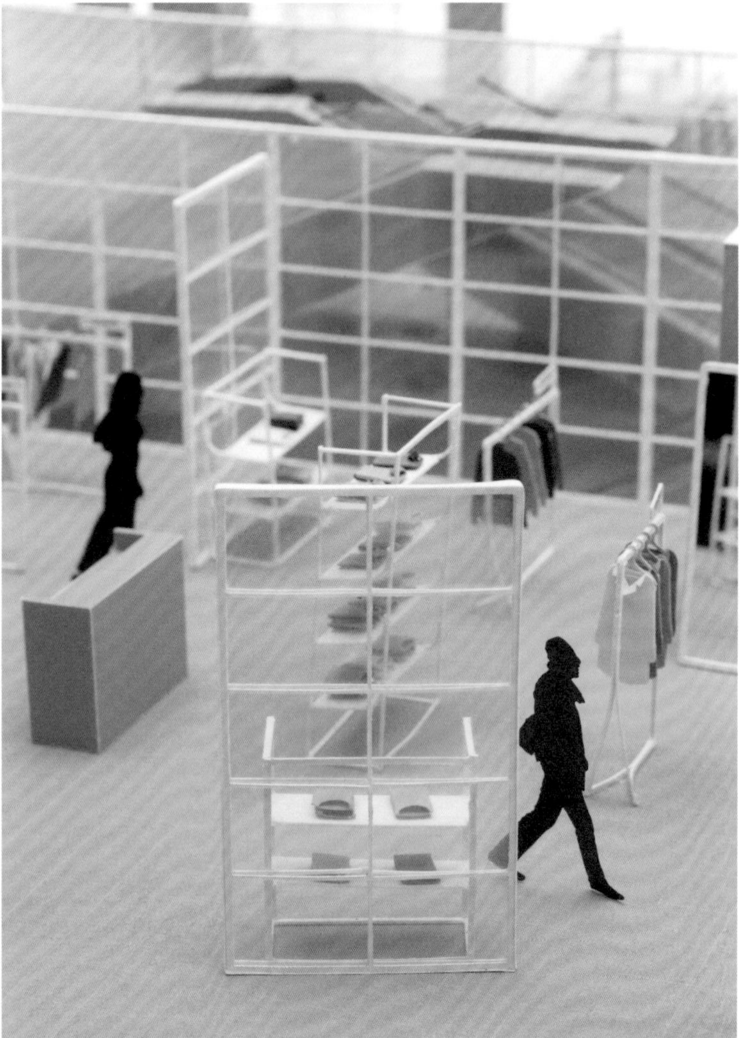

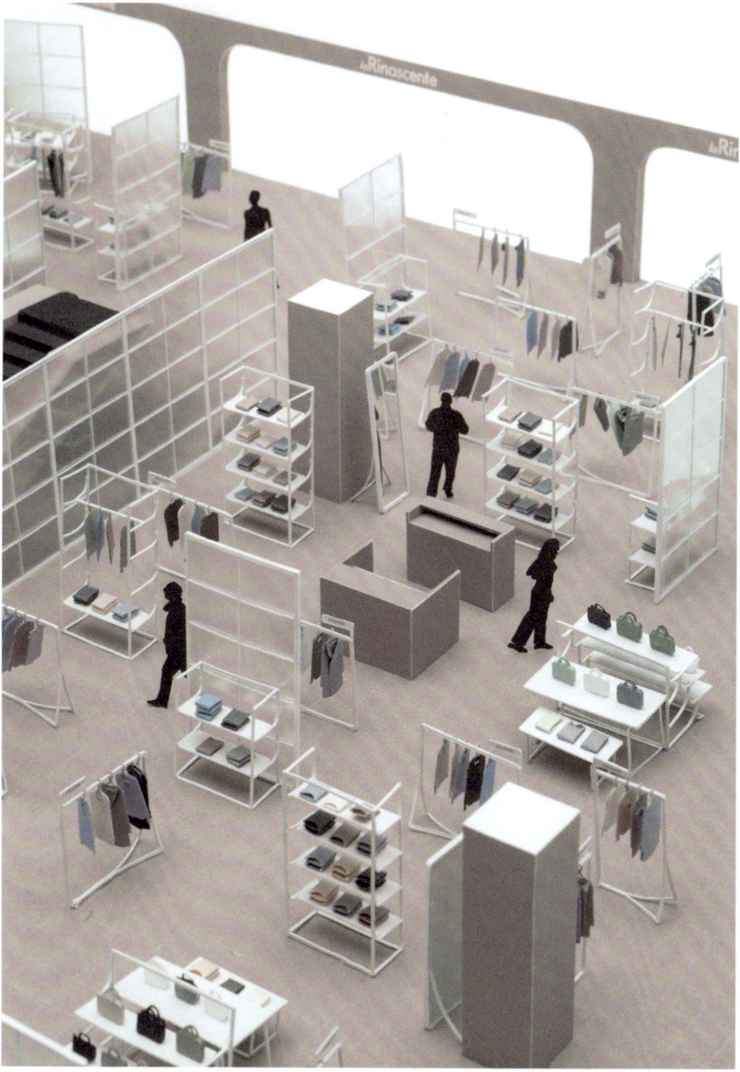
laRinascente

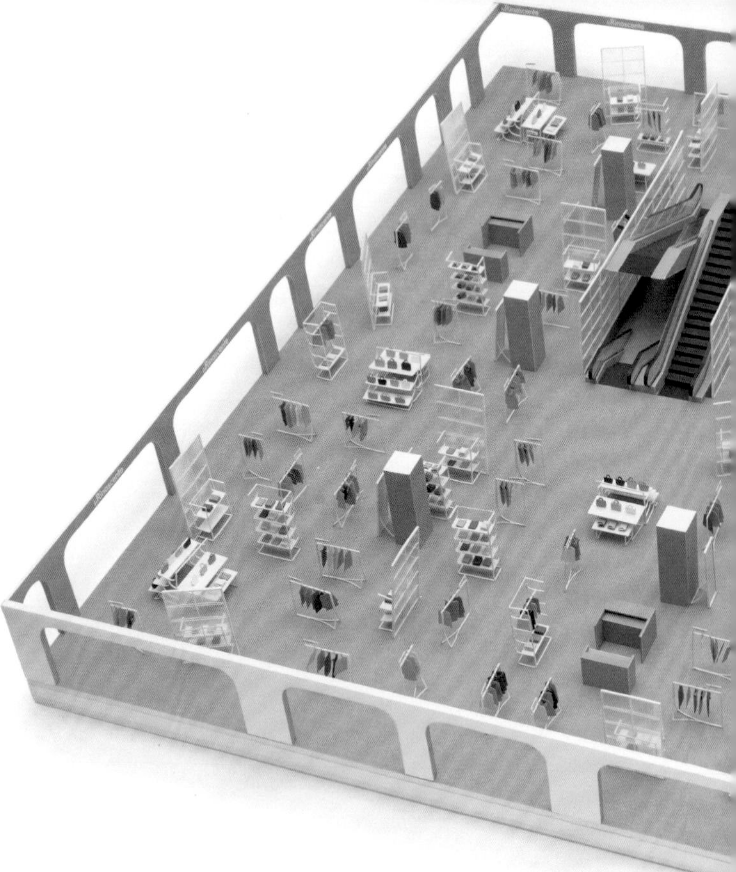

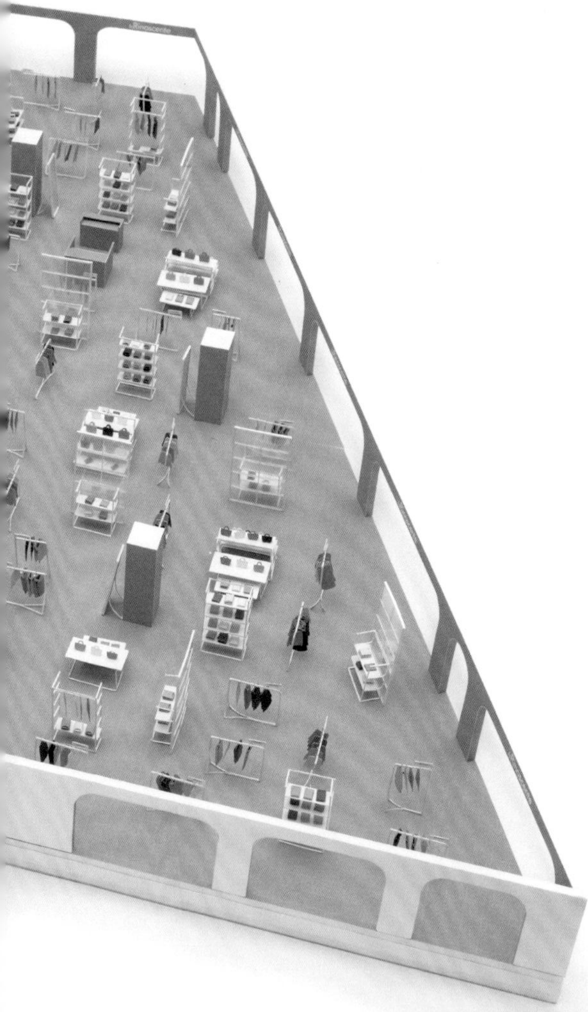
Rinascente

laRinascente
laRinascente
laRinascente
laRinascente
laRinascente
laRinascente

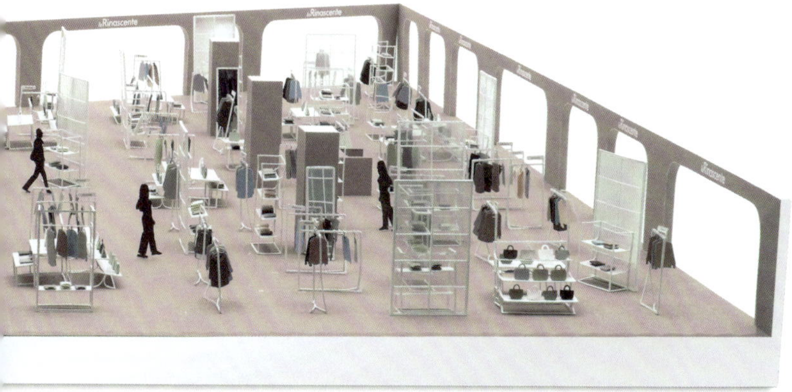
laRinascente
laRinascente

spicebox office

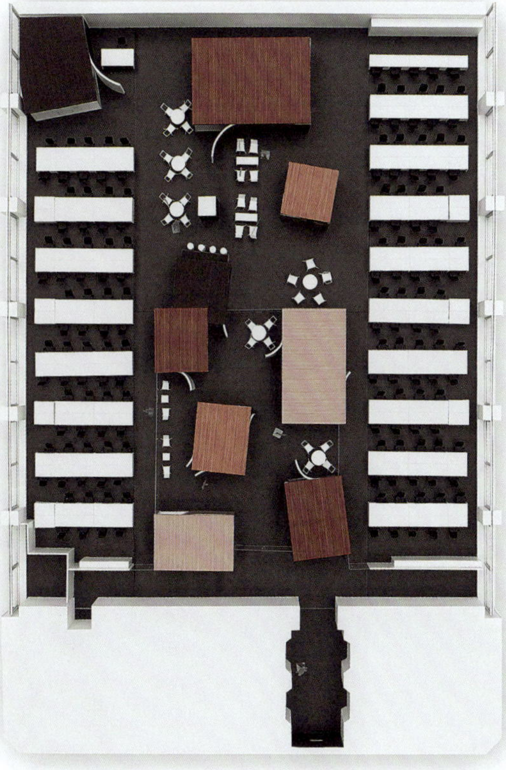

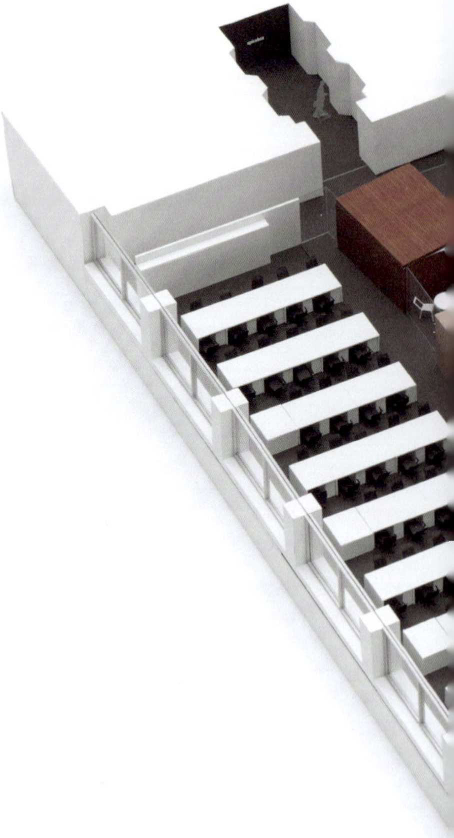

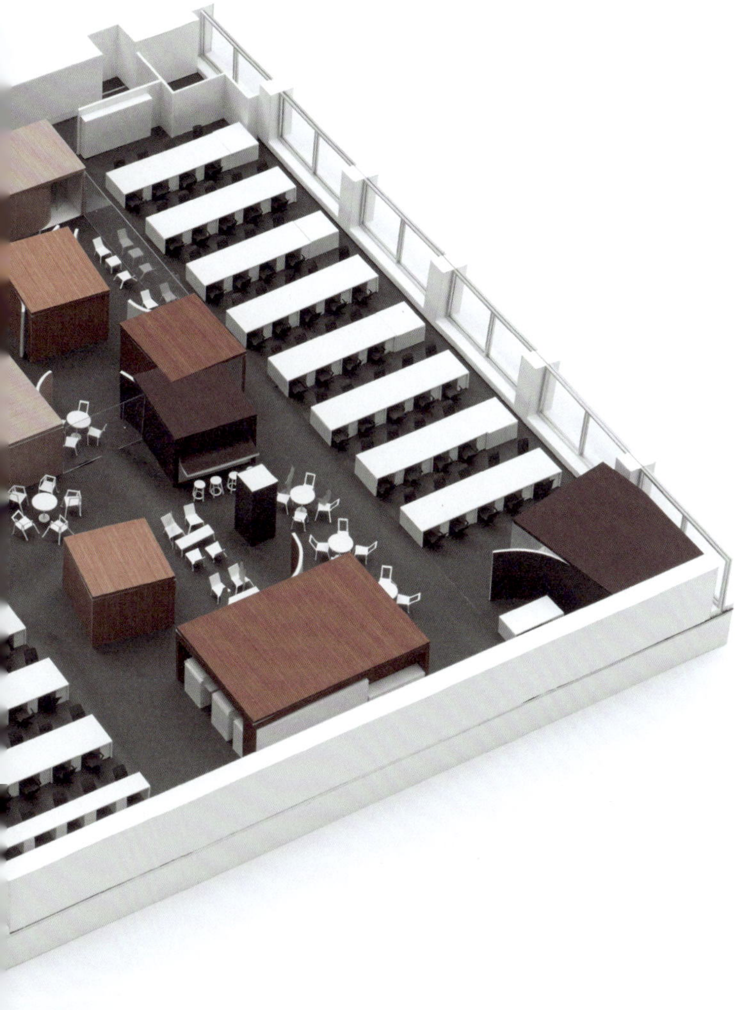

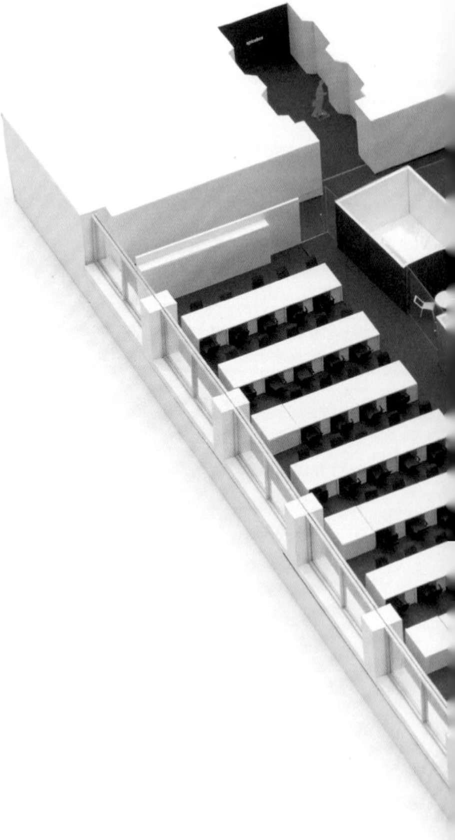

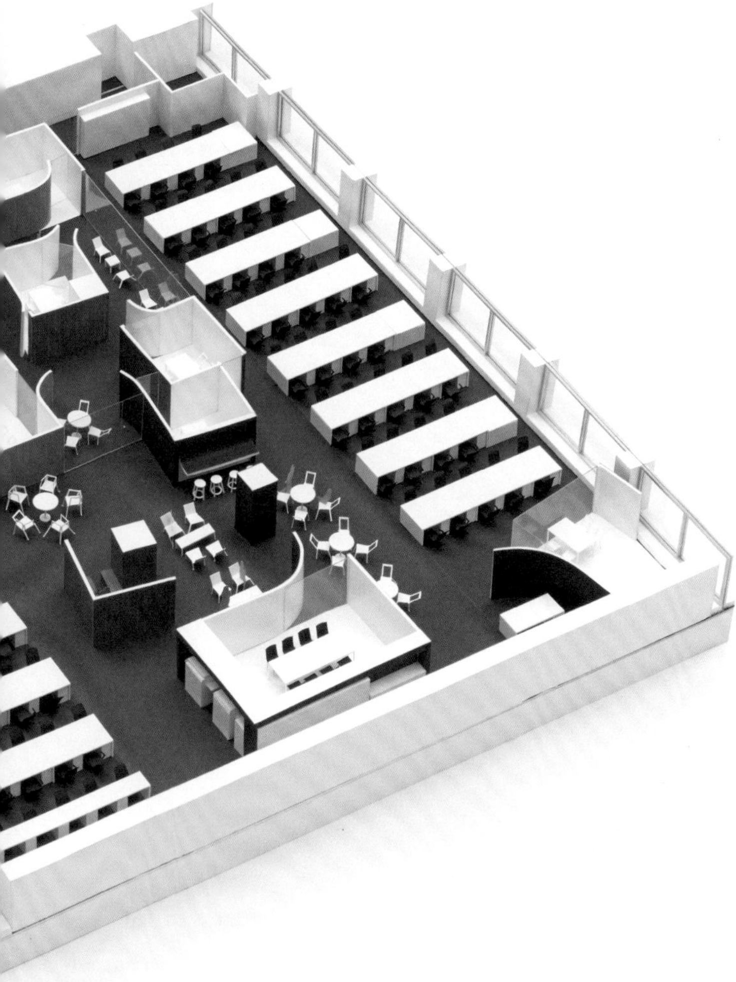

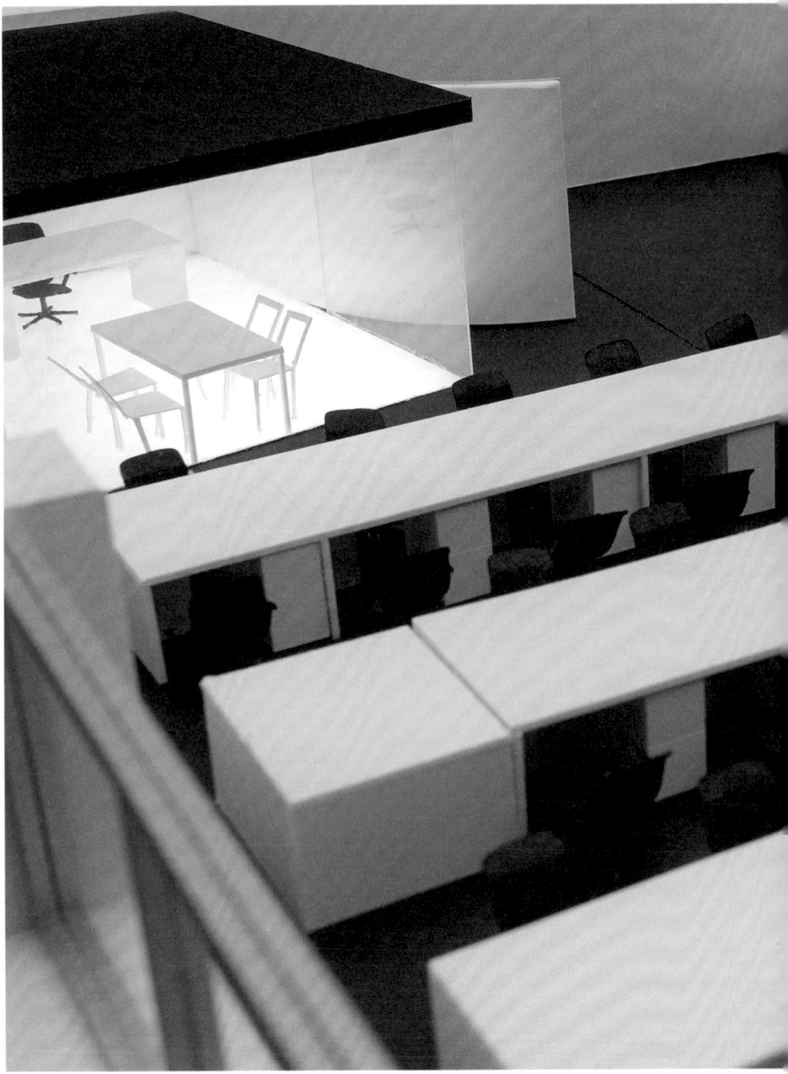

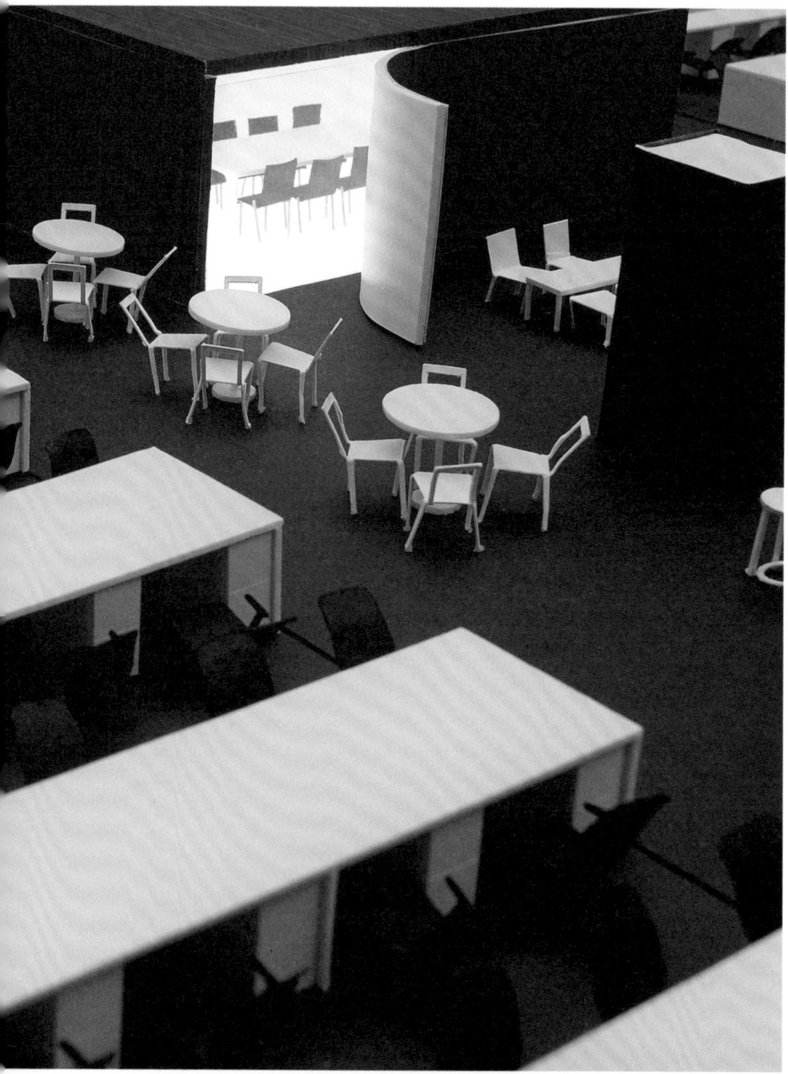

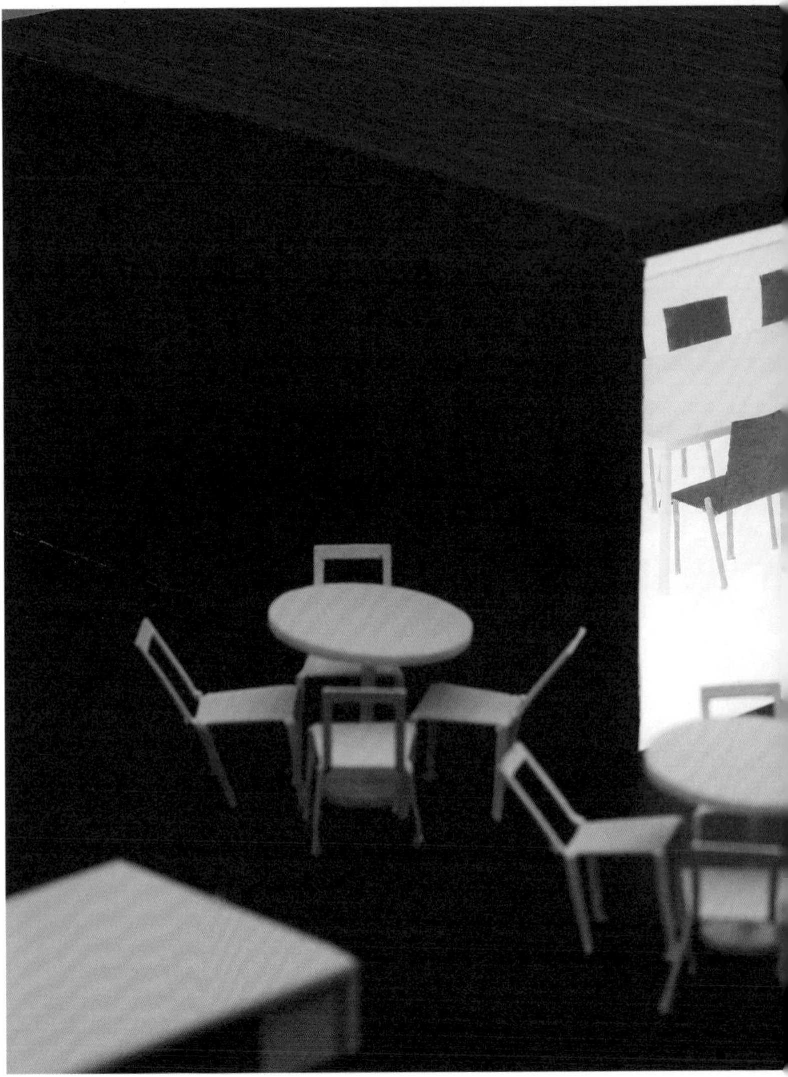

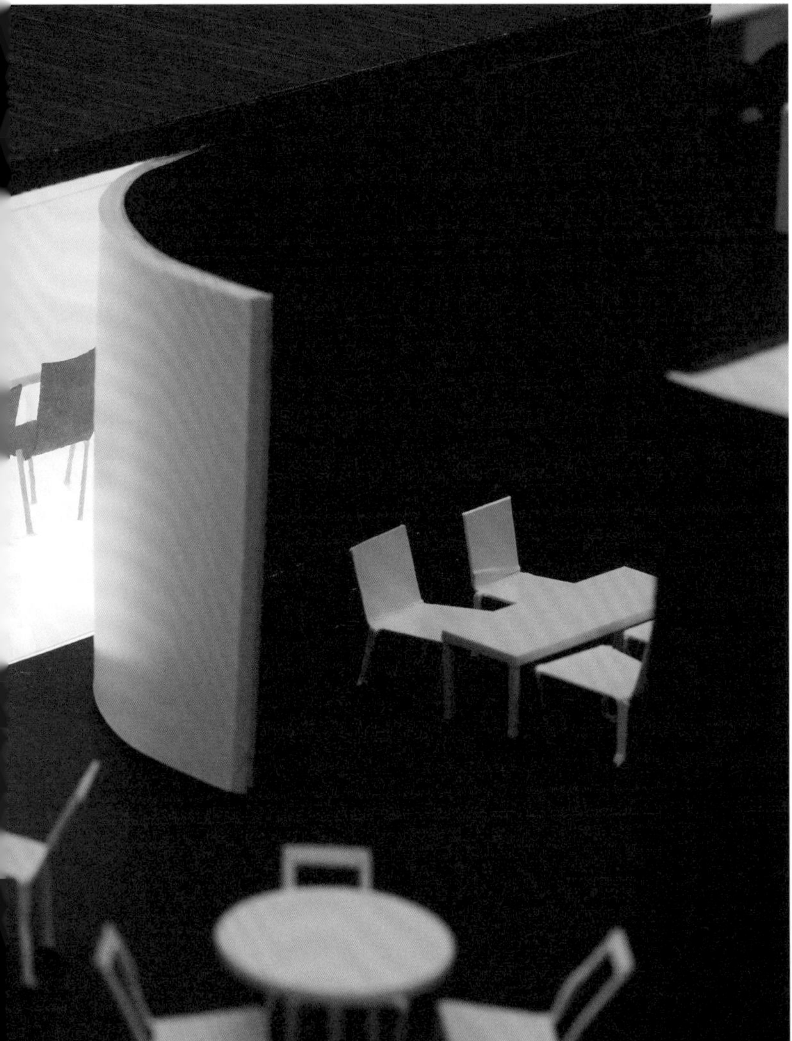

Starbucks Espresso Journey

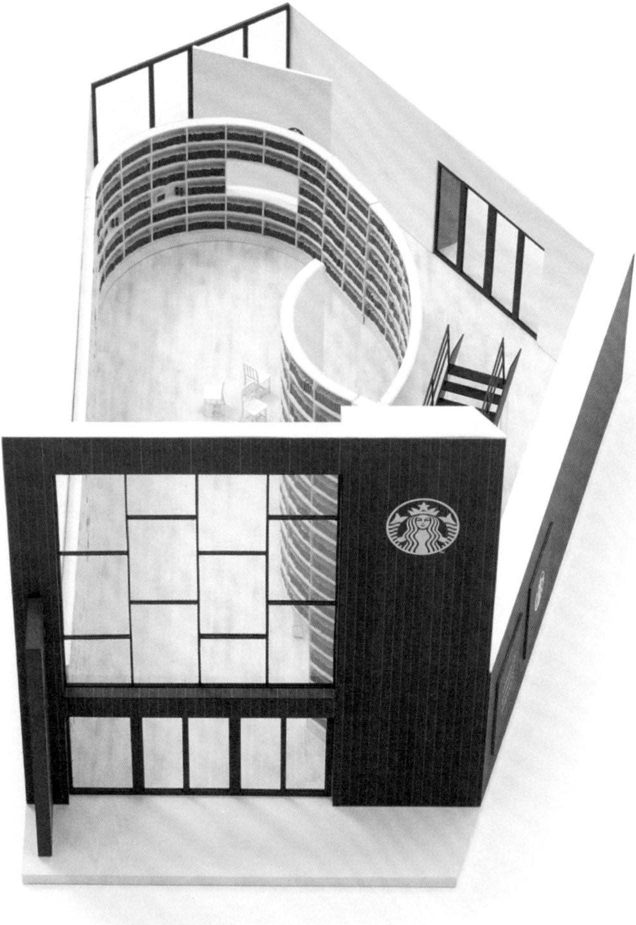

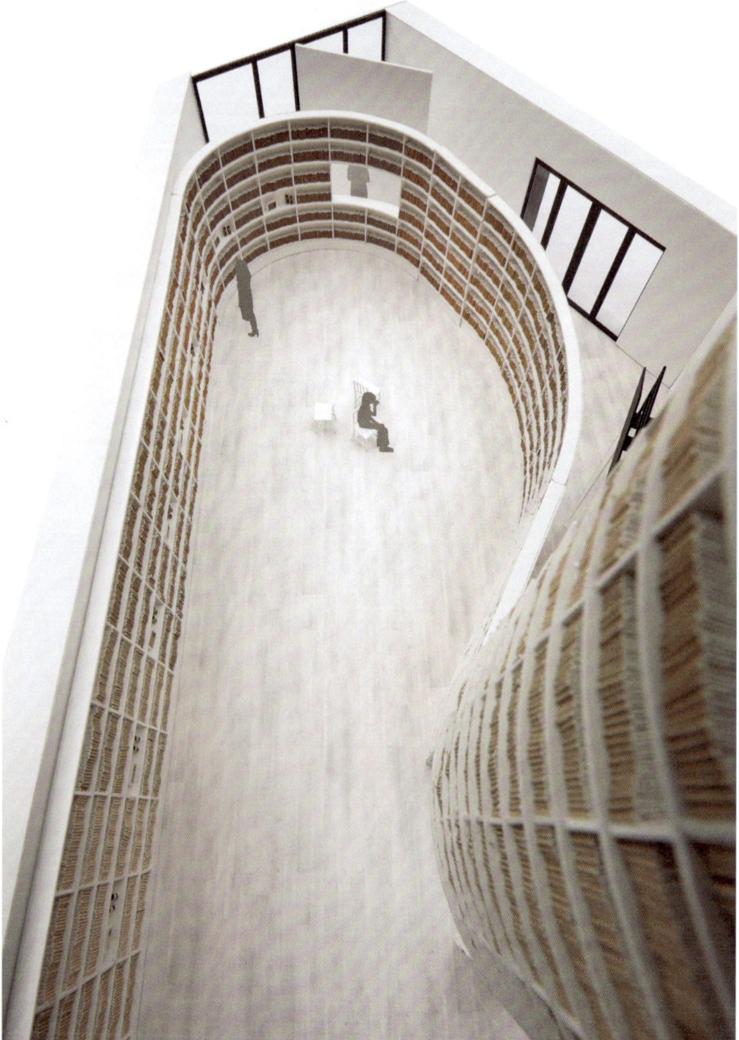

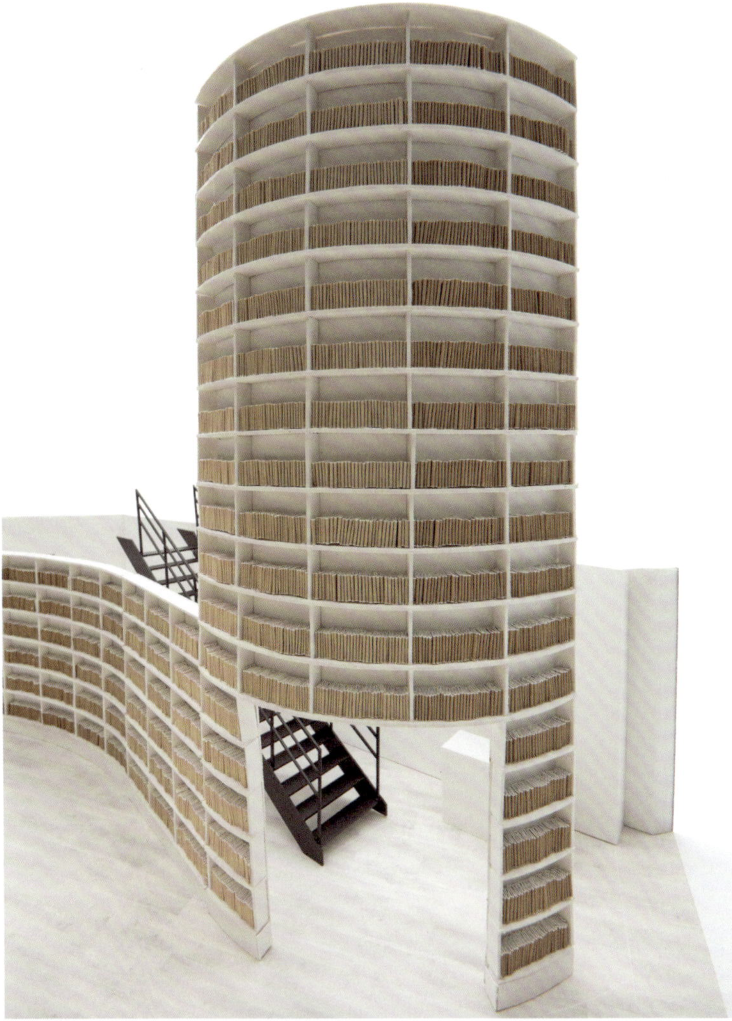

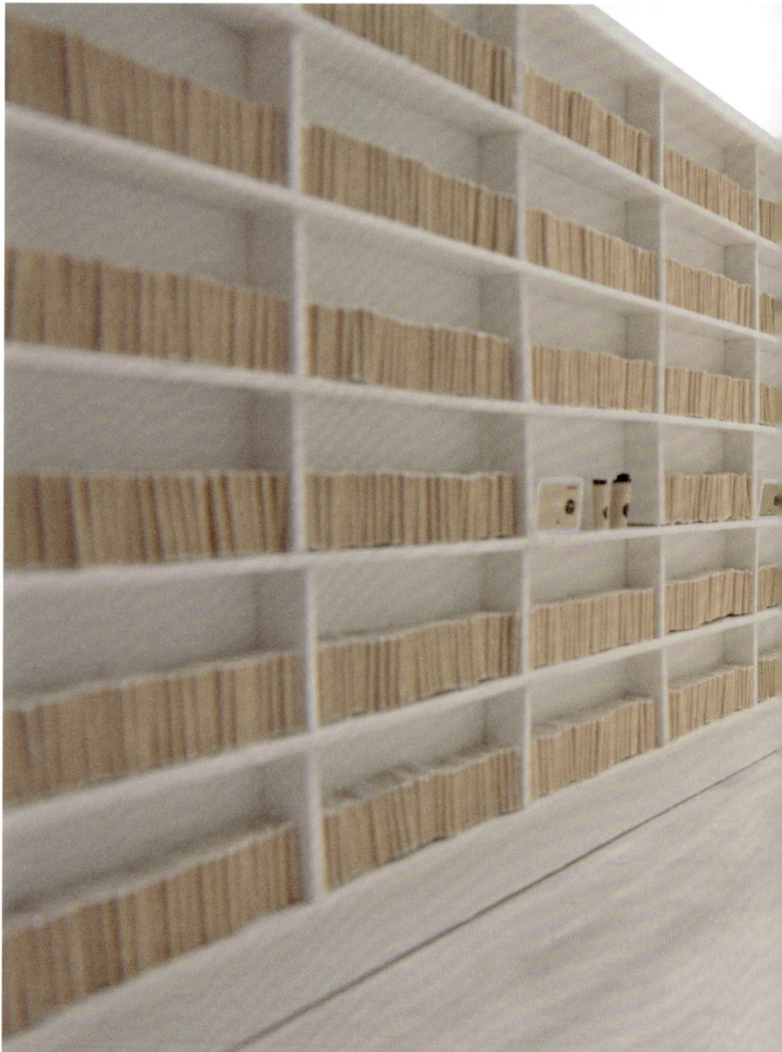

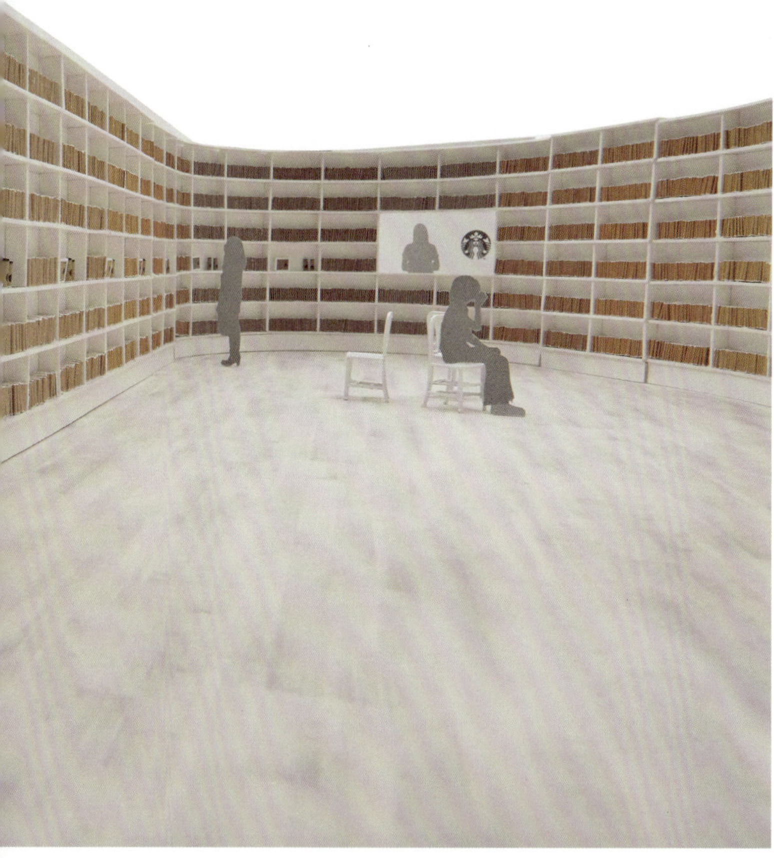

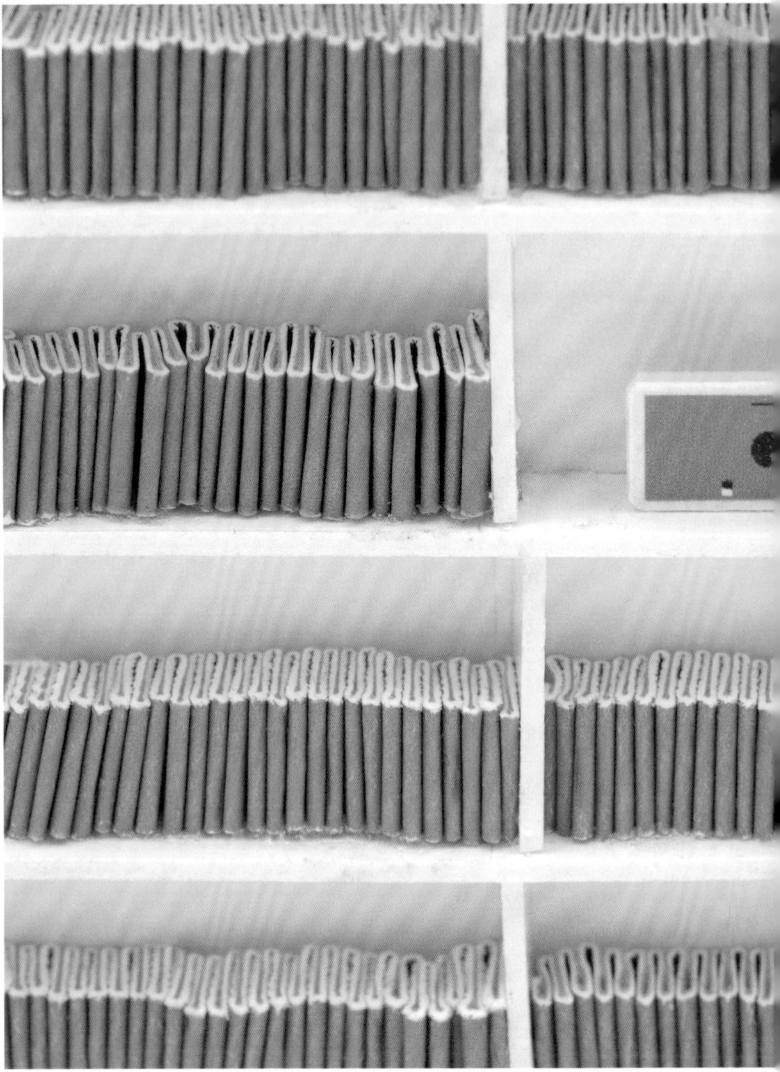

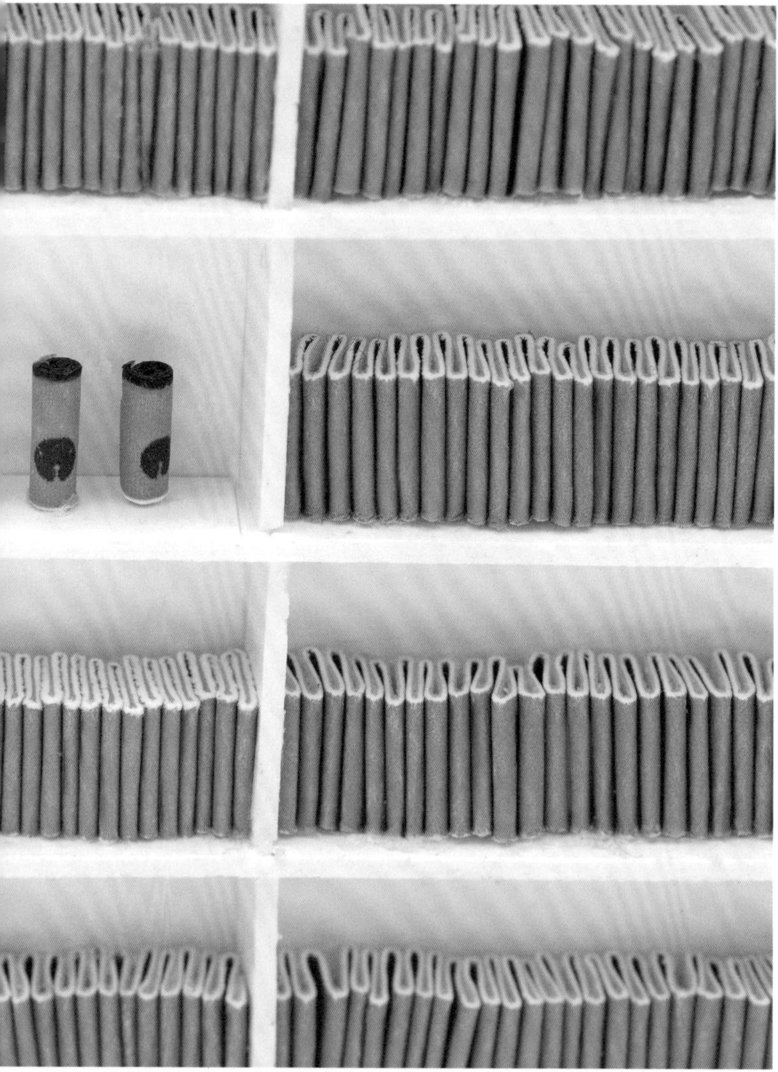

STARBUCKS ESPRESSO JOURNEY

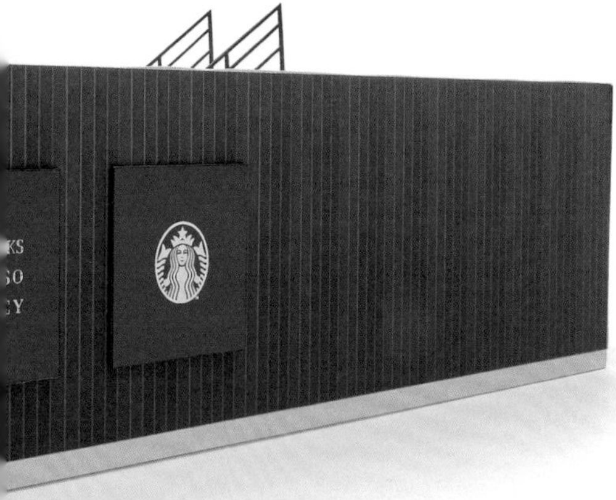

Theory

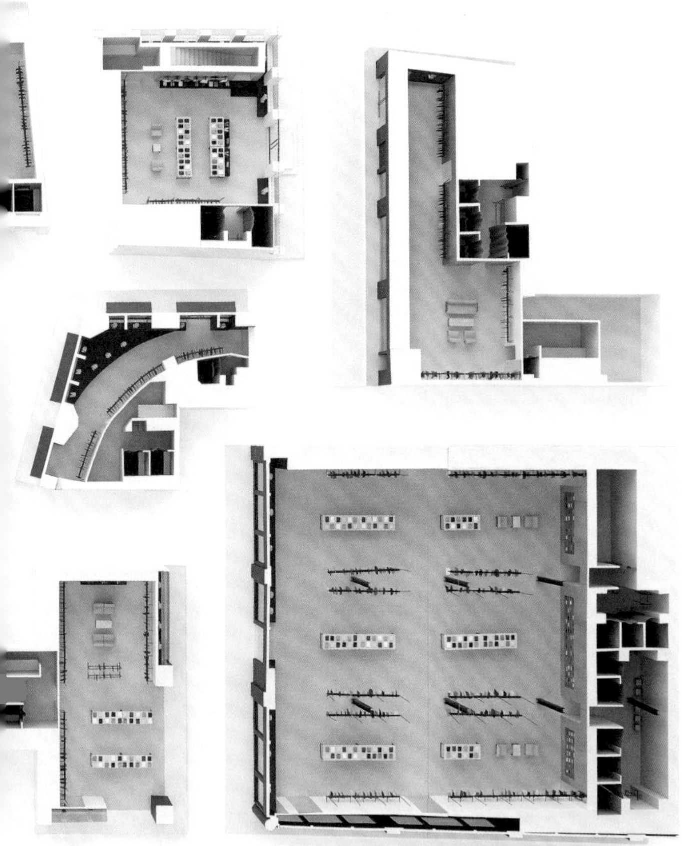

Theory Aoyama

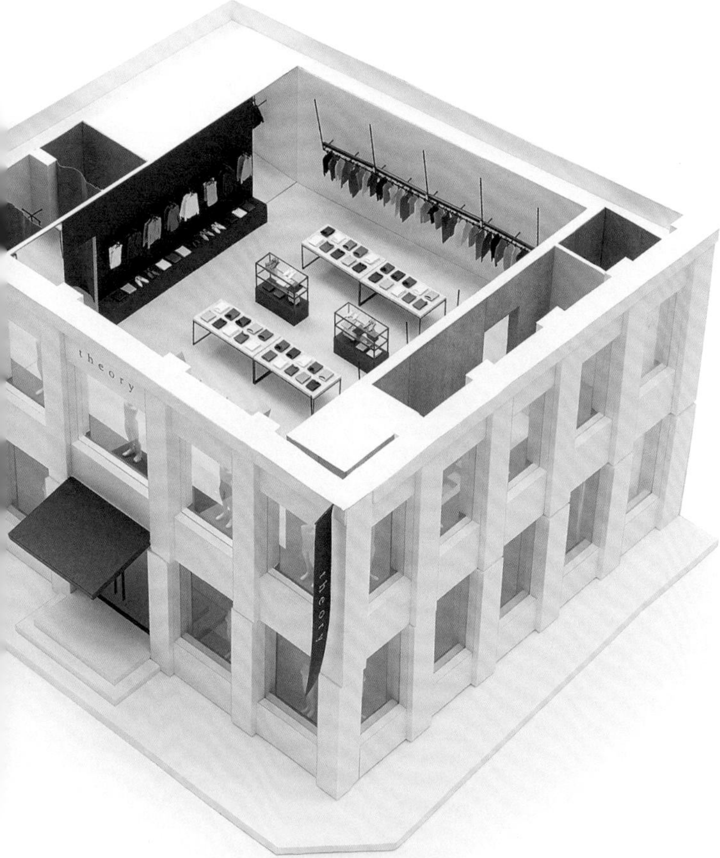
theory
theory

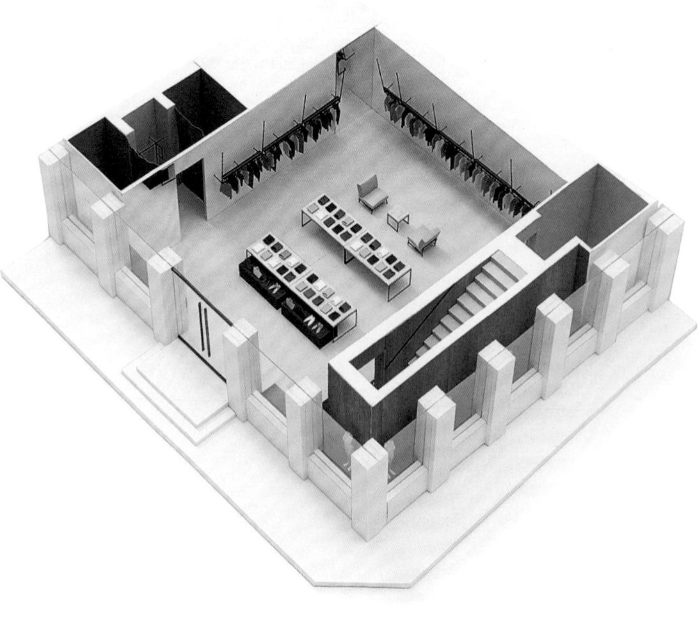

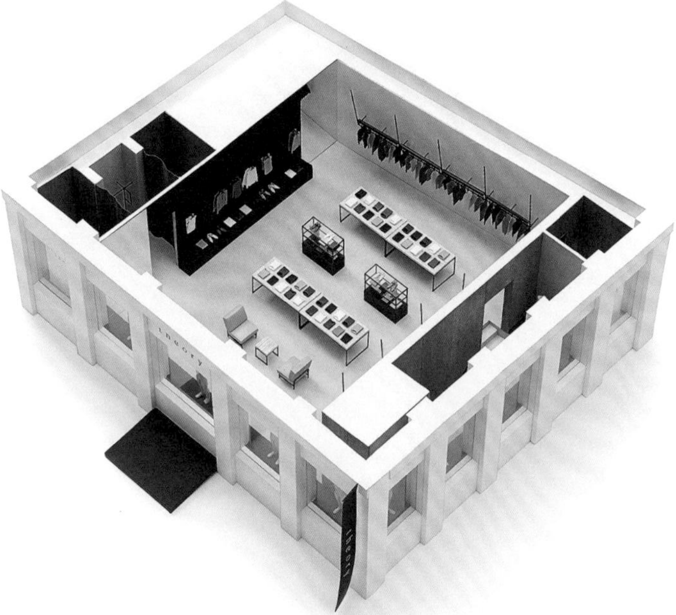

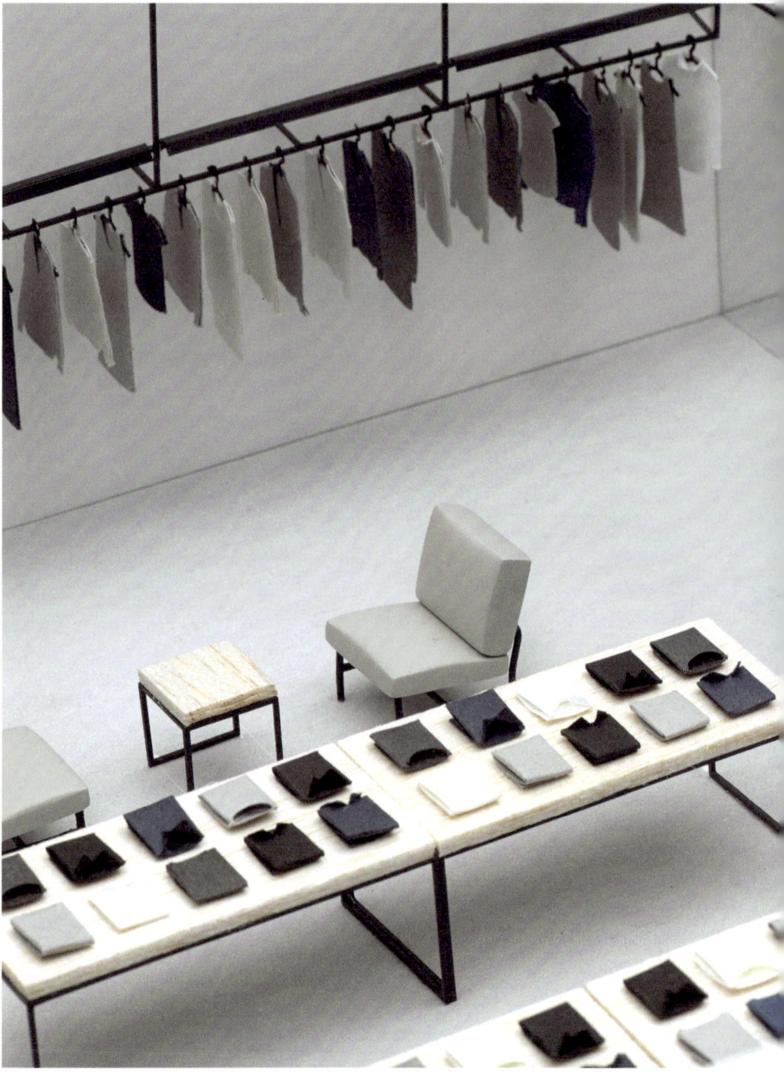

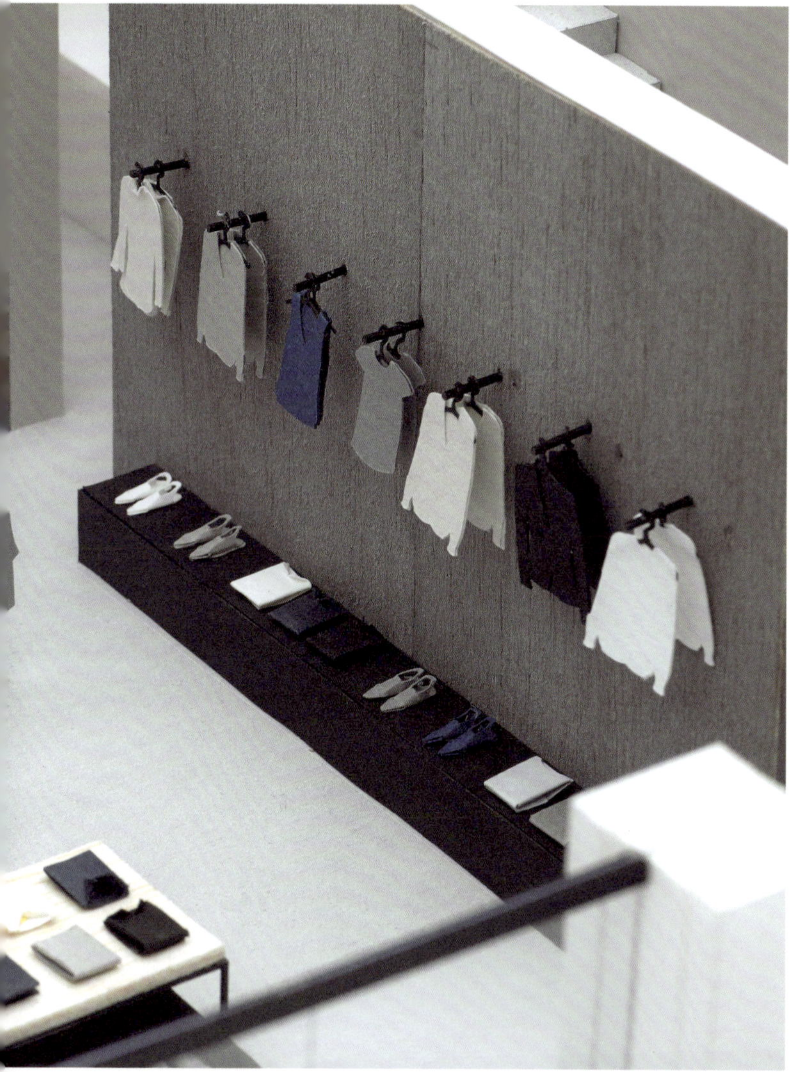

Theory Jiyugaoka

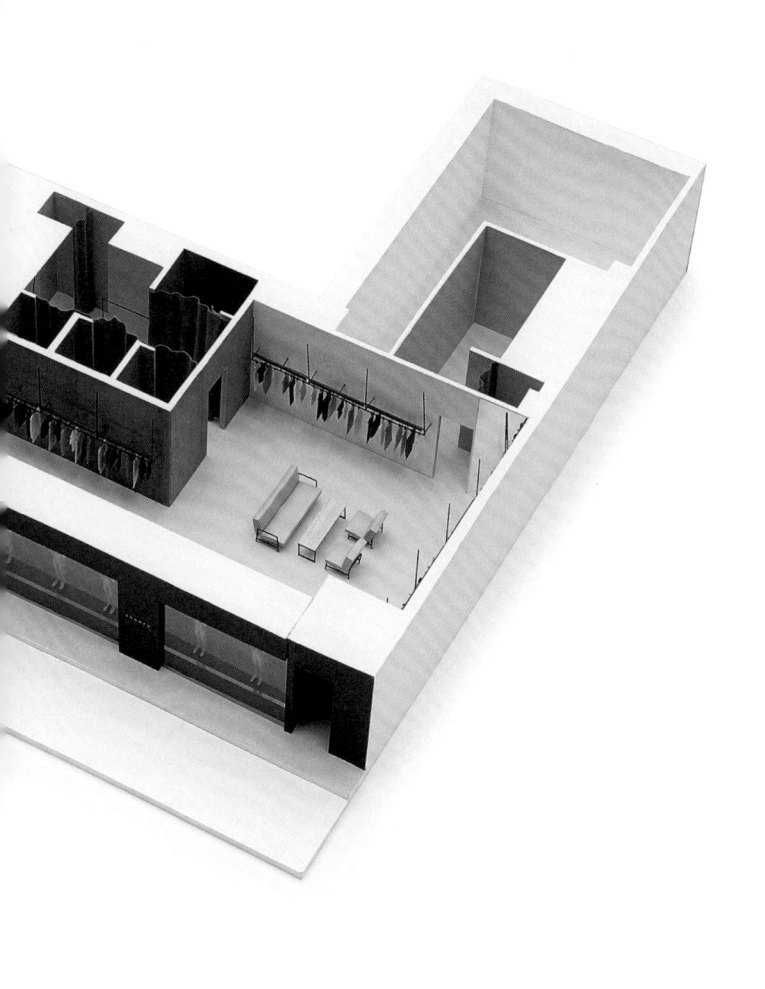

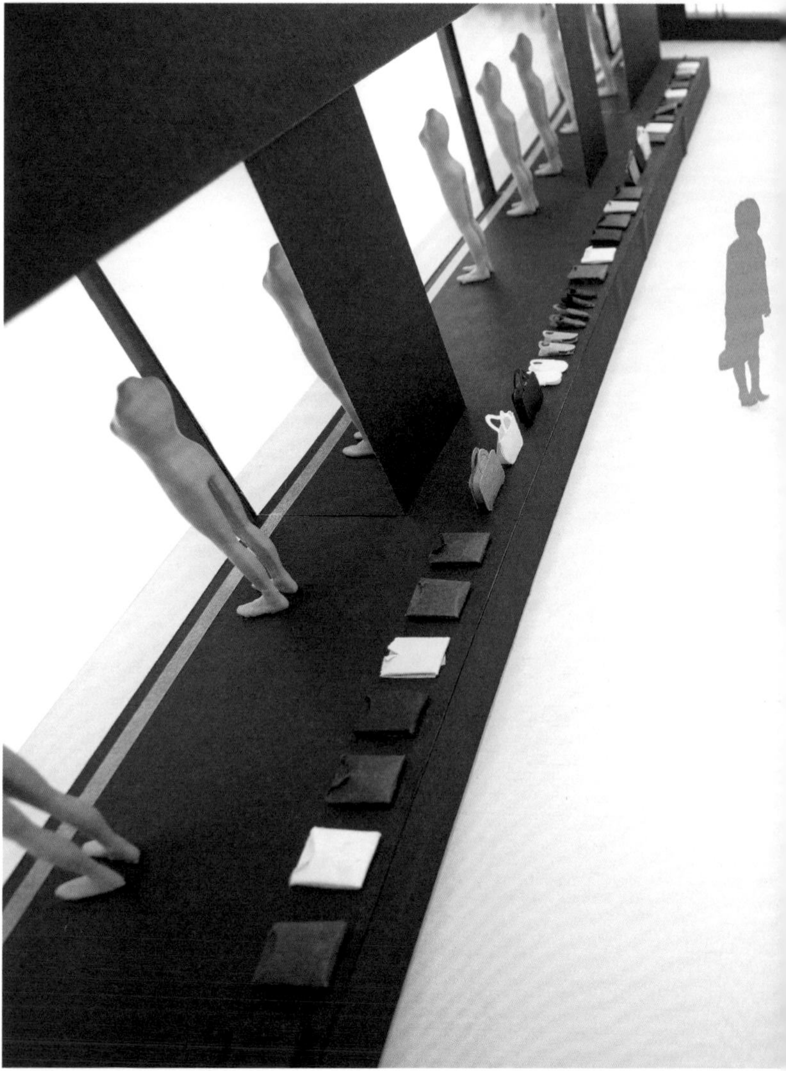

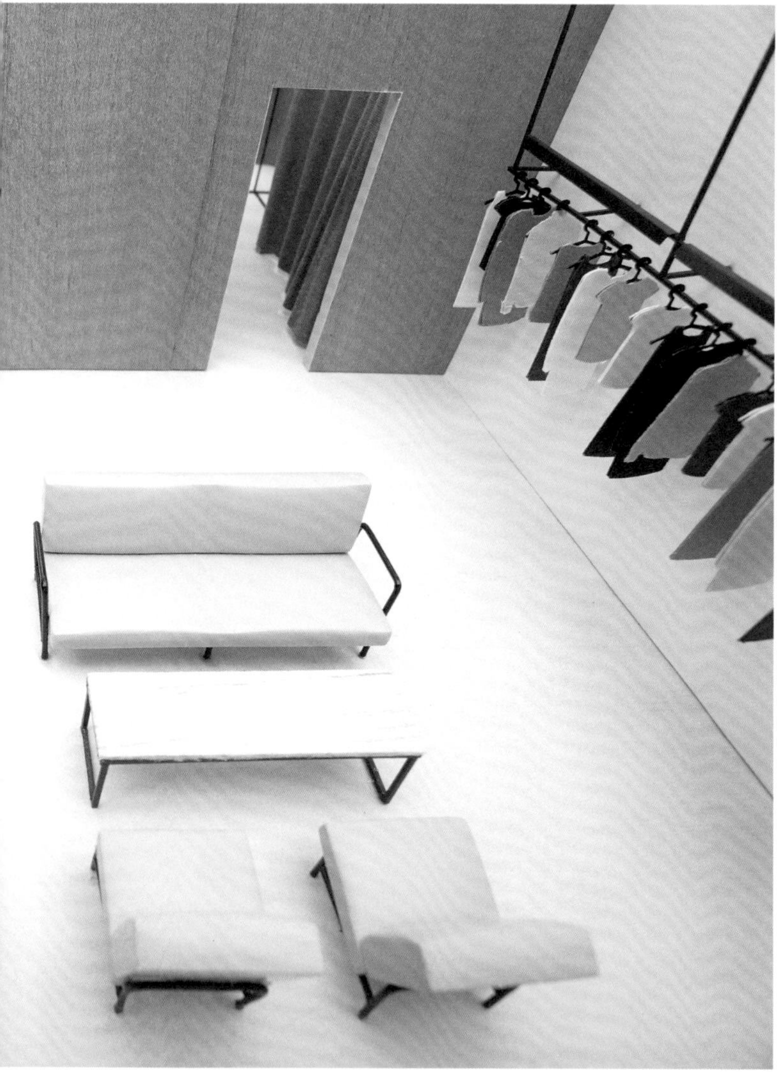

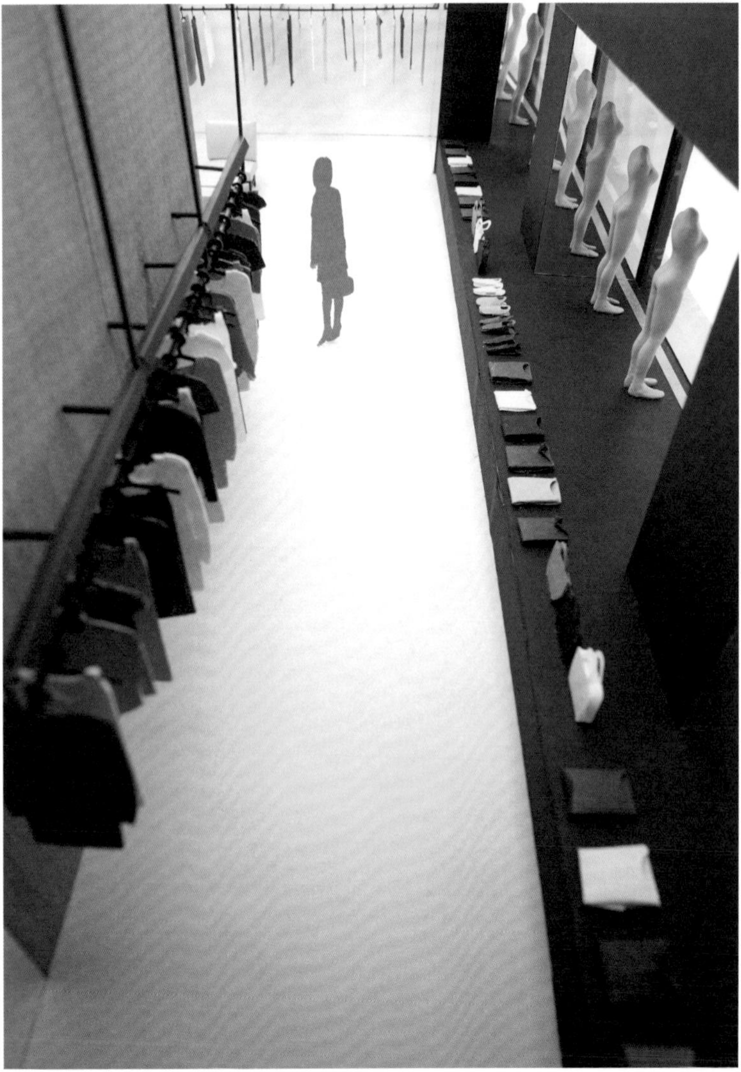

theory

Theory London

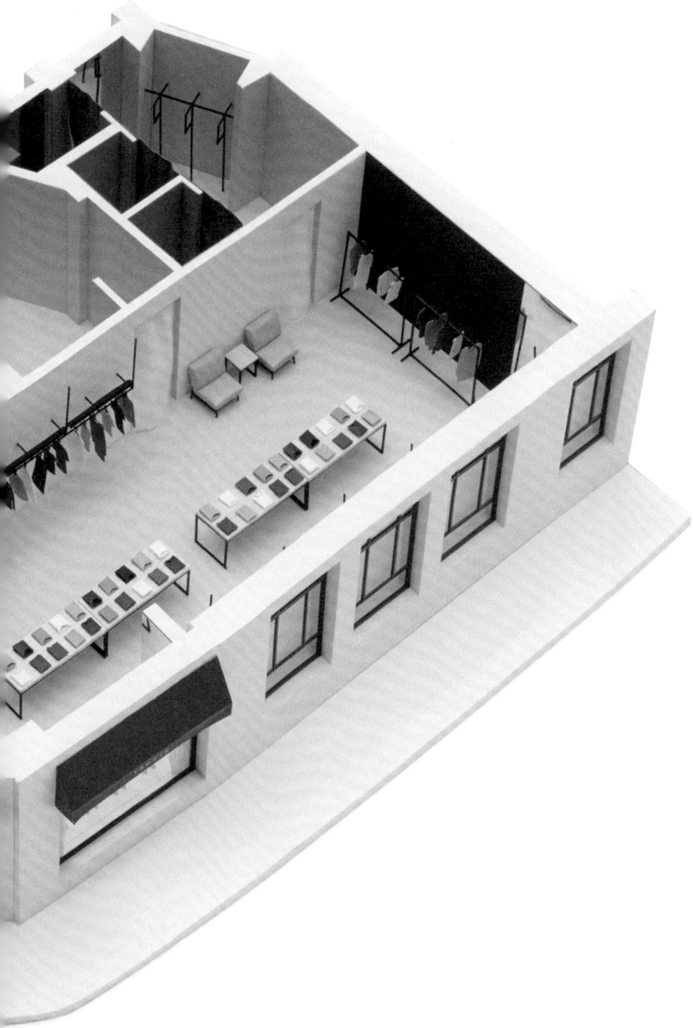

theory

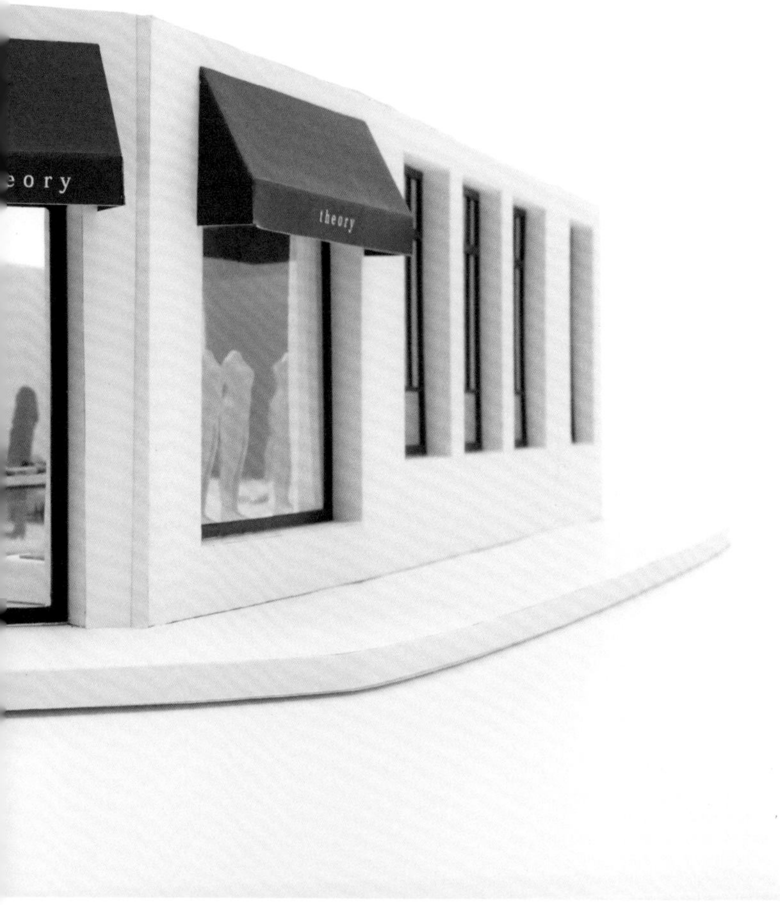
eory
theory

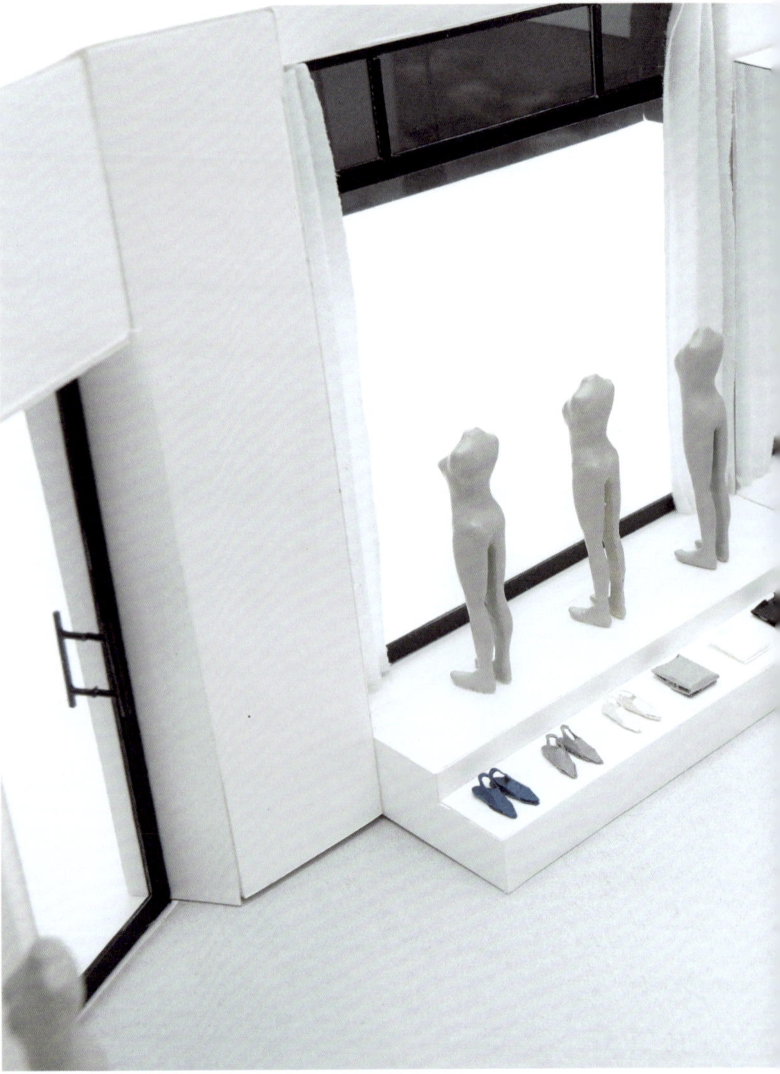

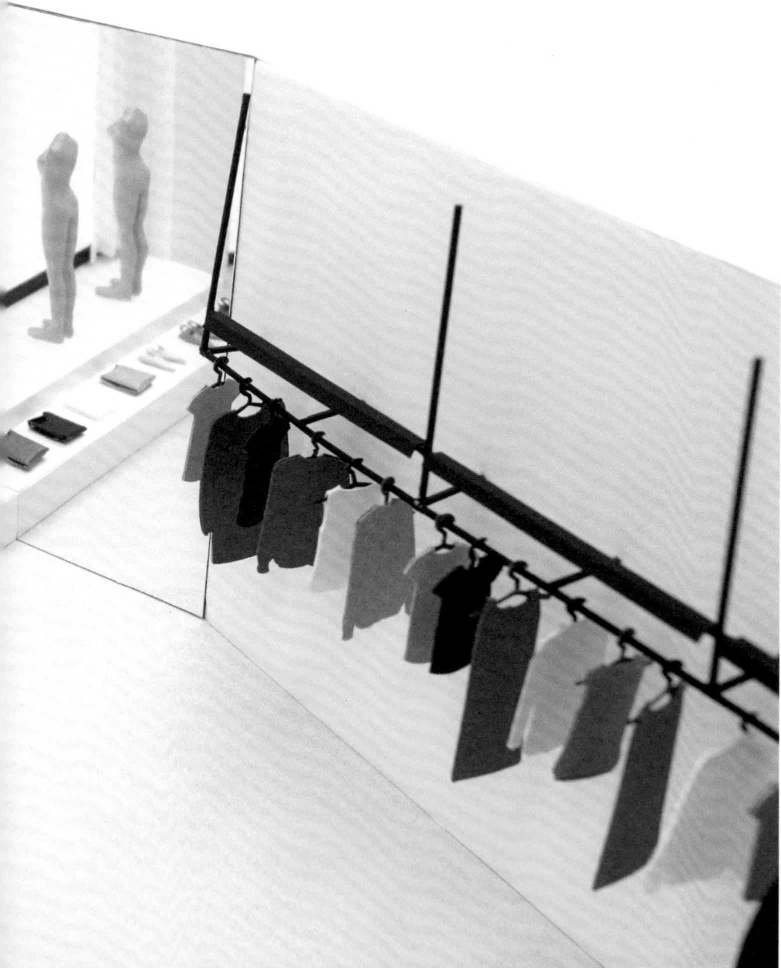

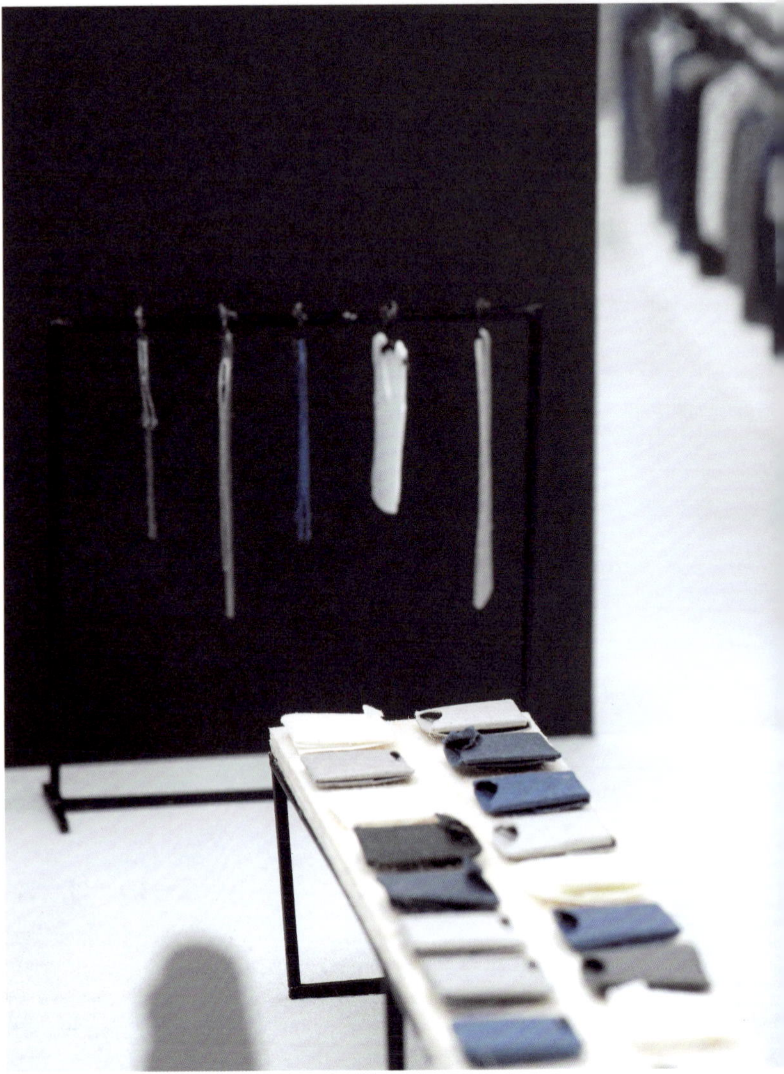

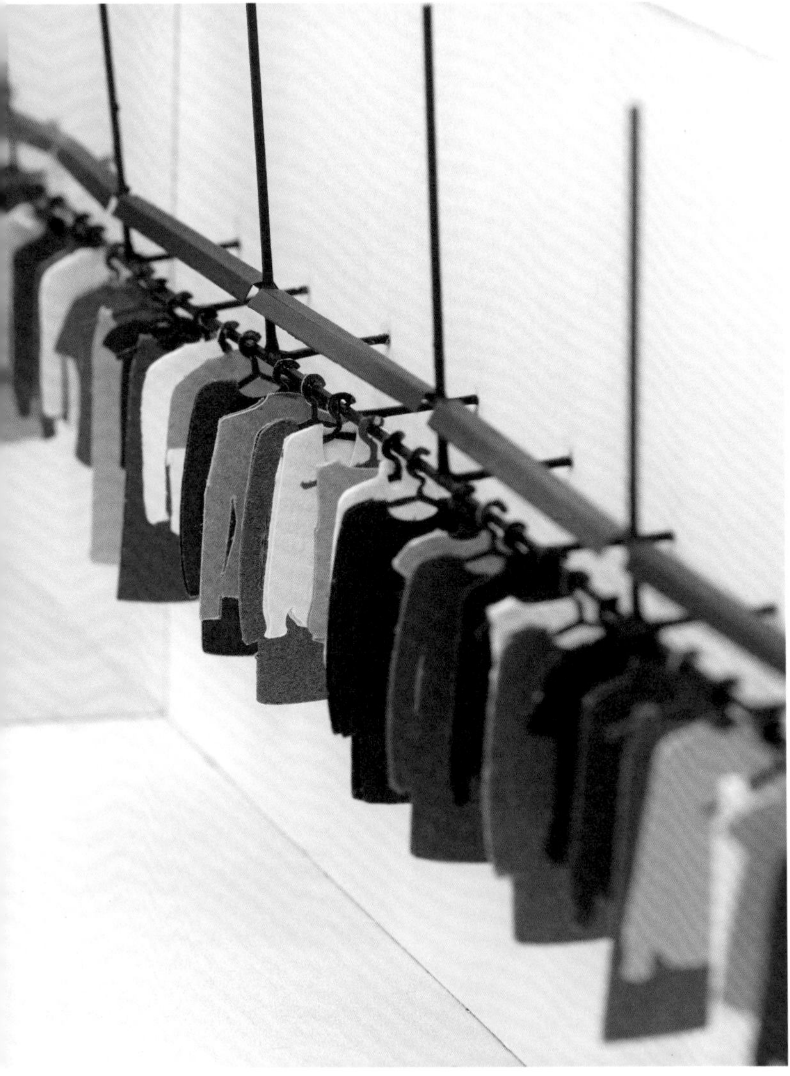

Theory Melrose

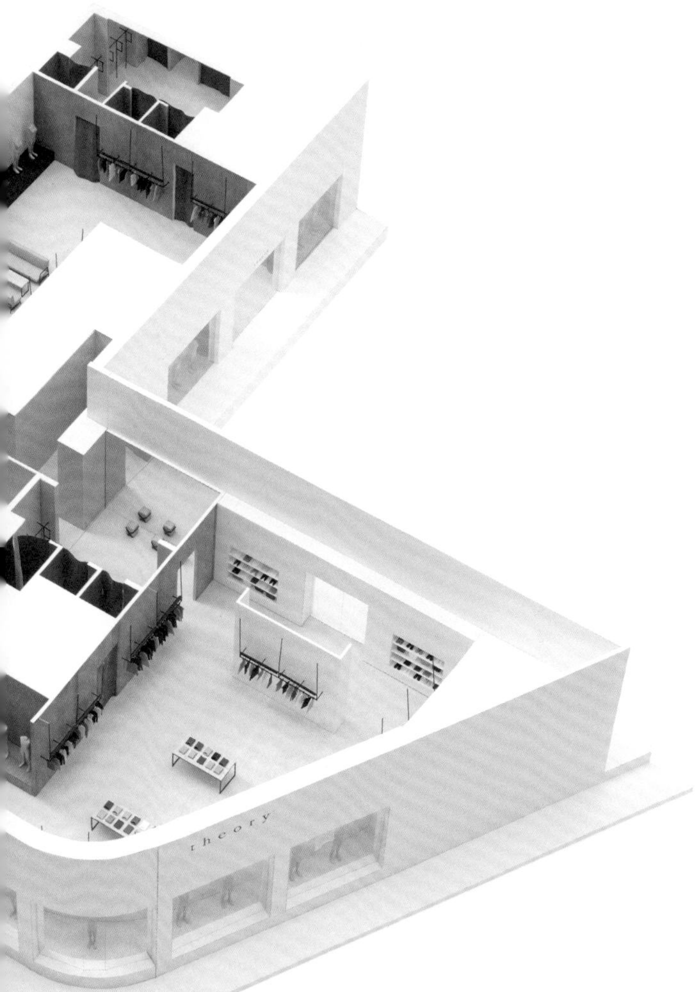
theory

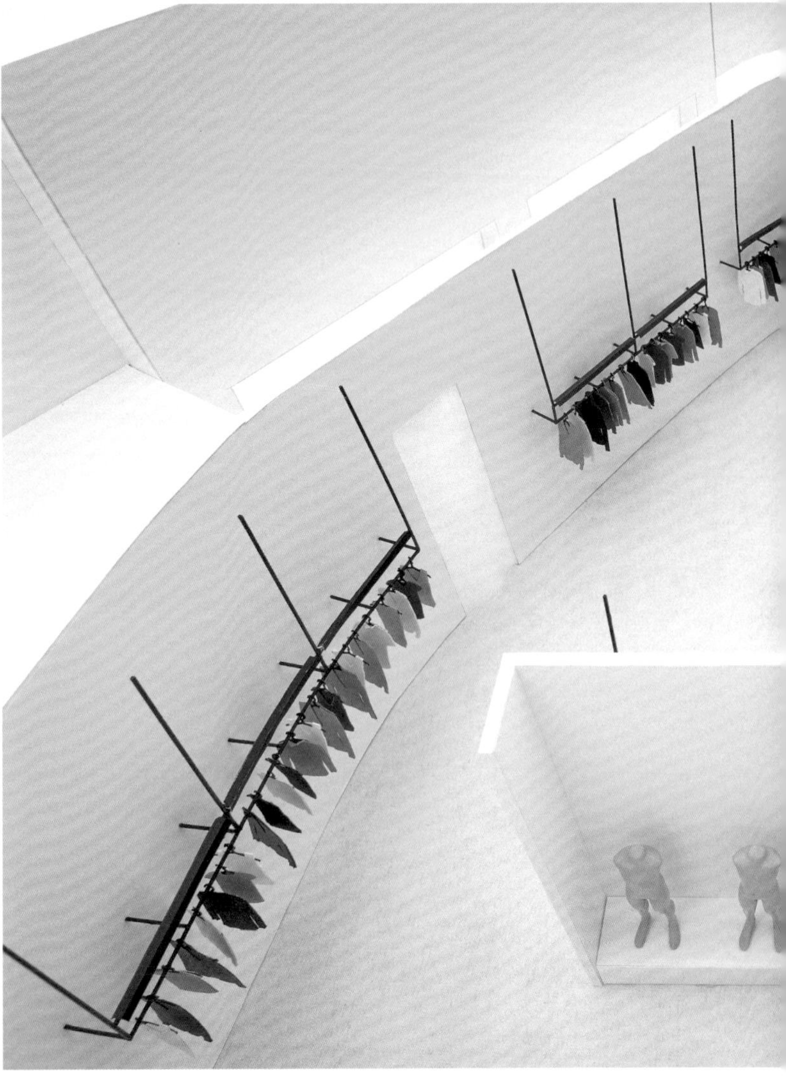

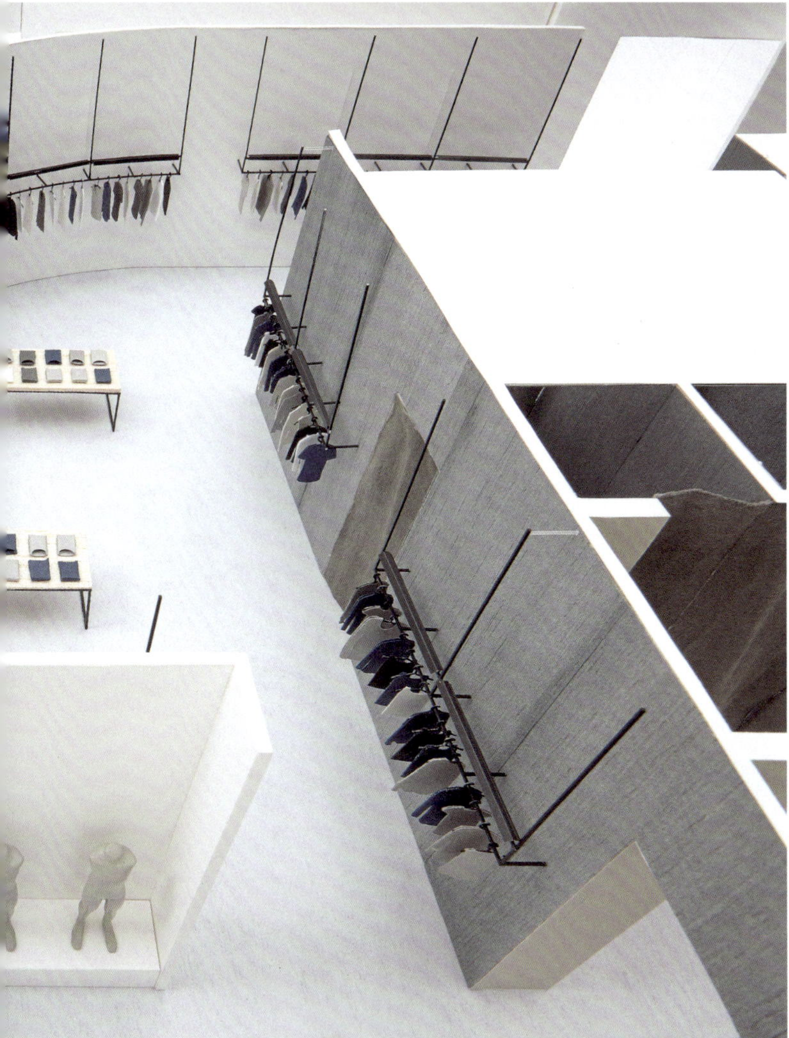

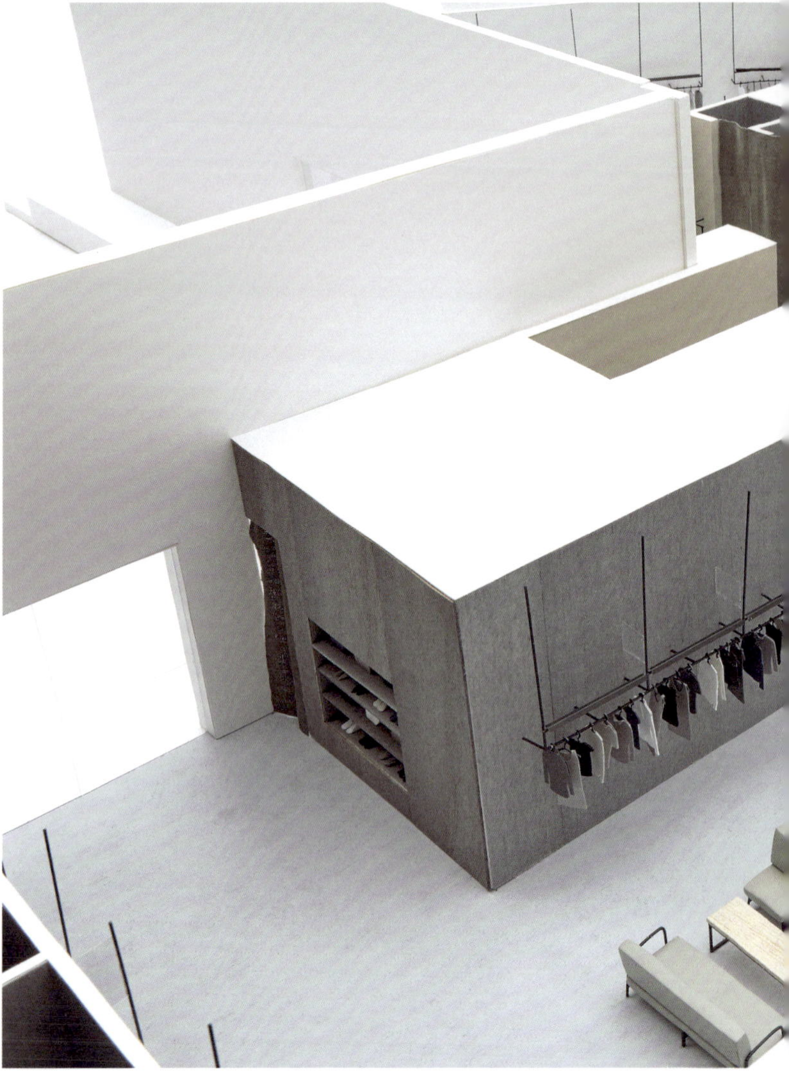

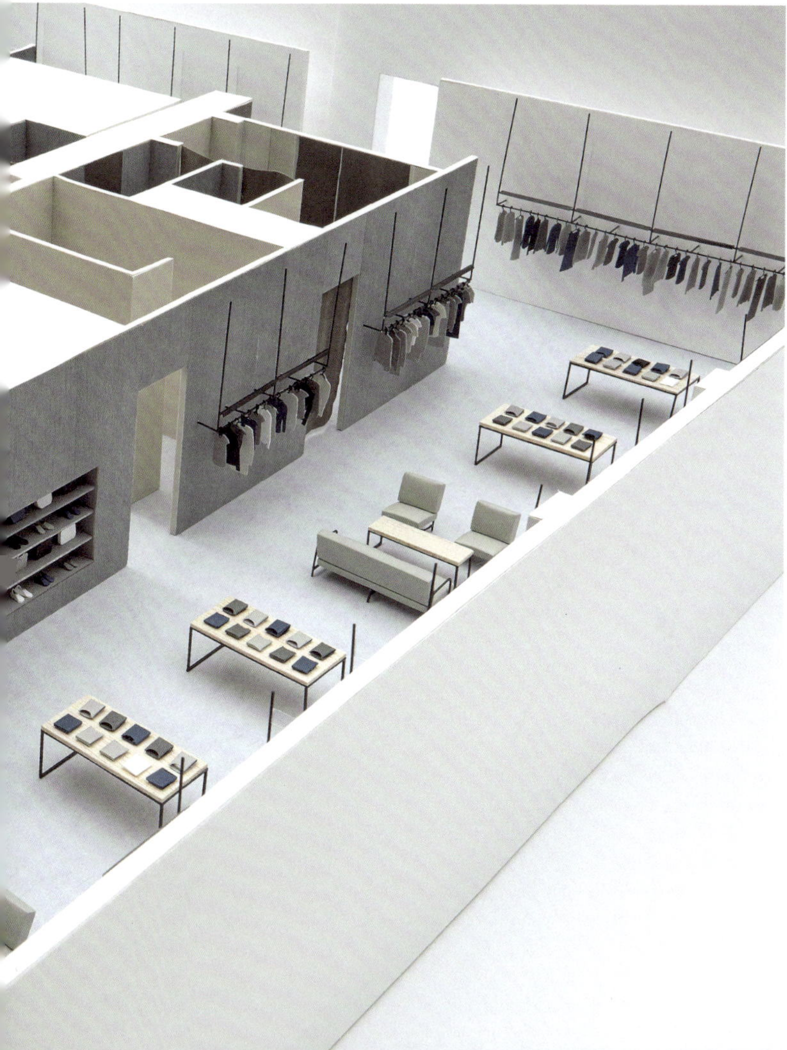

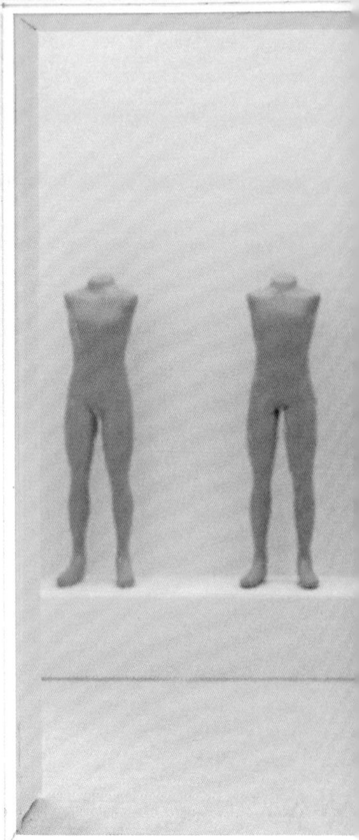

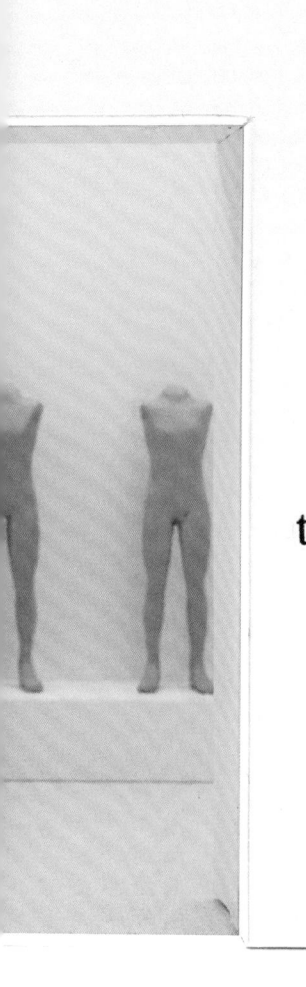

theory

theory

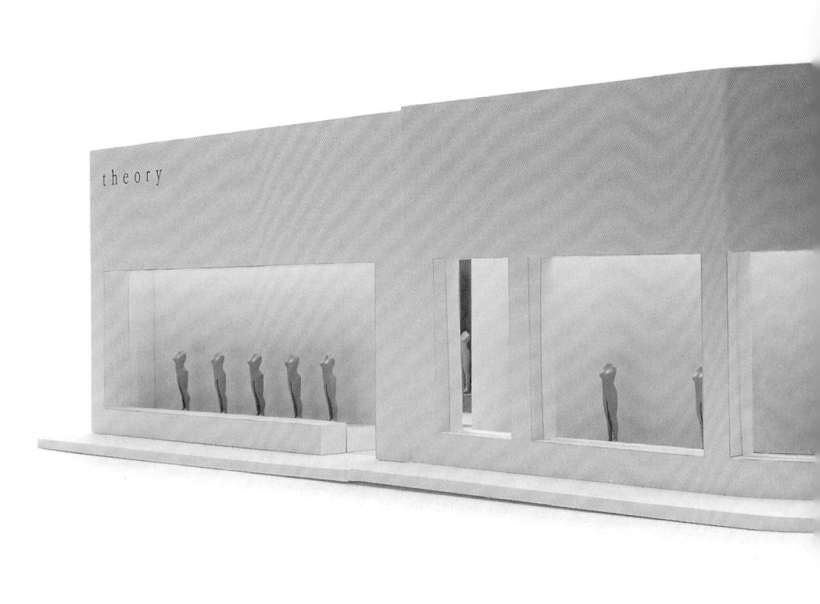

theory

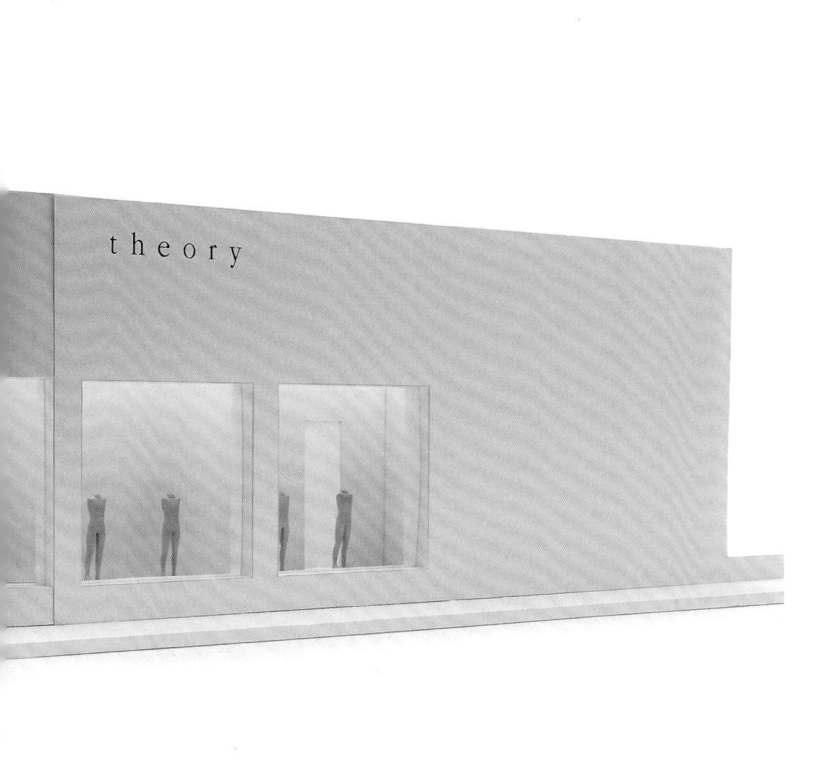

Theory North Beverly

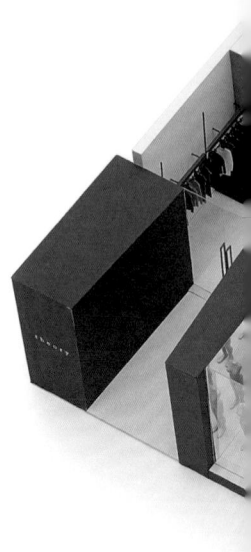

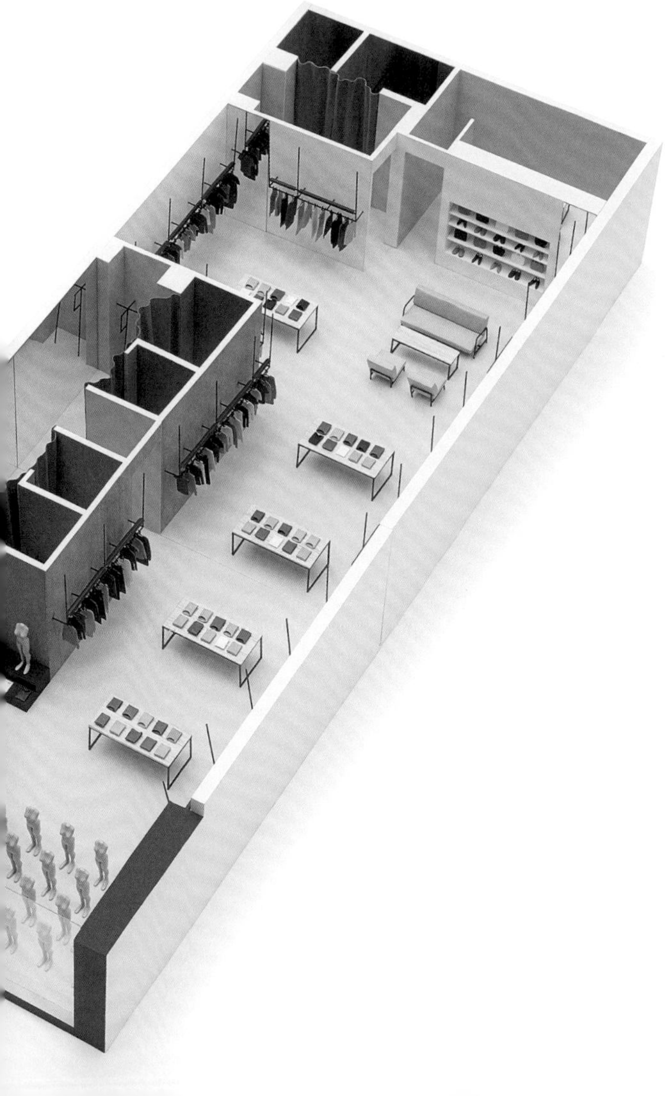

theory

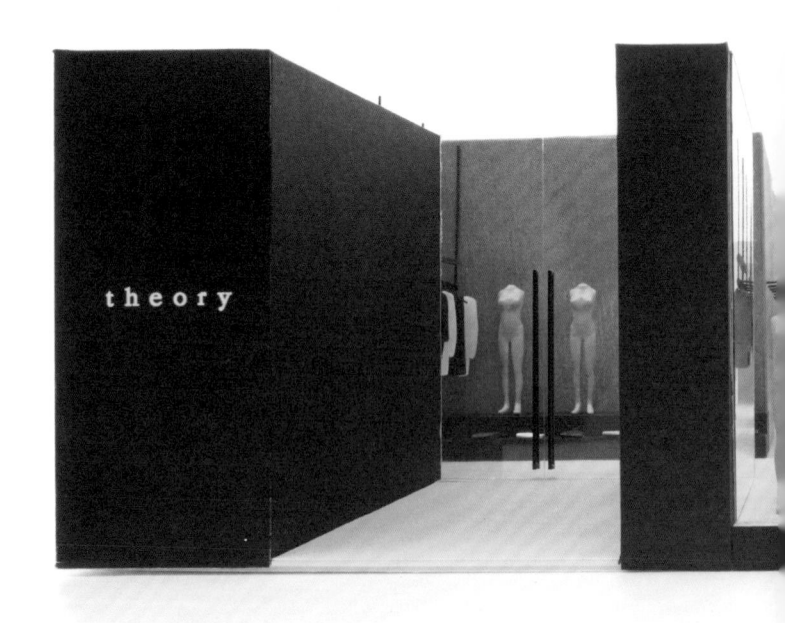

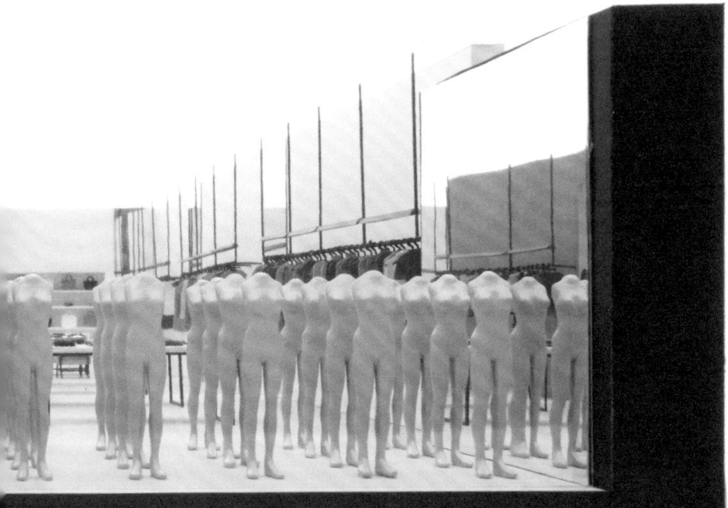

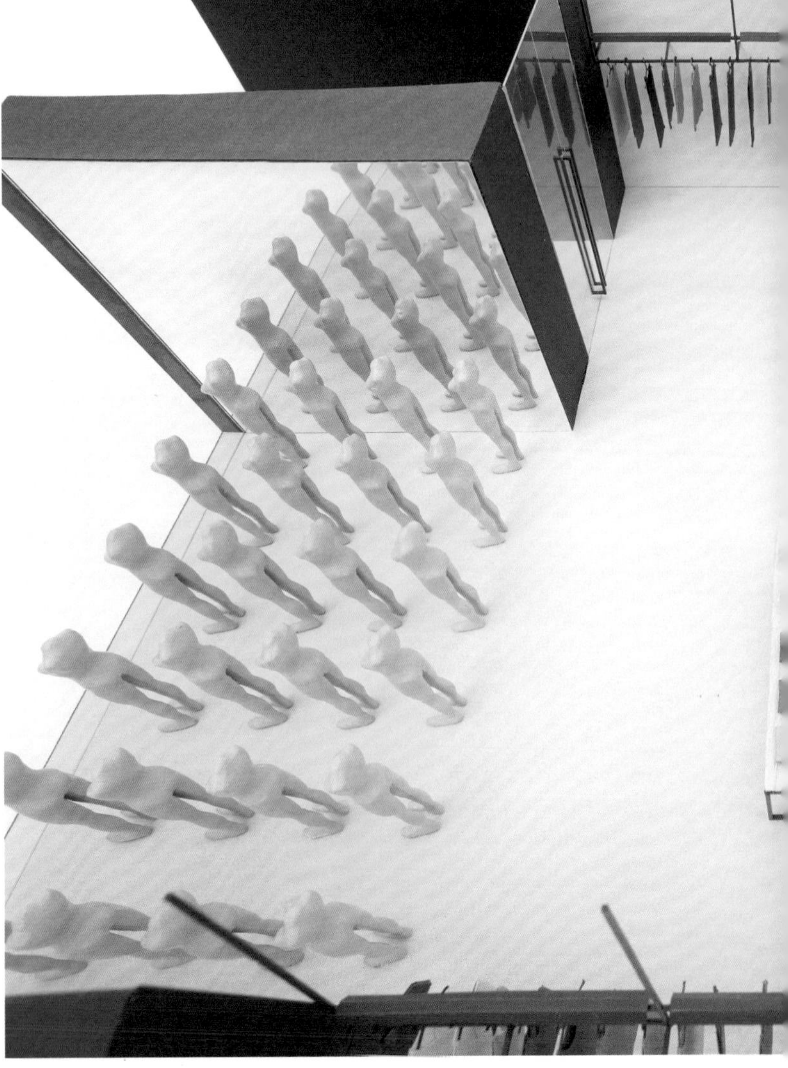

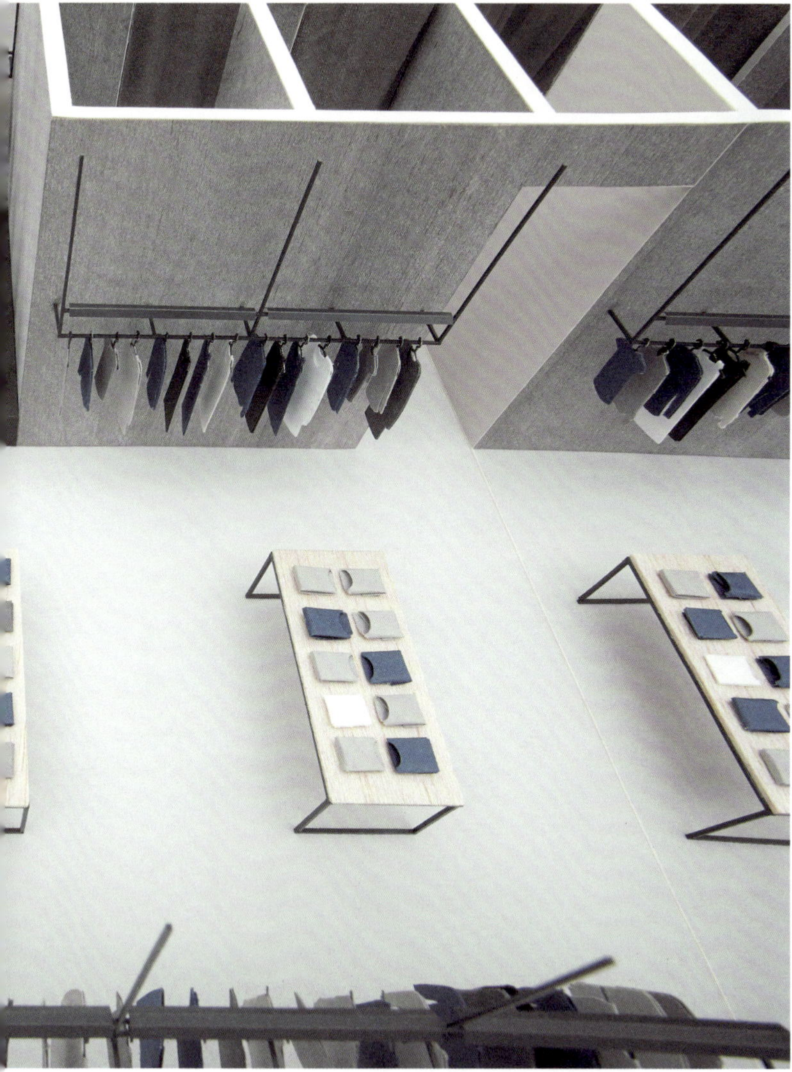

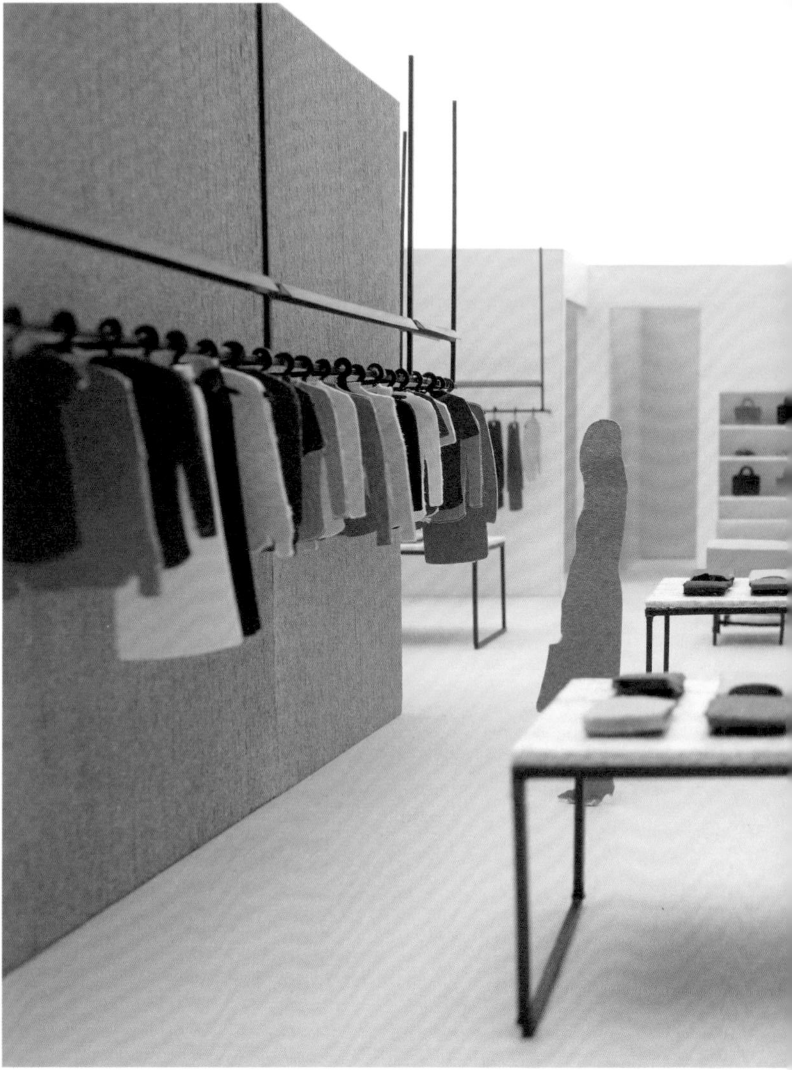

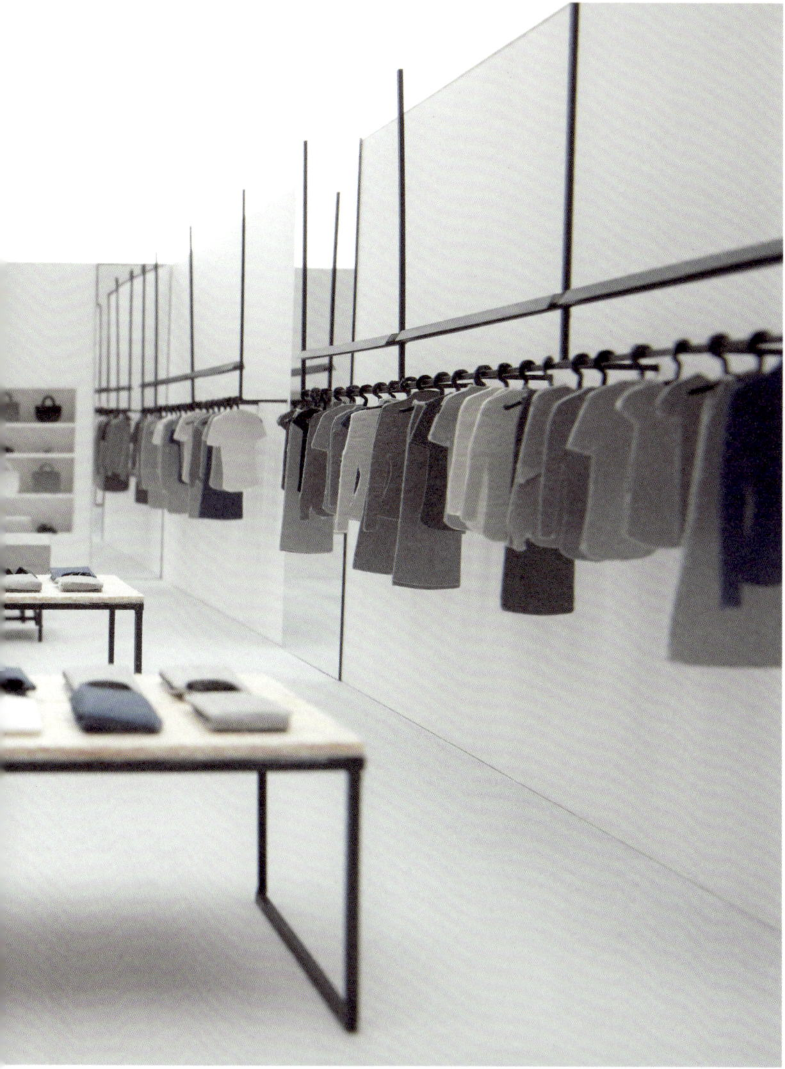

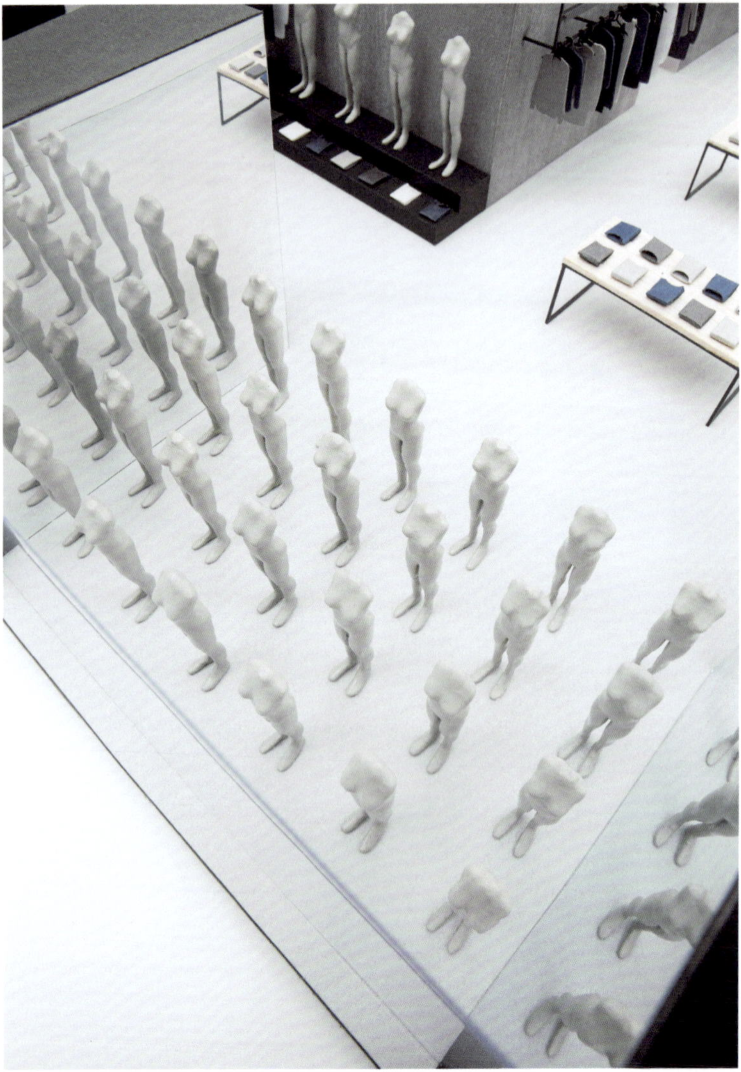

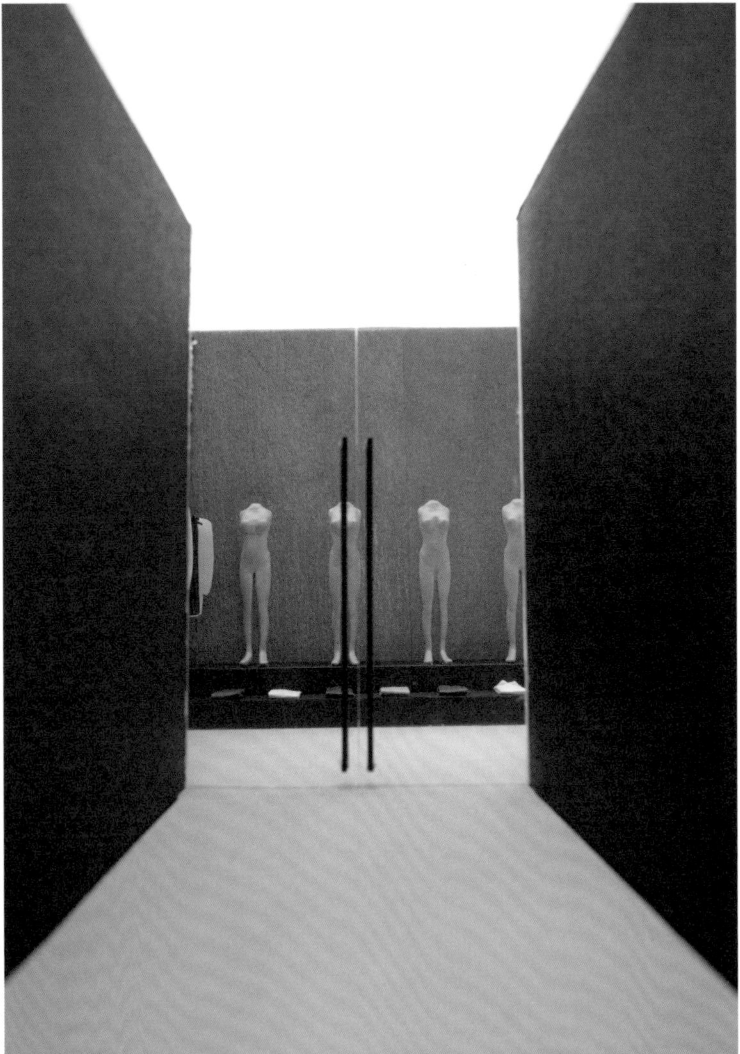

Theory New York Gansevoort

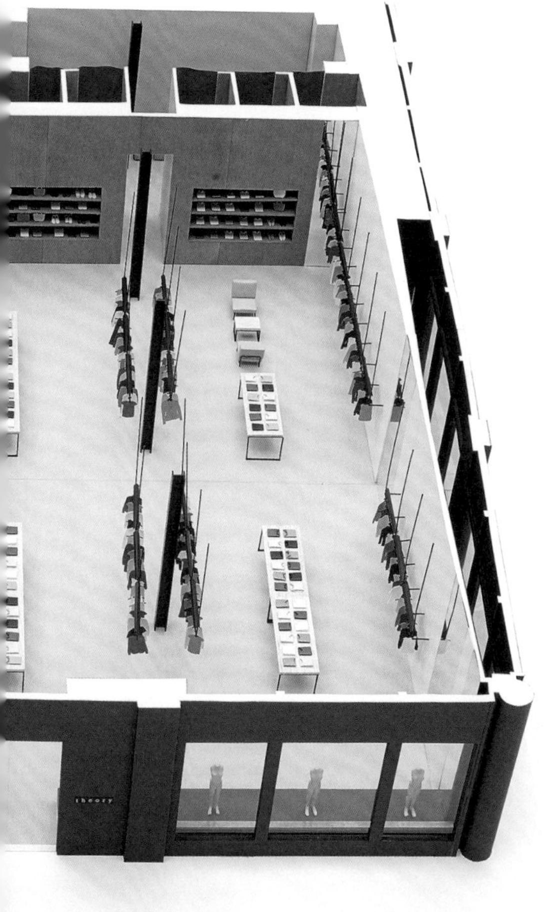
theory

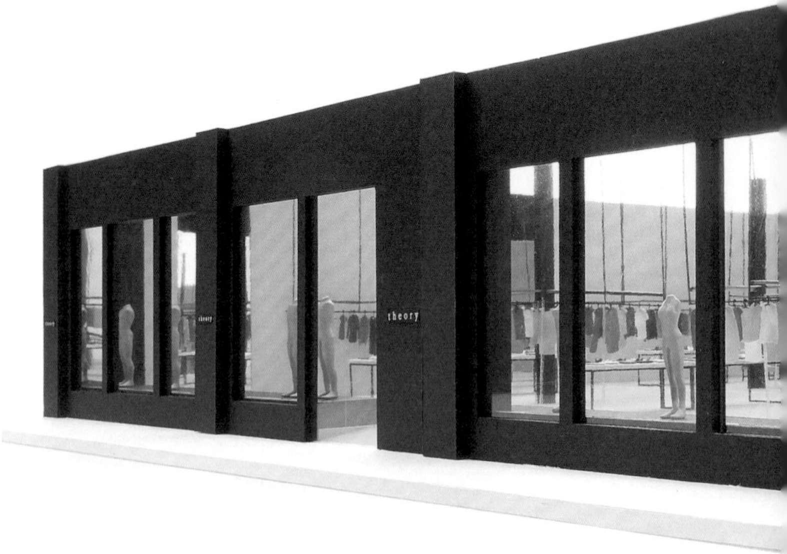
theory
theory

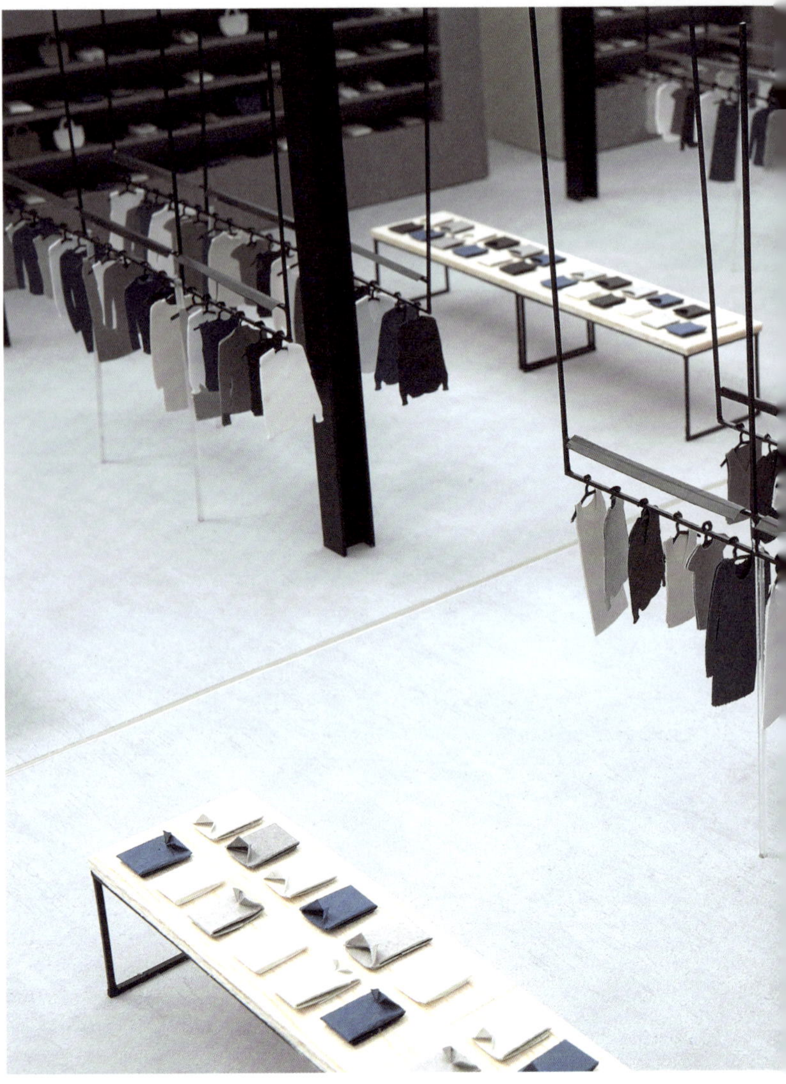

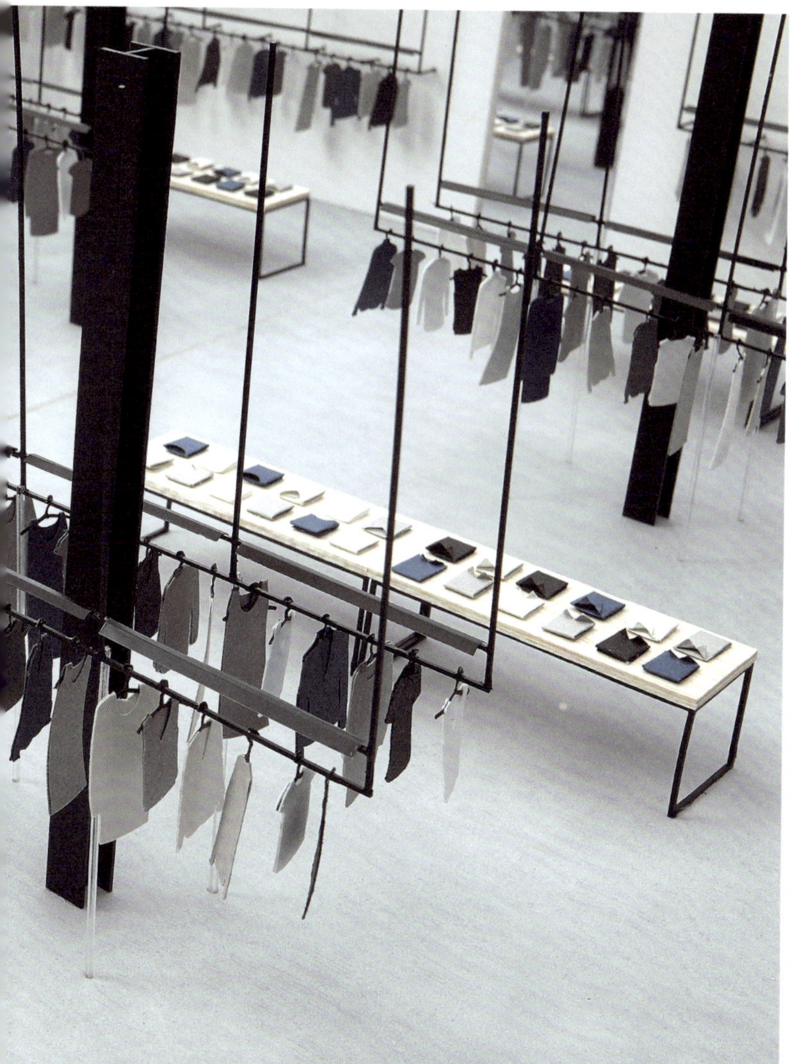

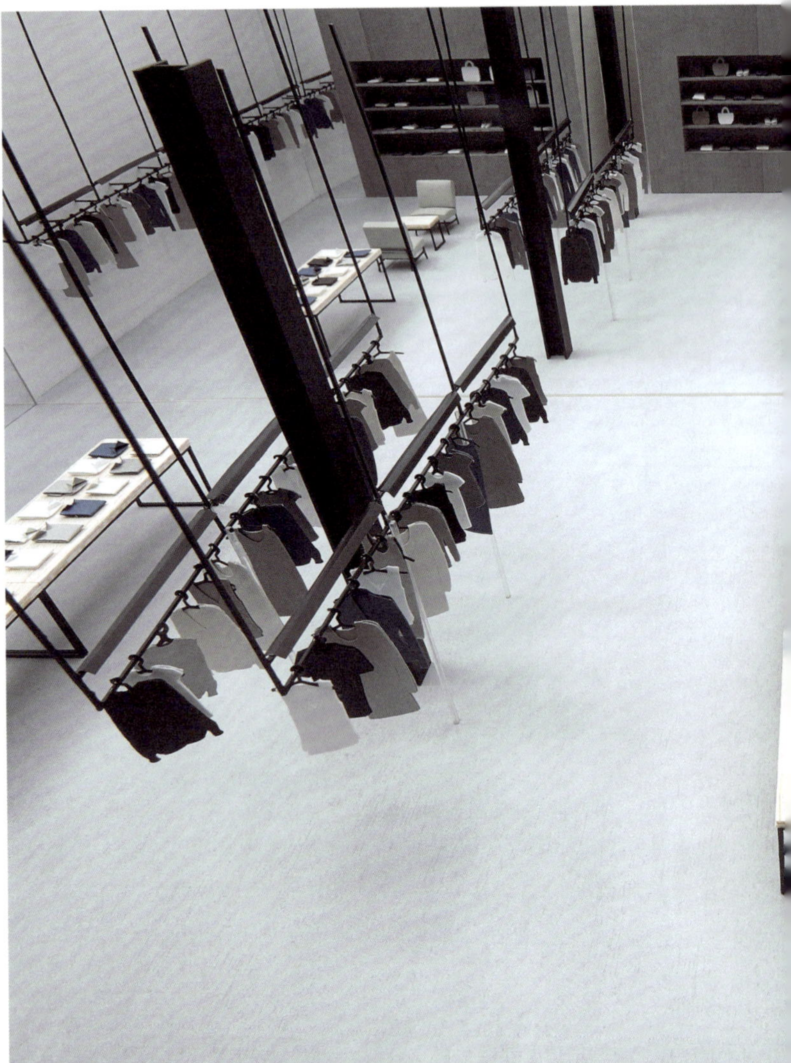

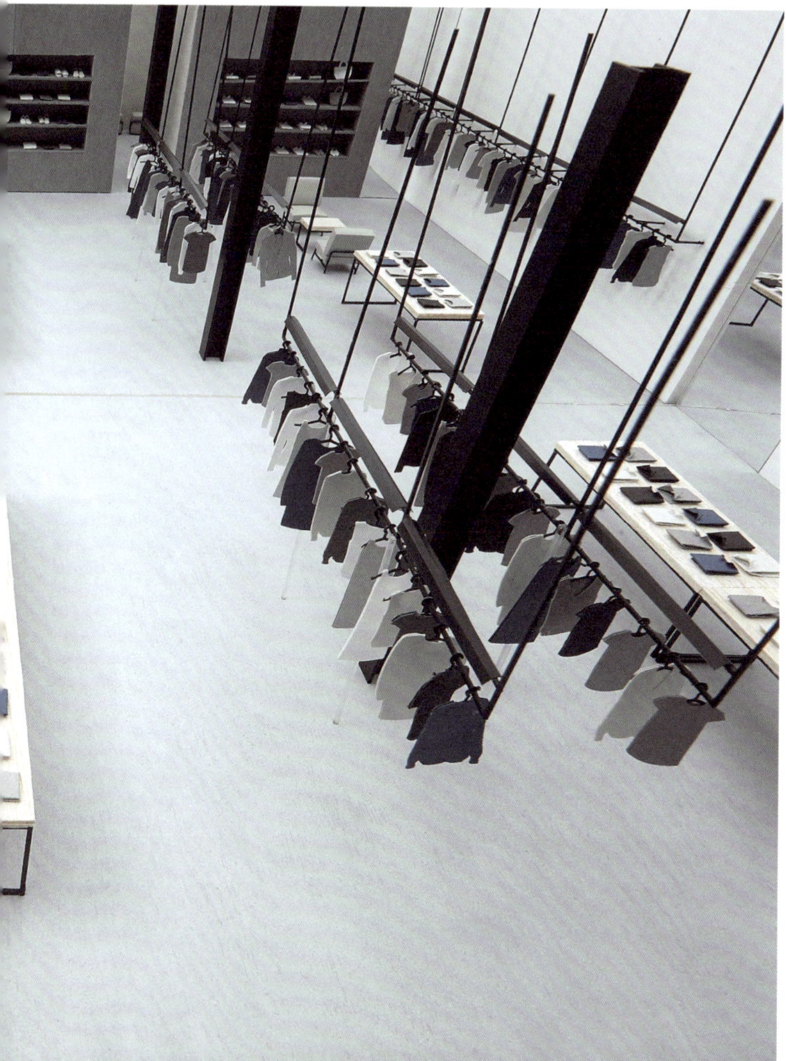

Theory Paris Saint Honoré

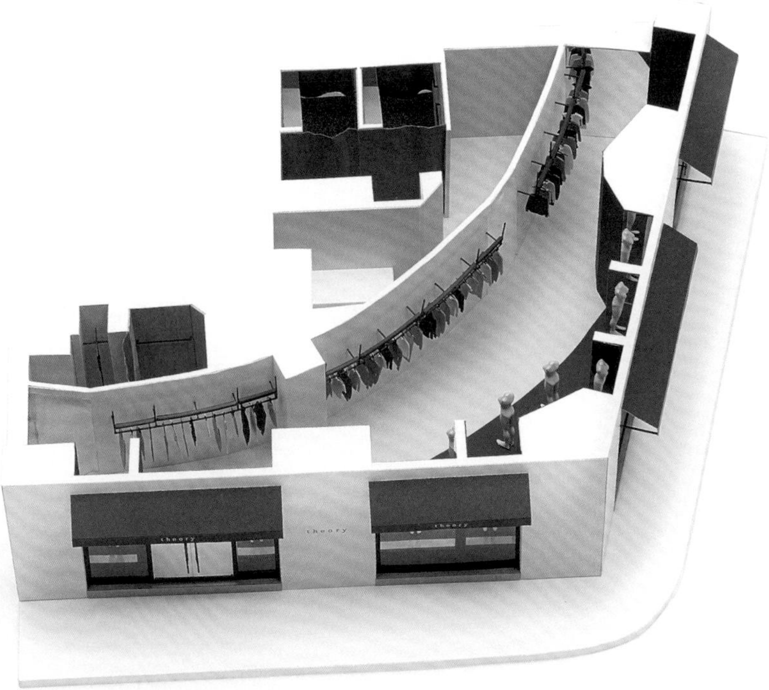
theory
theory
theory

theory

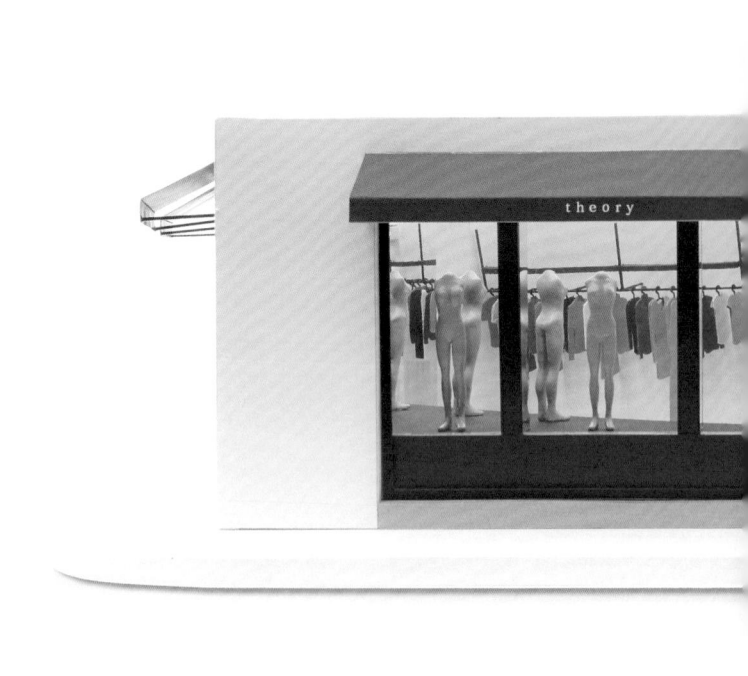

theory

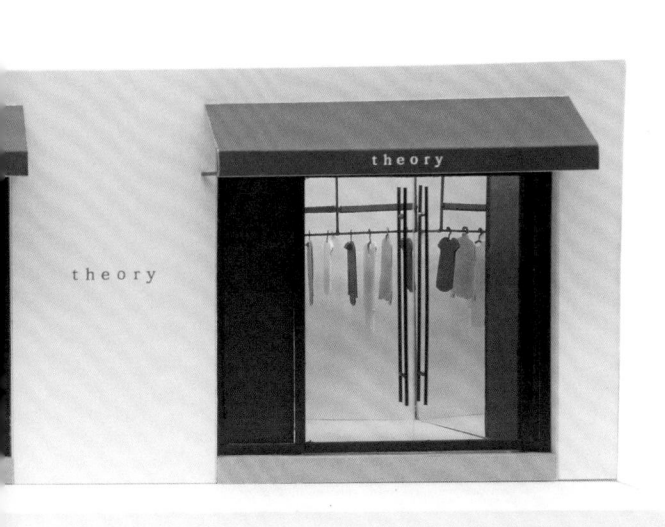

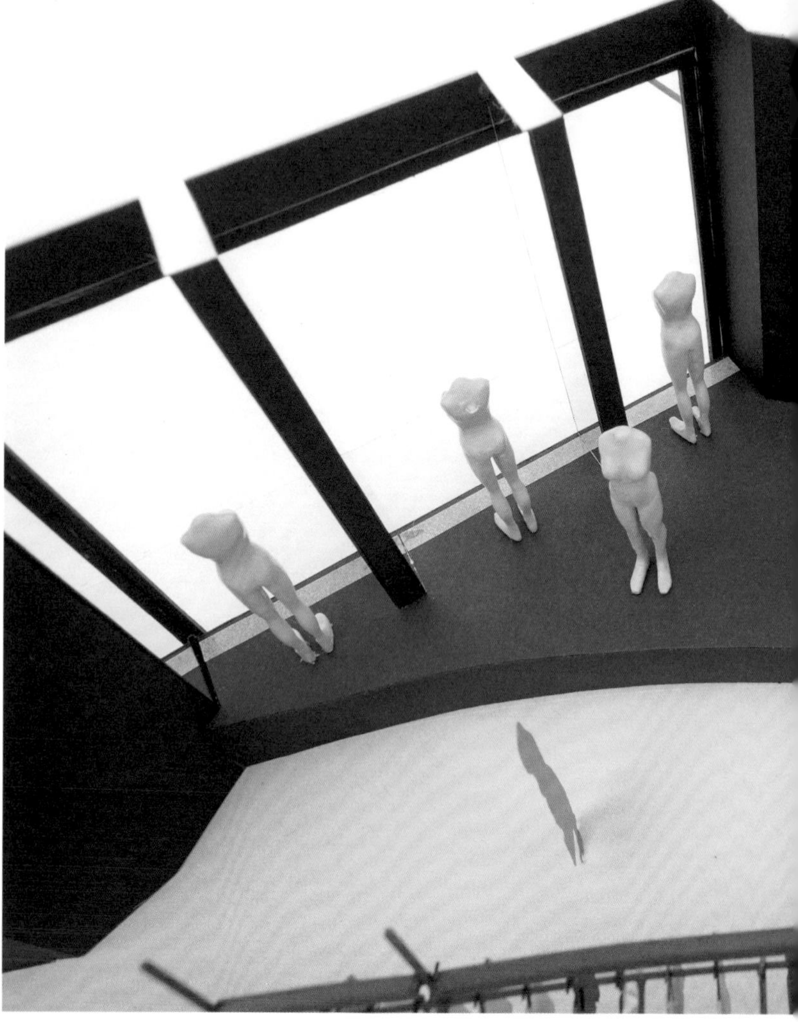

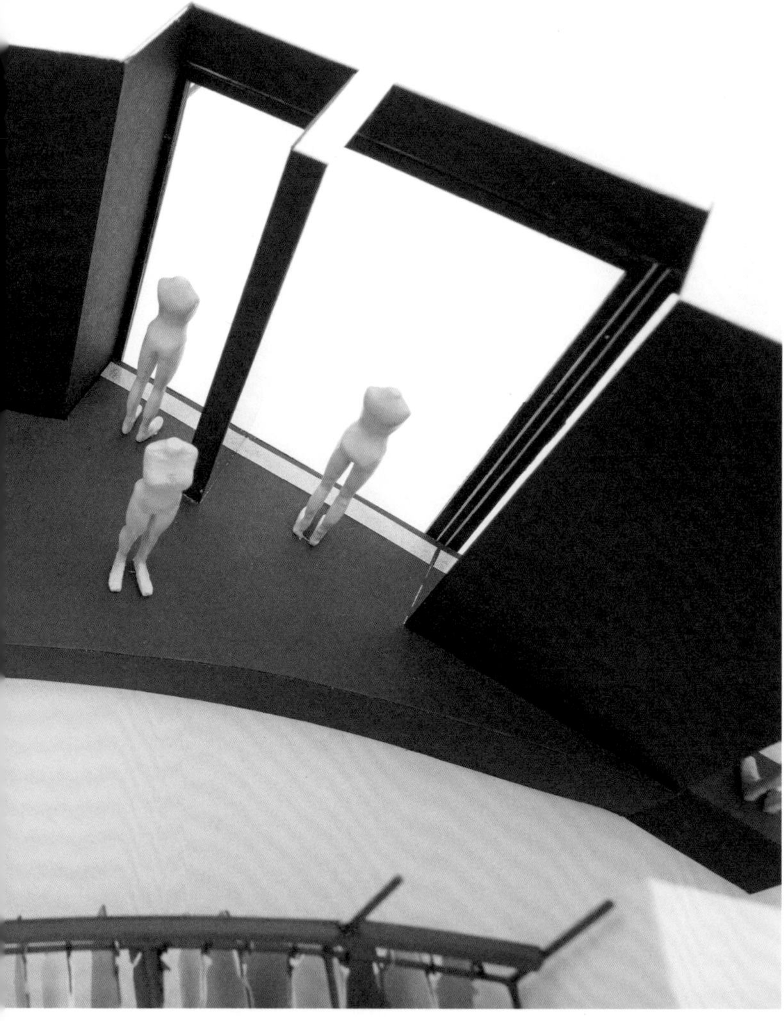

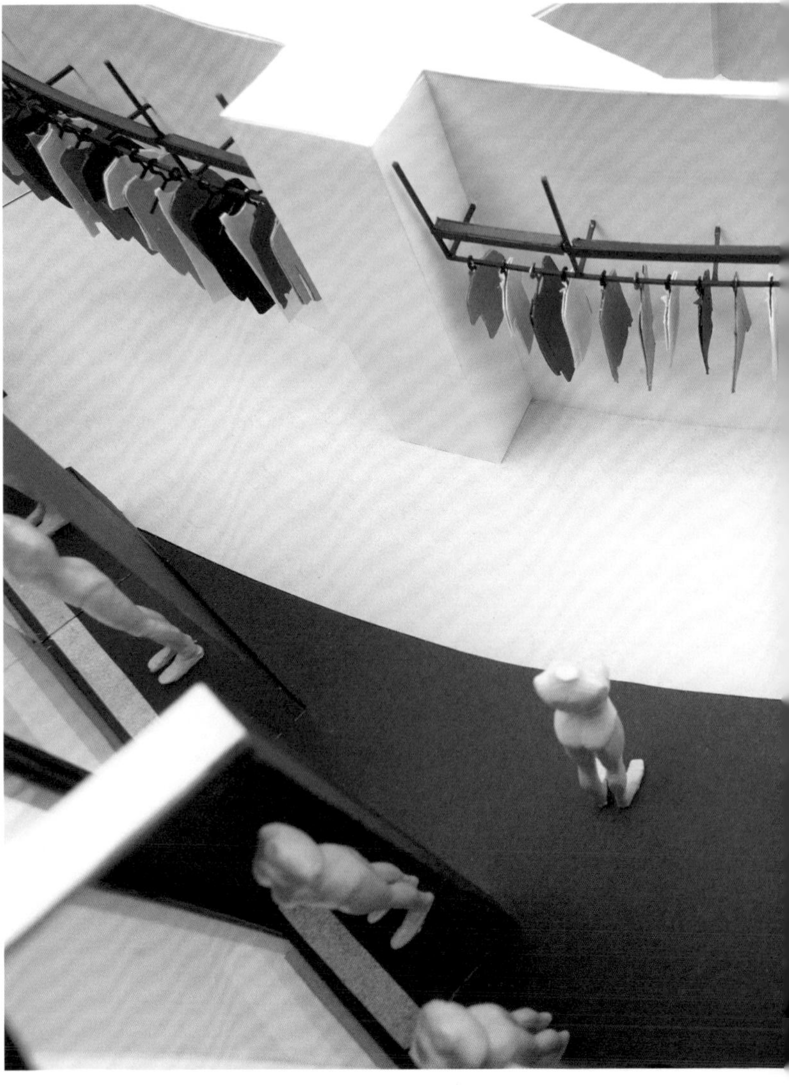

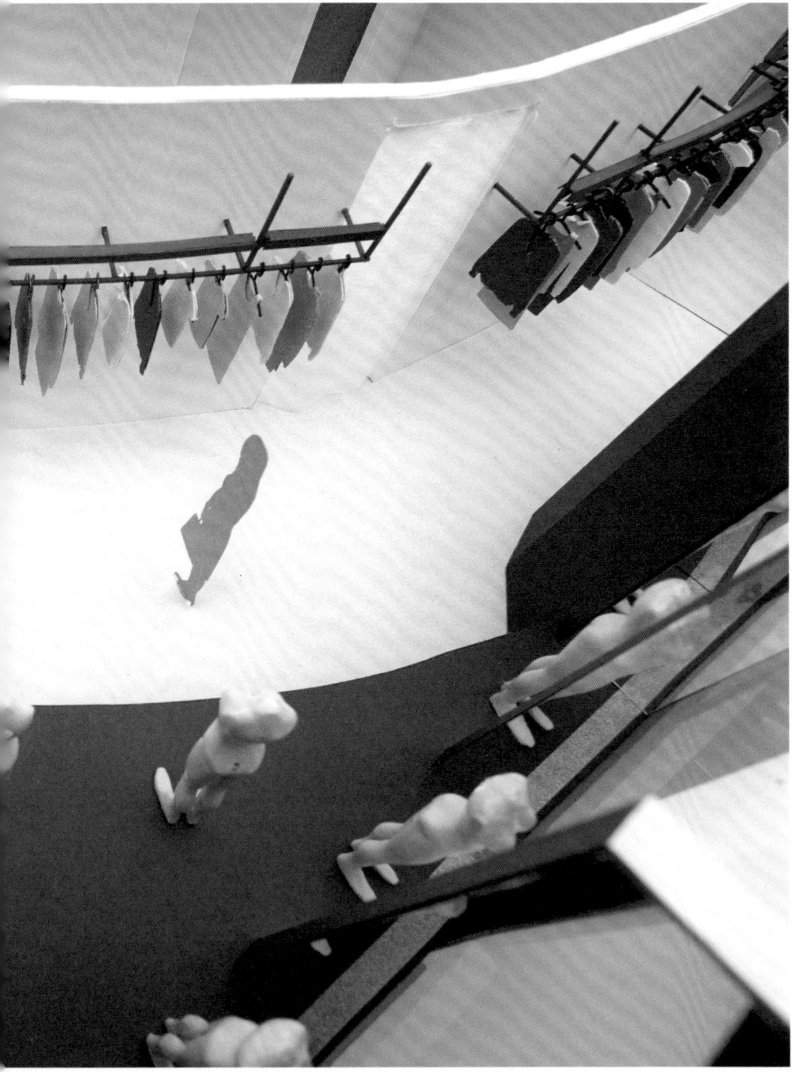

Theory Paris Saint Pere

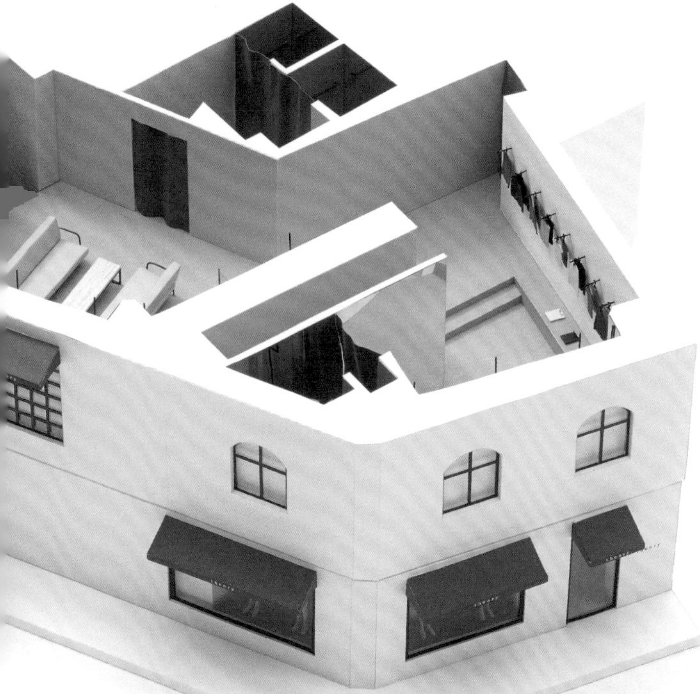

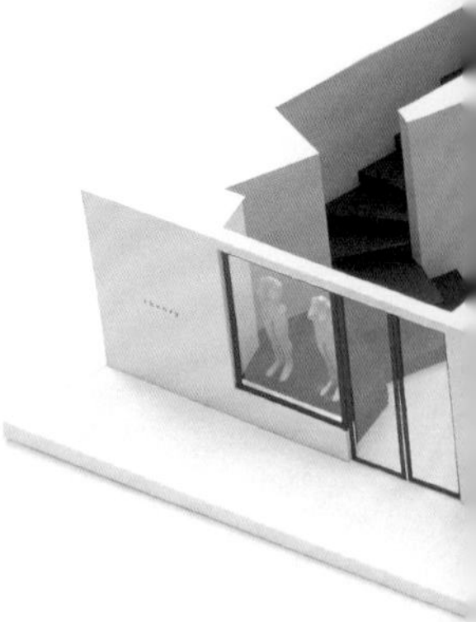

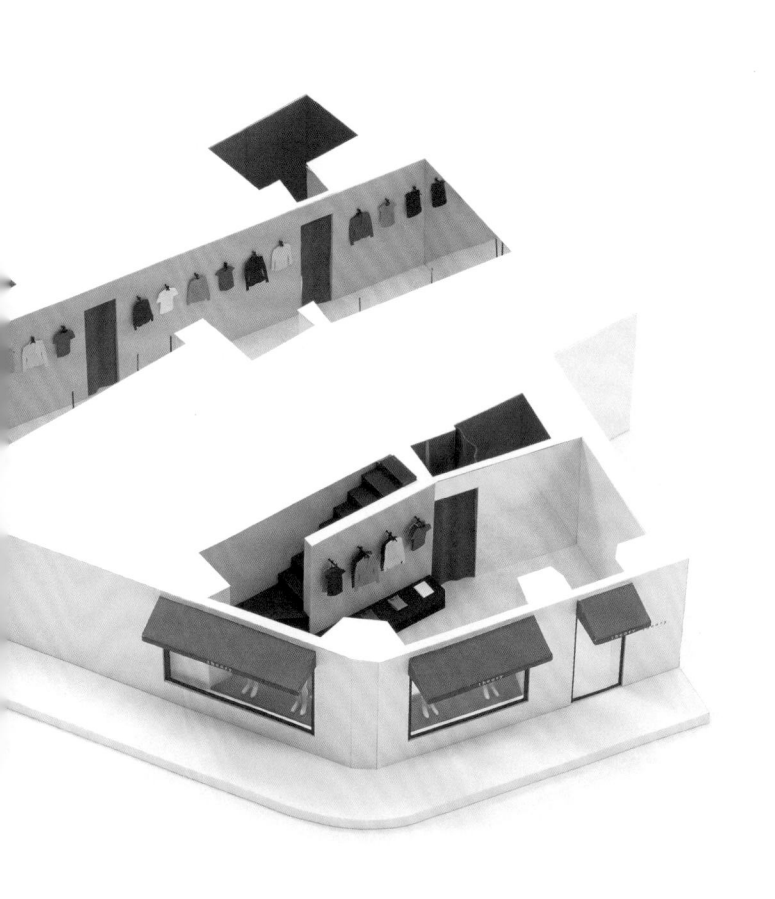

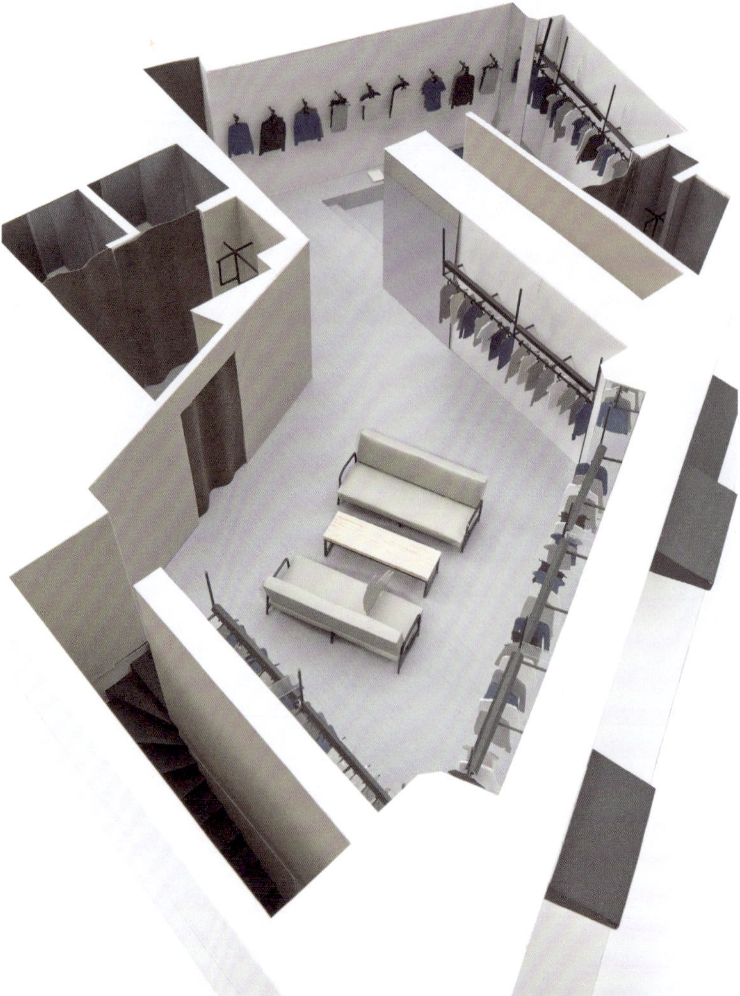

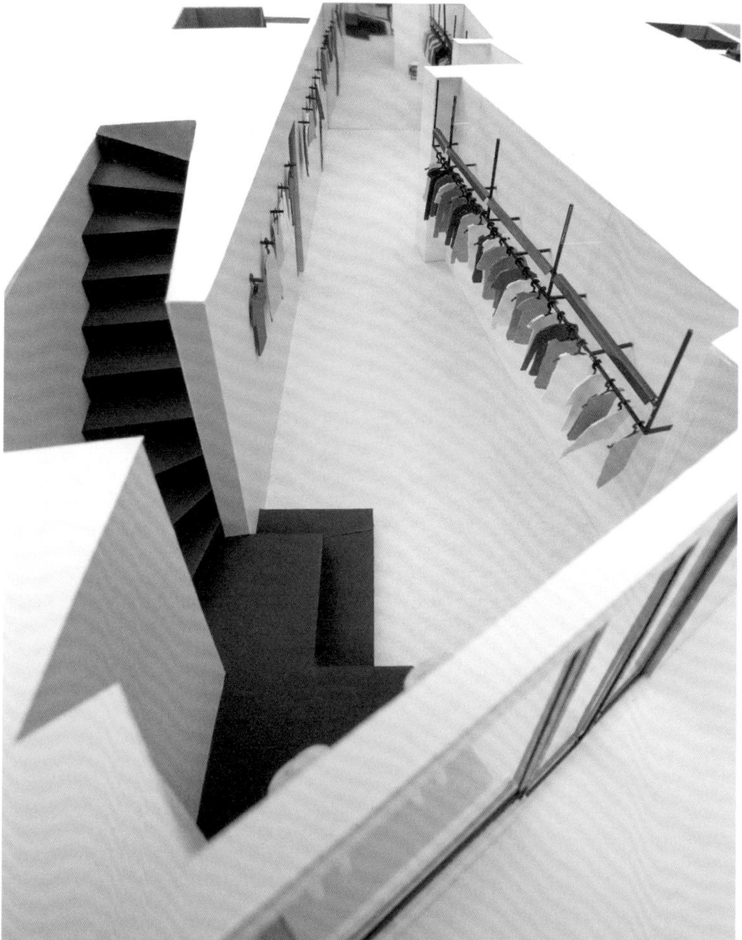

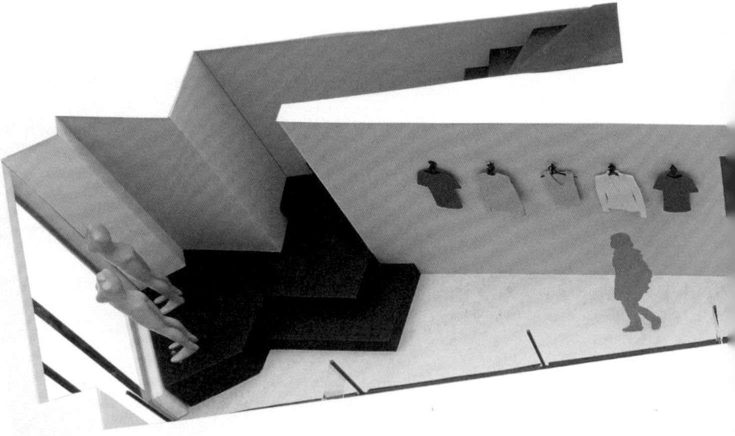

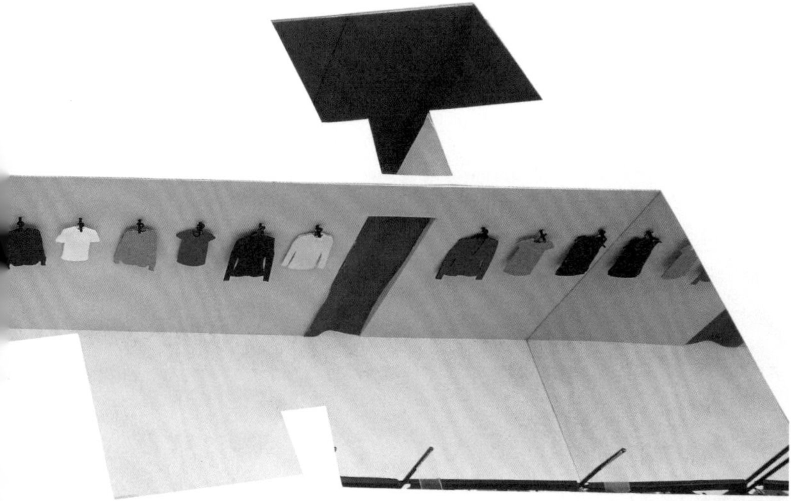

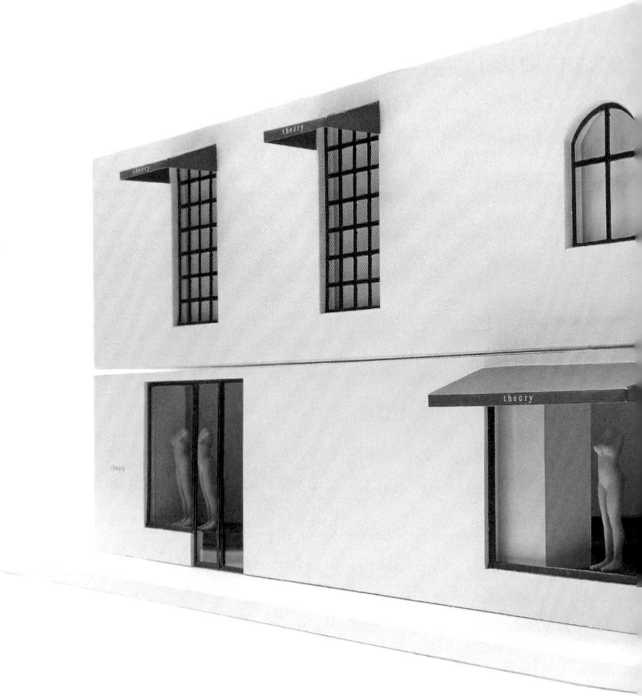
theory
theory
theory

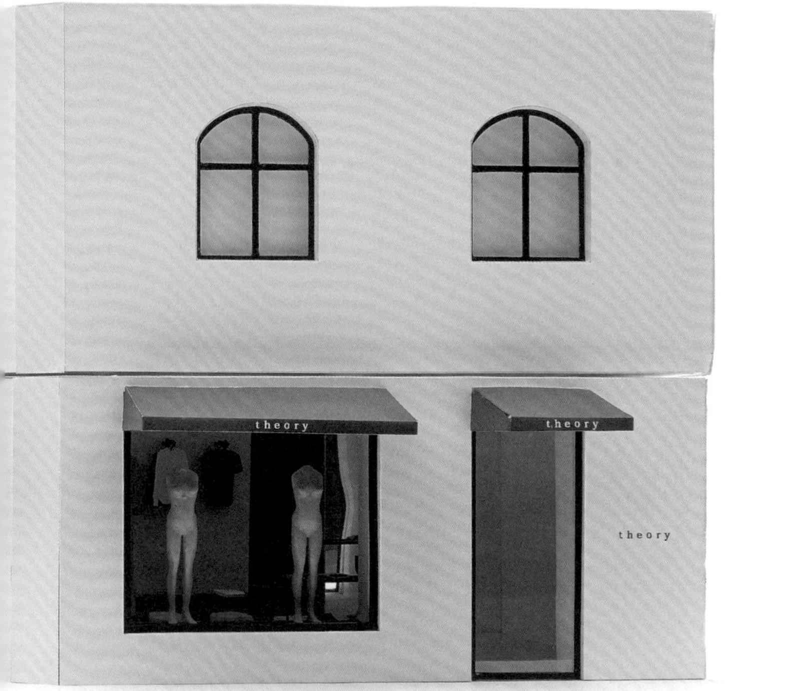
theory
theory
theory

Theory Shanghai REEL

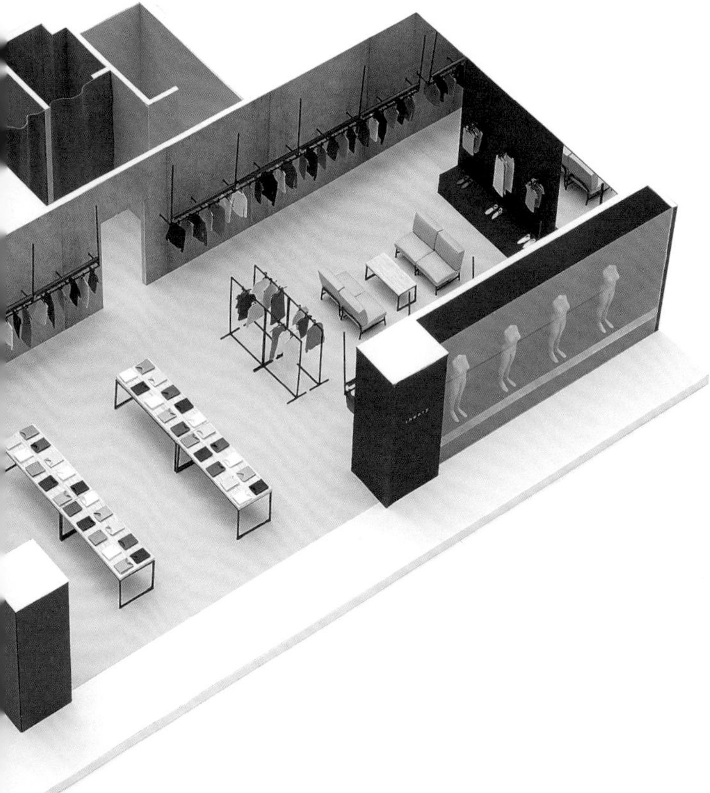

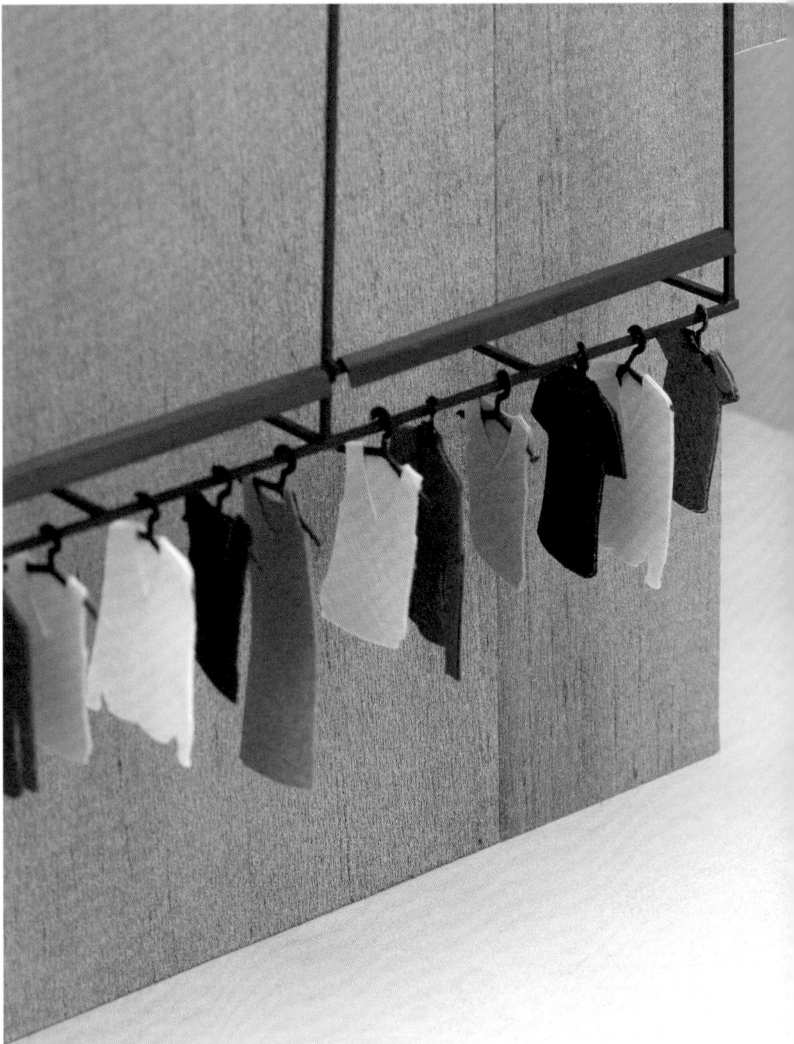

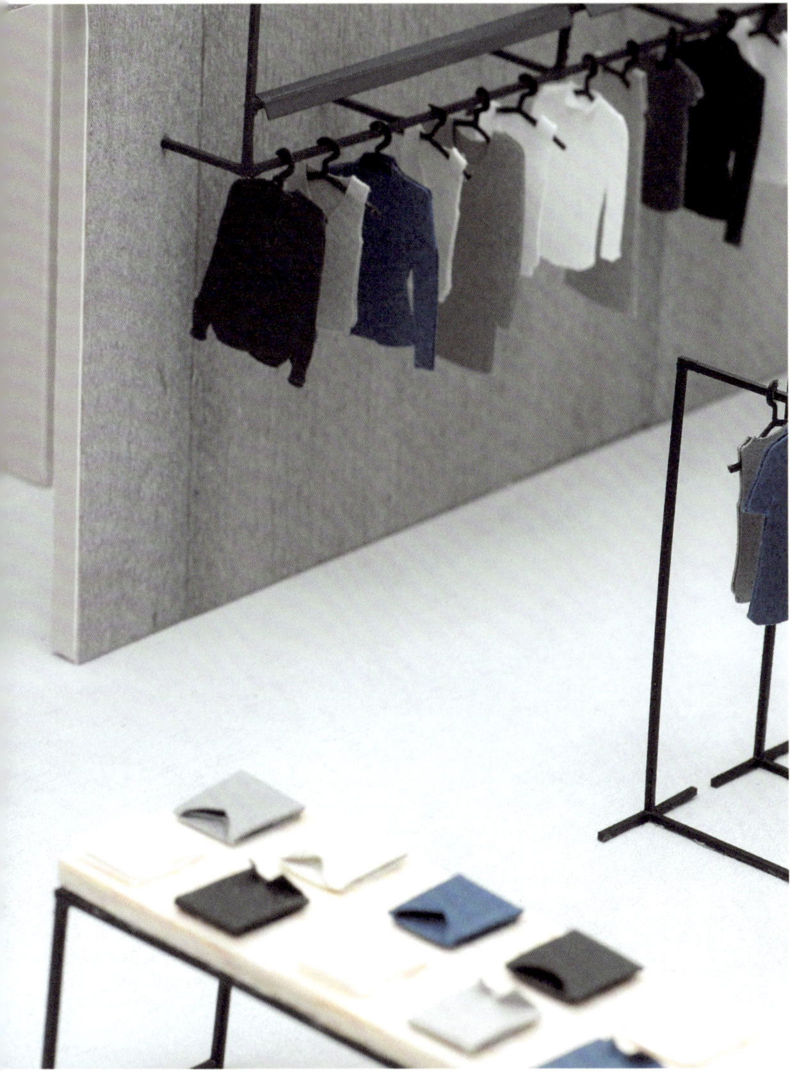

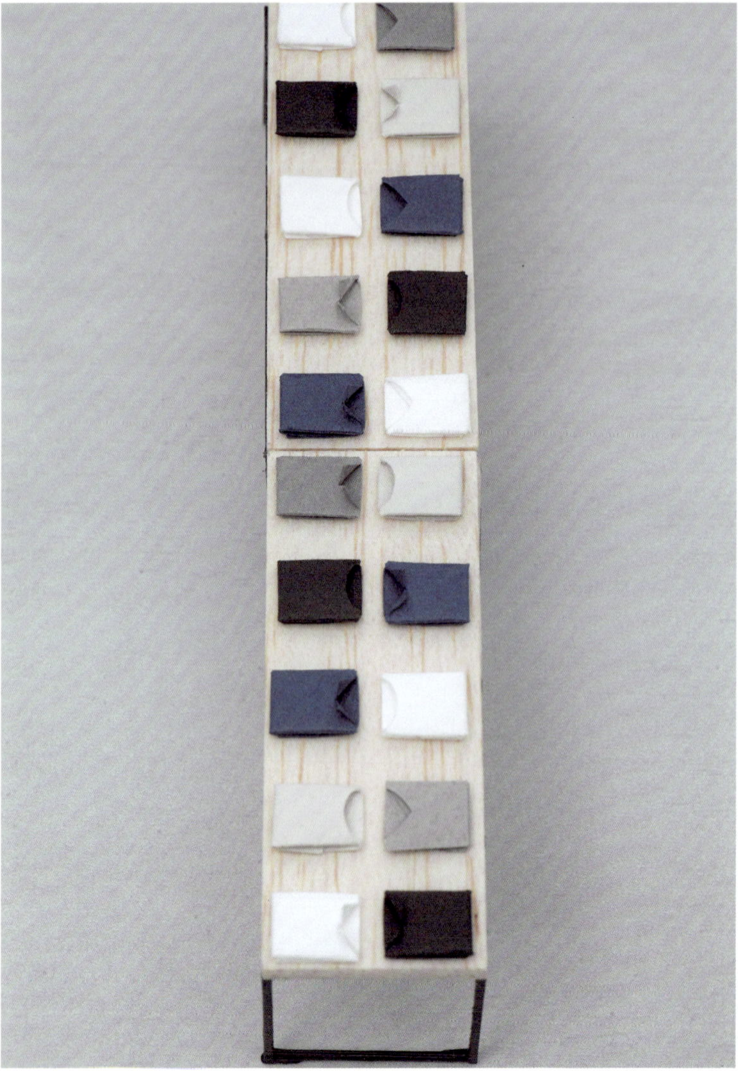

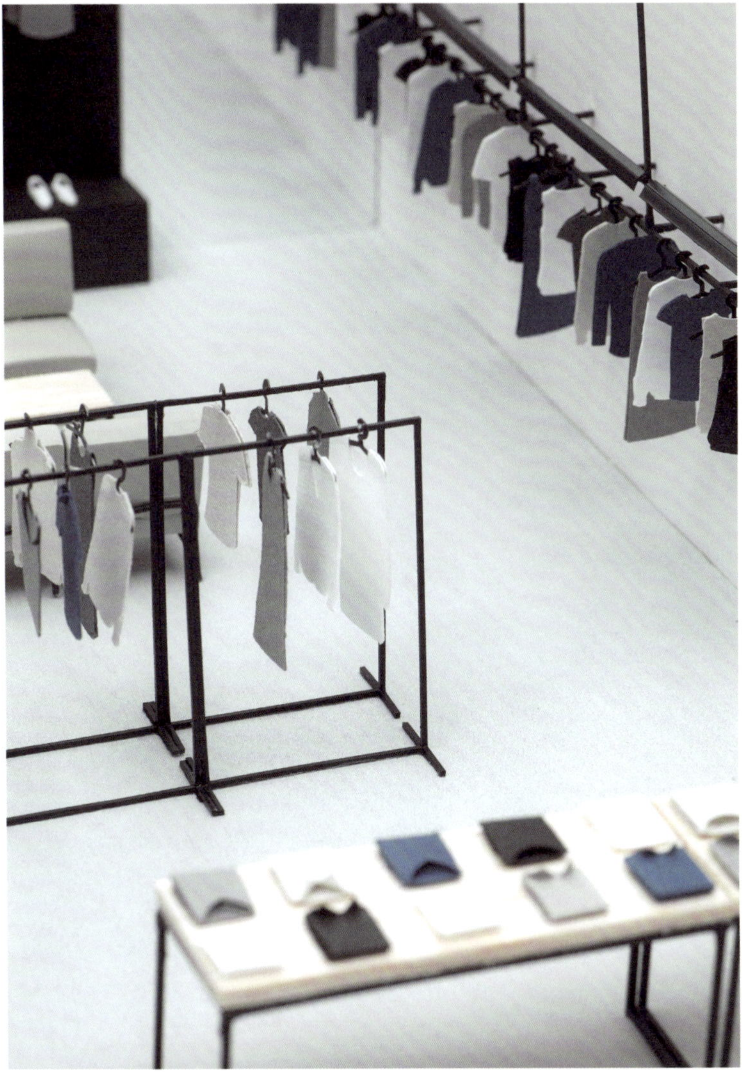

thin black lines + dancing squares

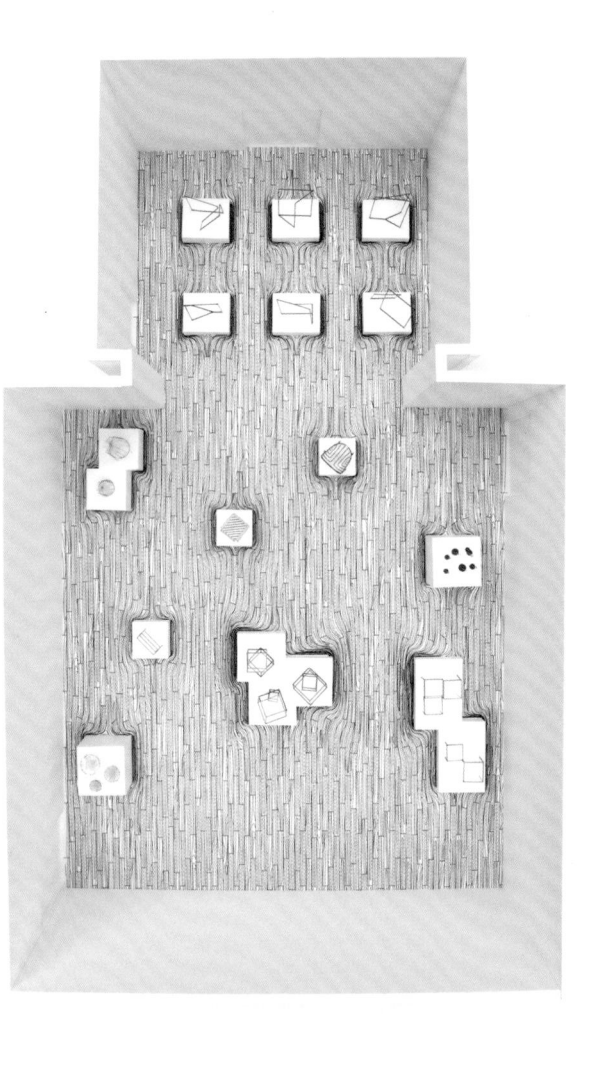

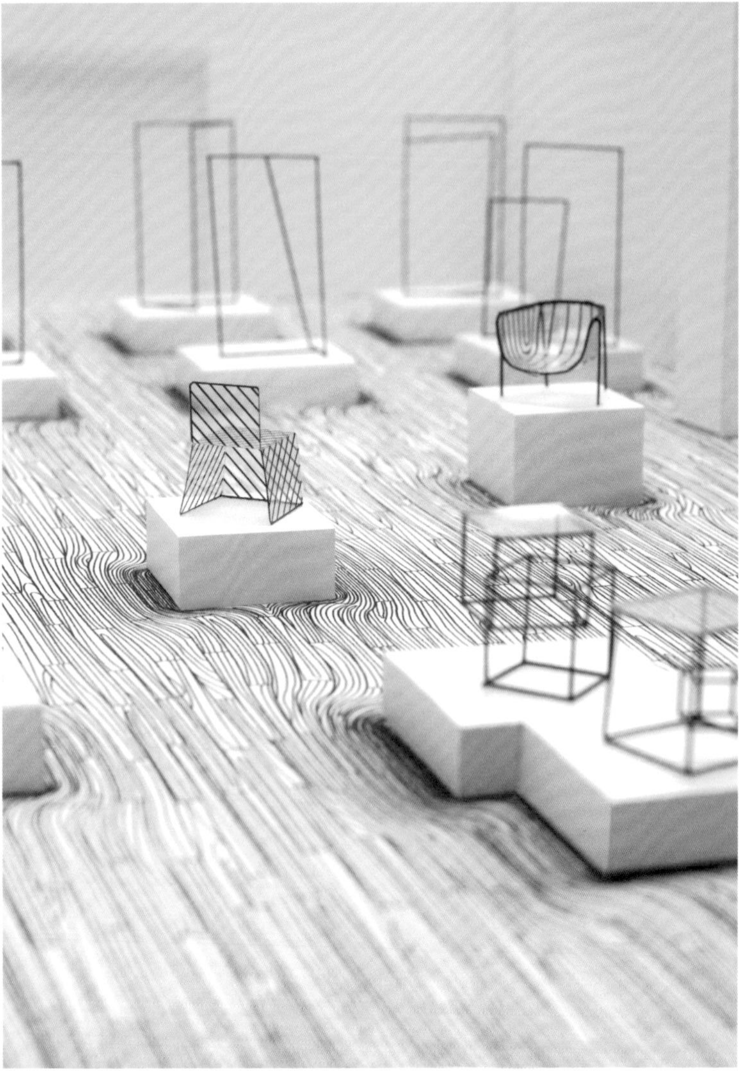

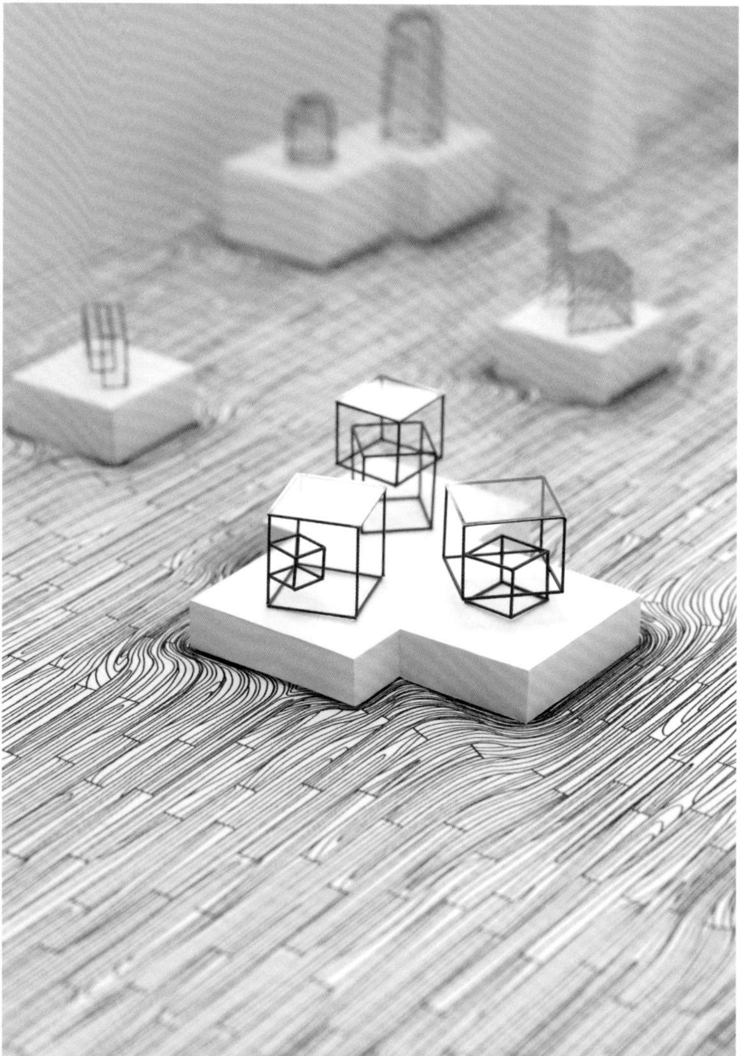

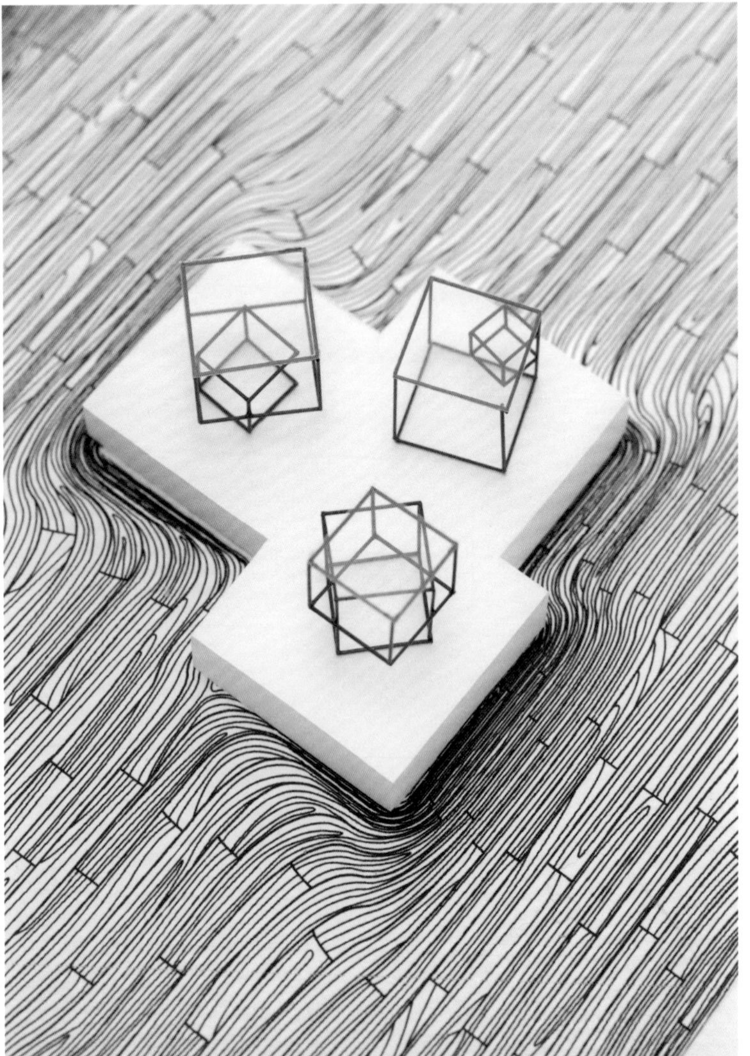

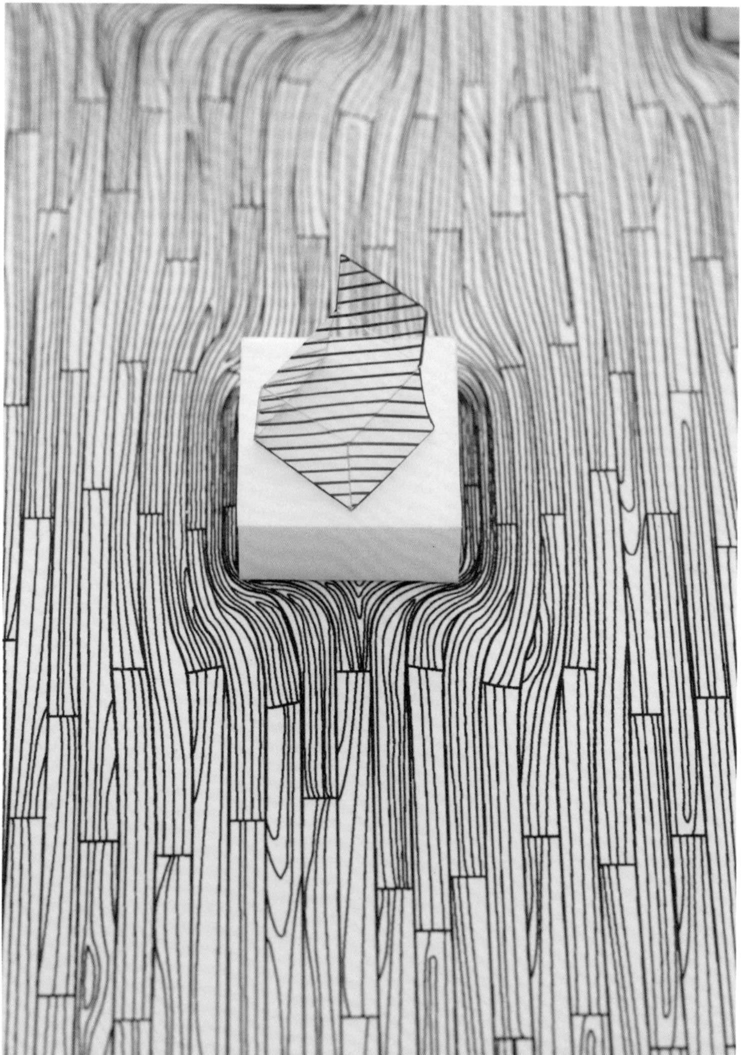

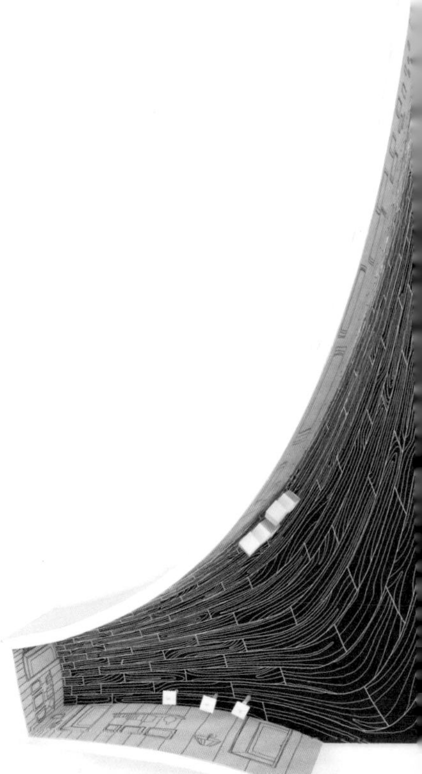

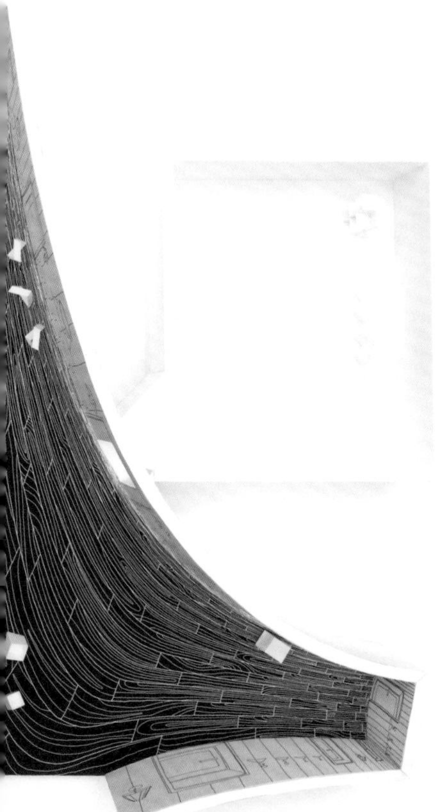

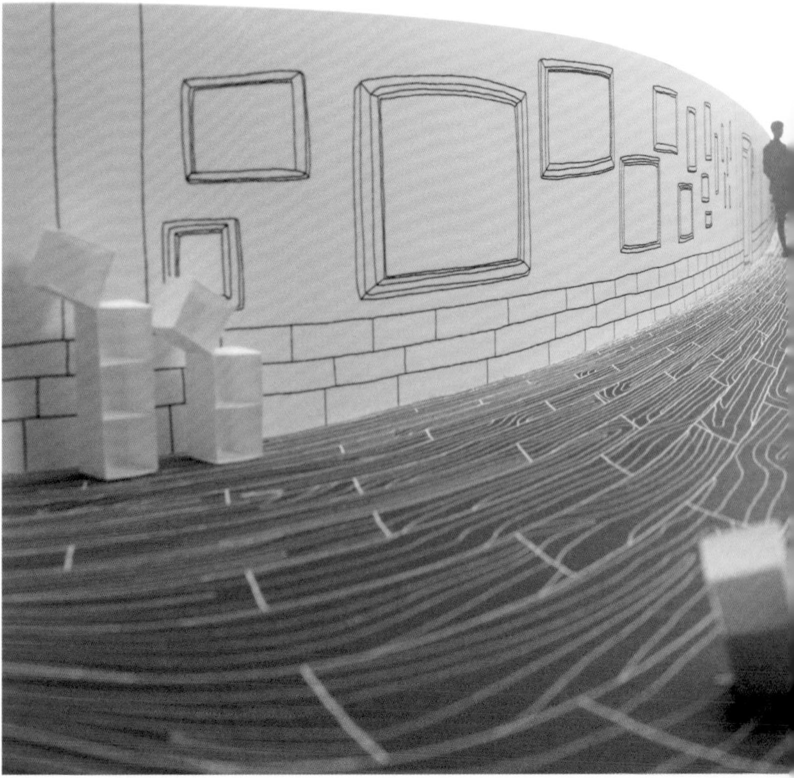

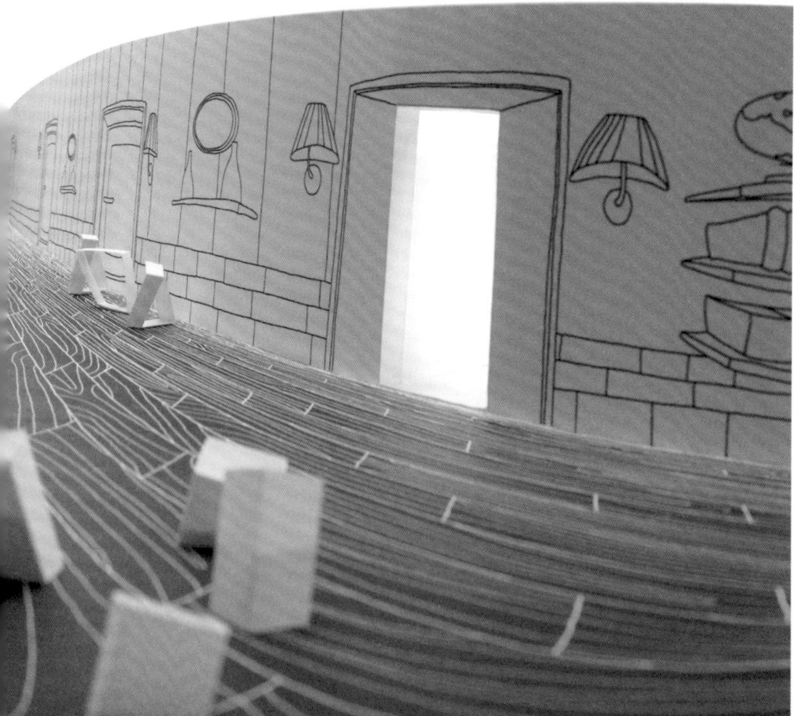

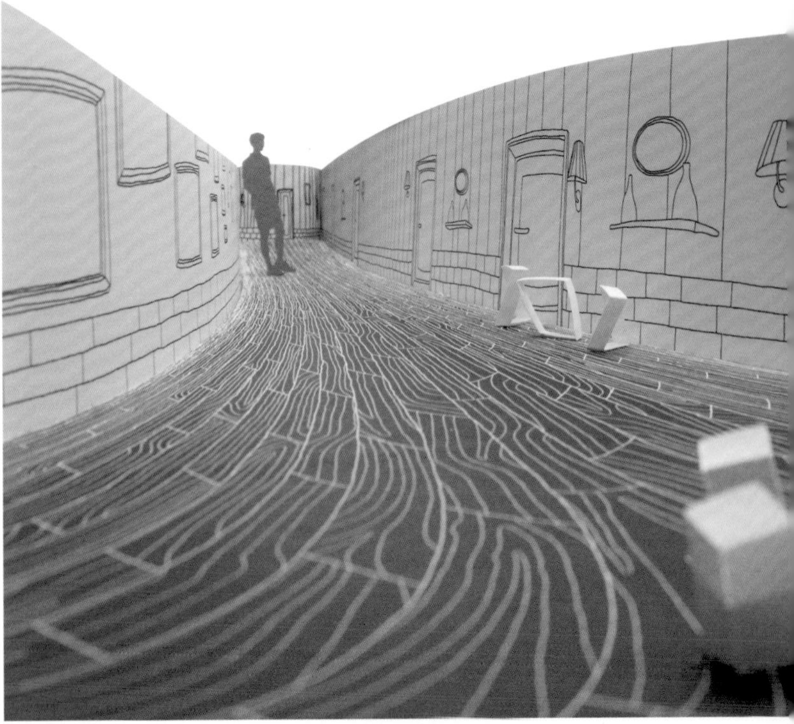

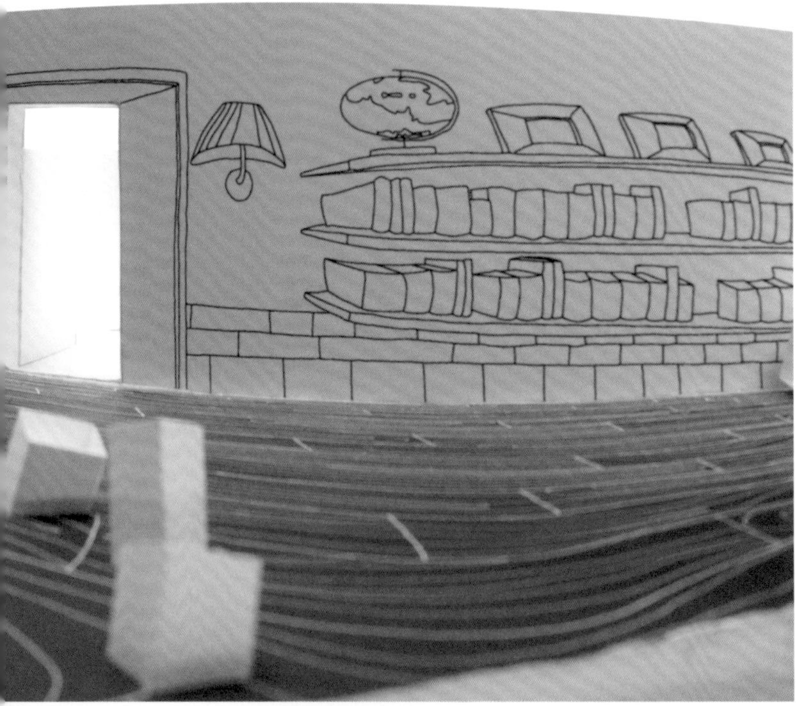

tokyo baby cafe

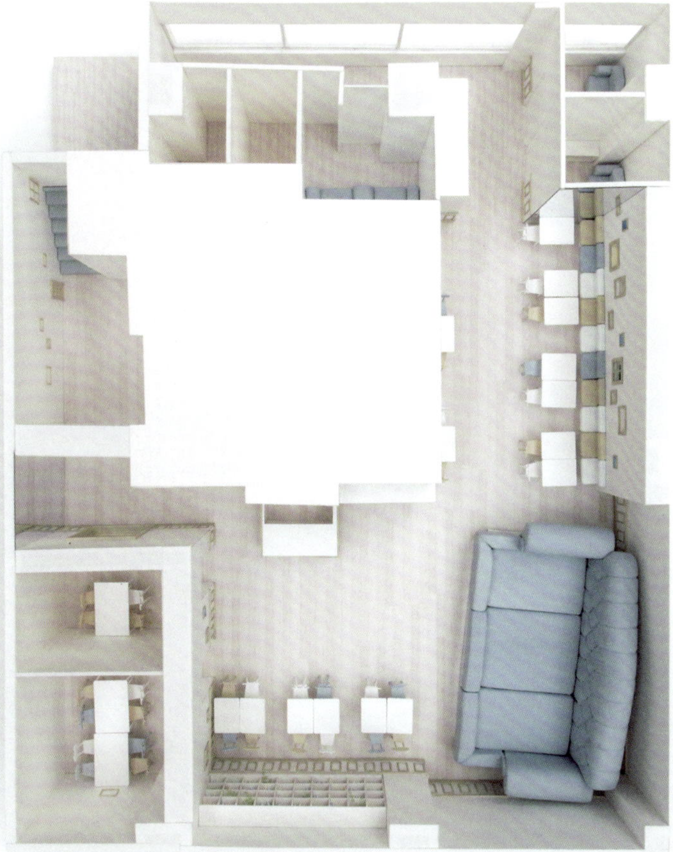

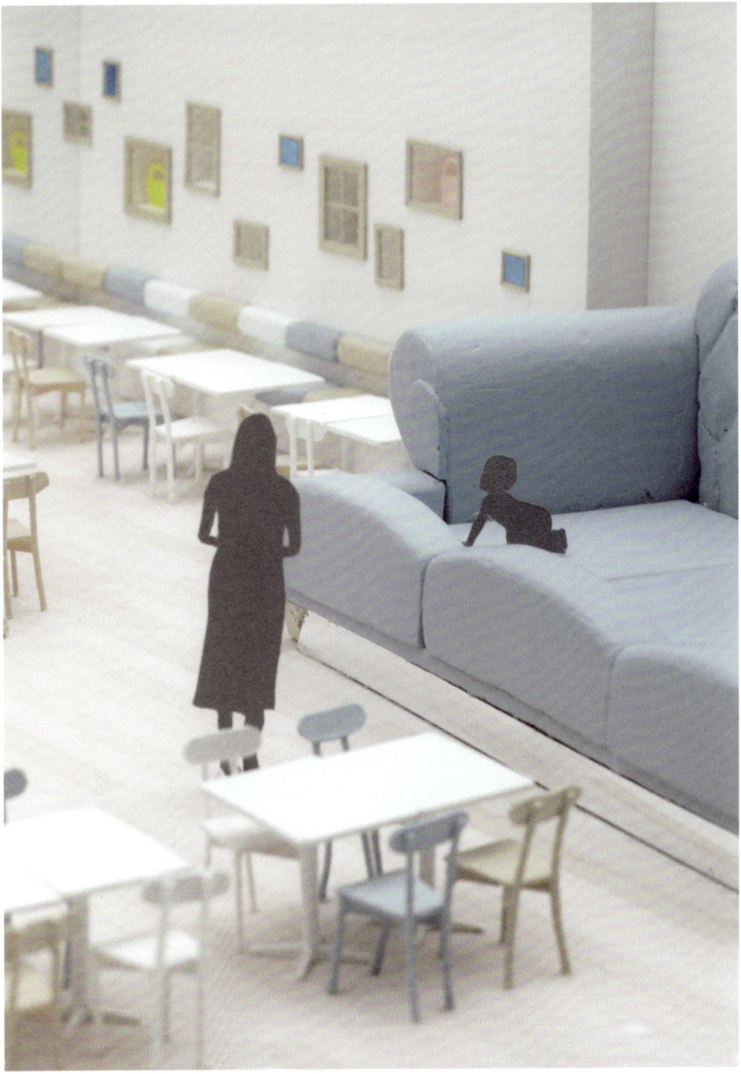

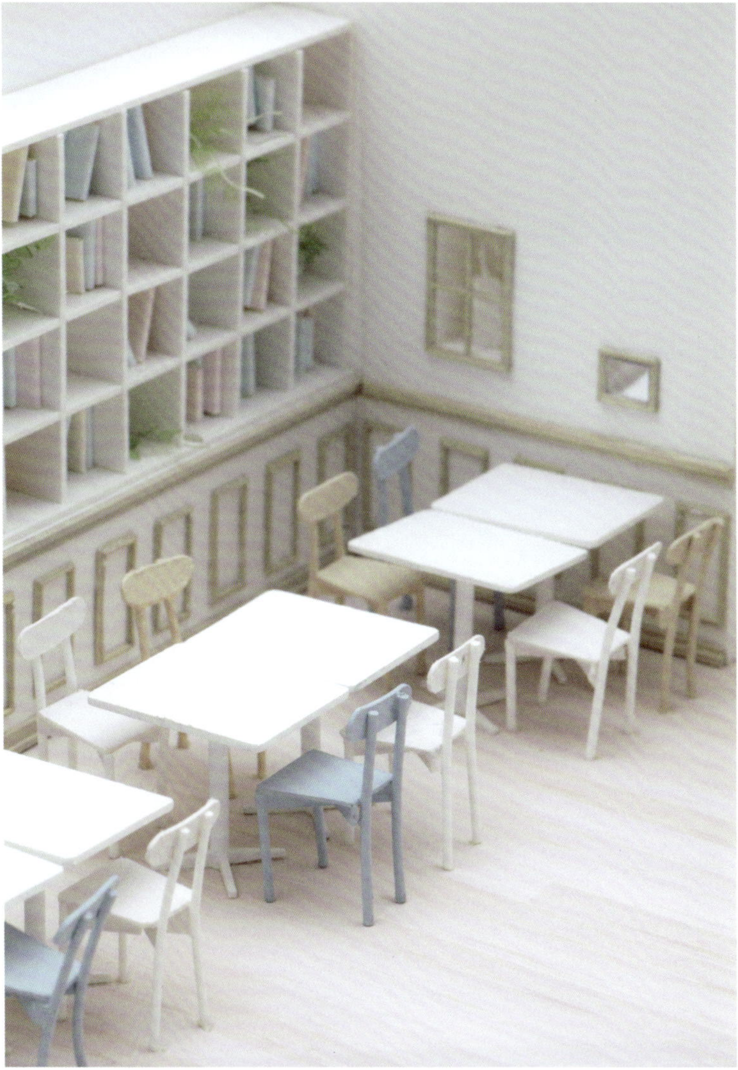

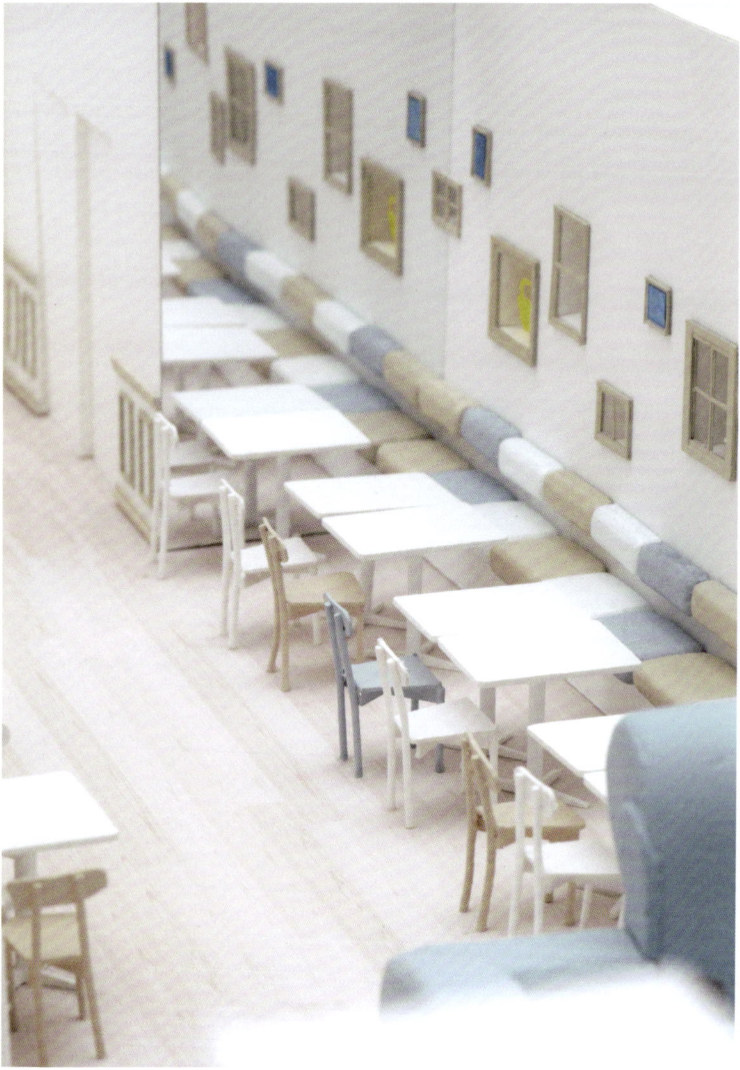

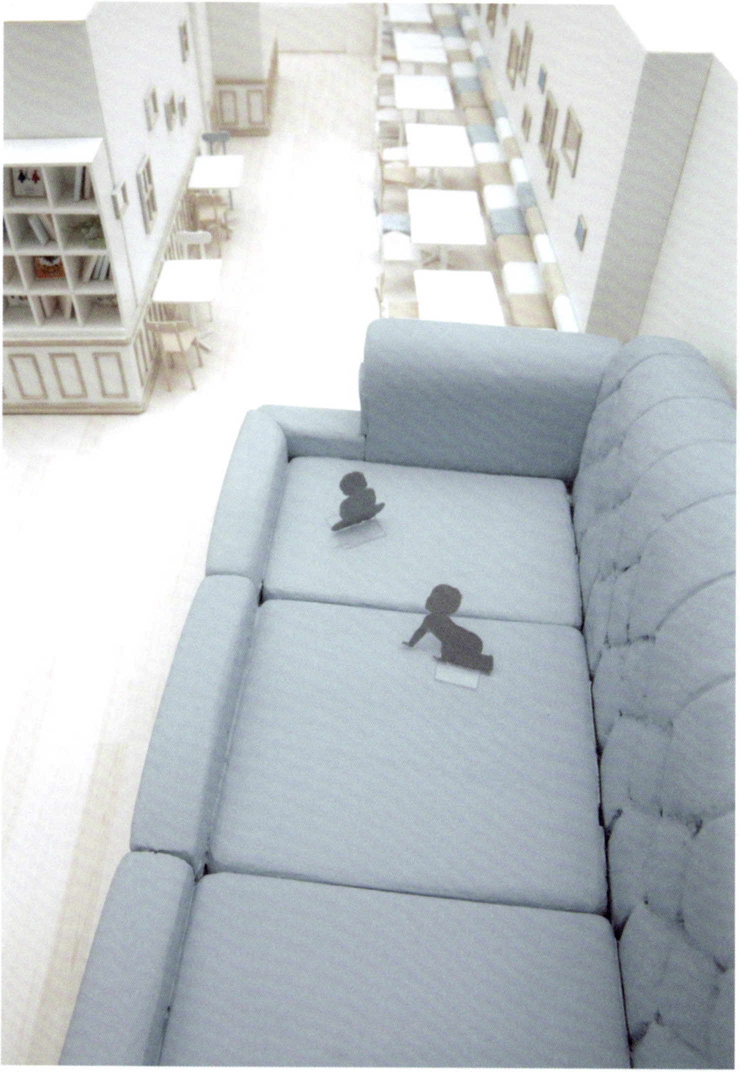

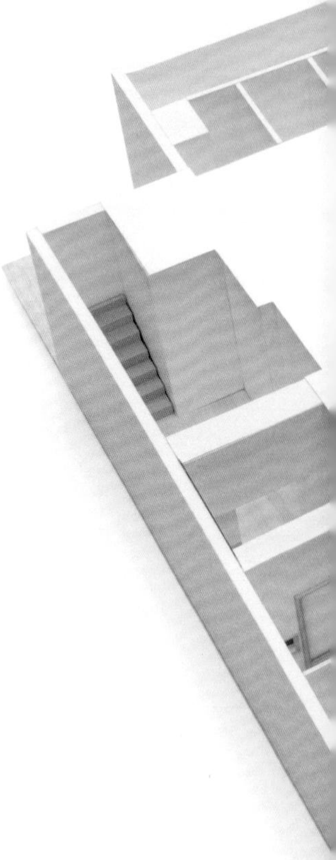

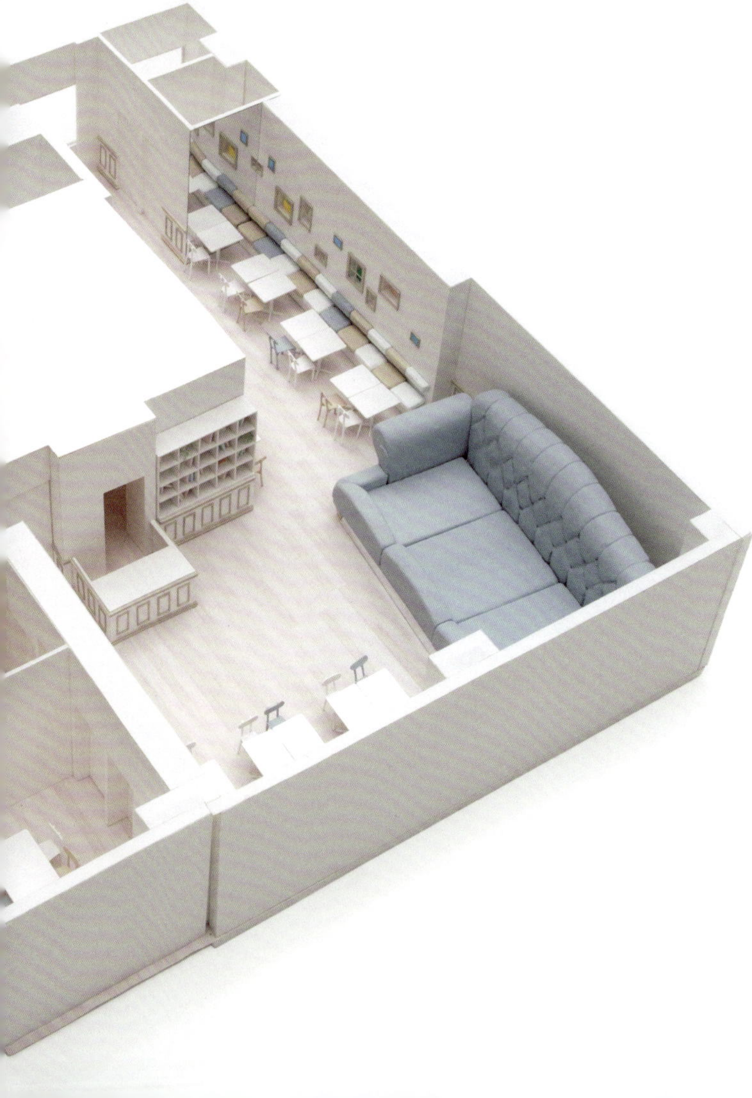

Yii exhibition

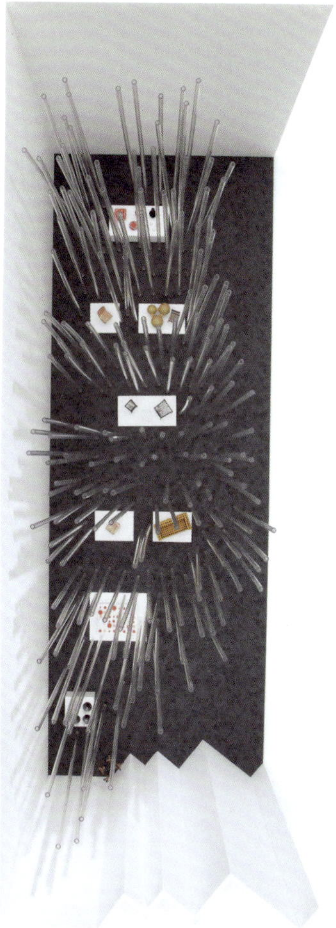

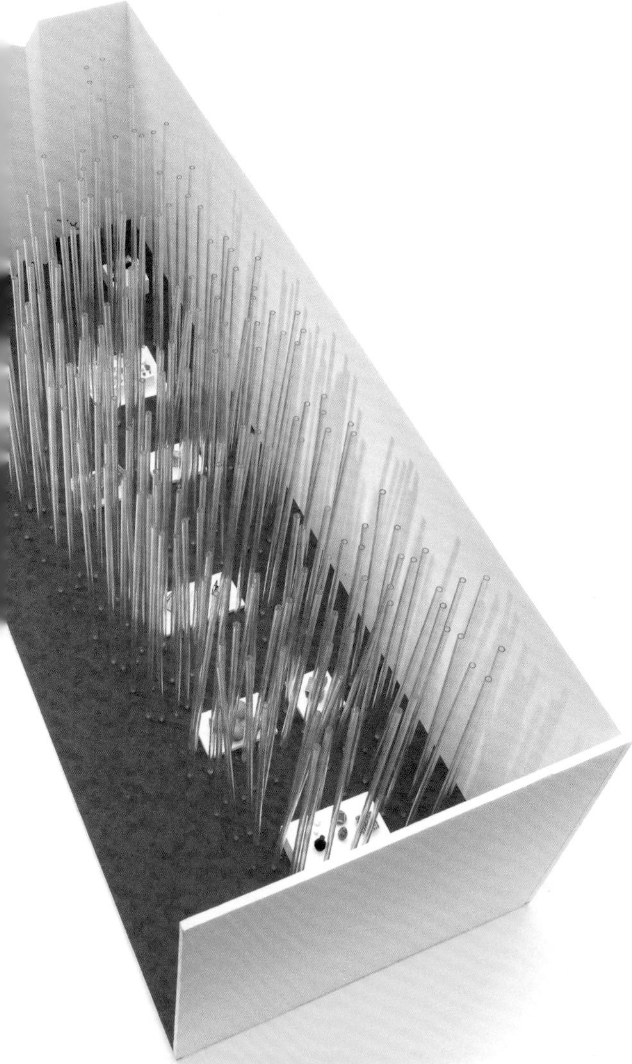

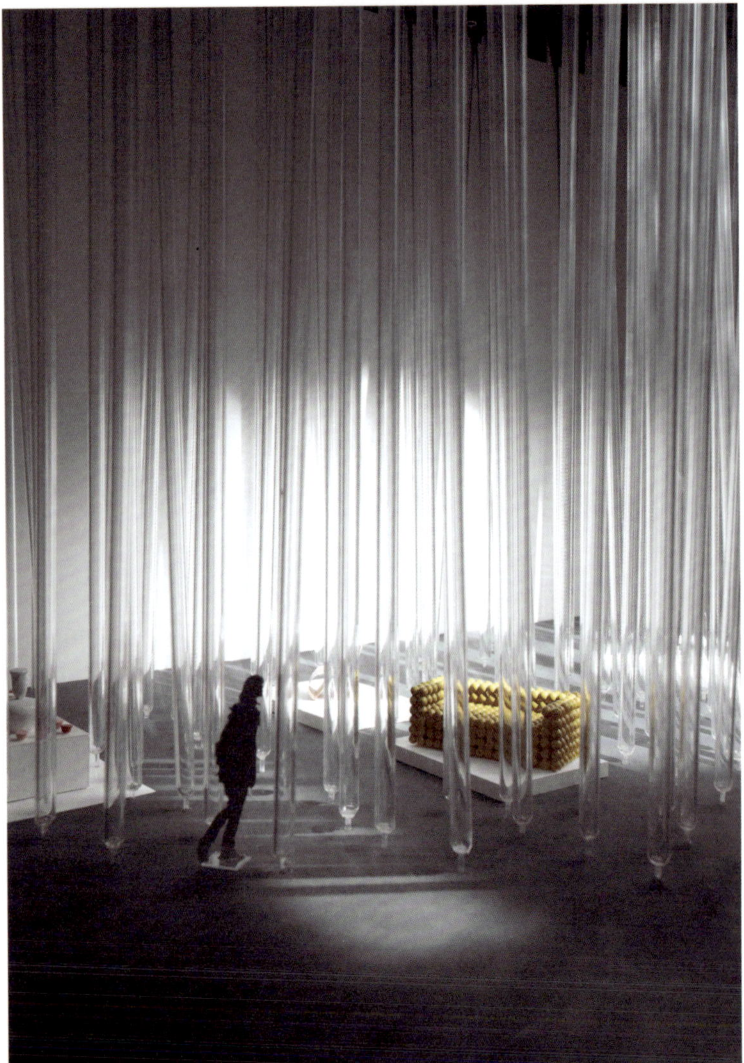

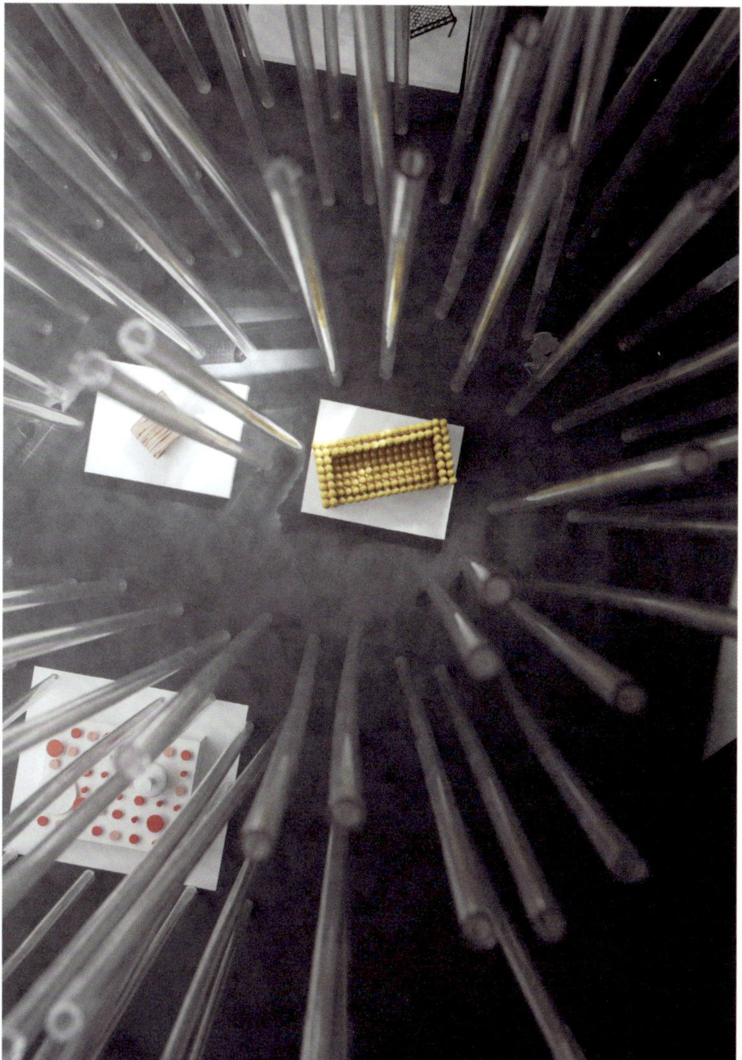

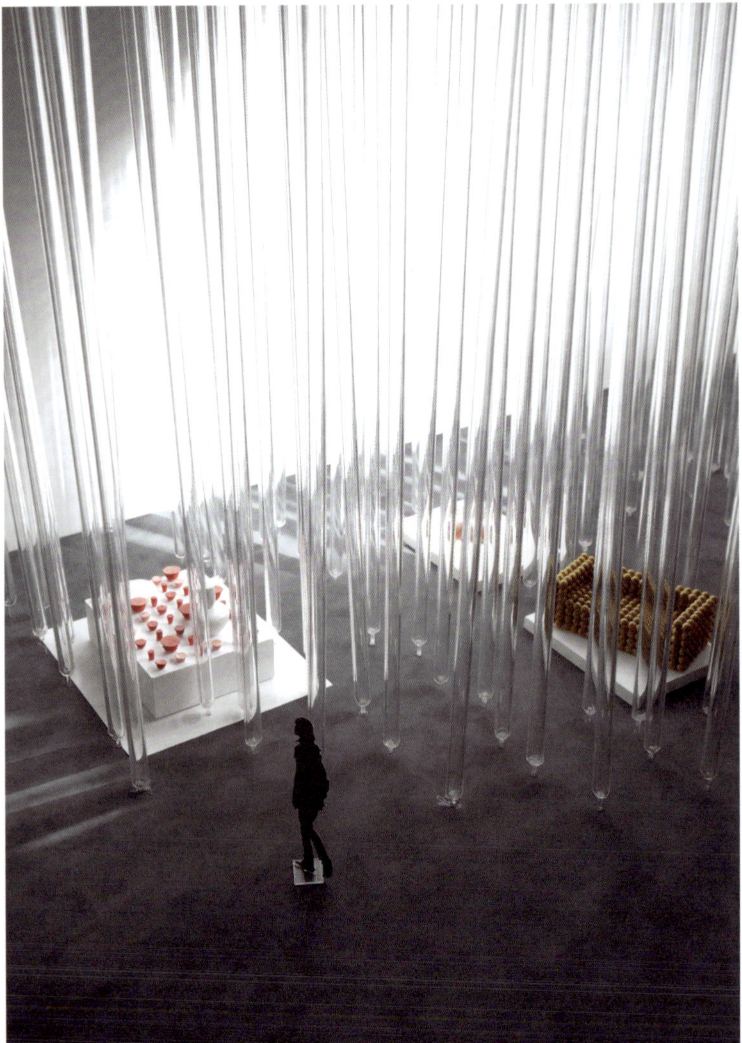

Yii exhibition

1% products@IFFT

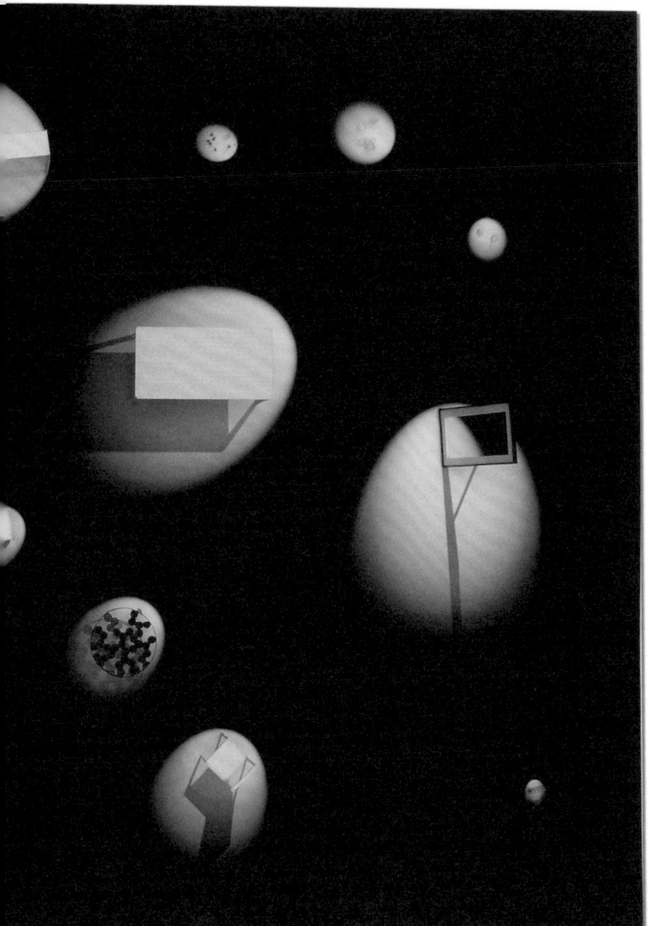

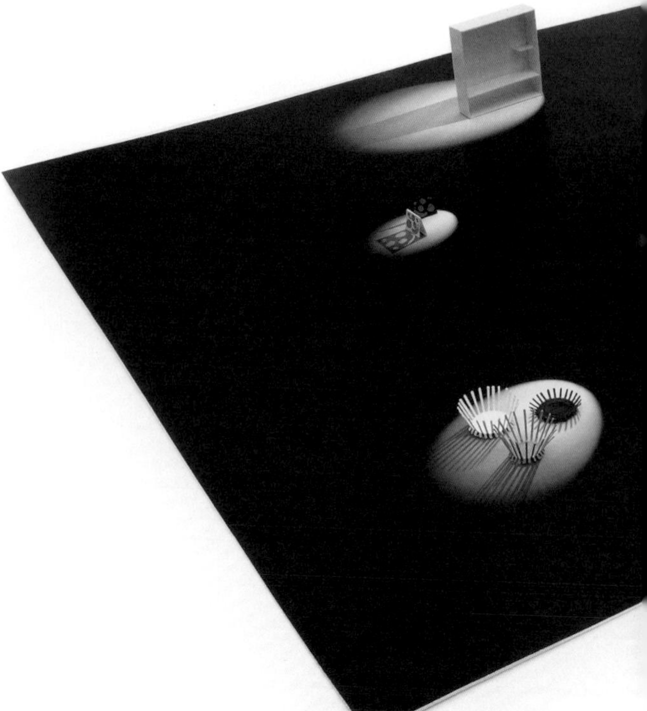

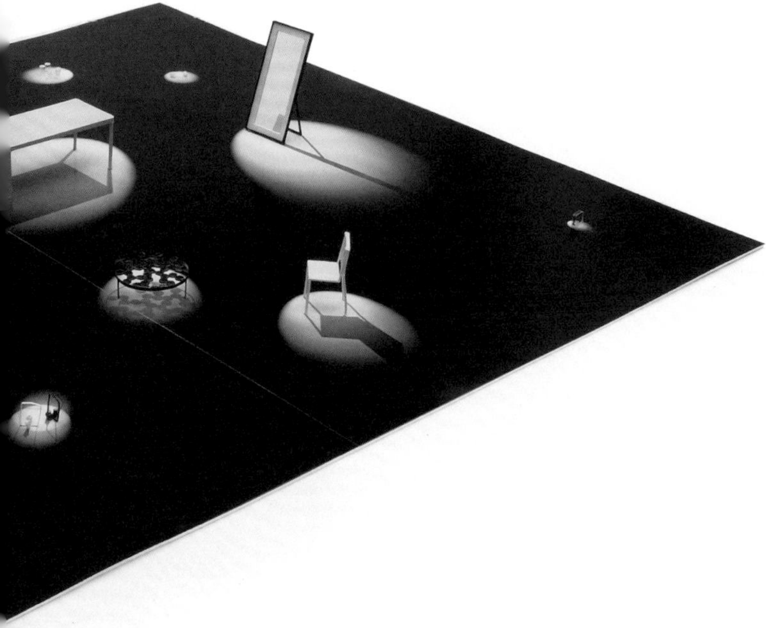

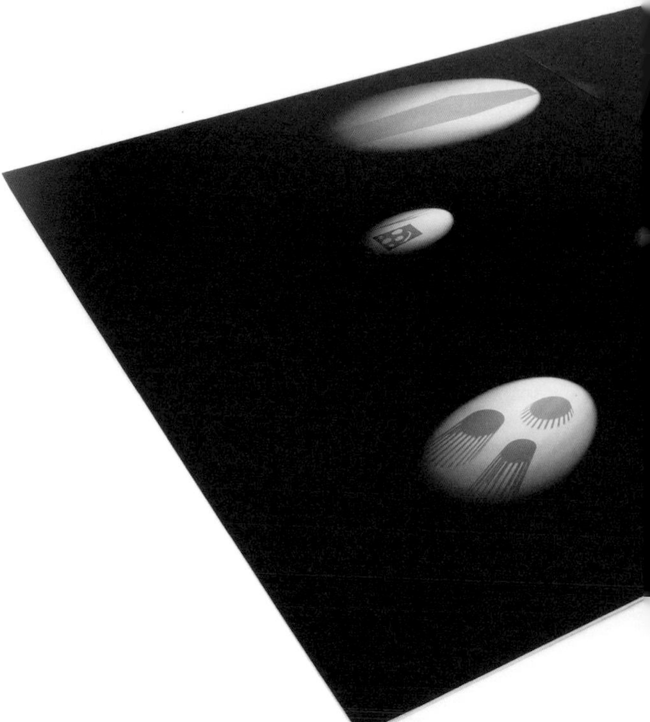

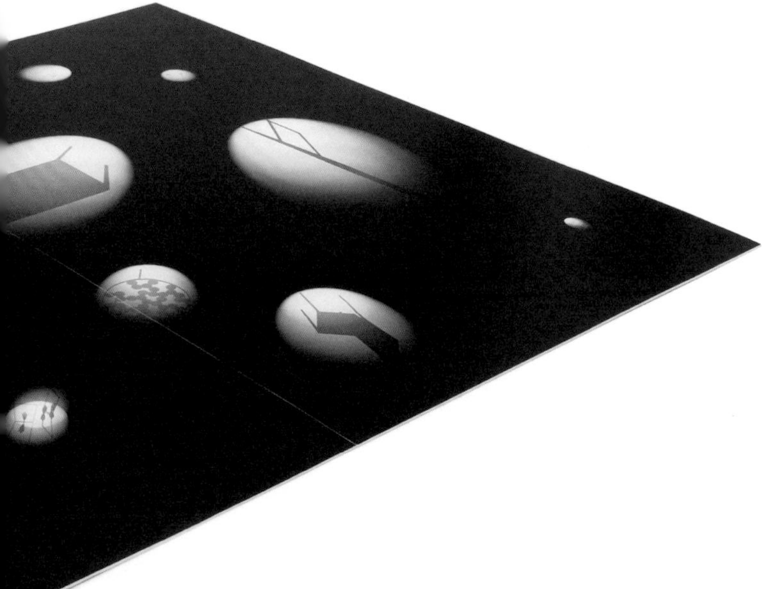

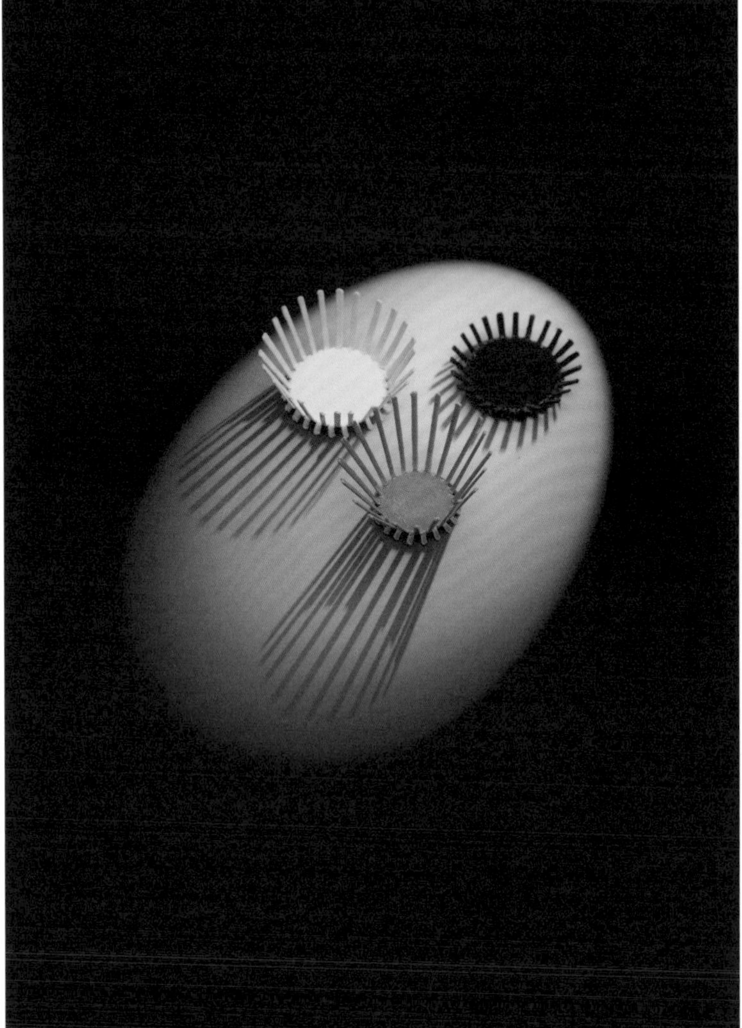

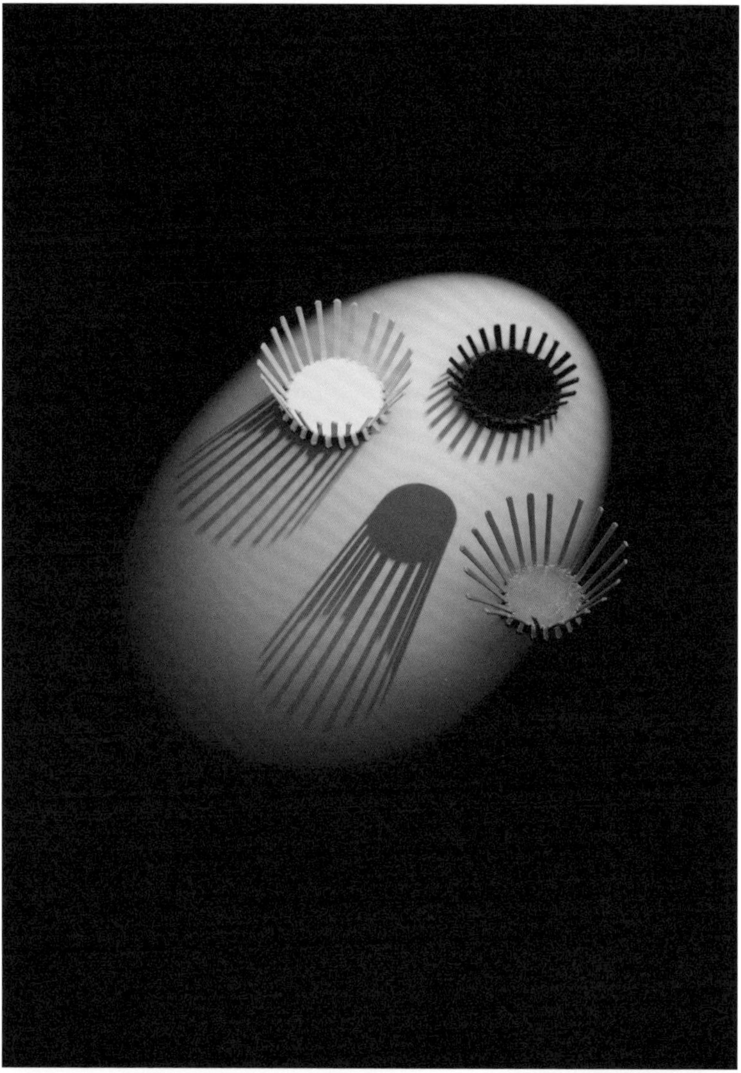

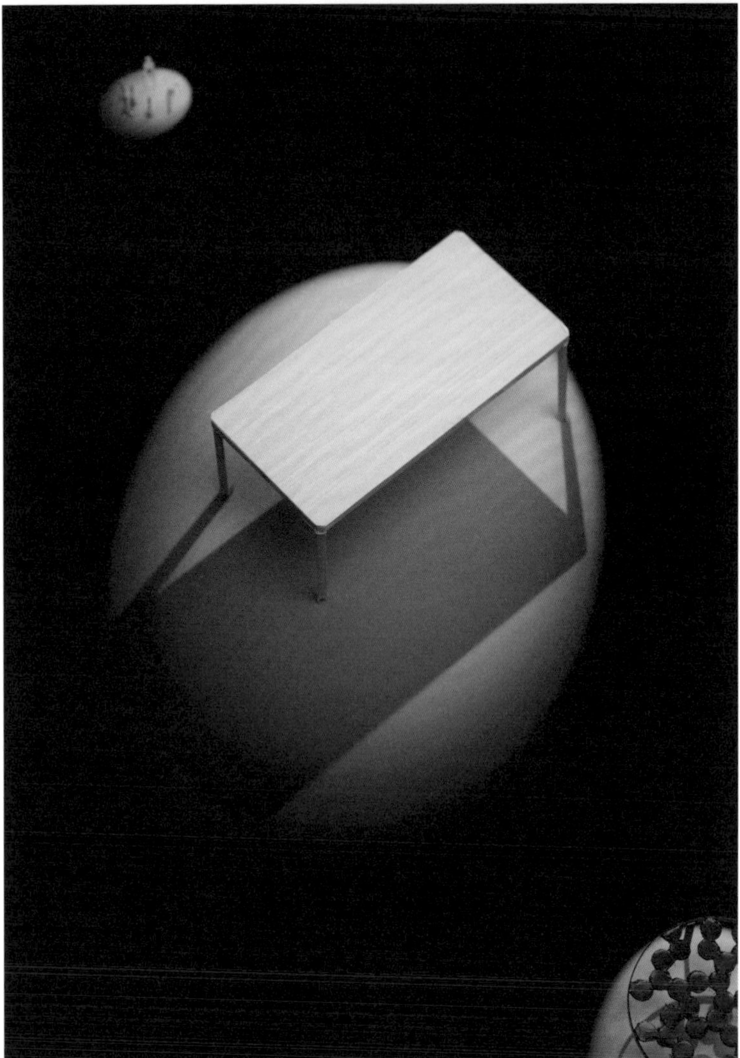

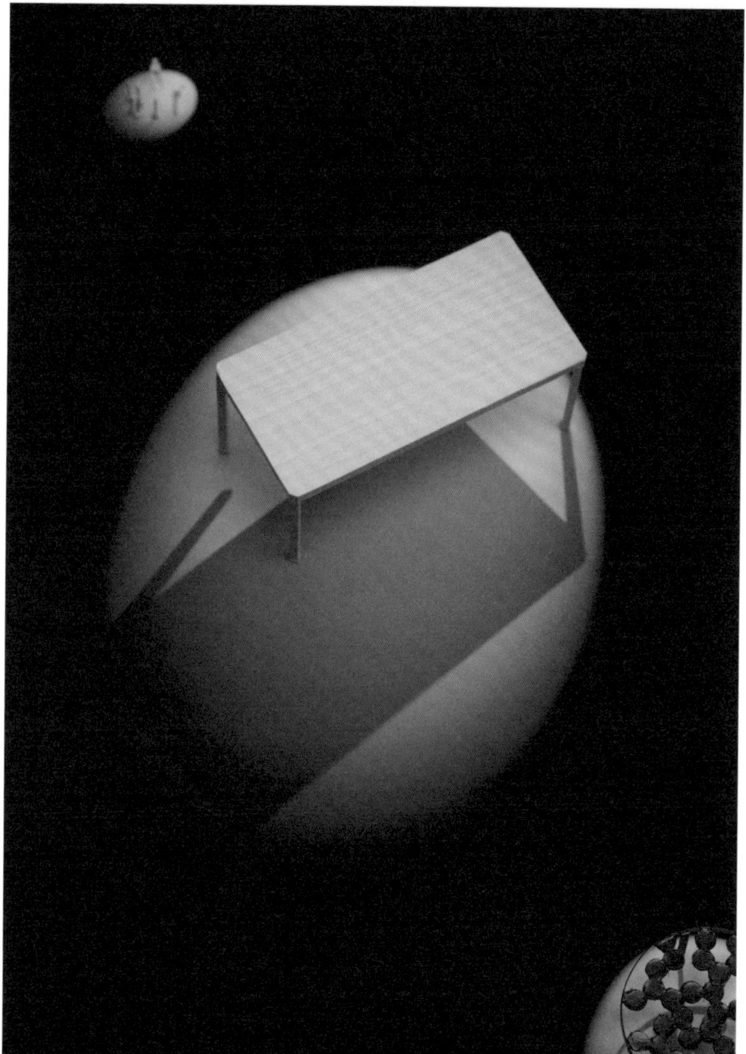

1% products@Interior Lifestyle

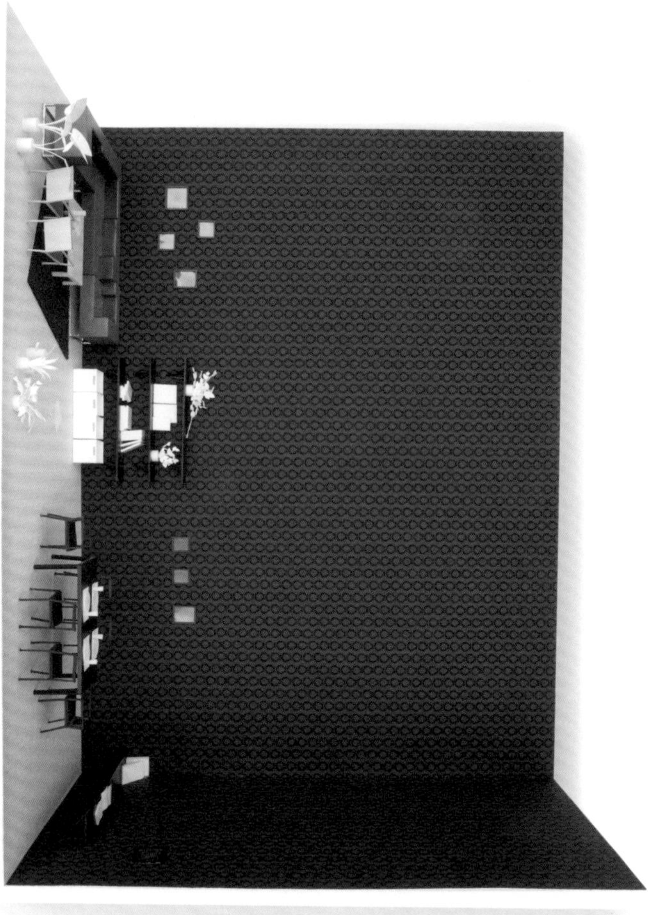

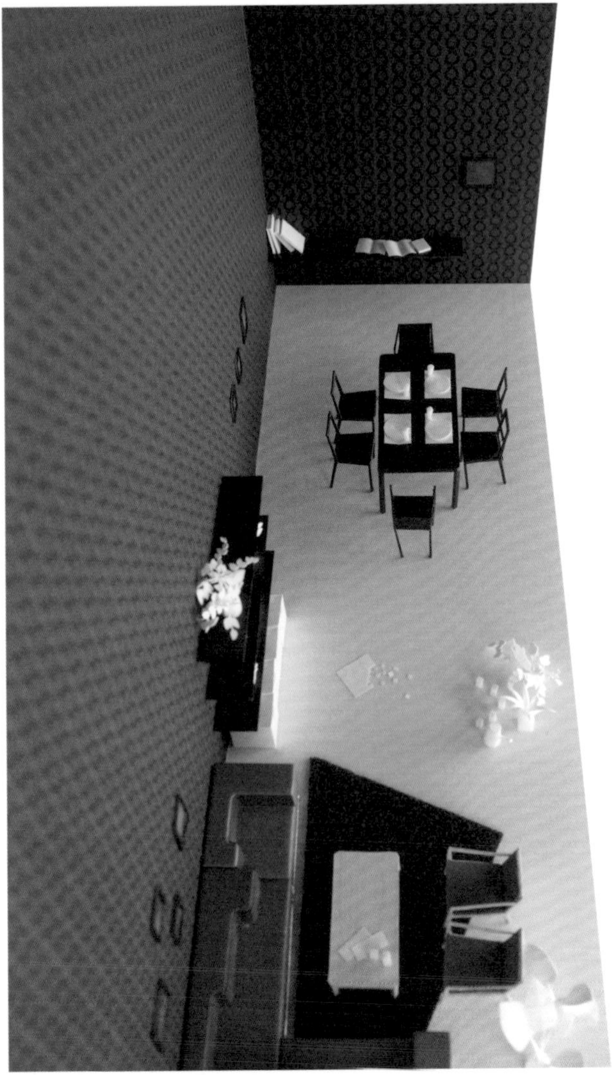

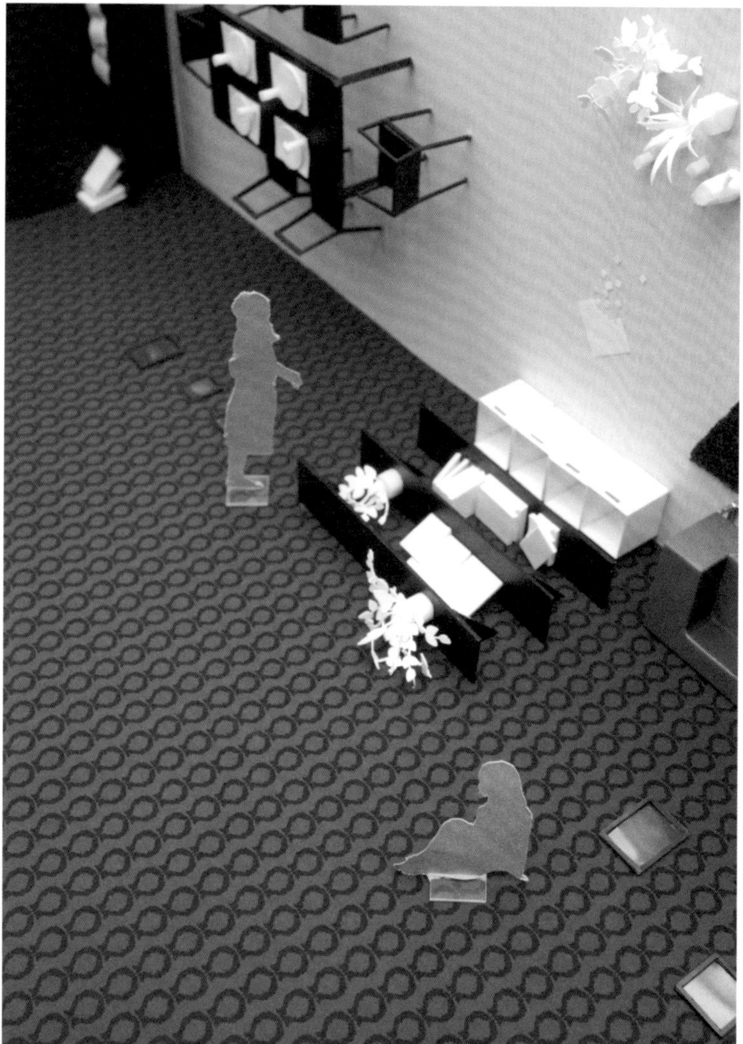

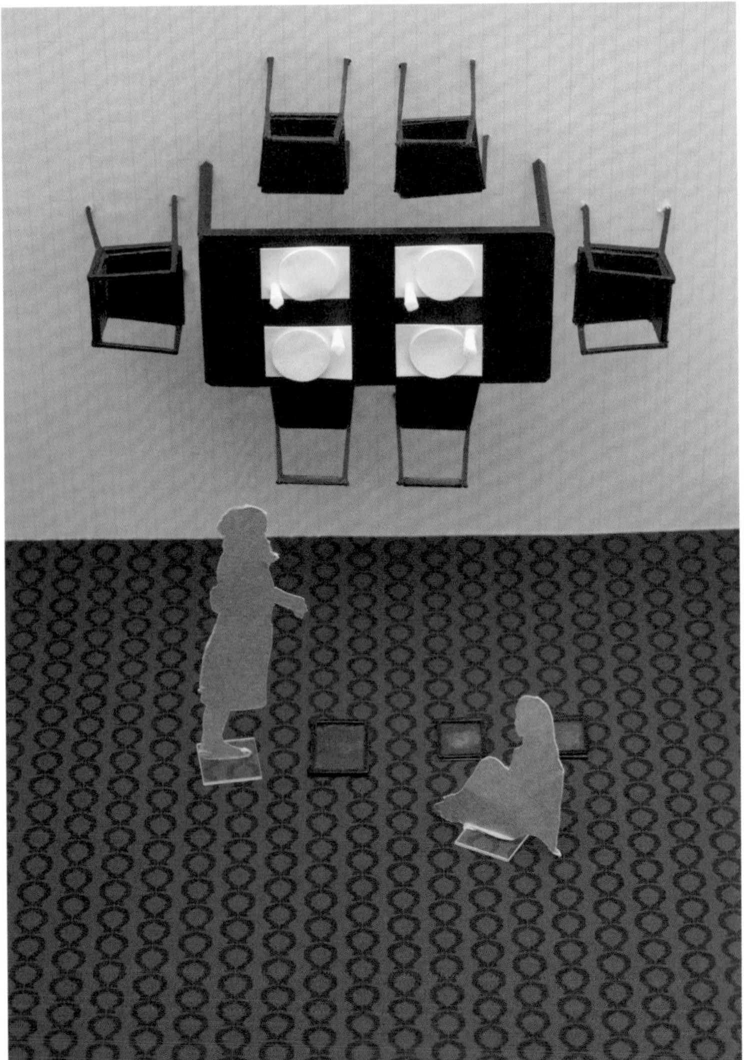

1% products@Interior Lifestyle

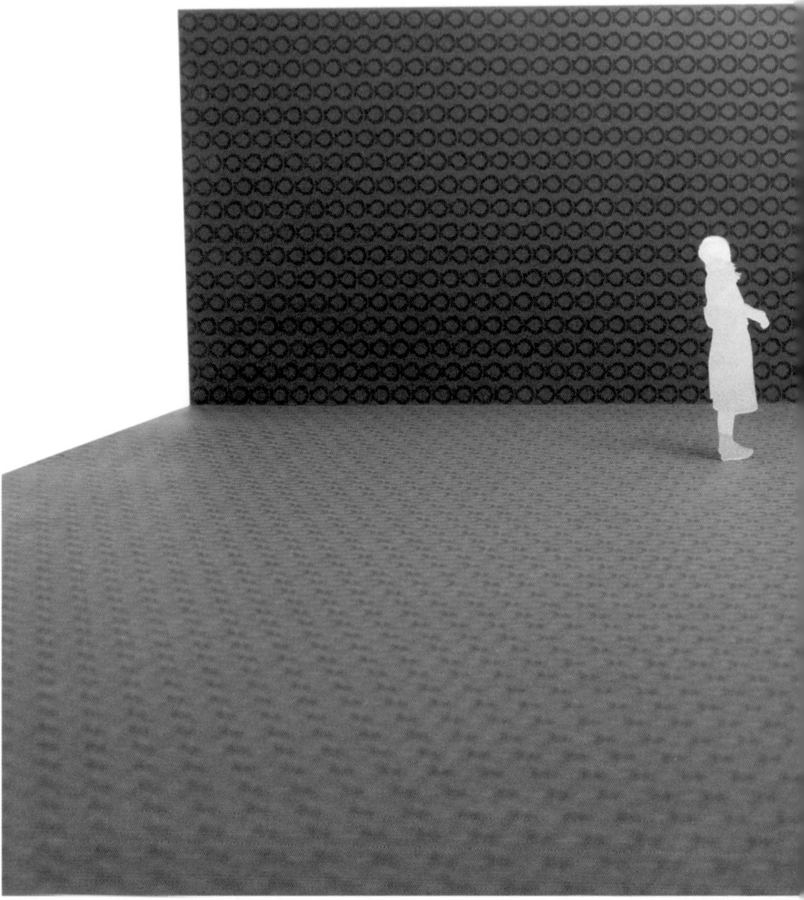

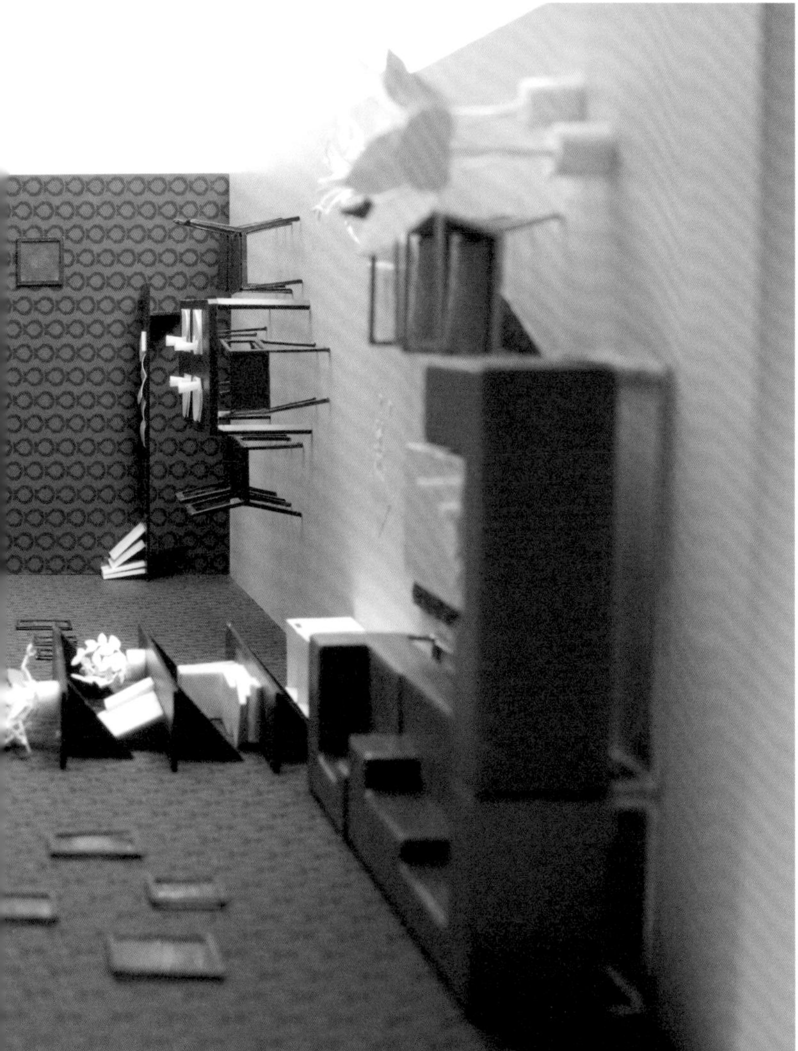

24 ISSEY MIYAKE

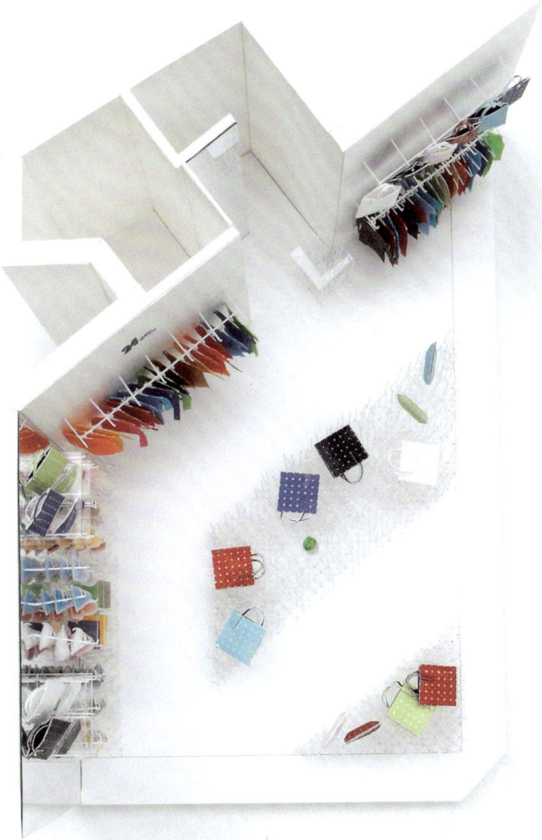

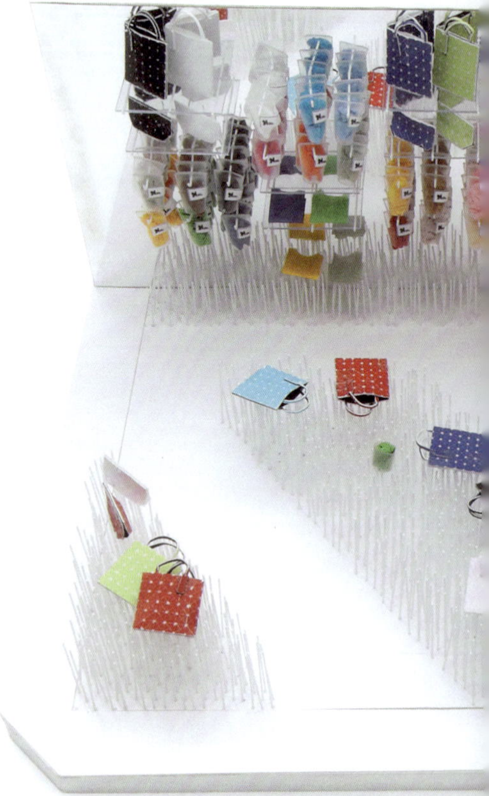

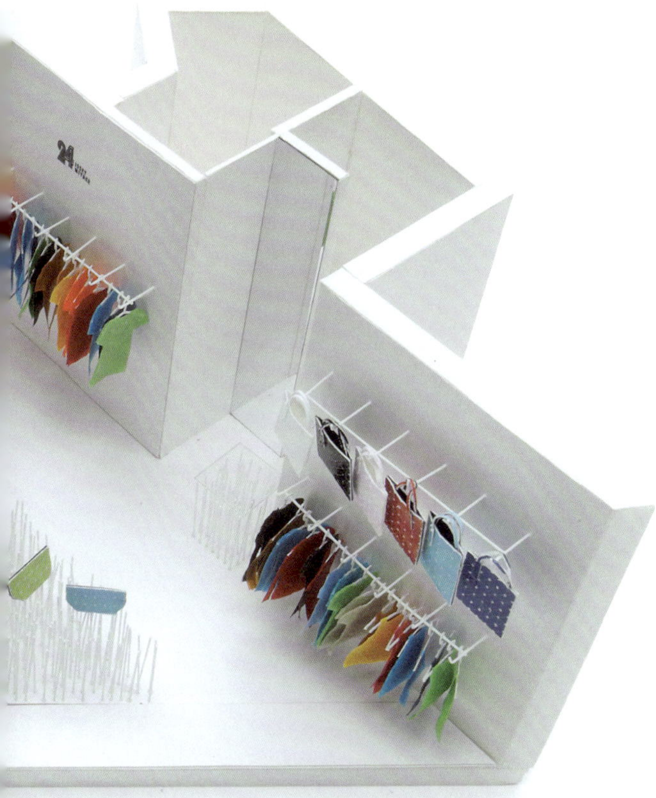

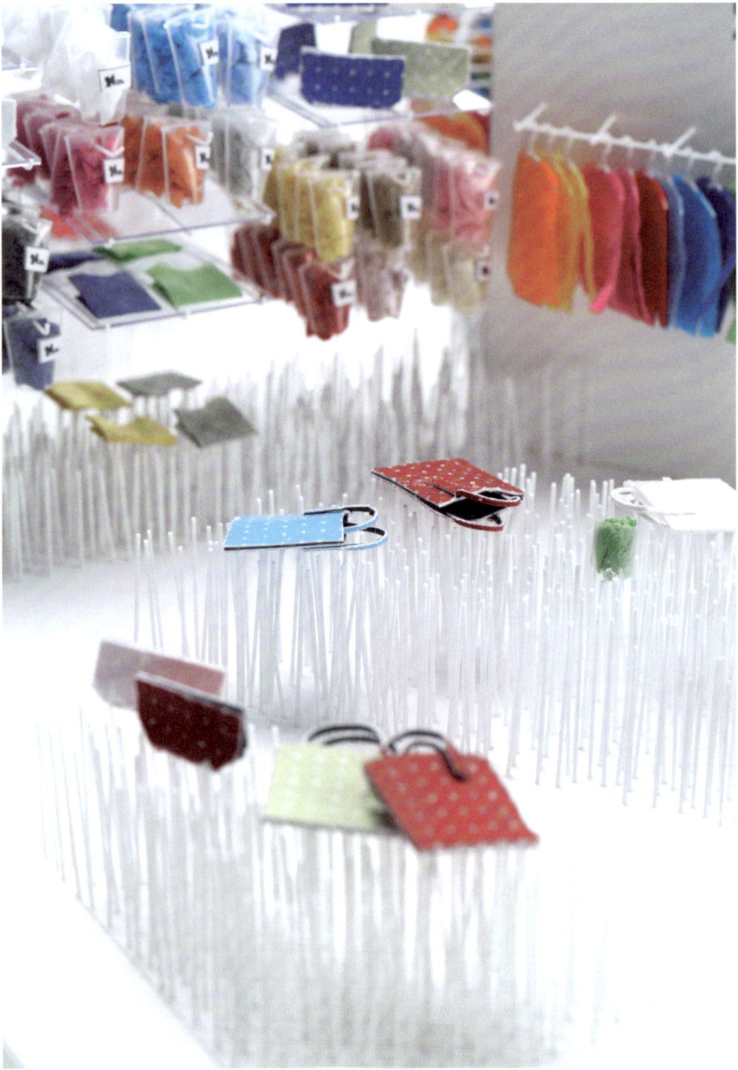

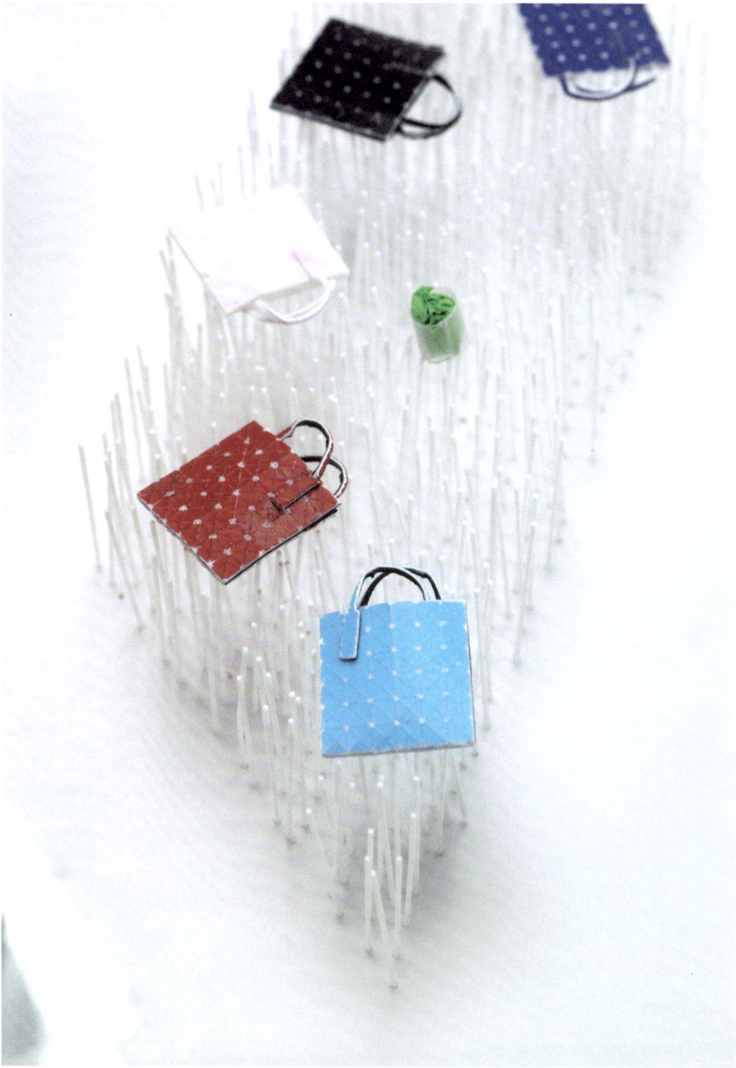

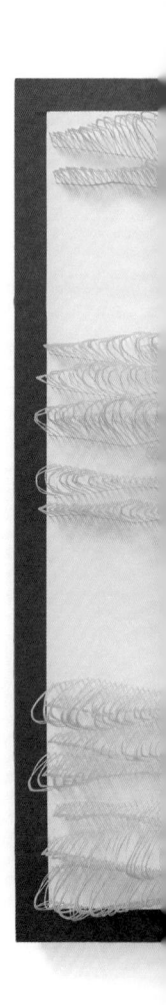

80 sheets of mountains

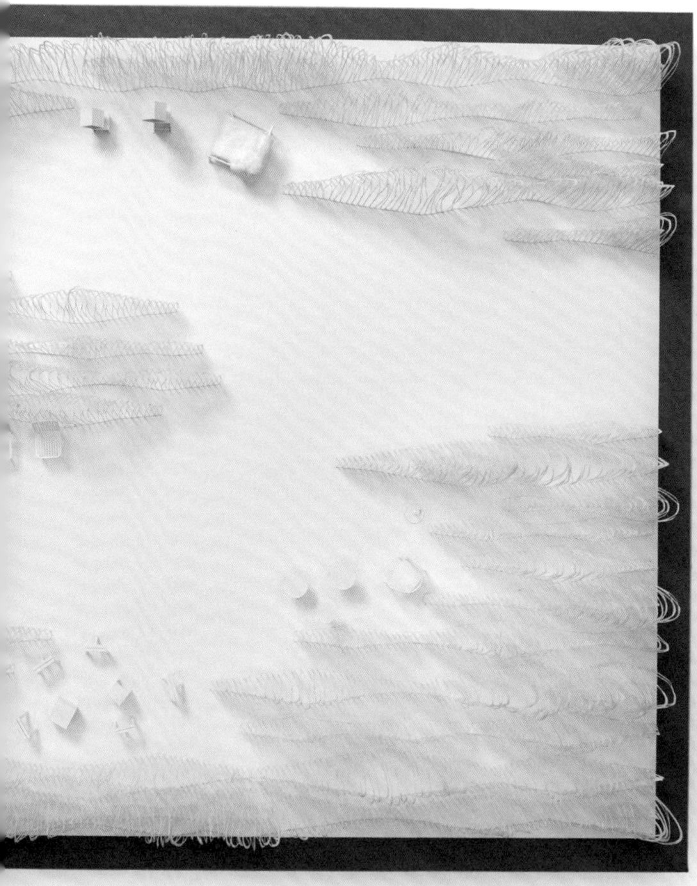

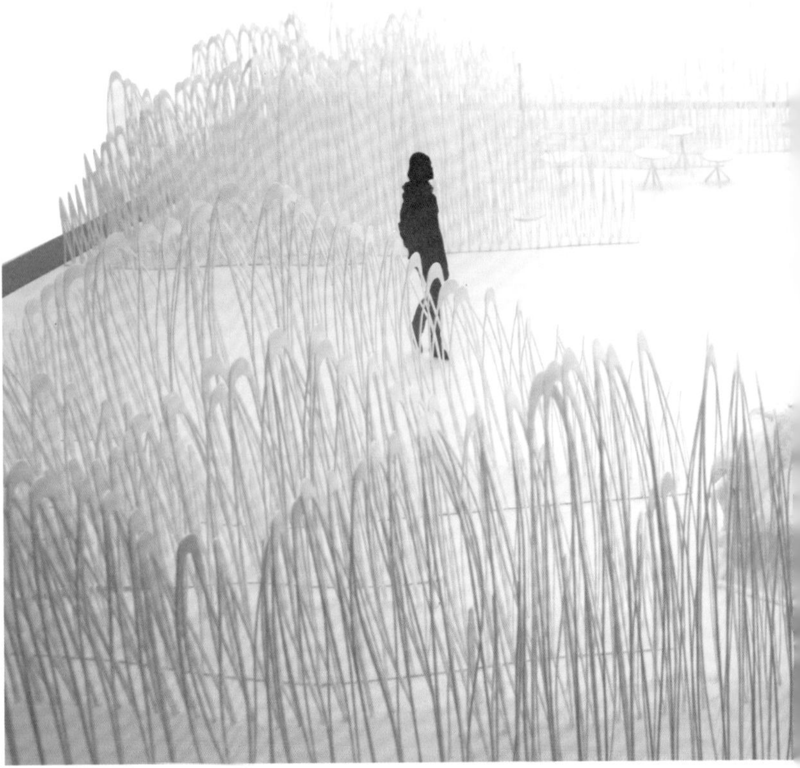

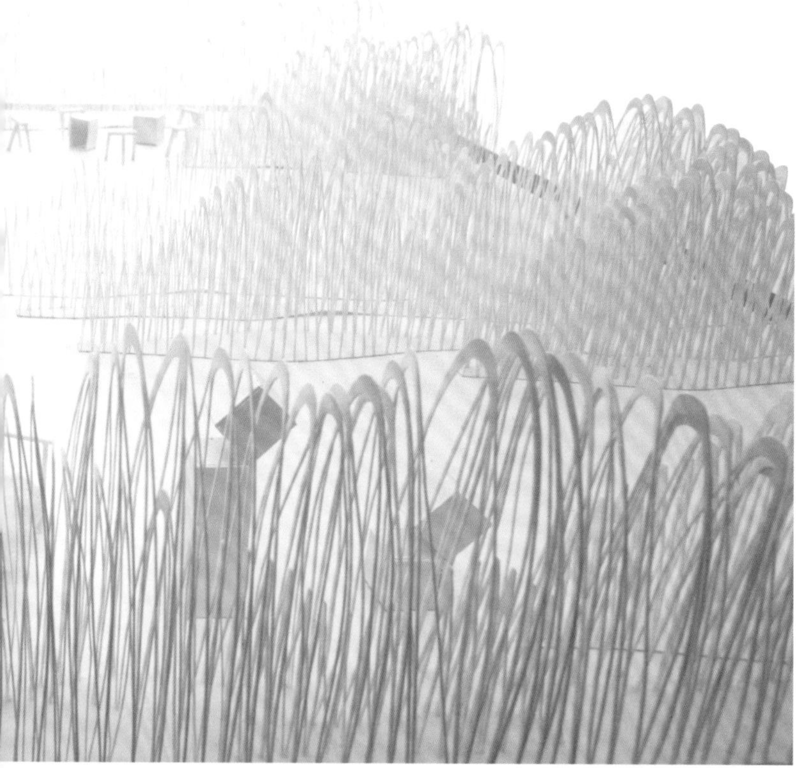

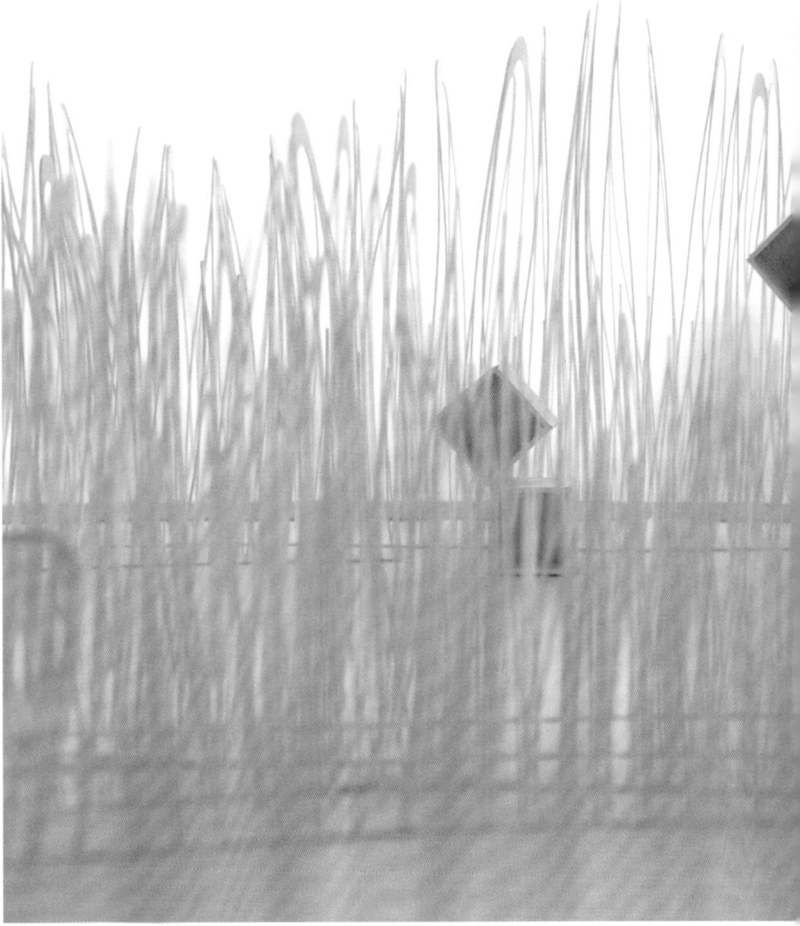

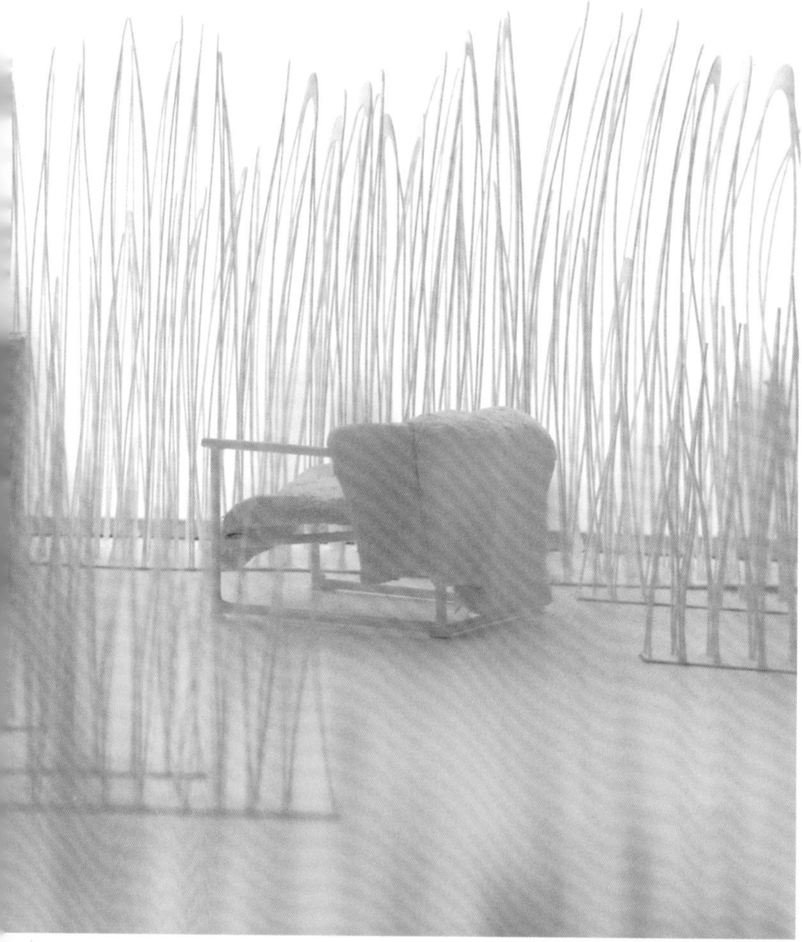

494 495

80 sheets of mountains

Index of models

Alice's Tea Party
pp. 10-17
Cafe | Lipton | Tokyo | 2006.07
model size 220 x 430 x 90 mm

Alice's Tea Party was held at Ozone Living Design Center in Tokyo, to celebrate the 100th anniversary of Lipton, English tea brand, for having a presence in Japan. We designed the cafe, inspired by the Mad Hatter's Tea Party in Alice in Wonderland. The installation changes in its scale, just like Alice gets bigger after eating cake. You feel you get bigger on some chairs, and you feel smaller on other chairs, hanging your feet over the chair.

紅茶ブランドLiptonの日本来航100周年を記念して東京・新宿で開催されたイベントで「不思議の国のアリス」に登場するティーパーティーをモチーフにしたカフェをデザインした。ずらりと並んだ椅子と長テーブルは遠近法に従って歪ませてあり、壁紙のパターンも同様に歪んでいることで、吸い込まれるように長く感じる空間に。体を押し込むようにしないと座れないくらい自分の体が「拡大」したり、座ると足が地面に着かずにブラブラするほど「縮小」したり、まるでケーキを食べたアリスのように身体スケールが変化していく。

ASOBIO Channel One
pp. 18-31
Shop | ASOBIO
Shanghai | 2009.06
model size
610 x 1680 x 120 mm
630 x 2580 x 130 mm

The first street-level store of ASOBIO, a fashion brand. The design concept of this shop was "focus". In two layered space, monotone photographs appeared on the floors and walls. They vary in size and gradation, which conjure up an effect of photography. Zoomed or defocused by the effect of the photographs, the space gives us a sense of depth and continuity, and thus transformation. In this way, we aimed to project an image that products are clearly focused and highlighted.

ASOBIO初の路面店。2層のゆったりとした店舗のテーマは「フォーカス」。壁や床にモノトーンの写真を配置し、そのサイズやボカシ加減を変えることで、カメラで撮影するときに拡大縮小する「ズーム」や、焦点が合わない「ピンぼけ」状態を擬似的に発生させた。それにより、空間の奥行き感や連続感を活かしながらも変化を与え、さらに、商品に「ピントが合っている」ような印象を与えて、商品を際立たせることを目指した。

ASOBIO Cloud Nine

pp. 32-39
Shop | ASOBIO | Shanghai | 2008.11
model size 600 x 430 x 110 mm

ASOBIO, a fashion brand based in Italy, opened its first flagship shop in Shanghai. The theme of the store was "reflecting yourself". Two types of mirrors were placed on the walls: "real/true mirrors" which people look themselves in, and "false mirrors" through which people can pass physically. In this way, products can be categorized for display by product type, without making the space seem smaller. With two kinds of mirrors, the space seems more spacious, creating continuity between sections. We aimed for shoppers to feel as though they're wandered into "another shop" that's hidden behind the walls.

イタリア発ファッションブランドASOBIOの中国初の旗艦店。店舗のテーマは「自分自身を映す」であることから、壁面に｜本物の鏡｜と、人が通ることが可能な｜偽物の鏡｜を組み合わせて配置することで、性質の異なる商品群を緩やかに区別した。2種類の鏡を使い分けることで、視覚的な広がりや連続性、壁の裏に隠れた「もうひとつの店舗」を散策するような空間体験を意図した。

BEIGE,
pp. 40-51
Shop | Onward | Tokyo | 2011.11
model size 420 x 270 x 120 mm

The shop design for BEIGE, women's fashion brand. The concept and name of the brand were inspired by a natural color of fabric, representing the philosophy of offering simple and functional designs. This philosophy was introduced to the design concept of the shop. Ordinary materials were used simply, still offering high functionality. Materials were reinterpreted and reshuffled, considering how they were related. This playfulness further enhanced an effect of various materials.

素材の「素の色」を意味する「BEIGE」をコンセプトにしたファッションブランドの店舗。
シンプルで機能的、しかもさり気ない遊び心で素材の魅力を引き出している商品ラインアップの考え方を、
そのまま店舗デザインに置換することを考えた。「C型鋼」「壁面」「カーテン」というありきたりの素材を
シンプルに扱いながらも高い機能性をもたせ、「関係性のシャッフル」というさりげない遊び心によって
素材の魅力を充分に引き出すこととなった。

bird-apartment
pp. 52-57
Treehouse | Ando Momofuku Center
Nagano | 2012.09
model size 200 x 200 x 300 mm

A tree house designed for the Ando Momofuku Center. This facility was built to promote outdoor & nature experiences. On one side of the tree house has 78 bird nests, on the other side has an entrance so that we can look at the nests from inside of the tree house. Our treehouse is collective housing for many birds and one person.

自然体験活動の普及と活性化を目的とした施設「安藤百福センター」のためにつくられたツリーハウス。長野県小諸市の森林の中に位置し、片面には鳥小屋78軒分が集中し、反対側から人が中に入ることで鳥小屋の内部が観察できるようになっている。「たくさんの鳥たち」と「一人の人間」がともに過ごすための小さな「集合住宅」。

Camper New York

pp. 58-67
Shop | Camper | New York | 2013.04
model size 470 x 560 x 160 mm

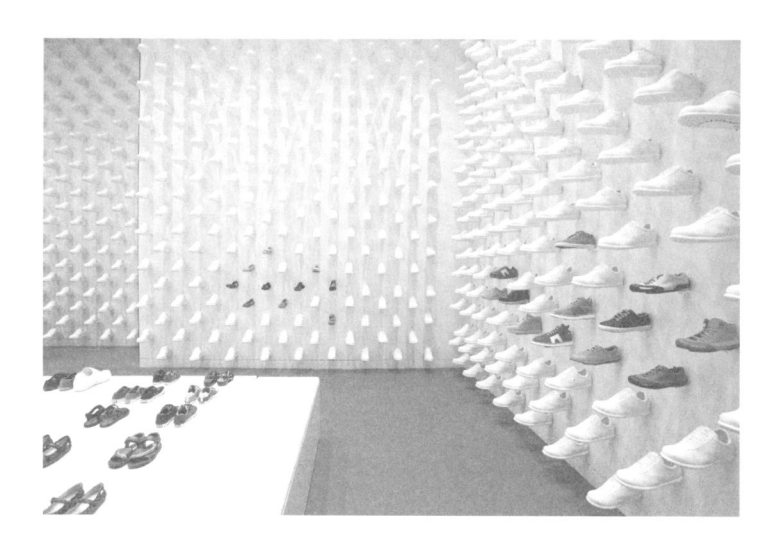

Index of models

The new design concept for Camper's large-scale store. In this large store,
the challenge is how to deal with empty upper space with high ceiling.
Our new approach was to produce a lot of pairs of "Pelotas", Camper's regular shoes,
made of white resin. Shoes are placed on the wall in the whole space.
This creates a sense of volume, space and order which conjures up a large storehouse.

Camperの大型店舗用デザインコンセプト。天井が高い既存の大型店では、カンペールの店舗の特徴である
「商品によるボリューム感」が出せないという課題があった。そこで、カンペールの定番商品「Pelotas」を
白い樹脂で大量に成型し、空間全体の壁面を覆うことによって、まるで「倉庫」のような整然とした雰囲気と
ボリューム感を空間に与えた。

Camper Paris

pp. 68-77
Shop | Camper | Paris | 2012.07
model size 580 x 230 x 130 mm

Camper shoes aren't for athletes trying to run faster or for people in search of a status symbol. They are made to simply enhance "the pleasure of walking". The shop displays shelves that conceptualize this, with thin pipes that run up from the floor to prop up the shoes, which appear to be floating freely in the air. A slow motion effect is created by slightly varying the angle of each mounted "foot print". The rest of the playfully designed Camper shop features various suspended shoes that seem to be taking an enjoyable stroll in the air.

Camperの靴は、アスリートが速く走るためのものでも、ステータスとして身に付けるものでもなく、純粋に「歩くことの楽しみ」を与えてくれる存在だと考え、靴が浮遊しながら自由に空間内を歩き回っているような店をデザインした。陳列された商品もまた、床から細いパイプで持ち上げられた「足跡」によって浮いているように見え、さらに、場所ごとにこの足跡の角度を徐々に変化させることで、上に乗った靴がスローモーションで歩いているかのような感覚が生まれた。

CATALOG Beijing

pp. 78-89
Shop | Swire | Beijing | 2011.12
model size 490 x 750 x 150 mm

The store's name, CATALOG, is a reflection of its philosophy: treat athletic wear brands with different outlooks equally, and actively assist customers with coordinating items from different brands. We wanted to recreate the characteristics and attraction of a catalogue in our store design. We "copy-pasted" the store windows over and over again, creating a spatial experience reminiscent of flipping through the pages of a catalogue. The result was a design in which the entire store became a series of show windows and every product was on display.

スニーカーを中心とした、スポーツファッションのセレクトショップ。世界観の異なる複数のブランドを
等価に扱い、コーディネート提案をしていくスタンスが、まさにショップ名の「カタログ」のようであることから、
「カタログ」の特性や魅力をそのまま空間に還元したいと考えた。店舗の「顔」となるショーウインドウを
何重にもコピー＆ペーストし続けることで、ばらばらとページをめくりながら読み進むような空間体験とともに、
「全てがショーウインドウ」となり、「全ての商品が主役」となるようなインテリアデザインが生まれた。

COMPOLUX

pp. 90-101
Shop | Seibu Shibuya | Tokyo | 2013.10
model size 560 x 660 x 130 mm

The ladies' apparel floor of Seibu Department Store, Tokyo. The ladies' apparel department must achieve consistency in the environment where multiple brands join but are loosely separated. Our design was inspired by wrought iron fences that surrounds the parks and squares in European cities. To be used as hanger racks, screens that look like the fence were suspended from the ceiling. The screens were easy to relocate, with built-in lighting for illuminating clothes. Came in six different patterns, they gave each brand a distinctive look.

西武渋谷店の婦人服売場及び共用部分のデザイン。複数ブランドが緩やかに区別された統一環境が求められた。また、什器の可変性も必須条件であった。そこで、ヨーロッパの公園を囲っている「フェンス」をスクリーンとして天井から吊るし、ハンガーラックとした。6種の「フェンス」をブランド毎に使い分け、「フェンス」は自由に移動させることができ、洋服を照らす照明も内蔵した。床はピータイルを複数種類カットしミックスして「石畳」のような貼り方をし、試着室の壁面は6色の「ツタ」で仕上げた。これらにより、まるで公園の中を自由に歩き回るような気持ち良さが生まれた。

Established & Sons@LDF
pp. 102-109
Installation | Established & Sons
London | 2011.09
model size 510 x 390 x 190 mm

Installation designed for Established & Sons, on exhibit in the British design company's showroom during the London Design Festival. The collection's theme was "My London", so we took 15,000 maps of London neighborhoods printed onto tracing paper and pasted them onto the walls, creating a design that conjures images of that characteristic phenomenon, the London Fog. The installation embodied the many small, personal memories of London that come together to form the dynamic and ambiguous face of the city.

英国の家具ブランド Established & Sons がロンドンデザインフェスティバル期間中にショールームで行った展示のデザイン。発表されたコレクションのテーマが「MY LONDON」であったため、ロンドン市内の地図を印刷したトレーシングペーパーを壁一面に約 15,000 枚貼ることで、ロンドンの特徴的な自然現象である「霧」を想起させるデザインにしたいと考えた。それは、一人一人がこの街に対して個別に抱く小さな想いが集積され、その結果として生まれる流動的で曖昧な「都市の表情」を体現するものとなった。

ghost stories 2nd chapter
pp. 110-117
Installation
Museum of Arts and Design
New York | 2009.10 - 2010.01
model size 500 x 800 x 140 mm

The design for the exhibition held at the Museum of Arts and Design in New York. Long rectangular windows run around the walls and ceiling of the gallery. Our decision was to avoid building any walls, so that visitors can enjoy viewing the windows and the light that change as time passes. The items, along with the sample of each production process, were placed on the gallery's white stands, which were surrounded with small, 5mm white stickers put on the floor. This created a gradation effect, as if the stand and the space had melted together, and became a larger object.

ニューヨークの美術館で行われた展覧会。展覧会場にはスリット状の窓が壁や天井に張り巡らされていた。それによって空間内に射し込む刻一刻と変わる光を、あえて壁で遮蔽しないことにした。 家具とその製作過程を示すサンプルの数々は既存の白い台に置くことになったが、これらの台の周辺の床に直径5mmの円形の白色シールを手で貼ることで、台と空間がグラデーション状に溶け合うような効果を生み出し、空間の特性を活かしながらも、作品の存在を一層引き立てる結果となった。

HALSUIT
pp. 118-135
Shop | Haruyama | Okayama | 2011.11
model size 1600 x 580 x 190, 600 x 400 x 740 mm

Index of models

The concept of mens' suit volume retailer, Haruyama. The fitting rooms are moved to the center of the store, which are surrounded with showcases. In the showcases, there are many different ways of coordinating suits. At the back of the fitting room, customers can take a seat and relax at the counter, reading a magazine or watching TV. The store exterior is created with louvers in two colors, which change the store impression depending on which directions the store is viewed from.

スーツ量販店の「ワークスタイルを楽しむ」というコンセプトを表現。フィッティングルームを店舗の中央に配置、その外周部はショーケースに。背面は同伴者がくつろげるように雑誌やテレビなどのあるカウンター席に。その周辺に小物やアクセサリー類を置き、ここを「拠点」にしてイメージを膨らませ買い物を楽しむことを意図した。主なスーツ着用シーンである「オフィス」にあわせて、照明に「デスクランプ」を、壁面には「オフィス用収納」をイメージした棚、ポスターの代わりに「液晶モニター」を、会計は「受付」で、「ラウンジ」や「会議室」のような空間も用意し、コンセプトを体現できる空間にした。外観は2色のルーバー仕上げで、道路の進行方向により店舗の印象が変化する。

Hermès wandering forest

pp. 136-143
Window display | Hermès
Tokyo, Yokohama | 2012.03
model size
330 x 90 x 210 mm
330 x 90 x 210 mm
330 x 90 x 210 mm
260 x 80 x 210 mm
260 x 80 x 210 mm
140 x 80 x 210 mm

Window displays designed for Hermès boutiques in Yokohama and Tokyo.
Looking closely at tools placed between the trees, tools are placed between the trees,
or divided by the trees. Tool at the front of the window disappear into the forest,
only to appear again from behind the tree, at the back of the display.
This creates a mysterious feeling. Depending on the angles, people would unexpectedly
feel a sense of inconsistency, contradiction and depth in the trees.
This shows our interpretation of Hermès and its playfulness.

エルメスのそごう横浜店と高島屋日本橋店のウインドウディスプレイ。木々の間に置かれているツールは、
よく見ると木の内部に入り込んでいたり、木と木の間で分断されていたり。さらに一部が奥にある木の後ろから
覗いていたり。「図と地を反転させる」ように作られた木々はそれぞれわずかに異なる色味や明るさで仕上げ、
ツールの形状も遠近法に従って歪ませることで、見る角度によって「矛盾」や「奥行き感」が突然立ち現れるような
不思議な感覚が生まれた。それはエルメスの遊び心への自分たちなりの解釈となった。

HIRATA NO BOSHI

pp. 144-153
Installation | Spiral Gallery
Tokyo | 2011.06.15 – 07.03
model size 610 x 2100 x 250 mm

Mr. Akio Hirata, an internationally famous hat designer, held the exhibition to show his 70 yeas of creative works. The mass-produced non-woven fabric hats are the antithesis of Hirata's carefully handmade hats. In contrast with these 4,000 hats, Hirata's hats stood out, with distinctive definition. The space with hats seemed as though they had been shrouded in a cloud, inviting people to come and see inside. Walking as they wish, they can enjoy finding and watching Hirata's creation.

国際的帽子デザイナー・平田暁夫氏の70年に及ぶ創作の歴史を凝縮した国内初の大規模な展覧会「ヒラタノボウシ」の会場デザイン。平田氏が手掛ける帽子が一点一点「手作り」であることから、あえて真逆の要素である「量産」された不織布の帽子を約4,000個使って空間をつくることで、平田氏の帽子がより際立ち、より活き活きと見えるように考えた。帽子によって満たされた空間は、まるで「雲」に覆われたようで、緩やかに来場者を内部に誘導し、自由に歩き回りながら作品を発見していくような展示環境となった。

hitogaki

pp. 154-161
Installation | Elle Decor | Tokyo | 2012.12
model size 570 x 800 x 160 mm

The design for the exhibition, the Elle Deco International Design Awards Japan.
Instead of separating the awarded works by 13 categories with stands and walls, they were
loosely divided with 60 human shaped panels. Where "people" gather, it's an exhibition
space. Where people do not gather, it's an aisle. Since "people" surround the display,
other people can not get a good view of them. People end up having to get closer
to watch over "people" out of curiosity.

Elle Deco International Design Awards Japanの展示デザイン。13部門の受賞作品をそれぞれ
展示台や壁で切り離すのではなく、「人型」に切り抜いた60体のパネル状の「人垣」によって 緩やかに仕切る
ことを考えた。人が集まるところは展示室に、そうではない場所は通路になった。離れた場所からは
「人垣」によって作品がよく見えないため、来場者は自然と近くまで吸い寄せられ、肩越しに鑑賞する。
まるで路上パフォーマンスを楽しむ時のような「興味を喚起する」デザインが生まれた。

ILLOIHA OMOTESANDO

pp. 162–169
Fitness club | ILLOIHA
Tokyo | 2006.12
model size 330 x 330 x 330 mm

Index of models

The interior design of a fitness club. The club is located at the second basement floor of the building. We chose to design and create a "rock-climbing" wall, utilizing two story hall, in order to represent the original brand concept of this club, "Let's do some exercise, let's be more healthy and beautiful". The idea was to use interior design elements such as tables, picture frames, bird cages, and even hard-to-find holds and unusually shaped finger grips. This makes the wall much tougher to tackle, than a regular, rough climbing wall.

フィットネスジムのインテリアデザイン。2層分の吹抜けに注目し、この空間ならではの機能を活かして「カラダを動かすことでキレイになる」というブランドコンセプトを表現するため、「ロッククライミング」ができる壁面装飾を施すことにした。これまでの無骨なクライミングウォールではなく、テーブルや額縁、鳥かごや花瓶などのインテリアの要素で構成し、機能面でも新しい提案になった。この競技に馴染みのない人への興味のキッカケとなり、より身近で新しいフィットネスのスタイルとなることを願った。

INDULGI
pp. 170-181
Shop | INDULGI | Kyoto | 2011.11
model size 330 x 1180 x 160 mm

This small clothing store situated in Kyoto, has a narrow entrance way that opens to reveal a wider interior. While some may favor an open kind of layout, this shop was designed with nooks and crannies on purpose, to produce a space that can never be seen in its entirety with a single glance. Its numerous doors and strong walls pique customers' curiosity, and are effective in enticing them to look for the neatly presented products, which seem to appear and disappear from view. Their experience of the shop changes as they move about it.

京都市の小さなアパレルショップ。間口が狭く奥行きのある「見通しの良い」空間であったため、あえて遮蔽物を加え、立つ位置により新たな要素が見え隠れする「全体が見渡せない」場所となることを考えた。「扉」を追加し、開き加減によって視線の遮蔽加減をコントロールした。「本当の扉」と「そうではない扉」が入り混じった不思議な状況が生まれ、ひとつの扉を開けたときの驚きと、また次の扉を開けたくなる好奇心を喚起する場所となった。

International KOGEI Triennale
pp. 182–195
Installation | Kanazawa City | Kanazawa | 2010.05–06
model size 2050 x 760 x 120 mm

The Rifare venue in Kanazawa, Japan was formerly the location of a large bookstore. Its temporary use as an exhibition venue necessitated that the furnishings be left more or less intact, and that no drastic changes be made to the interior. While working within a limited budget, we also needed to secure ample space for pieces selected by five curators. We decided that we would set up five pre-fabricated agricultural greenhouses made of plastic within the venue space and turn them into individual gallery spaces.

「工芸的ネットワーク」をテーマに金沢リファーレで開催された展覧会。5人のキュレーターが選定した作品のためのデザイン。書店であった居抜き物件を、手を加えず展覧会場とすることが求められた。限られた予算ながら、各キューレータに独立した空間を確保する必要があったので、既製品の農業用ビニールハウスを5つ設置し、それぞれをギャラリースペースとして使用した。金沢という特異な「土壌」から育ち、発展する工芸の姿を表すのに適した環境となった。

International KOGEI Triennale Pre-event

pp. 196–201
Installation | 21st Century Museum | Kanazawa | 2009.10
model size 870 x 910 x 160 mm

Design for an exhibition at the 21st Century Museum of Contemporary Art in Kanazawa, Japan. Object materials ranged widely and a variety of techniques were used in their creation. For the exhibition design, we chose the opposite strategy. Small, mass-produced home-use greenhouses give a sense of order to the space and provide visitors with a linear perspective from which to view the exhibition, allowing the rich variety of the objects to stand out. The greenhouses are made of glass, each with its own shelving and lighting. They are inexpensive, easily assembled with only a screwdriver and can be broken down and stored after the exhibition. This not only eliminates nearly all waste from the exhibition fixtures, but also allows for possible reuse.

金沢21世紀美術館で開催された工芸展の会場デザイン。作品は、ガラス、木、陶器、金属、布など、素材、技法、大きさがさまざまであることから、逆に空間は大量生産された均質な「観葉植物用温室」を展示ケースとして転用し整然と配置することで、鑑賞者はフラットな視点で全体を見渡すことができ、作品の多様性を際立たせることを考えた。温室は、全面ガラス張りで、棚板や照明用配線などが全てセットされ、しかも安価なため、限られた予算に収めることができ、また、1日で施工を完了できた。会期後の廃棄物も少なく、その後の再利用が可能となった。工芸の発展を願う気持ちと植物の成長を重ね合せた空間表現である。

JAPAN: Tradition. Innovation.
pp. 202–213
Installation | Canadian Museum of Civilization
Ottawa | 2011.05 – 10
model size 1830 x 780 x 180 mm

Exhibition design for "JAPAN: Tradition. Innovation." at the Canadian Museum of Civilization. The exhibition explores the relationship between Japanese culture and design. We decided to use "roofs" in a variety of sizes and heights to demarcate the different exhibits. Graphics on the floor that resemble a subway map allow visitors to identify the different zones. Areas under larger, lower roofs feel closed, while the light that falls between the many smaller roofs creates a semi-outdoor feeling. Visitors look out into "outside spaces" from underneath the roofs and conversely peer back into "inside spaces" from outside, producing a hybrid space in which the relationship between inside and outside is in constant flux. The space is subtly and carefully divided using the ancient Japanese concepts of "ma" and "shikiri" to define unseen spaces.

カナダ国立文明博物館の会場デザイン。交通、ロボット技術、社会的地位、消費文化、娯楽という５つのゾーンで日本文化とデザインの関わりを読み解く展示内容。970㎡の展示空間に壁を立てず、大小の屋根を異なる高さで空中に浮かべた。各ゾーンは「地下鉄の路線図」を模したグラフィックで床を色分けした。低い大屋根の下は「閉じた」空間に、複数の小屋根の下は隙間からの木漏れ日のような光で「半屋外」のような領域に。
屋根の下から「屋外の展示品を見る」、外から「屋内の展示品を覗き込む」といった内外の関係性が入れ替わる多様性のある空間となった。日本古来からある「間」や「仕切り」という「見えない領域を生み出す」手法で緩やかに空間を分節することを考えた。

karaoke-tub

pp. 214-217
Karaoke room | Tokyo | 2005.04
model size 100 x 150 x 190 mm

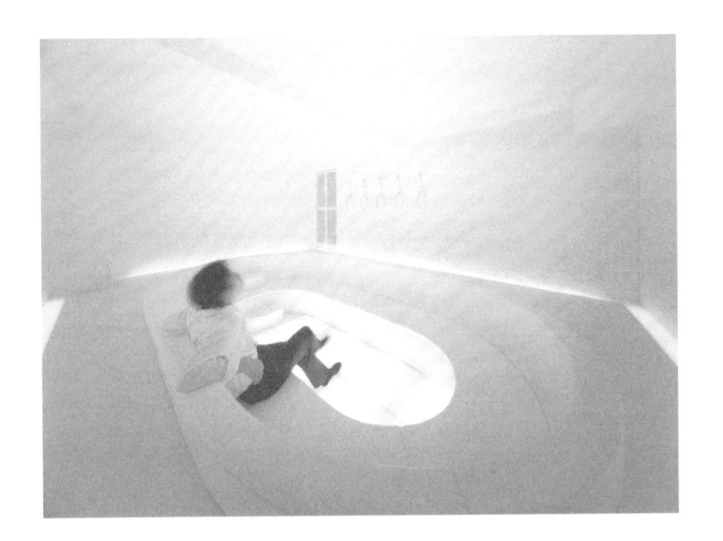

Karaoke-tub is inspired by the idea of singing in the bathroom. Open the folding door and step into the "bathroom", and you will find a bathtub like sofa. Sitting and singing side by side in a bathtub, people will feel relaxed and comfortably united. Showerheads are placed on the walls as coat hooks. Offering practicality, all the elements including floor tiles are just like a bathroom.

気持ちよく歌えるバスルームをイメージしたカラオケルーム。浴室の折戸を開けて中に入ると、肩を並べて座ることができる大きな浴槽のようなソファが低い位置に設置され、ゆったりとリラックスした感覚が使う人の一体感を高める。床のタイルや、コートハンガーとして使う壁面のシャワーヘッドもバスルームの雰囲気でありながらカラオケルームの機能の一部とした。

kisala

pp. 218–225
Restaurant | kisala | Tokyo | 2007.06
model size 950 x 540 x 200 mm

The restaurant is composed of four areas: Japanese food, Western food, a cigar bar, and a private dining room. We gave each space a different feel by varying the tone of the floorboards, and gradually increased the brightness of the floorboards to connect the space. With equal subtlety, the spaces for the cigar bar and private dining area are defined by lace curtains, and mirrored panels give discrete spaces the feeling of being connected. Textiles with colors chosen to match the tones of the floorboards enhance the sense of texture.

和食カウンター、洋食カウンター、シガーバー、個室という4つの異なる空間によるレストラン。部屋ごとにフローリング材の色味を決めることで特徴をもたせ、4つの部屋の色をグラデーション状に変化させることで、緩やかな繋がりが生まれた。バーや個室はレースカーテンで柔らかく仕切り、離れた部屋の気配をそれとなく感じさせるように鏡を使用。また、壁面にはそれぞれの空間の色味に合わせたテキスタイルを使うことで質感を与えた。

MD.net Clinic

pp. 226-231
Mental health clinic | MD.net | Tokyo | 2009.12
model size 500 x 230 x 140 mm

Interior design for a mental health clinic. The doors that line the walls of the clinic
do not open, while seemingly ordinary parts of the walls open up into new spaces.
Consultation rooms are accessed by sliding the bookshelves sideways.
By providing alternate perspectives for viewing the world and avoiding being trapped
by preconceptions, the interior allows visitors and staff members to experience
the opening of new doors in their hearts, one after the other.

「マイナス」を「ゼロ」に治療するだけでなく、充実した「プラス」の生活へのきっかけ作りをしたい、という
オーナーの想いを空間で表現しようと考えた。整然と並ぶ扉は開かず、扉ではない場所を開けて診察室に入る。
通路の突き当たりの扉を開けると、そこに部屋はなく、一面が自然光の入る窓になっており、開け加減で
光を調節できる。本棚は横に動き、治療室が現れる。既成概念に捕われない別の視点を提供することで、
心の中の「新しい扉を次々と開いていく」ことを体現できる空間となった。

meguro office

pp. 232-243
Office | Tokyo | 2007.11
model size 320 x 600 x 100 mm

The nendo Tokyo office is located on the fifth floor of an old office building.
We wanted to separate meeting spaces, workspaces, and storage space, yet still maintain
a sense of connection between them. To achieve this effect, we divided the spaces
with walls that appear to sag like a large piece of cloth held loosely between two hands.
In doing so, we were able to successfully enclose the various spaces more than the usual
office dividers, but less than traditional walls.

目黒川に近くに建つ古いビルの中に位置するnendoのオフィス。ミーティング、ワーク、収納といった用途を、
それぞれ独立させながらも繋がりをもった曖昧な空間にしたいと思い、だらりと「たるんだ」大きな布を
持ち上げたような形の壁で空間を仕切ることに。通常のオフィス用パーティションよりは閉じ、壁よりは開かれた
空間が生まれた。遮音性が求められる場所は、町工場などで使われるビニールカーテンを吊ることで
遮断しすぎず互いの気配を感じられるように。立って全体を見渡すと、人や棚、観葉植物といったモノが
波間に見え隠れするような風景が広がる。

mimicry chairs

pp. 244-317
Installation
Victoria & Albert Museum
London | 2012.09
model size
500 x 270 x 330 mm
600 x 180 x 230 mm
350 x 350 x 400 mm
620 x 170 x 60 mm
350 x 350 x 400 mm
400 x 220 x 190 mm
280 x 100 x 250 mm
370 x 550 x 190 mm
450 x 300 x 190 mm
1450 x 350 x 180 mm
600 x 300 x 200 mm

Installation for London's Victoria and Albert Museum. We pressed punched metal to create a transparent chair with a seemingly soft back rest, and placed it in the main entrance and ten other locations within the museum including galleries, staircases and corridors. For each location, we modified the chair to mimic the particular space and objects, so that it accords with its environment. We hoped that visitors might discover a new side to the museum's attractiveness, by sitting on and appreciating different chairs.

英国のビクトリア＆アルバート国立博物館で行ったインスタレーション。パンチングメタルに
プレス加工を施すことで、一見すると柔らかい背もたれのように見える透明性のあるイスをつくり、それらを
エントランスや展示室や階段室、回廊など11カ所に配置することにした。その際、それぞれの空間特性や
その場に展示されている作品に呼応するかのようにチェアを擬態化させた。チェアに腰掛けて休憩をしたり
作品鑑賞をすることで、来場者に博物館の新たな魅力に気付いてもらうことを考えた。

moss house
pp. 318-323
Private house | Tokyo | 2008.05
model size 110 x 140 x 200 mm

Renovating the old wooden house, we created a living and working space. Inspired by the moss vein outside the river bank, a dry moss was used on the walls as a decoration, in order to create a sense of continuity between the old and the new spaces, and between the inside and outside of the house. The moss pattern seems wallpaper, creating a texture that feels both artificial and natural.

木造家屋を住居兼アトリエにリノベーションするプロジェクト。増改築が繰り返されてきた家屋には不思議な廊下や小部屋、中庭などがあり、これらを生活形態に「馴染ませる」ようなデザインをすることにした。廊下は書斎に、小さな和室はアトリエに。窓の外の川沿いに見えるコケをモチーフに、内部と外部の環境をやわらかく「馴染ませる」ことを考え、コケを乾燥させたドライモスを使って、壁紙に使われるようなパターンを表現し室内壁面を覆うことに。これによって人工物と自然物の境界が曖昧なテクスチャーが生まれた。

PUMA HOUSE TOKYO
pp. 324-331
Showroom | PUMA | Tokyo | 2011.04
model size 450 x 780 x 350 mm

PUMA HOUSE TOKYO was created as the press room and event space. "Staircases" climb up on the wall and in the space as if they were covered with vines. "Staircases" also conjures up the stairs of stadium auditorium or podium. This represents the idea that we do exercise everyday, by going up and down stairs. This space makes us feel we are active in a pair of shoes. A three-dimensional display helps us fully experience the brand concept of PUMA.

プレスルームとイベントスペースとして東京・青山に誕生した「PUMA HOUSE TOKYO」。日常生活において体を動かしていることが実感できる場所であり、またスタジアムの観客席や表彰台などスポーツとの関連性も強い「階段」を、まるでツタが植生するように躯体に自由にまとわりつくように配置した。靴の動きを感じさせる空間が生まれ、立体的な商品展示が可能となり、PUMAブランドの世界観を存分に体感できる場所となった。

Rinascente Milan

pp. 332-341
Shop | Rinascente | Milan | 2012.09
model size 1000 x 1060 x 90 mm

To incorporate elements that would give visitors a tangible sense of the city, we installed 17 large windows, reminiscent of those seen around Milan, to function as subtle space dividers. We applied a film to the windows to make them opaque when viewed from an angle but transparent when viewed directly; this allows products to suddenly "appear" in front of shoppers' eyes as they move throughout the space. It also creates a constantly changing spatial experience, much like the constant but unpredictable "small surprises" of Milan itself.

ミラノを代表する百貨店をデザインするにあたり、ミラノの街を感じさせる要素が求められたため、市内で特徴的な「大窓」を17個配置することで空間を緩やかに仕切ることにした。この窓には「斜めから見ると不透明で、正面からは透明に見える」フィルムが貼られているため、歩いていると突然商品が現われたり、目の前の景色が次々と開けるといった、市内の路地裏を歩いているような空間体験を生み出した。
ハンガーや棚などの什器は「窓越しのめくれかけたカーテン」のような柔らかい印象にし、
「建物の間にケーブルで吊られている街灯」のような照明、「アーチ型」のショップエントランスによって、ミラノの街を歩く時のワクワクした気持ちを凝縮することを試みた。

spicebox office

pp. 342-351
Office | spicebox | Tokyo | 2013.05
model size 870 x 600 x 90 mm

The firm's name symbolizes the ability to deliver surprise and delight as if they were tumbling out of a box, so we placed seven box-shaped meeting rooms of differing sizes and finishes around the office. Each box "peels open" in a slightly different way, subtly connecting interior and exterior and altering line of sight to create a spatial experience in which each box reveals itself as you walk around the room. The peeled-open entrances turn the area around each box into a semi-open communication corner, transforming the area into a dynamic office environment where people can easily work and interact.

インターネットを用いた広告やプロモーションを手掛ける「spicebox」のオフィス。社名の由来が「刺激が次々と箱から飛び出してくるように、サプライズや喜びを提供すること」であるため、サイズや仕上げの異なる7つのボックス状のミーティングルームを配置し、それぞれのボックスの壁面を「めくる」ように開くことにした。めくり方は、一つひとつが異なり、それによってボックス内部と外部が柔らかく繋がる効果や、適度に視線を遮蔽することで、歩くとつぎつぎと新たなボックスが出現するような空間体験が生まれた。めくれた壁によって周辺はセミオープンなコミュニケーションコーナーとなり、動的なオフィス環境となるよう考えた。

Starbucks Espresso Journey
pp. 352-361
Pop-up shop | Starbucks | Tokyo | 2012.09
model size 520 x 360 x 200 mm

The design of Starbucks pop-up store. In the space like a library, the book shelves are lined up, filled with books about nine coffee drinks in nine colors. Browsing freely, customers make their coffee choice based on what each book says. At the counter, customers get a real coffee and a book cover in exchange of a book. Books and coffees play an important part in our daily life. In the store where books and coffees are connected, everyone finds a favorite coffee, just like they find a favorite book.

東京・表参道にできたスターバックスの期間限定店舗。ラテやカフェモカ、カプチーノなどのエスプレッソ
ドリンクの魅力を体験する場所として「書斎」のような空間をデザインした。本棚は9色の本で埋め尽くされ、
それぞれ9種類のエスプレッソドリンクに対応している。来場者は本棚の本を自由に手にとり、中の情報を
見比べながらドリンクを選ぶ。本をカウンターにもっていくと、そのドリンクとブックカバーが提供される。
自分にとって大切な一冊の本を見つけるように、自分にとって大切な一杯と出会う場所となることを願った。

Theory

pp. 362-435
Shop | Theory
model size
520 x 450 x 110, 450 x 380 x 160 mm
770 x 680 x 140 mm
570 x 390 x 140 mm
1160 x 1160 x 130 mm
470 x 350 x 300 mm
880 x 530 x 360 mm
550 x 470 x 140 mm
500 x 250 x 120, 330 x 250 x 120 mm
500 x 370 x 120 mm

Global stores of Theory, a fashion brand based in New York. Our idea was to adhere to the brand's existing combination of simplicity, functionality and a sense of ease, while adding a new concept: the flow of people. For this concept, we meet many different requests regarding the shop space. Keeping creating new flows of people, we aim that such flow of people goes out of the store and harmonize with the city.

ベーシックでありながら機能性とトレンドを取り入れたニューヨーク発のファッションブランドの店舗デザイン。パリ、ロサンゼルス、ロンドン、香港、北京、上海、国内では大阪、自由が丘、青山を手掛けた。既存店の特徴である、シンプルで機能的で無骨な印象の素材感は踏襲しつつ、新たなコンセプトとして「人の流れ」に重点を置いた設計を試みた。店舗毎に異なるさまざまな条件に対応しながら、新しい「人の流れ」を生み出し、それが店内だけでなく周辺にも染み出すことを目指した。

thin black lines + dancing squares
pp. 436-447
Installation
National Taiwan Craft Research Institute
Taichung | 2011.06 - 08
model size
670 x 410 x 160 mm
680 x 650 x 90 mm

Index of models

This solo show features two collections of monochromic furniture. In "thin black lines", the furniture is conceptualized from "still black" so the designer used "active black on white" in the exhibition space. Lines drawn on the floor appear to flow like water around the stands. The "dancing squares" collection is based on "active white" and its exhibit conveys the idea of "still white on black". On the wall, a full scale sketch of a room creates a fish eye effect, viewers experience seeing the room through a tiny drop of water.

台湾で開催された2つの個展。thin black lines が「静的な黒」で構成されている家具コレクションであることから、その空間はあえて「動的な黒と白」を使った表現にしたいと考え、「川の水が流れていく」ようなフローリングのスケッチを床面に施した。また、「動的な白」のdancing squares は、「静的な白と黒」の空間を「小さな水滴を覗き込んだ」ような魚眼レンズ効果をスケッチで再現した。

tokyo baby cafe
pp. 448-455
Cafe | tokyo baby cafe | Tokyo | 2010.04
model size 630 x 470 x 130 mm

The design for a parent and child cafe in Tokyo. Parents can spend a time with small children, without worrying too much about people around them. The cafe is designed for both parents and small children have a comfortable time, thus, difference in size plays an important role. Interior consists of "absolutely huge" items and "absolutely tiny" items, representing perspectives of both parents and children. A nursing sofa becomes a playroom when blown up on a massive size, and a diaper changing table when shrunk to minuscule proportions. Big windows pair with small ones, and big light bulbs with small ones. The floorboards vary in size. The undersides of tables, where parents' eyes don't reach, hide pictures of parent and baby animals. The cafe is all for "parents and children" always welcomes parent and children who want to have a good time.

東京・表参道にある親子カフェ。「大人」と「子供」というスケールの違う利用者が同時に楽しむ場所であることから、そのスケール感の違いをデザインの切り口とし、「子ども目線」と「大人目線」を活かした「すごく大きい」ものと「すごく小さい」もので構成されたデザイン。授乳用ソファが「すごく大きく」なってプレイルームに、「すごく小さく」なっておむつ替え用の台に。大きい窓と小さい窓。大きい電球と小さな電球。大小の床のフローリング材。「大人の目の届かない」テーブルや棚の裏には、動物の親子のイラストが隠れている。「親子」がたくさん散りばめられた、親子カフェとなった。

Yii exhibition
pp. 456-463
Installation | National Taiwan Craft Research Institute
Triennale di Milano | 2011.04
model size 1080 x 360 x 390 mm

On exhibit were traditional Taiwanese crafts repositioned in a contemporary context.
The installation consisted of 190 10m transparent vinyl balloons, minimizing waste,
manufacturing prices, shipping costs and allowing the installation to be reused
at subsequent venues should the exhibition travel in the future. As visitors walked along
the balloons, sightlines and lighting changed constantly. We hoped that this would allow
them to experience a kind of pleasant floating feeling as they viewed the exhibition.

台湾の伝統工芸の活性化を目的とした、ミラノ・トリエンナーレ美術館での展示。製造や運搬時のコストを
抑えながら、会期後の廃棄物も少なく、巡回時に繰返し使用が可能な点から、長さ10mのビニール製風船を
190本製作し空間内に林立させ、台湾に多い「竹林」がもつ空間の要素を再現したいと考えた。
竹越しの視線の抜け方と刻々と変化する光による浮遊感のある心地良さを体感する中での作品鑑賞を目指した。

1% products @ IFFT
pp. 464-473
Installation | 1% products | Tokyo | 2006.11
model size 510 x 390 x 190 mm

Since the hall has notoriously high ceilings, exhibition designers usually attach spotlights
to temporary walls and pillars to make sure each product is properly lit. This would also
make the space feel enclosed, so we covered the floor with a printed film whose pattern
mimics the light and shadows thrown by spotlights. As a result, each product stands out,
and the space feels masterfully illuminated without sacrificing its spaciousness.

会場の天井が高いために、通常は壁や柱を立てて個別にスポットライトを設置するが、会場全体に閉塞感が
出てしまうため、床を「スポットライトの光と影」を描いた出力シートで仕上げ、できるだけ開かれた
空間でありながらも、ライトアップされているかのように作品を浮かび上がらせることを試みた。
影はそれぞれのプロダクトの特徴を強調するべく調整し、説明的な要素となることも意識した。

1% products @ Interior Lifestyle
pp. 474-481
Installation | 1% products
Tokyo | 2007.05
model size 380 x 130 x 300 mm

The exhibition took place in an atrium that gave visitors a view from the second floor.
We put everything, from sofas to plants, on one wall, so that viewers looking down
from the second floor felt as though they were on the first floor, and viewers
on the ground floor felt as though they were looking down from above. Visitors were
essentially "walking on the walls", which heightened the topsy-turvy effect,
and made the visitors part of the display too.

2階からも見下ろされる可能性があるアトリウム空間での展示のため、家具や雑貨をすべて壁面に
固定することで、2階から見たときには「1階で見ているような」状態になり、逆に1階から見たときは
「2階から見下ろしているような」状態になった。また、来場者が会場内を歩きまわることでこの反転現象が
強調され、来場者自身も展示の一部となることを目指した。

24 ISSEY MIYAKE
pp. 482–487
Shop | ISSEY MIYAKE
Tokyo | 2010.05
model size 270 x 180 x 100 mm

Shop design for the "24 ISSEY MIYAKE". The Miyake team was seeking a new design concept for the store in Shibuya, as they were going to launch Miyake's new Bilbao bag which has no set, fixed form. To make a consistency with this design, we eliminated a standard, hard and flat fixtures, and created a set of variable-height fixtures made of thin steel rods that stand like a field of prairie grass. Supported by "points", the bags seem to waft in the air like flowers in a light breeze. The store looks as if they were a field of flowers.

「ビルバオ」という「形が定まらない」バッグを前面に打ち出す店舗であることから、什器も平滑なものではなく、スチール棒が高さを変えながら林立する「形が定まらない」ものにした。「点」で支えることで、その上をふわりふわりとバッグが形を変えながら漂う、まるで花畑のような店舗になった。

80 sheets of mountains
pp. 488-495
Installation | Stockholm Furniture Fair | Stockholm | 2013.02
model size 580 x 520 x 140 mm

An installation of the entrance hall at the Stockholm International Furniture Fair.
5mm polystyrene were laser-cut and stretched to make partitions shaped like mountains.
80 of them were arranged to make the space look as if they had been snow-capped
mountain. This represents the idea and philosophy of nendo design-expanding a small
idea. The delivery only needed one truck. The partitions were flattened when removed.
They can be recyclable, environmentally friendly.

ストックホルム国際家具見本市のエントランスホールで手掛けたインスタレーション。
5mm厚のポリスチレン板にレーザー加工で切り込みを入れ、引き延ばすことで山型のパーティションができる。
これらを80枚作成し配置していくことで雪に覆われた「山脈」のような風景が生まれた。小さなアイディアが
大きく広がる様子に似ており、nendoのデザイン観を表す空間に相応しいと考えた。ポリスチレン板は
板状で搬入され、現場で引き延ばされるために運搬は一台のトラックで済み、展示後は畳んで搬出され
再生利用も可能なため、展示による環境負荷は最小限に抑えられた。

in the box

I'm always carrying a white box.
Barcelona Airport. Piazza del Duomo in Milan. From chilly Prague to tropical Singapore.
I always have my white box in hand.

The box is made from taped-together 7mm-thick white styrene board, with a resin handle and bound by a white band. It travels with me on my flight, and remains tight within my arms even behind the wheel. And when I've arrived at wherever I'm staying for the night, I put the finishing touches on what lies within.

On the day of the meeting, I walk. I move with extreme care, avoiding sudden movements or a collision that might harm what lies within. Even so, I can't help but stop every now and then and take a peek inside. What lies within is not simply something I present to my client. What lies within is a small present for my client.

Asking someone what they want, and then giving them that exact thing – that's not a present. Forcing what you want upon them – that can't be called a present, either. Seeking out little bits and pieces of desire hidden within casual conversation, and then giving form to that desire and placing it right before their eyes, making them realize that this is what they truly wanted all along – this is what gives birth to true surprise and delight.

No two people want the exact same thing, and bringing someone the same thing that made them happy the first time doesn't work the second. This is why the size and shape of the box are different each and every time.

"I know that what I want is in the box."
This is the expectation that I work to create. This is the expectation that I work to live up to. And now I want to share with you my quest over the past 12 years to do just that – I want to share with you the world that lies in the box.

Oki Sato
April 2014

箱の中

いつも白い箱を持ち歩いています。
バルセロナの空港、ミラノのドゥオモ広場、
凍てつくプラハから常夏のシンガポールまで。
いつも手には白い箱があります。

7mm厚の白いスチレンボードをテープで貼り合わせて作った箱には、
白い結束バンドと樹脂製の持ち手が付けられています。
飛行機では必ず機内に持ち込み、車の中では抱きかかえながら移動します。
そして、到着した宿泊先で箱の中のものを仕上げます。
打ち合わせ当日は歩いての移動です。
何かにぶつかって中身が壊れないように、
揺れて歪まないように、常に細心の注意を払いますが、
ときどき不安になって立ち止まり、箱の中を確認します。
こうして持ってきた箱の中には依頼主への「プレゼン」用の資料が入っているのではなく、
ひとつの小さな「プレゼント」が入っているのです。

何が欲しい?と相手に事前に確認してから、
ずばりそのものをあげることはプレゼントではありません。
自分があげたいものを一方的に押し付けることもプレゼントとは呼べません。
相手との他愛のない会話の中から潜在化されている小さな欲求を探り当てていき、
それらをひとつの形として目の前に提示してあげることで、
相手が「本当に求めていたもの」に改めて気付かされることが本物の驚きと喜びを生むのです。
誰一人として同じものを求めていないからこそ、
そして同じ相手でも前と同じものでは決して喜んでくれないからこそ、
持ち歩く箱の形や大きさは毎回違います。
「箱の中にはきっと自分が欲しいものが入っている。」
そんな期待をしてもらいたくて、そして、そんな期待に応えたい一心で、
12年間作り続けた箱の中の世界をご覧ください。

2014年4月
佐藤オオキ

nendo / Oki Sato

Biography

1977	Born in Toronto, Canada
2002	M.A. in Architecture, Waseda University, Tokyo
	Established "nendo" Tokyo office
2005	Established "nendo" Milan office
2006	Lecturer for Showa Women's University, Tokyo
	"The 100 Most Respected Japanese" (Newsweek magazine)
2007	"The Top 100 Small Japanese Companies" (Newsweek magazine)
2008	Collection of works "nendo" (daab)
2009	Lecturer for Kuwasawa Design School, Tokyo
2010	Collection of works "nendo ghost stories" (ADP)
2012	Established "nendo" Singapore office
	"Designer of the Year" (Wallpaper magazine)
	"Designer of the Year" (Elle Deco International Design Award)
	Lecturer for Waseda University, Tokyo
2013	"Guest of Honor" Stockholm Furniture & Light Fair, Stockholm
	Collection of works "nendo 10/10" (Gestalten)
	Collection of works "nendo ghost shadows" (ADP)

Public Collections

The Museum of Modern Art, New York
Centre Pompidou, Paris
Les Musée des Arts décoratifs, Paris
Victoria and Albert Museum, London
Triennale Design Museum, Milan
Museum of Arts and Design, New York
Cooper-Hewitt, National Design Museum, New York
The Art Institute of Chicago, Chicago
High Museum of Art, Atlanta
The Montreal Museum of Fine Arts, Montreal
The Israel Museum, Jerusalem
Design Museum Holon, Holon
Los Angeles County Museum of Art, Los Angeles
Denver Art Museum, Denver

Hiroshi Iwasaki

Biography

1969	Born in Shizuoka, Japan
1990	Graduated from Tokyo Kogei Junior College
	Studied photography under Joe Akimoto and Ayumi Okubo
1998	Became independent

nendo／佐藤 オオキ

略歴

1977年	カナダ生まれ
2002年	早稲田大学大学院理工学研究科建築学専攻修了
	nendo東京オフィス設立
2005年	nendoミラノオフィス設立
2006年	昭和女子大学非常勤講師
	Newsweek誌「世界が尊敬する日本人100人」選出
2007年	Newsweek誌「世界が注目する日本の中小企業100社」選出
2008年	作品集『nendo』(独・daab)
2009年	桑沢デザイン研究所非常勤講師
2010年	作品集『nendo ghost stories』(ADP)
2012年	nendoシンガポールオフィス設立
	Wallpaper誌「Designer of the Year」選出(英)
	Elle Deco International Design Award「Designer of the Year」選出
	著書『ネンドノカンド 脱力デザイン論』(小学館)
	早稲田大学非常勤講師
2013年	Stockholm Furniture & Light Fair「Guest of Honor」選出(スウェーデン)
	作品集『nendo 10／10』(独・Gestalten)
	著書『ウラからのぞけばオモテが見える／10の思考法と行動術』(日経BP)
	作品集『nendo ghost shadows』(ADP)

作品収蔵美術館

ニューヨーク近代美術館(米)

ポンピドゥー・センター(仏)

パリ装飾美術館(仏)

ヴィクトリア・アンド・アルバート美術館(英)

トリエンナーレデザイン美術館(伊)

ニューヨークデザイン美術館(米)

クーパーヒューイット美術館(米)

シカゴ美術館(米)

ハイ美術館(米)

モントリオール美術館(加)

イスラエル美術館(イスラエル)

ホロンデザイン美術館(イスラエル)

ロサンゼルスカウンティ美術館(米)

デンバー美術館(米)

岩崎 寛

略歴

1969年	静岡生まれ
1990年	東京工芸大学短期大学部卒業
	写真家 秋元譲氏、大久保歩氏に師事
1998年	フリーランスとして活動開始

Photo Credits

Daici Ano: pp. 498, 500, 502, 505, 511, 513–516,
518–519, 521–527, 529, 532–534
Joakim Blockstrom: pp. 504, 507, 528, 535
Jimmy Cohrssen: pp. 499, 508, 517, 520, 530
Masaya Yoshimura: pp. 501, 506, 509, 512
Hermès: p. 510
Camper: p. 503

nendo: in the box

発行日：2014年4月16日

著者：nendo／佐藤オオキ
撮影：岩崎 寛
ブックデザイン：色部義昭、植松晶子
（株式会社日本デザインセンター 色部デザイン研究室）
プリンティングディレクション：浦 有輝（株式会社アイワード）

発行者：久保田啓子
発行所：株式会社 ADP／Art Design Publishing
〒165-0024 東京都中野区松が丘 2-14-12
Tel：03-5942-6011 Fax：03-5942-6015
http://www.ad-publish.com
郵便振替：0160-2-355359

印刷・製本：株式会社アイワード

©nendo 2014
Printed in Japan
ISBN 978-4-903348-41-4 C0072

本書の無断複写（コピー）は著作権上での
例外を除き、禁じられています。

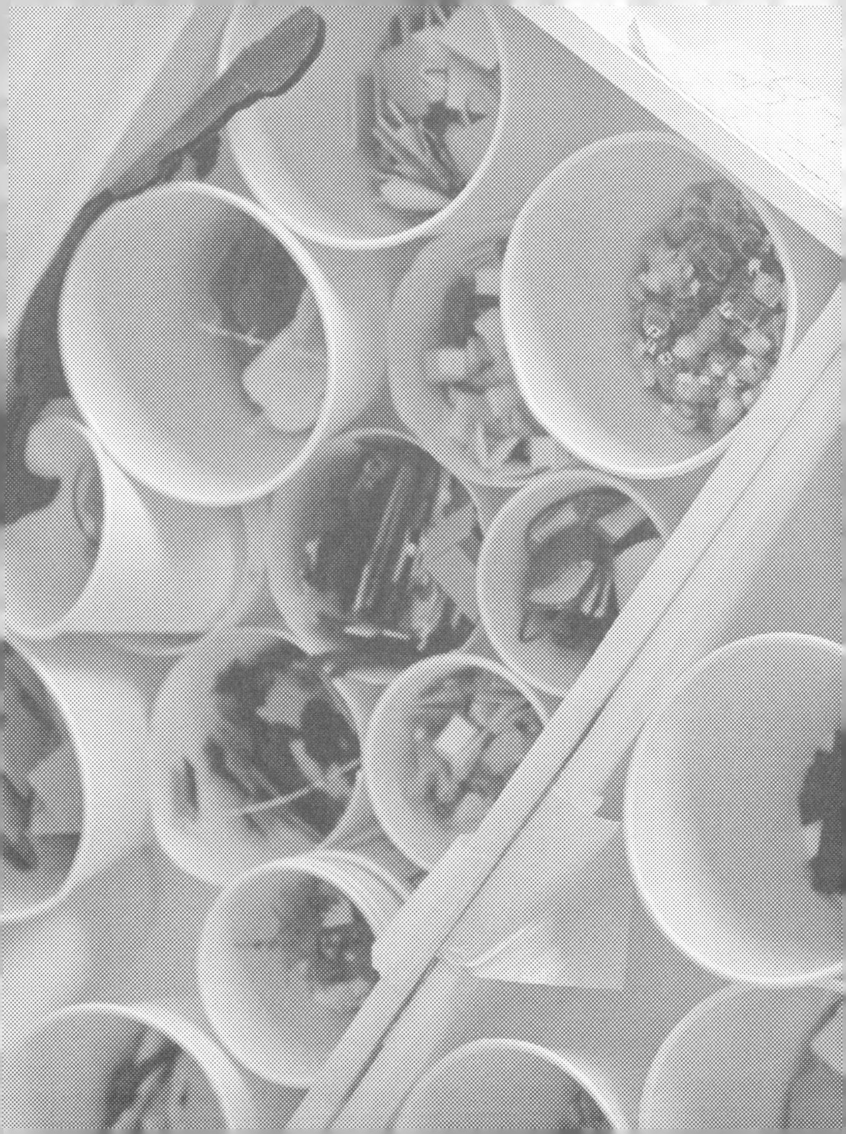

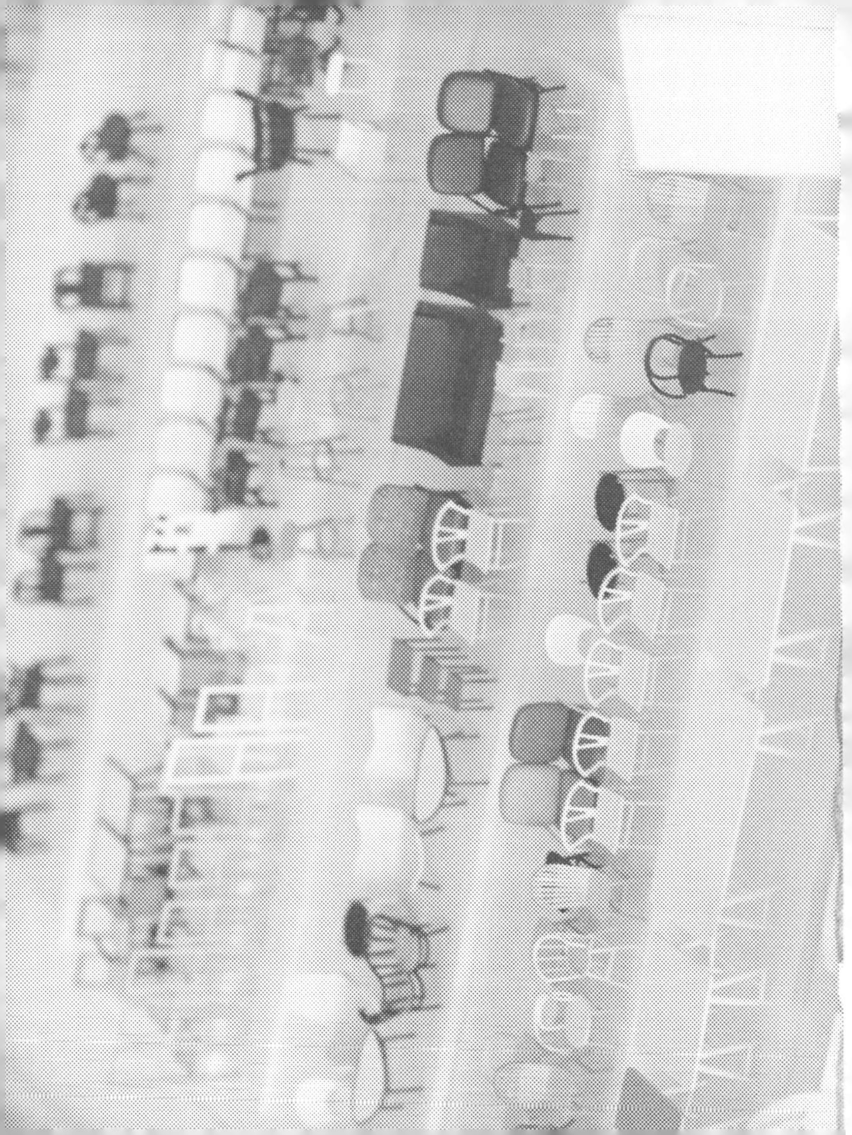

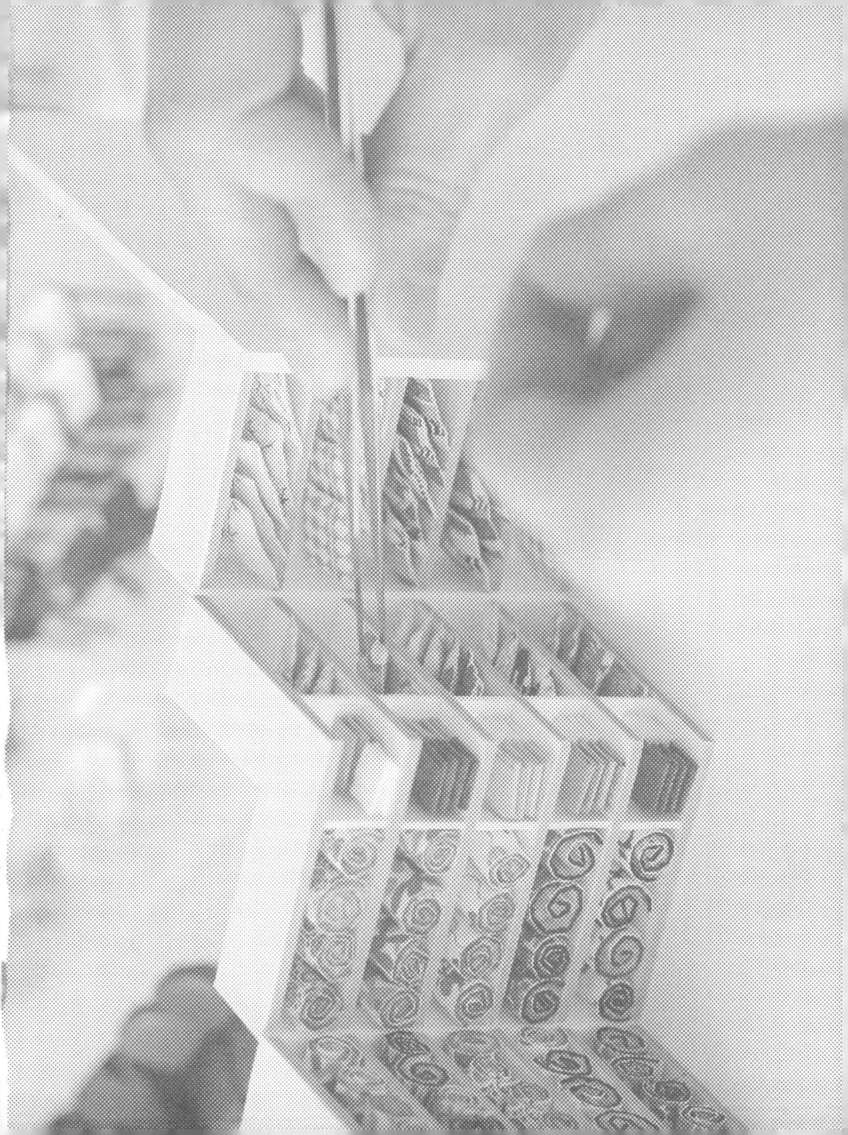

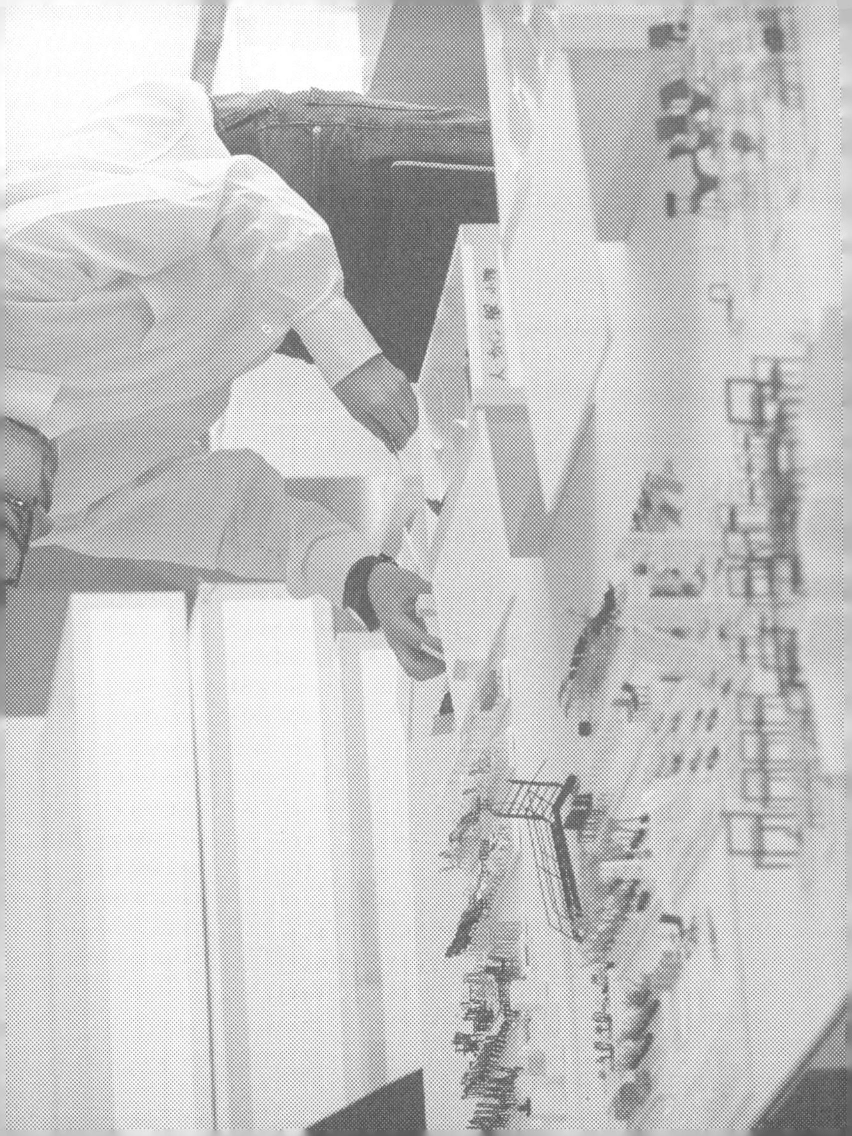